Dear

Happy Christmas

Lots of Love

Mum & Dad

xxx

The
CHEQUERED
FLAG

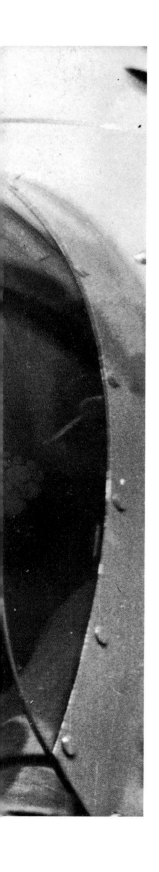

The CHEQUERED FLAG

The Complete History
of Motor Racing

IVAN RENDALL

WEIDENFELD & NICOLSON

Created by Media Eye Ltd, London

This edition produced for The Book People Ltd, Hall Wood Avenue,
Haydock, St Helens WA11 9UL

First published in 1993
by Weidenfeld & Nicolson Ltd
Orion House
5 Upper St Martin's Lane
London WC2H 9EA

Updated and reprinted, 1997, 2007

Designed by Ted McCausland; updates designed by Richard Carr

Index by Mike Darton; updated by Mark Kerr

Just before the 'Ste

500 Mi

ISBN 978-1-407-20683-7

A CIP catalogue record for this book is available
from the British Library.

Printed and bound in Italy

www.orionbooks.co.uk

CONTENTS

World Champion: Michael Schumacher, the only driver in the history of Grand Prix racing to win the World Championship seven times, at the Hungaroring in 2006. He retired at the end of the year, after sixteen seasons at the top of the sport.

INTRODUCTION

Motor sport has a natural ability to evolve; and evolve quickly. In over a century it has survived successive economic upheavals and used technological revolutions to adapt its mixture of extreme engineering and human competitiveness to meet new, commercial, cultural, sporting and international opportunities.

Now in its second century, road racing is in rude good health at the top of the evolutionary tree: the Formula 1 World Championship is a multi-billion pound, global business, a showcase for European and Japanese car makers, a laboratory for new technology and a television spectacle perfectly tuned to dynamics of global culture in the age of celebrity. The European road racing heritage and the American tradition of oval racing now mingle at the 'Brickyard', the oldest circuit in the United States where the Indianapolis 500 and the United States Grand Prix are run on different circuits.

However, America's open wheel equivalent to Formula 1, IndyCar and Champ Car, have been overshadowed over the last half century by NASCAR, a purely domestic stock car championship that has grown to dominate American racing culture. NASCAR's teams bear the names of America's big car-makers, such as Chevrolet, Ford and Dodge, and its drivers are household names. With over thirty races a year and seventy-five million regular fans, it is now challenging National League Football, America's number one sport on television.

Where NASCAR has grown huge in a domestic environment, the World Championship has grown by becoming more international. Grand Prix racing has evolved from its European heartland into Asia and the Middle East, to Kuala Lumpur, Bahrain, Shanghai and Istanbul where governments have invested in futuristic circuits to attract Bernie Ecclestone's flying circus.

Talent, money and technology now move around the world, cross-fertilising to produce new types of racing in a global marketplace.

A1GP, with its 'World Cup of Motorsport,' is a championship for national teams of highly-motivated individuals to express themselves through achievement and aspiration, but with one aim: to join the tiny number who have made it to the top.

Motor racing is a technology-based sport, but it is also one of the most human. The racing driver is already a twenty-first century icon: young, fit, attractive, a master of high technology who faces danger, even death, with equanimity. As the sport and the cars evolve, so does the driver, as each era produces its own generation of heroes who capture the spirit of their times. In 1895, it was Emile Levassor, whose sheer endurance in driving for over two days non-stop from Paris to Bordeaux and back, was marked by a statue erected in his honour. In 2006, the seven times World Champion, Michael Schumacher, retired as the most successful racing driver ever, ascending the top place on the podium ninety-one times; he was also a billionaire.

In between, the irrepressible Jimmy Murphy, the fearless Tazio Nuvolari, the gentle Juan Manuel Fangio, the gifted Jim Clark, the all-American A.J. Foyt, the dynastic Mario Andretti, the brash Nigel Mansell and the enigmatic Ayrton Senna all put their personal stamp on their time at the top while also showing the timeless qualities that are the soul of a racer: winning races, in different competitions, adapting their basic skills to new technologies and, the highest achievement of all, driving inferior cars to victory over the better-equipped opposition.

Racing drivers are born and made. Some started out in poverty and became millionaires and national heroes. Others started out as millionaires and became historical footnotes, having spent fortunes in pursuit of glory. Sometimes the sun shines on a whole generation of drivers until, suddenly, one stands out, putting the rest in the shade, as swift and ruthless a process of natural selection as any food chain in any jungle.

High Speed Service: The 2006 World Champion, Fernando Alonso, gets the attention of his dedicated pit crew during the 2007 United State Grand Prix at Indianapolis. Fractions of a second can make the difference between winning and losing; the race was won by his team mate, Lewis Hamilton.

Sometimes the margin of success is measured in a thousandth of a second, but today more than pure driving talent makes the difference. Watch the body language of any driver who has just won a race or a championship as he leaps over the fence to embrace his team of mechanics and shares his champagne with them; listen to what he says. It's not just about a ruthless determination, about winning at all costs, it's about being the rounded individual who cares about the detail, both technological and human. Every wise driver knows he must share his success, and that without generating a genuine bond of loyalty and shared technical expertise, he could not win. Moments after Lewis Hamilton took the chequered flag to win the 2007 United States Grand Prix at Indianapolis, and long before he came into the pits for the celebrations, he was on the team radio thanking the whole team, ending with the words 'I love you all.'

The evolution of the racing driver will continue to match that of the racing car as motor racing embarks on possibly the biggest technical challenge in its history: coming to terms with carbon footprints, global warming and green politics. Motor racing already offsets its carbon emissions, but it can also contribute to the development of cleaner and more efficient forms of engineering: recovering and retaining energy, especially under braking, experimenting with new fuels, new transmission systems, safer cars, becoming again what it was a century ago in its pioneering age, a proving ground for creative ideas. To achieve that, racing is more likely to develop the technical fix than to cut back on performance, but in doing so it may once again provide an evolutionary surge to the motor car as a humble means of transport.

That is the challenge for the future. But it won't happen without the people – the teams who make cars to win races and the drivers who race them to win.

IVAN RENDALL

9

CHAPTER ONE
PIONEERS, SPORTSMEN
& MR GORDON BENNETT

The technical revolution of the second half of the nineteenth century produced many new wonders – electric lighting, the telephone, steam turbines – but the invention that captured the popular imagination by going far beyond the merely practical, with its implications of individual freedom, modernity, and above all speed, was the 'horseless carriage': the automobile.

The internal combustion engine was invented in Germany, but – as in Britain – public opinion there was initially hostile to the motor car. It is no accident that the first recorded sale of a motor car was by a German company, Benz, to a Frenchman, M. Émile Roger of Paris, in 1888. France embraced the motor car with undisguised enthusiasm, and quickly established by far the largest industry in the world. Motor racing was born in France, first as a shop window for the motor industry, then as a technical laboratory. The rapid evolution of the motor car from fragile curiosity to robust, reliable replacement for the horse was driven by a curious and powerful merger of sporting ideals, natural human competitiveness and technical ingenuity.

Racing on public roads was banned in Britain and Germany, but in France it was largely unfettered. The combination of enthusiasm, rivalry, technical prowess, and miles of long, straight, open roads produced the first, heroic age of the sport, which was projected around the world by that other phenomenon of the late 19th century, the popular press. A decade later, it had been copied in America, Italy, Germany and Britain.

Accidents cast a shadow over the 1903 Paris–Madrid race. The contest attracted huge crowds and drew 316 entrants – the largest number that had ever been known; but high speeds made racing on public roads hazardous.

Count Jules de Dion's steam tractor pulled a passenger carriage in the 1894 Paris-Rouen run, and was the fastest vehicle in the event (**ABOVE**). The tractor weighed 2,500 kg fully laden and could develop about 20 hp; its front wheels were solid rubber and its back wheels were 'shod' with steel. De Dion (**RIGHT**), born in 1856 in Nantes, western France, was a wealthy playboy renowned for his love of gambling and a propensity for fighting duels.

At dawn on 22 July, thousands of people gathered at the Porte Maillot in Paris to see the start of a trial organized by *Le Petit Journal* to publicize the motor car. It was not a race. First prize would go to the vehicle which, in the opinion of the judges, covered the 80 miles from Paris to Rouen 'without danger, and was easy to handle and in addition was cheap to run.'

The magazine received 102 entries for vehicles powered by steam, petrol, compressed air, gravity, pendulums or hand-levers; some were described simply as 'automatic'. A prudent qualification required entrants first to cover 50 kilometres (30½ miles) in four hours – which reduced the field somewhat drastically to 21: eight steam cars and 13 petrol-driven, including five Peugeots and four Panhard-Levassors.

Nineteen made it to the start initially. The two missing cars belonged to Maurice le Blant, who was driving one of them, but who could not find a driver for his steam-powered Serpollet van. First off was a giant De Dion steam tractor driven by Count Jules de Dion. The others followed at 30-second intervals, accompanied by warm cheers and a swarm of cyclists. At the very last minute le Blant's brother Étienne agreed to drive his second car.

The De Dion had the most power, and the Count used his advantage to stay in front, drawing away from the less powerful Panhards and Peugeots, especially on the hills. Along the route, entire villages turned out to cheer and shower the cars with flowers and fruit. Many families set up their tables to picnic at the side of the road.

At 11 am the leaders arrived at Mantes, 30 miles from the start. De Dion crossed the bridge first; Georges Lemaître in a Peugeot was second, and Émile Levassor (>1895) driving a Panhard third. After a good lunch, they set off again, de Dion the last to leave. By the time the race reached Vernon, 15 miles farther on, he was back in front. At Gaillon the boiler of a steam-driven omnibus blew up. The driver, M. Scotte, jumped clear, grazing his hands and knees, and was picked up by le Blant. Le Blant and de Dion both had to have their heavy cars hauled out by spectators after grinding to a halt in a loose stone surface.

Taking a wrong turning at Igoville, de Dion found himself in a potato field – but he still finished first in a total time of 6 hours 48 minutes. Lemaître arrived 3½ minutes later in his Peugeot, and 13 minutes after that, Doriot arrived in another. Émile Levassor was fourth in the Panhard. Of the 21 starters 17 finished, including Maurice le Blant.

Officially it was not a race – but everybody wanted to know who was the fastest, and the unofficial winner was de Dion at 11.6 mph. Lemaître was second at 11.5 mph, and Doriot third at 11.1 mph. On Monday morning the judges disqualified de Dion from first position

and the prize of 5,000 francs (£200) because by requiring a stoker his machine did not comply with the outlined objectives. The prize went instead jointly to Peugeot and Panhard-et-Levassor for 'conforming so well to the rules without, as yet, fully realizing the dreams of the tourist or the businessman.'

De Dion had to be satisfied with the second prize of 2,000 francs (£80) for his 'interesting steam tractor which . . . develops a speed absolutely beyond comparison, especially when going uphill.'

The Paris–Rouen Trial did more than publicize the motor car – it brought motoring enthusiasts together and it also whetted their appetites for something more red-blooded: a full-blown race, in which speed was the criterion. On 2 November de Dion held a meeting at his house, assembling Count Gaston de Chasseloup-Laubat (>1898), Pierre Giffard of *Le Petit Journal*, Levassor, Peugeot, Serpollet, and other motoring luminaries. They formed a committee (>1895) to organize a race from Paris to Bordeaux and back – 732 miles – with no judges. The fastest car would be the winner. Motor racing had been born.

M. Michaud driving a Peugeot, No. 30, through Mantes at the end of the first stage of the Paris–Rouen trial. He was ninth fastest at an average speed of 9.4 mph.

MILESTONES

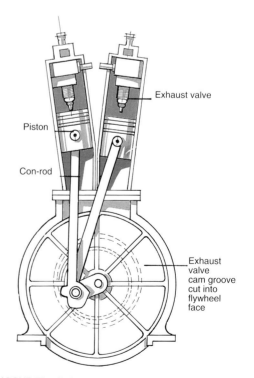

ABOVE: The Daimler V-twin engine produced by Panhard et Levassor; it ran at a constant speed of around 800 rpm, producing 3.5 hp. There was no accelerator; speed was controlled by changing gear; fuel was ignited by a hot platinum tube in the head, heated by a petrol burner.

Labels on diagram: Exhaust valve, Piston, Con-rod, Exhaust valve cam groove cut into flywheel face

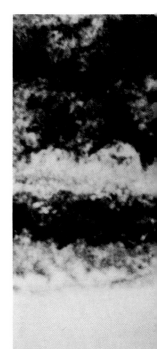

The idea of racing from Paris to Bordeaux and back had an epic quality. Regulations were kept to a minimum: cars had to carry more than two people and could be driven by more than one driver; riding mechanics could effect repairs en route under the supervision of a race official, but only with spares carried on the car; and there was a time limit of 100 hours. Wealthy sponsors, including two Americans – the newspaper publisher James Gordon Bennett (>1900), and William K. Vanderbilt (>1904) – contributed heavily to a prize fund that in all totalled 69,951 francs (£2,800), no less than half of which was to go to the winner.

The 21 competitors drove in procession from the Arc de Triomphe to the Place des Armes at Versailles for the start. Thirteen were petrol-driven, six steam-powered, one was electric, and there were two motorcycles. The first off was a Peugeot driven by M. Rigoulot, but it was Count Jules de Dion's steam car that took the lead, closely followed by a seven-seater Bollée steam omnibus. Both the steam vehicles broke down before they reached Tours, handing the lead to Émile Levassor for Panhard-Levassor.

Levassor reached Tours at 8.45 and led the race into the gathering dusk. The night was clear, and he managed an average speed of 15 mph with only oil-lamps to show the way. Stopping for fuel and for water, he reached Ruffec, 120 miles north of Bordeaux, at 3.30 am to find his relief driver still in bed. He had a sizable lead over his nearest rivals – Rigoulot and M. Doriot, both in Peugeots – but rather than wait, he drove on, and reached Bordeaux at 10.40 am, 3½ hours ahead of them. By the time they arrived, Levassor was well on his way back.

Levassor's rapport with the car and the demands of the race was so evident that he decided to drive the whole distance himself. Word of his epic drive spread before him, and a tumultuous reception greeted him at the Porte Maillot after just over two days at the helm – the winner of the first true motor race in history.

Of the eleven cars that reached Bordeaux, nine made it back to Paris. The second car, Rigoulot's Peugeot, arrived at 6.30 pm, and the last, the Bollée omnibus, at six the following morning. Émile Levassor was the hero of the hour – but because his car could carry only two people he was awarded the second prize of 12,600 francs. The first prize of 31,500 francs (£1,260) went to M. Koechlin in a Peugeot.

France had the most advanced automobile industry, and racing clearly promoted technical advances and public awareness. In the United States another wealthy newspaper owner, H. H. Kohlsaat, decided that the American industry should be given the same boost. In April 1895 he used the Chicago *Times-Herald* to back the first motor race in America. There

MILESTONES

Motor racing's first hero: Émile Levassor, winner of the 1894 Paris-Bordeaux race, is immortalized in the statue (**ABOVE**) at the Porte Maillot in Paris. Levassor (left, wearing sun helmet) drove Panhard et Levassor No. 5 in the race (**TOP RIGHT**). The car (**LOWER RIGHT**) used a two-cylinder 8-kg Phénix engine which produced about 4 hp at 800 rpm.

wind gusted to 60 mph. Making its way to the start the De la Vergne-Benz stuck in the slush and withdrew, and Jerry O'Connor in the Macy-Benz hit a horse-drawn bus, slid over a railway track, and collided with a sleigh carrying journalists, damaging its steering. In the race, O'Connor nonetheless set the pace. By the turning point at Evanston he had a two-minute lead over Duryea. But on the homeward run he had to retire because of the damaged steering, and Duryea took over.

In Chicago the crowd waited in the bitter cold. At dusk, with still no sight of the cars, most people began to drift home, so that as Duryea finally drove into town the streets were virtually deserted. When he crossed the finishing line to win the first motor race in America, only 50 people were there to see it. The prize was $2,000. Nearly half an hour later the Mueller-Benz drove into the park, the umpire, Charles King, steering with one hand while supporting Mueller, who had collapsed from exposure, with the other.

Motor racing was a heady mixture: futuristic vehicles, huge cash prizes, and competitions that made popular heroes of Frank Duryea and Émile Levassor overnight. What it lacked was organization. That changed in the closing weeks of 1895: on 1 November the American Motor League was established, and on 13 November Count de Dion (>1894) reconstituted his committee into the Automobile Club de France. Motoring – and motor racing – was gathering impetus.

BELOW: Frank Duryea (left, at the controls) in the Duryea Motor Wagon, winner of the Chicago-Evanston race.

were nearly 100 entries, but only two cars – a Duryea Motor Wagon, driven by Frank Duryea, and a Mueller-Benz, driven by the designer's son, Oscar – were ready by the original date of 2 November, so a 92-mile 'exhibition run' from 55th Street, Chicago, to Waukegan and back was held instead. The Duryea was faster, but it broke down, so Mueller took the prize.

The race itself was postponed until 28 November, at which time six vehicles arrived at Jackson Park: Duryea and Mueller again, a Morris & Salom electric car, a Sturges electric motorcycle, a Macy-Benz, and a De la Vergne-Benz. On the day, a foot of snow had fallen, temperatures hovered around freezing, and the

THREE YEARS' PROGRESS.

4th ANNUAL MEET

OF THE

MOTOR CAR CLUB.

GREAT RUN TO

BRIGHTON

Monday, November 13th, 1899.

All Motorists are cordially invited to participate and to communicate with the Hon. Sec., F. W. BAILY, 40, Holborn Viaduct, for full particulars.

Celebration: the run from London to Brighton on 14 November marked a new era for British motorists. The law requiring every car to be preceded by a man with a red warning flag had been repealed. Huge crowds gathered to see the cars at Reigate (*ABOVE*). The Motor Car Club, organizers of the run, issued a programme (*RIGHT*). *The Autocar* magazine produced a special 'red-letter-day' edition printed with red ink in recognition of 'throwing open the highways and byways of our beautiful country'.

Motor races were media events. They harnessed public interest in the novelty of the motor car and boosted newspapers' circulations at the same time. The second race in America was organized by *Cosmopolitan* magazine on 30 May: 52 miles from New York's City Hall to Irvington-on-Hudson and back. The $3,000 prize attracted 30 entries, but only six started. One lost a wheel, another a drive chain, a third collided with a bicycle, and the rest ground to a halt on Ardsley Hill – until the local country club came out and pushed. Frank Duryea (>1895) reached the top first, and went on to win.

In September the organizers of the Rhode Island State Fair, sited at Narragansett Park, Cranston, ran a series of races on a one-mile horse-racing track, the first motor race on a closed circuit. For once the crowd could watch the whole race from start to finish, and 50,000 turned out to see an electric Riker, driven by

A. L. Riker, win against five Duryeas. It was a form of racing very different from the long-distance competitions on public roads, and one innovation was crucial: there was a profit to it – spectators could be charged to watch.

Far from restricting the length of races for the benefit of spectators, in October the Auto Club de France (ACF) increased it. The Club organized a 1,062-mile race from Paris to Marseilles and back, in ten daytime stages to avoid night driving. Thirty-two drivers qualified. As they made the procession from the Arc de Triomphe to Versailles, the drivers had to battle against a tide of humanity, all eager for a glimpse of the cars. The crush caused a nasty accident in the Avenue de Paris when the first

LEFT: A Canstatt-Daimler (centre) following a Benz (right) in the London-Brighton run.

BELOW: the start of the run in central London.

MILESTONES

At London's Crystal Palace, Bridget Driscoll was run over on 17 August by a Benz driven by Arthur Edsell to become motoring's first fatality.

The first motorcycle race was run over 95 miles in conjunction with the Paris-Marseilles car race. M. Chevalier won, riding a Michelin-Dion.

The first motor insurance policy was issued on 2 November by the General Accident Co. The premium was 30/-, excluding damage caused by frightened horses.

In Britain the Locomotives and Highways Act, limiting cars to 4 mph preceded by a man carrying a red flag, was repealed in November.

On 13 November the first petrol-driven car built for sale in Britain, an Arnold-Benz made by W. Arnold & Son, was road-tested from Peckham to Bromley.

The most efficient racing car engine in 1896 was the four-cylinder Panhard of 8 hp. At 2.4 litres, its output was 3.3 hp per litre (>1904).

car, a Fisson driven by M. Ferté, ran over and badly injured a spectator.

A steam-powered De Dion, driven by Count Jules de Dion (>1894), made the running. It was fitted with pneumatic tyres for higher speed, but they were not up to the punishment they received in racing, and quickly disintegrated. With no spares, de Dion was out of the race. Émile Levassor, in the 6-hp Panhard he had used in 1895, was delayed when one of his solid tyres came off, but he was able to replace it. His works driver, Mayade, driving an 8-hp car, put up quite a reasonable time, but at Auxerre – the end of the first stage – M. Lejane was in the lead on his Bollée motor tricycle having recorded an average speed of 20 mph.

A violent storm swept across the country overnight. Driving head-on into the gale many cars were brought to a standstill; when the wind came from the side, some were blown off the road. Amédée Bollée hit a fallen tree, and a bull on the loose as a result of the storm charged another of the Bollées, damaging it beyond repair. Despite the hazards 18 drivers made it to Dijon, Levassor in the lead by nearly two hours.

Levassor continued to improve his position the following day – until he hit a dog near Avignon. The unstable car overturned, throwing him out. He was bruised and badly shaken, but after a delay insisted on continuing to Avignon, where he went to hospital (>1897). All 13 cars that had left Avignon arrived in Marseilles, putting up better times over the final stages as the wind veered to blow from behind them.

News of the race had been followed keenly in Paris, where the crowd started gathering long before the finish at the Porte Maillot. Six cars arrived before Mayade in the 8-hp Panhard, but he had been steadily pulling ahead throughout the return leg, and won on corrected time.

In Britain, racing was prohibited on public roads. In fact, every car travelling on the road had to be preceded by a man on foot carrying a red flag to warn pedestrians and horse riders. This law was repealed after pressure from enthusiasts in 1896, and to celebrate, the Motor Car Club organized a 'tour' from London to Brighton – a mere 90 miles. On 14 November 33 cars, the majority of them French – including Levassor's Panhard and a clutch of the tiny Bollée tricycles – assembled at Central Hall, Westminster. It was not a race, but those taking part were privately out to beat each other. First and second were two Bollées driven by the Bollée brothers.

After the epic long-distance races of the previous two years, the Auto Club de France (ACF) ran more, shorter, events in 1897. In search of good weather, the Club chose a 138-mile route along the winding roads of the Côte d'Azur from Marseilles to Nice, finishing with an 11-mile hill climb to La Turbie, a village atop a mountain behind Monte Carlo.

Émile Levassor was still suffering headaches after his crash (>1896), but he followed the race in a Panhard decorated with mimosa. The 26 heavy entrants were mostly Peugeots and Panhard-Levassors but included two steam De Dions, a pair of Benz, and three Landrey-et-Beyroux. The first signs that racing cars were developing as a distinct species separate from touring cars were already becoming evident. Professional drivers stripped off non-essentials, from mudguards to seat cushions, and manufacturers developed more powerful engines for them – a move resented by some amateurs.

One of the Panhard team, Fernand Charron (>1898), was driving flat out down a long hill near La Beausset when his fearlessness got the better of him. Approaching a right-angled corner too fast, he swung the steering tiller fully over, skidded, and overturned. His mechanic was thrown out before the car, turning over completely, landed back on its wheels with Charron still in his seat, his arm badly injured. But they made their repairs and completed the 96 miles to Fréjus.

The heaviest and most powerful car in the race was a steam-powered De Dion driven by

British manufacturers experimented with various means of powering cars, including electricity: an 'Electro Motor-Car' (**BELOW**) developed by C.P. Elieson of the Lumina Accumulator Syndicate in Camden Town, London. The car, powered by a battery in the rear, could run for about 40 miles.

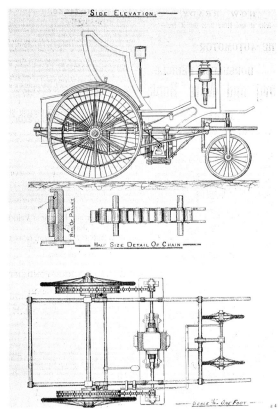

Following the success of the Brighton run, the Motor Car Club organized further non-competitive events on British roads: a De Dion steam carriage (**BELOW**) leading in one such run, between Coventry and Birmingham.

MILESTONES

Émile Levassor, the guiding hand behind the successful Panhard-Levassor racing cars, died on 14 April. He never fully recovered from his 1896 crash.

Britain's first motor race was scheduled for 27 May. Six cars turned up, but it was cancelled because none of them complied with the regulations as laid down.

On 30 May Alexander Winton won a race in Cleveland, Ohio, in a car of his own manufacture. He covered one mile in 1 minute 48 seconds: 33.8 mph.

On 28 July Alexander Winton arrived in New York in one of his own cars, having taken ten days to drive from Cleveland, Ohio, to publicize them.

The Automobile Club of Great Britain and Ireland (later the Royal Automobile Club), which represented British racing, was founded on 10 August.

The first British motorcycle races, at Richmond on 29 November, were won by F. T. Bidlake on a Clément and Charles Jarrott on a Fournier.

LEFT: Amédée Bollée, one of three brothers in a French family of motoring pioneers, who turned their minds to lightweight vehicles, challenging the larger machines then in vogue.

BELOW: Count de Dion, driving his steam-powered car in the Paris-Dieppe race. He won the four-seater category at an average speed of 24.6 mph. The De Dion produced about 20 hp.

Count Gaston de Chasseloup-Laubat. The power served him well on the hills, and despite having to stop to take on coal and water he was in the lead at the end of the first day. The second day was full of incident. Édouard Michelin's Mors broke down; Thibault hit a wall; and Lafitte, startled by André Michelin's overtaking him at speed in a Bollée, drove into the side of a bridge. Chasseloup-Laubat's axle seized on the outskirts of Nice, but his adept mechanic managed to fix it to retain the overall lead.

The third day was the day of the hill climb, in which once again the extra power of the two steam cars gave them a good advantage. André Michelin managed the best time, covering the 11 miles in 31 minutes 50 seconds. Chasseloup-Laubat was second in 37 minutes 55 seconds, but had done enough on the previous two days to ensure overall victory at an average speed of 19.2 mph – the only time a major race was won by a steam car.

In July, the ACF organized a one-day dash from Paris to Dieppe. Once the 59 entrants were on their way, the race officials and some lucky spectators boarded a special train chartered to get them to Dieppe for 12.30 – well before the finish. Viscount de Soulier went into the lead in a Bollée tricycle, until a tyre burst; Jamin then took the lead in another. Amédée Bollée, with Camille Bollée as passenger, took over first place at Gournay in their four-wheeler and seemed to be set for victory when, just four miles from the finish, a tappet broke. The brothers settled down to watch the other cars go through the village. After 20 minutes when none came, they started pushing their car to the finish.

Meanwhile at Dieppe, by 1 o'clock there was still no sign of the special train carrying the timekeepers. Worried officials listened out for the sound of the first cars. At 1.25 pm their worst fears were realized when they heard the first Bollée approaching. It was Jamin, closely pursued by de Dion, followed a quarter of an hour later by Charron and Gilles Hourgières in Panhards. Until the train finally did arrive, times were taken unofficially, giving the newspapers a great story – CARS BEAT TRAIN – and it quickly became the talking-point of France. Of the 59 starters, 41 duly arrived in Dieppe. The Bollée brothers pushed their car over the line for fourth place in their class. Jamin won, averaging 25.2 mph.

The shorter races of 1897 had been popular with the public and many drivers. But what the manufacturers and drivers at the top of the sport wanted was another epic race – and that was what the ACF planned for 1898.

BELOW: Motor racing's first fatal accident. Shortly after the start of a race at Perigueux, France, a Benz Parisienne (foreground) driven by M. de Montariol was forced off the road by the Marquis de Montignac. De Montariol leapt clear, but his mechanic was badly injured. The marquis, in a Landrey et Beyroux, lost control and ended up in the same field (background). The marquis and his mechanic died from their injuries.

Motor racing started out as a way of promoting the automobile for the benefit of the whole of the infant automobile industry. But individual car makers quickly realized that it was winning that mattered – it was beating their rivals that established their names and sold their cars. Only a few potential customers wanted to race, but most were attracted by the image of speed and believed that the fastest cars were also the best.

In the struggle to stay competitive, motor racing moved on from being simply a showroom for the industry to being a technical laboratory too: manufacturers invested in innovative engineering so as to stay ahead. Panhard-Levassor led the way. The success that they achieved in cooling down their engines using Grouvelle & Arquembourg gill-tubed radiators made to a specification drawn up by Léonce Girardot had been widely noted, and in 1898

such radiators were virtually standard. The same was true of pneumatic tyres, which had improved beyond recognition since Édouard Michelin first used them between Paris and Bordeaux in 1895. The most striking innovation came when Panhard and Bollée adopted the steering wheel in place of the tiller – an advance that enormously enhanced safety, and one that again was quickly copied.

Such technical improvements were vital, but in the quest for speed it was engine power that played the most important part, and the easiest way to get more power was to increase the overall cubic capacity of the engine. Whereas Panhard-Levassor touring cars still used variants of the 1,200-cc two-cylinder 3-to-4-hp Phénix engine, the company's racing cars had by 1898 moved on to the 2,408-cc four-cylinder Centaure – essentially two Phénix engines back-to-back – which gave 8 hp. Bollée went

As engines grew in size and power they needed more efficient cooling systems; the gill tube radiator (*RIGHT*) used rows of copper, or brass, tubes with wire helices soldered to them to dissipate the heat more quickly.

ABOVE: Amédée Bollée (right) in a Bollée car which shows early signs of streamlining (or 'windcutting' as it was known at the time); the radiator is built in an arrow shape, pointing forward, instead of being flat on to the direction of travel.

further, to 3,000 cc; and Peugeot went for 3,320. This trend, towards specialized monster cars built simply to promote a company's name by winning races, quickly and quite definitively established itself.

Second to start in the 1898 Marseilles-Nice race was Fernand Charron (>1897) driving a Panhard-Levassor painted white all over to attract maximum attention. He quickly took the lead. Behind him there were two more Panhards, driven by Gilles Hourgières and Count René de Knyff. A fine spray of rain all day turned the roads into a quagmire: cars and drivers were soon covered in a thick coating of mud. On the second day the rain was fiercer still, and drivers had to reduce speed to negotiate puddles the size of ponds. The wet caused particular problems for belt-driven cars and motorcycles – in particular for Madame Laumille on a De Dion motorcycle on which the peddling belt stretched and needed constant adjustment. The problems of belt trans-

mission – in comparison with relatively trouble-free gearboxes and chains – were duly noted by manufacturers, and another technical advance was added to the list of benefits to come from racing.

Marseilles-Nice was a triumph for Panhard. Charron arrived first, with Hourgières eight minutes behind, having battled through the mud with de Knyff, who came third. But the loudest cheers were reserved for Madame Laumille in reward for her perseverence when she finally made it to the finish.

On 1 May during the Course de Périgueux, a locally organized 90-mile race in south-west France, motor racing passed a milestone that had long been dreaded: its first fatality. As in the Marseilles-Nice race, light cars and heavier, more powerful cars were racing together in different classes. Shortly after the start M. de Montariol, driving a Benz Parisienne, heard the much heavier Landrey-et-Beyroux driven by his friend the Marquis de Montaignac coming up behind. Montariol moved over to let the faster car pass, and de Montaignac raised his hand in thanks, in a momentary lapse of concentration leaving the steering tiller unattended. His car swerved in front of the Benz, at once forcing Montariol off the road. Montariol shot up a little bank into a field, where he overturned. He himself was thrown clear, but his mechanic was crushed underneath the car, suffering severe head injuries.

Meanwhile de Montaignac compounded his error by turning to watch the crash, lost control again, and finished up rolling over several times in the same field, severely injuring himself and his own mechanic. The Marquis survived just long enough to take full responsibility for the crash before he died; his mechanic died shortly afterwards. Panhards finished up first and second, adding to their reputation, but their success was lost in the sombre mood at the finish.

The name Panhard-Levassor was further enhanced ten days later in a race from Paris to Bordeaux. Their cars were painted red, white and blue, representing French colours. Near Angoulême, Émile Mors collided with a horse and cart. He and his mechanic Toussaint were thrown out, and Mors broke his collarbone. Levegh, driving another Mors, stopped to assist, lost time, and later dropped out. Panhard took the first three places, de Knyff winning with a total elapsed time of 15 hours 15 minutes. (Three years earlier in 1895, Émile Levassor had taken as much as 22 hours 23 minutes to reach Bordeaux.)

In July came the race that all the drivers had been waiting for: the first-ever international

21

event – six days and 889 miles from Paris, via Belgium, to Amsterdam and back to Paris. But as the time for the start approached, the chief engineer of the Paris police, M. Bochet, intervened. No doubt unwilling to countenance the possibility of further fatalities, he informed the Auto Club de France (ACF) that under a local bylaw all the racing cars would have to submit to examination by him. When the drivers presented their cars to him, he rejected most of them. The outraged drivers announced that they would race anyway, whereupon Bochet called in the French army to provide a troop of cavalry to accompany him up to the start. Determined to race, the Club moved the start to Villiers in Seine-et-Oise, outside Bochet's jurisdiction. Drivers towed their cars to Villiers behind horses or put them on trains, and Amédée Bollée moved the original stock of fuel by horse and cart. Bochet retreated to Paris in thwarted impotence.

At 8.30 the next morning Charron started first; the rest of the 48-strong field followed at 30-second intervals. Charron set a cracking pace, Hourgières right on his tail, until a seized engine caused Hourgières a 15-hour delay and Léonce Girardot slipped into second place in another Panhard. After 183 miles at the end of the first day, Charron was leading Girardot by 12 minutes 44 seconds at an average speed of 32 mph.

Thirty cars set off the next morning for Nijmegen. On the day, Hourgières was fastest although he could never make up the time lost. François Giraud, for Bollée, was first to arrive in Amsterdam the following day, managing also the best time for the stage and so leading overall by 3½ minutes.

After a day's rest in Amsterdam they set off back to Paris. The race settled down into a battle between Charron and Girardot, with Giraud still a threat. At the end of day four Charron was leading. But by the end of day five Girardot had taken a 9-minute lead after a neck-and-neck battle with Giraud, who overturned – although he managed to right the Bollée and reach Verdun with only a fifth of a second between them for the stage.

At the start of the last stage the scene was set for a climactic finish. But the organizers had reckoned without the resolve of M. Bochet, who let it be known that any driver whose car had not passed his examination would be arrested on arrival. The ACF moved the finish to Montgeron, outside Paris.

The race was finally decided on punctures. Charron had four, making up 30 minutes on his rival Girardot who had many more, and came second; Giraud was third. When the dri-

ABOVE: Fernand Charron, in the Panhard-Levassor, No. 1, preparing to overtake François Giraud's racing Bollée during the Paris–Amsterdam–Paris race. Charron won the 889-mile race in 33 hours 4 minutes 53 seconds at an average speed of 26.9 mph, confirming his reputation as the leading driver of his day. His Panhard-Levassor was a new four-cylinder 8-hp model, one of the first racing cars to be fitted with a steering wheel rather than a tiller. Its victory was a great coup for the firm. Giraud was the first driver to arrive in Amsterdam, but finished the race third.

MILESTONES

The 100 kilometres record was broken on 22 July by Jamin driving a Bollée. He took 1 hour 53 minutes 15 seconds, an improvement of 3½ minutes.

The winner of the 1896 Marseilles race, Mayade, was killed on 17 September in a collision with a horse and cart in a touring car near Biarritz.

The first classification of cars came in the Marseilles–Nice race of 6–7 March: Heavy Cars were over 400 kilograms, Light Cars 200–400 kilograms.

The first American driver to race in Europe was George Heath, who lived in Paris, and who came 13th overall in the Paris–Amsterdam race.

Levegh won a 79-mile race specifically for Mors drivers on 20 October. The name was an anagram of the surname of Pierre Velghe that he used for racing.

On 27 November *La France Automobile* organized a 1.8-kilometre hill climb at Chanteloupe. Camille Jenatzy won in an electric car.

vers arrived at Montgeron, the officials wanted them to go on to Versailles for the benefit of the crowd, but most felt too tired and too wet. Charron and Girardot at first refused but, on hearing of the disappointment in the crowd, relented and put in an appearance. Possibly sensing that the arrest of such national heroes might be imprudent, Bochet stayed his hand. It was the climax of a great year's racing for Panhard-Levassor, whose name reverberated through the press boosting sales not only in France but throughout Europe.

On 18 December, Paul Méyan of *La France Automobile* magazine decided to organize a different kind of race – a timed run over a two-kilometre course marked out on a flat, straight stretch of road near Achères. The intention was to measure the top speed of the cars. Competitors were timed over the first kilometre from a standing start, then over the second with a flying start.

Count de Chasseloup-Laubat, driving a 40-hp electric car, was fastest at 39.3 mph – well ahead of Loysel in a Bollée. The innovation caught on immediately. On hearing of the Count's triumph, Camille Jenatzy – who had missed the trial – swiftly challenged him to a 'duel' over the same course, to be held within a month. Always the sportsman, de Chasseloup-Laubat accepted (>1899), and a new competition between drivers had begun – a competition that was to be for the land speed record, a race to see who could be the fastest man on Earth.

ABOVE: Fernand Charron, born in France in 1866, started his racing career as a cyclist on Clément bicycles. He crashed a Panhard in his first motor car race, the 1897 Marseilles–Nice–La Turbie contest. He won the 1898 Marseilles–Nice race, as well as the Paris–Amsterdam–Paris (*RIGHT*).

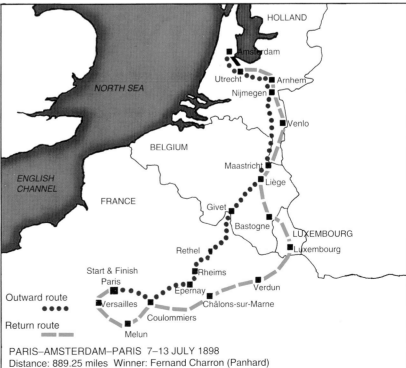

Outward route ••••

Return route – – –

PARIS–AMSTERDAM–PARIS 7–13 JULY 1898
Distance: 889.25 miles Winner: Fernand Charron (Panhard)

Le départ des automobiles pour la Course du tour de France

Deuxième année. — N° 31.   Huit pages : CINQ centimes   Dimanche 30 Juillet 1899.

LE PETIT MÉRIDIONAL
Supplément Illustré du Dimanche

ABONNEMENTS   ANNONCES
France, Algérie, Tunisie. 2 fr. • 3fr.50   POUR LA PUBLICITÉ S'ADRESSER
Étranger (Union postale). 2 fr. 50 / 5 fr.   Direction, Rédaction, Administration : Rue Henri-Guinier, MONTPELLIER   À Montpellier : Rue Henri-Guinier.
À Paris : 131, rue Montmartre.

mph. Jenatzy would not give up. He built a new car named 'Jamais Contente', embodying his restless spirit, and arrived – alone this time – on 1 April to try again. Unhappily, he started before the timekeepers were ready, and because his car could not manage more than one run on a single set of batteries he was obliged to pack up for the day. He came back again on 29 April – when everything went according to plan. Jamais Contente managed an overall speed of 65.75 mph.

The power of petrol engines was increasing.

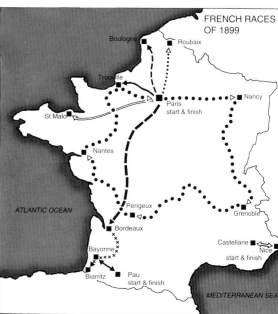

FRENCH RACES OF 1899

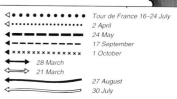

Tour de France 16–24 July
2 April
24 May
17 September
1 October
28 March
21 March
27 August
30 July

ABOVE: At 8 am on Sunday 16 July competitors line up for the start of the Tour de France. Fernand Charron was first away, in his 16-hp Panhard; the other 18 cars, four voiturettes and 25 motorcycles followed at 30-second intervals.

RIGHT: 'Avis' driving a 20-hp Bollée in the Tour de France. Four Bollées began the race, but only one finished; 'Avis' was among those forced to drop out.

The impending speed duel between Camille Jenatzy and Count de Chasseloup-Laubat (>1898) caught the public imagination, and on 17 January the course at Achères was lined with spectators. Jenatzy covered the standing kilometre in 68 seconds, and the flying kilometre in 54 seconds – beating de Chasseloup-Laubat's existing record by 7 seconds, with an overall speed of 41.4 mph. The Count replied with a total run of 1 minute 52 seconds (43.7 mph) even though his engine burned out 200 metres from the finish and he coasted to the line. Jenatzy repeated his challenge, and Chasseloup-Laubat accepted.

On 27 January Jenatzy managed a time of 1 minute 42 seconds – exactly 50 mph. But on this occasion de Chasseloup-Laubat's engine burned out on the start line. At the rematch on 4 March, de Chasseloup-Laubat brought the time down to 1 minute 27.4 seconds – 57.6

The cars in the 1898 Paris-Amsterdam race typically developed between 6 and 8 horsepower, but by early 1899 the cars attained between 16 and 20 hp – making it possible to race from Paris to Bordeaux in a day.

For this race the 28 entrants were to start en masse, instead of at timed intervals, but as they all rushed to snatch the best position on the road a huge cloud of dust shrouded them all. Georges Lemaître, unable to see properly, drove his Peugeot into the back of Gilles Hourgières' Panhard. Lemaître's mechanic was badly injured as he tried to jump clear.

The Panhards soon exerted their superiority, filling 11 of the first 13 places. Fernand Charron won, in 11 hours 43 minutes 20 seconds – just over half the time it had taken Émile Levassor to cover the distance in 1895.

In July the ACF held the longest race till then: the epic 1,378-mile Tour de France. Charron led the way during a week of relentless pressure for the drivers – not least in avoiding the packs of dogs that chased them through every village. The route was punctuated by level crossings, which damaged wheels and suspensions. Outside Nancy, at a hill known as Les Baraques, the road was unusable and the drivers had to find an alternative way into town.

Under such conditions the field thinned out steadily. Those who survived did so only by showing extraordinary stamina and ingenuity. When Léonce Girardot broke a wheel, he borrowed another from a farmer's cart. Charron arrived in Aix having driven for miles with both front springs broken. Jenatzy smashed a wheel at speed and finished up in a ditch; although he had no hope of finishing the stage in time he repaired the damage and pressed on. When a bearing cover broke on Charron's Panhard at Le Mans he was left with only reverse gear – and drove the next 25 miles backwards to finish the stage.

It was another triumph for Panhard: René de Knyff won, Girardot only five minutes behind, followed by de Chasseloup-Laubat.

LEFT: Camille Jenatzy with his electric car, 'Jamais Contente' ('Never Satisfied'), at Achères on 29 April. Two motors mounted on the rear axle were powered by batteries inside the car's cigar-shaped body. The motors drove the wheels direct.

MILESTONES

The first woman to take part in a motor race was Mme Labrousse, who came fifth in the three-seater class in the Paris–Spa race on 1 July.

On 30 August Freelan O. Stanley, driving his steam car, won the first Climb to the Clouds, an 8-mile hill climb up Mount Washington, New Hampshire.

In the Paris–Ostende race on 1 September, a massed start was tried. When all nine starters reached a bend together, one crashed, trying to overtake.

Alexander Winton challenged Fernand Charron – Europe's top driver – to a 1,000-mile race. Charron put up 20,000 francs, but the duel never took place.

The Automobile Club of America (ACA) was established as the official body to represent American racing at an international level.

On 25 February Marcel, Fernand and Louis Renault founded Renault Frères at Billancourt, near Paris, with a capital of 60,000 gold francs.

Up to the turn of the century, James Gordon Bennett was best known as the newspaper publisher who sent Henry Stanley to find David Livingstone in Africa. In 1900 he turned his attention to motor racing. By financing an international event he hoped to stimulate manufacturers outside France to improve their cars through racing, particularly in his native United States. Entries were limited to three cars from each country. They had to be built entirely in the country they represented, and entered by that country's national automobile club rather than by a manufacturer. The task of organizing the first race went to the Automobile Club de France (ACF), and the route chosen was from Paris to Lyons, but thereafter the country whose cars won had the right to stage the next race.

There was resistance to the idea in France, whose industry could produce several teams – whereas most other countries found it difficult to produce a complete car. The ACF balloted its members to select three drivers, rather than cars. They chose Fernand Charron, René de Knyff and Léonce Girardot – all Panhard enthusiasts – which caused immediate controversy as Mors, whose cars were increasingly competitive, felt slighted. Mors announced that it would enter unofficially and race alongside the Panhards. Belgium entered Camille Jenatzy in a Snoek-Bolide; Germany, Eugen Benz in a Benz; and America entered two Wintons driven by Alexander Winton and Anthony Riker (>1896).

The Gordon Bennett race was nearly cancelled before it was run. Public hostility to racing on public roads was growing, and it reached a peak as a result of a race from Paris to Roubaix. A large crowd – including the Deputy of the Department, M. Bos, and his wife – gathered at a right-angled bend just outside Paris, clustering on the outside of the corner. Disaster struck when two competitors approached almost together. The first, Martin, entered the corner too fast, going wide, and the second, Dorel, tried to pass him on the inside. Instead he collided with Martin. Both cars crashed into the crowd, injuring dozens of spectators including Mme Bos, whose leg was broken.

Two days later, the Prefect of Seine-et-Oise banned racing in the Department. Then the Secretary of the Interior, M. Demagny, circulated prefects throughout France, instructing them to submit any requests to hold races to him. Racing was effectively banned in France. But as the political influence of the motor industry and the huge popularity of racing were marshalled in its defence, the government's resolve weakened. French pride in a world-beating industry was at stake; Mme Bos' leg healed, a small race was run without mishap, and racing began again.

Five cars started in the Gordon Bennett race, plus the unofficial Mors being driven by Levegh. Benz withdrew because of tyre problems, and Riker's Winton was not ready. Embarrassingly for the organizers, Levegh took the lead and steadily increased it to half an hour over the three Panhards, who were

RIGHT: The dawn of a new century saw increasing public interest in motor racing. Michelin, the tyre manufacturer, recognized this by incorporating motor racing tiles as a motif in its headquarters building in London (now used partly as the restaurant, *Bibendum*). The illustration shows Levegh in a 24-hp Mors, winner of the Paris–Toulouse–Paris race of July 1900.

PARIS-TOULOUSE
1900

LEVEGH sur MORS

James Gordon Bennett (*RIGHT*), publisher of the *New York Herald*, donated the silver trophy (*BELOW*) to encourage international motor competition. It was a challenge to French domination, but the first winner was from France – Fernand Charron (*BELOW*) in a 24-hp Panhard-Levassor. National racing colours (*BOTTOM*) were established in this race.

followed by Jenatzy and, far behind, Winton. All the drivers had problems. Charron bent his rear axle driving over a gutter so that Henri Fournier, acting as his mechanic, had to keep a steady trickle of oil on the chains to keep going. Girardot's steering had to be repaired, then he lost his way near Orléans and fell back. De Knyff retired when his top gear stripped; Jenatzy was plagued with minor faults and retired too; Winton dropped out with a broken wheel; and Levegh had mechanical problems.

Charron took the lead. Suddenly, ten miles from the finish, a large dog charged his car as he was doing 60 mph downhill. It went under the front wheels and finished up jammed in the steering. The Panhard left the road, crossed a ditch and a field, then spun round on to the road again. Fournier removed the dead dog and restarted the engine, but the water pump had broken off its mounting, so he had to hold the drive against the flywheel to keep water circulating. They limped to the finish, Fournier alternately trickling oil on the chains and pumping water. But for their persistence the Gordon Bennett race would have been won by the maverick Levegh, who was second, well ahead of Girardot.

Levegh took his revenge in the main ACF race from Paris to Toulouse and back in July. His Mors outclassed the Panhards. With an average speed of 40.2 mph, he won from Pinson for Panhard, second at 37.7 mph. Panhard had been beaten at last.

MILESTONES

The first circuit race in France was held on 18 February from Melun, and was the Course du Catalogue – the six classes were organized according to price.

On 14 April a Ladies Race was staged at the Ranelagh Club, near London. Miss Wemblyn won in a 6-hp Daimler Parisienne from three other women.

A. L. Riker won the first road race on Long Island over 50 miles from Springfield to Babylon and back on 18 April in his electric car at 24.3 mph.

On 1 July a road race was held on a 136-mile circuit from Padua through Treviso and back to Padua. The winner was Coltelletti in a Panhard.

Vincenzo Lancia and Felice Nazzaro, in Fiats, were fastest in the Padua race, but were disqualified because spectators pushed them on a hill.

Total French car production in 1900 was 1,450: 400 De Dions, 350 Peugeots, 300 Panhards, 150 Richards, 150 De Dietrichs, and 100 Mors (>1903)

THE COMPETITORS' NATIONAL RACING COLOURS			
		GREAT BRITAIN	6
BELGIUM	2	GERMANY	3
FRANCE	5	UNITED STATES	4

1901

The trend towards more powerful, specialized racing cars accelerated. Panhard went to 7.4 litres and 40 hp, and Mors to 10 litres and 60 hp; weight increased from around 1,000-1,200 kilograms to 1,400-1,500. Critics pointed out that such monsters did little to advance the technology of the touring car. They were undoubtedly faster, but such big cars were hard on tyres – and the time lost in changing them was frequently greater than that gained by the extra speed.

Categories based on weight rather than engine size were introduced for the first time in the Paris-Bordeaux race. Heavy Cars weighed over 650 kg (and were typically 40-60 hp); Light Cars from 400 to 600 kg (closer to touring cars at 12-20 hp); Voiturettes from 250 to 400 kg (around 8 hp); and Cyclecars less than 250 kg. The advocates of smaller engines wanted to impose an upper weight limit, and on 15 June they posted a victory when the Commission Sportive decided that from 1902 the limit would be 1,000 kg.

Entries for the second Gordon Bennett race were very few, so the Auto Club de France (ACF) ran it at the same time as the Paris-Bordeaux race. The French team was Fernand Charron and Léonce Girardot, both of them in Panhards, and Levegh in his usual Mors. A German challenge was promised, but it petered out. Napier & Sons produced a huge 17-litre

MILESTONES

The Nice-Salon-Nice race over 243 miles on 25 March was won by the Daimler works driver Christian Werner in a 35-hp Mercedes at 36 mph.

The first track race in Britain was a one-mile handicap held on the Crystal Palace cycle track on 8 April. Charles Jarrott won in a Panhard.

Alexander Winton set a record of 57.8 mph for the new one-mile dirt track at Cleveland, Ohio, in the Winton Quad – a car of his own design.

Henry Ford won $1,000 for beating the favourite, Alexander Winton, on the Detroit Driving Club's one-mile oval track at Grosse Pointe in October.

Speaking about his victory later in life, Ford is reported to have said: 'Winning a race or breaking a record was the best kind of advertising.'

On 30 November, 25,000 people lined the Ocean Parkway in New York, to see Henri Fournier in a Mors win a measured-mile contest at 69.5 mph.

50-hp car for Selwyn Edge, but his British tyres proved inadequate for the job and he fitted French tyres instead, which disqualified him from the Gordon Bennett race – so he drove in the Paris-Bordeaux.

Levegh took the lead, followed by Girardot and Carl Voigt in Panhards, then Henri Fournier in another Mors. Edge managed fifth place in the early stages, until he dropped out with a faulty clutch; Levegh then had to give up following gearbox problems. Fournier took the lead, and won for Mors at 53 mph. Maurice Farman was second for Panhard at 49 mph. François Giraud won the Light Car class for Panhard at an average speed of 40.2 mph, with Paul Baras second. (Baras arrived in Bordeaux his engine lashed to the car with rope after the mountings failed.) Once Charron and Levegh were out, only Girardot remained in the Gordon Bennett race. He also finished ninth overall in the Paris-Bordeaux race – at 36.6 mph slower than Giraud in the Light Car class. Even the voiturettes of Louis and Marcel Renault managed 34 mph.

The big race of the year was another epic:

from Paris to Berlin – 687 miles over 3 days; 110 cars through 53 control points in France, Belgium and Germany. It was superbly organized. Soldiers lined much of the route to control spectators, but they could not control the dogs which caused numerous accidents. And dogs were not the only problem. Many drivers cornered far too fast, or lost control when a tyre burst at high speed, or collided with each other as one tried to overtake. At Monchenot, just outside Rheims, a small boy wandered into the middle of the road to watch a car disappear from view. The next car hit him at full speed and he died instantly.

The biggest problem was dust. Degrais, driving a Mercedes, was right up close behind Gilles Hourgières on a straight stretch of road, unable to see anything ahead for the dust cloud. Instead, he looked up, steering by the tops of the trees. Sadly they went straight on at a point where the road turned left, and he drove straight over the ditch into a field, rolling over several times and badly injuring his co-driver, Baron de Schwyter.

Fournier led throughout the race, followed closely by René de Knyff, Girardot and Maurice Farman in Panhards, until Farman dropped out after colliding with a private car at Spandau, just outside Berlin. Twenty-thousand spectators gathered to see Fournier finish on a horse-racing track. He did a single circuit at full speed, then pulled up at a dais where he was presented with a laurel wreath by the President of the German motoring association.

Amid all the celebrations, the death of the little boy in Monchenot was not forgotten. Deputies in the French parliament wanted the top speed of racing cars limited, but the government took even stronger action and altogether banned racing on the roads of France.

Fernand Charron's Panhard (**TOP LEFT**) has the road to itself in the Paris-Bordeaux race, and Chaucard, also in a Panhard, is untroubled by crowds as he passes through Florenville on the Belgian border in the Paris-Berlin race (**LEFT**). Both races were won by Henri Fournier (>1919) in a 60-hp Mors (**ABOVE**): he averaged 44.1 mph to Berlin and 53 mph to Bordeaux. Victory was by a slender margin: shortly after the finish one of the drive chains on his Mors broke.

BELOW: Engine size and horsepower increased steadily in the first six years of motor racing.

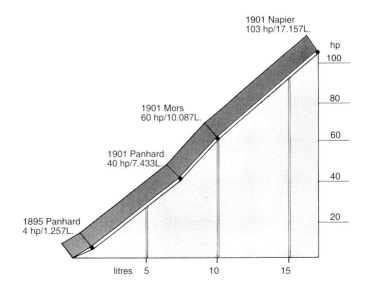

1901 Napier
103 hp/17.157L.

1901 Mors
60 hp/10.087L.

1901 Panhard
40 hp/7.433L.

1895 Panhard
4 hp/1.257L.

hp
100
80
60
40
20

litres   5   10   15

Britain's first success in motor racing came in 1902. Charles Jarrott in a 13.6-litre 70-hp Panhard (*RIGHT*) won the Circuit des Ardennes at an average speed of 54 mph. Selwyn Edge (*BELOW RIGHT*) won the Gordon Bennett Cup in a 30-hp Napier at an average 31.8 mph.

Despite the French government's total ban (>1901), the Auto Club de France (ACF) planned a motor race from Paris to Vienna. The Austrian government agreed, and the Swiss authorities allowed the competitors through their country – provided there was no racing. An ACF delegation then pleaded with the French government for just one more great race, and a 'tour' with neutral stages was eventually agreed. The Gordon Bennett race (> 1900) was run concurrently with the Paris-Vienna race, but the rules specified a maximum of 650 kilometres (396 miles), so the winner would be the fastest to Innsbruck.

The French Gordon Bennett team comprised Henri Fournier in a Mors (>1901), and Léonce Girardot and René de Knyff in Panhards. Britain challenged with Selwyn Edge in a 30-hp Napier, and Montague Graham-White and Arthur Callan in 45-hp Wolseleys. The field for the Paris-Vienna race totalled 137, the numbers swollen by entries for the Light Car class (>1901) and increased enthusiasm from wealthy amateur drivers such as Baron de Forest and Count Zborowski in Mercedes, the American William K. Vanderbilt (>1904) in a Mors, and his countryman George Heath driving a Panhard.

Fournier started first. Once he was on his

MILESTONES

Panhard's new car, built to conform with the weight limit of 1,000 kilograms, was not only 200 kg lighter but also 30 hp more powerful at 70 hp.

The American Automobile Association (AAA) was formed in Chicago in March. The AAA National Champion was elected each year by sports writers.

On 13 April the flying kilometre record (>1899) was raised to 75.06 mph on the Promenade des Anglais at Nice by Léon Serpollet in a steam car.

The Circuit du Nord on 15-16 May was designed to promote alcohol as a fuel. The results showed instead that petrol produced greater speed.

American interest in road racing increased after the Circuit des Ardennes: William K. Vanderbilt was third in a Mors, George Heath sixth in a Panhard.

Barney Oldfield, a racing cyclist, won the 5-mile Manufacturers' Challenge Cup on 23 October at Grosse Pointe in Henry Ford's car, the '999'.

way, spectators rushed to board a special train for Belfort at the end of the first stage. Near Nangis the railway ran alongside the road, and to the passengers' delight they arrived to see Fournier pass them at around 80 mph. Fournier then broke a gear shaft, however, and de Knyff took over the lead on the first day.

In the Gordon Bennett race, Girardot and the Wolseleys dropped out early, so when de Knyff's differential broke in neutral-stage Switzerland, Edge was alone. On the second racing stage from Bregenz to Salzburg (both in Austria), the amateur drivers did well against the professionals, and the Light Cars outperformed the Heavy Cars in the mountains. Louis Renault was leading when Baron Pierre de Crawhez collided with his car at the control in Innsbruck, breaking a wheel. Renault and his mechanic, François Szisz (>1906), made new spokes and rejoined the race but lost the lead. His brother Marcel, and J. Edmond in a light Darracq, finished the stage faster than all the Heavy Cars, although de Forest still led overall. Edge ran off the road before Innsbruck and had to be helped back on by spectators. A protest was lodged, but de Knyff sportingly brushed it aside – giving Britain victory in the Gordon Bennett Trophy.

Just after 2 pm, Marcel Renault arrived at the finish on a trotting track outside Vienna – but in his excitement drove around the track the wrong way. He went round again the right way, and finished just ahead of Count Zborowski. The Count's Mercedes was fastest overall, but he was penalized for not observing customs controls. So Renault won: a 16-hp Light Car had beaten a 40-hp Heavy Car.

There was no more racing in France, so the Belgian Automobile Club organized a new event, the Circuit des Ardennes. A road race but not between towns, it covered six laps of a 53-mile circuit near Bastogne, and attracted 49 starters, most of them Light Cars. De Crawhez led on the first lap in a Panhard; Fernand Gabriel in a Mors was second; and in third place was the British driver Charles Jarrott, also in a Panhard. De Crawhez continued in the lead until he collided with Coppée whom he was lapping at the time, breaking both front wheels. Jarrott and Gabriel then contended closely for the lead, only 1½ seconds separating them at the start of the last lap. A broken drive chain on Gabriel's car decided it: Jarrott won by nine minutes.

The Circuit des Ardennes was the first major race on a closed-road circuit, but it clearly offered advantages. With no controls and plenty of overtaking it was a safer and more competitive format, and both drivers and spectators loved it.

BELOW: Marcel Renault arrives in Vienna, winning the race from Paris at an average 38.9 mph. His 16-hp car was designed by M. Viet, who had moved to Renault from De Dion.

Louis Renault was one of the pioneers of the move from chain-drive to shaft-drive. The principles of the system on his 14-hp car (ABOVE) have endured to the present day: the gear box behind the engine connected to the differential by a prop shaft, with enclosed drive shafts to the wheels.

Road racing had never been allowed in Britain, but Selwyn Edge's victory in the Gordon Bennett race (>1902) gave the British motoring association an opportunity it was determined not to miss – even though it meant getting an Act passed by Parliament. Popular support was immense, and in the search for a suitable venue, Ireland – with its sparsely populated areas – was an obvious candidate. Supported by Irish members of parliament and business interests in the area, a circuit near Athy (18 miles south of Kildare) was suggested, and a huge petition presented by the club to Parliament, which passed the Bill on 14 March. The race date was set for June, on a closed circuit of roads following the Belgian model (>1902).

Closed-circuit racing was clearly the way ahead, but the Auto Club de France (ACF) continued to lobby for its epic tradition of racing from town to town. For 1903, the Club planned an even more ambitious event, from Paris to Madrid. King Alfonso of Spain consented, and because there had been no tragedies during the Paris-Vienna race (>1902), the French government finally gave way to the pressure. The race was planned in three stages: first to Bordeaux along the traditional route, then via Bayonne on the Atlantic coast, and Vitoria to Madrid.

Entries totalled a staggering 316, of which 275 started – 112 Heavy Cars, 64 Light Cars, 40 voiturettes and 59 motorcycles. To avoid weight, the cars were stripped to the barest minimum: the chassis were drilled with holes, and the drivers were expected to race for hundreds of miles sitting on a plank. Engine power was up, and stories of the speed of racing cars fuelled public interest. Three million spectators lined the route to Bordeaux, and more than 100,000 turned out for the start. When Charles Jarrott was waved away, the first to go, he was faced with a wall of humanity. He drove into it, and it parted and closed up again behind him.

The rest of the field left at one-minute intervals, but it was so large that by the time the final car set off the leaders were 135 miles on their way. Louis Renault took the lead early on in his lightweight 30-hp Light Car and, on the stretch into Chartres, averaged around 90 mph while all the star drivers of the day tried with every last ounce of power to catch him.

This time the ACF's luck ran out – accidents happened thick and fast. As Marcel Renault (>1902) was trying to pass Léon Théry at Couhé Verac, his view obscured by dust, he ran off the road, hit a tree at around 80 mph, and turned over. His mechanic was severely injured and died in hospital soon afterwards. The British driver Lorraine Barrow swerved to avoid a dog, also hit a tree at 80 mph, and although he survived, his mechanic Pierre Rodez was killed. Philip Stead and Joseph Salleron raced neck-and-neck for 150 miles, then collided near Montguyon. Both cars crashed, Stead was badly injured; Madame du Gast – the only lady in the race – stopped to render first aid. Approaching a level crossing too fast in his Wolseley, Leslie Porter aimed for a field instead; his car rolled over, hit a house, and caught fire. Nixon, his mechanic, was killed. Delayney overturned. Gras crashed into a level-crossing barrier. Beconnais and Jeandre collided. Lt-Col. Mark Mayhew's steering broke: he hit a tree and finished up injured in a ditch. Trying to avoid a spectator in the middle of the road, G. Richard also finished up in a ditch.

Spectators had difficulty allowing for the

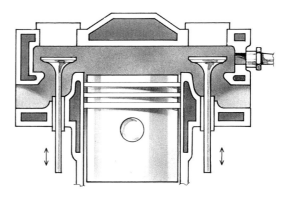

BELOW: Lorraine Barrow at the wheel of his 45-hp De Dietrich in the Paris-Madrid race. He was one of several drivers to crash during the race.

Up to 1901, inlet valves were opened by the suction of the piston's downstroke pulling against a spring, then closed by the upstroke; Mercedes introduced mechanically operated inlet valves (*LEFT*) which were more efficient over the increased rpm range which arose once engine speeds could be varied by a throttle valve on the carburettor.

ABOVE: Marcel Renault and his mechanic died from injuries sustained when they hit a tree at 80 mph in the Paris–Madrid race. They were driving a 30-hp Renault (LEFT: at speed earlier in the race). Marcel's brother Louis – who was the first driver to arrive in Bordeaux – withdrew the Renault team, but in any case the race was abandoned on safety grounds.

speed of the cars. In Angoulême, a small boy ran out from a group of spectators in the path of Tourand's car approaching at speed. A soldier on crowd-control duty darted out in an attempt to save him – but the car hit them head-on and killed them both, crashed, and Tourand's mechanic was also killed.

In Bordeaux another huge crowd was waiting, unaware of the deaths. Louis Renault arrived first, then Jarrott. But the loudest cheers were for Fernand Gabriel in a Mors, who had started in 168th position and arrived third. The mood changed as other drivers arrived bringing news of the carnage they had seen en route. Louis Renault withdrew his team and left immediately for his brother's deathbed. Other drivers also decided not to go on. But the decision was quickly taken out of their hands, as the French and Spanish governments banned further racing. The cars were not even allowed to be driven back to Paris:

MILESTONES

At the Daytona Beach Trials in Florida on 28 March, Alexander Winton achieved 69 mph for the flying mile in his Winton Bullet.

At the La Turbie Hill Climb at Monte Carlo, Count Zborowski was killed when he crashed, cornering too fast in one of the new 60-hp Mercedes.

Louis Renault gave up racing on his brother's death in the Paris-Madrid race. His mechanic, François Szisz, a Hungarian, took over as Renault's top driver.

Count René de Knyff announced his retirement from racing following his defeat by Camille Jenatzy in the Gordon Bennett race.

Barney Oldfield achieved the first circular mile in under one minute at the Indiana State Fair dirt track on 19 June; his speed was 60.4 mph.

Out of a world output of cars of 61,927, 30,204 were French, 11,235 American, 9,437 British, 6,904 German, 2,839 Belgian, and 1,308 Italian.

towed to the railway station by horses they came back by train.

Drivers blamed the spectators, but the lesson – clear for some time, and not only with hindsight – had had to be learned the hard way: after ten years of progress the speed of the cars, the competitiveness of the drivers, the enthusiasm of the spectators and the condition of the roads had together become an impossibly lethal combination.

In Belgium there were second thoughts about staging another Circuit des Ardennes (>1902), but the Auto Club de Belgique and the Belgian government agreed on stricter policing of the closed circuit, and racing went ahead. Instead of one race combining all the different classes, however, this time each class had its own race and the race meeting lasted two days. The voiturette class was run on a circuit at Arlon, rather than at Bastogne, at the request of local businesses.

In the race for Heavy Cars Baron Pierre de Crawhez – the instigator of the race – started first in a Panhard. He quickly discovered that some malicious person had strewn hundreds of nails on the track. Charles Jarrott, the previous winner, was a victim of the nails: he retired with tyre problems on the second lap. De Crawhez managed to avoid the worst of the nails, and led to the finish. In the Light Car race during the afternoon, Paul Baras in a 24-hp Darracq also led from start to finish. Comparisons between the two classes once again showed how the Light Cars were catching up. De Crawhez in the 70-hp Panhard drove the fastest lap in the Heavy Car class at

Camille Jenatzy (*RIGHT*, after the 1899 Tour de France). He won the 1903 Gordon Bennett race in Ireland in July driving a 60-hp Mercedes (*BELOW*), building up a huge lead and winning by almost 12 minutes.

LEFT: Louis Mooers of the United States passing underneath a grandstand erected at Ballyshannon, near Athy, for the Gordon Bennett Cup. All three American drivers dropped out of the race.

ABOVE: Barney Oldfield preparing to test the 65-mph '999' car designed by Henry Ford (right). It was the first car that Oldfield – a former racing cyclist – had driven; 'I'll try anything once,' he said.

56.55 mph; Baras was fastest in the Light Car at 53.63 mph. A further sign of progress in the smaller engines came in the Voiturette class at Arlon the following day, where the cars were fully 10 mph faster than those of their class the previous year.

The fourth Gordon Bennett race revived the flagging series. Selwyn Edge had earned his place in the British team by bringing the race to Britain, and Charles Jarrott for his victory in the Circuit des Ardennes (>1902). Napier was allowed two cars, but an elimination trial was held for the third place in the team. J. Stocks won in another Napier. The French team comprised René de Knyff and Henri Farman in Panhards, and Fernand Gabriel in a Mors. The American Club sent Alexander Winton (>1900) and Percy Owen in Wintons, and Louis Mooers in a Peerless.

Mercedes put up a strong team of cars and drivers, including two works drivers: Otto

Hieronymus and Christian Werner. But under the rules the drivers had to be members of the entering country's automobile club – and both had been refused membership of the German association, on purely social grounds: they were ordinary test drivers, employees. Herr Jellinek of Mercedes was adamant that his drivers should race, and eventually Hieronymus was accepted, but not Werner. Then the three 90-hp cars that had been prepared for the race were destroyed in a factory fire. They were replaced by three stripped-down 60-hp cars, and the final choice of drivers was Baron Pierre de Caters and Camille Jenatzy – both Belgians – and the American amateur Foxhall Keene.

Edge was first off – but was disqualified for a pushed start. Foxhall Keene was last away, but he put in the fastest first lap, a sign of what the Mercedes could really do. On lap 2 Jenatzy took over the lead, with de Knyff just behind. Jarrott's steering broke and he went through a hedge, crashed, and broke his collarbone. De Caters passed the scene of the accident, stopped, found Jarrott was in no mortal danger and drove on, but stopped again in front of the grandstand – at the expense of his own position in the race – to let the crowd know that Jarrott was all right. For this gentlemanly gesture and sportsmanship he was greeted with great applause. Stocks crashed in the third Napier. The American cars were not in the running. De Caters dropped out with back axle problems. And Keene retired at the end of lap 3 with tyre trouble. It was one Mercedes against the three French drivers, who kept up the pressure. But they could not catch Jenatzy, who went on to win by nearly 12 minutes from de Knyff.

Motor racing in North America had lagged a long way behind Europe. There were regular dirt-track races on one-mile circuits at Brighton Beach and Yonkers near New York, and at Grosse Point near Detroit, and they attracted large audiences, but road racing as a means of publicizing the motor car had never caught on as it had in Europe. Some manufacturers used speed records for publicity purposes, most notably Henry Ford who, on 12 January, drove his Arrow to a world record speed on 91.37 mph on the frozen Lake St Clair. It was not recognized by the Auto Club de France (ACF), the official custodian of the record book, but it attracted attention.

On 27 January, William K. Vanderbilt raised the record officially to 92.2 mph in a 90-hp Mercedes (>milestones). Vanderbilt was 26 years old, and very wealthy. He had raced in Europe, come third in the Circuit des Ardennes (>1902), and driven in the infamous Paris-Madrid race (>1903). He had seen how racing had improved cars in Europe, and realized how far behind the American car industry was. After breaking the world speed record in a European car, he ordered a silver cup from Tiffany's – the Vanderbilt Cup – and presented it to the American Automobile Association (AAA) for the winner of a new road race. The basic idea was the same as for the Gordon Bennett Trophy. The crucial difference was that the first two races had to be held in the United States. He presented the Cup to the AAA rather than to the Automobile Club of America (ACA) because the AAA was more energetic, and the ACA – the US body set up to look after racing – had singularly failed to organize the sport effectively.

The Gordon Bennett race had been reinvigorated by the event held in Ireland (>1903). Following Jenatzy's win then in a Mercedes, Germany was the host nation in 1904, and the German association chose a long circuit of closed roads near Homburg in the Taunus Forest. Eight national teams were entered – from Germany, France, Italy, Britain, the United States, Austria, Belgium and from Switzerland. Racing was at a standstill in France, so it was clearly going to be the race of the year in Europe, and German society rose to make it a truly grand occasion. His Imperial Highness Kaiser Wilhelm II decided to attend, and the date of the race – 17 June – was declared a local public holiday.

The Auto Club de France (ACF) was determined to bring the Trophy back to France. It had been stung by defeats at the hands of Napier (>1902) and Mercedes (>1903), and for 1904 the Committee decided that the best way to find the most competitive team to represent France was to hold an elimination race. The problem was that racing was banned in France (>1903). The Belgians offered the Ardennes circuit, but they had to set a time limit for a decision by 2 March. The ACF was determined to hold the eliminator in France, if possible, so they sent a deputation to see the Prime Minister, M. Combès, with only days to go. The Prime Minister had promised the Deputies that there would be no more racing on French public roads, so he had to have their support if there was to be a change of policy. Once again the political influence of the French motor industry won the day, and permission was given for just one race – on a closed circuit in a sparsely populated and inaccessible area of the Argonne.

RIGHT: The father of American motor racing. William K Vanderbilt, a New York socialite and a keen motorist, founded the Vanderbilt Cup race to encourage the development of cars in the United States.

BELOW: British trials for the Gordon Bennett Cup were held on the Isle of Man; Clifford Earp was successful driving a 55-hp Napier.

The British motoring club had a similar problem. The race at Athy had been a special case, permitted under an Act of Parliament. Rather than go for another Act, the club approached the House of Keys – the parliament of the Isle of Man – over whether it could hold eliminating races there. There was great commercial support for the idea, and permission was granted in a matter of hours. The trials produced few surprises: Selwyn Edge in a Napier, Charles Jarrott in a Wolseley, and Sidney Girling in another made up the team.

Public safety was much improved for the French elimination trials. The roads were sealed off by wooden barriers – and they were

Speed rivals: how French artist Edouard Montaut viewed the drama of the inaugural Vanderbilt Cup race (*ABOVE*). Racing drivers were capturing the imagination of the public, although the fastest men on earth were still the engineers who drove railway trains. The imaginary near-collision in Montaut's illustration features Fernand Gabriel in an 80-hp De Dietrich.

ABOVE: George Heath drives his 90-hp four-cylinder Panhard to victory in the 1904 Vanderbilt Cup at an average 52.2 mph. Heath was born in New York, but he lived in Paris, where he ran a tailor's shop.

MILESTONES

On 12 January Henry Ford reached 91.37 mph in his Arrow on the frozen Lake St Clair. The AAA recognized his record; the ACF did not.

The first man officially to exceed 100 mph was Louis Rigolly, who set a new world record of 103.56 mph at Ostende on 21 July in a Gobron-Brillie.

The first Coppa Florio at Brescia, Italy, on 4 September was won by Vincenzo Lancia in a Fiat. Count Vincenzo Florio was third in a Mercedes.

The most efficient racing car engine of 1904 was the 9.9-litre Richard-Brasier. At 80 hp, its output was 8.1 hp per litre capacity (>1896).

The first mass-produced car was the 'curved-dash Olds', built in Detroit: 5,508 were made in 1904.

It cost $650 and its top speed was 20 mph.

On 14 October *The Automobile* reported that drivers in the Vanderbilt Cup had to contend with nails and broken glass strewn by an ill-wisher on the road.

ABOVE: The 90-hp four-cylinder Mercedes. The German manufacturer supplied cars for both German and Austrian teams in the Gordon Bennett Cup race. Behind the car are: Camille Jenatzy (second from left), Pierre de Caters (fourth from left), Christian Werner (third from right) and Otto Hieronymus (second from right).

tarred. The field was France's finest – but the Panhards all had radiator problems: they overheated and gradually fell back. The first three were Léon Théry in a Richard-Brasier, Joseph Salleron in a Mors, and Henri Rougier in a Turcat-Méry.

Italy sent a team of three Fiats, driven by Vincenzo Lancia, Alessandro Cagno and Luigi Storero. The Belgian club sent Baron Pierre de Crawhez, Augières and Lucien Hautvast in three Pipes. Switzerland withdrew. In America the ACA, which officially entered the US team, never managed to organize an elimination trial and pulled out of the race, vindicating to some extent Vanderbilt's view of it as an ineffective body. Germany wanted to hold trials too, but the German club was fearful that any accident might jeopardize the race itself, so it selected Camille Jenatzy and Pierre de Caters, who had done so well at Athy (>1903), driving Mercedes, and Fritz von Opel driving an Opel which, although made in Germany to comply with the rules, was a very close copy of the French Darracq. The Austrian team included Christian Werner (>1903), John Warden and Edgar Braun, all driving Mercedes, which effectively thus had two teams in the race.

The competition was between Germany, France and Britain. After two laps, Théry led Jenatzy by just one second, the three British cars following until they all retired with mechanical problems. Jenatzy tried everything to pass Théry, but the Frenchman steadily

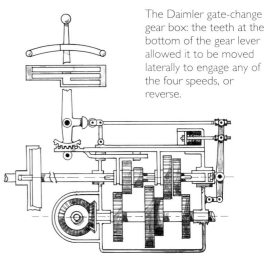

The Daimler gate-change gear box: the teeth at the bottom of the gear lever allowed it to be moved laterally to engage any of the four speeds, or reverse.

pulled ahead to win by 11½ minutes, and the much coveted trophy went back to France, restoring the country's slightly tarnished reputation as Europe's premier racing nation.

With no more races in France, the Circuit des Ardennes in Belgium attracted more than its fair share of entrants. Arthur Duray led on lap one for Darracq. Then Henri Farman passed him in a Panhard, closely pursued by the American driver George Heath, also in a Panhard. Heath took the lead on lap three. Georges Teste then took over in yet another Panhard until both back tyres burst on the last lap. Teste finished the race on bare rims, but Heath passed him to win by 55 seconds – the first American to win a major European race.

Heath returned to the United States something of a hero for the first Vanderbilt Cup. The race was held over ten laps of a 28.4-mile circuit on Long Island on 8 October. In the build-up there had been considerable hostility from local residents, who organized a People's Protective Association in protest. Many of their worst fears were realized when 50,000 boisterous and noisy spectators started looking for the best vantage points from early in the morning of the race.

Thirteen of the 18 starters in the United States' first international road race were European – although most of the drivers were American. The five Mercedes were driven by Al Campbell, George Arents, Alexander Hawley, Karl-Klaus Luttgen and Christian Werner (who had a 90-hp car). There were six French cars: Fernand Gabriel in a De Dietrich; three 90-hp Panhards for Heath, Teste and Henri Tart; an 80-hp Renault for Maurice Bernin; and an 80-hp Clément-Bayard for the 19-year-old Albert Clément. Giuseppe Sartori and William Wallace drove two 90-hp Fiats from Italy. The American cars were stripped-down stock cars, and much less powerful than the specialized European racing cars. Herb Lyttle's Pope-Toledo was 24 hp, as was Charles Schmidt's Packard; Joe Tracey's Royal was 35 hp; 'Spyder' Webb's Pope-Toledo was 60 hp; and Frank Croker's Simplex was 75 hp.

As the race got under way, the circuit was found to have been strewn with broken glass and nails. Campbell was first to go, but Teste took over in the Panhard and led for the first three laps, lapping at 70.9 mph on the first lap. Tracey's Royal broke a drive shaft on the first lap; he and his mechanic, Al Poole, left the circuit, persuaded a local blacksmith to open his shop and fashion a new one for them, then rejoined the race. Arents crashed on lap 2; Carl Mensel, his mechanic, was killed. Werner was delayed at a level crossing by a train, and protested loudly. Teste dropped out on lap 4, and Heath took the lead. In the closing stages Croker's Simplex started to sag in the middle: the chassis had been drilled so much in an attempt to lighten it that it was buckling under the strain – the gearbox was actually scraping along the road.

It was an exciting finish. The first two, Heath and Clément, raced to the end just 1 minute 28 seconds apart. Heath won, to great acclaim. Both at least managed to reach the finishing line. The crowd, which had become unruly, then invaded the circuit, bringing racing to a halt: no other cars succeeded in completing the full distance of the course.

BELOW: Léon Théry on his way to victory for France in the Gordon Bennett Cup race at an average 54.49 mph. He drove a 9.9-litre four-cylinder Richard-Brasier which produced 80 hp. The car was fitted with shock absorbers, which gave it a significant advantage over the second-placed Mercedes, driven for Germany by Camille Jenatzy.

LEFT: René Hanriot in a 30-hp Clément-Bayard light car. In the Circuit des Ardennes, Hanriot set the fastest average speed for this class of cars: 48.5 mph. Adolphe Clément, who founded Clément-Bayard in 1903, is behind the car.

The Automobile Club de France (ACF) had never made any secret of its hostility to the Gordon Bennett Trophy races. The Club still felt that it was unfair for France's huge industry only to have the same representation as the weakest countries, especially when – following the loss of its own epic inter-town races – the eliminator trials for the Gordon Bennett appeared to give the best racing on offer. It wanted a new event, to be known as the Grand Prix de l'Automobile Club de France, open to entry by manufacturers from any country. As a sop to international tradition established by the Gordon Bennett race, the Club suggested that national teams compete for the Trophy in the same race, and *L'Auto* magazine offered a prize of 100,000 francs for the Grand Prix. But when the ACF published its ideas, there were howls of protest from the other racing nations, most notably Britain.

The ACF convened an International Commission to settle the matter. It agreed that the two races would be run separately, and that after the 1905 season it would discuss the problem again. Because it was unlikely that the French government would permit two big races in one year, the ACF temporarily abandoned the Grand Prix – but let it be known that whatever the result of the Gordon Bennett race, the Club would not challenge for it again, and would support only its own Grand Prix.

The British eliminator trials, held again on the Isle of Man, produced a team of Clifford Earp in a six-cylinder Napier, and the Hon. Charles Rolls and Bianchi both in 100-hp Wolseleys.

In France the trials were held on the circuit that was to be used for the race, near Clermont-Ferrand in the Auvergne. The French industry took every advantage, building cars that suited the circuit. They came up with different ideas. Renault looked at the number of

corners and then built an ultra-low-slung car. Darracq built the lightest car he could. And de Dietrich went to the other extreme, building a 130-hp monster in the belief that power was the answer on the hilly circuit.

In the race, all cars finished the first lap; it was in the second that the accidents started. Henri Farman and his mechanic had a lucky escape when their car skidded and disappeared down a ravine: they managed to jump clear, landing in trees. Léonce Girardot and his mechanic had an equally lucky moment when both front wheels came off and they hit a tele-graph-pole. Léon Théry came first and Gustave Callois was second, both in Richard-Brasiers; Arthur Duray was third in a De Dietrich, and together they made up the team.

Mercedes managed to enter two teams again (>1904), one representing Germany – Camille Jenatzy, Pierre de Caters and Christian Werner – and the other representing Austria – Otto Hieronymus, Edgar Braun and Alexander Burton. The United States was represented by Joe Tracey in a Locomobile, and Herb Lyttle and Albert Dingley in Pope-Toledos. But the real challenge to France came from an unex-pected quarter – Italy, which produced three 110-hp Fiats driven by Vincenzo Lancia, Alessandro Cagno and a promising newcomer, Felice Nazzaro.

MILESTONES

On 25 January a British driver, A. E. MacDonald, covered the flying mile at the Daytona Speed Week at 104.65 mph in a 90-hp Napier.

On 24 June Guy Vaughan, driving a Decauville alone, covered 1,000 miles on the Empire City dirt track, New York, in a record 23 hours 33 minutes 20 seconds.

The first 24-hour race was won by the Soules brothers in a Pope-Toledo in July: 828.5 miles, at 34.5 mph on a driving track at Columbus, Ohio.

On 10 September Isotta-Fraschini – a new Italian firm – made its racing debut in the Coppa Florio. Neither of their 120-hp cars finished.

On 14 September the first Tourist Trophy was held on the Isle of Man on a fuel-consumption formula. J. S. Napier won in an 18-hp Arrol-Johnston.

On 17 November F. W. Clemens and Charles Merz drove a National for 24 hours on a dirt track at Indianapolis, Ind., covering a total distance of 1,094.75 miles.

Léon Théry was first to start, and the rest followed at five-minute intervals for greater safety. At the end of lap 1 Théry came past the grandstands first, but – to the horror of the French crowd – Lancia, who had started fourth, had overtaken Earp and Jenatzy and was only 13 minutes behind. This put him actually seven minutes in the lead. Moreover, Nazzaro and Cagno were in third and fourth place. All the Mercedes suffered from suspen-sion problems, and they gradually fell behind. At the end of lap 2, Duray had managed to pass Nazzaro and Cagno but was making no impression on Lancia.

On lap 3 Lancia's radiator was pierced by a stone, and he was out; he wept uncontrollably. Théry took the lead, and Duray dropped back with radiator problems, while Nazzaro and Cagno held on. And that is how the race fin-ished. France had certainly retained the Gordon Bennett Trophy – but the Italians had given them a nasty shock. One consolation for Lancia was that no one bettered his first lap

ABOVE: Vincenzo Lancia in the Gordon Bennett Cup race. His 16.2-litre Fiat developed 110 hp at 1,200 rpm and had a top speed of more than 100 mph. He was forced out by radiator trouble, but his average speed of 52 mph was the fastest in the race.

Léon Théry (**RIGHT**) on his way to a second successive victory in the Gordon Bennett Cup. The race was held on a winding course in the Auvergne region of France. Théry is seen (**ABOVE**) on the climb out of Rochefort. A highly consistent driver, Théry was nicknamed 'the chronometer' for his precision. Less kindly, a collision with a cow in the 1902 Circuit des Ardennes led to another name – 'Mort-aux-vaches' ('Cow-killer').

time, the fastest of the race at 53.93 mph.

The success of the Italians prompted a number of French drivers and manufacturers to enter the second Coppa Florio (>1904), run over a 104-mile circuit at Brescia in northern Italy. It was the brainchild of Count Vincenzo Florio, the son of a wealthy merchant in Palermo, Sicily. He was greatly in favour of individual drivers as entrants, rather than manufacturers, and entered himself, driving a Mercedes. In an extremely close race the French received another unwelcome shock when Carlo Raggio – an amateur, driving an Itala – won. Arthur Duray was second in a De Dietrich, and Lancia third for Fiat. There was an unpleasant scene when Victor Hémery, driving for Darracq, was given fourth place. He believed he had won, and became abusive – for which unsporting behaviour he was nearly banned from racing.

LEFT: Léon Théry drove an 11.3-litre four-cylinder Richard-Brasier in the Gordon Bennett Cup race. The car weighed 994 kg and produced 96 hp. He won at an average 48.46 mph, 16 minutes ahead of Felice Nazzarro in a Fiat.

ABOVE: Charles Rolls drives his 96-hp Wolseley through La Queville in the Gordon Bennett Cup. He was the best-placed British driver, in eighth position with an average speed of 40.4 mph. Rolls co-founded the renowned manufacturing company, Rolls-Royce, with Henry Royce in 1904.

The drivers and their teams then packed up for America and the Vanderbilt Cup. So well had the American manufacturers responded to William Vanderbilt's exhortation to build cars to beat the Europeans that the American Automobile Association (AAA) was forced to stage an eliminator race to pick a team of five. The winner was Albert Dingley in a Pope-Toledo; second was Joe Tracey in a 90-hp Locomobile. The assumption had been that the five fastest would make up the team – but the race commission replaced the third, fourth and fifth fastest on the day with a front-wheel-drive Christie, a steam-powered White, and another Pope-Toledo, causing much bitterness.

The French team consisted of Arthur Duray in a De Dietrich, Louis Wagner and Hémery in Darracqs, François Szisz (>1902, 1906) in a Renault, and the previous year's winner George Heath in a Panhard. Italy sent five

Fiats, for Lancia, Nazzaro, Giuseppe Sartori, Emanuele Cedrino and the American driver Louis Chevrolet. And there were four 120-hp Mercedes from Germany, for Jenatzy and three Americans: Foxhall Keene, Jack Warden and Al Campbell.

The crowd began gathering long before daybreak on 14 October to get to the good vantage points. Some of the farmers who had earlier protested against the race now cashed in, charging spectators up to $50 for the best places. By the time it was due to start there were an estimated 200,000 people lining the Long Island circuit.

Lancia reproduced the promise he had shown in the Gordon Bennett race. Taking the lead in the Fiat, he steadily increased it to 21 minutes over Heath in the Panhard by lap 7. Then he stopped for new tyres. As he prepared to rejoin the race he heard Walter Christie in his Christie approaching. It was no threat to him in the race, but it was notoriously difficult to pass because it had a tendency to swing from side to side at corners.

Lancia pulled out – but the Christie failed to reduce speed, collided with the rear of the Fiat, its front wheels leaping into the air and down again, breaking them both. The Fiat took 40 minutes to repair, and the delay cost Lancia the race.

Hémery won, Heath was second and Tracey third – but they were the only ones to cross the finish line. The huge crowd invaded the circuit, and racing had to be stopped.

According to the rules France should have gone on to stage the next race, now having won the Vanderbilt Cup twice. But the ACF was instead preoccupied with preparations for the first Grand Prix.

Chapter Two
Grand Prix, Brooklands & Building the Brickyard

The year 1906 was a watershed in top-level motor racing. The replacement of the Gordon Bennett races by the Grand Prix marked the end of the pioneering, heroic age, with its emphasis on creating an awareness of the motor car through sporting ideals, and the beginning of a brasher, more professional period in which the economic basis of the sport began to be recognized. The dominant position that France had enjoyed for more than a decade came under pressure from other countries, most notably Italy and Germany but also Britain and the United States, as the motor industries in those countries saw the benefits of racing and put resources into it.

That evolution brought about changes in the men who aspired to be racing drivers. The tradition of the wealthy, often titled, racing drivers continued, but the new stars of the sport were to be found in the increasing number of talented professionals – such as Renault's Hungarian-born mechanic François Szisz, Fiat's ex-apprentice Felice Nazzaro, the Mercedes shop-floor engineer Christian Lautenschlager, and Peugeot's test-drivers Jules Goux, Georges Boillot and Paolo Zuccarelli.

The style of racing changed too. Epic town-to-town road races had been killed off by the tragedy that occurred during the Paris-Madrid race in 1903, and although the Auto Club de France continued to think in terms of long distances on closed circuits, in Britain and America the first short purpose-built tracks were established at Brooklands and Indianapolis. From these futuristic concrete structures, with their banked corners and grandstands from which the spectators see the whole race, a new and separate tradition of track racing began to evolve.

But arguably the greatest change in the years leading up to the Great War was in the evolution of the racing car itself. Between 1906 and 1914 engine size was reduced by around 75 per cent – from 16 litres to 4.5 litres. Over the same period, speeds rose. The Grand Prix Peugeots and Mercedes cars of 1914 were the first real thoroughbred racing cars, and although many features have changed over the intervening years, modern racing engines with their computer controls and space-age materials can be traced directly back to the double overhead camshaft engines that were developed between 1911 and 1913.

Ready for the off: the line up for a 100-mile race on Indianapolis' new brick surface.

Three new races in 1906 marked it as a year of change in motor racing. The most controversial was the Grand Prix, organized by the Auto Club de France (ACF) in an endeavour to reassert France's pre-eminent position in the sport after the extinction of the Gordon Bennett Trophy (>1905). The most innovative was the Coupe de l'Auto, run by *L'Auto* magazine, the first major race staged specifically for voiturettes – cars much smaller than the monsters that had dominated the sport for more than a decade. The most imaginative was the Targa Florio, organized by Count Vincenzo Florio (>1904). To boost the prestige of Italy in motor racing, he created one of the toughest races ever, for production cars, and commissioned its trophy of solid gold.

In the Madonie mountains of his native Sicily, Florio had reconnoitred a 92-mile circuit that started at sea level on the northern coast at Campofelice, then rose 3,600 feet up narrow, twisting roads before descending again to the coast. Three laps put maximum strain on men and machines.

Ten cars made it to the start: a Fiat driven by Vincenzo Lancia; five Italas driven by Alessandro Cagno, Ettore Graziani, George Pope, Victor Rigal and Pierre de Caters; two Clément-Bayards driven by Achille and Maurice Fournier; a Berliet driven by Paul Bablot; and a Hotchkiss driven by Hubert le Blon, whose wife was his riding mechanic.

Lancia led the way, but his brutal driving together with the rough conditions ruptured his petrol tank, and his engine then gave up under the strain. He was not the terrain's only casualty: George Pope's car lost petrol through a fractured fuel pipe and he had to wait until fresh supplies could be delivered. And Achille Fournier hit a boundary stone, smashing his rear axle. After one lap Cagno was leading, but he was constantly under pressure from team-mate Graziani. On the second lap Graziani pulled ahead. The more experienced Cagno recovered on the third lap, to win by 32 minutes after 9 hours 33 minutes of strenuous racing.

In numbers of competitors it was a small race: only six cars finished. Last home were the le Blons, who took more than 12 hours. But the harsh conditions and the remoteness of the Targa Florio captured the imagination of both the public and the racing fraternity – one of motor racing's enduring legends had been born (>1973).

Entries for the Grand Prix in June were far more numerous, and – as the ACF hoped – reflected the strength of the French industry. France fielded ten teams against two from Italy

ABOVE: François Szisz preparing for the start of the ACF Grand Prix. He won the race in a 90-bhp four-cylinder Renault, averaging 62.88 mph over 769.3 miles.

(Fiat and Itala), and one from Germany (Mercedes). The cars represented the culmination of the era of specialized, monster racing cars. Weight was limited to 1,000 kg, but there was still no limit on engine size, and both Panhard-Levassor (>1895) and Lorraine-Dietrich had capacities well over 18 litres. Fiat, Darracq, Itala, Mercedes and Hotchkiss all weighed in at between 14 and 16 litres, and Renault, Clément-Bayard and Brasier at around 12 litres. The smallest was Grégoire, at 7.5 litres one of the first indications of a trend towards smaller cars.

The Grand Prix was to put the city of Le Mans on the motor racing map forever. Eager for the publicity, the city council and hoteliers put up £5,000 to persuade the ACF to run the

ABOVE: François Szisz was born in Hungary in 1873, and came to France in 1900. He joined Renault as a mechanic, riding with Louis Renault in the 1903 Paris–Madrid race before becoming chief tester and the company's principal racing driver (>1970).

The triangular circuit at Le Mans (*BELOW*), used for the first Grand Prix, linked the town with motor racing for ever. The scene in the pits before the race (*BELOW*). With the race held over two days, the cars were kept overnight in a *parc fermé*, guarded by members of the ACF Commission Sportive against sabotage or unauthorized work.

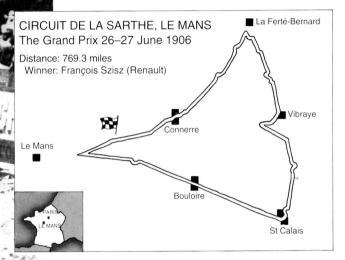

CIRCUIT DE LA SARTHE, LE MANS
The Grand Prix 26–27 June 1906

Distance: 769.3 miles
Winner: François Szisz (Renault)

La Ferté-Bernard

Vibraye

Connerre

Le Mans

Bouloire

St Calais

PARIS
LE MANS

race over a 60-mile circuit to the east of the city. The ACF then spent £14,000 building grandstands and a pit area, erecting paling fences, improving the road surface, and laying wooden roadways to bypass two villages.

The first Grand Prix was run over twelve laps on two days, starting at 6 am on 6 June. René de Knyff, the official starter (>1903), flagged off his old chum Fernand Gabriel, but sadly Gabriel's huge Lorraine-Dietrich stalled on the line and Vincenzo Lancia's Fiat was first out on to the circuit. He maintained this position for the first lap, with Arthur Duray in another Lorraine-Dietrich second, and François Szisz third for Renault (>1903).

Tar had been applied to parts of the surface to improve it, but once the sun was up, the tar melted and the surface broke up. The cars – some of which reached around 100 mph on the long straights – threw up clouds of debris, showering drivers and mechanics with melted tar and pebbles, so much that many required medical treatment afterwards to their battered and swollen faces.

The fastest cars were the Brasiers, but as the day wore on it was Szisz who steadily took the lead. The reason was simple – everybody was going through tyres at a prodigious rate due to

The 1906 Renault

Renault's Grand Prix car, driven by François Szisz (*ABOVE*), used lightweight wire wheels in practice; the tyres had to be slashed off with a knife, then a new inner tube and outer casing fitted and inflated. For the race, Michelin offered all the companies its new system of detachable rims which had a fully inflated tyre and tube fitted, and could be removed and replaced by undoing eight nuts. The new system was heavier, so only the lighter cars could use them without breaking the 1,000-kg weight limit; on balance the 10-minute saving on each tyre change more than compensated for the extra weight and tyre wear.

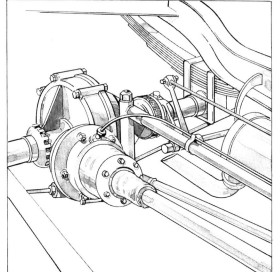

Renault, together with six of the other eleven teams, used shaft drive to replace the traditional chain drive as a means of transmitting power to the rear wheels; Renault used a three-speed gearbox. Both rear wheels were driven continuously, Renault's engineers having decided that with few sharp corners on the Le Mans circuit, a differential would not be needed; double-action hydraulic dampers were also fitted.

the appalling surface. Most had to slash off each old tyre with a knife, then put on a new inner tube and outer casing, using levers, before inflating it. But Renault and Fiat had both fitted a new system of Michelin detachable rims which could be unbolted and bolted back on complete, reducing the time taken by around 10 minutes. Once Szisz was in the lead he made the best use of his advantage by driving consistently, and at the end of the first day he was ahead by more than 17 minutes.

The sixteen cars that finished the first day were locked up in a *parc fermé* for the night, guarded by members of the Commission Sportive to make sure that nobody worked on them or tampered with them. On the second morning some drivers withdrew because they could not face the conditions. The remainder started at intervals equivalent to their positions at the end of day one, with an allowance for their original starting times, so the leader was the first car round each time and the winner would be the first over the finish line.

Driving conditions certainly were worse. The surface was already badly broken up and the roadside was soon littered with more shredded tyres. Tyre changes decided the race. Ever the professional, Szisz used the advantage of the detachable rims to the full again, driving

just fast enough to give him final victory by 32 minutes. The battle for second place between Felice Nazzaro and Albert Clément was closer: they exchanged positions several times before Nazzaro pulled 3 minutes ahead at the finish.

When it was all over, the organizers agreed that two days had been too long, and that the strain of doing all the work themselves had

ABOVE: Georges Sizaire in the 18-bhp Sizaire-Naudin that took him to an impressive victory in the Coupe des Voiturettes at Rambouillet, to the west of Paris. The race followed a gruelling six-day endurance test in

been too great on drivers and mechanics. There was also a feeling that the race had been won by a technological aid, and that the Grand Prix had yet to prove a worthy replacement for the purely sporting ideals of the Gordon Bennett races. Renault demurred. Its name was splashed all over France, and that had a direct effect on sales – between 1906 and 1907 production at the Billancourt factory nearly doubled from 1,600 cars to more than 3,000, and by 1908 it topped 4,600.

The Coupe de l'Auto was held on 12 November. The editor of *L'Auto* was keen to promote engineering innovation rather than engine size, so all voiturettes had to conform to a formula: a cylinder bore of 120 mm for single-cylinder engines, 90 mm for two-cylinder, and a *minimum* weight of 700 kg, to prevent designers from seeking an advantage by making their cars dangerously light.

As a test of stamina the Coupe de l'Auto was more formidable even than the Grand Prix. It lasted a week. For six days drivers had to complete 8 laps of the 20-mile course at Rambouillet, and average a speed of 30 mph over each day. On the seventh day, those who had come through the ordeal qualified for the race proper. Georges Sizaire led from start to finish in his Sizaire-Naudin; Ménart Lucas was second in a Delage, just five minutes behind; and Giosue Giuppone was third for Lion-Peugeot.

The names of Sizaire-Naudin, Lion-Peugeot and Delage were to dominate voiturette racing for the next six years as it grew in prominence. With their highly skilled and very competitive drivers the little cars drew huge crowds, and in their technology they provided a hotbed of innovation that was to transform motor racing at the top level – including the Grand Prix.

BELOW: Arthur Duray and his mechanic cling on to a spare tyre which had worked loose during the Vanderbilt Cup race. Duray finished third in his 130-bhp De Dietrich at an average 60.3 mph.

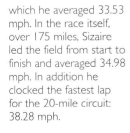

MILESTONES

The ACF accepted Fred Marriot's 121.57-mph record over the flying kilometre in the Stanley Steamer Rocket – but not a 127.6-mph run over a mile.

Following the Florida Speed Week in January, several drivers took part in the first-ever race in Cuba: Demogeot won in a 1904 80-bhp Renault.

which he averaged 33.53 mph. In the race itself, over 175 miles, Sizaire led the field from start to finish and averaged 34.98 mph. In addition he clocked the fastest lap for the 20-mile circuit: 38.28 mph.

To qualify for 'production' status in the Targa Florio, cars had to cost less than 20,000 French francs and be one of at least ten vehicles built.

On 17 August, L. L. Whitman and L. S. Corris arrived in New York having covered the 4,100 miles from San Francisco in a record 15 days 2 hours 12 minutes.

The Tourist Trophy – run on a fuel-consumption formula – was won by the Hon. Charles Rolls in a Rolls-Royce on 27 September with 0.131 gallon left.

When the Italian government refused to provide soldiers to police the Brescia circuit, the meeting was cancelled. Fans rioted in protest.

On 6 October Louis Wagner won the Vanderbilt Cup in a Darracq. Once again the circuit was invaded by the crowd and racing had to be stopped.

In November Vincenzo Lancia founded his own company to build touring cars and racing cars. He continued to drive for Fiat (>1909).

France's position as the foremost country in motor racing had gone more or less unchallenged for a decade. The Auto Club de France (ACF) and the French motor industry had worked together to sustain that position, most notably by sabotaging the Gordon Bennett races (>1905), but in 1907 Europe moved into recession and that coalition began to come under strain. The industry – which bore the cost of producing the specialized cars on which the sport was based – wanted more control. Rival industrial organizations were formed, one headed by the racing pioneer Count Jules de Dion (>1894), to try to wrest power from the ACF. The moves failed, but weakened the French position at a time when it was under challenge from other quarters.

The first challenge to top-class racing came from within France: the growing interest in voiturette racing. The cars were closer in size to those that people could buy, and the names Sizaire-Naudin and Lion-Peugeot were receiving huge publicity. There was an even greater challenge from abroad. Italian cars, most notably Fiat, had given the French industry a nasty shock in the first Grand Prix (>1906) by coming second, and clearly it was only a matter of time before they became even more competitive. Companies such as Fiat, Mercedes and Benz could see the benefits of racing, and wanted races on their own soil. Even in Britain, where racing on public roads was banned, a specially-built race track was under construction at Brooklands (*see* box).

Countries that had their own races could set their own rules and tailor them to the interests of their own industries. In Italy and Germany those interests were perceived to be to bring racing cars closer to touring cars, rather than to compete with the French monsters. When

Moment of victory: Felice Nazzaro and his mechanic Fagnano crossing the line to win the Targa Florio, the first of Nazzaro's three great victories in 1907. The car was a modified 7.4-litre chain-driven Fiat tourer, with a four-cylinder overhead valve engine that developed approximately 60 bhp at 1,200 rpm.

MILESTONES

In January, Fred Marriot crashed at over 190 mph on Daytona beach during a record attempt in the steam-powered Stanley Rocket. He was badly injured.

On 30 May the Tourist Trophy (>1905) was won by E. Courtis in a Rover.

He completed the 241 miles on 9.75 gallons of petrol at an average 28.8 mph.

The first-ever race at Point Breeze, Philadelphia, went to Robert Maynes and J. Brown in an Autocar – 791 miles at an average 33 mph.

In June, Frank Kulick and Bert Lorimer won a 24-hour stock car race at Detroit, averaging 47.29 mph over 1,135 miles in a Model K Ford.

On 25 July John More-Brabazon won the Kaiserpreis class in the Circuit des Ardennes in a

Minerva by 27 seconds from Koolhoven in another.

On 1 September Ferdinando Minoia won the Coppa Florio for Isotta-Fraschini, also in the Kaiserpreis class, over 8 laps of the new 38-mile Brescia circuit.

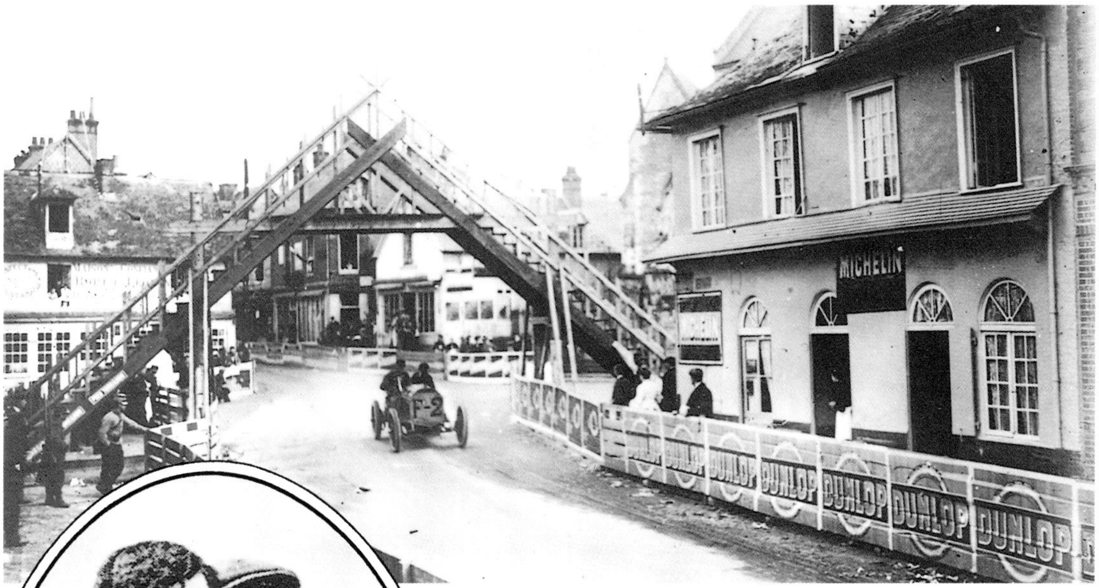
MICHELIN
DUNLOP

LEFT: Nazzaro leading the Grand Prix through Envermeu, a village on the Dieppe circuit; the pedestrian bridge was temporary, put up purely for the race. The racing Fiat was much more powerful than the production car he drove in the Targa Florio; its 16.3-litre engine developed around 130 bhp at 1,600 rpm, giving it a top speed of around 98 mph.

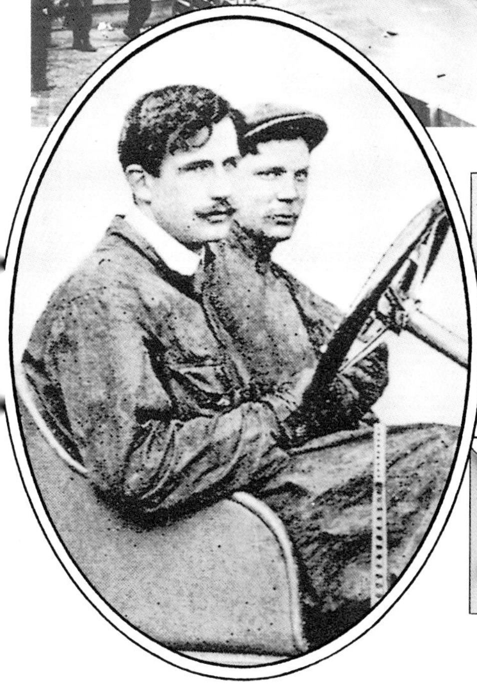

FAR LEFT: Felice Nazzaro, Italy's first great racing driver, came from Turin. He was Count Vincenzo Florio's chauffeur-mechanic before the days of the Targa Florio, and began his career racing against his employer at Favorita Park in Palermo.

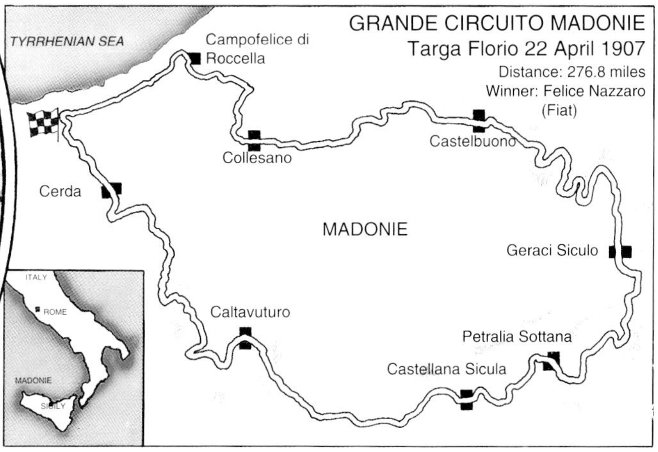
GRANDE CIRCUITO MADONIE
Targa Florio 22 April 1907
Distance: 276.8 miles
Winner: Felice Nazzaro (Fiat)
TYRRHENIAN SEA
Campofelice di Roccella
Collesano
Castelbuono
Cerda
MADONIE
Geraci Siculo
Caltavuturo
Petralia Sottana
Castellana Sicula
ITALY
ROME
MADONIE
SICILY

LEFT: Arguably the toughest road racing circuit in the world, the 92.44-mile Madonie circuit in Sicily. Vincenzo Lancia set the lap record in 1907 at 2 hours 43 minutes 8 seconds: 33.99 mph. There was only 20 seconds' difference between his second and third laps.

the German automobile club announced the Kaiserpreis, a new race for 1907 to be attended by the Kaiser, it set an upper limit on engine size of 8 litres. For the Targa Florio, the formula was more complicated, allowing the bigger cars in but limiting them to four cylinders with a bore of between 120 mm and 130 mm, and a weight of 1,000 kg with an allowance of 20 kg extra for every millimetre above 120 mm.

The season opened with the Targa Florio on 22 April. The stature of the mountain race had been built on the headlines that it had generated the previous year, and the French companies could not afford to stay away. Of the 45 cars lined up at Campofelice, 19 were Italian, 16 French and 10 German.

The dominant theme for the year was clearly going to be rivalry between France and Italy. The Italians made a great start. Vincenzo Lancia shot into his customary lead for Fiat (>1906), holding it for the first lap with Alessandro Cagno just 14 seconds behind in an Itala. Then came Vincenzo Trucco in an Isotta-Fraschini, followed by Felice Nazzaro in another Fiat (>1906) and Ferdinando Minoia for Isotta-Fraschini. The best French performance came from Louis Wagner driving a Darracq in fifth position.

On the second lap Nazzaro took the lead. Wagner began to carve his way through the Italians, including Lancia, to within three minutes of Nazzaro. The French challenge and the closeness of the racing caused great excitement among the spectators – until the Darracq broke a half-shaft and was out of the race, leaving Italian cars to take the first three places: Nazzaro and Lancia for Fiat, and Maurice Fabry for Itala.

The number of entries for the Targa was high, but the ADAC was taken by surprise at the 78 who entered for the Kaiserpreis.

There was strong German representation from Benz, Mercedes, AEG and Opel (one of the cars was driven by Fritz von Opel himself). And as expected, there was a large contingent from France, several Pipes from Belgium, and a single Napier from Britain, driven by Lord Glentworth. The circuit was one of the longest ever closed off for racing – 73 miles through the Taunus forest, starting near Homburg. To cope with the numbers the club decided to hold two heats of two laps on one day, the first 20 in each going through to a final on a second day over four laps.

The Kaiser started the first heat at 4 am in

Hait pages : CINQ centimes

Le Petit Parisien

SUPPLÉMENT LITTÉRAIRE ILLUSTRÉ

DIRECTION : 18, rue d'Enghien (10e) PARIS

Terrible Accident sur le Parcours du Circuit de Dieppe

light rain. Vincenzo Lancia took the lead, followed closely by Fritz von Opel who, much to the delight of the German spectators and the Kaiser, gave the Italian a race. But Lancia steadily pulled ahead and won the first heat by five minutes. The other two Fiat stars, Nazzaro and Wagner (who had recently joined Fiat), dominated the second heat, which was much faster. They were followed closely by C. Deplus, who was third in one of the Pipes.

The race proper, on 14 June, followed the pattern of heat two: Nazzaro and Wagner led, and Lucien Hautvast challenged for Pipe. Lancia was slow at the start, and although he steadily improved his position, he could not catch the leaders. Hautvast briefly took the lead at one point, but Nazzaro took it back to win by less than five minutes.

Three weeks later, the second Grand Prix was run at Dieppe. The ACF had made an overall loss of £3,000 the previous year, so when Dieppe's council guaranteed £4,000 the race was run near by over ten laps of a 47-mile circuit. Rivalry between Italy and France was at a peak, and this was the race to win. National racing colours (>1900), which had not been used since the last Gordon Bennett race (>1905) were revived, adding to nationalist fervour. A shadow was cast over the race during practice when two French drivers, Albert Clément and Marius Pin, were killed in separate crashes; there was a move to call off the race, but to no avail.

The ACF used a formula based on fuel consumption: 30 litres per 100 kilometres (9.41 miles per gallon). Seventeen teams were represented: eleven were French, two Italian, one German, one Belgian, two British cars, and a lone American Christie. There was a slight shift towards smaller cars. Germain used the smallest engine, at 5 litres, but at the other end of the scale there was also the biggest engine ever raced, the Christie, at nearly 20 litres. Some innovation was manifest too: Dufeaux, Porthos and the British Weigels were using eight-cylinder engines.

Lancia went into his customary lead early on for Fiat. Arthur Duray challenged closely in his Lorraine-Dietrich, eventually taking the lead, and keeping it for half the race against repeated challenges from Lancia. There was French dismay when Duray's gearbox seized. Thereafter attention shifted to another Franco-Italian battle between François Szisz in the Renault and Nazzaro, both of whom succeeded in passing Lancia.

The racing was close, the rivalry was thrilling for the spectators, but because of the formula drivers had to be careful with fuel.

Szisz was a conserver; Nazzaro was all flair. The Frenchman carefully husbanded his supply, while the Italian put his foot down and hoped for the best – which paid off. French gloom was intense when Nazzaro roared to victory and Szisz's tank was found to have fuel in reserve.

It was a momentous year for Italy: Felice Nazzaro became a national hero; Fiat became the name to beat, with all the implications for car sales at home and abroad; and Italy was set on a course that led eventually to replacing France as the world's foremost racing nation.

Italian enthusiasm quickly spread to voiturette racing. Count Florio had seen the opening in the market, and he organized the first Coppa delle Vetturette on the Madonie circuit in April. It was won by Louis Naudin, the other half of the Sizaire-Naudin partnership; Florio himself was second. In a Palermo park in August he staged the first Corsa Siciliana Vetturette, which he won, driving a De Dion. Yet another voiturette race on the Madonie circuit in October was won by Paolo Tasca, also in a De Dion.

In France it was left to Georges Sizaire and Louis Naudin to lift French hearts in the last race of a disastrous year for France. This was the second Coupe de l'Auto (>1906) at Rambouillet. Amid a huge entry the two men fought it out together, Sizaire just managing to outwit his partner to win.

Brooklands

The world's first motor racing track was built by Mr H. F. Locke King on his estate in Surrey at a cost of £150,000. It opened on 28 June 1907, when Selwyn Edge (>1901) broke the 24-hour distance record, covering 1,581 miles at an average speed of 65.905 mph in a Napier. He made world headlines, but spectators were not impressed with the racing at first: cars appeared slow against the expanse of concrete, and although Brooklands achieved its aim of improving British cars, it never enjoyed the popularity of road racing on the Continent (>1929, 1939).

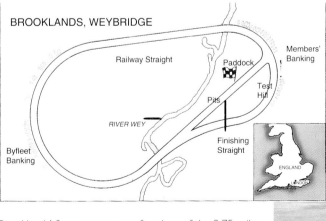

Brooklands' first race was the Marcel Renault Memorial Plate (>1903). The prize money was 400 gold sovereigns. The winner was H. C. Tryon in a Napier (*RIGHT*), over four laps of the 2.75-mile circuit (*ABOVE*). The Brooklands Automobile Racing Club (*TOP*) was exclusive: its unofficial motto was 'the right crowd and no crowding'.

In 1895 the top speed of the winning Panhard-Levassor in the Paris-Bordeaux race had been around 20 mph. By 1908, speeds of 100 mph were commonplace, partly due to improvements in engine technology. But most designers had taken the easier route to more power – simply increasing the size of the engines – so that by 1908 engines were approaching 20 litres. Worse: to keep weight down, the engines were mounted on the flimsiest of chassis, and although much loved by their drivers, the big racing cars had become dangerous freaks, adding little to the development of the touring car which had always been the rationale behind racing.

Several attempts had been made to check the trend by limiting weight, piston size and fuel consumption, but each country had adopted a different formula. In 1907, an International Commission agreed an international formula limiting the bore of four-cylinder engines to 155 mm, and of six-cylinder engines to 127 mm. It also set a *minimum* weight of 1,100 kg without tyres, water, fuel and oil, so that designers could not compensate by making the chassis even lighter and more dangerous.

Setting an international racing formula led indirectly to a new contest in the United States – the American Grand Prize. The Automobile Association of America (AAA) and the Automobile Club of America (ACA) had long been rivals for the control of American racing. The ACA was similar to European clubs, run by wealthy men of standing in the automobile industry. The AAA was a more populist body and controlled America's premier road race, the Vanderbilt Cup (>1904). But its supervision of the circuit was poor: every year enthu-

siastic spectators invaded the track at the finish. Things got so bad that the race was cancelled after the 1906 event. But the AAA revived it for 1908, ignored the international formula, and set its own upper weight limit of 1,200 kg. European clubs protested, but to no avail – so they boycotted the race. The ACA, seeing its opportunity, announced the American Grand Prize, to be run under the international formula at Savannah, Georgia, on Thanksgiving Day. European manufacturers responded with enthusiasm.

Despite its huge success the previous year, the Targa Florio in 1908 attracted only 13 entrants, 11 of them Italian. The high cost of going to Sicily in the recession kept many manufacturers away, so to boost interest, Count Florio put on a voiturette race the day before the Targa. Louis Sizaire and Georges Naudin – the stars of French voiturette racing (>1907) – entered, but both crashed, leaving the race for Giosue Giuppone to cruise home first in a Lion-Peugeot.

In the Targa Florio, Felice Nazzaro and Vincenzo Lancia expected to build on their triumph for Fiat the previous year, despite challenges from Isotta-Fraschini and a newcomer, SPA (Società Ligure-Piemontese Automobilista). The rivalry between the Italian firms led to close racing, and at the end of the first lap only 19 seconds separated the first four cars. Nazzaro led, with Lancia just behind, followed by Trucco for Isotta and Ernesto Ceirano for SPA. When Nazzaro's steering broke, Lancia took the lead. But when he stopped to change a tyre, Trucco was close enough to take over and give Isotta its first taste of victory.

ABOVE: German driver Christian Lautenschlager won the Grand Prix at Dieppe at an average 69.05 mph. His 12.8-litre, four-cylinder, 20-bhp Mercedes had a maximum speed of 98 mph. Lautenschlager drove a steady race and slowed at corners to conserve his tyres in order to save time changing them in the pits.

MILESTONES

Flying kilometre and flying mile record attempts were not staged during the Florida Speed Week due to the poor condition of Daytona Beach.

February 12 saw the start of the New York–Paris race via Russia. Montague Roberts and George Shuster won, covering 13,431 miles in 170 days.

The first motor race in Russia was from St Petersburg 438 miles to Moscow on 19 May.

Victor Hémery won the Heavy Car class in a Benz.

The first supercharged car was a Chadwick. Willie Haupt took 21 seconds off the record for the Giant's Despair Hill Climb in it on 30 May (>1923).

Just before the ACF Grand Prix, Hall Watt – an Englishman who had bought the Renault that won the 1906 race – was killed driving it on the Dieppe circuit.

On 19 October the International Commission met and decided on a formula to be introduced into racing in 1909: a maximum weight of 900 kilograms and a maximum cylinder bore of 130 millimetres.

On 24 October the Vanderbilt Cup was won by the American driver George Robertson in a Locomobile, the first American car to win the race (>1904).

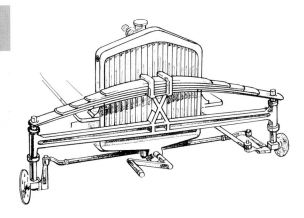

The great French voiturette designers Georges Sizaire and Louis Naudin adopted independent front suspension to improve the roadholding of their cars in 1908, but the design was not copied widely and few racing car manufacturers adopted it until the mid-1930s (>1934).

BELOW: Albert Guyot in a single-cylinder Delage in the Grand Prix des Voiturettes at Dieppe. Guyot drove with remarkable consistency, his lap times varying barely a minute throughout the 5 hours 45 minutes of the race. His average speed was 49.74 mph.

ABOVE: Christian Lautenschlager (centre) and his mechanic with pit staff after the Dieppe Grand Prix. It was Lautenschlager's first race as a driver; he was Otto Salzer's mechanic in the 1906 Circuit des Ardennes. Born in 1877, he was apprenticed to a locksmith before joining Daimler as a foreman-inspector in 1900.

The ACF chose Dieppe for the Grand Prix, largely because the local council agreed to subsidize it again (>1907). The formula's limit on piston size had some effect: the Clément-Bayards and Opels were the biggest, at just under 14 litres – around average for the previous year. Of the 48 cars entered, 24 were French. Their main threat came from Fiat and Mercedes, although Britain entered the lists with a modified, six-cylinder Austin tourer.

Like Count Florio, the ACF recognized the attraction of voiturette racing and staged a Grand Prix des Voiturettes the day before the big race. It attracted a staggering 64 entries. Lion-Peugeot fielded single- and twin-cylinder cars but, taking advantage of a change in the formula which allowed voiturettes to have four cylinders, Isotta-Fraschini arrived with an exquisite four-cylinder engine that had overhead valves and a four-speed gearbox.

At the start Sizaire-Naudin stole the show. Sizaire led on the first lap and Naudin on the second. Then Sizaire dropped back with plug trouble, and Albert Guyot moved into second place for Delage. The Delage carried enough fuel for the whole race, so that after Naudin was obliged to stop to refuel, Guyot won by 16 minutes.

If French voiturettes were thriving on the competition, it was soon evident that their Grand Prix cars were outclassed. As the leaders thundered past the grandstands after the first lap, they were very close and – to the horror of the French spectators – Otto Salzer was in the lead for Mercedes. He was followed by three French cars: Paul Bablot and Léon Théry for Brasier, and François Szisz for Renault. Behind them came Louis Wagner for Fiat and Paul Baras in another Brasier. French hopes rose briefly on the second lap as Salzer fell back and eventually retired, but then Felice

Broadway, New York: the start of the longest race yet staged – from New York around the world to Paris along a route that crossed the United States and Siberia before approaching Paris from the east. The winning car was American: a four-cylinder 60-bhp Thomas Flyer, driven by Montague Roberts and George Shuster. Second was a 40-bhp four-cylinder Protos, entered in the name of Germany's Kaiser and driven by Lt. Hans Koeppen of the 15th Prussian Infantry.

BELOW: Frenchman Louis Wagner in the 120-bhp Fiat which he drove to victory in the Grand Prize of the Autumobile Club of America at Savannah,

Nazzaro for Fiat and Christian Lautenschlager for Mercedes started carving their way through the pack to take first and second positions, with Théry third and Wagner fourth. The lead swapped back and forth on lap 3 between Nazzaro, Wagner and Victor Hémery in a Benz, but the furious pace took its toll. Szisz dropped out on lap 2, followed by the Darracqs and Lorraine-Dietrichs, and on lap 3 Fiat's hopes of another great victory were dashed when Nazzaro and Wagner both dropped out with mechanical trouble.

The surface was in a terrible state, largely due to the voiturette race on the previous day. While he was in the lead, a stone smashed Hémery's goggles – the glass pierced his eye – but he drove on to the pits for medical treatment, then got back into the race and chased Lautenschlager who had taken over the lead. Despite his bleeding eye he managed to close on the Mercedes. Théry kept French hopes alive by contriving to stay with the leaders as Lautenschlager had to reduce his speed because the Mercedes pit had run out of tyres. But Lautenschlager still won. Hémery was second and René Hanriot, in another Benz, third. France had been humiliated again (>1907), and the recriminations started even before the band had finished playing *Deutschland, Deutschland über Alles*.

The American Grand Prize was superbly organized on a 25-mile circuit near Savannah. The roads had been improved and the verges cleared by convict labour, and on race day they were lined with well-armed policemen, backed up by soldiers with strict instructions to keep the volatile spectators under control.

Georgia. His average speed of 65.11 mph included the fastest 'flying mile' at 90 mph. Wagner, born in 1882, raced for Darracq from 1903–1907 before joining Fiat.

Six American drivers – Ralph Mulford, Joe Seymour, Bob Burman, Willie Haupt, Len Zengle and Hugh Harding – were driving American cars, ranged against the cream of European cars and drivers. Nazzaro and Wagner were there for Fiat, with a third car for the American driver, Ralph de Palma, supported by Vincenzo Lancia's riding mechanic, Pietro Bordino (>1923). Hémery and Hanriot were there for Benz, and Henri Fournier, Alessandro Cagno and Giovanni Piacenza made up a strong team for Itala. François Szisz was there for Renault, backed up by an American driver, Lewis Strang. Arthur Duray was there for Lorraine-Dietrich, and Victor Rigal and Lucien Hautvast for the Clément-Bayard team.

Ralph de Palma went into the lead on the first lap, holding it for two more before mechanical problems slowed him and Hanriot took over. The fastest cars were evenly matched and only a few seconds covered Hanriot, Szisz, Wagner, Hémery and Nazzaro. It was a fight between Benz and Fiat, and neither the American nor the French cars were really in contention. Going into the last lap Nazzaro was leading, but 15 miles from the finish a tyre burst. Hémery crossed the line first, but it was Wagner for Fiat who was fastest on corrected time – by 57 seconds after more than six hours of neck-and-neck racing. None of the American cars finished: the best performance came from Seymour in a Simplex, who retired on the fifteenth lap.

The racing was close and exciting, the setting was new and exotic, the organization smooth, the hospitality marvellous, and there had been no track invasions. It was America's greatest road race to date – but it demonstrated yet again the superiority of European racing cars. Henry Ford, who served on the ACA Technical Committee, saw that American manufacturers would never be able to compete unless they built the same type of highly specialized racing cars: it was no use adapting touring cars. He added that he would only do so when he had spare capacity in the factory that he had just committed to mass-producing the Model T.

During the year, the ACF announced that the 1909 Grand Prix would be held at Anjou. The club prudently added that if fewer than 40 entries were received, they would cancel it. Renault had already announced that it would pull out of racing, and faced with recession and having suffered defeat in all the major races in 1908, most of the other French manufacturers wanted to do the same. But few of them wanted to do so alone, and so leave the field to their competitors. Instead they decided to abstain collectively, and a document was prepared for all to sign. Fiat, Itala and the French company Mors did not sign, but twelve French companies did – and on the last day of the year, with only nine entries, the ACF cancelled the Grand Prix.

While motor racing was declining in Europe due to recession, it was expanding in America. On 10 October, there were five races in the inaugural meeting on the Long Island Motor Parkway circuit in Nassau County, Long Island, New York (*LEFT*). Stock-car veteran Herb Lytle won the first race, the 'Motor Parkway Sweepstakes', in a 7.9-litre Italian Isotta-Fraschini 50 at 64.3 mph. The circuit was used for the Vanderbilt Cup two weeks later.

1909

Motor racing in Europe was in a crisis, but in America it was booming. In addition to the high-profile road races, such as the Vanderbilt Cup (>1904) and the American Grand Prize (>1908), promoters put on events on horse racecourses, at fairgrounds, and on dirt tracks. Some venues, like Brighton Beach on Coney Island, staged races throughout the year. It was not racing at the frontiers of technology, but it made money for the sponsors and the drivers, and it entertained spectators who could now sit and watch each race from start to finish.

Making money and providing entertainment were the two main ideals embodied in the Indianapolis Motor Speedway, a 2.5-mile oval track conceived and built by businessmen to improve the quality of American racing cars by providing good competition and cash prizes. Unfortunately, during the inaugural race the track's surface of crushed stone and asphalt broke up, causing several crashes. One driver, two riding mechanics and two spectators were killed. The race's winner – Louis Schwitzer, driving a Stoddard Dayton – was given a medal. By the time the three-day meeting (*see* box) ended, the surface was utterly ruined. The owners, undaunted, paved the entire circuit with 3.2 million bricks, so giving the track its famous nickname: the Brickyard.

In Europe, suspension of the Grand Prix caused attention to shift to voiturette racing. The 1909 voiturette formula limited the stroke of the cylinder as well as the bore, in an effort to encourage engine designers to utilize multicylinder engines. But such technical advances required time to put into effect, and most designers opted for cylinders with the longest stroke they could obtain. The result was some extraordinarily tall single-cylinder engines, the tallest more than 3 feet high. Italian drivers and spectators were enthusiastic supporters of voiturettes, and despite the recession – and an earthquake in Sicily – the tireless Count Florio organized another Corsa Vetturette Madonie three days before the Targa Florio. Only six cars took part – the professional Lion-Peugeot team of Jules Goux, Georges Boillot and Giosue Giuppone, against three amateurs all driving De Dions. Goux won; Giuppone was second, but he was demoted a place for refuelling outside the prescribed area, putting one of the amateurs, Norman Olsen, into second place.

There were only eleven entries for the Targa Florio, including Count Florio in his Fiat. Reduced to one lap, it was still the only significant race for the big cars in 1909. Vincenzo Lancia (>1908) had set up his own team and,

TOP: Giosue Giuppone won the Coupe des Voiturettes at an average 47.46 mph. The single-cylinder engine of his Lion-Peugeot had a remarkably long stroke and was over three feet tall.
ABOVE: A.J. Hancock set two speed records in his 20-bhp Vauxhall at the recently completed Brooklands track (>1907). He covered half a mile from a flying start at 88.62 mph and averaged 81.33 mph over ten laps of the banked track.

MILESTONES

From 1909 the AAA National Champion was selected by the Association rather than by sports writers. The first title went to George Robertson (>1916).

On 12 June a road race for stock cars up to a value of $1,600 was held on a new course at Portland, Oregon. The winner was H. Corey in a Cadillac.

On 1 July Count Florio staged a voiturette race over 100 laps of a 0.93-mile (1,637-yard) circuit in Favorita Park, Palermo. He himself won in a De Dion from two others.

The Vanderbilt Cup was run on the Long Island Motor Parkway with an engine-size formula of 301–600 cu. in. Harry Grant won in an Alco.

At Brooklands on 8 November, the world land speed record was raised to 125.95 mph by Victor Hémery driving the 21.5-litre 200-bhp Benz No. 1.

In November, Senator F. L. Maytag invested in a new factory for the Duesenberg brothers at Waterloo, Iowa, and the cars became known as Maytags.

seeing the trend towards smaller racing cars, produced a 2.5-litre model, driven by Guido Airoldi. It was a close race – just 12 minutes covered the winner, Baron Ciuppa (a private entrant in his own SPA), Florio and Airoldi.

On 26 May voiturettes competed in the first motor race of any standing in Spain: the Copa de Cataluña, at Sitges near Barcelona, attended by King Alfonso XIII. The Lion-Peugeots and Sizaire-Naudin (struggling in the recession but still competitive) were there, but local interest centred on the four-cylinder Hispano-Suizas, designed and built in Barcelona by a Swiss engineer, Marc Birkigt, and driven by an Italian mechanic, Paolo Zuccarelli (>1910), and a Frenchman, Louis Pilleverdier.

The race itself nearly became a Spanish fairytale. Nobody was surprised when Goux took the lead, or when his team-mate Georges Boillot took over on the second lap. But few expected Zuccarelli's move into the lead on the third lap, and certainly not that he would hold off the Frenchmen for three laps, until his clutch failed. Sizaire fell back after break-

ing a wheel; Boillot's Lion-Peogeot and one of the Hispanos turned over; and Goux won by well over an hour from Sizaire. A De Dion-powered Werner was third, and Pilleverdier was fourth for Hispano.

The Coupe des Voiturettes at Boulogne in June was the main event in France. Goux drove the new V-twin Lion-Peugeot whereas Boillot and Giuppone still had single-cylinders. Zuccarelli and Pilleverdier were again driving the much squatter, four-cylinder Hispano-Suizas. Zuccarelli finished the first lap in front, although Goux was leading on time and the other two Lion-Peugeots were second and third. Boillot stopped to change plugs on lap five and took 20 minutes to restart the engine. But Goux continued serenely on to win; the two Hispanos were finally fifth and sixth. The Spanish cars were clearly a challenge to French dominance in voiturette racing, but for the rest of 1909 Lion-Peugeot kept its unbeaten record: Boillot went on to win the Coupe de Normandie, and Giuppone won the Coupe d'Ostende.

Indianapolis

The Indianapolis Motor Speedway Corporation was founded by local industrialists on 9 February: Carl Graham Fisher, whose Prest-O-Lite company made carbide headlamps, his partner James Allison, Arthur Newby of National Motors and Frank Wheeler of Wheeler-Schebler carburettors. Its purpose was twofold: as a race track and test track for America's automobile industry. It was completed six months later and the first race was held on 19 August; with the exception of the years when America was engaged in the World Wars, racing has taken place there every year since, making it the world's longest-established race venue still in use.

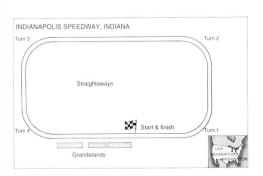

Louis Schwitzer taking the chequered flag in the first-ever race at the Indianapolis Speedway on 19 August – a two-lap, five-mile dash. Schwitzer later became a prominent Indianapolis businessman.

The Speedway's surface was paved with bricks before the 1910 racing season; the first race on bricks was won by Lewis Strang in a Fiat, one of 42 races over three days in May. There was another

meeting on the Fourth of July and another on Labor Day (6 September) before Carl Fisher hit on the idea of having one long race a year with the richest prize in motor sport – the Indianapolis 500 (>1911).

Motor racing in America continued to grow and to spread westwards. In Los Angeles, investors built the Playa del Rey Motordrome, a steeply-banked one-mile oval surfaced entirely with wood. The owners of the first 'board speedway' invited Barney Oldfield, who had just set a new world speed record of 131.72 mph in his Blitzen Benz at Daytona, to make the inaugural run. On 8 April he set the first track record of 99 mph before a capacity crowd. Five days later, Ralph de Palma won a 50-mile race in a Fiat, and Ray Harroun a 100-mile event in a Marmon.

Meetings at Indianapolis were linked to three great public holidays: Memorial Day, Independence Day and Labor Day. Each meeting had 10-mile, 50-mile, 100-mile, and 200-mile races, and cash prizes were offered by sponsors, giving the cream of American drivers every incentive to try to master the new brick surface. Indianapolis soon gained its first stars: Ray Harroun, Joe Dawson, Bob Burman, Eddie Hearne, Johnny Aitken and Howdy Wilcox. The meetings were successful, but they lacked the epic quality the owners wanted. So they decided that in 1911 they would hold just one 500-mile race – to be the longest and most lucrative race in America. The Indianapolis 500 had been born.

In road racing, the AAA and ACA tried to reconcile their differences (>1909) by jointly forming The Motor Club Holdings Company to run the Vanderbilt Cup (>1904) and the Grand Prize (>1908) on Long Island. The Cup, held on 1 October, was no better organized than in the previous years. During practice, George Robertson took a newspaperman for a ride, but the timorous reporter's nerve gave out just as they approached a tricky corner – he grabbed the wheel. Robertson struggled with him, but the car overturned: Robertson was badly injured. He never raced again.

In the race, Louis Chevrolet led from the start in a Marquette Buick, but crashed on lap 9, killing his mechanic Charles Miller. Joe Dawson took the lead in his Marmon, and stayed in front until spectators started straying on to the track with two laps still to go. He ploughed straight into a group of them, stopped to offer assistance to the injured, and thereby handed the lead to Harry Grant in an Alco, who won by 25 seconds. In all, the race claimed three dead and 20 injured.

The Grand Prize had been cancelled, but the Savannah Automobile Club – which had run the first Grand Prize (>1908) – lobbied hard to restage it, and a new date was set for 12 November. Fiat sent Felice Nazzaro (>1907) and Louis Wagner, Benz sent Victor Hémery –

Warning note: a race official alerts spectators to the approach of cars during the Coupe des Voiturettes at Boulogne in September (**RIGHT**).

BELOW: The flamboyant American driver Barney Oldfield (>1903) toured dirt tracks with the 21.5-litre 'Blitzen' Benz ('Lightning' Benz) in 1910. The German car was capable of 140 mph and was used to set many speed records.

MILESTONES

Barney Oldfield raised the world speed record to 131.724 mph in a 200-bhp Benz he called the 'Blitzen Benz'. The ACF decided it would not recognize the record.

Brooklands became the home of British aviation as well as motor racing in 1910, with the opening of an airfield inside the race track.

The first Elgin road races were held on 26 August on an 8.5-mile circuit to the west of Chicago. Ralph Mulford won the first race in a Lozier.

Count Jules de Dion (>1894) resigned from the ACF in the feuding over the Grand Prix. The French government awarded him the Légion d'Honneur.

Victories over 100 miles at Playa del Rey and over 200 miles at Atlanta and Indianapolis ensured that Ray Harroun became National Champion.

In December the Association Internationale des Automobile Clubs Reconnus (AIACR) took over administration of speed records from the ACF.

and both firms sent cars for American drivers: Fiat took on Ralph de Palma, Benz hired David Bruce-Brown and Willie Haupt.

First away was Arthur Chevrolet in a Marquette Buick, but the European cars steadily pulled ahead, despite a series of mishaps. Hémery burst a tyre while in the lead; Nazzaro went into a ditch; Wagner broke a spring shackle; and Haupt – briefly in the lead – crashed into a tree. Nazzaro surged ahead again, but had to quit after his car shed too many tyres due to a bent axle. And de Palma retired with a cracked cylinder. The victory was either Hémery's or Bruce-Brown's. Hémery crossed the line first but, to tremendous local jubilation, the clock showed that Bruce-Brown was ahead by 1.4 seconds. An American driver had won America's premier road race: Bruce-Brown was paraded at shoulder height through the cheering crowd. Bob Burman was third in a Marquette Buick, and American cars filled the next three places – a great improvement on previous years.

In Europe, the Grand Prix was still in abeyance (>1908) and heavy car racing was in the doldrums. The entry for the Targa Florio was so poor that Count Florio amalgamated it with the voiturette race that had traditionally preceded it. When the Lion-Peugeot team of Georges Boillot, Jules Goux and Giosue

Giuppone entered, however, Italian manufacturers were discouraged, and the field was reduced to eight. It was a clean sweep for the Frenchmen: Boillot first, then Giuppone and Goux. The first of the big cars – a Franca driven by Tullio Cariolato – was fourth, nearly 50 minutes behind Goux.

In the Copa de Cataluña, the Peugeots were again challenged by a strong team from Hispano-Suiza (>1909). Goux won and Giuppone was second, but Carreras was third for Hispano, only six minutes behind. The rivalry climaxed in the Coupe des Voiturettes. Peugeot introduced two new models – one model with a tall, 280-millimetre-stroke twin-cylinder engine for Goux and Giuppone, and a squatter version with a four-cylinder engine for Boillot. Just two days before the race, Giuppone crashed on a test drive and was killed outright.

In the race, Goux and Boillot put Peugeot in a strong position from the start. Then Goux had a puncture and Boillot's engine started overheating. Paolo Zuccarelli in his Hispano saw his chance. Once in the lead he made no mistakes, the car behaved quite perfectly – and France's premier voiturette race was won by an Italian driving a Spanish car.

ABOVE: An arena for modern-day gladiators. The Playa del Rey Motordrome, America's first 'board speedway', opened in Beverly Hills on 8 April. The track was the idea of Fred E. Moscovics, an engineer and motoring enthusiast who had managed the Mercedes team in the 1904 Vanderbilt Cup. The Motordrome, built entirely of wooden boards, cost $75,000 to construct. It was hailed as the world's safest, as well as its fastest, race course.

The first signs of a revival in European racing began to appear in 1911. The Auto Club de France (ACF) declined to stage another Grand Prix, but supported the Auto Club de l'Ouest (ACO) in organizing a 'Grand Prix de France' on a 33-mile circuit south-east of Le Mans (>1924). And fifteen cars entered the Targa Florio, among them two new names from Italy: SCAT (Società Ceirano Auto Torinese), as driven by Ernesto Ceirano himself, and two ALFAs (Anonima Lombarda Fabbrica Automobili) from Milan.

At the start of the Targa, Nino Franchini led the first lap in one of the ALFAs. But heavy rain had turned the mountain roads into rivers, and his car threw up a continuous spray of mud against which he had little protection. He retired on lap 2, physically exhausted. Only five hardy souls completed all three laps. Ernesto Ceirano finished first, after 9½ hours.

In France, a revolution was taking place at Peugeot. Possibly because of the success of Hispano-Suiza in 1910, and certainly despite it, Robert Peugeot was prepared to invest to put the company back on top. Jules Goux, whose family had worked for the Peugeots for generations, persuaded him that racing car production should be separated from the main factory under the direction of Georges Boillot – a bold idea, and one bound to upset senior Peugeot engineers who naturally had little time for amateurs.

While Peugeot was rethinking its strategy, Hispano-Suiza was also undergoing change. A strike at the Barcelona factory had soured relations between Marc Birkigt (the car's designer) and Paolo Zuccarelli and Louis Pilleverdier, the latter of whom was now running Hispano's Paris office. Birkigt decided to pull out of racing.

That left Zuccarelli without a job. But following the death of Giosue Giuppone there was a vacancy at Peugeot, and it did not take long for him to get together with Boillot and Goux. This growing team of amateurs was christened 'the Charlatans' by the senior staff at Peugeot. Robert Peugeot eventually put a proposition to the Charlatans: they were to be independent entrepreneurs, rather than employees, with a contract from Peugeot to build a prototype car at a fixed price of £4,000. In Georges Boillot they had a gifted driver, an engineer, and a natural leader. In Goux they had a brilliant driver with the ear of Robert Peugeot. In Zuccarelli they had another gifted driver and engineer – and one with inside knowledge of Hispano's secrets. Together they believed they could construct a world-beating car, so they agreed, taking on Pilleverdier as general administrator. They also hired Ernest Henry, a quiet, self-effacing Swiss engineer who was experienced in advanced combustion chamber design and valve layout from his previous work on power-boat engines built by Lucien Picker in Switzerland. Henry was to turn out to be a key member of the team.

To cover himself, Peugeot offered the same deal to another untrained but intuitive engineer, Ettore Bugatti, an Italian who had settled in France. The Charlatans' and Bugatti's prototypes would be run off against each other, and the team with the faster car would produce racing cars for Peugeot under contract (>1912).

In America, the first Indianapolis 500 lived up to the owners' expectations. The grandstands were packed with 77,000 people, and the 40 cars were driven by the cream of American talent – a roll-call that encompassed former and future national champions,

RIGHT: Fiat's monster racing cars culminated in the S.76; its 28.35-litre engine produced 800 bhp at 1,900 rpm; in 1911 Arthur Duray reached 137 mph in it in a speed record attempt at Ostende.

BOTTOM RIGHT: Lion-Peugeot's long-stroke voiturettes culminated in the 1.9-litre car; the engine was so tall that the driver had to peer round it.

BELOW: Ralph Mulford, winner of the 1911 Vanderbilt Cup in a Lozier at an average 74.21 mph; he was also the year's National Champion.

RIGHT: Italian winner. The Fiat S74 was a powerful force in 1911. David Bruce-Brown drove it to victory in the American Grand Prize at an average 74.45 mph. The 4-litre, two-cylinder engine produced 190 bhp at 1,600 rpm. The car, which weighed 1,500 kg fully laden, had a top speed of 102 mph.

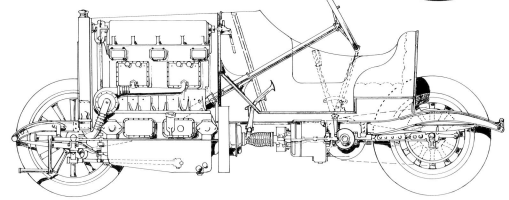

including David Bruce-Brown, Ralph de Palma, Spenser Wishart, Ralph Mulford, Joe Dawson, Howdy Wilcox, Gil Anderson, Bob Burman, Arthur Chevrolet, Johnny Aitken and Eddie Hearne. All except Ray Harroun, who was driving a single-seater Marmon, carried riding mechanics. To keep an eye on the traffic behind him – one of the tasks of a mechanic – Harroun fitted a rear-view mirror: the first time the device had been used.

The racing was close, fast, and full of incident. Arthur Griener lost control of his Amplex on the back straight on lap 13 when a front wheel rim came off. As the car spun round, he and his mechanic Sam Dickson were thrown out; Dickson hit the protective wall and was killed instantly. The steering on Joe Jagersberger's car broke in front of the grandstands at the 300-mile mark. He slowed down in the middle of the track, both front wheels wobbling, but as his mechanic Anderson leapt from the car to try to turn the wheels by hand, Jagersberger accelerated towards the pits. Anderson was crushed under the rear wheel and left stranded in the path of Harry Knight's Westcott, approaching at 80 mph. Anderson tried to get up but stumbled. To avoid him, Knight swerved towards the pits and crashed into Herbert Lyttle's stationary Apperton. Nobody was killed, but for a moment the race was in total confusion. An AAA official gesticulated to the other cars to slow them down while the track was being cleared.

MILESTONES

The first Monte Carlo Rally was held in January, cars starting from several European capitals. Henry Rougier won, in a Turcat-Méry.

In April, Bob Burman raised the speed record to 141.732 mph in the Blitzen Benz he had bought from Barney Oldfield. The record was unofficial.

To assert control over American racing, the AAA banned several drivers – including Barney Oldfield – for competing in non-AAA-sanctioned races.

Isotta-Fraschini was the first company to introduce front-wheel brakes. The first time they were used in a race was in the Indianapolis 500.

One of the worst racing accidents in America happened at the New York State Fair on 16 September: Lee Oldfield ploughed into the crowd, killing eleven.

The Vanderbilt Cup at Savannah on 27 November was won by Ralph Mulford in a Lozier; he went on to become National Champion.

63

Harroun – leading from the 200-mile mark – won, covering the 500 miles in 6 hours 42 minutes 8 seconds: an average speed of 74.59 mph. Second, less than two minutes behind, was Mulford in a Lozier. But controversy immediately surrounded the result after Mulford claimed that he had not been credited with a lap during all the confusion caused by the pile-up. The result stood – a decision that rankled with him for the rest of his life.

The first Indianapolis 500 set a pattern that has endured ever since: big crowds, big money (the drivers shared a purse of $27,550), high drama, human tragedy and controversy, all in a gladiatorial setting.

In third place was Bruce-Brown driving a Fiat S61, one of the few European cars in the race. Fiat's Chief Engineer, Guido Fornaca, had persisted in building big, chain-driven racing cars since taking the post in 1906. While most European manufacturers abstained from racing, or were pursuing smaller, more efficient engines, Fiat was the leader in producing bigger racing cars, among which the S61 was more than competitive.

At the other end of the scale, *L'Auto* magazine was still encouraging innovation with smaller engines. The Coupe des Voiturettes was run concurrently with a new race for light cars of up to 3 litres, and it was this new class that attracted most manufacturers. Delage made a comeback with four new cars for

Victor Rigal, Paul Bablot, Albert Guyot and René Thomas. Peugeot, whose new car was still at the design stage, relied on a version of its 1910 V-4 engine, and the three Charlatans were joined by the ex-Grand-Prix driver René Hanriot. Newcomers came from Britain, where the Brooklands circuit (>1907) had encouraged companies to build racing cars. Fred Burgess, Harry Robinson and Russell Fletcher drove Calthorpes, James Reid and Dario Resta were at the wheels of Scottish Arrol-Johnstons, John Hancock drove a Vauxhall, and Richards a Sunbeam.

Boillot led from the first lap; Burgess was second, followed by Goux, three Delages and Hancock's Vauxhall. The British cars put up a good showing, but as Bablot in his Delage battled to the front to challenge Boillot, they were left behind. Then Peugeot had problems. Zuccarelli overturned, Hanriot found the smaller cars difficult, Goux's engine started running badly, and a burst tyre cost Boillot five minutes, letting Thomas's Delage into second place. Boillot managed to pass Thomas again but could not catch Bablot, who won by a minute, giving Delage a great day.

Enthusiasm for the Grand Prix de France had initially been strong, but it dwindled as manufacturers estimated the cost and remembered their 1908 agreement. In the end, the ACO was left with what the French press unkindly called the Grand Prix des Vieux

Tacots ('of the old crocks'), a mixture of voiturettes and old Grand Prix cars. Arthur Duray was driving a 1906 Lorraine-Dietrich; Anthony a 1908 Porthos; Fernand Gabriel, Victor Rigal and Fauquet were in newly-built Rolland-Pilains; Victor Hémery had an S61 Fiat; Maurice Fournier a Corre-la-Licorne; and, right at the other end of the scale, Ernest Friedrich drove a comparatively tiny 1.3-litre Type 13 Bugatti.

The press was right. Fournier led until his steering failed. Fauquet took over until his rear axle broke, while Anthony dropped out with a cracked cylinder. Having repaired his steering, Fournier was racing Hémery down a long straight when his axle broke and the car somersaulted into a field, killing him and his mechanic. Duray then led until his differential seized, bequeathing his position to Hémery whose gearbox was stuck in top gear. The Fiat nonetheless managed to hang on to the end to give Hémery victory, followed ten minutes later – to great applause – by Friedrich's Bugatti. The race bordered on farce, but it proved one thing – that good racing required investment in new and reliable technology.

The reputation of road racing was kept alive – even enhanced – by the American Grand Prize at Savannah. Fiat and Benz sent teams to compete against increasingly competitive American cars, such as Bob Burman and Cyrus Patschke's Marmons, Ralph Mulford's Lozier and Lou Disbrow's Pope. Fornaca had produced a 14-litre monster Fiat, the S74, sending a team of three for Louis Wagner and the American drivers David Bruce-Brown and Caleb Bragg. Benz sent Hémery and cars for Erwin Bergdoll and Eddie Hearne. Bragg led at the start, followed then by Bruce-Brown and Hémery. As the lead swapped back and forth in the early stages, Patschke briefly took the lead, making Marmon the first American car ever to lead the Grand Prize. But although more competitive, American cars were still no match for the latest Fiat, and the race ended with a second consecutive victory for Bruce-Brown: a last hurrah for the era of the monster racing car.

ABOVE: Ray Harroun, winner of the first Indianapolis 500 race, was born in 1879 and began his racing career on New York's Harlem dirt track in 1905. He joined the Marmon company in 1908 as an engineer and test driver, and went on to win the American National Championship in 1910 in a Marmon. He worked as a consulting engineer in the car industry after the 1914–1918 war and was a frequent and welcome visitor to the Indianapolis speedway. He died in 1968.

LEFT: The Marmon badge. Indianapolis-based Howard Marmon built his first car in 1902, in the corner of his father's mill-machinery works. Serious racing began with the 318-cu. in. (5.2-litre) Model 32, on which the Wasp was based.

As recession eased in Europe, the revival in motor racing there turned into a full-blown renaissance. In France, voiturette racing burgeoned, filling the vacuum left by the absence of the Grand Prix. British racing cars produced to compete at Brooklands (>1907) had by 1911 become more competitive in light car races. Meanwhile, the American Grand Prize – which had kept alive the idea of a supreme test of man and machine – now threatened to steal the limelight from the Grand Prix. Reviving the race was the obvious way for the ACF to put itself back at the heart of the sport – so it announced that the Grand Prix would be run in 1912 at Dieppe, after a gap of three years.

In America, the first specially-built racing cars began to emerge, challenging European dominance. Three names – Mercer, Stutz and Mason – appeared more frequently in the headlines as they consistently beat the modi-fied stock cars that were the backbone of American racing. The Masons were built in Des Moines, Iowa, by the Duesenberg broth-ers, Frederick and August (>1921), and took their name from a local lawyer who had backed the company. The basis of the broth-ers' success was their enthusiasm for building smaller, more efficient engines.

All three names appeared among the cars entered for the 1912 Indianapolis 500. The Duesenbergs entered a 226-cu.in. (3.703-litre) Mason against the more traditional Nationals, Fiats and Mercedes that had engines more than twice the size. Sadly, their driver Lee Oldfield failed to qualify after a cylinder cracked during practice. The British driver Hugh Hughes qual-ified in a 300-cu.in. (4.916-litre) Mercer, and Charles Merz likewise qualified in a Stutz.

For most of the race it looked as if Ralph de Palma would win in his Mercedes, but his engine failed with two laps to go. He and his mechanic Rupert Jeffkins pushed the car towards the finish, but they were overtaken by Joe Dawson in a National, who won. Second was Teddy Tetzlaff in a Fiat. But third and fourth places were taken by Hughes for Mercer – only 2.4 mph slower than the winner – and Merz for Stutz.

In the competition to build prototypes for Peugeot's new racing cars, the Charlatans and Ettore Bugatti settled the matter with a run-off. The Bugatti reached 99 mph – but the Charlatans' creation managed a superb 114 mph to win the contract. Their four-cylinder double overhead camshaft 7.6-litre engine, with four valves per cylinder and hemispheri-cal combustion chambers, was an engineering breakthrough. At 148 bhp it produced nearly 20 bhp per litre at 2,200 rpm, compared with the just over 13 bhp per litre at 1,600 rpm of its rival, the 190-bhp 14.1-litre Fiat S74.

The best of the old cars was pitted against the shock of the new in the Grand Prix, for which the ACF had decided on an epic format: 954 miles over two days. Worried that com-petitors might be a little thin on the ground, however, the Club decided on an open formula for the Grand Prix, and ran the Coupe des Voiturettes concurrently. Fourteen of the total entry of 47 cars were Grand Prix cars, and 33 were voiturettes. Peugeot had put its effort into the Grand Prix cars, and Georges Boillot gave a hint of the potential of the L-76 by returning the fastest practice lap at 35 minutes 55 sec-onds – 79.77 mph. Facing the Peugeots were three S74s, driven by the stalwart Louis Wagner and the Americans David Bruce-

Brown and de Palma. Peugeot's emphasis on the Grand Prix diminished its effort in the voiturette class, and although France was well represented by the presences of Sizaire-Naudin, Grégoire, Schneider and Darracq, most interest in the class focused on the British teams Calthorpe, Arrol-Johnston, Singer, Sunbeam and Vauxhall.

The first ACF Grand Prix for four years started at 5.30 am on 25 June. Victor Rigal in a Sunbeam led the way for the voiturettes, and Victory Hémery in a huge Lorraine-Dietrich was first off in the Grand Prix class. Hémery made a good start, but before long Bruce-Brown was lapping at 37 minutes 18 seconds in the lead, ahead of Boillot, with Wagner third. The Fiats were slightly faster, but were delayed by protracted pit-stops: Fiat mechanics refuelled using churns and a funnel whereas Peugeot utilized a pressure system, and the Fiats' wooden artillery wheels with detachable rims took much more time to change than the Peugeots' detachable wheels with knock-off hubs. Both teams lost members. Jules Goux was disqualified for refuelling outside the pit area after a leaking fuel pipe emptied his tank. Paolo Zuccarelli dropped out with ignition problems. And de Palma was disqualified for working on the car outside the pit area.

At the end of the first day Bruce-Brown was

MILESTONES

The Targa Florio was moved to a 651-mile circuit round Sicily after damage to the Madonie circuit by the weather and by the 1911 race.

Gil Anderson in a Stutz drew pole position for the Indianapolis 500. The fastest practice lap was driven by David Bruce-Brown in a Fiat (>1915).

With no hope of winning, Ralph Mulford completed the Indianapolis 500 at a leisurely 56 mph to qualify for starting money. He even stopped for lunch.

The 250-mile 'Free-for-All' in the first Montemara Fiesta road races at Tacoma on 5 July was won by Teddy Tetzlaff in a Fiat at 65.8 mph.

On 5 July Ralph de Palma won two of the five Elgin road races in his Mercedes, which helped him towards the AAA National Championship.

Sunbeam broke a total of 44 records at Brooklands: distance records from 1 hour to 12 hours, and time records from 50 to 1,000 miles.

The total prize money for the Indianapolis 500 nearly doubled from $27,550 in 1911 to $52,225 in 1912; Joe Dawson's share was $20,000.

The first race outside France to use the title Grand Prix was in Belgium; as a reliability trial for touring cars, there was no outright winner.

leading by two minutes from Boillot; Wagner was third. But in fourth place – causing a mild sensation – the Sunbeam driven by Dario Resta had beaten the rest of the Grand Prix cars. One Lorraine-Dietrich finished the first day but caught fire overnight, and the Grégoires withdrew, so French hopes rested on Boillot to rescue their premier event from an Italian car driven by an American.

The second day was much like the first, except that the weather was poor and Boillot started more slowly in the wet. As the day wore on he speeded up, gaining on Bruce-Brown. Then on lap 15 the Frenchman spied the American stranded at the side of the road, a fuel pipe broken. Well aware that he would be disqualified if he fixed the pipe and refuelled outside the pit area, Bruce-Brown – ever the sportsman – saluted Boillot with a wave as he went past him and into the lead.

Boillot was way ahead of Wagner, and was well placed to win unless a similar misfortune befell him. On the penultimate lap, disaster struck – a universal joint seized and his gearbox jammed. It took Boillot and his mechanic Charles Prévost all their ingenuity to fix it, but 20 minutes later they were off again, albeit with only second and fourth gears. Boillot won by 13 minutes from Wagner, and so became a national hero – the first Frenchman to bring a French car to victory in the Grand Prix since as far back as 1906.

Equally sensational was the finish of the Coupe des Voiturettes. Rigal crossed the line just 40 minutes after Boillot in the first of the Sunbeams, followed by Resta and Médinger in two more – a first, second and third that put Britain on the international motor racing map.

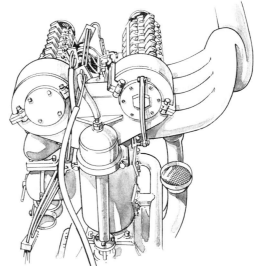

ABOVE: Lieutenant Knapp's Fiat taking part in the 'Battle of the Flowers' which followed the second Monte Carlo rally. Ninety cars entered the rally, heading for Monte Carlo from Austria, Russia, France, Germany and Holland. Prizes were awarded for speed, distance covered, the number of passengers carried and the condition of the cars at the finish.

At the same time as the ACF Grand Prix was revived, the American Grand Prize was looking for a new home. After three superb races, the Savannah club had come under criticism both for using convicts to prepare the circuit and local militia to police it, and for closing off local roads for long periods during practice. This year the club declined to sponsor it.

A new home – and backers for both the Grand Prize and the Vanderbilt Cup – was found at Greenfield, Milwaukee. Once the venue was announced, however, land sharks and speculators – some using dubious methods – moved in and bought up all the land for grandstands and parking. Rather than letting them cash in, an alternative circuit was found at Wauwatosa.

Of the eight cars that entered the Vanderbilt Cup, only two were modified stock cars – Ralph Mulford's Knox and Duke Nelson's Lozier – confirming the trend towards specially-built cars. Gil Anderson's Stutz and Hugh Hughes' Mercer challenged the four European cars: Tetzlaff's Fiat and three Mercedes driven by George Clark, Spenser Wishart and de Palma. De Palma won – the first Mercedes victory in seven attempts in the Cup (>1914).

During practice runs for the Grand Prize, America lost arguably its greatest racing driver. David Bruce-Brown, twice the winner of America's most coveted trophy and driving the S74 Fiat in which he had come close to winning the French Grand Prix, asked for permission to do one extra lap before the roads were reopened to traffic. On a narrow section of road a worn tyre burst at high speed. The Fiat rolled over, killing Bruce-Brown and his mechanic, Tony Scudelari.

American drivers had all but taken over the Grand Prize, although most still drove European cars. Of the 13 entries there were three Mercedes driven by Wishart, de Palma and Clark; three Benz driven by Bob Burman, Erwin Bergdoll and Joe Horan; and three Fiats driven by Tetzlaff, Caleb Bragg and Barney Oldfield. Anderson drove the Stutz he had used in the Vanderbilt Cup, Hugh Hughes the Mercer, Ralph Mulford the Knox, and Fountain a Lozier.

Tetzlaff, Bragg and de Palma fought for the lead from the start. Tetzlaff prevailed, and stretched his lead to 12 minutes by the half-way mark. But his furious driving tore the rear axle off the car and Bragg took over, with de Palma only seconds behind. Trying to overtake Bragg, de Palma drew alongside and the two cars touched – the Mercedes cartwheeled into a field. De Palma escaped with a broken leg; his mechanic was only slightly injured. Bragg went on to win, giving Fiat its third victory in the Grand Prize. Bergdoll was second for Benz, and Anderson third in the Stutz – a feat that represented the best-ever result until that time for an American car.

The race was the high water mark of American road racing. It was expensive and difficult to promote against the attractions of track racing and the lucrative Indianapolis 500. No promoter could be found to back the Vanderbilt Cup and Grand Prize in 1913, so, ironically, in the year that the ACF Grand Prix was revived, America's premier road races both went into abeyance.

ABOVE: The Grand Prix is back. After a three-year gap, the Automobile Club de France proclaims the return of its prestige race.

It was Peugeot's year. For the first time since 1906 France looked to the future with some confidence. The Charlatans' high-performance engine was producing just over 20 bhp per litre, and in the hands of Georges Boillot, Jules Goux and Paolo Zuccarelli it was clearly a world-beater. The giant Fiats disappeared from the scene after their valiant rearguard action at Dieppe (>1912), and Peugeot was determined to make the most of its technical advantage at home and abroad.

In March Jules Goux was despatched with an L-76 to England where, at Brooklands, he raised the record for the flying half-mile to 109.99 mph – an increase of 7 mph. He then went on to break the absolute record for any vehicle travelling for one hour by completing 106.003 miles, breaking the previous record of 104.27 miles held by Jules Vedrines in a Deperdussin monoplane!

The Vanderbilt Cup and Grand Prize in abeyance, the Indianapolis 500 was the premier race in North America. Carl Fisher, moving force behind the Indianapolis Speedway, sent a personal envoy to Peugeot asking them to send a team. Peugeot responded by sending Goux and Paolo Zuccarelli with two L-76s, Goux's car the one in which Georges Boillot had won at Dieppe the year before. The limit on engine size had been reduced from 600 cu.in. (9.832 litres) to 450 cu.in. (7.734 litres), so the Peugeot engines had to be linered down. The drivers had problems adapting to the brick surface and banked corners, and destroyed large numbers of tyres before Fisher put them in touch with Johnny Aitken, who was not driving that year and who became their consultant for the race.

The move towards cars built specially for racing had gathered pace in America. In the Indianapolis 500, Spenser Wishart and Ralph de Palma were both driving Mercers. Charles Merz had a Stutz. Three Masons (>1912) qualified: Jack Towers set a new qualifying speed record of 88.5 mph in one, and Robert Evans even led the race itself for the first few laps in another. But they were no match for Goux in the Peugeot. Towers overturned, breaking his leg in what was the only serious accident of the race, and Zuccarelli retired with main engine bearing failure, but the result was another jewel in Peugeot's crown: a resounding victory for Goux. Wishart was second for Mercer, and Merz third for Stutz. Back in France Goux and Zuccarelli were feted on arrival at Le Havre, and Goux was accorded national hero status at the Gare St Nazaire in Paris, where the other Charlatans – including Ernest Henry, the man behind the engine – gathered to greet him.

BELOW: The Bugatti 'Baby', a light car prototype, used a tiny 0.85-litre, 7-bhp T-head engine with bore and stroke of just 55 × 90 mm. Bugatti completed the prototype in 1911 and it went into production with Peugeot the following year. The 'Baby' was a significant landmark in the development of Ettore Bugatti's touring cars and racing cars (>1924).

Peugeot produced a smaller 5.6-litre engine for the Grand Prix three weeks later. It was run under a fuel consumption formula of 20 litres per 100 kilometres (14.5 mpg) and a weight limit of 800 kilograms. The team set off for the new circuit at Amiens in high spirits. Their preparations were then overshadowed by tragedy when Zuccarelli, driving at full speed

set off again. Boillot finished the first lap in the lead; Goux was second and Jean Chassagne in a Sunbeam was third. Suddenly, Boillot had ignition problems, letting Albert Guyot into first place for Delage. Boillot then drove superbly and overtook him once more, before the same thing happened again and Guyot regained the lead. This time Boillot could not catch him: he was forced back into the pits, his car clouded in steam. Fortunately the problem was only a burst radiator hose, and he was soon back chasing Guyot. Guyot's own bad luck came on the ninth lap, when a tyre burst. In his haste to fix it, his mechanic leapt out while the car was still moving and was run over. Guyot was obliged to lift him gently back into the car and drive cautiously back to the pits to get him medical attention. Meanwhile, Boillot slipped back into the lead and went on to win. Goux was second, and Chassagne for Sunbeam third. Boillot was carried shoulder-high through the crowd.

The year ended as it had begun for Peugeot – with success. Boillot won the Coupe des Voiturettes and Goux was second.

After years of frustration and wallowing in the doldrums, France was back on top of the sport once more. Most people in the business believed that, for the moment at least, Peugeot was unassailable.

ABOVE: The railway bridge at Boves, near Amiens. Paul Bablot on his way to fourth place in the ACF Grand Prix in a 7-litre Delage. The race was held over a short, 31-kilometre (20-mile), circuit near the town in order to attract more spectators.

LEFT: Georges Boillot won the ACF Grand Prix for the second successive year and consolidated his position as a national hero. Boillot, born in 1885, began racing for Peugeot in 1908. His first victory was in the Normandie Cup at Caen in 1909.

MILESTONES

The ACF announced that for the first time the Grand Prix at Amiens would be run clockwise on the circuit, rather than anticlockwise.

Jules Goux was reported to have consumed six bottles of champagne on his way to victory in the Indianapolis 500. His winnings were $8,750.

Entry for the Grand Prix was restricted to manufacturers. Théodore Pillette, Mercedes' Belgian agent, challenged the rule but was refused.

Pillette entered five Mercedes in the ACO's Grand Prix de France instead. Two came third and fourth, the last chain-driven cars to race at Grand Prix level.

The Grand Prix Peugeots' wheels were the first to be held on by single locking nuts with 'ears', making them quick to knock off with a hammer.

The first Corona road races were held near Los Angeles. Earl Cooper won two events, helping him to his first AAA National Championship (>1915, 1917).

in practice, hit a farm cart that was crossing the road and was killed instantly.

There was no shortage of incident in the race itself, either. On the first lap Antonio Moriondo overturned his Itala, jumped out unhurt, and with his mechanic Giulio Foresti heaved the car upright, changed a broken wheel, straightened the steering column, and

Two highly successful races had restored the prestige of the Grand Prix, and several towns were eager to stage the 1914 race. With the promise of over £10,000 in subsidies from the local council, the ACF chose a new circuit at Lyons. And the Club set a maximum engine size of 4.5 litres for the race – the first time cubic capacity was part of the Grand Prix formula. At the Mercedes headquarters in Stuttgart, Paul Daimler decided that the time had come to challenge French motor racing pride and to rub some of the shine off the prestige that had accrued to Peugeot in 1913. He entered the maximum of five cars. Peugeot responded by entering four new cars with a new 4.5-litre double overhead camshaft engine. The battle-lines in 1914 were as clearly drawn as they had been before in 1908: France versus Germany.

In America, road racing was declining in the face of the growing popularity of the dirt and board speedways (>1910) that were springing up across the country. Track racing generated profits for the owners and cash prizes for the drivers, which in turn encouraged the makers of the new breed of specially-built racing cars in the United States: Stutz, Mercer and Mason (Duesenberg). The cars became increasingly competitive, although European cars still re-tained their overall superiority. Indeed, one of the only clouds over American racing was the rueful memory that Peugeot had walked off with the cash and the honours at Indianapolis in 1913.

In February there was an attempt to breathe life into American road racing by reviving the Vanderbilt Cup and the Grand Prize at Santa Monica in California. The Cup was billed by the press as a grudge match between Barney Oldfield and Ralph de Palma. De Palma had resigned as Mercer team captain when the company hired the brash, extrovert Oldfield without consulting him first. De Palma was determined to drive, so he borrowed the 1911 Mercedes that had carried him to victory in the Cup in 1912.

Eddie Pullen in a Mercer and Gil Anderson in a Stutz made the early running, until Pullen lost a front wheel at the corner known as Death Curve. Racing neck-and-neck, Oldfield and de Palma both managed to pass Pullen, but de Palma was finding it difficult to make any real impression on Oldfield's Mercer and seemed stuck in second place. Then he noticed that Oldfield's tyres were in poor shape. His own were fine, but, passing his pit, he signalled he would stop for tyres on the next lap, and he held back. Oldfield saw the signal and, think-

LEFT: The Death Curve on the Santa Monica circuit, near Los Angeles, was notorious. British driver John Marquis, in a Sunbeam, overturned while leading in the American Grand Prize.

BELOW: Ralph de Palma (>1912) won the 1914 American National Championship in a Mercedes. Born in Italy in 1883, he came to the USA aged 10 with his parents.

ing he was safe to stop for tyres as well, stopped at the pits next time round. De Palma roared on without stopping – and won by 80 seconds from Oldfield. Billy Carlson was third in a Mason.

Two days later, an estimated 250,000 people lined the same circuit for the Grand Prize. For the first time there was a real possibility that an American car would win America's premier road race, and the crowd vociferously cheered Spenser Wishart as he led for the first 22 laps in a Mercer. Then his engine failed. De Palma took over the lead in the venerable Mercedes, until engine trouble put him out of contention too, and a British driver, Marquis, took over in a Sunbeam. Under pressure from Pullen, he held the lead for three laps before overturning at Death Curve, leaving the first three places filled by American cars driven by American drivers: Pullen in a Mercer, Ball in a Marmon, and Billie Taylor in an Alco. They finished in that order.

American euphoria at the first home victory in the Grand Prize was short-lived. Eager for a second triumph in the Indianapolis 500, Peugeot sent Georges Boillot and Jules Goux. There was also a team of French independents – René Thomas and Albert Guyot in Delages, and the Belgian Arthur Duray in a 3-litre Peugeot voiturette. Boillot was fastest in practice, setting a new lap record of 99.86 mph, but pole position was decided by drawing lots and it went to Jean Chassagne in a Sunbeam. Boillot and Goux made the running until one of Boillot's tyres broke up, the wrecked outer casing wrapping itself round the brake lever, sending him spinning off the track. Peugeot

ABOVE: W.O. (Walter Owen) Bentley, one of the pioneers of motoring in Britain. Born in 1888, he grew up in London and, after a spell as an apprentice to the Great Northern Railway, took up motorcycle racing in 1908. From 1912–1914 he and his brother H.M. Bentley managed the London agency of the French car company, DFP (Detroit Flandrin et Parant).

LEFT: Grand Prix power. The Mercedes' engine used a mixture and benzol; there were two spark plugs on the inlet side of each cylinder, a third on the exhaust side and a space for a fourth if needed.

ABOVE: Mercedes museum piece. The 1914 Grand Prix cars were raced long after the First World War (> 1922); this one survived the Second World War, and is now at the Daimler-Benz museum in Stuttgart.

was effectively defeated by tyre problems – Goux stopped so often that he fell well back.

There was only one serious accident. Ray Gilhooley crashed his Isotta, and as his mechanic Nino Zinani was crawling out from under the wreckage, Joe Dawson (>1912) in a Marmon swerved to avoid him, turned over, and was severely injured. He never raced again. The 500 finished with a crushing victory for the independent French team. Thomas carried off the winner's purse of $37,000, Duray was second, and Guyot third. Goux was fourth. The best American performance came from Barney Oldfield in a Stutz, who was fifth.

In tenth place was Eddie Rickenbacker in a Duesenberg; Willie Haupt was twelfth in another. The Duesenberg brothers had moved their factory to St Paul, Minnesota, and the cars were no longer known as Masons. Rickenbacker was racing captain, and with Fred Duesenberg he built up a strong team, training drivers and planning ahead. Stutz, Mercer and the European cars might have taken the major prizes, but Duesenberg established a firm grip on dirt speedway racing. On 4 July, Rickenbacker scored the company's first major success, winning the inaugural 300-mile race at the new Sioux City Speedway by 48 seconds from Spenser Wishart in a Mercer. Out of 73 starts in 1914, Duesenbergs gained 34 firsts, 7 seconds and 14 thirds.

When René Thomas and the victorious independent drivers arrived home from Indianapolis, they found Europe in the dark shadow of war. On 28 June Archduke Francis Ferdinand was assassinated in Sarajevo. A week later, with French and German armies mobilizing and nationalist sentiment rising, the ACF held the Grand Prix.

The Peugeot team – three new L-45s driven by Boillot, Goux and Victor Rigal – was defending its 1913 title against 33 challengers.

François Szisz (>1906) was driving an Alda; Felice Nazzaro (>1907) was driving a car of his own manufacture; and there were teams from Opel, Sunbeam, Vauxhall, Fiat, Delage and Schneider, virtually all of them now sporting double overhead camshaft engines. But the main challenge came from a well-disciplined Mercedes team led by Christian Lautenschlager, the man who had humbled France in 1908. He was backed up by Max Sailer (>1938), Otto Salzer, Louis Wagner and Mercedes' Belgian agent, Théodore Pillette. Little had been left to chance. Mercedes' team managers and technicians had twice gone over the circuit during the spring, examining the circuit in detail. They set up a racing headquarters in Lyons, and the team made full use of the two official practice periods three weeks before the race. It was reported that the minutes of one of their board meetings stated that 'for reasons of propaganda, Mercedes has decided to win the Grand Prix this year.'

Lyons was seething with spectators on the night before the race; estimates put the total at 300,000. The following morning, the 12 miles of road from Lyons to the start was jammed with would-be racegoers, and many of them missed the start at 8 am. It was a race of tactics. Boillot was the first to complete a lap, but the first lap-times that went up on the board showed that Sailer was ahead on time. He set a furious pace – forcing Boillot and Goux to push their Peugeots to the limit simply to keep up – with the very intention of acting as a hare in the hope that they would break their cars

BELOW: Tactical racing. Max Sailer forced a fast pace for Mercedes in the ACF Grand Prix, leading for the first five laps and setting a lap record of 20 minutes 6 seconds: 69.8 mph. Sailer retired on the fifth lap, but his job was done – the leading Peugeots broke down, leaving the way clear for the other Mercedes drivers.

MILESTONES

The first mica-insulated spark plugs were used by Sunbeam in 1914. They were KLGs, named after the British driver Kenelm Lee Guinness.

Delage, Peugeot and Fiat all used four-wheel brakes in 1914. Mercedes fitted them to one Grand Prix car but did not use them in the race.

On 24 June at Brooklands, L. G. Hornstead was the first to break the speed record under new AIACR rules which averaged the speed over two runs: 124.1 mph.

On 4 July Eddie Rickenbacker beat Spenser Wishart by 48 seconds in the inaugural race at Sioux City to give Duesenberg its first important victory.

Spenser Wishart was killed in a crash while leading in the Elgin National Trophy race. Ralph de Palma won, and became National Champion.

On 27 December there was a race over 50 miles between Barney Oldfield and Bob Burman at the Ascot dirt track. Burman won in a Peugeot.

ABOVE: Christian Lautenschlager (>1908), winner of the ACF Grand Prix at Lyons. He used the 25,000-franc prize to build a house in Germany.

LEFT: The victorious Mercedes team at the Daimler factory at Untertürkheim near Stuttgart in Germany after the ACF Grand Prix. From left to right: Christian Lautenschlager, Otto Salzer and Louis Wagner. The mudguards and lights had been removed for the race, but were replaced for the long drive home from Lyons.

chasing him. His car lasted five laps before the big-end bearings failed. Boillot then led, although with Lautenschlager only a minute behind; Goux was in third place under similar pressure from Salzer and Wagner. For the next 13 laps Boillot drove the race of his life, before Lautenschlager – under orders from the pits – put on maximum pressure, moving into a 23-second lead with one lap to go, while Salzer and Wagner overhauled Goux.

Boillot never gave up: he drove beyond the call of duty for the honour of France. But the Peugeot could not take the strain; it was practically wrecked. Just 14 miles short of the fin-ish line a valve failed, and Lautenschlager swept past to win. Wagner came in second and Salzer third – the most crushing victory that Mercedes could have hoped for. Goux was placed fourth.

France had been humiliated, and Lautenschlager was greeted in silence.

A month later Europe was at war and motor racing abruptly stopped. The pioneering age of the sport was over.

The epic quality of the racing since 1894, and the extraordinary technological advance of the racing car that accompanied it, would never be repeated.

CHAPTER THREE
ENGINES, AEROPLANES &
DIRT TRACK CHAMPIONS

Twenty years of competition between rival car manufacturers in Europe came to an abrupt halt with the outbreak of war in 1914. The process of technological evolution – which had helped the racing car change from a 15-mph adaptation of the touring car into a 112-mph thoroughbred dedicated to racing – went into abeyance.

The most advanced developments in racing technology (particularly the double overhead camshaft engine) had been effected in European road racing, culminating in the Peugeots and Mercedes which had fought for supremacy in the 1914 Grand Prix. American racing cars were less competitive. While the United States was not at war, racing there continued – and American drivers eagerly sought to acquire the European cars. Dario Resta had one of the 1913 Peugeots. The Italian-American driver Ralph de Palma bought the Mercedes that had won the 1914 Grand Prix. And Carl Fisher – the man behind the Indianapolis 500 – bought two of the 1914 Peugeots and shipped them to the United States. As soon as they arrived, he handed them over to the Premier Motor Corporation and ordered three replicas.

The legacy of 20 years of development in Europe, the most advanced racing cars in the world crossed the Atlantic and gave a boost to American motor racing just as it entered a period of rapid advance. Long-distance road races – such as the Vanderbilt Cup and the Grand Prize – were in decline, and without the participation of European manufacturers and drivers, that decline accelerated. Promoters, drivers and spectators increasingly preferred the shorter, more spectacular events on small, purpose-built, oval tracks. The most popular were the board speedways: one- and two-mile 'speedbowls' that could be built quickly and relatively cheaply out of wood. Racing on them was fast and full of incident. Spectators could see the whole race from the grandstand and, more importantly, could be charged for entry. Between 1915 and 1916 seven new speedways were built, at Chicago, Omaha, Tacoma, Des Moines, Sheepshead Bay (Brooklyn), Cincinnati and Uniontown, Pennsylvania.

On those tracks, and at Indianapolis, the distinctive American racing tradition – short, fast, close, populist and commercial – continued to evolve. In 1915, ten road races were included in the AAA National Championship; in 1916 only two were included; by 1917 they had disappeared altogether: the Championship was made up of 14 oval-track races.

Speedway racing continued in America through the war: the 100-mile race at Cincinnati in 1918 was won by Ralph de Palma in a Packard.

OFFICIAL PROGRAMME

LIBERTY HANDICAP
JULY 4, 1918
CINCINNATI SPEEDWAY

With racing at a total standstill in Europe, Peugeot shipped its L-45s to America where a freelance driver, Bob Burman, had already started the year well for them on 3 January by winning a 50-mile race at the Bakersfield dirt track. Then in February, the Vanderbilt Cup (>1904) and the American Grand Prize (>1908) formed part of the great Panama-Pacific Exposition in San Francisco. The plan was to stage them both on a 3.84-mile (6.18 kilometre) road circuit with some specially-built board sections within the Exposition grounds.

The Cup was postponed because of severe weather, but despite high winds and driving rain the Grand Prize went ahead. It had a strong field of 30 entrants, three of whom were European: Dario Resta was in a 1913 Peugeot, Ralph de Palma in a Grand Prix Mercedes, and Newhouse in a Delage. Eddie Rickenbacker had moved from Duesenberg to Maxwell to lead a team that included Barney Oldfield and Billy Carlson; Eddie Pullen headed Tom Alley and Eddie O'Donnell in the Mercer team; and there were three Stutzes, one each for Howdy Wilcox, Gil Anderson and Earl Cooper.

Resta took the lead, and held it as the field thinned out due to the weather. Wilcox stuck with the Peugeot – but Resta maintained the lead and won by seven minutes. Only five cars made it to the finish.

Resta went on to win the Cup on 6 March, and Peugeot became very much the marque to beat in 1915.

Most of the drivers who had raced at San Francisco met again at the Indianapolis 500. Resta was driving one of the 1914 Peugeots, and the race became a struggle between him and de Palma in the Mercedes. The Peugeot was faster on the straights, but the Mercedes was quicker at the corners. Although Resta

managed to hold de Palma off for 100 miles, he had to make an extra pit stop for tyres and never made up the time. De Palma won, but the pressure showed: a con-rod broke, and he took the flag with his Mercedes firing on three cylinders and with large, gaping holes in the crankcase.

The era of board speedway racing began in earnest on 26 June at Maywood, close to Chicago. Peugeot reasserted its superiority as Resta won the 300-mile inaugural race at 97.58 mph.

That was followed shortly after on 5 July by the inaugural race at Omaha, in which Eddie Rickenbacker led from start to finish.

As speedway racing gathered momentum, there were even complaints that too many races were being staged. On 7 August drivers actually had to make a choice between a second meeting at Maywood and an inaugural race at Des Moines.

At Des Moines a capacity crowd saw for the first time how lethal the board speedways could be. On the 28th lap a tyre burst on Joe Cooper's Sebring. His car smashed through the

ABOVE: Another victory for Mercedes – Ralph de Palma in the 1914 Grand Prix car in which he won the Indianapolis 500. European cars took the first two places, with Dario Resta's Peugeot slightly less than four minutes behind in second place. American cars finished in the next three places. Norwegian-born Gil Anderson was third in a Stutz, Earl Cooper was fourth in another Stutz and Eddie O'Donnell was fifth in a Duesenberg.

RIGHT: Earl Cooper, the year's AAA National Champion. Driving a Stutz, Cooper won five major races, including the inaugural 500-mile contest on the concrete speedway at Fort Snelling, Minneapolis, the sixth Elgin road race (301 miles) in Illinois, the Point Loma Road Race (305 miles) at San Diego, California, and the Phoenix Road Race (150 miles) at Phoenix, Arizona, which was stopped after 109 miles due to nightfall.

MILESTONES

In May Erwin 'Cannonball' Baker set a record of 11 days 7 hours 15 minutes for the 3,728-mile drive from San Diego to New York in a Stutz.

The first 100-mile race won in less than an hour in America was at Maywood, Chicago, on 7 August. Dario Resta won for Peugeot at 101.86 mph.

The Vincent Astor Cup – the inaugural race at the Sheepshead Bay board speedway on Long Island, N.Y. – was a victory for Gil Anderson in a Stutz.

Earl Cooper won four road races and one track event during the year to earn the AAA National Championship. All his victories were in a Stutz.

In Italy the mining engineer Nicola Romeo bought a controlling interest in the Milan car-maker ALFA: it became Alfa-Romeo in 1919.

On 25 November Ralph Mulford set a record of 76 mph for Class B (231-300 cu.in. capacity) stock cars over 50 miles at Sheeps-head Bay, Long Island.

Cincinnati, Ohio: the 2-mile oval speedway under construction. It was the seventh speedway to be built out of wood. The surface was made of 16-foot-long 4 × 2-inch planks laid edge to edge; it took more than 1.5 million feet of timber to build the track. It opened in September 1916.

fencing at the top of the turn, rolled over in the air, and hit the ground many feet below. Louis Pelo, his mechanic, was thrown clear, but Cooper was crushed beneath the car and was killed. In a macabre twist to the novelty of board track racing, many souvenir hunters descended on the car, carrying off pieces of timber that had pierced it on impact. On the 237th lap, Billy Chandler – Ralph Mulford's ex-mechanic – also burst a tyre, turned over, and his mechanic Morris Keeler was killed. Mulford himself won the $3,000 first prize in a Duesenberg.

The following morning drivers and mechanics assembled at a local funeral parlour to pay their respects to their dead colleagues before moving on to the next race.

RIGHT: Moment of victory. Ralph de Palma waves as he takes the chequered flag in the Indianapolis 500. De Palma's 115-bhp Mercedes finished at a record speed of 89.84 mph, 7.37 mph faster than the previous year's record, which had been set by René Thomas in a Delage. De Palma's fastest qualifying lap was 98.6 mph, which put him in second place on the grid. His prize was $20,000.

In 1916 the American Automobile Association (AAA) officially changed the way it awarded the National Championship, from a selection to a points system. Peugeots were the best cars around, and the best drivers were eager to drive them. Dario Resta, Howdy Wilcox, Johnny Aitken and Ralph Mulford made it Peugeot's year.

At Indianapolis, the replica Peugeots that Carl Fisher had put on order (>page 76) were ready. Called Premiers, they looked identical to the Peugeots, but they were slower than the real thing. In the 500 (which for this year was over 300 miles), Resta took the lead in his thoroughbred and never lost it. The highest-placed Premier was 17th, the one driven by Howdy Wilcox.

Ralph de Palma missed Indianapolis but appeared two weeks later at Maywood board speedway for a 300-mile wheel-to-wheel race with Resta that lasted almost three hours. With only four miles to go, a plug failed on the Mercedes – and Resta accordingly won by 1 minute 54 seconds.

Competition between French, German, American, and occasionally British cars was used to promote board track races to international status, adding to their appeal. At Omaha on 15 July, Resta won the 150-mile event for Peugeot and de Palma the 200-mile race for Mercedes. Johnny Aitken won all three races at a second meeting at Indianapolis in September for Peugeot, and Resta put the final gloss on Peugeot's performance on the board tracks by winning at Maywood in the following month.

The carnage continued too. At Omaha, Aldo Franchi and his mechanic were killed when a burst tyre caused a crash. On 2 December a new board track was opened at Uniontown, Pa., featuring a 100-mile inaugural race. Hughie Hughes crashed on the 98th lap, but escaped unhurt. He had just taken refuge in a press box by the side of the track when Frank Galvin lost control of his Premier and hit the box, demolishing one corner of it and smashing into Hughes, who finished up along with the car 100 feet down the track upside down. Galvin, his mechanic Gaston Weigle, and Hughes were all killed. Louis Chevrolet won the race in a new and promising American car, the Frontenac, but his victory went almost unnoticed amid reports of the deaths.

The 'roaring boards', with their drama and danger, were taking over American racing. But before they finally eclipsed America's last two great road races, the Vanderbilt Cup and the Grand Prize provided their own tragedy – and some farce.

The two events were held in November at Santa Monica. Resta won the Cup, giving him an edge on points over Aitken for the championship. The outcome depended on the Grand Prize. Lew Jackson, a novice driving an old Marmon, lost control and hit a concession stand, killing himself, a photographer and two spectators. When Aitken's own Peugeot broke down on the first lap and Resta's failed too, Aitken took over Wilcox's Peugeot while Wilcox was leading. Changing the drivers was against the rules, but Resta – believing his championship chances were being threatened –

BELOW RIGHT: Drivers, cars and mechanics pose before the start of the Indianapolis 300. The race was shortened from 500 to 300 miles because the speedway management was worried that there would be a shortage of entries as a result of the war in Europe. Cars on the front row of the grid, from left: Dario Resta's Peugeot, Gil Anderson's Premier, Eddie Rickenbacker's Maxwell, and Johnny Aitken's Peugeot. Resta won the race at an average 84.001 mph.

MILESTONES

Bob Burman, his mechanic Erick Schroeder, and a track guard were killed when Burman crashed his Peugeot in the Corona Grand Prix on 8 April.

On 10 April at Daytona Beach, Florida, Ralph Mulford drove a Hudson Super 6 to a flying mile speed record for stock cars of 102.5 mph.

At Indianapolis Eddie Rickenbacker and Peter Henderson both wore steel crash-helmets – the first drivers to use head protection in the race.

In a match race between Dario Resta and Ralph de Palma at Maywood on 11 June, Resta's Peugeot averaged 105.1 mph against the Mercedes' 104.5 mph.

France's racing hero Georges Boillot, who had joined L'Armée de l'Air as a fighter pilot, was killed in action flying over Verdun on 21 May 1916.

Duesenberg had 68 starts during the year, and six victories. Peugeot achieved 15 wins from 48 starts.

accosted Earl Cooper in the pits and tried to buy his Stutz 'price no object'. But Cooper declined, and went on to finish second behind Aitken. The AAA awarded the race to Wilcox and Aitken . . . but the championship went to the relieved Resta.

William K. Vanderbilt watched the races from the stands. They had become a pale shadow of his original concept of long-distance road races encouraging Americans to construct cars to beat the Europeans (>1904). With Peugeot on top, an Anglo-Italian as American National Champion, and the board tracks taking over, he must have thought that his mission had failed. In fact the seeds he had sown were simply taking time to bear fruit.

Ralph Mulford (Peugeot, No. 9) leading Dario Resta (Peugeot, No. 19) at the Sheepshead Bay track in Brooklyn. Resta won at an average 83.26 mph. The track, on the site of an old horse-racing course within easy access of the heart of New York City, attracted fans in their thousands.

ABOVE: Dario Resta, the year's AAA National Champion with five victories including Indianapolis. Resta, dubbed 'the speed king of America', was born in Italy but brought up in England; he started racing at Brooklands.

The motor racing season was well under way when the United States declared war on 6 April. There was no edict from the government to stop motor racing, and although the American Automobile Association (AAA) announced that no further points would be awarded towards the National Championship, the decision was later quietly reversed. At Indianapolis, Carl Fisher cancelled the 500 and turned the speedway over to the government. Cars continued to be tested on the track, while inside it the area was made into an airfield for the rapidly expanding US Army Air Corps.

Military leaders in Europe had in 1914 been slow to grasp what an impact aircraft would have on warfare – but once it was realized, demand for aircraft grew, giving a huge boost to high-performance engine development. One of the great legacies of the war was aero engines such as the 360-bhp Rolls-Royce Eagle and the 400-bhp US Liberty: engines on which postwar civil aviation was founded.

Aircraft engines were too big for racing cars, but the expertise attained in developing them also found its way into motor racing. One such engine was the Bugatti U-16. When Ettore Bugatti's factory at Molsheim was over-run by the Germans in 1914, he moved nearer to Paris, where he produced a straight-8 14.5-litre 200-bhp aero engine. With the U-16 Bugatti was aiming at 500 bhp, and to achieve it he effectively put two eight-cylinder engines side by side driving a single propeller, with space between for a canon that could be fired through the propeller boss. As part of the team, Bugatti took on Ernest Henry, the man behind the Peugeot double overhead camshaft racing engine – the very man whose expertise in design some years previously had given the Charlatans the edge over Bugatti in the closely-

contested run-off for the Peugeot contract (>1911, 1912).

When the United States entered the war, the government selected the Bugatti U-16 for further development under the direction of another racing enthusiast, Charles E. King (>1895), and it became known as the Bugatti-King. King in turn contacted another racing engineer, Fred Duesenberg, to build and test the engines, and the new Duesenberg factory at Elizabeth, N.J., was equipped at government expense to do the work.

For carburettors Duesenberg turned to another name in US motor racing – Harry Miller, a one-time racing mechanic who went on to make his fortune manufacturing spark plugs and carburettors in Los Angeles. Miller had perfected a way of casting lightweight aluminium carburettors that were ideal for racing, and also had an intimate knowledge of

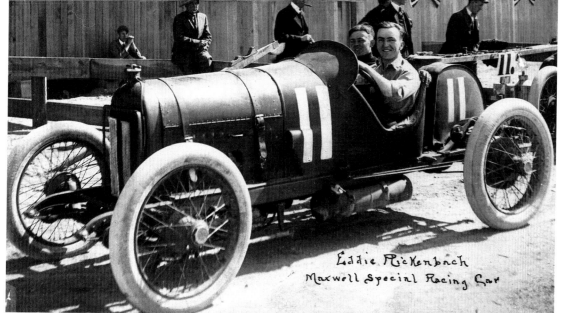

Eddie Rickenbach
Maxwell Special Racing Car

LEFT: Eddie Rickenbacker led the Maxwell team until he joined the army in 1917. He was never successful in the Indianapolis 500, retiring after 103 laps in 1915 and after just nine laps in 1916, but he finished up buying the speedway from Carl Fisher (>1927).

Peugeot's secrets from an engine that Bob Burman had asked him to overhaul. As speedway racing grew, Miller supplied carburettors to all the top drivers. At one time a banner above his factory proclaimed: '75% of all Speedway cars Miller equipped'.

The U-16 project produced one engine that flew – and Duesenberg produced a 55-litre 800-bhp derivative that never flew – but at the end of the war all the expertise gained (at government expense) was available to the racing world through the involvement of Bugatti, Henry, Duesenberg and Miller. They had all individually come to the same conclusion that an eight-cylinder double overhead camshaft engine would be ideal for racing, and laid plans to produce one after the war.

When the armistice was signed on 11 November 1918, Carl Fisher was eager to get the Indianapolis Speedway back in business.

The prewar Peugeots were still in racing condition, and the board speedways had produced a crop of competitive American cars such as the four-cylinder Frontenacs built by Louis Chevrolet. But to add glamour to the 500, Fisher wanted European competition, and he approached the French driver and winner of the 1913 500, René Thomas, who was keen to compete at Indianapolis again.

Thomas had no car, so he went to Ernest Ballot – another engine manufacturer – to finance an altogether new car to be designed by Ernest Henry. Looking ahead to publicizing touring cars under his own name, Ballot agreed, and on Christmas Eve 1918 Henry was put under contract. For the cars to be ready for the 500 at the end of May, they would have to leave France by ship on 29 April 1919. This left 120 days to design, build and test a completely new car.

MILESTONES

Eddie Rickenbacker became America's leading fighter pilot, achieving 26 kills, the Congressional Medal of Honor and the Légion d'Honneur.

Barney Oldfield drove Harry Miller's first car, the enclosed-cockpit 'Golden Submarine', to 80 mph over 1 mile at St Louis on 9 August 1917.

In 1917 Dario Resta fell out with Peugeot. He drove a Frontenac at Sheepshead Bay in 1917, and a Resta Special in 1918 – without success.

On 1 July at Sheepshead Bay Speedway, Long Island, N.Y., Ralph de Palma won the 100-mile Harkness Trophy in a Packard at an average 102 mph.

Louis Chevrolet's Frontenac cars won eight races in 1917, and eight more in 1918. The drivers were Chevrolet, Ralph Mulford and Eddie Hearne.

The 1917 AAA National Championship was won by Earl Cooper for Stutz: his third title. Ralph Mulford took it in 1918 driving for Frontenac.

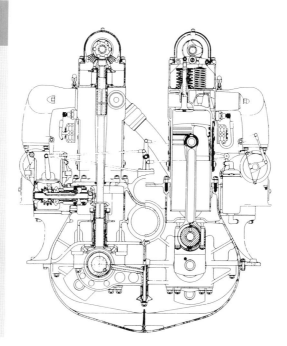

LEFT: The Bugatti-King U-16 engine. In tests it produced 410 hp at 2,000 rpm – instead of the 500 hp at which Bugatti was aiming. The engine was ready to go into production at the end of the war – 2,000 were planned for June 1919 – but within days of the Armistice in November 1918 the order was cancelled. By then 40 had been built.

CHAPTER FOUR
SUPERCHARGERS, SINGLE-SEATERS &
ROARING BOARDS

Four years of war left Europe exhausted. Whole economies, particularly their engineering industries, had been harnessed to produce weapons. The French automobile industry was in no condition to support motor racing, at least not in the short term, and the French Automobile Manufacturer's Association and the Royal Automobile Club in Britain made an agreement not to do so. The only two races run in 1919 were the Targa Florio, in Sicily, thanks to the tireless Count Vincenzo Florio, and the Indianapolis 500, for which Carl Fisher announced prize money of $55,275.

Indianapolis was won by a Peugeot, but from 1920 onwards, American cars and drivers recaptured their premier race. During the war years, American designers had not only caught up with Europe, they had moved ahead. The evidence came when Jimmy Murphy won the first postwar ACF Grand Prix in 1921 in a Duesenberg – a complete reversal of the prewar days when European cars and drivers habitually won the American Grand Prize.

War had not dislocated the American economy nearly as much. Motor racing expanded rapidly: between 1920 and 1925, nine new board speedways were built. They created a demand for specialized racing cars, optimised for the 'roaring boards', and a small high-technology industry grew up to meet their needs. At the heart of that process was Harry Miller, who built the first thoroughbred single-seaters. They were built purely for speed, and with function and form in harmony, they were some of the most beautiful cars ever built.

As the European economies revived, and racing restarted, a new order emerged. France lost its pre-eminent position. Italy ran its own Grand Prix. Fiat won the 1922 ACF Grand Prix, then built the first supercharged Grand Prix cars. Sunbeam, Bugatti, Alfa-Romeo and Delage picked up the challenge, producing fast and exquisitely crafted two-seaters. But as fierce competition brought about a brief golden age, most of the new cars were in the red of Italy.

Art captures the drama of motor racing. In the 1920s, French races were held on both specially built tracks and road circuits. The Grand Prix d'Ouverture was held at the Miramas Autodrome near Marseilles in 1925.

L'Autodrome

REUNION DU 17 MAI 1925

Grand Prix d'Ouverture

PRIX : **1** fr.

Howdy Wilcox (*RIGHT*) had raced in the Indianapolis 500 every year since it started in 1911. His persistence was finally rewarded in the 1919 race when he won as a member of the Indianapolis Motor Speedway team, driving a Peugeot at an average 88.05 mph. Wilcox died following a racing accident at Altoona, Pa., in 1924.

There were only two top races in 1919: the Indianapolis 500 and the Targa Florio.

The line-up for the Indianapolis 500 was a mixture of the new and the old: four prewar Peugeots for Jules Goux, Howdy Wilcox, Art Klein and Ray Howard; a 1914 voiturette to be driven by André Boillot, younger brother of Georges Boillot (>1916); and two 1915 Stutzes, entered as Durant Specials by Cliff Durant and driven by Earl Cooper and Eddie Hearne. Another five cars had the trusty Duesenberg four-cylinder engine: Eddie O'Donnell's Duesenberg, Arthur Thurman's Special, Wilbur d'Alene's Shannon Special, and the Roamers of Kurt Hitke and Louis LeCocq. Three new straight-8 single overhead camshaft Duesenbergs were completed in such a rush that only Tommy Milton had time to qualify in one. The new Frontenacs of Gaston and Louis Chevrolet, Ralph Mulford and Joe Boyer made extensive use of aluminium and were consequently very much the lighter – 1,600 pounds, compared with the Peugeots' 2,200 pounds. Ralph de Palma was driving a new V-12 Packard. Omar Toft and Roscoe Sarles had new four-cylinder Millers (>1917–18).

Foremost among all these new cars were the four straight-8 double overhead camshaft 4.9-litre Ballots (>1917-18), completed at a cost of £30,000, and driven by René Thomas, Paul Bablot, Albert Guyot and Louis Wagner. Practice showed they were overgeared, but by using smaller locally-made wheels and tyres Thomas was the first to break the 100-mph barrier, and qualified at 104.78 mph.

In the race, de Palma went straight to the front, challenged by Gaston Chevrolet, with Wilcox third. After 150 miles de Palma fell back with valve trouble. Chevrolet took the lead, but reduced speed because of tyre problems and his brother Louis took over. At the 200-mile mark Thurman misjudged a turn, overturned, and was killed; his mechanic suffered a fractured skull.

Then LeCocq overturned his Roamer, which caught fire, burning him and his mechanic Nicholas Milonero to death. At 300 miles Wilcox took the lead. The challenge from the Ballots faded. Thomas's tyres disintegrated under the punishing high speeds on the bricks. Bablot became ill from the strain, and retired. Jean Chassagne – whose Sunbeam had been

ABOVE: Howdy Wilcox in the Peugeot he drove to victory in the Indianapolis 500. He had qualified at 100.01 mph; in all, seven drivers broke the 100-mph barrier in qualifying – René Thomas, Louis Chevrolet, Louis Wagner, Joe Boyer, Ralph Mulford, Gaston Chevrolet and Wilcox, whose share of the $55,275 purse was $20,000.

The start took place amid snow and high winds. Drivers wore gauze masks, but goggles had to be discarded because of the snow. Thomas led on the first lap. Driving with a mission, Boillot left the road several times but still managed to gain on Thomas – and as Thomas refuelled going into lap 4, he was astounded to find that Boillot, in a car with half the cubic capacity, was 7 minutes ahead. Boillot did not wait to refuel. Instead, his mechanic grabbed a can from the pits and refuelled on the move.

Thomas pushed as hard as he knew. Then he pushed too hard, and crashed. As Boillot approached the finish, the crowd surged on to the road to greet him. He braked hard, and spun into the grandstand just short of the finishing line, injuring three people. Spectators started to push the car back on to the track, until a journalist pointed out that Boillot would be disqualified unless he and his mechanic did it. They were exhausted, but managed it, and Boillot reversed over the line.

Then Ernest Ballot reminded everyone that reversing over the line was also against the rules. So they were lifted back in, drove down the road, turned round, and recrossed the line forwards. Shattered Boillot collapsed over the wheel sobbing: 'C'est pour la France!'

disqualified for being oversize – took over his car and promptly crashed. Guyot then retired through fatigue; and Wagner, whose own car had lost a wheel, took over Guyot's car. The old thus triumphed over the new. Wilcox won, Hearne was second, and Goux was third – all in prewar cars.

In Europe, Count Vincenzo Florio managed to arrange the first postwar Targa Florio in November. Most of the 17 entries were Italian: Alfa-Romeos for Giuseppe Campari and Nino Franchini, CMNs driven by Enzo Ferrari (>1988) and Ugo Sivocci, and a pair of 1914 Grand Prix Fiats driven by Antonio Ascari and Count Giulio Masetti. Against them, home from Indianapolis, were Thomas in the Ballot and Boillot in the Peugeot voiturette.

MILESTONES

On 12 February Ralph de Palma set an unofficial land speed record of 149.87 mph in a V-12 Packard over a flying mile on Daytona Beach.

The AIACR announced a new international formula of 3 litres (183 cu.in.) and 800 kilograms (1,763.7 pounds) for 1920. It was accepted by the AAA.

The Duesenbergs sold the rights to their four-cylinder engine to J. N. Willys of the Rochester Motor Co. to finance their new eight-cylinder engine.

Leo Goosen joined Harry Miller to work as a draughtsman on the T4 engine. He stayed with the company and its successors until his death in 1974.

On 1 September Jimmy Murphy, Tommy Milton's former mechanic, entered his first race at the Uniontown board speedway. He drove for Duesenberg.

In Paris, Henri Fournier died on 12 December. He raced bicycles before cars, dominating the sport at the turn of the century driving for Mors.

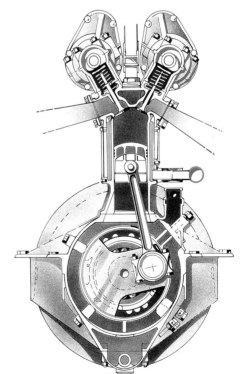

ABOVE: A cross-section of the 3-litre Ballot engine designed by Ernest Henry for the 1919 Indianapolis 500. The eight-cylinder engine had twin overhead camshafts, four valves per cylinder, and hemispherical combustion chambers. The illustration is based on a re-drawing in the 1960s of the original blueprints.

Two years after the war there was still no Grand Prix in France. Because the American Automobile Association (AAA) had adopted the international 3-litre formula, the French companies that had built new cars to its specifications therefore went to Indianapolis instead. It promised to be an exciting race – and a lucrative one. A new system of prizes awarded $100 to the leader of each lap, in addition to a $20,000 first prize. Peugeot looked strong, with its new, if complicated, triple overhead camshaft engine and a team of formidable drivers including two former 500 winners, Jules Goux (>1913) and Howdy Wilcox (>1919), and André Boillot. As drivers, Ballot had two former winners too, René Thomas (>1914) and Ralph de Palma (>1915), backed up by Jean Chassagne, all in new 3-litre cars.

American companies responded vigorously. Louis Chevrolet was sponsored by William Small to produce a team of four-cylinder double overhead camshaft cars to be called Monroes after his company, and to be driven by Louis Chevrolet, his brother Gaston, Joe Thomas and Roscoe Sarles. Chevrolet built three more as Frontenacs, driven by Art Klein, Bennett Hill and Joe Boyer. Duesenberg was late again (>1919), but their three new cars were qualified by Eddie Hearne, Tommy Milton and Jimmy Murphy.

There was confusion at the start of the race, when Barney Oldfield driving the Marmon pace car went off early. Most of the field followed, but de Palma had not yet started his Ballot and was late in getting away. Then he had to go into the pits with a faulty tyre after one lap. He rejoined the race one lap behind the leading bunch of Klein, Chassagne, Gaston Chevrolet and Thomas, in front of whom Boyer was just in the lead, making it a Monroe/Frontenac-Ballot duel.

The lead changed with the pit stops, and although Boyer predominated, de Palma man-

BELOW: Gaston Chevrolet in the Monroe Special. The Chevrolet brothers, Louis and Gaston, were unable to build cars under their own name because Chevrolets were produced by General Motors, with whom the brothers had parted company in 1916.

BOTTOM LEFT: Giuseppe Campari (left) in an Alfa-Romeo 40-60 hp.

GASTON CHEVROLET, WINNER 1920

MILESTONES

On 11 April racing restarted at Brooklands with the Short Essex Easter Handicap. It was won by Malcolm Campbell in a Lorraine-Dietrich.

On 27 April Tommy Milton raised the land speed record unofficially to 156.03 mph in a Duesenberg powered by two eight-cylinder 330-cu.in. engines.

Prior to the record attempt, Jimmy Murphy drove the Twin Duesenberg to 151 mph in testing. Milton was furious, and it created a rift between the drivers.

Two new board speedways were opened in California in 1920, at Beverly Hills and Fresno. Both inaugural races were won by Jimmy Murphy.

In June Sunbeam acquired the assets of Talbot and Darracq. The headquarters of STD was in Paris; Louis Coatalen was its racing director.

On 25 November Gaston Chevrolet and Eddie O'Donnell collided and crashed at Beverly Hills. Chevrolet was killed, and O'Donnell died the next day.

LEFT: Ralph de Palma in the 251-mile Elgin road race on August 28, which he led from start to finish in a 3-litre Ballot. His average speed of 79.0 mph smashed the seven-year-old course record. De Palma's riding mechanic was his nephew, Peter de Paolo, who went on to become a successful racing driver himself (>1925).

The French-born Chevrolet brothers chose the name Frontenac for their cars in memory of the 17th-century governor of French colonies in North America. The engine (*ABOVE*), one of the first to be built partly of aluminium, was engineered by Cornelius W. van Ranst, and was inspired by Ernest Henry's Ballot design. The cylinder block, head and upper part of the crankcase were a single, integral iron casting.

aged to wrest the lead from him by the half-way mark. A series of disasters had by then whittled down the Monroe/Frontenacs. On lap 58 Klein spun into a wall. Then Sarles did the same. On lap 94 it happened again to Louis Chevrolet. The accidents were all caused by steering arms that had been badly cast. Sarles took over Hill's Frontenac, and it happened yet again – but this time, as he slewed sideways down the track, Chassagne and Thomas were coming up behind him in their Ballots. Thomas went to the right and slipped past, but Chassagne had to head for the infield and had a terrifying ride over the bumpy ground at 100 mph before rejoining the track farther down.

On lap 192 Joe Boyer's steering arm broke altogether. De Palma was leading, and Gaston Chevrolet was second, driving a car that had a major steering fault and was under pressure from Chassagne and Thomas. Then, with just four laps to go, de Palma's car caught fire out on the track: one of the magnetos had failed. He fixed it, drove to the pits, and started off once more in fifth place. It happened again. In the pits he found that the fires were caused by an accumulation of petrol in the cylinders served by the faulty magneto. He cut off the fuel to those cylinders, and rejoined the race firing on only four. Meanwhile, over the last few laps, Chassagne had been putting pressure on Chevrolet. The crowd bellowed as the Ballot gained on the Monroe. Then Chassagne misjudged a turn and went into the wall. Thomas tried next – but Chevrolet's steering arm held out, and he crossed the line in front: the first American car to win since 1912.

Against such epic racing in the United States, the Automobile Club de l'Ouest (ACO) staged what in effect corresponded to the race cancelled because of the war – the Coupe des Voiturettes over 250 miles at Le Mans on 29 August. The field of 26 included many cars that had been prepared in 1914.

Pierre de Vizcaya, Ernest Friderich and Michele Baccoli took up first, second and third places for Bugatti, and nobody could catch them. De Vizcaya had the race sewn up at three-quarters distance. He went into the pits for oil, where Ettore Bugatti – never a man to pass up an opportunity for a grand gesture – went forward to check the water too. He unscrewed the radiator cap . . . and de Vizcaya was promptly disqualified for receiving outside assistance. Friderich won.

89

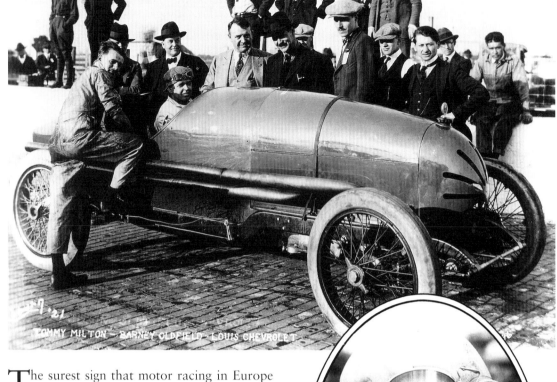

RIGHT: Tommy Milton (seated) savours victory in the Indianapolis 500. To his right is riding mechanic Henry Franck; to his left, Barney Oldfield (bare-headed); behind the car alongside Oldfield are Louis Chevrolet (with moustache and hat) and Cornelius van Ranst (wearing flat cap). Van Ranst, Chevrolet's engineer, occasionally drove in races himself.

RIGHT: Tommy Milton, AAA National Champion in 1920 and 1921, was the first driver to win the Championship in successive years. Blind in his left eye from birth, he passed the eyesight test for qualification as a racing driver by first memorizing the standard eye charts.

The surest sign that motor racing in Europe was reviving came when the Automobile Club de France (ACF) announced that the Grand Prix would be held at Le Mans in July. There were in addition to be four voiturette races: the Coupe des Voiturettes also at Le Mans, the 'Grand Prix de Boulogne', the 'Grand Prix de Penya Rhin' organized by the Barcelona club in Spain, and the 'Junior Car Club 200' at Brooklands. In Italy, seven major races were planned, including the first Italian Grand Prix (Gran Premio), to be run under the international formula, which inaugurated the Brescia Speed Week, a festival of motor racing in September.

In May there was a huge entry for the Targa Florio. The Formula Libre rules produced a mixture of Italian Grand Prix cars, hotted-up tourers, and voiturettes from SCAT, Itala, Ceirano, Diatto and Chiribiri. Count Giulio Masetti (>1919) had a Fiat 451, and Fiat entered two 801s for Pietro Bordino and Ferdinando Minoia. Alfa-Romeo was out in force with a lightened version of their 60-bhp sports car for Giuseppe Campari, and three ES sports models for Enzo Ferrari, Ugo Sivocci and Antonio Ascari. Germany was still not welcome in races in France, but Italy took a rather more relaxed view. Daimler sent Max Sailer (>1914) in a 7.4-litre Mercedes which he drove to the start from Stuttgart.

Sailer finished the first lap in the lead by 21 seconds from Masetti, but Masetti's skill in mountain driving enabled him to move ahead on lap 2. Sailer then closed the gap – but

Masetti rose to the challenge and won by more than 2 minutes.

At Indianapolis, American drivers were set to demonstrate anew that the previous year's American victory had been no fluke. Louis Chevrolet entered two new eight-cylinder Frontenacs, replacing his brother Gaston (>1920) with Tommy Milton, who had split with Duesenberg, and also taking on Ralph Mulford. Duesenberg fielded seven straight-8s for Roscoe Sarles, Eddie Miller, Albert Guyot, Bennett Hill, Joe Boyer, Jimmy Murphy and Joe Thomas. Ira Vail was driving a Special with a straight-8 Miller engine. The only real European challenge came from the Ballots of Jules Goux (>1919), Louis Wagner, Jean

MILESTONES

On 22 May, the racing motorcyclist Tazio Nuvolari tried his hand with motor cars: he came third in the Circuito del Garda in northern Italy in an Ansaldo.

On 24 July Alfa-Romeos driven by Giuseppe Campari, Enzo Ferrari and Ugo Sivocci took the first three places in the Circuito di Mugello.

During the Brescia Speed Week, Ernest Friderich took the Gran Premio delle Vetturette, and Count Conelli won a race for private entrants, both in Bugattis.

Italy's Baroness Maria Antonietta d'Avanso won the Coppa delle Dame at Brescia in a 20/30 Alfa-Romeo. She continued racing until 1939.

The 'Gran Premio Gentlemen', a race run especially for private entrants at Brescia, was won by Count Giulio Masetti in a 1914 Mercedes.

Germany's first purpose-built track, the 12.3-mile AVUS circuit, opened on 24 September. Fritz von Opel won the inaugural race in an Opel.

Chassagne and Ralph de Palma, the latter of whom set the fastest qualifying time for the third successive year.

De Palma had it all his own way for the first half of the race, leading Milton by three laps at the 100-lap mark. Then he became embroiled in a personal duel with his ex-team-mate René Thomas, now driving for Sunbeam. Thomas posed no threat, but de Palma damaged his engine in the tussle and had to retire. Milton went into the lead, with Sarles second. Fred Duesenberg sent frantic messages to Sarles from the pits: GO GET MILTON, and, even less subtly, FASTER. Sarles was exhausted, and quite content with second place, but Milton wanted to ram home his point to Duesenberg. He gave Sarles just enough room to come through on the inside of a turn. Sarles took it, and as they went round the corner wheel-to-wheel Milton twisted in his seat, took one hand off the wheel and patted his Frontenac on the rear, smiling all the way. Milton had judged the corner perfectly, and accelerated out of it back into the lead. Sarles did not try again, and Milton won – another all-American victory.

Seven years and one World War after Germany had humiliated France on the racing track (>1914), the Grand Prix was back again. German entries were not invited. Ballot's new 3-litre cars, in the hands of Goux, Wagner, Chassagne and de Palma, were the clear favourites. Ernest Ballot was keen to have a Frenchman win, which naturally caused friction between him and de Palma. The Anglo-French conglomerate Sunbeam-Talbot-Darracq (STD) entered seven cars, for Kenelm Lee Guinness, Henry Segrave and Count Louis Zborowski, all Brooklands drivers, and Dario

Motor sport could still be the preserve of the gifted amateur. Count Giulio Masetti (**TOP LEFT**), a Florentine aristocrat, won the Targa Florio in a Fiat in a record 7 hours 25 minutes 5.25 seconds (>1922, 1926). Count Louis Zborowski (**LEFT**) set two speed records at Brooklands in an early Aston Martin. He reached 66.82 mph over a mile and 60.09 mph over a kilometre, both from standing starts. Zborowski was born in England of a Polish father and an American mother.

Resta, André Boillot, René Thomas and André Dubonnet (heir to the apéritif fortune). But ten days before the race, Louis Coatalen – technical director of STD – realized that his cars would not be ready in time, and pulled out. The drivers protested, and he agreed they could race if they could get the cars ready. Only Segrave, Guinness, Thomas and Boillot made it.

When the official entry list closed, the race looked rather thin. Then Fred Duesenberg sent a cable entering four cars. He had been unable to afford the trip over to Europe until the French-born spark plug manufacturer Albert Champion stepped in with $60,000 in sponsorship. The entry was accepted, and the drivers were named as Jimmy Murphy, Joe Boyer, Albert Guyot and Louis Inghibert. The functional-looking Duesenbergs provoked a lot of interest in Europe, especially their all-round hydraulic brakes – the first time they had been used in a Grand Prix. The brakes proved a problem at first, causing Murphy to crash and

ABOVE RIGHT: Jimmy Murphy crossing the line to triumph in the ACF Grand Prix, the first time an American car had won a major race in Europe. His mechanic, Ernie Olson, celebrates by raising his arm to the sullen French crowd.

RIGHT: Murphy (background) on his way to victory. All the drivers in the Grand Prix had been offered cash incentives to use French-made Claudel carburettors; Murphy was the only member of the Duesenberg team to refuse, sticking instead to his trusty Miller carburettor.

FAR RIGHT: Murphy was orphaned by the 1906 San Francisco earthquake. He began his motor-racing career riding as mechanic with Eddie O'Dowd and Tommy Milton before making his debut as a driver in 1919. In the following year he came fourth in the Indianapolis 500 and won a 200-mile board track race at Fresno.

The badge that shook the French racing establishment. The Duesenberg brothers, Fred and August, started out building bicycles in Rockford, Iowa, at the turn of the century. They built their first car in 1907 and used racing to publicize their luxury touring cars.

lapping at 7 minutes 43 seconds in the lead. On lap 10 he went in for tyres, and managed to rejoin still in the lead. But Chassagne passed him in his Ballot, and pulled ahead, only to have to retire shortly afterwards because of a split petrol tank.

Then the surface started breaking up, and as Murphy passed Segrave and his mechanic Nicholas Moriceau, working on their troublesome Sunbeam, a flying stone knocked poor Moriceau unconscious. Both de Palma and Boyer suffered punctured radiators, although de Palma managed to race on. The STD challenge faded, and the battle was left to the Ballots and Duesenbergs. Murphy's radiator was also punctured by a stone, then a tyre burst. He made it to the pits, his engine steaming. Then with just 8 miles to go, another tyre burst and he had to finish on the rim. There were no cheers as he crossed the line, the first American car ever to win a premier European race. France had been humiliated again, and although de Palma was given a half-hearted welcome for bringing his Ballot in second, the real cheers were reserved for Goux, third in another. European racing was back on the world stage – but the United States had stolen the limelight.

There were only six entries for the Italian Grand Prix: Ballots for de Palma, Goux and Chassagne, and new Fiat 802s (which had been prepared for the French Grand Prix but had missed it because of an industrial dispute) for Pietro Bordino, Louis Wagner and Ugo Sivocci. Bordino set the pace, leading for the first twelve laps, but then had to retire with mechanical problems. De Palma – his relationship with Ernest Ballot at an all-time low – did no more than he had to. But Goux drove with his usual skill and flair to give Ballot his first Grand Prix victory. Even so, having failed over three years to win any of the top prizes, Ballot pulled out of racing in order to find cheaper ways to publicize his production cars.

break a rib, and Inghibert similarly to be injured badly enough to put him out of the race. The difficulty was that as the car's weight shifted forward under braking, the brakes affected mainly the rear wheels, which then locked up. Ernie Olson, Murphy's mechanic, noticed that the Ballots had smaller brakes at the back, and suggested sawing 2 inches off the rear brake shoes. This greatly improved the Duesenbergs' performance.

In the race, de Palma led on the first lap for Ballot, completing the lap in 8 minutes 16 seconds. Behind him, Boyer's Duesenberg lapped at exactly the same time. Murphy, swathed in bandages, was third. The hydraulic brakes enabled the Duesenberg drivers to slow down later going into the corners, giving them a clear advantage, and by lap 7 Murphy was

RIGHT: Count Giulio Masetti on his way to victory in the Targa Florio. His privately entered car was the 4.5-litre Mercedes that had won the 1914 ACF Grand Prix.

BELOW RIGHT: Jimmy Murphy and mechanic Ernie Olson, after winning the Indianapolis 500 at an average 94.48 mph. Their car, the 'Murphy Special', was the Duesenberg in which they had won the 1921 ACF Grand Prix re-engined with a 181-cu. in. Miller.

The renaissance of motor racing in Europe continued. In a move intended to limit top speeds, the international formula was changed – maximum engine size was reduced from 3 litres to 2 litres – but manufacturers responded with their usual ingenuity and produced new cars with an emphasis on lightness and stream-lining, and new engines with higher output per litre capacity. Bugatti and Rolland-Pilain built new eight-cylinder engines; Fiat opted for six cylinders in its 804; and Ballot and Sunbeam both used four cylinders. But in Germany, Mercedes went down an even more innovative route, one that was to have the most far-reaching effect on top-level motor racing: super-charging.

Mercedes and Benz, who were gradually easing their way back into the sport after the war, both sent teams to the Targa Florio which, under Formula Libre rules, had no restrictions on engine size. There were three types of Mercedes: three 1914 Grand Prix cars, driven by the winner of the 1914 race Christian Lautenschlager, Otto Salzer and Count Giulio Masetti; two of the 7.4-litre 28/95s for Christian Werner and Max Sailer (>1921); and two smaller 10/40/60PS for Paul

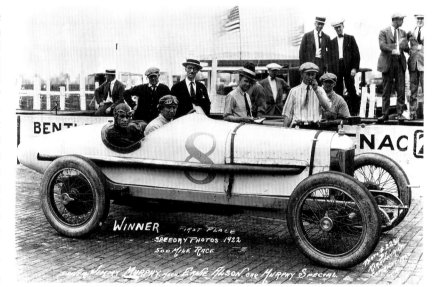

Sheef and Ferdinando Minoia. The last two types both had superchargers that could be engaged by the driver when he needed extra power, in the case of the 10/40/60PS raising power very significantly, by more than half again, from 54 to 82 bhp. They were the first supercharged cars to take part in real racing (>1908).

RIGHT: Line-up for the Indianapolis 500. On the front row of the grid, from left to right: Ralph de Palma, Harry Hartz, Jimmy Murphy. Murphy won; Hartz was second; de Palma finished fourth.

Another highly innovative car was the tiny 1.1-litre Austro-Daimler Sasha designed by Ferdinand Porsche, a man with an almost missionary zeal to build small, efficient cars (>1934). The project was financed by Count Sasha Kolowrat, a wealthy Austrian film producer, who was to drive one of them. Another was driven by Alfred Neubauer (>1934). There were several privately-entered Fiats, but the sole official entry was a 1921 3-litre Grand Prix car from Fiat's expanding and innovative design department run by Guido Fornaca. It was driven by Biagio Nazzaro, nephew of Italy's greatest driver till then, Felice Nazzaro. Alfa-Romeo chose the familiar quartet of Antonio Ascari, Enzo Ferrari, Ugo Sivocci and Giuseppe Campari (>1919) to drive their specially prepared ES sports cars; the Baroness Antonietta d'Avanso drove another, privately entered. The French challenge was a single Ballot 2LS sports car, to be driven by Jules Goux, and one privately-owned Type 22 Bugatti driven by Raymond Tornaco.

But for all the technical innovation, it was the driving – as always – that counted in the Targa Florio. Masetti knew the circuit, and went into the lead on the first lap in his 1914 Mercedes. Goux followed for Ballot, and Nazzaro for Fiat. Sailer and Werner in their supercharged cars started well ahead of Masetti, but he soon overtook them. Not only were the German drivers less familiar with the circuit, they were also unable to make good use of their superchargers around the tight hairpin bends. With a masterly display of controlled driving, Goux managed to overtake Masetti on lap 2, and held the lead until the last lap – by which time the Ballot's brakes were wearing thin and operating only on the front wheels. They faded altogether on a corner, and Goux finished up in a bank with a damaged chassis member and punctured radiator. He succeeded in getting back into the race only for a front tyre to burst, and he noticed then that the rear tyres were worn through to the canvas. Having no more spares, he drove slowly to the finish – letting Masetti catch up and win his second Targa Florio, and win Mercedes' first. It was only the second time (>1919) in the 13 races that it was won by other than an Italian car. The best result for the supercharged cars was the sixth place of Max Sailer in his 28/95; the first Sasha home was Neubauer in 19th place.

The American Automobile Association (AAA) stuck to the previous year's 3-litre formula, for which Harry Miller (>1917–18) built a superby crafted 183-cu.in. double overhead camshaft engine that produced 125 bhp – that is, 42 bhp per litre capacity. Following his success in the French Grand Prix of 1921, Jimmy Murphy bought the winning Duesenberg from

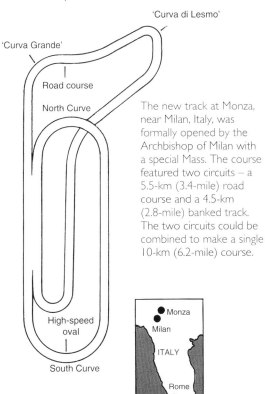

MONZA Lap distance: 6.2 miles

'Curva di Lesmo'

'Curva Grande'

Road course

North Curve

High-speed oval

South Curve

Monza
Milan
ITALY
Rome

The new track at Monza, near Milan, Italy, was formally opened by the Archbishop of Milan with a special Mass. The course featured two circuits – a 5.5-km (3.4-mile) road course and a 4.5-km (2.8-mile) banked track. The two circuits could be combined to make a single 10-km (6.2-mile) course.

the company and, looking for more power, took it to Miller to have one of his new engines fitted. He called the car a Murphy Special, and in qualifying for the Indianapolis 500 he set a new lap record of 100.5 mph. Starting from pole position he led for most of the race against a field dominated by Duesenbergs and Frontenacs. He won; Duesenbergs filled six of the next seven places. Murphy went on to win a 225-mile race at the Uniontown board speedway which, with other victories in Duesenbergs, gave him the AAA National Championship. More importantly for the future of American racing, he showed what Miller's engines could do, and other drivers beat a path to Miller's Los Angeles factory.

Because of the formula difference, Murphy and Duesenberg could not defend their title in the French Grand Prix held over a triangular 8.3-mile circuit near Strasbourg. The field included three teams from France: 90-bhp Type 30 Bugattis for Ernest Friderich, Pierre de Vizcaya, Jacques Mones-Maury and Piero Marco; Rolland-Pilains for Louis Wagner, Victor Hémery and Albert Guyot; and Ballots for Goux, Masetti and Giulio Foresti. Britain was represented by Clive Gallop and Count Louis Zborowski in Aston Martins, and three Sunbeams for Henry Segrave, Kenelm Lee Guinness and Jean Chassagne. But the sensation of the race was the team of three new Grand Prix Fiats which had the slim, sleek look of pure thoroughbreds. Underneath the bonnet was a completely new six-cylinder double overhead camshaft engine, with two valves per cylinder and triple valve springs. The pistons were of light alloy, the cylinder blocks of steel; the crankshaft ran on eight main roller bearings; as a unit it produced 96 bhp – 48 bhp per litre capacity. The cars reached 108 mph in practice, and were the fastest there. The drivers of these technical marvels were Felice and Biagio Nazzaro and Pietro Bordino.

Race day was wet, and the roads were muddy. The Auto Club de France (ACF) finally dropped the timed-interval start in favour of an American-style rolling mass start. The cars were paraded in front of the grandstands, then driven out of sight to form up in a grid. They did not adopt the system by which the fastest driver in practice was given pole position, but Felice Nazzaro was number 1, so he was in front.

They started in the distance, roared up to the grandstands – 18 exhausts blaring in unison – and burst into the view of the spectators in a cloud of mud, each driver eager to be in front before the first corner. The Fiat's extra power kept Nazzaro ahead, but he was closely followed into the Entzheim hairpin by Friderich, Guyot and Goux. The other Fiats gradually worked their way through the field. Pietro Bordino made it into third place by lap 3, and by lap 8 the three Fiats were in first, second and third places. In the struggle to keep up, most of the other cars dropped out. At just over half-way through, only three Bugattis were left to challenge the Fiats, which were well ahead. It looked as if France was in for another humiliation until lap 51, when tragedy struck.

Coming out of the Entzheim hairpin Biagio Nazzaro accelerated to full speed down the long straight – when his rear axle snapped and a rear wheel came off. The car somersaulted end-over-end at 100 mph, and Nazzaro and his mechanic were killed. Five laps later, exactly the same thing happened to Bordino, but fortunately it happened at a slow corner, and he survived the crash. Unaware that his nephew was dead, Felice Nazzaro went on to win. When his car was examined later, it was

Shape of things to come

The Benz *Tropfenwagen* (literally, 'tear-drop car') had many of the characteristics of a modern racing car: the engine was situated between the driver and the rear wheels, in what is known as the mid-engined position; it had independent suspension all round; and great attention was paid to making it aerodynamically efficient. It was designed by a team of engineers under Max Wagner, Benz's chief engineer, and Dr Edmund Rumpler, who had started designing aeroplanes before the First World War. Its racing career was cut short by lack of resources at Benz and it was dropped after only one season.

ABOVE: The car's sleek lines were broken by the radiator scoop, above the engine.

BELOW: The futuristic *Tropfenwagen* appeared in only one Grand Prix, at Monza on 9 September 1923. Driven by Ferdinando Minoia, it finished fourth. It had a maximum speed of nearly 115 mph. The top speed of the Fiat 805-405, which won the race, was 136 mph.

LEFT: The car's six-cylinder 2-litre engine produced 80 hp at 4,500 rpm. One of the great advantages of the mid-engined position was the reduction in mechanical losses by having engine, gearbox and drive shafts all in one unit.

Rising star of Italian motor racing: Pietro Bordino in the ACF Grand Prix. Born in 1890, Bordino started racing aged 14 as a Fiat mechanic, and rode with Vincenzo Lancia, Felice Nazzaro and Ralph de Palma. He won his first race as a driver at Château Thierry (France) in 1908, in a Fiat. He toured the United States with a 3-litre Fiat early in 1922 and drove the fastest lap in a 250-miler at Beverly Hills, before being forced to retire from the race. British driver Henry Segrave thought Bordino 'the best road driver in the world'.

MILESTONES

At the Easter meeting at Brooklands, G. A. 'Tony' Vandervell (>1956) entered in a single-seater Model T Ford Special. He retired after three laps.

On 15 May Felice Nazzaro and Vincenzo Lancia formally cut the first turf for the Monza Autodrome; it was completed on 15 August.

On 22 June the Royal Automobile Club held the last Tourist Trophy for cars on the Isle of Man. Jean Chassagne won in a Sunbeam at 55.78 mph.

Ernest Henry joined STD to design a new four-cylinder double overhead camshaft engine. Unsuccessful, its failure ended his career.

The Italian Grand Prix at Monza was the first to be given the extra title 'European Grand Prix' – a move deeply resented by the ACF.

On September 17 the 300-mile inaugural race at the newly-built Kansas City board speedway was won by Tommy Milton in a Leach at 108.8 mph.

found to be cracked in the same place at which the other two cars had broken. He was undoubtedly saved by his relaxed driving style, which put less strain on the car. Nazzaro returned to Italy a national hero for the second time in his life (>1907), but in mourning for his nephew.

Italy was now the top racing nation in Europe, displacing France. Not only did Italy have the finest Grand Prix cars and drivers, in 1922 it added the finest circuit too. Road racing was flourishing in Italy, but it was not a commercial proposition. So the Milan automobile club took a bold step and bought a 30-year lease on part of the gardens at Monza Palace, which had just been handed over by the King of Italy to the state. The club built a track following the model of Brooklands (>1907), Indianapolis (>1909) and AVUS (>1921), but instead of creating a simple speedbowl the designers combined an oval with a 6.2-mile (10-kilometre) road circuit that also had bends and gradients to simulate road conditions. Spectators could watch the whole race, they could be charged for entry, and for the first time in Europe huge cash prizes

(300,000 lire for the Italian Grand Prix, for example) could be awarded.

For the Grand Prix to be held at Monza in September, the circuit had to built in four months. In fact it was ready in 101 days, and 200,000 people came to see the first race, the Gran Premio delle Vetturette. The crowd was wildly enthusiastic . . . but the racing was not very exciting. Apart from the Fiats, only five other cars (three Chiribiris and two Sashas which had competed in the Targa Florio) took part. The remainder of the 23 original entries were frightened off by Fiat's obvious superiority in the Grand Prix, suspecting that their voiturettes were just as competitive. Fiat did indeed take the first four places: the drivers were Pietro Bordino, Enrico Giaccone, Evasio Lampiano and Carlo Salamano. Bordino set the first lap record at 90.2 mph.

Competition was even less evident in the Italian Grand Prix. Out of an entry list of 39, 31 withdrew, including all the British and French teams with the one exception of de Vizcaya, who drove his Bugatti from the factory in Molsheim, near Strasbourg, to Monza. When he tried the car out on the

RIGHT: Guido Fornaca, one of the key men behind Fiat's emergence as a powerful force in motor racing. Born in Italy, he trained as a railway engineer in Romania and was appointed Fiat's chief designer in 1906. A stern man who was not immediately popular, he was renowned as a superb administrator.

RIGHT: The programme for the 1922 ACF Grand Prix at Strasbourg. The French national automobile club still regarded their Grand Prix as the Grand Prix despite the fact that the Italians had adopted the same title for their premier motor race.

track, however, it was soon clear that the tyres were not up to the high speeds, and he was on the point of withdrawing too when Fiat offered him wheels and tyres, simply to give them some competition. Apart from the Fiats which, since the French Grand Prix, had had their power output raised to 112 bhp, there were two Diattos driven by Alfieri Maserati and Guido Meregalli, and two Heims from Germany with Franz Heim and Reinhold Stahl at the controls respectively.

Nazzaro and Bordino shot into the lead, but Giaccone's Fiat remained on the start line, its transmission broken. The Heims retired quite early on. Maserati then crashed, and Meregalli withdrew through mechanical problems. De Vizcaya gave the Fiats a race until he lost a full lap changing spark plugs. But the real sensation for the Italian crowd was that the old master, Felice Nazzaro – the driver who had put Italy on the international racing map and, moreover, the winner of the year's French Grand Prix – was being given a lesson by Bordino, who won by two laps, to a storm of acclamation. Italians had the finest circuit in the world, they had the finest cars, and now they had a new hero.

ABOVE: Two of motor racing's greatest names in the early 1920s – Fiat and Bugatti – locked in combat, in this painting of the ACF Grand Prix by British artist Gordon Crosby. The veteran Felice Nazzaro (Fiat, No. 4) is overtaking Pierre de Vizcaya (Bugatti, No. 12). Nazzaro was 42 years old (>1907). He finished nearly an hour ahead of de Vizcaya.

99

RIGHT: Kenelm Lee Guinness, in a Sunbeam, at the start of the ACF Grand Prix at Tours. Following are Albert Guyot in a Rolland-Pilain (No. 3) and Ernest Friderich in a Bugatti Type 32 (No. 6). The eight-cylinder Type 32 reflected early aerodynamic styling and was known as 'The Tank' because of its all-enveloping body. The leader, Pietro Bordino, had already passed the camera.

The surge of technical innovation continued on both sides of the Atlantic. In Italy Fiat's chief designer, Guido Fornaca, led the way with the 805-405, the first Grand Prix car to be supercharged; and in Germany, France and Britain – the other major racing nations – Benz, Bugatti, Mercedes, Sunbeam, Voisin, Delage and Rolland-Pilain were all working on new ideas.

Change was also in the air in America. Carl Fisher, the man who had made the prestigious Indianapolis 500 what it was, announced that he wanted to give it up (>1927), and before he went he exerted pressure on the American Automobile Association (AAA) to adopt a 2-litre formula in the fond hope of attracting European cars to US tracks – his way of ensuring competitiveness in the 500. Building an engine and car to a new formula from scratch was expensive, but the AAA obliged. At the same time it announced that carrying a riding mechanic would in future be optional. In the face of the mounting cost, Louis Chevrolet pulled out. Other American designers went back to their drawing boards, either scaling down their 3-litre engines or building something new. Fred Duesenberg went for a new engine, using a double overhead camshaft for the first time. Harry Miller went a stage fur-

ther. Jimmy Murphy's win at Indianapolis (>1922) had boosted interest in his engines, and since then he had been experimenting also with lightweight chassis. Free now, for the first time, to build a single-seater, he produced the first racing cars ever designed for just the one occupant.

From the outset the Millers were conceived for the needs of oval track racing. Horsepower played an enormously important part, and the new 122-cu.in. engine produced 120 bhp at 4,500 rpm – 60 bhp per litre capacity. He put it into a razor-thin body: the result looked like a jewel and ran like a handmade watch. Cliff Durant (>1919) bought six Miller 122s to be run as Durant Specials, and Harry C. Stutz ordered two more that were to become known as HCS Specials.

Miller 122s dominated the 500, making up eleven of the 24 starters in different guises. Against them were three Packards, for Dario Resta, Ralph de Palma and Joe Boyer, and a 'Fronty-Ford' (a Ford with a Frontenac engine) for L. L. Corum. Duesenberg was late as usual: a single car arrived for Wade Morton only two days before the race. European opposition came from five Type 30 Bugattis fitted with single-seat bodies for Prince de Cystria, Count Louis Zborowski, Pierre de Vizcaya, Raoul

Riganti and Martin de Alzaga, who had previously helped finance the Bugatti team. Max Sailer, Christian Werner and Christian Lautenschlager (the only driver to carry a mechanic) drove three supercharged Mercedes 10/40/65PS, the first supercharged cars to compete at Indianapolis.

The Millers put their stamp on proceedings even before the race. Tommy Milton broke the qualifying record at 108.7 mph to take pole position in his HCS Special. He went on to win the race itself from Durants driven by Harry Hartz, Jimmy Murphy, Eddie Hearne, Frank Elliot and Cliff Durant himself. The Miller 122s' dominance was broken only by L. L. Corum in the Fronty-Ford in fifth place. In eighth place was Max Sailer in his super-charged Mercedes. It was a magnificent result for Milton, the first driver ever to win twice, but it was even more significant for Miller, for it led ultimately to his cars' dominating all aspects of American racing until the end of the decade.

There was a dazzling array of new ideas in the line-up for the French Grand Prix at Tours in July. Bugatti stuck with his eight-cylinder engine, scaled down to the new formula, but he shortened the Type 32's wheelbase and put a more futuristic, streamlined body around it. Delage had a conventional body, but experimented with a high-revving twelve-cylinder engine. The aircraft maker Voisin entered the fray with a very light semi-monocoque body.

ABOVE RIGHT: Tommy Milton, the first two-time winner of the Indianapolis 500. He won $9,600 in lap money as well as the $20,000 winner's prize. He finished the race with badly injured hands: when sweat caused the immaculate white kid leather driving gloves that he was wearing to shrink, blistering his skin, Milton decided to drive bare-handed; but then glue leaking from the adhesive tape covering the steering wheel stripped the skin from his palms.

ABOVE: Milton's winning car, a Miller 122 entered by automobile manufacturer Harry C. Stutz. Every Miller car was meticulously finished and represented around 6,500 man-hours' work. A Miller cost approximately $15,000 – ten times the price of a good touring car at the time; the engine alone accounted for half that price.

RIGHT: The 122-cu.in. Miller engine powered eleven of the 24 starters in the 500.

But Fornaca's 805-405 was the sensation. He could have scaled down the successful 112-bhp engine from the previous year, but instead he decided to construct a completely new straight-8 double overhead camshaft supercharged engine that produced 130 bhp at 5,500 rpm. Unlike the Mercedes', the compressor in the Fiat ran permanently, rather than engaging via a clutch, although the mechanic could dump the extra power by operating a lever to open an outlet valve.

In Britain, Ernest Henry had left to live in quiet obscurity (>1950). To replace him, Louis Coatalen approached one of Fornaca's finest design engineers, Vincenzo Bertarione, who had been largely responsible for the 1922 Fiat engine. Bertarione joined Sunbeam-Talbot-Darracq, bringing with him – according to some reports – a full set of blueprints. He built a virtual copy of the six-cylinder Fiat engine, so similar to it in fact that when the Sunbeams arrived at Tours they were promptly christened by the pit-lane cognoscenti 'Fiats in British Racing Green'.

In the race, the massed start was used again, and as the cars roared past the grandstands, Pietro Bordino – who had started in the second row of the grid in his Fiat – was already threading his way past René Thomas in the Delage and Kenelm Lee Guinness in a Sunbeam, By the time they reached the first corner Bordino was leading. The Bugattis, with their short wheelbase, were very fast round the corners, but they proved difficult on the straight at full speed. On the first lap, de Vizcaya lost control of the car approaching La Membrolle corner, scythed through the newly erected fence and hurtled into the crowd, injuring 16 people, some seriously.

The race was a battle between the Fiats and their British cousins, the Sunbeams. When the

RIGHT: The first Italian manufacturer to achieve international racing success. Founded in 1899 in Turin, F.I.A.T. (Fabbrica Italiana Automobili Torino) changed the styling of its name to Fiat in 1906.

leaders came past the grandstand for the first time, Bordino was leading the pack at 100 mph with Guinness not very far behind. Enrico Giaccone had fought his way into fourth position for Fiat; after him came the Sunbeams of Albert Divo and Henry Segrave. Bordino led for nine laps, then the public address system announced: 'Bordino has stopped'. Suddenly it was 'Bordino is off again', then 'Bordino has stopped again' – and when Guinness came past the grandstands in the lead it was confirmed: Bordino was out. The air intake for the supercharger was too close to the ground; unprotected, it had ingested dust, stones and other debris: the engine was wrecked.

Guinness made a pit-stop but managed to get back on to the road just ahead of Giaccone in his Fiat, who was now second. Then Guinness's clutch started slipping, making it impossible to use full power. His mechanic Perkins tied a piece of rope to it and pulled it back to engage it, but to effect this improvisation they had to stop, and in the process Giaccone took the lead. Guinness gradually slipped back to sixth place, and then came into the pits with poor Perkins unconscious. He had been hit on the head continually by flying stones because of the position he had had to adopt to pull on the rope.

Then Giaccone came into the pits – and remained there. Nothing he or his mechanic could do would persuade the engine to start again; it had the same problem as Bordino's. Carlo Salamano, who had been lying second, took over the lead. Divo managed to make some impression on him but he had to stop and fill up his reserve fuel tank on every lap because the filler cap on the main tank was stuck fast.

Segrave took up the challenge, moving into second place, but it looked as if Fiat would triumph. On lap 30 Salamano failed to appear, and Segrave came round in the lead. Then Salamano's mechanic Feretti appeared running back down the track. He shouted for petrol, and Coatalen sent a new man out on a bicycle. Officials pointed out that mechanics could be changed only while the cars were in the pits, so Feretti climbed on to the bicycle and wobbled off with the fuel to an accompaniment of boos and hisses aimed at the officials. It was all to

MILESTONES

On 15 April Alfa-Romeo took the first two places in the Targa Florio. Ugo Sivocci won in a bored-out 3,154-cc RLTF sports car in 7 hours 18 minutes.

After the failure of a project to build a de luxe Frontenac touring car in Indianapolis, Louis Chevrolet went bankrupt in April.

At Fanø in Denmark, Malcolm Campbell, driving a 350-bhp Sunbeam, set a two-way record for the mile of 137.72 mph; it was not recognized officially.

The total purse for the Indianapolis 500 was $50,000 of which the winner took around half; the average industrial wage in 1923 was $1,500 p.a.

The first spectator killed in the 500 was Bert Schoup. He was watching unofficially through a hole in a fence when Tom Alley crashed into it.

Albert Divo won the Spanish Grand Prix on a new oval circuit at Sitges, near Barcelona. The circuit was poorly designed, and closed soon afterwards.

no avail: the Fiat failed to start, and Segrave duly won. Divo came in second. Ernest Friderich just managed to get past Guinness on the last lap to stop Sunbeam taking all three top places.

Britain had never won a Grand Prix before, so it was a great triumph. But it was also an ironic one, in that the Sunbeams' design was inherited from Turin and that it was a Fiat design fault that had given Sunbeam victory. Nonetheless, it was the greatest moment to date in British motor racing history, and that was all that counted to the British press and racing public (>1957).

Despite the initial air intake problems, the Fiat 805-405 was clearly in a class of its own. Redesigned for the Italian Grand Prix (Gran Premio), and on Monza's smooth surface, it would be unbeatable. Sunbeam and most of the French manufacturers – except Rolland-Pilain and Voisin, who sent one car each – knew it, and stayed away again (>1922). Benz sent its revolutionary mid-engined car, the *Tropfenwagen*, driven by Ferdinando Minoia. The most promising competition came from America: Jimmy Murphy and Count Louis Zborowski were driving a pair of Miller 122 single-seaters adapted so a riding mechanic could just squeeze in. In practice, Fiat had strong, home-grown opposition from Alfa-Romeo, who entered three new P1s driven by Ugo Sivocci, Antonio Ascari and Giuseppe Campari. But this challenge evaporated when

Sivocci was killed the day before the race, and the team was withdrawn.

Fiat's problem was drivers. Two weeks before the race, Bordino had been testing a car with Giaccone in the mechanic's seat. They overturned: Giaccone was killed, and Bordino broke his arm.

On the day of the race, Bordino used his good arm while his mechanic changed gear. At the start, he repeated his performance at Tours, showing a clean pair of heels to Salamano and to Felice Nazzaro (>1907, 1922) who had replaced Giaccone. Between them, the three Fiats never lost the lead.

ABOVE: American challenge. Count Louis Zborowski in his privately entered Miller 122 at Monza. He retired on lap 15. Jimmy Murphy was third in a similar car.

Bordino drove the fastest lap at 99.86 mph and led for 45 out of the 80 laps before exhaustion overcame him. Nazzaro took over the lead in some pain from hot oil that dripped persistently on to his leg. When Nazzaro stopped for water, Salamano took over to win. Nazzaro was half a minute behind in second place. Murphy was third in his Miller, after a superb drive in a car that was sadly lacking in the roadholding characteristics appropriate to road-type racing.

The Italian Grand Prix marked the high point for Fiat's racing department. Having lost Bertarione to Sunbeam, Fornaca lost another of his gifted engineers, Vittorio Jano, to Alfa-Romeo. It was Enzo Ferrari (>1919, 1988),

nominally still a driver but establishing his reputation as a great fixer in the sport, who approached Jano and lured him away to Milan – a coup of recruitment that was to have profound effects in 1924.

One of the main consequences of the rapid evolution of different types of car was that road racing and track racing, with their different needs, went their separate ways. For road racing in Europe, cars had to be fast, but they also needed good braking, transmission, suspension, and overall handling for the variety of corners and gradients. The Millers – perfectly adapted for oval track racing but uncompetitive in road races – ushered in a new golden age of the sport in America.

LEFT: Innovation at the Italian Grand Prix. In the foreground: André Lefebvre's monocoque Voisin, which retired on lap 29. Behind, left to right: Ferdinando Minoia in the mid-engined Benz *Tropfenwagen*, Felice Nazzaro and Carlo Salamano in their supercharged Fiats.

BELOW LEFT: Historic car – the Fiat 805-405, the first supercharged car to win a Grand Prix. In 1922, Pietro Bordino set a lap record for Monza of 91.3 mph in an unsupercharged six-cylinder Fiat; Salamano raised it to 99.8 mph a year later in the supercharged car.

BELOW: Historic engine – the Fiat 405, Guido Fornaca's 2-litre supercharged masterpiece, which produced 130 bhp at 5,500 rpm, giving it a top speed of 132 mph. The Wittig supercharger (front) forced a fuel-air mixture into the carburettor under pressure. For the Italian Grand Prix, it was fitted with a more powerful Roots-type supercharger, which produced 140 bhp and a top speed of 136 mph, making it the fastest car of the day by a large margin.

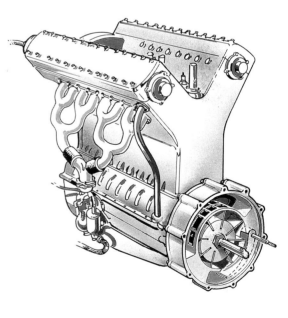

LEFT: Carlo Salamano and his winning Fiat 805-405 in the pits during the Italian Grand Prix. Salamano's total time was 5 hours 27 minutes 38.4 seconds: an average of 91.03 mph.

Two racing car designers – Vittorio Jano and Ferdinand Porsche – changed employers in 1924. Both were to have a profound influence on the development of the European racing car, an influence that lasted well into the 1950s.

Having been with Guido Fornaca at Fiat since 1911, Jano joined Alfa-Romeo and, with the greater freedom of a more senior position, his genius flowered. He experimented with a supercharger on the P1 (>1923), from which he evolved a new and innovative Grand Prix car, the P2.

Ferdinand Porsche left Austro-Daimler after 15 years to work for Daimler in Stuttgart; Alfred Neubauer (>1922) went with him. The performance of his Sasha had been recognized at Mercedes, where he developed the 2-litre supercharged Targa Florio from previous models, while at the same time designing an eight-cylinder 2-litre Grand Prix car that he called the Monza.

The first clash between the products of these two minds came in the Targa Florio. Alfa-Romeo fielded three 88-bhp RLTF sports cars driven by Antonio Ascari, Giuseppe Campari and Louis Wagner; Count Giulio Masetti (>1921, 1922) entered his own. The Mercedes team was Christian Lautenschlager, Christian Werner and Neubauer. Fiat fielded Pietro Bordino, Carlo Salamano and Cesare Pastore in a trio of 805-405s. Three other German companies – Steyr, Steiger, and AG für Automobilbau (AGA) – had also entered cars, and more than 50,000 German fans journeyed to Sicily, where they packed out the Palermo hotels and the grandstands.

At the end of the first lap, Masetti was leading in his Alfa, but by the end of the second lap Werner had taken the lead and Ascari had moved up to second place in the works Alfa. Werner established a 3-minute lead, but German and Italian spectators were on the edges of their seats as on the last lap he lost it with a bad pit-stop, putting him neck-and-neck with Ascari. Werner crossed the line first, but Ascari – who had started 28 minutes behind him – could still win. When he had just three miles to go, a gun was fired to let the crowd know he was approaching: it seemed certain he

RIGHT: British export. John Duff and Frank Clement storming to victory in a Bentley at Le Mans in 1924. Their six-cylinder 3-litre car was fitted with stone guards to protect the radiator and the petrol tank. The painting was commissioned for a Bentley promotional catalogue.

Centesimi 80

ILLVSTRAZIONE DEL POPOLO

Supplemento della Gazzetta del Popolo

Anno IV. N. 33   Torino, via IV Marzo   17 Agosto 1924

Vittoria italiana nel secondo Gran premio automobilistico d'Europa sul Circuito di Lione — Giuseppe Campari, su "Alfa-Romeo", arriva primo battendo una formidabile coalizione straniera (Disegno di Alfredo Ortelli)

had won. Then just 50 yards from the line the Alfa spun round and stopped. The engine had seized, and all efforts to push-start it failed. Ascari and his mechanic eventually dragged the car bodily over the line into third place, behind second-placed Masetti. Werner was the first German driver to win a major race since the war, and he duly returned to Stuttgart a hero. Porsche was similarly feted: he was awarded an honorary degree by Stuttgart Technical University.

For the first time in its history, there were no European cars in the Indianapolis 500. It was a competition between the ubiquitous Miller 122s and Duesenberg, and while Miller continued to develop his existing car, Fred Duesenberg fitted superchargers to three cars for Joe Boyer, L. L. Corum and Ernie Ansterberg. There was a fourth, 'unblown' car for Peter de Paolo, Ralph de Palma's nephew and former riding mechanic.

Boyer started well down the grid, but with the extra power he stormed through to take the lead by lap 2. Then Ansterberg hit the wall, and the drive on Boyer's supercharger sheared, leaving Jimmy Murphy in the lead, followed by Earl Cooper, Bennett Hill and Harry Hartz, all in Millers, ahead of Corum. When Corum came in for new tyres, Fred Duesenberg replaced him with Boyer, commanding him forcefully: 'Put that ship in front or burn it up!'

Boyer quickly overhauled Hartz and Hill, but Murphy and Cooper were made of sterner

ABOVE: Italy's Giuseppe Campari in the eight-cylinder Alfa-Romeo P2. Campari won the ACF Grand Prix at Lyons-Givors in 7 hours 5 minutes 34.8 seconds: an average speed of 70.97 mph. Albert Divo upheld French pride by finishing second in a twelve-cylinder Delage, just over a minute behind.

ABOVE: Christian Werner (left), winner of the Targa Florio in a supercharged four-cylinder 2-litre Mercedes at an average 41.02 mph. He also won the Coppa Florio (>1927), which this year was decided by an extra lap of the 67-mile Targa course. Born in Stuttgart in 1892, Werner spent his entire racing career with Mercedes. He died in 1932.

BUGATTI

Racing-car artistry. Ettore Bugatti was born in Milan in 1881, the son of a cabinet-maker and artist. He set up his car-manufacturing concern in 1910. His light cars were successful in voiturette races in the early 1920s, and the larger cars were well-placed in Grands Prix: Bugattis were second, third and fourth in the 1922 French Grand Prix. In 1924 came the 2-litre Type 35.

stuff. Both nonetheless had well-worn tyres, and Boyer steadily gained on them, finally managing just to get ahead and win.

For its Grand Prix, the Automobile Club de France (ACF) selected the circuit at Lyons-Givors, the site of France's humiliation in 1914. Sunbeam (>1923) boosted the power of its engines from 105 bhp to 138 bhp with a Roots-type supercharger that forced a fuel-air mixture into the engine, rather than forcing air into the carburettor – the first company to use the method. The Sunbeam drivers were Kenelm Lee Guinness, Dario Resta and Henry Segrave. Fornaca used the same system in the Fiat 805, giving it 145 bhp. The team was led by Felice Nazzaro; other members comprised Pietro Bordino, Cesare Pastore and Onesimo Marchisio. But the focus of pre-race attention was the quartet of Alfa P2s driven by Ascari, Giuseppe Campari, Louis Wagner and Enzo Ferrari. (Ferrari, however, suffered a nervous breakdown shortly before the race and returned to Italy.)

French designers eschewed supercharging. Delage had experimented with it, but dropped it for the Grand Prix, improving the V-12 engine and streamlining the body for the team of Albert Divo, Robert Benoist and René Thomas. The public relations sensation of the race was the debut of the Type 35 Bugatti, a straight-8 engine in a new chassis with light-alloy wheels cast in one piece with the brake drums. It was a dream to look at – but at 105 bhp outclassed by the supercharged cars.

It was a three-cornered race between Sunbeam, Alfa-Romeo and Fiat. Segrave went into the lead from the front row of the grid, closely pursued by Ascari. On the second lap, Guinness moved up into third place, and Bordino came through in the Fiat to pass him and, after a struggle, Ascari too. Segrave managed to hold him off until lap 3, when the Sunbeam started misfiring badly and he was obliged to stop to change plugs. Two duels now developed, one between Bordino and Ascari for the lead, and the other between Guinness and Campari. In the fierce competition, the lap record fell steadily: Bordino 71.41 mph, Campari 72.94 mph, Bordino 74.60 mph, Ascari 75.47mph – it was Segrave who drove the fastest lap of the race at 76.11 mph.

The Fiat challenge faded as first Bordino

Death of a hero: Jimmy Murphy (**ABOVE**), seconds before his fatal crash at the New York State Fair in Syracuse. Murphy was vying for the lead with Phil Shafer in a 100-mile National Championship contest when he crashed through the inside fence; one of the boards went through the radiator and into his body. Tommy Milton accompanied Murphy's corpse back to the West Coast of the USA.

MILESTONES

Jimmy Murphy was killed in an accident at the Syracuse board speedway, the first driver to become AAA National Champion posthumously.

The Alfa-Romeo P2 made its debut in the Formula Libre Circuito di Cremona. Antonio Ascari won at 98.3 mph, 54 minutes ahead of his nearest rival.

At Brooklands, Dario Resta driving a Sunbeam lost a tyre at 113 mph on the straight, crashed, and was burned to death before help arrived.

In the San Sebastian Grand Prix, Kenelm Lee Guinness was injured when his car left the road and crashed into a ravine; his mechanic, Barrett, was killed.

The first Coppa Acerbo near Pescara was won by Enzo Ferrari in an Alfa-Romeo RL; he was awarded the title *Commendatore* by Premier Mussolini.

In August, Joe Boyer – millionaire playboy and Indianapolis winner – was killed in a crash at Altoona board speedway

went into the pits for attention to his brakes – allowing Ascari through into the lead once again – and Nazzaro's brakes then also gave trouble. The Sunbeams' challenge dwindled when Guinness dropped out with a failed main bearing. Segrave manage to haul his way back into sixth place, but his car was still misfiring extremely badly.

On lap 32 of the 35, Ascari slowed down noticeably, and he was passed both by his Alfa team-mate Campari and by Divo before going into the pits where the car refused to start

again. Campari won from Divo and Benoist for Delage; Wagner was fourth in the other Alfa P2.

It was a great race – but another humiliation for France, for whom there could be only small consolation in the fair performance of the Delages.

The Italian Grand Prix had been scheduled for 7 September, but after Salamano injured his arm in practice, and Bordino's old injury caused problems, Fiat pulled out. Mercedes asked for a postponement to get its Monza cars ready, and the race was deferred until 19 October. Fiat did not reappear: Fornaca was exasperated at losing promising talent to other companies.

In the race it was Mercedes against Alfa-Romeo. Porsche had adopted a permanently engaged Roots-type supercharger for the Monza, which produced 170 bhp at 7,000 rpm, and although this resulted in a top speed of 130 mph, the P2 with 145 bhp at 5,500 rpm was faster at 139 mph. The Mercedes team was Werner, Masetti, Neubauer and Count Louis Zborowski. The Alfas were driven by Wagner, Ascari, Campari and Ferdinando Minoia. Ascari led from start to finish. Masetti was briefly in second place for Mercedes, but the Alfas all overtook him, forming a procession up at the front. Then tragedy struck. Zborowski ran off the road at the Lesmo Curve, was thrown against a tree, and was killed outright; the rest of the Mercedes team was withdrawn out of respect. Alfa-Romeo was left with a clean sweep.

LEFT: Riding mechanic Giulio Ramponi trying to push-start Antonio Ascari's Alfa-Romeo P2 in the French Grand Prix. His efforts were fruitless.

ABOVE LEFT: Harry Miller, designer of a string of superb engines, brought an intuitive flair to his work. He was born in Wisconsin in 1875, the son of a German schoolteacher. His first successful engine was produced in 1916, the four-cylinder 289-cu.in. (4.7-litre) unit which Barney Oldfield used in his record-breaking car, the 'Golden Submarine'.

After the 1924 Indianapolis 500, Jimmy Murphy mused that if 2.5 seconds could be shaved off each turn 'without ruining your rubber', the average speed for the race might rise by 10 mph. One way to achieve faster cornering was to make the car lower, but the problem was that the driver's seat had to be above the propshaft that drove the rear wheels. Harry Miller suggested using front-wheel drive to create a much lower-slung car, and Murphy ordered one just before he was killed. Miller built it not only with front-wheel drive but with a supercharger too, producing 200 bhp. He also supercharged his rear-wheel-drive cars, and existing Miller owners were offered a retro-fitted blower for $1,100.

From 1925 the Indianapolis 500 counted towards a new international innovation: a World Championship for manufacturers. In the line-up were two Duesenbergs, driven by Peter de Paolo and Phil Shafer, and 17 Millers, 11 of them supercharged, one driven by de Paolo's uncle, Ralph de Palma. The front-wheel-drive Miller was entered by Cliff

MILESTONES

European racing followed the American example and banned riding mechanics in Grands Prix, but a second seat and a driving mirror were obligatory.

The American driver George Stewart, using the pseudonym Leon Duray, set a new record of 113.196 mph in qualifying for the Indianapolis 500.

A Benz *Tropfenwagen* (>1923) driven by Franz Horner won the inaugural race at the Solitude circuit near Stuttgart in Germany.

Malcolm Campbell, complying with strict new AIACR rules, set a new world speed record of 150.869 mph in a Sunbeam on Pendine Sands, South Wales.

At Brooklands, J. G. Parry Thomas (>1927), driving the 7.3-litre Thomas-Leyland, beat the 21.7-litre Fiat Mephistopheles in a match race.

The Delage driver Paul Torchy was killed when he crashed into a tree trying to overtake Giulio Masetti's Sunbeam in the Spanish Grand Prix.

TOP: Vittorio Jano, designer of the Alfa-Romeo P2. Born in 1891, he started in the motor industry aged 18 working for STAR, the *Societá Torinese Automobili Rapide*, and joined Alfa in 1923 after twelve years with Fiat. He was one of the top designers in Italian motor racing for 40 years until his death aged 74 (>1965).

ABOVE LEFT: Alfa-Romeo's P2 was unbeatable in 1925, achieving easy victories in

the Belgian and Italian Grands Prix.

ABOVE: Alfa-Romeo added a laurel wreath to their badge to mark victory in the 1925 World Championship.

Durant (>1919) as a 'Junior 8', and driven by Dave Lewis. Miller in fact entered a second front-wheel-drive car for Bennett Hill, but after trying it, Hill reverted to a rear-wheel-drive car.

In the race, de Paolo took the lead for Duesenberg, swapping it with his team-mate Shafer. Ever higher speeds on the brick surface exhausted many drivers, and when de Paolo needed a rest he was relieved by Norman Batten. Batten lost ground to Lewis, who took the lead, so after a break de Paolo took over again, forging through the field to second place. Then Lewis came back into the pits exhausted, and Hill – whose car was out – took over. Starting more than a lap behind de Paolo, he quickly found an affinity with the front-wheel-drive Miller, and with 11 laps to go he overtook the Duesenberg, putting him on the same lap. He made up half the lap before de Paolo took the chequered flag, averaging 101.3 mph – the first time the 500 had been won at over 100 mph (>1932).

In Europe, the season started in February with a new Formula Libre race, the Premio Reale di Roma. Count Giulio Masetti won in a Type 35 Bugatti – the first time the Type 35 had been raced in Italy.

Building on his success, Bugatti entered three Type 35s in the Targa Florio, to be driven by Bartolomeo Costantini and the de Vizcaya brothers, Pierre and Édouard. The entry was small: four Peugeot sports cars, driven by André Boillot, Christian d'Auvergne, Louis Wagner and Victor Rigal, some privately-entered Alfa-Romeos, an Itala, a Fiat and an OM. Peugeot dominated the early part of the race, Boillot leading, followed by Wagner and d'Auvergne, with Costantini behind for Bugatti. Costantini drove a faultless race to win from Wagner. In two races, the Type 35 had established a striking reputation for Italian private entrants.

The Belgian Grand Prix was added to the calendar in 1925, run on a road circuit at Spa. Only Alfa-Romeo and Delage made it there, the V-12 Delages, now supercharged, driven by Albert Divo, Robert Benoist, René Thomas and Paul Torchy, the Alfas by Antonio Ascari, Giuseppe Campari and Count Gastone Brilli-Peri. It was a straight fight between France and Italy. The Belgian crowd cheered the French entrants, and was conspicuously silent towards the Italians. Ascari established a huge lead for Alfa, followed by Campari and Brilli-Peri. The Delages languished in disaster: Benoist had to drop out with a fuel tank problem, Torchy retired, and Thomas's car caught fire. Divo managed to pass Brilli-Peri, but had to retire with supercharger problems.

ABOVE: Antonio Ascari in his Alfa-Romeo P2 at Spa-Francorchamps after winning the first Belgian Grand Prix. His average speed was 74.56 mph. He died later the same year after crashing his P2 in the French Grand Prix. Ascari was born in 1888 at Casteldario, near Mantua, the son of a corn merchant, and began racing in 1919 in a modified 4.5-litre 1914 Grand Prix Fiat.

LEFT: Peter de Paolo, winner of the Indianapolis 500. Born in America in 1898, de Paolo started racing as a mechanic for his uncle, Ralph de Palma. De Paolo retired at the end of his first season as a driver, 1922, following three serious crashes in Frontenacs, but returned to racing in 1924, for Duesenberg.

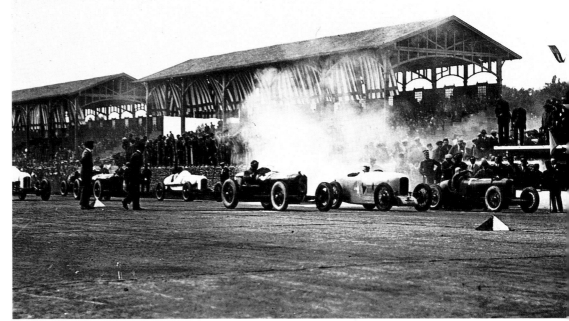

RIGHT: Alfa-Romeo dominated the Italian Grand Prix. Gastone Brilli-Peri won in a P2 in 5 hours 14 minutes 33.3 seconds, followed by a second P2 shared by Giuseppe Campari and Giovanni Minozzi just under 20 minutes behind. Alfa's reserve driver was a rising star of motorcycle racing, Tazio Nuvolari (>1930), but he crashed and was injured in practice and took no part in the race. Indianapolis-winner Peter de Paolo was a guest driver in the Alfa team, coming fifth in another P2.

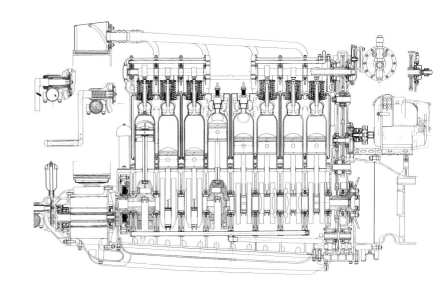

LEFT: Bartolomeo Costantini in the eight-cylinder 2-litre Type 35 Bugatti at the ACF Grand Prix. Race winners were Robert Benoist and Albert Divo, who shared a Delage, finishing in 8 hours 54 minutes 41.2 seconds. Costantini came fourth.

The power behind the P2: the eight-cylinder 1.98-litre supercharged engine (*LEFT*) which took Alfa-Romeo to victory in the first World Championship for manufacturers. In 1925 it produced 155 bhp at 5,500 rpm, up from 145 bhp at 5,500 rpm the previous year. Bench tests on the first P2 engine began in March 1924 and the first car was rolled out on 2 June 1924. Giuseppe Campari and Antonio Ascari then put it through its paces at Monza.

The three Alfas lapped serenely on until Vittorio Jano (>1923) decided to rub in Italian superiority. He had a superb lunch laid out in the pits. Then – to boos and hisses from the crowd – he called in his drivers and they all sat down to a meal while the mechanics polished the cars. After lunch they went back to racing, and the inevitable clean sweep: the finishing order was Ascari, Campari, Brilli-Peri.

Economics finally forced French race organizers to build artificial circuits. Two *autodromes* modelled on Monza, each with a road circuit and a high-speed oval, were opened at Montlhéry, outside Paris, and at Miramas, near Marseilles. The French Grand Prix was held at Montlhéry, the first outing on an artificial circuit. The French President was invited and a huge crowd was expected – but many enthusiasts stayed away, fearing further French humiliation after the disastrous performance of the Delages at Spa.

Benoist and Divo were joined at Delage by the veteran Louis Wagner. There was a works team of three Bugattis, still unsupercharged, for Costantini, Pierre de Vizcaya and Jules Goux; and a pair of private Type 35s for Ferdinand de Vizcaya and Giulio Foresti. Alfa sent its victorious team. Sunbeam was represented by Henry Segrave and Counts Masetti and Conelli. The start was bungled: the flag was dropped when some drivers were not looking. Pierre de Vizcaya went into the lead, followed by Ascari and Segrave, but by the time they came into view after one lap, Ascari was leading from Divo. Ascari increased his lead and Campari moved up into third place. Just as it seemed the crowd was indeed in for another demonstration of effortless Italian superiority, disaster struck. Ascari clipped the fencing with his front wheel; the P2 over-turned, and rolled several times. Ascari died before reaching hospital.

When his death was announced over the public address system, the crowd bared their heads in respect. The Alfa team was then withdrawn. Benoist won for Delage, and the crowd cheered themselves hoarse in acclamation of the first Frenchman to win the Grand Prix since 1913. Benoist and Louis Delage were congratulated by the French President, and Benoist received a huge bouquet of flowers. On his lap of honour he stopped where Ascari had crashed and placed the flowers by the side of the road.

Delage knew the P2s were unbeatable, and he refrained from entering the Italian Grand Prix a month later. The starting grid at Monza was enhanced by two Duesenbergs, driven by Tommy Milton and Peter Kreis. Peter de Paolo took over Ascari's place in the Alfa-Romeo team. Kreis shot into the lead for the first two laps before crashing at the Lesmo curve. Campari then took over, followed by the other two Alfas. But with a masterly display of driving, Milton overhauled de Paolo, putting the Duesenberg in third place. He held it until lap 32, when he went into the lead as the Alfas went in for fuel. Brilli-Peri had a good pit-stop and came out in second place, behind Milton. Campari had a bad pit-stop and rejoined well down the field. Then Milton came in for fuel: another long pit-stop meant he failed to catch the leaders – Brilli-Peri won from Campari.

Alfa did not go to San Sebastian for the Spanish Grand Prix. Seeing his opportunity, Delage took it: Divo won, from Benoist and Thomas. But this race did not count towards the manufacturers' World Championship and Alfa took the title, adding a laurel wreath to its badge.

CHAPTER FIVE
RED CARS, BLUE CARS &
THE WALL STREET CRASH

As the Roaring Twenties turned into recession, motor racing went through a period of rapid change. It was driven by the unseen hand of economics, but it was triggered by a new formula. Speeds had risen, leading to concern for safety. Antonio Ascari's fatal crash in 1925, coming on top of the deaths of Jimmy Murphy, Joe Boyer, Dario Resta and Louis Zborowski, turned concern into alarm, and in response the AIACR reduced engine size in competition to 1.5 litres.

The change did not have the intended result – designers simply strove to get the same power from smaller engines – but it did have an unintended effect. Faced with the cost of producing new engines, many manufacturers pulled out of racing. They did so just as the number of races was proliferating. Britain and Germany announced Grands Prix, but the real growth came not in formula races for a supreme prize at the frontiers of technology, but in Formula Libre races in which a variety of cars could compete. By 1927 top-level formula racing in Europe was faltering, and by 1928 it disappeared completely.

In the process, privateers replaced manufacturers as entrants, and this change provided a growing market for companies like Bugatti and Alfa-Romeo who sold racing cars. Ettore Bugatti maintained a small works team to ensure winning, but he sold hundreds of Type 35 variants: a Bugatti brochure in 1926 claimed that the company's cars had won 503 competitions. Such statistics gave his name great prominence which he then used to sell high-quality touring cars.

In America, the formula lasted until 1929, when the AAA introduced a stock car formula – quickly dubbed the 'Junk Formula' – at Indianapolis, in an attempt to lure the manufacturers back. Aided and abetted by the Wall Street Crash, the age of the state-of-the-art racing car was temporarily brought to a close.

Grand Prix racing comes to Britain. Albert Divo in a Talbot (third from left) leaving the Delages of Robert Sénéchal and Louis Wagner on the line at the start of the first British Grand Prix in 1926. Wagner won the race after taking over Sénéchal's car when Sénéchal retired with burned feet. Malcolm Campbell was second.

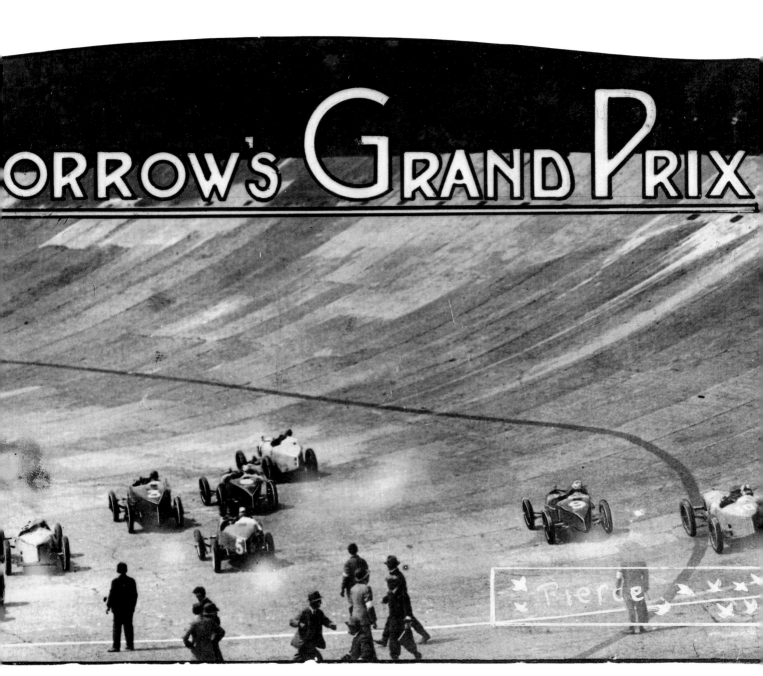

ORROW'S GRAND PRIX

Alfa-Romeo and Sunbeam followed Fiat out of Grand Prix racing under the new formula. Louis Delage stayed, building a complex engine for the new 15-S-8. Bugatti built the 1.5-litre Type 39A. Vincenzo Bertarione (>1923) moved from Sunbeam within the consortium to Talbot, to build a new Grand Prix car. All were supercharged.

In America both Fred Duesenberg and Harry Miller constructed new eight-cylinder supercharged 91.5-cu.in. (1.5-litre) engines. Duesenberg entered two cars for Indianapolis: a conventional one for Peter de Paolo (>1925) and an experimental two-stroke car for Ben Jones. Days before the race, one Miller driver, Peter Kreis, went down with flu and nominated an unknown dirt-track driver, Frank Lockhart, to replace him. On lap 71 rain stopped the race for just over an hour, but when racing resumed, the record crowd of 145,000, was thrilled by a duel between Lockhart and Harry Hartz, also in a Miller. At 400 miles the rain started again and, with the track awash, the race was stopped. Lockhart won, splitting winnings of $34,000 with Kreis.

The French Grand Prix at Miramas – the new, artificial road and oval circuit near Marseilles – marked an ultimate low in the history of the race. Neither Delage nor Talbot was ready; only three Bugattis started, driven by Jules Goux, Bartolomeo Costantini and Pierre de Vizcaya. De Vizcaya and Costantini dropped out with supercharger problems, leaving Goux circling the vast autodrome alone.

By contrast, the first German Grand Prix, held two weeks later under an open formula at AVUS, attracted a mixed bag of 46 sports cars, Grand Prix cars and voiturettes. Two 2-litre

Mercedes (>1924), although works-backed, were privately entered by Rudolf Caracciola (>1934) and Adolf Rosenberger. Rosenberger took the lead. It poured with rain, and he lost control on the North curve, crashing into the timekeeper's box, killing the three occupants. Many drivers retired because of the rain, but Caracciola was curiously at home in the wet: he won, earning himself the title *Regenmeister* ('Master of the Rain').

For the Spanish Grand Prix, Delage sent Robert Benoist and Edmond Bourlier against Goux, Costantini and de Vizcaya for Bugatti. The temperature at San Sebastian was 110°F (44°C), and with the exhaust pipes inside the Delage bodywork, the drivers were unbearably hot. Moreover, the airflow over the Delage body sucked fumes into the cockpit. Mechanics bored holes in the cars, but before long all the Delage drivers were out. Bourlier lay prostrate in the pits, his legs covered in burns. Robert Sénéchal, a Bugatti driver in the crowd, found Louis Delage, who put him in Bourlier's car in which he showed the superiority of the Delages, beating Costantini into second place but failing to catch Goux.

The Delages were rebuilt for the first British Grand Prix at Brooklands. Sénéchal joined Benoist and Louis Wagner, with André

BELOW: Rudolf Caracciola (>1933), winner of the first German Grand Prix. His eight-cylinder 2-litre Mercedes M218 produced 150 bhp at 7,000 rpm. He was born at Remagen in Germany in 1901 at the Hotel Caracciola, which was owned by his father. He made his racing debut in 1922, driving a Mercedes at the AVUS circuit.

RIGHT: Major F. B. Halford in a Halford Special leading Robert Sénéchal's Delage in the British Grand Prix on 7 August. Halford retired on the 82nd of the 110 laps of the Brooklands circuit; Sénéchal handed over to Louis Wagner who won in 4 hours 0 minutes and 56 seconds. Sandbanks were built to make the circuit represent a road race.

Dubonnet (>1921) in reserve. The Talbots made their debut, the drivers Jean Moriceau, Albert Divo and Henry Segrave. The 'home team' was Malcolm Campbell in a Bugatti 39A, J. G. Parry Thomas in a Parry Special, Frank Halford in a Halford Special, and George Eyston in an Aston Martin. Divo took the lead, but the race was a disaster for the Talbots. They were fast, but not ready. The Delages fared better but Wagner dropped out. Benoist took the lead. Then Sénéchal's exhaust box blew, the hot gases blasting straight on to the cockpit side. When his shoes began to

burn, he came in and stood in a bucket of water. Wagner took over his car and managed to pass Benoist, who then came into the pits trailing smoke. Dubonnet then took over his car, but Campbell passed him to finish second behind the Sénéchal/Wagner car.

In the three-sided battle between Talbot, Delage and Bugatti, the Talbots were the fastest but least reliable; the Delages were slower, more reliable, but lost time changing roasted drivers. The Bugattis were also slow but reliable, and for their consistency won the second manufacturers' World Championship.

LEFT: Early stages of the British Grand Prix. Henry Segrave and Albert Divo lead in Talbots; Robert Benoist is behind in a Delage.

BELOW: Harry Miller's Type 91 fwd (front-wheel-drive) car, unveiled in 1926. The 91-cu.in. (1.5-litre) engine used a centrifugal supercharger and produced a remarkable 154 bhp: 102 bhp per litre. Miller continued to work on the engine over the following years, and by 1930 it produced 252 bhp at 8,000 rpm: 169 bhp per litre capacity.

MILESTONES

Bartolomeo Costantini won the Targa Florio in a Bugatti for the second time; a third of all entrants in the race were Bugattis (>1925).

Count Giulio Masetti, the only other man to win the Targa Florio twice, was killed in the 1926 race when he overturned his Delage on a corner.

The first German Grand Prix, run at AVUS, was won by Rudolf Caracciola driving one of Dr Porsche's 2-litre Grand Prix Mercedes (>1924).

The Italian Grand Prix at Monza was won by the French driver Jean Chaverel under the pseudonym 'Sabipa' in a Bugatti; Costantini was second.

Herb Jones crashed and was killed qualifying for the Indianapolis 500. His car was rebuilt for the race and driven to ninth place by John Duff.

Jules Goux retired after winning the French and San Sebastian Grands Prix. His first race had been the Coupe des Voiturettes in 1906.

The withdrawal of Fiat and Alfa-Romeo from racing, coupled with Bugatti's win in 1926 in both the Targa Florio and the Italian Grand Prix, had left the top level of the sport in Italy in a parlous state. Against that background the year opened with the birth of another legendary race in Italy, open to all manner of cars, and run to a format that had disappeared a quarter of a century earlier (>1903). A race from Brescia to Rome and back via a circuitous route, it covered precisely 1,000 miles: the Mille Miglia ('one thousand miles' in Italian).

Four young men in Brescia – once the home of Italian motor racing but now overtaken by Monza – wanted to re-establish the town's position. Count Aymo Maggi, Count Franco Mazzotti, Renzo Castegneto and Giovanni Canestrini conceived an epic race on public roads, which would not even officially close. The idea appealed to Italy's leader, Benito Mussolini, who saw motor racing as a forward-looking force for modernization which he considered essential for Italy, and permission was immediately forthcoming.

Italian motor racing had been very success-ful, but individual ownership of cars in Italy remained low and the roads were poor. The attraction of the Mille Miglia was that it popularized production cars. There were 77 entries, the vast majority of them Italian. Two days were allocated for the race, 26–27 March, but in reality nobody knew how long it would take.

The first car, a straight-8 Isotta Fraschini driven by Count Maggi, was flagged off at 8 am, followed by the others at regular intervals. Count Gastone Brilli-Peri drove an Alfa-Romeo RLSS sports car. Ferdinando Minoia was in a similar OM. Vincenzo Lancia (>1907) entered a team of six Lancia Lambda production cars. Tazio Nuvolari entered in a Bianchi. There were luxury V-12 Fiat 519 tourers at one end of the spectrum, and 990-cc Fiat 509s at the other.

The sports cars did far better than the tour-ers. Brilli-Peri took the lead, and stretched it to 14 minutes by the time the race reached Rome. As the cars went into the night, spectators lined the route with torches to show drivers the way. Brilli-Peri retired with a broken oil pipe. Attilio Marinoni and Giulio Ramponi (formerly Antonio Ascari's riding mechanic) in another Alfa dropped out too, leaving three OMs in front, led by Ferdinando Minoia. Minoia arrived back in Brescia first after 21

SAINT-BRIEUC 17 Juillet 1927

PROGRAMME PRIX OFFICIEL 3 FRANCS

LA COUPE FLORIO

GRANDE COURSE INTERNATIONALE AUTOMOBILE

Organisation Générale: Journal L'Ouest-Eclair
Pouvoir Sportif: Automobile Club des Côtes du Nord

hours 4 minutes 48 seconds' racing, and Italian cars filled the first ten places. OMs were second and third, Lancias fourth and fifth, Maggi's Isotta-Fraschini sixth, and Nuvolari's Bianchi tenth.

Italian cars had triumphed in the first Mille Miglia, and Bugatti tightened his grip on the Targa Florio. Bartolomeo Costantini returned in 1927, not to race but to organize works backing for the huge number of private entrants racing their own Bugattis. Bugatti himself entered three supercharged 2-litre Type 35s driven by Emilio Materassi, Ferdinando Minoia, and André Dubonnet. In the race, Dubonnet took on André Boillot's Peugeot in the early stages, until both cars collapsed under the strain. Minoia took the lead until he broke a universal joint. Materassi took over, to win, giving another great overall boost to the Bugatti name.

There were 29 Millers and five Duesenbergs on the grid for the Indianapolis 500. The 91.5-cu.in. (1.5-litre) Miller now developed 230 bhp – 153 bhp per litre capacity – easily the most powerful engine in racing. Frank Lockhart broke the one-lap qualifying record in a Miller at 120.918 mph, then led the race for 120 laps before a con-rod broke. All but ten of the cars dropped out. George Souders won, having driven a comparatively unspectacular race in an old Duesenberg that he had bought for as little as $1,500.

In Europe, Grand Prix racing diminished further as costs rose and entries dropped. The competition was between Delage, Talbot and Bugatti. Ettore Bugatti improved the Type 39A with a larger supercharger, although not enough to match the Talbot. Louis Delage made expensive modifications to the 15-S-8, replacing the twin superchargers with one, and sorting out the heat and exhaust fumes problem (>1926). The engine block was reversed

ABOVE: The Coppa Florio was established by Sicilian Count Vincenzo Florio in 1905. Under its rules, the manufacturer with most victories after seven races would keep the trophy. The contest was held irregularly; after the seventh, in 1924, there was no clear winner. Peugeot won the eighth race in 1925 to keep the cup. In 1927 Peugeot held one last race in France for *La Coupe Florio*. The winner was Robert Laly in a 3-litre Aries.

MILESTONES

On 29 March Henry Segrave was the first to break the 200-mph barrier, setting an official land speed record of 203.793 mph in a Sunbeam Slug.

Otto Merz (Archduke Francis Ferdinand's chauffeur at Sarajevo in 1914) won the German Grand Prix at the Nürburgring in a 6.7-litre Type S Mercedes-Benz.

The AIACR finally dropped the requirement for two seats in Grand Prix cars, and drivers at last drove unaccompanied by riding mechanics (>1923).

Two of the redundant Grand Prix Delages were bought by the British driver Malcolm Campbell and the rising star from Monaco, Louis Chiron (>1928).

Louis Wagner retired from racing following the French Grand Prix, the last active driver to have driven in the first Grand Prix (>1906).

Eddie Rickenbacker, prewar racing driver and war hero (>1917–18), bought the Indianapolis Speedway from Carl Fisher and Jim Allison for $700,000.

When Robert Benoist was unable to race after crashing into Leon Duray's car during practice at Miramas, the crowd invaded the Talbot pit.

The Le Mans 24-hour race was won by Dudley Benjafield and Sammy Davis in a 3-litre Bentley, the first of four successive Bentley victories in this race.

and the engine offset, a practice initiated by Talbot, so that the exhaust was farther away from the driver. The result was one of the finest Grand Prix cars of its day – and in Robert Benoist, Delage found the driver to match it. Another promising sign came when Fiat announced a comeback to Grand Prix racing in the form of a twelve-cylinder single-seater, the 806.

There were ten entries for the French Grand Prix at Montlhéry: Benoist, Edmond Bourlier and André Morel for Delage; Materassi, Count Conelli and Dubonnet, fresh from their success in the Targa Florio for Bugatti; Talbots for Albert Divo, Louis Wagner and W. Grover-Williams; and George Eyston in a Halford Special from Britain. At the last minute, Ettore Bugatti withdrew his team, claiming that his cars were beaten before they started. The 100,000 crowd shouted its disapproval, but they were then thrilled by the rivalry between Benoist and the favourite, Divo, who went into the lead, followed by Benoist and Williams. These three pulled ahead of the rest, until Divo had a succession of engine problems in the troublesome Talbot. Benoist took the lead on lap 4, and held it to the end despite repeated challenges from Divo, to win by 11 minutes, followed by his team-mates Bourlier and Morel. Soon after the race, Talbot withdrew from racing.

Benoist and Delage went from victory to victory. Bugatti contested the Spanish Grand Prix, which Benoist won after some trouble from Materassi until the Italian crashed while in the lead. Bugatti withdrew from the Italian Grand Prix at Monza, so with Talbot already out, the only serious competition came from America – George Souders in the Indianapolis-winning Duesenberg, and Earl Cooper and Peter Kreis in front-wheel-drive Millers. The American cars had the power for flat-out racing, but lacked the handling for road racing. Delage was unconvinced that they represented serious opposition and sent only Benoist, who won.

The British Grand Prix at Brooklands was a Delage procession. Benoist won, followed by Bourlier and Divo, who had joined Delage from Talbot. Delage won the World Championship for manufacturers, but the cost had been too high, even for Louis Delage. Having spent most of his family fortune building racing cars, and despite his great successes, he pulled out.

Top-level racing came to an end at the end of the year. The sign of revival signalled by Fiat's re-entry into the sport petered out after the Gran Premio di Milano. Fiat entered the 806 – at 187 bhp, the most powerful Grand Prix car of the age – and Pietro Bordino won it easily, giving a tantalizing glimpse of what might have been.

Fiat's board was, however, horrified at the rising cost of producing state-of-the-art cars, and abandoned racing again, this time for good. Instead of the cars' being sold into private hands, they were destroyed as they

RIGHT: Fiat's last Grand Prix car. The twelve-cylinder 806 Corsa had a top speed of 155 mph and produced 187 bhp at 8,500 rpm. Pietro Bordino drove the car to an emphatic victory in the Milan Grand Prix, at an average speed of 94.57 mph.

were, together with their predecessors, the 804 and 805 (>1922, 1923).

The AIACR dropped the formula for 1928: the only restrictions that remained were on weight and the length of the race. In doing so, it was merely acknowledging the reality that manufacturers were no longer going to pay for the extraordinary pace and scope of technical progress that had characterized what with hindsight can be seen as one of motor racing's golden ages.

BELOW: World Champions. From left, drivers Edmond Bourlier, Robert Benoist and Albert Divo with the 1.5-litre Delages, winners of the World Championship for manufacturers. The car's engine developed 170 bhp at 8,000 rpm. Its top speed was 130 mph.

ABOVE: Louis Delage founded his company in 1905 and began racing the following year. He is reported to have spent £36,000 developing the 1927 Grand Prix car.

The Nürburgring

The Nürburgring, in the Eifel Mountains, was Germany's most famous road racing circuit. It was built in the 1920s as a scheme to create work for Germany's unemployed (BELOW), and opened in 1927. The circuit centred on the village of Nürburg, where the medieval castle looked down on the pits area. The twisting course had 89 left-hand bends and 85 right-handers; its highest point – the pits – was 620 metres (2,034 feet) above sea level, and its lowest point – at Breidscheid, near Adenau – was at an altitude of 320 metres (1,050 feet). Racing began in June 1927: the first race was won by Rudolf Caracciola in a Mercedes 680. The first German Grand Prix, held at the Ring on 17 July, saw another home win: Otto Merz in a Mercedes at an average 63.39 mph.

The Nürburgring was 14.7 miles (22.8 km) in length, including a start/finish straight of 1.4 miles (2.2 km). A 4.8-mile (7.7-km) south loop was added but was seldom used.

NORTH LOOP   Karussel

Flugplatz

Nürburg village

Schwalbenschwanz

Start & finish

SOUTH LOOP

GERMANY
Nürburg
Koblenz

ABOVE: Louie Meyer, winner of the Indianapolis 500 and the year's AAA National Champion. At Indianapolis he drove Alden Sampson II's eight-cylinder Miller, with Sampson himself as mechanic. Meyer was born in 1904 and was mechanic and relief driver for Wilbur Shaw's fourth-placed Jynx in the 1927 500.

ABOVE RIGHT: Giuseppe Campari driving over the Raticosa Pass on his way to victory in the second Mille Miglia. His co-driver in the six-cylinder 1.5-litre supercharged Alfa-Romeo 6C was Giulio Ramponi.

The racing authority AIACR set a maximum car weight of 550–600 kilograms (1,102–1,323 pounds) and a minimum race distance of 600 kilometres (372.8 miles). The British Grand Prix was abandoned, and most other organizers adopted Formula Libre. This brought about a revival of private interest in older Grand Prix cars – the Talbots, Delages, Bugattis and Alfa-Romeo P2s (>1925).

The first Mille Miglia had been a great success, and Ettore Bugatti responded by sending a team of 2.3-litre supercharged Type 43s to add the Mille Miglia to his crown. He exchanged his French drivers for Italians: Pietro Bordino, Count Gastone Brilli-Peri, and Tazio Nuvolari. The opposition was a masterpiece from Vittorio Jano – the 1,500-cc Alfa-Romeo 6C sports car. Alfa entered eight 6Cs, one of them supercharged and prepared in great secrecy for Giuseppe Campari and Giulio Ramponi. The Bugattis led from the start. Nuvolari, Brilli-Peri and Bordino were first, second and third when the race reached Bologna. But they were not suited to the conditions, and lost a lot of time with mechanical problems. Back in Bologna after 780 miles, Campari was in the lead for Alfa-Romeo, and held it to the end. The first Bugatti home was Brilli-Peri in sixth place.

Following the decline of the French Grand Prix, the Targa Florio became Europe's premier race. It was another battle between hordes of Bugattis and two supercharged 6C Alfas driven by Giuseppe Campari and Attilio Marinoni. Albert Divo set the fastest time in practice, and led from the start for Bugatti. Campari and Elizabeth Junek in a Type 35B fought for second place. Junek took the lead at one point, but then fell back with engine problems. Campari crossed the line first, to a delirious reception from a crowd who believed an Italian had broken Bugatti's grip on the race. But Divo, who had started later, managed to win by 97 seconds; Junek was fifth.

MILESTONES

On 22 April Ray Keech raised the land speed record to 207.553 mph in a White Triplex powered by two 13.5-litre V-12 Liberty aircraft engines.

On 25 April Frank Lockhart attempted to beat Keech's record in a Miller-engined Stutz-Blackhawk Special; he crashed at 210 mph and was killed.

The French Grand Prix was run as a handicap sports car race; William Grover-Williams won for Bugatti, the only works car in the race.

In May Fritz von Opel drove his rocket-powered car, Rak-2, to 121.2 mph at the AVUS circuit; it accelerated from 0–100 km/h (0–62.13 mph) in 8 seconds.

The German Grand Prix at the Nürburgring was won by Rudolf Caracciola in a 7.1-litre Mercedes SS; Christian Werner shared the driving.

Two weeks before the Targa Florio, Pietro Bordino was killed in practice. The Bordino Prize race in his memory was won by Tazio Nuvolari.

In the United States, Eddie Rickenbacker (>1917) had bought the Indianapolis Speedway from Carl Fisher and his associates. For the first race under the new ownership, Leon Duray set a record in qualifying at 124.018 mph. He also led the early part of the race, but pushed his car too far, overheated, and dropped back. Jimmy Gleason took over in a Duesenberg until a mechanic poured water over the magneto, leaving Tony Gulotta to lead until a blocked fuel pipe put him out. The next driver to inherit the lead was Louie Meyer, driving his first 500 in a Miller: he completed the distance without mishap and won (>1933, 1936).

The Italian Grand Prix was the only formula race in Europe. Twenty-two cars started, among them many ex-Grand-Prix cars including eleven Bugattis: a works team of W. Grover-Williams, Nuvolari, Giulio Foresti and Guy Bouriat, and Louis Chiron, the favourite, in a privately entered car. Emilio Materassi was driving his own ex-Grand Prix Talbot, Luigi Arcangeli and Brilli-Peri were in two more Talbots. Achille Varzi drove his own Alfa-Romeo P2.

The Grand Prix cars produced close racing, reminiscent of earlier times. Williams led from the start, hotly pursued by the Talbots, then Varzi, Nuvolari and Chiron. When Williams slowed with engine problems the lead swapped back and forth between Nuvolari, Varzi and Materassi. Then tragedy struck. Materassi was challenging for the lead when his steering failed; he swerved across the track, hit the barrier, and died instantly. The disintegrating car killed 22 spectators and injured a good number more. All the Talbots were withdrawn immediately, but the race continued, keenly fought to the end by Chiron and Varzi: another Bugatti-Alfa battle, which Chiron just won.

It was Chiron's year – on top of winning the only Grand Prix of real stature, he won the Marne Grand Prix at Rheims, the Rome Grand Prix and the San Sebastian Grand Prix, all driving for Bugatti.

ABOVE LEFT: Bugatti champion Louis Chiron. Born in 1900 in Monaco of French parents, he started his racing career with Bugatti. He spent the First World War as an army driver and was personal driver to Marshal Foch in 1919.

LEFT: Louis Chiron overtaking Bugatti team-mate Gastone Brilli-Peri in the Rome Grand Prix. Chiron finished first in 3 hours 5 minutes 48.6 seconds, and Brilli-Peri was second, just under five minutes behind. Both men were driving Type 35Cs, which developed 135 bhp at 5,300 rpm.

Two famous names reached a peak of ascendency in 1929: Miller and Bugatti. But both were under threat. In America, the American Automobile Association (AAA) was considering a stock car formula in the hope of luring manufacturers back into racing. In Europe, Bugatti was under direct challenge from the developing technologies of Alfa-Romeo and Maserati.

The duel between Bugatti and Alfa was the theme of the year. Vittorio Jano developed a 1.7-litre engine for the 6C (>1928), and Giuseppe Campari and Giulio Ramponi took first blood in it in the Mille Miglia. It was something of a hollow victory: Bugatti was not competing. The Mille Miglia was held on the same day as the first Monaco Grand Prix, and Ettore Bugatti made Monte Carlo – with its customer potential – his priority. Half the 16 entries were Bugattis: W. Grover-Williams led the works drivers. Alfa managed to race at both events, sending Goffredo Zehender and Victor Rigal in 1.7-litre 6Cs. Germany was represented by Rudolf Caracciola in the 7.1-litre SSK Mercedes sports car. The feature of the race was the struggle between Caracciola and Williams. They swapped the lead back and

forth until Caracciola had a bad pit-stop and rejoined too late to catch Williams, who thereupon won.

After these early skirmishes, Bugatti and Alfa squared up to each other fully in the Targa Florio. Bugatti was defending his four consecutive victories with four Type 35Bs for Albert Divo, Ferdinando Minoia, Louis Wagner and Count Conelli, against three Alfa 6Cs driven by Campari, Achille Varzi and Count Gastone Brilli-Peri.

Divo's starting position was twelve minutes behind Campari, but Divo slowly gained, passing the Alfa on lap 3. He husbanded his car right up to the end – making it five wins in a row for Bugatti.

Bugatti continued winning the major races. Williams took the French Grand Prix at Le Mans, and Chiron the German Grand Prix at the Nürburgring. At the same time it was the Alfa drivers who continued to win on home ground: Brilli-Peri won the Circuito di Cremona in a P2, and Varzi took the Rome Grand Prix, the Coppa Ciano and the Monza Grand Prix in his P2.

The Indianapolis 500 was the crowning glory of the career of Harry Miller. Frank Lockhart had bought two front-wheel-drive Millers, developing them even further before he died (>1928). They were bought by two rich men and raced by Ray Keech and Louie Meyer, who dominated the 500. Meyer led until he lost all his oil pressure. Keech took over and established an unbeatable lead before Meyer rejoined to take an extremely creditable second place.

Leon Duray took two other front-wheel-drive Millers to Montlhéry, where he broke

BELOW: Grover-Williams' Bugatti 35B taking a sharp corner in the first Monaco Grand Prix. Grover-Williams, who raced under the name 'Williams', finished first in 3 hours 56 minutes 11.0 seconds, a little over a minute ahead of his Bugatti team-mate Georges Bouriano in a Type 35C. Williams was born near Paris in 1903, the son of a French mother and an English father. He started racing in 1926 in a Hispano-Suiza and the same year began a long association with Bugatti (>1943).

RIGHT: Monte Carlo. The novelty of racing on the streets of Monaco was enormously popular with spectators. One of the safety measures taken was to paint kerbstones white so that the drivers could see them more clearly.

MILESTONES

Louis Chiron qualified for Indianapolis in a 1927 Delage at 107 mph and finished seventh; Miller drivers were qualifying at around 120 mph.

Two weeks after winning the Indianapolis 500, Ray Keech died in a crash on the Altoona board speedway, the last board track still running races.

The 'Bentley Boys', a 'works team' of wealthy enthusiasts, took the first four places in the Le Mans 24-hour race for sports cars (>1930).

The Bugatti works team dominated the German Grand Prix at the Nürburgring. Louis Chiron won, breaking Mercedes-Benz's hold on the race.

More than 500,000 people lined the Ards circuit for the Ulster TT for sports cars. Rudolf Caracciola won for Mercedes out of 65 entries.

In November Erwin 'Cannonball' Baker (>1915) took 2 days 21 hours 31 minutes to drive from Los Angeles to New York in a Franklin.

several speed records – the fastest the one-kilometre at 143 mph (230 km/h) – demonstrating the matchless power and speed of the Millers. Duray then entered the Monza Grand Prix, racing Varzi's Alfa P2 wheel-to-wheel until his car's main bearings went and he retired. After the race, Duray swapped the Millers for three Type 43 Bugattis. Bugatti examined the engines and finally adopted the Miller double overhead camshaft and hemispherical combustion chambers, coming to the conclusion that they would produce an extra 50 bhp (>1931).

Several factors now pointed towards Miller's incipient decline. The Wall Street Crash took away much of the money that had sponsored the drivers who raced his cars. The board speedways, for which they were designed, were no more; they had rotted, and most were closed. The final blow was the AAA formula for 1930: 366 cubic-inch (6-litre) engines, only two valves per cylinder, no superchargers, two seats, and an obligatory riding mechanic. It was designed for stock cars, not the thoroughbred racers of which Miller was the master. The purists christened it the 'Junk Formula', but it was evidently the way ahead.

Harry Miller, with no production car business to fall back on, after a struggle went bankrupt (>1933).

LEFT: Woolf Barnard and Sir Henry Birkin's 6.5-litre Bentley on its way to victory in the Le Mans 24-hour race for sports cars.

They finished 71 miles ahead of the second-placed car – a 4.4-litre Bentley driven by Glen Kidston and Jack Dunfee.

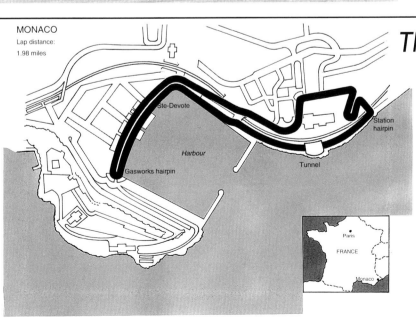

MONACO
Lap distance:
1.98 miles

Ste-Devote
Harbour
Gasworks hairpin
Station hairpin
Tunnel

Paris
FRANCE
Monaco

The Monaco road circuit

The 'round the houses' circuit in Monte Carlo is one of the most enduring in motor racing. It was conceived by the President of the Automobile Club de Monte Carlo, Anthony Noghès, in 1928 and was first used in 1929. Starting from the harbour, the circuit climbs into the town to pass the famous casino, then descends via a hairpin bend to the shore. Here the cars plunge into a tunnel that takes them back to the pits and start area. The narrow, twisting roads of the city mean that overtaking is extremely difficult, and make Monaco's 1.5-mile course one of the most testing Grand Prix circuits in the world.

RIGHT: Achille Varzi and mechanic Tabacchi taking their modified Alfa-Romeo to victory over the tortuous and demanding road circuit of the Targa Florio. Their average speed was 48.52 mph, although the car's maximum speed was 118 mph.

The 'Junk Formula' at Indianapolis (>1929) was partly successful in influencing the American motor industry more towards racing. Among the 38 starters in the 500 were specials made with engines from Chrysler, Buick, Stutz, Studebaker and Duesenberg – but most were emasculated Millers, thoroughbred racing cars adapted to the new rules.

Louie Meyer took the lead in a 'Samson' powered by two Miller engines. On lap 3 he was overtaken by a front-wheel-drive Miller hybrid, its 91-cu.in. (1.5-litre) engine bored out to 152 cubic inches (2.5 litres), and its cockpit widened to take Billy Arnold and his mechanic, Spider Matlock. Cy Marshal's Duesenberg crashed on a curve, and his brother Paul, riding as mechanic, was killed. Arnold won at an average speed of 100.448 mph – tantalizingly close to the track record (>1925). Reworked Millers took the first four places.

The Alfa team for the Mille Miglia was Tazio Nuvolari, Achille Varzi, Count Aymo Maggi and Giuseppe Campari. Mercedes sent Rudolf Caracciola and the veteran Christian Werner (>1931). Luigi Arcangeli took the lead in a Maserati, then crashed, so that it became a three-cornered race between Nuvolari, Varzi and Caracciola. As dawn on the second day approached, Varzi was three minutes ahead of Nuvolari on the road, although Nuvolari was well ahead on time. It was still dark when Nuvolari saw his rival ahead. He switched off his lights and crept up on him unawares, flashing them on again as he swept by, to win – a hat trick of Mille Miglia wins for Alfa.

Three weeks later, the pair met again in the Targa Florio. The Alfa team was managed by Enzo Ferrari (>1924). He had 6Cs for Nuvolari and Campari, and a bored-out P2 for Varzi which, with a top speed of 140 mph, was not suited to the twisting Madonie circuit. Ferrari decided it was too dangerous, but Varzi – who had won the Bordino Prize in it – protested, and got his way. Proving his point,

BELOW: The Indianapolis 500 sold itself as an all-American day out. Attractions included marching bands before the start of the race.

he overtook all the Bugattis and Maseratis, breaking the lap record on the first lap. Only Louis Chiron in his Bugatti stayed with him, but he crashed, losing time. Varzi then also fell back, nursing a fuel leak, and Chiron caught up. So on the last lap Varzi's mechanic took the fuel with him, pouring it in on the move – and spilling some on the exhaust. It caught fire, but Varzi raced on, his mechanic beating the flames with his cushion, to rapture in the stands when he finally took the chequered flag. At last Bugatti's stranglehold (>1929) on the Targa Florio had been broken.

Bugatti lost the Targa, but his cars continued to win important races. René Dreyfus, a private entrant, won the Monaco and Marne Grands Prix, Chiron the European Grand Prix at Spa, and Philippe Etancelin the French Grand Prix. In Italian domestic races the new 8C-2500 Maseratis – their first new cars since 1927 – were increasingly competitive. Emilio Arcangeli won the Rome Grand Prix in one, and Varzi drove them to victory in the Coppa Acerbo and the Spanish Grand Prix.

Alfa, Bugatti and Maserati met again at the Monza Grand Prix. There were heats for 1-litre, 2-litre, 3-litre and bigger cars, with a final between the fastest four of each group. The Alfas fared badly in the heats and, seeing that they were outclassed by the Maseratis, the team wanted to withdraw. The Monza management, in an attempt to dissuade the Alfas from leaving, cabled Rome for political support. At once back came a message under Premier Benito Mussolini's own hand to the Alfa team: 'Your proposed action does not meet with my approval.'

They raced, the rivalry focusing on Nuvolari, Campari and Baconin Borzacchini for Alfa, and Arcangeli, Varzi and Ernesto Maserati for Maserati. Arcangeli took the lead, but Nuvolari managed to pass Varzi into second place before the Alfas developed tyre problems and pulled out. Varzi, lying second, went into the pits for plugs. When he rejoined, something of the spirit that had claimed him in Sicily took over. He passed both team-mates to win by one-fifth of a second.

MILESTONES

The Indianapolis winner Billy Arnold in his Miller/Hartz won two races at the Altoona board speedway, at 111 and 113 mph, to take the AAA National Championship.

Woolf Barnato and Glen Kidston won the Le Mans 24-hour race in a 4.4-litre Bentley, the British company's third successive win in the race.

Henry Birkin came second in the French Grand Prix in a stripped-down 4.4-litre Bentley. When Louis Chiron blocked his path, he sounded his horn.

Tazio Nuvolari's third place in the Masaryk Grand Prix in Brno, Czechoslovakia, was the last racing appearance of the Alfa-Romeo P2 (>1925).

After many years working for Alfa-Romeo, Enzo Ferrari began to run the company's racing activities through his own team, Scuderia Ferrari.

The economic situation in Germany forced Daimler-Benz publicly to renounce racing – but Rudolf Caracciola continued to receive covert support.

ABOVE LEFT: Billy Arnold (right), winner of the Indianapolis 500 in a Miller/Hartz at an average speed of 100.448 mph, and the year's AAA National Champion. Support came from riding mechanic Spider Matlock (right).

ABOVE: The Mercedes-Benz badge. German companies Daimler and Benz merged in 1926; Mercedes-Benz was the name used for marketing. The badge's heraldry represented engines manufactured for land, sea and air.

RIGHT: Moment of triumph in the Indianapolis 500 – Louis Schneider and riding mechanic Jigger Johnston taking the chequered flag. Schneider won $29,500 out of a total purse of $81,800.

BELOW RIGHT: In the pits at the Italian Grand Prix. Tazio Nuvolari and Giuseppe Campari shared the winning Alfa 2300, covering 967.94 miles in the race's ten-hour limit.

The second year of the so-called 'Junk Formula' at Indianapolis came tragically close to the truth. Crashes started in practice when Joe Caccia hit the track wall and flipped over it, killing himself and his mechanic, Clarence Grover. In the race, Billy Arnold (>1930) took the lead in the Miller/Hartz as the accidents continued: Harry Butcher went over the wall in his Buick on lap 7, Wilbur Shaw followed him on lap 61 and Bill Cummings on lap 70, both in Millers. All were injured, but survived, and the race then settled down until lap 163 when Arnold's rear axle broke. He slewed across the track and Luther Johnson in a Studebaker hit him broadside. Arnold went over the wall, and both he and his mechanic, Spider Matlock, were injured. More tragically, a wheel from his car flew into the air and landed outside the track, killing an 11-year-old boy, Wilbur Brink, who was playing in his garden. Louis Schneider inherited the lead in a Bowes/Miller, and went on to take the chequered flag.

As Indianapolis moved back to production-based cars, specialized racing cars started a renaissance in Europe. Bugatti and Alfa-Romeo, spurred on by Maserati's 8C-2500 (>1930), both brought out new cars. Bugatti developed two more variants on the Type 35B: the 2.3-litre supercharged double overhead camshaft Type 51, and the 4.9-litre Type 54. Alfa developed the eight-cylinder Monza from the successful 6C-1750 sports car (>1929), and – as Indianapolis regressed to riding mechanics – Vittorio Jano unveiled Europe's first true single-seater, the Tipo A Monoposto, powered by twin 6C-1750 engines.

The new Alfas did not make it to the Monaco Grand Prix, in which Goffredo Zehender faced 16 Bugattis, and Rudolf Caracciola for Mercedes, alone in a 6C-1750. The race was hard fought. Carracciola, Luigi Fagioli in a Maserati, and Achille Varzi in a Bugatti chased Louis Chiron (also in a Bugatti) around the streets of his home town. Nobody could catch him, to the great delight of his fellow Monégasques.

The first real trial between Alfa and Bugatti came in the Targa Florio as the race celebrated

IMP. ARTE PARIS · MUSÉE DE L'AUTOMOBILISTE

LEFT: No Grand Prix had more glamour than Monaco. This year's race saw a home win – Monégasque Louis Chiron in a Bugatti 51 in a total of 3 hours 39 minutes 9.2 seconds. Second was Luigi Fagioli in a Maserati, 4 minutes behind.

MILESTONES

On 5 February, Malcolm Campbell broke the land speed record at 245.733 mph in his car 'Bluebird', powered by a twelve-cylinder Napier aero engine.

Rudolf Caracciola and co-driver Wilhelm Sebastian won the Mille Miglia in a Mercedes SSK sports car, the first non-Italians to win the race.

Two British drivers, Earl Howe and Tim Birkin, won the Le Mans 24-hour race in an Alfa-Romeo Monza. Bugatti withdrew after their tyres broke up.

The first major motor race to be held in Switzerland was the Geneva Grand Prix on 7 June; the winner was Marcel Lehoux in a Type 51 Bugatti.

On 7 September Shorty Cantlon, driving a Miller, won the final board speedway race at Altoona, Tipton, Pa., the last wooden track to hold races.

The man who built Britain's first racing car, Montague Napier, died aged 60; his aero engines also powered Malcolm Campbell's 'Bluebird'.

its 25th anniversary (>1906). Bugatti did not enter officially, but Varzi begged a Type 51 from him and the ensuing battle with Nuvolari in a Monza was worthy of the occasion. Varzi led for three laps until it rained and his front wheels, which lacked mudguards, sprayed him with thick mud. He threw away his caked goggles but had to slow down, and Nuvolari and Baconin Borzacchini – both protected by mudguards – overtook him. Nuvolari took the flag.

The AIACR's fuel consumption formula was ignored by promoters and eventually abandoned for Grands Prix lasting a minimum ten hours, two drivers per car. The first such marathon was the Italian Grand Prix at Monza, where Bugatti unveiled the Type 54 for Varzi and Louis Chiron to challenge Borzacchini and Giuseppe Campari in Monzas, and Nuvolari and Luigi Arcangeli in Tipo As. That changed when Arcangeli was killed in practice, and Jano withdrew the Tipo As. Varzi held the lead for the first two hours, then Chiron took over until the Type 54's engine failed. Campari, partnered by Nuvolari, completed the ten hours in turns to win.

The Auto Club de France (ACF) celebrated the 25th anniversary of the first Grand Prix

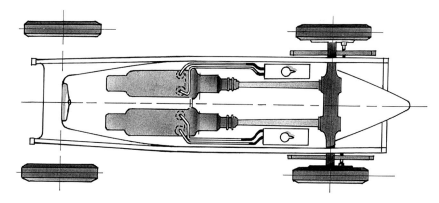

with a lunch at Le Mans attended by François Szisz and Felice Nazzaro (>1906, 1907). The Grand Prix at Montlhéry attracted 23 entries. Bugatti, Alfa and Maserati sent strong teams and, as German cars were allowed for the first time since 1914, Caracciola brought his Mercedes. Chiron and Varzi covered 782.1 miles in their Bugatti to win from Campari and Borzacchini, who clocked 755 miles for Alfa.

Caracciola won the German Grand Prix at the Nürburgring, but Bugatti ended the year on a high note: Chiron won the Belgian and Czechoslovakian Grands Prix.

ABOVE: The Alfa-Romeo Type A. It was powered by two front-mounted six-cylinder parallel engines with a total capacity of 3,504 cc; maximum output was 115 bhp at 5,200 rpm for each engine, giving a total of 230 hp. Its top speed was 149 mph.

129

After two years, the change to a formula based on stock cars for Indianapolis seemed to be successfully luring the American automobile industry back into motor racing. Studebaker entered a team of five superbly finished racing cars based on their luxury touring car, the President. The 336-cu.in. (5.5-litre) side-valve engine produced 196 bhp, giving the drivers Cliff Bergere, Zeke Meyer, Tony Gulotta, Peter Kreis and Luther Johnson a top speed of 130 mph. Against them the favourites were Billy Arnold (>1930, 1931) and Fred Frame, driving the latest Miller-based specials produced by Harry Hartz. Harry Miller himself was close to bankruptcy, but he produced a pair of 307.9-cu.in. V-8 four-wheel-drive cars and a 308-cu.in. V-16 for the race.

Two men died in practice. Benny Benefield hit the track wall on a turn, soared over it into trees, and crashed to the ground; he was injured, but his mechanic Harry Cox was killed. Then Milton Jones did the same, killing himself, although his mechanic survived. Lou Moore's Miller was fastest in qualifying, at 117.363 mph, and he took pole position. Edsel Ford drove the Lincoln pace car, setting the 40 starters off at 70 mph, with Moore in the lead. But Billy Arnold stormed through the pack to overtake him on lap 2; Bryan Saulpaugh was third in the V-16 Miller. The leaders, mostly Miller variants, set a fast pace, and the best the Studebakers could manage was tenth. Gus Schrader did well in his four-wheel-drive Miller until he crashed on lap 7, but at the 100-mile mark, Arnold was still leading at an average speed of 111.494 mph, compared with 104.733 mph at the same point the previous year. Then he lost concentration going into the main straight to turn 3, hit the wall hard, wrecked the car, and injured himself and his mechanic, Spider Matlock.

Bob Carey then inherited the lead and held it to nearly half way, when he hit the wall and broke a wheel. With pit-stops, retirements and accidents, the lead swapped back and forth, but after 400 miles Fred Frame in the second Miller/Hartz showed he was fastest and won at 104.144 mph, breaking Peter de Paolo's record of 1925. Howdy Wilcox II (no relation to the 1919 winner) was second in another Miller, and Bergere was third for Studebaker. The prize money for the race had increased to a total of $93,900.

In Milan, Vittorio Jano had been working on a new single-seater Alfa Romeo since September 1931. With limited funds, he was unable to design a new engine from scratch, so he took the eight-cylinder 2.3-litre engine from the Monza sports car (>1931) and

ABOVE: Leading figures of the American motor industry at the Indianapolis 500. Standing at the left: Eddie Rickenbacker, the contemporary owner of the Indianapolis Speedway, and Henry Ford, the automobile magnate. Ford's son Edsel is seated in the 500 pace car, a Lincoln KB Sports Roadster. At the far right is Harvey Firestone Senior, the tyre manufacturer.

increased it to 2.6 litres, adding two superchargers to produce 215 bhp, or 81 bhp per litre – low, compared with the 123 bhp per litre achieved by Fiat in the 1.5-litre 806 (>1927), but higher than many contemporary cars. Power was transmitted to the back wheels by two prop-shafts, one to each wheel. It was a light car – around 700 kilograms (13.8 hundredweight) – and lightness was crucial, for it would be competing against cars with much greater power. They would have the edge on the straights, but the Tipo B Monoposto, as it was known officially, would have the advantage on the corners. Light cars not only made more use of the power, turning it into more speed, they also followed the contours of the ground more closely, increasing traction and so improving cornering.

Enzo Ferrari continued to manage the Monzas that raced in the Mille Miglia and the

MILESTONES

Baconin Borzacchini won the Mille Miglia in a Scuderia Ferrari Alfa Monza in a record 14 hours 55 minutes 19 seconds. Alfas took the first seven places.

At AVUS, Manfred von Brauchitsch, driving an SSK Mercedes sports car, beat Mercedes' former driver, Rudolf Caracciola, driving an Alfa Monza.

On 19 September Ab Jenkins driving a Pierce Arrow won the first 24-hour Speed Run on the Bonneville Salt Flats, covering 2,710 miles at 112.94 mph.

One of America's racing pioneers, Fred Duesenberg (>1912) died from pneumonia recovering from injuries received in a crash in his own car.

The AIACR, concerned at the increasing engine size and speed of racing cars, announced a weight limit of 750 kg for Grands Prix for 1934, 1935 and 1936.

On 1 November, in response to the new formula, Dr Ferdinand Porsche (>1924) formed his own company to design and race cars under its name.

ABOVE: Fred Frame, winner of the Indianapolis 500 in 4 hours 48 minutes 47.46 seconds. Frame was born in 1894 and started racing in the late 1920s. He finished second at Indianapolis in 1931.

ABOVE: The Indianapolis 500 on 30 May. Entry numbers were steadily increasing (40 in 1932 and 42 the following year) but in 1934 the race organizers decided to restrict the field to 33 – a limit that is still in force today. Detailed lap times were registered for every car by an individual scorer. From 1927, when radio commentaries began, the scorers each wore a number pinned to their backs – and as 'their' car changed position, they swapped seats so that the radio commentators could see the race order at a glance.

ABOVE: Rudolf Caracciola driving an Alfa-Romeo P3 to victory in the German Grand Prix, ahead of his Alfa team-mates Tazio Nuvolari and Baconin Borzacchini. Caracciola's family had lived in Germany – where his father was a hotelier and wine merchant – for several generations since emigrating from Sicily in the nineteenth century. He was renowned as a sensitive driver who never overworked his car or his tyres. He won the German Grand Prix six times – in 1926, 1928, 1931, 1932, 1937 and 1939.

Targa Florio, but Jano looked after the Tipo B team himself, taking on the two finest drivers of the day in Tazio Nuvolari and Rudolf Caracciola. Mercedes, suffering in the acute economic conditions in Germany, finally gave up racing completely; Caracciola left the company with a promise to Alfred Neubauer to return if ever they started again (>1934). Before the debut of the new car on 5 June at the Italian Grand Prix, the pair had already made a brilliant start to the season in Monzas: Nuvolari won the Targa Florio and Caracciola the Eifelrennen at the Nürburgring. To maximize the chances of an Italian win, Nuvolari and Giuseppe Campari drove the two Tipo Bs, while Caracciola and Baconin Borzacchini

TOP: Vittorio Jano's second masterpiece, the Tipo B 'Monoposto'. Between 1932 and 1934 the car won every Grand Prix for which it was entered. Six Tipo Bs were built in 1932, and a further seven were made in 1934, modified to comply with the new Grand Prix formula which imposed a weight limit of 750 kilograms.

ABOVE: The Tipo B's eight-cylinder engine had a light-alloy block with pressed steel cylinder liners. The capacity of the 1932 unit was 2.6 litres, but by 1934 it was up to 2.9 litres. The engine had two valves per cylinder.

drove Monzas. The beautiful new car was promptly christened the P3 because many racing enthusiasts and journalists saw it as a natural successor to Jano's previous masterpiece, the P2 (>1924).

The opposition came from two works Type 54 Bugattis driven by Achille Varzi and Louis Chiron, and Luigi Fagioli in a formidable 16-cylinder Maserati which used two eight-cylinder engines in line (>1930), producing 330 bhp from the 4.9 litres.

In the race, Chiron took the lead early on, but he and Varzi suffered from engine problems and retired. Caracciola retired with magneto problems. Borzacchini was hit by a stone

ABOVE: Benito Mussolini, the Fascist leader of Italy (seated), meeting Alfa-Romeo directors and drivers, including Tazio Nuvolari (centre, in white suit). Mussolini saw success in motor racing as a symbol of a resurgent and modern Italy.

and came in, and Caracciola then took over his Monza. But the real race was between Nuvolari and Fagioli. The Maserati was faster than the P3, and Fagioli broke the lap record at 112.07 mph. With Nuvolari's expertise at the wheel, the Alfa's superb cornering, and much faster pit work by Jano's team of mechanics, Nuvolari nonetheless took the P3 to victory in its debut race. Fagioli was second, and Caracciola third.

The French Grand Prix was held at Rheims for the first time. It was a straight fight between Bugatti and Alfa, for Maserati could not afford to take its team to France. Alfa brought three P3s for Nuvolari, Borzacchini and Caracciola. Bugatti fielded Varzi and Albert Divo in Type 54s, and Chiron in a Type 51. After pressure from racing promoters and the public, the AIACR had cut the length of Grands Prix from ten hours (>1931) to five hours. The start was at midday.

Caracciola took the lead, followed by Varzi. Then Nuvolari came charging through the field into third place by lap 4, and four laps later he had passed Varzi; on lap 11 he passed Caracciola. Borzacchini had already moved into third place, and the P3s were now in first, second and third places. The Alfa drivers fought amongst themselves, Caracciola taking the lead back from Nuvolari on lap 20, Nuvolari getting back in front ten laps later – by which time the three Alfas had lapped most of the field, some of them twice over. By lap 65 they had lapped Chiron, and as five o' clock approached, the Alfa drivers arranged themselves in the order in which they wished to finish – Nuvolari, Borzacchini, then Caracciola – for Alfa, Mussolini and Italy expected the Italians to win.

Two weeks later the unseen hand of politics intervened again, at the German Grand Prix at the Nürburgring, when the trio arranged themselves in a different order – Caracciola, Nuvolari, Borzacchini – and on this occasion Germany was delighted. Chiron then won the Czechoslovakian Grand Prix at Brno for Bugatti when all the Alfas had mechanical problems. But with that one exception, the P3s won every race they entered: Nuvolari the Coppa Ciano and Coppa Acerbo, after another furious struggle with Fagioli in the Maserati, and Caracciola the Monza Grand Prix. It was the kind of impact by one name not seen since Alfa had won everything in sight in the P2 in 1925. In 1932, at the end of the season, history repeated itself when the Alfa board stopped any more racing because it was simply too expensive. Instead of handing the cars over to Enzo Ferrari for his Scuderia, they put them into storage and he had to continue with the Monzas . . . which were becoming decidedly long in the tooth.

LEFT: Italian greats. Count Vincenzo Florio, founder of the Targa Florio race (>1906), with Tazio Nuvolari, the finest Italian driver of the 1930s. Nuvolari was born on 18 November 1892 at Casteldario near Mantua in northern Italy. He started racing on motorcycles, and his first victory was in the 1922 Circuito di Belfiori, riding a Harley Davidson.

Alfa-Romeo's decision to pull out of racing left some top drivers looking for a new job. Tazio Nuvolari went to Scuderia Ferrari with Baconin Borzacchini; Rudolf Caracciola formed a partnership with Louis Chiron, who had been fired by Bugatti, and they bought three Alfa Monzas; Giuseppe Campari bought an 8C-2800 Maserati. The only works team left was Bugatti, whose drivers were Achille Varzi, William Grover-Williams, Albert Divo and René Dreyfus.

At the Monaco Grand Prix, racing nearly lost one of its greatest drivers when Caracciola crashed in practice, smashing his leg badly enough to put him out of racing for a year. The race itself was a memorable one. Nuvolari in a Monza and Achille Varzi in a Type 51 Bugatti raced wheel-to-wheel for 99 of the 100 laps. Then, with only yards to go, and Varzi leading, Nuvolari's engine expired under the strain; he pushed it to the finishing line.

In the French Grand Prix at Montlhéry, Nuvolari put in a final practice lap of 141.242 mph, compared with Chiron's best of 137.446 mph. In the race, Nuvolari led, while Chiron challenged him in his own Alfa, until both cars suffered failures in their rear axles. Campari in his Maserati and Piero Taruffi in a Scuderia Ferrari Monza then treated the crowd to a great battle, until Taruffi came into the pits. Enzo Ferrari replaced him with Nuvolari, who managed only a few laps before the car broke down, leaving Campari to win the race for the second time in nine years (>1924).

The Scuderia cars were showing their age. Remaining within the team, Nuvolari changed to a Maserati which he had strengthened to take the punishment he was prone to handing out. At the Belgian Grand Prix he gave a

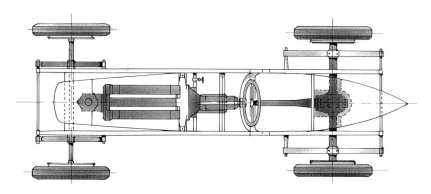

ABOVE: Italy's second single-seater, the Maserati 8CM, was built to challenge Alfa-Romeo's P3. It was the beginning of an intense rivalry between the two great Italian firms that would continue until after the Second World War. In its original form the 2.9-litre engine developed 220 bhp at 5,500 rpm, but this was subsequently raised to 240 bhp at 5,500 rpm. Top speed was 155 mph. Tazio Nuvolari drove the 8CM to victory in the 1933 Belgian Grand Prix.

ABOVE: Giuseppe Campari. Born near Milan in 1892, he joined Alfa-Romeo as a test driver in his teens and had a long career with the company. Campari was married to the singer Lina Cavalleri; he had a great love of music and was noted for singing operatic arias while he was racing.

MILESTONES

LEFT: Black day at Monza. Giuseppe Campari's overturned Alfa-Romeo (left) and Baconin Borzacchini's Maserati after their fatal crash in the second heat of the Monza Grand Prix. Count Czaikowski was killed at the same spot in the final race. Distraught at the tragedy, Tazio Nuvolari kept vigil through the night with the drivers' widows.

BELOW: Marquis Antonio Brivio in the Italian Grand Prix, driving one of the great Alfa-Romeo sports cars, the 8C-2600 Monza. He handed over to Eugenio Siena, who finished fifth.

The Monaco Grand Prix was the first to allocate grid positions in order of fastest practice times, pole position going to the fastest driver.

Five men were killed and one seriously injured in three crashes at Indianapolis, more evidence of the folly of risking mechanics in the cars.

At Indianapolis drivers went on strike when Howdy Wilcox II was disqualified for fainting through diabetic attacks. They resumed racing when Mauri Rose replaced him.

Louie Meyer won the 500 at a record 104.162 mph, his second victory (>1928, 1936). The Depression nearly halved the total purse to $54,450.

Tazio Nuvolari won the 24-hour sports car race at Le Mans partnering Raymond Sommer in an Alfa Monza; the winning margin was no more than 10 seconds.

On 6 November Raymond Mays founded English Racing Automobiles Ltd (ERA) to build British racing cars based on his modified Riley engine.

seater. Ferrari hired Chiron (his partnership with Caracciola dissolved) and Luigi Fagioli – lately of Maserati – to replace them.

At the Nice Grand Prix, Nuvolari took the lead, closely challenged by the younger blood from France and Italy – Philippe Etancelin, Jean-Pierre Wimille and Guy Moll in Alfas, and René Dreyfus and Marcel Lehoux in Bugattis. He pressured them into mistakes, and won by 1½ minutes from Dreyfus. His performance did not go unnoticed at Alfa-Romeo, and after pressure from Ferrari, the board released the P3s to him, after which Nuvolari's star began to wane. A week after Nice, he met Chiron and Fagioli in P3s at the Coppa Acerbo at Pescara. He led for part of the race, but not even Nuvolari in his 8CM could beat the P3: Fagioli won by 2 minutes.

There was a carnival atmosphere at Monza, where the Italian drivers were burning to win on their home ground, and Campari announced that he would retire after the day's two events to pursue a career in opera. In the first heat of the first race, oil was spilled on a corner. When Campari and Borzacchini braked on it in the second heat, both crashed and died instantly. In the final, Count Czaikowski hit the same patch in his Bugatti, crashed, and was killed too. The second race, the Grand Prix, was an all-Italian battle between Fagioli in the P3 and Nuvolari in the 8CM, which Fagioli won, but the day was remembered more for the death of the three drivers just as Grand Prix racing was looking to a new era.

virtuoso performance, sweeping away the opposition to win at an average speed of 89.23 mph – more than 1 mph faster than the previous lap record, which he raised to 92.33 mph. But in exasperation with the ageing machinery, Nuvolari formed a team with Borzacchini and bought two 8CMs, Maserati's new single-

135

CHAPTER SIX
STOCK CARS, SILVER ARROWS &
VORSPRUNG DURCH TECHNIK

Motor racing provided entertainment and an escape from the miseries of the Depression. The sport grew, but, like every other activity in the early 1930s, it was starved of investment, and the expansion was based on old technology.

Racing car design stagnated, particularly chassis design. What investment there was went into engines, finding more power by increasing size. Speeds at Indianapolis and in Grands Prix rose, and the AAA and AIACR both moved to curb it. In 1934 a fuel-consumption formula of 45 US gallons (37.47 UK gallons; 170.34 litres) was introduced for the 500, and a weight limit of 750 kilograms (1,653½ pounds, 14.74 hundredweight) was introduced for Grands Prix.

In January 1933, a few months after the new Grand Prix formula was announced, Adolf Hitler was elected to power in Germany. The new German Transport Minister announced a fund of 450,000 Reichsmarks (£45,000) for companies to build Grand Prix cars, plus bonuses for winning. Hitler wanted to use motor racing as a propaganda platform for the Nazi Party and to show the superiority of German engineering. Mercedes decided to build a car to the new formula. Dr Ferdinand Porsche (>1924, 1932), who had been working on such a car for more than a year, teamed up with Auto Union. The subsidy was split between the two.

Hitler's money funded a revolution in chassis design. Both companies used light alloys and independent suspension on all four wheels, improving traction and cornering at a stroke. Mercedes used a conventional in-line eight-cylinder engine in the front, Porsche put the engine behind the driver. Within months of their introduction, the cars were winning virtually everything they entered. They spawned a process of development that culminated in speeds approaching 200 mph. The logic of the stated intention that restrictions would curb speeds was never more clearly stood on its head. The 750-kilogram formula ushered in an age of rapid evolution in the technology, power and speed of racing cars, and in the spectacle of racing.

One of Germany's 'Silver Arrows': Auto Union's Type C, the car Bernd Rosemeyer drove to victory in the 1936 German Grand Prix.

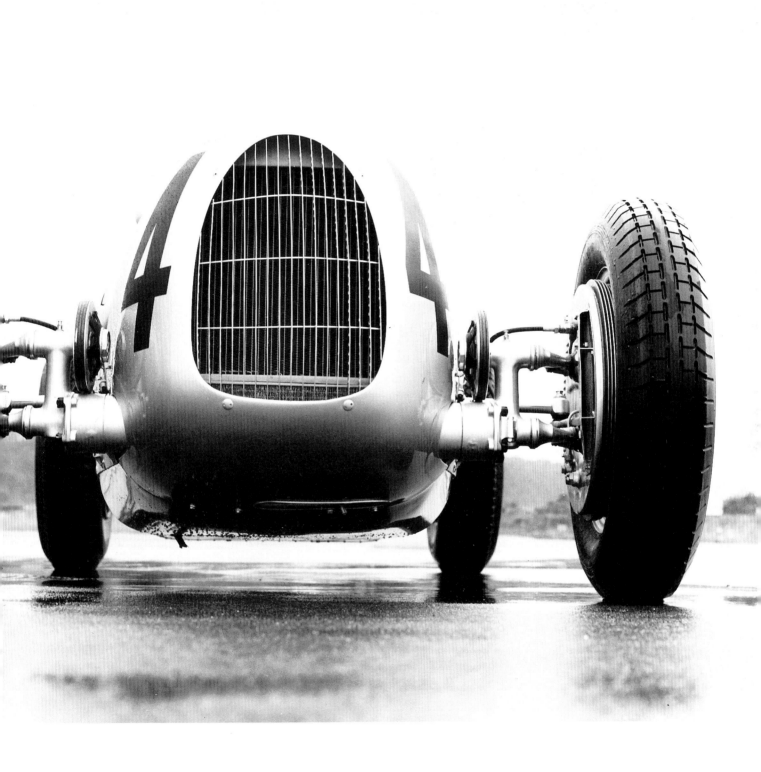

One of the effects of the change in the formula, and the resurgence in Germany which it provoked, was the return to works-backed teams at the top level, replacing the entrepreneurial partnerships that had thrived during the years of free-for-all racing. Tazio Nuvolari, the top driver in 1933, remained independent. His greatest rival Achille Varzi went over to Scuderia Ferrari to drive Alfa-Romeos. So did another former Bugatti driver, Louis Chiron, joining Guy Moll, a young man from Algeria, whom Enzo Ferrari had discovered. Hans Stuck, Auto Union's top driver,

was joined by two German amateurs, August Momberger and Prinz zu Leiningen. Mercedes re-engaged Rudolf Caracciola, although he was still limping and far from fit to race (>1933), and also took on Manfred von Brauchitsch, a Prussian aristocrat. To complete his team Alfred Neubauer (>1924), the Mercedes racing manager, engaged the fiery Italian driver Luigi Fagioli, who had shown great form in the Alfa P3 during the closing months of 1933.

In January, Auto Union tested its Type A at the Nürburgring. On 6 March Stuck took it to AVUS and broke the 1-hour record by 2 mph, reaching 164 mph on the long straights. The Mercedes W25 prototype was tested at Monza in February – but von Brauchitsch crashed it. It was rebuilt and went back to Monza in March. In April Caracciola took it to AVUS where he did one lap at 143 mph. For patriotic reasons both teams wanted their car's debut to be in Germany, so they missed the Monaco Grand Prix, which was won by Moll in an Alfa P3. On 27 May a crowd of 220,000, including the Führer himself, gathered at AVUS to look them over for the first time. Caracciola put in some very fast practice times, which pleased the crowd, but the Mercedes were running rough, and Neubauer withdrew the team rather than risk a debacle. Auto Union faced

MILESTONES

The first purpose-built circuit in Switzerland was opened at Bremgarten. Hans Stuck won the first international Grand Prix there for Auto Union.

In the Indianapolis 500, 'Wild' Bill Cummings won in a Boyle Special at a new record speed of 104.863 mph – despite the AAA fuel consumption formula.

Peter de Paolo (>1925) brought a two-seater four-wheel-drive Miller Special from America to compete in the AVUS Grand Prix – but retired.

René Dreyfus won the Belgian Grand Prix, the last major Bugatti victory; the Germans withdrew because of punitive Belgian taxes on their special fuel (>1956).

In the Coppa Acerbo at Pescara, Guy Moll driving an Alfa P3 was killed trying to overtake Ernst Henne's Mercedes at 150 mph on a long straight.

Hans Stuck ended the year breaking records at AVUS: 101.37 mph for the standing kilometre, 116.73 mph for the mile, and 152.18 mph for the 100 kilometres.

LEFT: Two of the great figures in Italian motor racing in the 1930s – Enzo Ferrari (standing) and Achille Varzi. Ferrari, born in 1898, was a farrier in the First World War, shoeing mules for the Italian Army. He raced for Alfa-Romeo in the 1920s, leaving in December 1929

to set up the Scuderia Ferrari in Modena. The company made its own cars and prepared private entrants' Alfa-Romeos for competition. Varzi joined the Alfa-Romeo team in 1929. In 1934 he won the Tripoli Grand Prix and the Targa Florio in Alfa-Romeo Tipo Bs.

BELOW: Hans Stuck in the Auto Union Type A at the French Grand Prix at Montlhéry on 1 July. He retired after 32 laps when the car's fuel system developed problems. In 1934 Stuck won the German, Swiss and Czechoslovakian Grands Prix for Auto Union.

the Alfa-Romeos of Varzi, Chiron and Moll alone. Stuck blasted into the lead from the start, pulling ahead of Chiron in the first of the Alfas. Momberger and von Brauchitsch were not in the same class as Varzi, Moll and Chiron, who fought for second place, still 1 minute 25 seconds behind Stuck. Varzi moved to lead the Alfas, but he could not catch Stuck until – to the dismay of the crowd – Stuck's clutch failed. Suddenly the Alfas were all at the front . . . until Chiron lost power and fell back. Moll won, Varzi was second, and Momberger came third.

Two weeks later both German teams were ready for the Eifelrennen at the Nürburgring. Caracciola was not fit, so it was left to von Brauchitsch and Fagioli to make Mercedes' debut. They went straight into the lead, ahead of both Auto Union and Alfa. Fagioli was faster than von Brauchitsch, and nothing Stuck or Chiron could do could catch them. With Mercedes cars firmly established in first and second place, politics intervened. It was not in the script that Mercedes' first victory in the new era should be at the hands of an Italian. Neubauer signalled to Fagioli to give way to von Brauchitsch. The Italian obeyed, but the next time he came into the pits for tyres, Fagioli and Neubauer had a blazing row. Fagioli wanted to win. Out on the track again, he harried von Brauchitsch mercilessly, making it plain he was being held back on orders. Neubauer called him in again and the row continued. This time when Fagioli got out to the track again, he parked his W25 at the side of the road and walked back, denying Mercedes a 1-2 victory and giving Stuck second place for

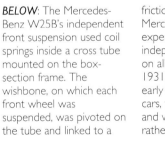

BELOW: The Mercedes-Benz W25B's independent front suspension used coil springs inside a cross tube mounted on the box-section frame. The wishbone, on which each front wheel was suspended, was pivoted on the tube and linked to a friction damper (below). Mercedes-Benz had been experimenting with independent suspension on all four wheels since 1931, but on most of the early independently sprung cars, transverse leaf springs and wishbones were used rather than coil springs.

ABOVE: German champion Hans Stuck was born on 27 December 1900 in Warsaw, while his German parents were there on a business trip. He served in the artillery during the First World War and began his racing career in 1924. Mercedes signed him as a driver in 1931 but he moved to Auto Union in 1934 (>1963, 1978).

Auto Union behind von Brauchitsch – a dream result for Führer Hitler.

A month later, excitement at the French Grand Prix at Montlhéry was at fever pitch. Past French humiliations at the hands of Mercedes (>1908, 1914) were still fresh in many memories, and they were rekindled when Mercedes came to practise before the race. The Montlhéry lap record was held by Nuvolari at 5 minutes 19 seconds. Von Brauchitsch quickly brought it down to 5 minutes 16 seconds, before Fagioli broke it three laps in a row, reducing it to 5 minutes 11 seconds. When official practice started, Stuck took another five seconds off it, then Chiron – on whom French hopes rested – equalled Stuck's new record, as did Fagioli, before von Brauchitsch brought it down again by some margin to 5 minutes 5.6 seconds.

In the race, Chiron took the lead, with Fagioli, Stuck and Caracciola close behind. Then Stuck passed Fagioli and Chiron, and French hearts began again to sink. But von Brauchitsch had to retire with engine problems on lap 9, and soon afterwards Stuck's Auto Union faltered and he had to go into the pits, putting Chiron back in the lead. French despair turned to hope first when Fagioli drove up a bank while challenging Chiron and dropped out with damaged brakes, and then again when Caracciola's engine gave up and he retired. Stuck raced on, but the Auto Union was now very slow, and he was no threat. The challenge had evaporated: Alfa romped home to a 1-2-3 victory: Chiron, Varzi, and Count Carlo Trossi.

The Germans had been well beaten – but nobody believed it would stay that way. Two weeks later, on their home ground at the Nürburgring for the German Grand Prix, Stuck and Fagioli set the pace, Chiron and Varzi fighting for the third place in Alfas. Caracciola, looking for his old form, burst through to take the lead briefly, then retired with engine problems. This time his retirement did not spark a general retreat. Stuck won for Auto Union, Fagioli was second for Mercedes, and Chiron third for Alfa.

The German works teams then enjoyed a relentless run of victories. Fagioli won the Coppa Acerbo at Pescara and the Spanish Grand Prix, and Stuck took the Swiss and Czechoslovakian Grands Prix for Auto Union. After the tragedies of 1933, the Italian authorities insisted on chicanes on the fast stretches at Monza for the Italian Grand Prix, making a total of 100 corners per lap. Caracciola led until all the braking and cornering caused his leg too much pain. Then Varzi and Nuvolari,

who was driving a new 3.2-litre Maserati, had a brief all-Italian duel. Fagioli went into the pits with supercharger problems, took over Caracciola's car – and duly went on to beat his two countrymen.

The message was clear: driving as an independent was not going to lead to victory. A driver who wanted to win had to join one of the German teams. Nuvolari had lost his position at the top of the league of drivers, and decided to join up. Mercedes had Caracciola, who despite his bad leg was not about to be dropped; they had von Brauchitsch and they already had one Italian, Fagioli. Auto Union was short of top drivers, and so Nuvolari approached them. In December he received a letter saying that the 'other drivers' did not want him. Auto Union had signed up Varzi, and Varzi had vowed he would never drive in the same team as Nuvolari; Stuck did not want the greatest driver of the age in the team either. So Nuvolari next approached Enzo Ferrari. At first Ferrari declined, remembering the way Nuvolari had walked out on him (>1933) – but politics intervened again. Premier Mussolini wanted Italian drivers in Italian cars, and he made it plain to Ferrari that Nuvolari should be brought into the Scuderia.

Ferrari obliged.

ABOVE: The poster for the French Grand Prix held at Montlhéry. Mercedes chose the ACF race for the debuts of their new Grand Prix cars in 1914, 1934 and 1954. In 1914 and 1954 the Mercedes won, but in 1934 France held the German invasion at bay – Louis Chiron winning in an Alfa-Romeo P3.

RIGHT: The eight-cylinder Mercedes W25 developed 354 bhp at 5,800 rpm and had a top speed of around 175 mph. Mercedes works drivers scored 16 international victories in the W25 between 1934 and 1936.

LEFT: The old and the new. Rudolf Caracciola in a Mercedes W25 leading Achille Varzi in an Alfa-Romeo P3 and Tazio Nuvolari in a Maserati 8CM through the chicane at Monza in the Italian Grand Prix. Luigi Fagioli won the race after taking over Caracciola's car.

BELOW: The first of the new Mercedes W25s was completed in January 1934, when it was inspected by Nazi leader Adolf Hitler at the Mercedes-Benz works in Stuttgart. The first tests were held in March at the high-speed AVUS and Monza circuits.

For 1935 the German motoring association (the ADAC) suggested a European Drivers' Championship. Many national clubs agreed, but the Automobile Club de France (ACF) – hostile to most things German – declined to take part. It went ahead anyway, including the German, Swiss, Belgian, Italian and Spanish Grands Prix. The top six drivers were spread evenly between Mercedes (Rudolf Caracciola and Luigi Fagioli), Auto Union (Hans Stuck and Achille Varzi) and Alfa-Romeo (Tazio Nuvolari and Louis Chiron).

Both German companies modified their cars. Mercedes put a 4.9-litre engine in the W25B, increasing power to 400 bhp. Auto Union produced the Type B, which had torsion-bar rear suspension rather than leaf-spring. To counter the German threat, Alfa-Romeo resorted to independent front suspension and brute force. Its 'Bimotore' had two engines, one behind the driver and one in front; a vehicle with two 3.2-litre engines producing 540 bhp was tested on a Milan *autostrada* at 212 mph. Auto Union did not make it to Monaco, where Mercedes filled the front of the grid. Caracciola's engine blew up at the start, but Fagioli led most of the race to register a comfortable win.

The Bimotores were tricky to handle on Monaco's streets, but their power was more usable in the Tripoli Grand Prix, on the fast Mellaha circuit with its long straights. Fagioli went into the lead, followed by Caracciola, when suddenly Nuvolari overtook them with 20 mph in hand. Nuvolari's punishing driving, and the heat, took a heavy toll on the

ABOVE RIGHT: Early in the season, Mercedes-Benz and Auto Union traditionally gave Berlin motor racing fans a look at the year's new cars at the AVUS track, where Formula Libre races were held each May. There were two heats and a final. In heat one, Bernd Rosemeyer (front right, in an enclosed Auto Union Type B of the kind used for speed record attempts) made his debut on the AVUS track, but was forced to retire; Hans Stuck (front left, in an open-cockpit Type B) won at 155.5 mph.

RIGHT: Tazio Nuvolari, winning the German Grand Prix in an Alfa P3 before a silent home crowd, after the greatest drive of his illustrious career.

Bimotore's tyres. He made a total of 13 stops, while Caracciola – finding his old form – drove a careful race, conserving his tyres, to win: his first victory since his bad accident (>1933). Later, after a titanic struggle with Auto Union's discovery, Bernd Rosemeyer, Caracciola also won the Eifelrennen by the slight margin of 1.9 seconds.

The ACF put a series of chicanes on the straights at Montlhéry in order to slow the German cars. In the Grand Prix, Stuck took the lead, but Nuvolari's greater skill showed in the chicanes and, in his 3.2-litre P3 Monoposto, he overtook Stuck by the end of lap 1. Caracciola then found his form and passed both Stuck and Nuvolari. Stuck and Rosemeyer dropped out with carburettor problems, and Caracciola and Nuvolari had a brief battle until Nuvolari's transmission broke. Jubilant, Caracciola and Manfred von Brauchitsch then circled serenely to the end, to catcalls from the grandstands. Revenge was never more sweet.

Fagioli won at Penya Rhin, and Caracciola won the Spanish and Belgian Grands Prix following the established theme of the year – Caracciola supreme among the Germans, with Nuvolari a constant thorn in his side, prevented from doing any real damage to German progress only by having to drive inferior cars. Caracciola won the important races, and with them the European Drivers' Championship.

Then came the German Grand Prix at the Nürburgring. More than 300,000 spectators were expecting a race between Mercedes and Auto Union. Nuvolari was driving an Alfa P3 Monoposto with independent front suspension, bored out to 3.8 litres, giving it 330 bhp. Caracciola took the lead, but both he and the crowd were astonished to find that at the end of the first lap Nuvolari was only 12 seconds behind, ahead of Rosemeyer, Fagioli and Chiron. By lap 9 these three had overtaken Nuvolari, and he then had a bad pit-stop. But Nuvolari fought his way through again to second place, even as von Brauchitsch took the lead. Nuvolari drove the race of his life, putting pressure on von Brauchitsch until, on the last lap, a tyre burst on the Mercedes – and Nuvolari won before a silent crowd. It was one of the most remarkable drives in Grand Prix history: a driver of sublime skill triumphant over the latest technology in an obsolete car.

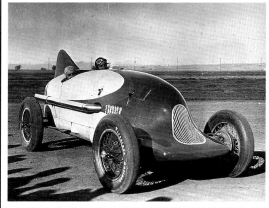

The 'Catfish Special' was built in 1932 by Art Sparks and Paul Weirick, who worked with Harry Miller in developing its 220-cu.in. engine. The bulbous body was an attempt to improve aerodynamic efficiency, calculated by two professors from Stanford. Its best position in the Indianapolis 500 was 14th in 1932, driven by Stubby Stubblefield.

MILESTONES

ABOVE: A caricature of Italy's top driver Tazio Nuvolari, by British motoring artist Gordon Crosby. Nuvolari had a very colourful driving style and was renowned for sitting up high in the seat and pulling faces while racing. He was extremely superstitious and always raced in a yellow shirt, leather jerkin and blue trousers. Born near Mantua, he was nicknamed the 'Flying Mantuan'.

When Dr Hans Nibel – designer and Director of Mercedes' Grand Prix project – died of a stroke aged 54, he was replaced by Max Sailer (>1914).

In practice for the Monaco Grand Prix, a young Mercedes mechanic, Hermann Lang, was given an opportunity to drive, but not to race (>1937).

The Mille Miglia was won for Alfa by Carlo Pintacuda and the Marquis della Stufa in a specially-adapted Tipo B Monoposto Grand Prix car.

Kelly Petillo won Indianapolis using an Offenhauser engine – Fred Offenhauser, Miller's foreman, had bought his boss's bankrupt business (>1980).

In September Sir Malcolm Campbell broke the 300-mph barrier taking the land speed record at 301.129 mph in 'Bluebird' at the Bonneville Salt Flats.

The first Grand Prix in Britain since 1927, at Donington Park on 6 October, was won by the British driver Richard Shuttleworth in an Alfa P3.

Daytona Beach in Florida was too short and too rough for the land speed record breakers as they approached 300 mph. When they moved to the Bonneville Salt Flats in Utah, local businessmen were dismayed at the loss of business. They turned for ideas to a former LSR driver, Sig Haugdahl, who suggested cutting breaches in the sand dunes 1½ miles apart, creating a circuit out of the beach and the road that ran behind. The American Automobile Association (AAA) sanctioned a 250-mile race for stock cars on the 3-mile circuit on 6 March. The $5,000 prize attracted a field including the Indianapolis 500 winner, Bill Cummings. A huge crowd grabbed every good vantage point for a race that started fast, but slowed as the soft sand at the turns was churned up. Fords filled the first five places. The winner was Milt Marion. In fifth place was Bill France, the man who was later to establish Daytona as the world capital of Stock Car racing (>1959).

Eddie Rickenbacker made improvements to the Indianapolis Speedway, widening the turns, making them smoother, and reducing the banking. The outside wall was rebuilt at an angle inwards to stop cars going over it in crashes (>1931, 1933), and although there

RIGHT: Milt Marion leading in a Ford at the North Curve during the first race on the combined beach and road circuit at Daytona Beach, Florida. The race was scheduled for 250 miles but the surface was so badly broken up after 200 miles that it was stopped at that point (>1959).

BELOW RIGHT: The British Empire Trophy Race was held on the 2.55-mile road circuit in Donington Park, near Derby. It was the first time the Empire Trophy had been held on a road circuit – having previously been run at Brooklands.

MILESTONES

The Vanderbilt Cup (>1915) was revived on a road and dirt circuit at Roosevelt Field, Long Island. Tazio Nuvolari won the 300-mile race for Alfa.

International oil sanctions against Italy for invading Abyssinia nearly caused the cancellation of the Mille Miglia; some cars raced using charcoal-burning systems.

At Indianapolis, Magnaflux tests were used for the first time. Parts were magnetized then dipped in oil containing iron filings to reveal cracks.

The Donington Park Grand Prix attracted continental entrants. The winner was the Swiss amateur Hans Reusch, with the British driver Richard Seaman (>1938).

R.1A – the first ERA racing car, a supercharged voiturette – won the Nuffield Trophy at Donington Park. It was driven by Raymond Mays (>1949).

Tazio Nuvolari's victory in the Coppa Ciano was the last time that an Alfa-Romeo beat both the Mercedes and Auto Union team cars.

were three crashes in practice, nobody was killed. In a further effort to reduce speeds, the AAA limited fuel to 37.5 gallons (>1934), making the race an even more careful balancing-act between winning and finishing. Rex Mays was fastest in a Gilmore Special, qualifying at 119.644 mph, and he set a cracking pace for 20 laps before slowing to conserve fuel. Babe Stapp took the lead, then Wilbur Shaw, both in Offenhauser-powered cars, before Louie Meyer (>1928, 1933) went to the front. As the finish approached, seven cars ran out of fuel, including Mays – but Meyer finished with three gallons of fuel unused. The restriction did nothing to reduce speeds: his winning speed was 109.069 mph, a new record, and the first five cars were all faster than the 1935 winner's time.

In Europe the German teams continued their dominance, only Alfa's Nuvolari giving them any trouble. Following their relatively poor performance in the previous year, Auto

Union lengthened the Type C by 4 inches (10.2 centimetres) to improve roadholding. Mercedes shortened the W25 by 11 inches (27.9 centimetres) and increased engine size to 4.7 litres, resulting in a total of 494 bhp. Alfred Neubauer took on Louis Chiron – a move that had to be sanctioned by Führer Hitler – and Hermann Lang (>1935) was given a chance to race. Alfa-Romeo produced a Tipo C with all-round independent suspension.

The Auto Club de France (ACF) was not prepared to see France humiliated again, so it opted out of true Grand Prix racing, reverting to a sports car formula on the flimsy excuse that spectators preferred production cars. The entry was a huge 37, but the crowd was thin.

Rudolf Caracciola started the season well, with wins at Monaco and Tunis, and Tazio Nuvolari gave the German cars some problems, getting the better of them at the Penya Rhin, Brno and Milan Grands Prix and the Coppa Ciano. But once Bernd Rosemeyer got into his stride in the Auto Union, he dominated in the major races, winning the Eifelrennen, the German Grand Prix and the Coppa Acerbo – in which he was timed at 183 mph. Caracciola saw his European title slipping away, and although he took the lead when the two met at the Swiss Grand Prix at Berne, Rosemeyer was right behind him, shaking his fist at what he regarded as Caracciola's blocking tactics. The Clerk of the Course gave Caracciola a blue flag, instructing him to let Rosemeyer through. Rosemeyer won. The two did not speak to each other for weeks. Rosemeyer went on to take the Italian Grand Prix and with it the European Drivers' Championship.

The 750-kilogram formula for Grands Prix was extended for 1937. Auto Union made few basic changes to their Type C, preferring to wait for the introduction of a new formula. After their rather poor performance in 1936, Mercedes reorganized their racing activities, creating a racing department under the direction of Rudolf Uhlenhaut, a gifted young engineer, while Alfred Neubauer continued to run the racing team and hire the drivers. Under Uhlenhaut's direction, Mercedes brought out a completely new car, the W125. It was a masterpiece – longer than the W25, built using specially hardened materials, with improved suspension, and powered by a 5.6-litre supercharged engine that produced 610 bhp. Alfa-Romeo took over Scuderia Ferrari to form Alfa Corse ('Alfa Racing') – still part of the company, and still under Enzo Ferrari – while Vittorio Jano planned the new 12C-37.

Achille Varzi had left Auto Union; he had become unreliable following an addiction to morphine in 1936. Auto Union took on Ernst von Delius and Luigi Fagioli – who had left Mercedes discontent with his team status (third in priority behind Rudolf Caracciola and Manfred von Brauchitsch). Neubauer took on the British driver Richard Seaman (>1936) and the Italian Goffredo Zehender. Tazio Nuvolari stayed with Alfa, although he was increasingly frustrated with the poor quality of their cars.

Hermann Lang showed what the new W125 could do in its first outing at the Tripoli Grand Prix. He led almost from start to finish at an average speed of 134.42 mph – 5 mph faster than Varzi's record for Auto Union the previous year. Before the Grand Prix season was fully under way, both German companies went to the Formula Libre AVUS Grand Prix. The North Curve had been steeply banked – reportedly at the instigation of Führer Hitler – making lap speeds of 180 mph possible. The constructors both prepared special cars with streamlined bodies. Caracciola won the first heat by no more than 1 second from Bernd Rosemeyer's Auto Union; von Brauchitsch won the second heat. Lang won the final.

In America the worst effects of the Depression were easing. Eddie Rickenbacker further improved the Indianapolis Speedway, laying asphalt on the turns. There were also changes to the regulations, taking the 500 back towards pure racing cars. Engine size remained at 336 cubic inches (5.5 litres), but superchargers were permitted again, and the fuel consumption limit was lifted, although the lethal cocktails of alcohol, benzol and acetone were banned.

RIGHT: Avusrennen, 30 May. Rudolf Caracciola in a Mercedes-Benz W125 overtaking Bernd Rosemeyer in an Auto Union Type C on the North Curve of the AVUS circuit. Caracciola won the heat, but Hermann Lang in another W125 won the final. After each major race, the W125s were taken back to the Mercedes works and completely overhauled. The cars were constructed to last around 500 miles - not much more than the 300-400 miles of a single Grand Prix.

LEFT: Hermann Lang was born in Germany in 1909, and began racing motorcycles in 1928. He started with Mercedes as a racing mechanic in 1934. A reserved man, he won his place in the driving team in 1935 on pure ability.

MILESTONES

On 1 January Pat Fairfield won the South African Grand Prix at East London at 89.17 mph in R.4A, the first ERA built for a private customer.

The Targa Florio changed from Formula Libre to a voiturette race, and moved from the Madonie circuit (>1906) to Favorita Park in Palermo.

In October Bernd Rosemeyer, driving an Auto Union on the Darmstadt-Frankfurt autobahn, was the first to exceed 400 km/h (248.5 mph) on the road.

In November George Eyston raised the land speed record to 312 mph in a British car, the 4,700-bhp 'Thunderbolt', on the Bonneville Salt Flats.

In bench tests, the Mercedes W125 engine produced 646 bhp, an output not equalled until 1965 at Indianapolis and until 1981 in Grands Prix.

At the end of the season Auto Union fired Hans Stuck; the reason was that he had shown Bernd Rosemeyer his contract and salary details.

BELOW: The cockpit of Rudolf Caracciola's Mercedes W125 while the car was being prepared for the Donington Grand Prix. The W125's steering wheel was detachable to give the driver easy access to the cockpit. A quick-release mechanism ensured that the steering wheel could be removed swiftly in the event of an accident.

approached by a young engineer, Art Sparks, who had designed a six-cylinder supercharged engine with finance from an industrialist, Joel Thorne. The result was the Sparks-Thorne, which produced 450 bhp. Jimmy Snyder designed a streamlined chassis for it, and qualified for the race with a one-lap speed of 130.49 mph, so breaking the nine-year-old record set by Leon Duray.

Snyder set the pace in the race, but retired on lap 27 with transmission problems. Wilbur Shaw, who had built his own streamlined car around a four-cylinder Offenhauser ('Offy') engine, and Ralph Hepburn in another Offy-powered car treated the crowd to some very close racing. Shaw established a lead that began to disappear when his car started leaking oil. As his oil pressure dropped, Shaw slowed. Hepburn advanced, but Shaw just managed to stay ahead, finally to win by only 2.16 seconds.

The revived Vanderbilt Cup road race was run for a second year on a circuit of dirt tracks linking the runways at Roosevelt Airfield on Long Island. The date clashed with that of the Belgian Grand Prix, so the German teams split their effort. At Roosevelt Field Caracciola and Seaman represented Mercedes, Rosemeyer Auto Union. The new Alfas were not ready, but Nuvolari and Giuseppe Farina arrived with year-old cars, and Rex Mays drove an Alfa he had modified himself. Caracciola took the lead first, followed by

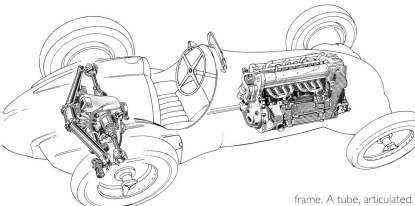

ABOVE: The Mercedes-Benz W125. Gear ratios could be changed to optimize the car's performance: with the highest ratios it was capable of 200 mph. Rear suspension was based on the De Dion system, designed by Georges Bouton for Count Jules de Dion in the 19th century.

The wheels were driven by open shafts with universal joints from a bevel box mounted on the frame. A tube, articulated at the centre and with hubs at both ends, supported the wheels independently of the drive shafts.

Harry Miller, America's world-renowned builder of racing engines, had gone bankrupt, but his business had been bought by his machinist Fred Offenhauser and his draughtsman Leo Goosen, and they produced the four-cylinder engine that had won Indianapolis in 1935. For the 1937 race, Offenhauser was

ABOVE: Bernd Rosemeyer winning the British Grand Prix at Donington on 2 October in an Auto Union Type C. He finished in 3 hours 1 minute 2.2 seconds, just 37.8 seconds ahead of Manfred von Brauchitsch in a Mercedes W125. The German teams made astonishingly fast pit-stops: on lap 31, Rosemeyer refuelled and changed all four tyres in just 31 seconds, and on lap 40 Mercedes' Rudolf Caracciola did the same in 26.6 seconds. Auto Union won the team prize, with Bernd Rosemeyer in first place, Hermann Müller fourth and Rudolf Hasse fifth.

Rosemeyer. Nuvolari blew up his engine trying to pass Rosemeyer. He took over Giuseppe Farina's car for another ten laps before that car failed too. When Caracciola's Mercedes also expired, Seaman took on the challenge, gaining to within 9 seconds of Rosemeyer. But it was not enough: Rosemeyer won, with Seaman second and Mays third.

Meanwhile Lang for Mercedes and Hans Stuck for Auto Union were battling it out at Spa. After both had lengthy pit-stops they fell back, and a new Auto Union driver, Rudolf Hasse, won; Stuck came in second. With the French Grand Prix once again restricted to sports cars, the German Grand Prix at the Nürburgring was the premier European event of the season – and after two defeats by Auto Union, Mercedes put on maximum effort.

Rosemeyer was fastest in practice, but Lang took the lead in the race, passing him on lap 2. Then Caracciola moved up through the pack and put pressure on Rosemeyer, who hit a bank, damaging a wheel. When he went into the pits Caracciola took the lead, followed by a Mercedes procession: von Brauchitsch, Lang and Seaman; von Delius for Auto Union was fifth. When von Delius challenged Seaman, both cars left the road and crashed. Von Delius was mortally wounded, Seaman quite severely injured. Rosemeyer, his wheel repaired, moved

ABOVE: Manfred von Brauchitsch's Mercedes W125 taking off on the hill up from Melbourne Corner during the Donington Grand Prix. Von Brauchitsch and Bernd Rosemeyer shared the £100 prize for fastest lap after tying with exactly the same speed, at 85.52 mph.

up again. When Lang had a burst tyre he took over third place, but could advance no further. Caracciola won, with von Brauchitsch in second place.

In the Monaco Grand Prix, Caracciola and von Brauchitsch had a fierce duel, which von Brauchitsch won. Caracciola then won the Coppa Acerbo, and the Swiss, Italian and Czechoslovakian Grands Prix, thus asserting Mercedes' supremacy – and winning his second European Championship.

The German team's record in these races only highlighted the shortcomings of Alfa-Romeo. Making its debut at the Coppa Acerbo, the new 12C-37 was slow and unreliable – and to show his disgust, Nuvolari handed it over to Farina. He was still not prepared to leave Alfa, but he accepted an invitation to drive for Auto Union in the Swiss Grand Prix. He did not start in the race, but when Fagioli dropped out from exhaustion, he took over, until Rosemeyer took over from him. It was a demonstration to Alfa that alternatives were open to him if they could not come up with a

car to match his skills. At the Italian Grand Prix, moved from Monza to a street circuit at Livorno (Leghorn), the best he could do in the Alfa was twelfth. Alfa's response was swift: they withdrew from racing for the rest of the season – and fired Vittorio Jano.

The last race of the 750-kilogram formula was the Donington Grand Prix, at which a British crowd witnessed full-blooded Grand Prix racing for the first time. The Auto Unions and Mercedes looked even faster on the small circuit, and the sheer noise of the engines had spectators covering their ears. There was support for Seaman, Britain's finest driver, but also for Raymond Mays and three other British drivers who took on the Germans in ERA voiturettes. The Germans left the ERAs well to the rear on lap 1, the four Mercedes leading, three Auto Unions just behind, until Rosemeyer began picking his way through the Mercedes. It became a battle between von Brauchitsch and Rosemeyer. Rosemeyer won, salvaging something for Auto Union from what had undoubtedly been a Mercedes year.

LEFT: Tragedy at Indianapolis. Overton Phillips crashed his Duesenberg-engined Mannix Special into the pits at the end of the practice week, killing his mechanic George Warford and Otto C. Rhode, the chief engineer of the Champion Spark Plug Company who was working in the pits.

ABOVE: Wilbur Shaw (>1939, 1940-41), winner of the Indianapolis 500. Born in 1903 in Indianapolis he started racing on dirt tracks in 1924. He came fourth in his first 500 in 1927 but retired from racing the same year, distraught at the death of of his young wife in childbirth. He made his comeback in 1929.

The year started with a tragedy. On 27 January Mercedes and Auto Union drivers met on the Darmstadt-Frankfurt autobahn to attempt various class speed records. Rudolf Caracciola made the first run, and recorded 432.69 km/h (268.86 mph). On his first run, Bernd Rosemeyer managed to reach 429.92 mph (267.14 mph). Then he prepared to go again. The Auto Union flew out of control, crashed, and Rosemeyer was killed.

He was given a military funeral in Berlin, and his wife – the aviatrix Elly Beinhorn – received thousands of letters from ordinary Germans in addition to official commiserations from the hierarchy of the Nazi Party.

The loss of Rosemeyer left Auto Union without top drivers. Hans Stuck had been dismissed (>1937), and Tazio Nuvolari – despite many conversations and although he was very unhappy with Alfa-Romeo – decided to stick with Alfa for at least the start of the season. Auto Union had also lost Professor Ferdinand Porsche, who had moved on to develop Führer Hitler's other great motoring dream, the Volkswagen. The team of engineers he left behind, led by Professor Robert Eberan von

Eberhorst, updated the basic design to the Type D.

A new formula was adopted on both sides of the Atlantic – a sliding-scale relationship between engine capacity and weight, up to a maximum of 3 litres supercharged, 4.5 litres unsupercharged, and a limit of 850 kilograms. Mercedes, Auto Union, Alfa-Romeo, Maserati

BELOW: World-beaters. The legendary Mercedes-Benz team after its 1-2-3 triumph at the Swiss Grand Prix. From left: Rudolf Uhlenhaut, design engineer; drivers Manfred von Brauchitsch (third), Rudolf Caracciola (first), and Richard Seaman (second); Max Sailer (with glasses, >1914), a director of Daimler-Benz; Alfred Neubauer (wearing greatcoat), the team manager. Hermann Lang was having his eyes examined after a stone had smashed his goggles.

LEFT: *LEFT*: Ferdinand Porsche in 1935. He was born in Bohemia in 1875, the son of a tinsmith, and worked for Austro Daimler, Mercedes and the Vienna-based firm Steyr before setting up as a freelance designer in 1930. He was hired by Auto Union from 1933 to 1937, developing the German company's mid-engined car. He died in Stuttgart on 30 January 1951.

LEFT: René Dreyfus's Delahaye Type 145, winner of the Pau Grand Prix – the first victory of a French car in a major race since the 1934 Belgian Grand Prix. Dreyfus was born in Nice in 1905, the son of a linen merchant, and began racing in a Mathis in 1925. He was a driver in the US Army in the Second World War, and after the war settled in the United States, where he ran a number of successful restaurants.

ABOVE: The Auto Union Type D at the Donington Grand Prix. Swiss driver Chris Kautz (right) drove car No. 3, but retired on the second lap after an accident at Melbourne Corner. Tazio Nuvolari won in another Type D.

Auto Union was not ready for the first Grand Prix of the season at Pau in France. It was normally a small event, but because this time it was the first race under the new formula, Mercedes and Alfa both decided to try out their cars. Mercedes sent Rudolf Caracciola and Hermann Lang, Alfa dispatched the long-suffering Nuvolari in the untried Tipo 308. In practice, Nuvolari's fuel tank split and the car caught fire. He was badly burned, furious at the poor workmanship, and walked out on Alfa for the second time (>1933). He then announced his retirement and went on a long holiday to America with his wife.

Alfa, Talbot, Bugatti and Lang's Mercedes all withdrew from the race and only eight cars started. Once Caracciola had established a good lead, he eased off – only to find that René Dreyfus in a Delahaye was catching him. He opened up again, but Dreyfus stuck to him. At the half-way mark Caracciola came in for fuel; Dreyfus's car was capable of completing the whole race on a single tank. Lang took over from Caracciola, but Dreyfus still managed to stay ahead. It was difficult for the Mercedes drivers to use all their power on such a small circuit, and Dreyfus won – to resounding cheers.

Anybody who thought that the might of Germany had been seriously dented had only to wait for the Tripoli Grand Prix. Dreyfus arrived in a new, streamlined version of the Delahaye, but he made not the least impression on the Mercedes drivers, who took the first three places: the order was Lang, Manfred von Brauchitsch, Caracciola.

The Type D Auto Unions were ready for the French Grand Prix at Rheims, but the marque was still short of drivers and sent

and most other designers went for the supercharged option. Mercedes and Auto Union both used V-12 engines: the new Mercedes W154 produced 468 bhp (158 bhp per litre capacity), the Auto Union Type D gave 420 bhp (140 bhp per litre). Alfa-Romeo, now without Vittorio Jano (>1937), improved the 12C-37 chassis but worked on a range of three different engines, the eight-cylinder Tipo 308 at 295 bhp, the twelve-cylinder Tipo 312 at 350 bhp, and the V-16 Tipo 316 at 440 bhp. Unable to match the Germans in Grands Prix, they were also working on a 1.5-litre voiturette, the Tipo 158 (>1946, 1950). Maserati, which had been bought by the Orsi family, invested in a new car, the supercharged 8CTF, which produced 350 bhp. In France, Delahaye and Talbot conversely decided against supercharging, and instead went for the unblown 4.5-litre option.

three inexperienced men, Rudolf Hasse, Hans Müller and Christian Kautz. Hasse and Müller crashed in practice, and Kautz and Hasse again crashed in the race, leaving Mercedes the first three places once more: this time von Brauchitsch, Caracciola, Lang.

The day after the race, Dr Feuereissen, the Auto Union team manager, rang Hans Stuck and, after some haggling, signed him up again. He also contacted Nuvolari who, refreshed from his holiday, signed up too, ready for the German Grand Prix at the Nürburgring. The front row of the grid suggested that Mercedes might be in for a shock. Von Brauchitsch, Lang, Richard Seaman, Caracciola and Tazio Nuvolari were on the front row. Nuvolari was the only threat to Mercedes – until he spun into a bank on lap 1. Von Brauchitsch took the lead, followed by Seaman and Lang. Caracciola dropped out with a stomach complaint. Seaman was about 10 seconds behind von Brauchitsch when they both came into the pits at the same time. The pit crew overfilled von Brauchitsch's fuel tank, and when he started, the exhaust ignited the overflowing fuel. Alfred Neubauer managed to drag von Brauchitsch out with his overalls on fire. He was quickly doused, and the fire brought under control, but in the chaos Seaman had rejoined the race in the lead. Von Brauchitsch got back in his car and sped off after Seaman, but three miles farther on he crashed, leaving a British driver to win the German Grand Prix. In the highly-charged political atmosphere there were mixed feelings as Seaman was

wreathed in laurels bearing the swastika, and gave the Nazi salute.

The Italian Grand Prix, at a resurfaced Monza, was held against the background of rising political tension as Hitler demanded the Sudetenland region from Czechoslovakia. The Mercedes team was out in force. Giuseppe Farina was there in a Tipo 316 Alfa, and Nuvolari was at the wheel of his Auto Union, so the crowd had split loyalties between Alfa and Nuvolari. Müller shot into the lead for Auto Union, then Lang overtook him. But by lap 7 Nuvolari had the measure of the car, and he passed Lang. All the Mercedes retired except Caracciola. Farina worked his way up into second place but could not catch Nuvolari, who won.

Doubt hung over the Donington Grand Prix. It was originally planned for 2 October, and the German teams arrived a week earlier to start practice – right in the middle of the Munich crisis, when Prime Minister Neville Chamberlain went to parley with Hitler and Mussolini. In case war broke out the Germans returned home quickly from Harwich, and the

The Maserati company was established in 1920 by Alfieri, Bindo and Ernesto Maserati, three of a family of six brothers. The Diatto firm hired the brothers to build a 2-litre Grand Prix engine, and when Diatto stopped racing in 1926 Maserati took over the design. The three arms of the badge represented Neptune's trident.

MILESTONES

The Italians made the Coppa Ciano, Coppa Acerbo and Tripoli Grand Prix voiturette races in which Alfa-Romeo and Maserati had a distinct advantage.

During the Mille Miglia a Lancia left the road at a level crossing near Bologna and ploughed into the crowd, killing ten people, seven of them children.

On 18 April Prince Bira of Siam won the Campbell Trophy at Brooklands in an ERA. He was one of the most successful ERA drivers.

On 6 June the band-leader Billy Cotton won the second Whitsun Handicap at Brooklands in his ERA; it had been built for Richard Seaman.

On 7 August Emilio Villoresi and Clemente Biondetti came first and second in the Coppa Ciano in Alfa 158 'Alfetta' voiturettes, the cars' debut race.

On 15 September John Cobb raised the land speed record to 350.2 mph in his Railton Special. The next day George Eyston raised it to 357.5 mph in 'Thunderbolt'.

ABOVE: Bernd Rosemeyer. He was born in 1909 in Germany, the son of a car dealer, and began racing motorcycles in 1931. One theory on what caused his fatal crash during a record attempt in January 1938 is that his streamlined Auto Union was caught by a

crosswind. Dr Ferdinand Porsche – the car's designer – was not at the scene, but when he was told the news he said: 'I am sure I would not have let him start had I known it was windy, especially since the car was so sensitive to side winds.'

race was cancelled. Then, once Chamberlain had returned with 'Peace in our time', it was rescheduled for 22 October, and they came back again.

The Duke of Kent started the race with a Union Jack. Nuvolari went into the lead and stretched it to 14 seconds before a long pit-stop put him back to fourth place behind the Mercedes. Then on a downhill section of road approaching a hairpin, a British Alta broke a con-rod and oil splashed all over the track. Nuvolari went broadside over the grass and rejoined at the hairpin. Von Brauchitsch and Seaman both spun on the oil and lost time. After another pit-stop for tyres, Nuvolari rejoined in third place behind Lang and his team-mate Müller. Nuvolari then gained several seconds a lap on them, passed Müller, then Lang, eventually to win comfortably by 1 minute 48 seconds.

Nuvolari's genius had put Auto Union back in the forefront of the sport, but Mercedes had won the major races and he was too late to take the European Championship away from Caracciola.

BELOW: Tazio Nuvolari's Auto Union Type D hit a stag at 80 mph during practice for the Donington Grand Prix when the animal leapt out of the trees at McLean's Corner.

Nuvolari had the head of the deer stuffed and sent back to his home in Mantua as a trophy. The impact damaged his ribs, and he wore bandages for the rest of practice and

the race. Yet he drove a superb practice lap of 2 minutes 11.2 seconds and was beaten to pole position by Hermann Lang's Mercedes W154 by just 0.2 seconds.

LEFT: The Maestro – Tazio Nuvolari, winner of the Donington Grand Prix in an Auto Union Type D. He joined Auto Union in July for the German Grand Prix, and gave the German firm their only two Grand Prix victories of the year – at Monza in September, then at Donington. Nuvolari had been trying for some time to join the team; despite his remarkable ability, Auto Union showed no interest in hiring him until the tragic death of Bernd Rosemeyer in January left them without a top-class driver.

RIGHT: Rudolf Caracciola in a Mercedes W154/163 at the French Grand Prix at Rheims. He ran off the track shortly afterwards.

ABOVE: Pit-stop for Hermann Müller's Auto Union Type D in the German Grand Prix on 23 July. Müller finished second, 58 seconds behind the Mercedes of Rudolf Caracciola after 22 laps of the Nürburgring. Conditions on the mountain circuit were wet, slowing the race down and forcing some cars – including Hermann Lang's Mercedes – to drop out with carburation problems. Caracciola, who was nicknamed the Regenmeister ('Master of the Rain'), thrived in the wet, but even his speed – 75.12 mph – was the slowest winner's average recorded in the German Grand Prix since 1935.

The Germans now occupied the remains of Czechoslovakia; France, Great Britain and Poland agreed to come to each other's aid if attacked; Hitler and Mussolini countered with 'the Pact of Steel', committing Germany and Italy to mutual support. Against that background, a full programme of international motor racing was planned.

Mercedes updated the W154 with a new engine, raising output to 485 bhp (162 bhp per litre capacity). Auto Union used a two-stage supercharger to boost the Type D's output to just about the same power. The season opened at Pau on 2 April. Mussolini banned Italian drivers from going to France, and without Tazio Nuvolari Auto Union did not go to Pau. Mercedes sent along Rudolf Caracciola, Manfred von Brauchitsch and Hermann Lang to face very weak opposition from Talbot-Darracqs driven by Philippe Etancelin and René Carrière. The German cars had no difficulty in establishing a commanding lead. Caracciola had an oil leak and retired, but Lang won, with von Brauchitsch second.

At the Tripoli Grand Prix for voiturettes (>1938) on 7 May, the Italians were shocked to find that Rudolf Uhlenhaut (>1937) had built a voiturette, the W165, a scaled-down version of the W154 with a new V-8 super-charged 1.5-litre engine. The starting grid consisted of 28 Italian cars and the two Mercedes;

Caracciola and Lang shared the front row of the grid with Alfa's star driver, Giuseppe Farina (>1950), and Maserati's Luigi Villoresi. Lang won; behind him Caracciola was second, and Villoresi third.

The Eifelrennen at the Nürburgring two weeks later was the first confrontation of the year between Mercedes and Auto Union. Caracciola's Mercedes was fastest in practice, but the race was between Lang (Mercedes) and Nuvolari (Auto Union). Lang managed to win by just 11 seconds over the 'Maestro'. Lang's third victory in a row caused resentment in the Mercedes ranks: Caracciola saw a challenge looming to his fourth European Championship, while the aristocratic von Brauchitsch begrudged the success of a humble mechanic risen to national hero.

For the first time in over a decade, the same formula applied on both sides of the Atlantic. European cars were thus eligible to enter Indianapolis. The Chicago industrialist Mike Boyle bought three Maserati 8CTFs, contracting Wilbur Shaw – the 1937 500 winner – to drive one. It was a race of champions: Louie Meyer was looking for his fourth victory in the Bowes Special, Floyd Roberts looking for his second in an Offenhauser-powered Special. Joel Thorne entered three six-cylinder Sparks-powered cars, one for himself, the others to be driven by Rex Mays and Jimmy Snyder.

Snyder set a new one-lap qualifying record of 130.757 mph, and in the race led from the start, with Meyer second and Shaw third. When Snyder went into the pits Shaw took

over. Snyder rejoined back in fifth place, but charged his way through to the lead again, Meyer just behind. Then Snyder had to make a second pit-stop, and Shaw went ahead of Meyer. At the 400-mile mark, Meyer was back in the lead, one lap and 2 seconds ahead of Shaw. But Shaw overtook Meyer on the road and began to eat away at the one-lap deficit. The crowd rose to acknowledge the effort of the underdog, and with 16 laps to go, as the pair came into the main straight, Shaw just passed Meyer. As they went into the next turn Meyer spun and burst a tyre, continued on the flat, to more cheers, restarted, and set out after Shaw. Two laps from the finish, Meyer crashed into the wall and was out:

BELOW: Wilbur Shaw (>1939, 1940-41), winner of the Indianapolis 500 for the second time. He qualified third fastest at 128.977 mph, behind Jimmy Snyder and Louie Meyer. Shaw's winnings were $27,375 out of a total purse of $87,050.

ABOVE: Mercedes voiturette. Hermann Lang's eight-cylinder W165 on its way to victory in the Tripoli Grand Prix at the Mellaha circuit on 7 May.

Lang led from start to finish; his time was 1 hour 59 minutes 12.36 seconds, a record average of 122.91 mph; he also drove the fastest lap at 133.5 mph.

Only 12 of 30 starters managed to finish the 244-mile event, which was staged in conditions so hot that some drivers collapsed.

MILESTONES

The Indianapolis four-lap qualification record fell three times: Cliff Bergere 123.835 mph; Louie Meyer 130.067 mph; Jimmy Snyder 130.167 mph.

Floyd Roberts was killed in the Indianpolis 500 in a crash with Bob Swanson and Chet Miller. The other two drivers survived with injuries.

Louie Meyer retired from racing after the 500; he continued in partnership with Fred Offenhauser in the engine business (>1946, 1964).

Jean-Pierre Wimille and Pierre Veyron won the Le Mans 24-hour race in a Type 57C Bugatti. Ettore Bugatti's son Jean was killed testing the same car in August.

The last race at Brooklands was on 3 August. The circuit was taken over by Vickers who built Spitfires during the war; it never reopened.

On 23 August John Cobb raised the land speed record to 369.74 mph in the 1,250 bhp Railton Special at the Bonneville Salt Flats (>1947).

Shaw coasted through to his second victory.

In Europe, the Grand Prix circus arrived at Spa for the Belgian Grand Prix. It took place in torrential rain. Hans Müller took the lead for Auto Union, but the Mercedes of Lang and Richard Seaman (>1938) advanced steadily, both passing him, then Seaman pulled ahead of Lang. Driving too fast for the conditions, Seaman left the road, hit a tree, and was knocked unconscious. The fuel tank split and the car caught fire; seriously burned, he died that night in hospital. Lang wanted to withdraw, but Alfred Neubauer insisted he continue. He did so, and despite all the efforts of Nuvolari to dislodge him, Lang won.

There were no Italian cars in the French Grand Prix at Rheims. Caracciola took on Nuvolari from the start and paid for it on the first corner, finishing up in a wall with a split fuel tank. Nuvolari took the lead, Lang doing everything he knew to get past. The lap record fell three times in two laps. On lap 5, on a long straight, Lang drew level and, as they came out of the next corner, accelerated into the lead. Nuvolari charged after him until his engine expired two laps later, leaving Lang 38 seconds ahead of the next Auto Union, driven by Müller. Von Brauchitsch dropped out with engine problems, leaving Lang the only Mercedes in the race. Lang steadily extended his lead over Müller to 1 minute 35 seconds, then a thin trail of blue smoke started to come from his exhaust. Müller gained quickly and went on to win his first Grand Prix.

By 23 July political tension was high as Hitler looked east, to Gdansk (Danzig), claiming it for the Reich. The German Grand Prix at the Nürburgring nonetheless went ahead as planned. The only foreign competition came from two Maseratis and two Delahayes. Lang took the lead, and by the end of the first lap had opened up a 27-second gap between himself and von Brauchitsch. Müller was in third place for Auto Union, then Paul Pietsch in a red Maserati. On lap 2, Pietsch managed to pass both Müller and Brauchitsch, and Lang had to go in for plugs, so for a time the Maserati was leading – until Pietsch had to go into the pits for brakes. Nuvolari took the lead, now followed by Müller and Caracciola. There was consternation in the Mercedes pit when the carburation on Lang's car was found to be faulty. Neubauer signalled the fourth team member, Heinz Brendl, to come in to the pits so that Lang could take over his car, but Brendl crashed before he could comply, so leaving Lang fuming. Von Brauchitsch then dropped out with a fuel leak. Caracciola, in the only raceworthy Mercedes, rose to the occasion. On lap 6 he passed Nuvolari – and won from Müller and Pietsch. It was his last Grand Prix victory. On 20 August, after a titanic struggle with him in the Swiss Grand Prix, it was Lang who won, and who took the European title with it (>1946, 1952, 1959).

On 1 September Germany and the Soviet Union invaded Poland. France and Britain issued an ultimatum, which expired on 3 September. The Yugoslav Grand Prix was scheduled for the afternoon of that day, and

BELOW: Mercedes out in front at the Tripoli Grand Prix. Hermann Lang's winning car, the W165, was designed and built in just eight months. Its eight-cylinder 1.495-litre engine had twin Roots-type superchargers and developed 256 bhp at 8,000 rpm; the top speed was 170 mph.

although the ultimatum expired in the morning, the race went ahead. The finale to six years of development, which had seen Auto Union and Mercedes transform motor racing beyond recognition, was played out between five drivers: an unsuspecting Yugoslav named Milenkovic in an ancient Type 51 Bugatti, Nuvolari and Müller for Auto Union, and von Brauchitsch and Lang for Mercedes. The two

Mercedes scrambled for the lead, eager to settle old scores, and in the process a stone from under von Brauchitsch's car hit Lang's face, smashing his goggles, glass piercing his eye. Von Brauchitsch then spun twice, letting Nuvolari through. Once in the lead Nuvolari drove immaculately, to give the final victory of that extraordinary period to Auto Union and Italy.

LEFT: The Mercedes W154/163. Its twelve-cylinder 2.96-litre engine gave the car a top speed of just under 200 mph. Its power output of 161.33 bhp per litre compared favourably with the 101.79 bhp per litre produced by the much larger-capacity 1937 car, the 5.6-litre W125.

Auto Union Type D

The Type D was the culmination of Auto Union's mid-engined cars which began with the Type A in 1934. The Type D's 3-litre V-12 engine was originally fitted with a Roots-type supercharger and produced 460 bhp at 7,000 rpm. A two-stage supercharger replaced the single-stage unit for the 1939 French Grand Prix, and with this fitted, the engine developed 500 bhp at 7,500 rpm under test conditions. The Type D first appeared in the 1938 German Grand Prix. Its first victories came later in the year in the Italian and British Grands Prix.

An Auto Union Type D at Silverstone in 1990, driven by John Surtees (*FAR LEFT*). Ferdinand Porsche's design for the earlier mid-engined cars was improved by Robert Eberan von Eberhorst for the Type D (*BELOW*). The new engine was shorter in length, allowing it to be moved farther back, which improved the car's handling.

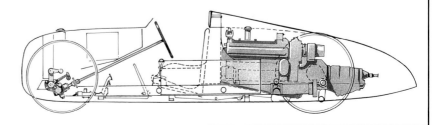

Once war had broken out, racing stopped in Germany, France, Belgium and Britain. But Italy was still neutral in 1940, as was the United States, and racing continued in both of those countries.

The Mille Miglia was revived in a different form (>1938). Instead of an inter-town race from Brescia to Rome and back (>1927), the organizers proposed a 1,000-mile race around a circuit near Brescia. Permission was granted, and Alfa-Romeo put up a strong team of sports cars to be driven by Giuseppe Farina (>1950), Clemente Biondetti, Carlo Pintacuda and Count Carlo Trossi. Against the Alfas Germany fielded a team of BMWs specially prepared for the race and led by a Waffen-SS officer, Huschke von Hanstein, partnered by Walter Baumer, whose Grand Prix career with Mercedes had been cut short by the war. At 135 bhp and 140 mph, the BMWs were faster: von Hanstein led from start to finish, followed for most of the way by his team-mates. They would have finished in the first four places, except that as the finish approached the German drivers let Farina's Alfa into second place and Biondetti's into fourth.

After the setback of the previous year, the Tripoli Grand Prix was an all-Italian race under the 1.5-litre voiturette formula. The Alfa-Romeo team of Farina, Biondetti and Trossi, in beautiful Tipo 158s, were up against Luigi Villoresi and Franco Cortese (>1951) in Maserati 4CLs. Villoresi took the lead, but Farina soon passed him, and Alfa took the first three places: the finishing order was Farina, Biondetti, Trossi.

ABOVE: Giuseppe Farina taking the flag in the Tripoli Grand Prix. His eight-cylinder 1.5-litre Alfa-Romeo Tipo 158 'Alfetta' developed around 220 bhp at 7,200 rpm and had a top speed of 144 mph. It was designed by Gioachino Colombo, Vittorio Jano's replacement as designer at Alfa-Romeo.

Alfa did not enter the Targa Florio voiturette race in Favorita Park, Palermo (>1937). Maserati took the first three places: Villoresi, Cortese, Giovanni Rocco.

As these races were being run, Hitler launched his Blitzkreig across the Netherlands, Belgium and France. Mussolini declared war on the Allies on 11 June, and Italian racing came to a halt.

With war raging across much of Europe, the *Indianapolis Star* had two headlines on its front page on 29 May, the day before the 500-

MILESTONES

Prevented from using his own vehicles for four years by agreement with Alfa, Enzo Ferrari named his first sports-car plant Auto-Avio Costruzzione.

Ferrari entered two cars in the Mille Miglia, one driven by Alberto Ascari, son of Antonio Ascari (>1925). He retired with a broken valve.

Britain's first successful racing driver, Selwyn F. Edge (>1902), died having spent his fortune on various motor car projects and pig breeding.

Foxhall Keene – one of the first Americans to race in Europe, including the 1901 Paris-Berlin and 1903 Gordon Bennett races – died in poverty.

Louis Chevrolet (>1919) died in poor health in 1941 having reportedly worked as a mechanic in a Chevrolet plant during the Depression.

The last competitive event before America entered the war on 7 December was the Pikes Peak Hill Climb. Louis Unser won in a Maserati.

mile race: 33 SPEED KINGS AWAIT RACE and DEFEATED ALLIES FLEE FLANDERS – in that order. Among those 'speed kings' was Wilbur Shaw, driving the Maserati in which he had won the race the previous year. His rivals were Rex Mays in the Bowes Seal-Fast Special, and Mauri Rose in an Offenhauser-powered Elgin Piston Special. The three battled for the lead, until rain brought out the yellow flag with 50 laps to go, and everybody had to hold their positions. Shaw, who was fortunate enough to be leading at the time, coasted home – much to the frustration of Mays and Rose – to victory, joining Louie

Meyer as a three-time winner (>1937, 1939).

Race day for the 1941 Indianapolis 500 started with a fire in the garages at the track that destroyed three cars, including a Harry Miller-designed mid-engined car modelled on the Auto Unions in which George Barringer had already qualified. The race was dominated by the same three names as in 1940 – Mauri Rose, who took pole position in a Maserati, Wilbur Shaw in another, and Rex Mays in the Bowes Seal-Fast Special. Rose led from the start, but had to retire with carburettor problems. On lap 72, when Shaw was in the lead, he took over another car – the Offy-powered Noc-Out Hose-Clamp Special currently in twelfth place and until then driven by Floyd Davis. Shaw led for most of the race until lap 152, when he crashed. Rose took over the lead and, although Mays spurted to try to catch him, stayed in front to win his first 500 (>1947, 1948).

BELOW: The six-cylinder 2-litre BMW 328 Coupe, winner of the 'Gran Premio della Mille Miglia', as the 1940 race was called. The winning drivers, Huschke von Hanstein and Walter Baumer, finished in 8 hours 54 minutes 46 seconds – an average 104.2 mph.

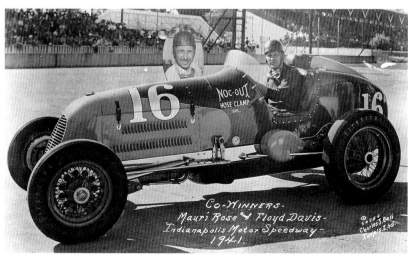

LEFT: Floyd Davis (seated) and Mauri Rose (inset), joint winners of the 1941 Indianapolis 500 after Rose took over Davis's car under orders from their sponsor Lou Moore. The winning time was 4 hours 20 minutes 36.24 seconds, a minute and a half ahead of Rex Mays. The winners' cut of a total purse of $90,925 was $29,200.

ABOVE: One of the Indianapolis 500's great triers. Babe Stapp raced in the 500 every year from 1927 to 1940, with just two breaks – in 1932 and 1934. He achieved two good positions: sixth in a Miller in 1928, and fifth in an Alfa-Romeo/Weil in 1939, but every other time he finished well down the field.

CHAPTER SEVEN
CLOSEDOWN, REBIRTH &
THE CASUALTIES OF WAR

The rapid evolution of the racing car in Europe in the 1930s, spurred on by six years of Nazi investment, stopped dead with the outbreak of war. Auto Union had shown the way ahead. Their mid-engined layout was already being copied: Harry Miller produced the Gulf-Millers in America (>1941), and Wilfredo Ricart the Alfa-Romeo Tipo 512 in Italy. But that line of development was suspended when Auto Union's factories were first turned over to war production, then flattened by concerted Allied bombing.

As war destroyed, so it also sowed the seeds of new technical advances. Wartime research sparked off all manner of technical innovation to cope with high speeds and stresses, particularly in aircraft construction. Radial tyres, cast alloy wheels, disc brakes, fuel injection, turbochargers, monocoque construction, high-octane fuels, even the jet engine – all these, and many more, were either invented or proven in the war, and eventually found their way into motor racing.

In 1945 the sport had to be reborn with the cars that had survived the war. Foremost among them were Gioachino Colombo's 1.5-litre supercharged Alfa-Romeo Tipo 158 voiturettes (>1939) which, since the Germans took over Italy in 1943, had been hidden in a cheese factory. They ruled Grand Prix racing almost effortlessly in the 1940s against the Maserati 4CLs, ERAs, a lone Delahaye and some three or four 4.5-litre unsupercharged Talbots.

The Fédération Internationale de l'Automobile (FIA) – which replaced the AIACR as the international competition-governing body after the war – took a pragmatic view, setting its Formula A (which quickly became known as Formula One) to fit the cars available: 4.5 litres, or 1.5 litres supercharged.

In the United States, the American Automobile Association was equally practical. It retained the prewar formula of 4.5 litres or 3 litres supercharged to encompass the existing cars, but reduced the weight limit to encourage large numbers of Offenhauser-engined dirt track cars and drivers to compete at the Indianapolis speedway.

Racing reborn: the Coupe de Paris was a series of three races held in the Bois de Boulogne in September 1945 to raise money for French prisoners of war and deportees. An estimated 100,000 people attended, paying between 100 and 1,000 francs (10 shillings and £5) for entry.

COUPE DE PARIS
AUTOMOBILE 1945 MOTOCYCLISTE
★

Just one month after the atom bombs fell on Hiroshima and Nagasaki, racing restarted. On 9 September 1945 the Coupe de Paris was staged in the Bois de Boulogne. The names incorporated carried echoes of the war: the Formula Libre Coupe des Prisonniers, won by Jean-Pierre Wimille in a Type 59 Bugatti; the Liberation Trophy for 2-litre cars, won by Henri Louveau in a Maserati; and the Robert Benoist Trophy for cars of 1.5 litres and under, won by Amédée Gordini in a car he built himself from Simca and Fiat parts.

Robert Benoist (>1927) was hailed as a war hero in France. He worked in the Resistance, was captured, and was executed by the Germans. Another Resistance fighter, William Grover-Williams ('Williams'; >1929), was captured by the Gestapo at Benoist's house on 2 August 1943, and later executed.

Rudolf Caracciola (>1938) was too old for military service and lived in Switzerland for the duration of the war. Manfred von Brauchitsch was also rejected for military service and spent the war as secretary to a German general. Alfred Neubauer continued to work for Mercedes-Benz, managing repair shops for damaged Luftwaffe and Wehrmacht vehicles. Dr Ferdinand Porsche adapted the Volkswagen into the Kübelwagen, a military utility vehicle for the German army; he was imprisoned by the French after the war.

Enzo Ferrari moved his engineering company to Maranello, not far from Bologna, producing machine tools for the Italian government. The company flourished, and as the war in Italy came to a close, he turned once again to racing cars and sports cars.

Eddie Rickenbacker (>1973), the owner of the Indianapolis Speedway, had diversified into the airline business, raising $3.5 million with others for Eastern Airlines. During the war he worked for the Military Air Transport Service, flying as the personal envoy of the Secretary for War, Henry Stimson. He crashed on a flight over the Pacific and survived 24 days on a life-raft before being rescued. Wilbur Shaw worked in the aircraft division of the Firestone Tyre Company at Akron, Ohio. In 1944 he was sent to test a new synthetic rubber in a 500-mile run at Indianapolis and found the Speedway in a run-down condition. He contacted Rickenbacker, who confirmed the track was for sale. Shaw found a buyer in Anton 'Tony' Hulman, an Indiana businessman with interests in oil, brewing, and distribution. In November 1945 Hulman duly bought the Speedway for $700,000, made Wilbur Shaw president, and authorized millions of dollars' investment in the track.

In Britain, there was no such benefactor for Brooklands (>1907). During the war it was taken over by Vickers to extend their aircraft factory, and by 1945 it was in a lamentable state. When the club members tried to get it back, the Ministry of Supply demurred, and Vickers bought it for £330,000. Donington, Britain's first road racing circuit, was turned into a military vehicle park; in 1945 it was

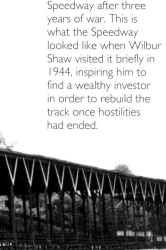

BELOW: Closedown – the Indianapolis Motor Speedway after three years of war. This is what the Speedway looked like when Wilbur Shaw visited it briefly in 1944, inspiring him to find a wealthy investor in order to rebuild the track once hostilities had ended.

LEFT: The start of the Coupe de Paris, 9 September 1945.

FAR LEFT: Robert Benoist, born France 1895; died Buchenwald 12 September 1944. Benoist started racing in 1921, joining Delage three years later. He won the French, Spanish, Italian and British Grands Prix in 1927, giving Delage the World Championship and earning him the Légion d'Honneur.

ABOVE: Enzo Ferrari prospered during the war, making engines under military contracts for the Italian government. At the end of the war, his title Commendatore, awarded by Mussolini for victory in the 1924 Coppa Acerbo, lapsed – as did all honours granted under the Fascist regime.

MILESTONES

Mercedes cars were dispersed across Germany during the war for safety. One 1939 W154/163 was hidden in Czechoslovakia.

The Mercedes W165 (>1946–47) voiturettes were in Switzerland when war broke out. Under international law they were interned for the duration.

Raymond Mays kept his ERA near his home during the war, from where he drove it on many fund-raising appearances for the Red Cross.

Harry Miller, who built the world's first pure single-seater racing car (>1923), died in poverty of facial cancer in Detroit in 1943.

Bartolomeo Costantini, Alfa's 1940 Mille Miglia team manager and once one of the greatest Bugatti drivers (>1926), died of lung cancer in 1941, aged 52.

The Sports Car Club of America (SCCA) was formed by seven sports car enthusiasts in Boston, Mass., on 26 February 1944 (>1948-49).

covered in trucks which took years to shift (>1971, 1993). But as two circuits disappeared in this way, the wartime airfield building programme provided absolutely ideal places for racing, and two more – Silverstone and Goodwood – replaced them.

In Italy, Monza was also used to store military vehicles, and was badly damaged by Allied bombing (>1948). In France, the Le Mans circuit was taken over by the Luftwaffe, turned into an airfield, bombed by the Allies, then destroyed by the Germans as they retreated (>1949). Montlhéry fell into disrepair during the war and never reopened.

Following the defeat of Germany, the Soviet, United States, British and French governments divided the country. In Berlin, the boundary between the Soviet sector and West Berlin went straight through the South Curve at AVUS (>1959).

163

As motor racing struggled to revive in a dislocated world, the greatest problem on both sides of the Atlantic was a shortage of tyres, fuel, oil and spares. In Europe there was also a shortage of cars and of places to race, so the first races were run as Formula Libre on ordinary street circuits. The new owner of the Indianapolis Speedway, Tony Hulman, was committed to refurbishing it, but that would take time. For the 1946 race the best that could be done was a clean-up and several coats of paint.

The cars for the first postwar 500 were mostly prewar models, but they were still competitive: Ralph Hepburn raised the four-lap qualification record to 133.944 mph in a Novi Governor. The purse was also a record at $115,450, and attracted a full field of 33 cars. Rudolf Caracciola crossed the Atlantic hoping to drive one of the Mercedes W165 supercharged voiturettes, but they were held up by Swiss bureaucracy. He qualified in a Thorne Special at 118 mph, but was struck by a bird and crashed, suffering severe concussion, his life saved by a crash-helmet that he had declined to wear at first. In the race, Mauri Rose crashed on lap 41, and only nine cars were still racing as the end approached. George Robson finally drove a Sparks-engined Thorne (>1937) to victory – Joel Thorne's first 500 win in a decade of trying.

LEFT: Mauri Rose (>1941), winner of the 1947 Indianapolis 500. Rose was a part-time driver, who fitted in his racing around a job in the automobile industry. In 1947 he was working for Studebaker.

ABOVE: Louis Chiron winning the 1947 French Grand Prix at Lyons in a Lago-Talbot. Chiron was the second fastest qualifier at 3 minutes 18.3 seconds, 0.4 seconds behind Henri Louveau's Maserati.

MILESTONES

The first postwar race in the United States was for stock cars at Daytona Beach on 14 April 1946; Red Byron won in a Ford (>1936).

Louie Meyer, the first Indianapolis three-times winner, and his riding mechanic Dale Drake, bought the Offenhauser engine business.

On 16 September 1947 John Cobb drove the Railton Special to a new land speed record of 394.196 mph at Bonneville (>1939, 1963).

In 1947 the British Motor Racing Research Trust was formed to build a British Grand Prix car, the BRM (British Racing Motors; >1950).

On 21 August Ettore Bugatti died, aged 66 (>1912, 1924, 1956, 1963). His great adversary Louis Delage died on 14 December (>1914, 1926).

On 14 December the National Association of Stock Car Auto Racing – NASCAR – was formed in Daytona. Bill France was president (>1936).

LEFT: Racing in Switzerland, a country untouched by war, was restarted soon afterwards.

BELOW: Count Carlo Trossi (Alfa-Romeo 158, No.30) on his way to

victory in the 1947 Italian Grand Prix at an average 70.29 mph. The race was held on a road circuit in Milan – since the war-damaged track at Monza had not yet been repaired – and was a triumph for

Alfa-Romeo, whose Tipo 158s finished 1-2-3-4: Trossi was just a length ahead of Achille Varzi (No.16), after a stirring contest; Consalvo Sanesi was third and Alessandro Gaboardi fourth.

The first postwar Grand Prix in Europe was held on the streets of St Cloud, outside Paris, on 9 June. On the front row of the grid were Raymond Sommer in a Maserati 4CL and Jean-Pierre Wimille and Giuseppe Farina in Alfa-Romeo 158s. Just behind them was Tazio Nuvolari in another Maserati, his health visibly declining from a lung disorder contracted after years of inhaling petrol and exhaust fumes. The Alfas were fastest, but both dropped out with transmission problems; Sommer won for Maserati. It was the last time Alfa was beaten on the track until July 1951. The superb prewar voiturettes won 27 consecutive races – and Maserati, Talbot, ERA and Ferrari only got a look-in when Alfa was not racing.

The Maserati brothers decided to quit the company of their own name, and to set up an independent company of their own, making racing and sports cars. Based in Bologna, the new firm went under the name OSCA.

The 1947 Indianapolis 500 saw a new car on the grid. Lou Moore had signed a sponsorship deal with the Blue Crown Spark Plug company which enabled him to build two superb front-wheel-drive cars, both of them with Offenhauser ('Offy') engines at a cost of $32,000 each. They were designed by Leo Goosen, Harry Miller's former draughtsman, and to drive them Moore signed up Mauri Rose and Bill Holland. Holland led for most of the race. He lost it when he spun in front of Shorty Cantlon, who crashed into the wall and was killed. Rose took the lead; then Holland took it back, and the two looked clear to cruise to a 1-2 victory. They did, but not in that order. Rose crept up on Holland and passed him in the dying laps to win by 32 seconds. Holland was furious: he had thought Rose was a lap behind.

In 1947 Grand Prix racing was once again under a formula: 4.5 litres or 1.5 litres supercharged. Jean-Pierre Wimille won the Swiss and Belgian Grands Prix, and Count Carlo Trossi the Italian Grand Prix. Alfa did not contest the first postwar Grand Prix run by the Auto Club de France (ACF) at Lyons, and French hopes were pinned on a new French 1.5-litre supercharged car produced in an old arsenal outside Paris by the 'Centre d'Études Techniques de l'Automobile' (the CTA Arsenal), designed by Albert Lory. The hopes died when the clutch broke and Sommer was forced to retire, leaving the race to Louis Chiron (>1928) in a 4.5-litre Talbot. A French car had won the ACF Grand Prix, but only because the Alfettas – as the 158s were known – were not there.

After the war, Enzo Ferrari was released from his obligation to Alfa-Romeo and could use his own name (>1940–41), and in August 1945 he took on Gioachino Colombo, the man behind the Alfettas. Colombo later returned to Alfa, but while he was with Ferrari he designed a new V-12 engine; development on it continued under the designer Aurelio Lampredi.

The result of this was that Lampredi was able to enter two V-12 Tipo 166 sports cars in the Mille Miglia for Clemente Biondetti and Tazio Nuvolari.

Nuvolari's health was poor but his skill and determination had not deserted him. In the race he built up a 29-minute lead over Biondetti, virtually wrecking his car in the process – he even lost the seat, which he replaced with a box of oranges. When he reached Maranello, Ferrari saw that Nuvolari was exhausted, coughing and spitting blood, and tried to persuade him to retire, but Nuvolari pressed on until the Ferrari's brakes gave way near Parma. Unable to get out of the car by himself, he was found by a priest and put to bed (>1953).

Biondetti won, having in addition already won first postwar Targa Florio in Sicily in the same year, adding an immediate lustre to the Ferrari name.

Alfa-Romeo uprated the Alfettas to 310 bhp at 8,000 rpm, but did not enter the Swiss or Monaco Grands Prix, leaving them for Giuseppe Farina to win in a Maserati.

Every time the Alfas did actually enter a race, it was to continue their unbroken record. Carlo Trossi won the European Grand Prix at Berne, then they moved to Rheims for the Grand Prix organized by the Auto Club de France, where Jean-Pierre Wimille and Consalvo Sanesi were joined on the front row of the grid by Alberto Ascari, who had moved from Ferrari (>1940–41). Behind them were seven Talbots and a Delahaye, four Maseratis, a lone 2-litre Ferrari, and – making his Grand Prix debut – Juan Manuel Fangio, driving a Simca.

Wimille came close to breaking the lap record, despite wet conditions, and the Alfas utterly dashed hopes of a revival in French fortunes, taking the first three places: the order was Wimille, Sanesi, Ascari.

Ferrari's first Grand Prix car, the Tipo 125, made its debut in the Italian Grand Prix at Turin with a team of three, driven by Giuseppe Farina, Raymond Sommer and Prince Bira of

RIGHT: Ferrari's first Grand Prix car. Raymond Sommer in the new Ferrari Tipo 125 (right, No.28) just behind Luigi Villoresi in a Maserati 4CLT/48 (No.40) during the 1948 Italian Grand Prix, run on 5 September in the wet at Valentino Park, Turin. The Tipo 125's supercharged 1.5-litre engine developed 225 bhp at 7,000 rpm; it was called 125 because each of the twelve cylinders had a capacity of 125 cubic centimetres.

Juan Manuel Fangio's first car: a Model T Ford which he rebuilt and raced in 1934. Fangio was born in June 1911 in Argentina and raced for the first time – as a mechanic – aged 17. He drove Chevrolets from 1940 to 1948, and was Argentine National Champion in 1940 and 1941. His first European season in 1949 was funded by the Argentinian Automobile Club and govenment: he won six regional Grands Prix in France.

RIGHT: Louis Rosier in a Lago-Talbot heading for victory in the 1949 Belgian Grand Prix at Spa-Francorchamps. Rosier finished in 3 hours 15 minutes 17 seconds, ahead of two Ferrari Tipo 125s driven by Luigi Villoresi and Alberto Ascari. The unsupercharged 4.5-litre Lago-Talbot was relatively slow, but reliable – in this race its low fuel consumption gave Rosier a crucial advantage over the fast but thirsty Ferraris. Rosier did not make a single pit-stop.

LEFT: The start of the 1948 Indianapolis 500. Mauri Rose (>1947), winner for the second consecutive year, took $42,800 out of a total purse of $171,075. Rose was the third fastest qualifier at 129.129 mph; pole position went to Rex Mays in a Kurtis-designed Bowes Seal-Fast Special at 130.577 mph. Veteran Indianapolis driver Ralph Hepburn was killed in practice when he crashed his Novi Grooved Piston car.

Thailand. Farina gave the Alfas a race in the early stages, but then crashed. Wimille yet again won for Alfa; this time Luigi Villoresi was second in a Maserati, and Sommer came in third.

The Ferrari 125's first victory came shortly afterwards when Farina won a minor race, the Circuito del Garda.

At the peak of its success, Alfa Romeo pulled out, mainly because of the cost but also because of the death of two more of their top drivers: Wimille died in Argentina when he crashed avoiding spectators on the track, and Trossi died after a long illness. In their absence, Louis Chiron drove a new 4.5-litre Talbot to victory in the 1949 Grand Prix de France at Rheims, and Louis Rosier won the Belgian Grand Prix in another. Emanuel de Graffenried won the British Grand Prix in a Maserati – but it was Ferrari that benefited the most. Ascari rejoined Ferrari and promptly won the Swiss Grand Prix; Villoresi won the Dutch Grand Prix.

Then Ferrari boosted the 125 to 300 bhp with a two-stage supercharger, in which Ascari won the 1949 Italian Grand Prix at a reopened Monza. The British driver Peter Whitehead later went on to win the Czechoslovakian Grand Prix also for Ferrari – it was truly Ferrari's year.

At Indianapolis, Mauri Rose and Bill Holland continued their success in the Blue Crown Specials. Rose won again in 1948, then Holland won in 1949 after Rose dropped out with a faulty magneto. This let Johnny Parsons into second place in a car designed by Frank Kurtis.

Kurtis' reputation as a builder of dirt track cars and Indianapolis cars was growing, and in the following decade the innovations in design for which he was responsible completely transformed racing at the Speedway.

MILESTONES

The Argentinian driver Juan Manuel Fangio won the Pau Grand Prix in a Maserati 4CL/48, the first of six victories in regional Grands Prix in 1948.

On 1 July Achille Varzi (>1930) was killed in practice for the European Grand Prix in Switzerland; he went into a corner too fast in the wet.

In 1948 the FIA announced a 2-litre Formula B (which became known as Formula Two); a 500-cc supercharged option was never used.

The 1949 Mille Miglia attracted 303 entries; 182 cars finished. The winner was Clemente Biondetti for Ferrari – his third MM victory in three years.

In 1949, the first postwar Le Mans 24-hour sports car race was won by Luigi Chinetti and Lord Selsdon in a 2-litre Ferrari Tipo 166.

American road racing was revived at Watkins Glen, New York, on 2 October 1948 with a race run by the Sports Car Club of America (>1961).

Chapter Eight
Little Cars, Big Cars &
World Champions

At the start of the new decade there was a new sense of purpose and of promise in motor racing. In May 1950 25 new drivers passed their tests at Indianapolis, where the wooden grandstands had been pulled down and replaced with a structure of reinforced concrete. Such renovation continued, and by 1956 there was a new control tower, more seats, a tunnel underneath the track, and a new pit area. Attendances boomed accordingly, and the total purse for the 500 reached the magnificent figure of $300,000.

In the same period the Indianapolis car was transformed. In 1952 Frank Kurtis built a diesel-powered car for Cummins, a truck engine manufacturer. To accommodate the engine, he laid it on its side in a lightweight tubular chassis. He further developed this 'laid-down' position, tailoring his cars specifically for Indianapolis – where all the corners are left-handers. By positioning the engine on the left of the car he found that when the weight transferred to the outside of the turn, the car was in balance and able to corner faster. These 'roadsters' (as they became known) were perfect for Indianapolis – but uncompetitive anywhere else.

In Grand Prix racing, the most important development was the introduction of the World Drivers' Championship in 1950, which provided a clear focus for the sport. The Grand Prix car evolved dramatically too in the 1950s. The first changes came in Italy, from where supercharged cars had dominated the postwar era. Within two years supercharging had disappeared, overtaken by new normally-aspirated engines pioneered by Enzo Ferrari. At the same time there was an even more fundamental change taking place. In 1950 the FIA introduced Formula 3 for 500-cc cars, acknowledging a class of racing dominated by tiny mid-engined vehicles built by the British garage owner Charles Cooper. He steadily moved up the formulae, and in the process provoked a revolution in the design of the racing car. It was a revolution that had nonetheless been signposted as early as in 1934: the universal adoption of the mid-engined layout.

Italian cars continued to dominate the top level of motor racing after the withdrawal of Alfa-Romeo. Maserati and Ferrari set Grand Prix standards and attracted the world's best drivers. The 1953 French Grand Prix was a glorious duel between Mike Hawthorn (Ferrari, left) and Juan Manuel Fangio (Maserati).

RIGHT: The final of the International Trophy at Silverstone. Giuseppe Farina (No.1, left) was the winner in an Alfa-Romeo Tipo 158; British driver Cuthbert Harrison (No.11, far right) did very well to finish fourth in an outdated 1937 ERA.

BELOW RIGHT: Italy's Giuseppe Farina, winner of the first Drivers' World Championship.

The new spirit in motor racing was captured to the full at the British Grand Prix at Silverstone on 13 May. It was the first race in the new World Drivers' Championship, and it had been awarded the honorary title of the European Grand Prix. To mark the occasion, King George VI and Queen Elizabeth attended. The race was billed as 'Royal Silverstone', and the organizers began to dream that motor racing would join horse racing at Ascot, rowing at Henley, and tennis at Wimbledon as part of The Season.

There were cheers for Their Majesties, but there were more and louder cheers when Raymond Mays gave a demonstration in the BRM, the car that was intended to be the British answer to Italian domination of motor racing at the top level. The crowd thrilled to the eerie sound of its V-16 engine with two-stage superchargers at high revs.

On the front row of the grid were four Alfettas. Their factory resources and slender finances had been largely tied up in producing a new range of sports and touring cars, but with new support to tackle the prestigious Drivers' Championship, Alfa was back with the three top drivers of the day: the veteran Giuseppe Farina, the newcomer Juan Manuel Fangio, and the 52-year-old Luigi Fagioli (>1934). The fourth car was driven by the British driver Reg Parnell.

The rest of the field was mainly trusty Maserati 4CLs, driven by Louis Chiron, Emanuel de Graffenried and Prince Bira of Thailand, and 4.5-litre unsupercharged Lago-Talbots driven by Philippe Etancelin, Louis Rosier, Georges Martin and Yves Giraud-Cabantous. There were no Ferraris: they were still being prepared for the Monaco Grand Prix to be held the following week.

Farina went straight into the lead, the other three Alfas right behind him, pulling ahead of the rest of the field led by Prince Bira. Fangio was in second place, Fagioli third, then Parnell, his car easily recognizable through a smashed radiator grille after hitting a hare. Fangio disputed the lead briefly with Farina, then slid on some oil, damaged an oil pipe, and retired. The Alfas finished 1-2-3, with Farina in first place, Fagioli in second and Parnell in third. The fourth-placed car, Yves Giraud-Cabantous' Lago-Talbot, was more than two laps behind.

At Indianapolis there were four of Lou Moore's Offenhauser-powered front-wheel-drive Blue Crown Specials looking for a third successive victory; in the team were Mauri

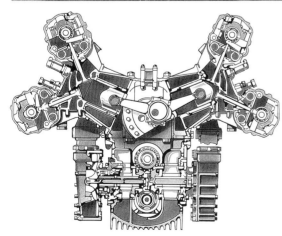

ABOVE: After working all night to get the car ready, mechanics help Raymond Sommer and the new BRM on to the Silverstone track for practice prior to the International Trophy – but the great British hope took no part in the race after a drive shaft failed on the starting grid. The BRM was designed by Peter Berthon, Stuart Tresilian and Raymond Mays. Maximum power in 1950 was 495 bhp at 12,500 rpm but by 1952 this was up to 525 bhp at 12,000 rpm – the highest power output of any racing car under the 1.5-litre formula.

ABOVE: The BRM V-16's two banks of cylinders were angled at 135 degrees. Each row of cylinders had two overhead camshafts and the valves were set at 90 degrees to each other. The engine had a two-stage supercharger.

Rose and Bill Holland plus Tony Bettenhausen and Lee Wallard. The field contained many new cars built round the Offenhauser ('Offy') engine, among them a number designed by Frank Kurtis (>1948–49) with welded tubular frames and independent front suspension. One such was the Wynne's Friction Special, driven by Johnny Parsons who had finished second to Holland in a Kurtis-Offy in 1949.

The race was dogged by rain: when the final yellow flag came out, Parsons was leading, a full lap ahead of Holland. He eventually won after completing 345 miles. Rose crashed, and after the race formally announced his retirement from motor racing.

Meanwhile in Europe, the Alfas continued on their unbeaten way through the season. At Monaco Alberto Ascari, driving a Ferrari Tipo 125, challenged them and came in second. Ferrari was already experimenting with normally-aspirated engines, moving away from the complicated and highly stressed supercharged units. Aurelio Lampredi was masterminding the development of the 4.5-litre V-12 sports car engine for Grand Prix racing.

In the Belgian Grand Prix at Spa, Ascari came fifth in a Tipo 275 using a 3.3-litre version of it. For the Swiss Grand Prix, he used a 4.1-litre version and succeeded in worrying the Alfa team by harrying Fangio before he himself had to retire.

For the Grand Prix organized by the Automobile Club de France, which had returned to full Formula One status, the Alfas turned out in force; this time, however, Ascari withdrew and Fangio won.

The final 4.5-litre version of the V-12

171

Ferrari Tipo 375 was ready in time to make its debut in the Italian Grand Prix at Monza on 3 September. It was said to develop 300 bhp – compared with the Alfa's 350 bhp – and in unofficial practice it was already giving the Alfa team something to think about. Ascari managed to break the lap record by lapping Monza in 1 minute 59 seconds, breaking Consalvo Sanesi's 1948 record in the Alfa of 2 minutes 0.4 seconds. In official practice he brought it down further, to 1 minute 58.8 seconds, although Fangio managed to clip another two tenths of a second off that to take pole position. It was not just the speed of the Ferraris that worried the Alfa drivers: it was the fact that their own thirsty, supercharged cars would have to stop twice to refuel during the 312-mile race, whereas the Ferraris could complete the whole race distance on a single tankful of fuel.

Alfa fielded five cars: Sanesi and Piero Taruffi joined the regulars, who took the lead from the start. Within a lap Ascari had forced his way into second place behind Farina, and the crowd roared its pleasure in anticipation of a great race between two Italian names. They got it. Ascari – never more than seconds behind Farina – managed to pass him, demonstrating how much the unsupercharged cars had progressed. Then Farina took the lead back, but before Ascari could challenge again, the Ferrari engine packed up and he had to walk back to the pits. Fangio's Alfa also gave way under the strain.

The crowd roared again when Dorino Serafini came into the Ferrari pit for tyres and Ascari took over his car, setting off after Farina and Fagioli. Farina had made his last

BELOW: Race-winner Juan Manuel Fangio in an Alfa-Romeo Tipo 158 leading the Monaco Grand Prix. Bob Gerard (following, No.26) finished sixth in an ERA, more than six laps behind Fangio.

MILESTONES

The World Drivers' Championship covered the British, Monaco, Swiss, Belgian, French and Italian Grands Prix, and the Indianapolis 500.

German drivers and manufacturers were readmitted to Grand Prix racing for the first time since the war; Mercedes planned a return.

The RAC Tourist Trophy for sports car at Dundrod, County Antrim, in Northern Ireland, was won by 21-year-old Stirling Moss in a Jaguar XK120.

Lee Petty led NASCAR's Grand National Championship for stock cars, but he was stripped of his points for driving in non-NASCAR events.

On 9 December Ernest Henry (>1911) – the man who had given the racing world the double overhead camshaft engine – died alone in Paris.

On 31 December a 6-hour sports car race inaugurated the airfield circuit at Sebring, Florida. Fritz Koster won in a Crosley.

British Racing Motors (BRM) – Britain's attempt to build a Grand Prix car capable of matching the best that the rest of Europe could offer.

LEFT: Johnny Parsons, winner of a rain-shortened Indianapolis 500. His total time was 2 hours 46 minutes 56 seconds: an average 124.002 mph over the 345 miles he completed.

ABOVE: Alberto Ascari in the new model Ferrari 166 F2/50, on his way to victory in the Formula Two Modena Grand Prix on 10 May. Mario Tadini was second in a 1949 model Ferrari Formula Two car; Piero Carini third in an OSCA MT4. Alberto Ascari, the son of the great Italian driver Antonio Ascari (>1927), was born in 1918 in Milan; he won his first car race at Modena in 1947 and joined Ferrari in 1949.

fuel stop but Fagioli still had to come in – and when he did, Ascari took second place. He failed to catch Farina but finished second, giving Alfa-Romeo yet another nasty shock.

The Alfa drivers won all eleven races they entered in 1950, and with second and third places they filled the top three slots in the World Drivers' Championship: Farina became World Champion, followed by Fangio and Fagioli.

One non-Championship race that they entered and – inevitably – won (finishing order: first Farina, second Fangio) was the International Trophy at Silverstone. It was notable for the publicity that surrounded the racing debut of Britain's supercharged challenger, the BRM.

The BRM was the brainchild of Raymond Mays and his friend Peter Berthon, both of whom had been behind the ERA in the 1930s. After the war they gathered support from the British motor industry in cash or kind to build a world-beating car.

To do so, the project was heavily publicized – and much was expected of it. They built a V-16 engine with two-stage supercharging designed to produce more than 600 bhp, but by 1950 it was still producing only 330 bhp at 10,250 rpm. Raymond Sommer drove it on its debut, starting at the back of the grid. When he let the clutch in, the car shot forward – and then stopped: a drive shaft had broken. As it was pushed off the track spectators booed and hissed and threw pennies at it, a gesture of frustration and derision at what had then turned into a costly British failure.

The BRM team had aimed too high. They had tried to achieve in a few years what even experienced companies like Alfa had failed to do over a much greater period of time. Reg Parnell won two minor races at Goodwood later in the year, against insignificant opposition, and gradually some pertinent lessons were learned.

BRM eventually came good (>1962), but by then other British makers had overtaken it and established Britain well to the forefront of the sport (>1958).

173

RIGHT: Italian manufacturers locked in battle at Monza. Juan Manuel Fangio's Alfa-Romeo Tipo 159 (No.38) leading from Alberto Ascari's Ferrari Tipo 375 (No.2) during the Italian Grand Prix on 16 September. Fangio dropped out with piston trouble on lap 39; Ascari won in 2 hours 42 minutes 39.3 seconds. Fangio's Alfa team-mate Giuseppe Farina drove the fastest lap at 120.97 mph and finished third.

Racing cars on both sides of the Atlantic were in a period of transition. At Indianapolis the dirt track cars had been continuously refined through the late 1940s, and by 1951 performance was improving steadily. Lap speeds had risen from around 120 mph in 1946 to 140 mph in 1951, but top speeds had risen by only around 10 mph over the same time, betokening much better handling in the corners. Improvements in power came from fitting fuel injection to the trusty 4-cylinder Offenhauser ('Offy') engine. Handling was improved by making the cars lighter. In 1951 14 of the 33 starters in the Indianapolis 500 had lighter, stiffer, triangulated tubular space-frame chassis built by Frank Kurtis, pointing the way ahead.

There was also a new breed of driver challenging at Indianapolis – young drivers whose careers were year-round in the expanding roster of dirt track races, who raced every week at local tracks.

One such driver was Lee Wallard, driving a Kurtis-Offy combination, the Berlanger Special. He took hold of the race from the start, and although he practically wrecked the car over the distance, he won in 3 hours 57 minutes 38.05 seconds at a new record speed of 126.244 mph – the first occasion on which the 500-mile race had been completed in less than four hours.

In Europe the battle-lines for the year were clearly drawn between the two major Italian manufacturers.

At Ferrari, Aurelio Lampredi had managed to boost the power of the 4.5-litre V-12 engine in the Tipo 375 to 380 bhp.

At Alfa-Romeo, Gioachino Colombo squeezed the last drops of power and performance from his 13-year-old Alfettas: he raised the supercharger pressure, improved the brakes, and adopted De Dion suspension on the rear wheels. The eight-cylinder engine peaked at 425 bhp on the test bed (corresponding to 287 bhp per litre capacity), but in racing condition it produced around 400 bhp. In this form they were fast but thirsty, doing only around 1.5 miles to the gallon. Colombo fitted extra fuel tanks, but even then they needed two fuel stops in a 300-mile race, whereas the Ferraris could manage the shorter races without stopping for fuel at all.

BRM was getting 525 bhp out of the supercharged V-16 (325 bhp per litre) but the car was still unreliable and no real threat to the Italians. With the 4.5-litre/1.5-litre formula extended to the end of 1953, Mercedes-Benz decided that it would return to Grand Prix racing with a new version of the W165 supercharged voiturettes, the only cars that had ever soundly beaten the Alfettas, in Tripoli in 1939.

The rivalry between Alfa-Romeo and Ferrari produced the best season of Grand Prix racing in Europe since the war.

It started with the Alfas looking invincible: Juan Manuel Fangio won the Swiss Grand Prix, and the reigning World Champion Giuseppe Farina the Belgian Grand Prix – although Ferraris driven by Alberto Ascari and Luigi Villoresi were only just behind in second and third.

Then came the Grand Prix organized by the Automobile Club de France at Rheims on 1 July. Alfa fielded Farina, Fangio, Luigi Fagioli and Consalvo Sanesi, while Ascari and Villoresi were joined by another Argentinian driver, Froilan Gonzalez, and a British driver, Reg Parnell. In the audience were veterans Alfred Neubauer and Hermann Lang, whose 117.5-mph lap record at Rheims had stood since 1939. It was to be broken many times, such was the quality of the competition.

Fangio was fastest in practice, and Italian cars filled the first seven places on the starting grid. The fastest French car was Louis Chiron's Talbot.

Ascari passed Fangio on the first lap to take the lead, with Villoresi for Ferrari in third place. In trying to catch Ascari, Fangio broke the lap record again on lap 2, then both drivers broke it on lap 6. Fangio broke it again on lap 8.

FAR LEFT: The rising star of British motor racing – Stirling Moss at Monza, where he tested the 16-cylinder BRM in 1951. Moss, born in London in 1929, began racing in 1948 aged 18. His first major victory was the 1950 Tourist Trophy in Northern Ireland driving a Jaguar XK120 (>1962).

BELOW: Lee Wallard's Kurtis-Offy, the Belanger Special (No. 99), overtaking Duane Carter's Mobilgas Special on the way to victory in the Indianapolis 500. Carter finished eighth. Just four days after his 500 triumph, Wallard had a serious crash in a sprint car event at Reading, Pa., and never raced again.

Such furious racing took its toll, and on lap 10 Ascari retired with brake failure. Then Fangio's engine started misfiring and he dropped back. Farina took over the lead for Alfa and reduced the lap record a further four times by lap 18, Villoresi at this stage a minute behind in second place.

In the pits, Fangio took over Fagioli's car and promptly put in the fastest lap of the race at 2 minutes 27.8 seconds (corresponding to 118.29 mph). Ascari then took over Gonzalez's car and the battle continued. By the half-way mark Fangio was lying second to Farina, Ascari was third, and all three had lapped Villoresi in fourth place.

Then Farina lost the tread on one tyre, and Fangio took over the lead. He made a final fuel stop and managed to get back ahead of Ascari to win a classic victory – the 47th overall for the Alfetta, and its 27th consecutive Grand Prix win since the war. But behind him came three Ferraris: a sure sign that there were imminent changes to come.

Two weeks later came the British Grand Prix at Silverstone. The Alfettas had had even larger fuel tanks squeezed into the engine compartment, and Fagioli had been replaced by Felice Bonetto. Ferrari was represented by Ascari, Gonzalez and Villoresi, with a fourth 1950-vintage Ferrari Tipo 375 racing in green rather than red as a Thinwall Special. It was owned by Anthony 'Tony' Vandervell, a British industrialist whose firm manufactured Thinwall bearings.

Vandervell was one of the backers of the BRM, but he was keen to learn about racing cars and the organization of racing teams, and by racing the Thinwall Special he began developing the expertise in Britain.

The battle between the two Italian marques started in practice. Gonzalez's 100.65 mph smashed Farina's lap record of 97.19 mph on the previous year to take pole position. Alfas and Ferraris filled the first two rows of the grid; then came Lago-Talbots, ERAs, an Alta, two Maserati 4CLT/48s and an even older 4CL, and, right at the back, two V-16 BRMs driven by Reg Parnell and Peter Walker. They had arrived at the circuit too late to be able to practise.

The Argentinians Fangio and Gonzalez went away together, but Farina came from behind to squeeze between them. Yet by the end of the first lap Bonetto was leading for Alfa, followed by Gonzalez, Farina, Ascari, Fangio, Villoresi, and Sanesi in a continuous red blur, followed by the green of Peter Whitehead's Thinwall Special.

A lap later, Gonzalez was leading and Parnell had managed to get one of the BRMs up into seventh place.

The Alfas were heavy with fuel and not handling at their best, but by lap 10 they had

RIGHT: Powerhouse – the Alfa-Romeo Tipo 159's supercharged 'straight-8' engine (comprising eight cylinders in a line).

RIGHT: End of an era. The Alfa-Romeo Tipo 158/159, or Alfetta, set the standard for Grand Prix racing cars, but by 1951 its prewar chassis and engine had been developed as far as they could go. It ended its career on a high note, taking Giuseppe Farina in 1950 and Juan Manuel Fangio in 1951 to the Drivers' World Championship. Fangio's victory at the 1951 French Grand Prix was the Alfetta's 27th consecutive Grand Prix win since the war.

lightened and Fangio managed to get past his countryman into the lead. The two battled away, never more than 5 or 6 seconds apart, often as close as four-tenths of a second. In the struggle Gonzalez hit a boundary marker, went over it, and ploughed through a line of straw bales – but he barely noticed the disruption and immediately chased off again after Fangio.

The two BRMs were well behind the leading Italian cars, their drivers suffering burns from the cockpit sides which were too close to the engine.

Fangio came in for fuel on lap 49 and Gonzalez took the lead, stretching it to 1 minute 13 seconds by the time Fangio was back in the race. Ascari's gearbox had failed and he had retired.

On lap 61 Gonzalez came in for fuel. In the pits he leapt from the car, expecting Ferrari's No.1 driver, Ascari, to take over – but Ascari gestured him back in, unwilling to spoil his chance of victory. After a 23-second pit-stop, Gonzalez rejoined without losing the lead, still retaining his lead of a minute ahead of Fangio.

Fangio did everything he knew to catch Gonzalez, and he closed the gap by 10 seconds, but the burly Gonzalez was in sublime

MILESTONES

The 374-mile French Grand Prix is the longest World Championship race to date; Rheims (>1932) was later modified (>1966) to by-pass Gueux village.

The first time disc brakes were used in a race was by the Conze brothers in the Indianapolis 500; they were developed for aircraft.

Tony Bettenhausen took over the Berlanger Special after the 500, winning eight dirt track races in it to become AAA National Champion.

Production of 500-cc Coopers for Formula Three races reached a peak of production in 1951 at slightly more than one car a week (>1958, 1959).

Jack Brabham became Australian national speedway champion for the fourth time driving a midget car of his own design (>1959).

Talbot's last Grand Prix appearance was in the Belgian Grand Prix, in which Louis Rosier and Yves Giraud-Cabantous came fourth and fifth.

ABOVE: In its ultimate form in 1951, the Alfa-Romeo Tipo 159's 1.5-litre supercharged engine produced 425 bhp at 9,300 rpm – almost 285 bhp per litre – a remarkable figure which would remain unmatched for a quarter of a century. It gave the Alfetta a maximum speed of 189 mph. A De Dion rear axle and transverse leaf spring were introduced to replace the swing-axle rear suspension on the later and most powerful versions of the car, which because of very high fuel consumption required extra tanks around the body – increasing the weight considerably to about 710 kilograms (1,562 pounds). The 159 ran on 98 per cent methanol fuel. Even with the capacity to carry 66 gallons of methanol, it needed to stop twice for refuelling in a Grand Prix's 300-mile length. The curious-looking 'elephant's trunk' (right foreground) is the carburettor air intake.

form and it fell to him to end Alfa's five years of victory. Villoresi was third, two laps behind the leaders, and the scorched BRM drivers, Parnell and Walker, between them managed fifth and seventh.

It was the greatest British Grand Prix ever till then, and it marked a turning-point in Grand Prix history: the end of the super-charged era and the beginning of a new epoch. It settled an old score between Enzo Ferrari and Alfa-Romeo which had started before the war in the already distant days when the Alfetta was a new car.

But Ferrari was supremely gracious in victory, personally cabling the Alfa Managing Director, 'I still feel for our Alfa the adolescent tenderness of first love . . .'

Ascari won the first postwar German Grand Prix at the Nürburgring, then the Italian teams moved back to their home ground at Monza once more for the Italian Grand Prix.

The Alfas were fastest in practice, but during Sanesi's practice fuel stop the valve on the fuel hose stuck open, spraying Sanesi with fuel

ABOVE: Argentine invasion. Second-placed Juan Manuel Fangio congratulates fellow-Argentinian and race-winner Froilan Gonzalez after the British Grand Prix at Silverstone on 14 July. Gonzalez finished in 2 hours 42 minutes 18.2 seconds, 51 seconds ahead of Fangio after 270 miles of racing.

TOP: Gonzalez's 4.5-litre Ferrari 375 coming out of Stowe Corner at Silverstone on the way to a memorable victory. The burly Argentinian, nicknamed 'The Pampas Bull', was popular with the British crowd and loved the Silverstone circuit, where he was particularly successful. He led the race from lap 49 to the finish.

which caught fire. A mechanic pulled him out, and both were immediately taken to hospital with severe burns. The car was completely destroyed.

The BRMs arrived for practice but the RAC refused to license one of the drivers, Tony Richardson, so Hans Stuck (>1934), who was in the crowd, was offered a chance to drive. The cars then developed gearbox problems and were withdrawn anyway.

There were two Alfas and two Ferraris on the front row of the grid: Farina and Fangio, Ascari and Gonzalez. Behind them were Villoresi and Piero Taruffi in two more Ferraris, and Bonetto in the third Alfa. Farina and Fangio managed to leave the others at the start, but Ascari managed to get into second place behind Fangio. They disputed the lead until Fangio's first pit-stop, when a tyre exploded as he came in. Farina then fell back, and there were three Ferraris in the lead. When Ascari came in for fuel, the hose stuck again and he too was sprayed with fuel, but he accelerated back into the lead without catching fire.

Fangio's car then broke a valve and he retired, leaving Farina by himself to tackle the four Ferraris.

Ascari appeared to be coasting to victory. Then the crowd noticed a slight change in the note of his engine as it started misfiring due to a faulty magneto. Farina gained slowly – then approaching the pits he ran out of fuel, coasting in silently. He re-started, then the pit crew saw that his fuel tank was leaking.

Both men nursed their cars to the end. Ascari won, with Gonzalez second, followed by Farina, Villoresi and Taruffi – four Ferraris in the first five.

The Italian result meant the honours in the top races were even, with three each. Fangio was leading the World Championship, but by only two points from Ascari, so there was absolutely everything to race for in the final race of the season, the Spanish Grand Prix at Barcelona.

Alfa had Fangio, Farina and Bonetto, and Ferrari had Ascari, Gonzalez and Taruffi. The Ferrari team opted for a full load of fuel to run the whole race without stopping, but they chose wheels and tyres that for them were smaller than usual.

Ascari was fastest in practice, and he led from the start, with his team-mate Gonzalez in second place.

Then Fangio got into his stride and passed Gonzalez and started to challenge Ascari. Ascari held him off until lap 8, when a tyre lost its tread.

Fangio never looked back: all the Ferraris suffered tyre problems, and he roared home the winner in the Alfetta's final race – taking the World Championship too, in a fairy-tale ending to its career.

LEFT: The British Grand Prix at Silverstone. Giuseppe Farina's Alfa-Romeo 159 on the grass at the Abbey Curve after it caught fire during the race.

1952

The relentless advance of the Offenhauser engine, and of cars built by the Southern Californian designer Frank Kurtis, continued at Indianapolis. Of the 33 cars on the grid, 29 had Offy engines and 20 were built by Kurtis. Most were quite conventional derivatives of dirt track cars, but two built by Kurtis attracted particular attention. In pole position was the Cummins Diesel Special, driven by Fred Agabashian.

Cummins had come to Kurtis wanting to build a racing car around their 401-cu.in. supercharged diesel engine, and the only way Kurtis could see to accommodate it was revolutionary: to lay it on its side. This held extra advantages, especially at Indianapolis which had only left-hand corners. With the engine in this position, the crankshaft on the left, the weight of the engine was also concentrated on the left, then as the car cornered, the weight transferred to the outside, keeping the car broadly in balance and making it faster through the corners.

The result was a low, sleek, and very fast monster of a car.

BELOW: The combination of the Ferrari Tipo 500 and Alberto Ascari (**BELOW RIGHT**) were unbeatable in 1952. Ascari drove the 500 to victory in twelve races, including the Belgian, British, Dutch, Italian, German and French Grands Prix, and won the World Drivers' Championship.

ABOVE: Heading into the first turn of the Indianapolis 500. Jack MacGrath leads in a Hinkle Special, followed by Jim Rathmann in a Grancor-Wynn and Duane Carter in a Belanger Special. Alberto Ascari is fifteenth, having come off the seventh row of the starting grid after qualifying at 134.408 mph.

ABOVE RIGHT: Troy Ruttman (centre left), winner of the Indianapolis 500, with wealthy team-owner J. C. Agajanian (centre) and members of the Agajanian family.

In eighth place on the grid was an Offy-engined Kurtis, the KK500A, sponsored by Fuel Injection Engineering, which adopted the same principle except that the engine could only be tilted at 36 degrees. It was driven by Bill Vukovich, who had put up the fastest time in qualifying. Next to him was a more conventional Offy-engined car designed by a one-time employee of Kurtis, Eddie Kuzma, and driven by 22-year-old Troy Ruttman. Way back on the grid in 19th place was Alberto Ascari in a Ferrari Tipo 375, the only one of four to qualify. One reason they were slow by comparison with the American cars was that the driver had to change gear twice on every lap, whereas the Offy-engined cars went round in top gear.

The KK500A lived up to its promise, and Vukovich took hold of the race from the start although Agabashian and Ruttman kept up well. Ascari managed to advance to 12th place before a wheel on his Ferrari broke and he was out. On lap 71 the supercharger on the Cummins Diesel gave problems and Agabashian was out too. Vukovich continued serenely on his way, with Ruttman never far

behind – a race between the best of the old faced with the shock of the new. It looked as if Vukovich would win until the crowd suddenly saw him slide it along the wall and jump out; the steering had broken. Ruttman, who was only 19 seconds behind, coasted easily to victory.

A traditional car had won, but Kurtis had shown the way ahead. Somebody jokingly compared the KK500A to a 'track roadster', modified stock cars used by amateur dirt track drivers, and the name caught on and stuck. The roadster era, after something of a false start, had finally begun.

In Europe the World Championship was in some confusion at the start of the season. Alfa-Romeo had pulled out at the end of 1951 because they could not hope to get anything more out of the Alfettas. That left the Ferrari 375 the only competitive car, and race promoters worried that without real competition, attendances would fall. Their fears for Formula One were borne out in a non-Championship event at Turin, when BRM pulled out before the race and Ferrari had a walkover.

Promoters turned to Formula Two, which had been flourishing since 1948, and bowing to the inevitable the FIA agreed that for the 1953 and 1954 World Championship points would be awarded in Formula Two races. Formula One went into abeyance for two years, giving manufacturers plenty of time to build new cars to the new formula of 2.5 litres, or 750-cc supercharged.

In the surge of interest from the Formula Two fraternity, a new range of cars and drivers rose to face top-class competition. Ferrari was still the most competitive. Aurelio Lampredi had been developing its 2-litre Formula Two

Cooper cars gave many British drivers their start in racing. The International Trophy race at Goodwood (*BELOW*) was won by Bob Gerard in a Mark VI Cooper with a Norton motorcycle engine. Rising star Mike Hawthorn (*BOTTOM*) drove a Cooper-Bristol to a superb third place in the British Grand Prix.

car – the Tipo 500 – since 1948. Its twin camshaft four-cylinder engine produced 190 bhp, and with De Dion rear suspension it had superb roadholding. For 1952 Ferrari took on Alberto Ascari, Giuseppe Farina, Luigi Villoresi, Piero Taruffi, and the Frenchman, André Simon. A Swiss private entrant, Rudolf Fischer, was also a regular competitor.

Ferrari's most competitive opponent was Maserati. After a career that spanned time with both Alfa and Ferrari, Gioachino Colombo had moved to Maserati in 1951 to mastermind the 2-litre A6GCM, a six-cylinder Formula Two car that was less powerful than the Ferrari at 160 bhp and, with a rigid rear axle, less competitive on the corners. Maserati hired the services of the reigning World Champion, Juan Manuel Fangio, fellow-Argentinian Froilan Gonzalez, and Felice Bonetto.

The switch to Formula Two stirred great interest in Britian, where a number of companies were already building cars to the formula – Connaught, Frazer-Nash, HWM and Cooper among the most competitive. Cooper was the furthest advanced, breaking away from its mid-engined Formula Three cars with the Bristol-engined 2-litre T20. They were driven by Mike Hawthorn, Alan Brown and Eric Brandon. HWM used an Alta engine and De Dion rear suspension, and its drivers were Stirling Moss, Lance Macklin, Peter Collins, and one of the founders of the firm, an ex-bomber pilot, George Abecassis. In France, Amédée Gordini produced a car on a shoe-string budget; and from Germany, Alex von Falkenhausen's AFM with a BMW engine was driven by Hans Stuck (>1934).

The British, French and German teams were hopelessly uncompetitive compared with the Italians, but they made up for that with enthusiasm for an opportunity to experience top-level racing that was not to be missed. When the season opened at Berne with the Swiss Grand Prix, Ascari was away at Indianapolis, but even without him Ferrari demonstrated its superiority. Piero Taruffi won, with Rudolf

MILESTONES

On the Mille Miglia's 25th anniversary, a record 501 drivers took part: 275 finished, and the winner was Giovanni Bracco for Ferrari.

Luigi Fagioli (>1934) crashed a saloon car in a curtain-raiser for the Monaco Grand Prix. Badly injured, he died in hospital three weeks later.

Rudolf Caracciola crashed a Mercedes 300SL in practice for a sports car race at Berne, smashing his leg seriously for a second time (>1933); he then retired.

Mercedes 300SLs came first and second in the 24-hour sports car race at Le Mans. The winners were Hermann Lang and Fritz Riess.

In the 1,900-mile Carrera Panamericana road race in Mexico, Karl Kling won the sports car class in a Mercedes 300SL at 103.07 mph.

Chuck Stevenson won the Carrera Panamericana saloon car class in a Lincoln at 91.41 mph; he went on to become the year's AAA National Champion.

BELOW: The BRM makes progress – Froilan Gonzalez winning the Woodcote Cup at Goodwood.

BOTTOM: BRMs (No.5 and No.6) burning rubber at Goodwood. The car's power could not be used effectively through the narrow tyres, resulting in wheelspin.

Fischer second. When Ascari returned, he won the Belgian, French, German and Dutch Grands Prix with Farina second, and the British with Taruffi second – and Hawthorn third in a Cooper-Bristol.

For the Italian Grand Prix, Colombo had uprated the Maserati A6GCM to produce 180 bhp, giving Ferrari some competition for the first time and resulting in the best race of the season. On the front row of the grid were three Ferraris driven by Ascari, Villoresi and Farina. Next to him was Maurice Trintignant in a

Gordini, followed by Gonzalez in the new Maserati. Farther back were seven British drivers in British cars, including Stirling Moss in a Connaught and Mike Hawthorn in the Cooper-Bristol.

Gonzalez put in one of his virtuoso performances, leading for the first 36 laps. His Maserati was unable to complete the full 80 laps, or 312 miles, on a single tank, so Gonzalez had set off with a light fuel load, hoping to build up a sufficient lead to come into the pits, refuel, and get out again. But in nearly half the race he only managed to build up a 20-second lead over the Ferraris, and after a lengthy 35 seconds spent in the pits he rejoined in fifth place. The crowd roared its approval as he charged ahead and challenged for the lead. In the battle that followed, Ascari broke the lap record for Formula Two cars at 111.77 mph – which Gonzalez promptly equalled.

It was not enough. Ascari won by 47 seconds, making it seven Grands Prix in a row for Ferrari, and the World Drivers' Championship for himself.

The British drivers, mechanics, manufacturers and teams won few laurels, but the experience they gained was invaluable and whetted their appetite for more top-level racing.

RIGHT: British triumph. Mike Hawthorn is mobbed after his victory in the French Grand Prix at Rheims – the first win by a Briton in the World Drivers' Championship. Hawthorn finished the year fourth in the World Championship table with 19 points, behind Giuseppe Farina (third, 26 points), Juan Manuel Fangio (second, 28 points) and Alberto Ascari (first, 34½ points).

The 37th Indianapolis 500 produced a record crowd of 200,000, a record purse of \$246,300, and a record temperature on race day of 130°F (54°C). Bill Vukovich was fastest in qualifying in the Kurtis-Offy KK500A at 138.392 mph – slightly under the record set by Chet Miller the previous year – but competition for the 33 places on the grid was fierce, almost gladiatorial, the slowest qualifier only 3 mph behind the fastest. The overall average of those who made it into the 500 itself was 136.409 mph, the fastest ever. Unhappily, Miller was killed in qualifying.

Vukovich put his stamp on the race from the start: he led on the first lap, pulled 3 seconds ahead on the second, and was 9 seconds in the lead on the third.

Incidents started early in the race. Andy Linden lost control on lap 4 – his car hit the wall and burst into flames, but he was uninjured. Then Jim Davies lost his brakes; he made two unsuccessful attempts to get into the pits by sliding sideways to slow the car down. On his third attempt, he scraped his wheels and tyres down the pit wall for much of its length to stop.

On lap 76, the steering arm on Bob Freeland's Watson-Offy (>1956) broke and he spun violently into the wall.

All the drivers suffered from the heat – the drivers of cars using nitromethane fuel proportionately more from fumes and the extra heat generated. Many of them had to be relieved. Crashes leaving many others back in the pits, there were plenty of volunteers.

Linden drove as relief for two other drivers. When Tony Bettenhausen came in exhausted, his car was taken over by Chuck Stevenson who had crashed earlier. Then Gene Hartley crashed, and when Stevenson came in to be relieved, Hartley took over from him, only to crash a second time later in the race. Cale Yarborough also retired exhausted, but as he got out of his car, he collapsed; he was taken to hospital where, afterwards, he died. Johnny Parsons and Fred Agabashian also made use of relief drivers.

But in the lead Vukovich never faltered. He lost the lead for only five laps during his three pit-stops. Each time, the pit crew poured cold water down the back of his shirt. He steadily built up his lead and won with three laps in

RIGHT: Bill Vukovich (>1955), the winner of the Indianapolis 500, flanked by Speedway president Wilbur Shaw (>1937) and actress Jane Greer in Victory Lane. The presence of celebrities at the 500 became an established Indianapolis tradition in the years after the Second World War. Prize money was rising all the time – Vukovich won a record $89,496 and even Andy Linden, placed last after covering just three laps, won $2,126.

LEFT: Italian dominance at the Dutch Grand Prix. Alberto Ascari (No. 2, Ferrari) leads from Luigi Villoresi (No. 4, Ferrari), Giuseppe Farina (No. 6, Ferrari), Juan Manuel Fangio (No. 12, Maserati) and Mike Hawthorn (Ferrari), with Stirling Moss following in a Connaught. Italian cars took the first five places: Ascari first, Farina second, Felice Bonetti and Froilan Gonzalez joint third in a Maserati, Hawthorn fourth and Emanuel de Graffenried fifth in another Maserati.

hand – a victory that marked the beginning of a new era at Indianapolis: the era of the 'roadsters' (>1952).

In Europe, Grand Prix cars remained largely unchanged from the previous year as manufacturers prepared for the introduction of the new formula in 1954. The two top names – Ferrari and Maserati – were very evenly matched on the track. The Maserati A6GCM was rather faster, giving it an advantage on the straights, whereas the Ferraris, with their De Dion rear suspension, were faster through the corners.

The best drivers were also spread between the two top names: in their cars Ferrari had Alberto Ascari, Luigi Villoresi and Giuseppe Farina, plus the fastest of the young British drivers, Mike Hawthorn; Maserati had the two top Argentinians, Juan Manuel Fangio and Froilan Gonzalez, to which they added a third Argentinian, Onofre Marimon, and the Italian Felice Bonetto.

The opening race of the season was in Buenos Aires, acknowledging the growing interest in the sport in Argentina, not least on the part of President Peron, in the wake of the success of Argentinian drivers. With three of them, including Fangio, in the Maserati team, the crowd was hoping for, if not actively expecting, a home win – but it was not to be. Ascari won for Ferrari; Villoresi was second, and the first Argentinian home was Gonzalez in third.

Ascari went on to establish a lead in the World Drivers' Championship with two more wins, in the Dutch and Belgian Grands Prix. Then came the French Grand Prix, at Rheims. No fewer than the first four rows of the grid were filled with the red cars of Italy. Behind them were seven green British cars, Coopers and Connaughts, with just a single Italian

The Le Mans 24-hour race for sports cars was the scene of another British success, the six-cylinder 3.5-litre Jaguar C Type finishing first, second and fourth. Duncan Hamilton and Tony Rolt drove the winning car (No. 18), covering 2,540.58 miles at an average 105.85 mph – the first time the winner's average had topped 100 mph. Stirling Moss and Peter Walker came second and Peter Whitehead and Ian Stewart were fourth; third place was taken by a 5.45-litre Chrysler-engined Cunningham from America. The C Type developed 220 bhp at 5,200 rpm and was the same type that won at Le Mans in 1951, driven by Peter Walker and Peter Whitehead. Jaguar's use of more efficient disc brakes gave its drivers a crucial advantage over the rest of the field, by enabling them to brake later going into the corners.

OSCA among them. Finally, right at the back, there were four blue Gordinis representing the host country.

Bonetto just managed to hold Ascari at the start and, as the pair pulled away from Villoresi, Gonzalez found his way into the gap and somehow succeeded in passing all three. It was Gonzalez in the lead by 2.8 seconds at the end of lap 1. He had started with a light fuel load, intending to build up a lead that would in due course enable him to refuel without losing it. Making good use of the marginal speed advantage and lightness of the Maserati, he steadily extended his lead over the four Ferraris behind him – Ascari, Villoresi, Hawthorn, and Farina. Fangio was holding sixth place for Maserati.

Gonzalez's plan did not work. When he came in for fuel on lap 27, his stop lasted an interminable 27 seconds, and when he rejoined he was well down, in fifth place, so close was the racing.

Fangio now found his old form, and at 30 laps – the half-way mark – he was leading in a terrific battle with Hawthorn. The duel

between these two was the highlight of the race. Their cars were rarely more than a length apart, the lead ever swapping back and forth, Fangio occasionally stretching it from the front and narrowing it from behind on the straights. Behind them, Ascari and Gonzalez were having an equally epic Ferrari-Maserati battle for third place. Each time they came round, the crowd in the grandstands rose to their feet in anticipation of a change in their fortunes.

Going into the last lap, Fangio and Hawthorn were neck and neck. Hawthorn braked a little later going into the Thillois hairpin at the end of the straight, and with a little more power at the 'bottom end', accelerated out of the corner in the lead – which he held to the end.

After 314 miles and 2 hours 44 minutes of racing, 1.4 seconds covered the first three cars: Hawthorn beat Fangio by 1 second, and Gonzalez, who had finally managed to break away from Ascari, was only 0.4 second behind Fangio. A British driver had won the French Grand Prix – and was only the third ever to do so (>1923, 1929).

Ascari returned to form for the rest of the season, winning both the British and Swiss Grands Prix to put him in an unassailable position in the Drivers' Championship well before the last race of the season, which was the Italian Grand Prix staged, as usual, at Monza.

Of the 30 starters there, six were Ferraris

ROUEN CIRCUIT: 1 LAP: 3.17 MILES

Pits

Virage Sanson

Start & Finish

Hairpin

Rouen holds a special place in motor-racing history as the finishing point of the world's first motor competition, the Paris-Rouen trial in 1894. A short course existed at the Rouen-Les Essarts track before the Second World War but in 1950 the Automobile Club Normand created a new circuit. The first meeting was held on July 30, 1950, Louis Rosier winning the main contest in a Talbot. The track was used for the 1952 ACF Grand Prix, won by Alberto Ascari in a Ferrari.

ABOVE: The Rouen-Les Essarts circuit lies in a wooded valley to the south-west of Rouen, Normandy. It was extended to 4.06 miles in 1955.

ROUEN
PARIS

FAR LEFT: President Peron of Argentina congratulating Alberto Ascari, the winner of the Argentine Grand Prix. Peron insisted that his 'children' be allowed to watch the race and more than half a million of his citizens packed the Buenos Aires circuit. Tragedy struck when Giuseppe Farina's Ferrari collided with some spectators who had strayed onto the track, killing ten and injuring 36. Ascari's winning time was 3 hours 1 minute 4.6 seconds: 78.14 mph. It was the first time the Argentine Grand Prix had been included in the World Drivers' Championship.

BELOW: Juan Manuel Fangio in a typically relaxed, straight-arm driving position during the Swiss Grand Prix at Bremgarten. Fangio finished fourth in a Maserati A6GCM, around 2.5 minutes behind the winner, Alberto Ascari in a Ferrari Tipo 500.

and six more Maseratis. Maserati had improved its suspension, but one way or another Ferrari still seemed to have the edge overall. Ascari was fastest in practice, although Fangio was no more than a mere half second behind him.

In the race, Ascari went into the lead, but at the end of the first lap only 3 seconds covered the first four cars: Ascari (Ferrari), Marimon (Maserati), Farina (Ferrari) and Fangio (Maserati). In fifth place there was something of a surprise: Stirling Moss, who was determined to drive a British car, in a specially prepared T24 Cooper-Alta with De Dion rear suspension, fuel injection, disc brakes, and nitromethane fuel.

The four leading cars continued flashing past the grandstands in a blur of red at 160 mph, the lead swapping occasionally. Moss was pretty well as fast, but he was bedevilled by mechanical problems and was obliged to drop back, while the Italian cars continued faultlessly on their way.

Ascari was leading by a length from Farina as they went into the last lap, Marimon behind them, then Fangio. Coming into the last bend, the pressure got the better of Ascari, and he spun. Marimon hit him, putting both of them out.

Farina swerved to avoid the melée, allowing Fangio a small gap – into which he shot, roaring down the straight to an unexpected but no less welcome victory.

LEFT: Mike Hawthorn's Ferrari (left), neck-and-neck with Juan Manuel Fangio's Maserati during the French Grand Prix at Rheims. The thrilling struggle between these two drivers – and third-placed Froilan Gonzalez – made it one of the most competitive races in the history of the sport. Ferraris and Maseratis took the first nine places: Jean Behra was tenth in a Gordini, five laps behind the leader; Bob Gerard was eleventh in a Cooper-Bristol.

MILESTONES

The Sports Car World Championship was introduced by the FIA, and covered mainly endurance races, such as the 24-hours race at Le Mans.

On 15 February Bill Blair won the 160-mile NASCAR Daytona Beach and road race in an Oldsmobile at an average speed of 89.5 mph.

Felice Bonetto was killed in the Carrera Panamericana; Fangio won the sports class for Lancia, Chuck Stevenson the saloon class for Lincoln.

Louis Chiron made his last appearance in the French Grand Prix. He first appeared in 1930, winning it five times, in 1931, 1934, 1937, 1947 and 1949.

On 11 August Tazio Nuvolari died after a long illness (>1948). He was buried in his leather helmet, yellow shirt and blue trousers (>1935).

Stirling Moss was the first driver to use disc brakes in Grand Prix racing in his T24 Cooper-Alta in the Italian Grand Prix at Monza.

187

After two years' racing under Formula Two, the World Drivers' Championship returned to a new Formula One: 2.5 litres, or 750 cc supercharged – although no serious contender took the supercharged option.

Ferrari and Maserati both developed their existing models for the new season. Faced with the cost of funding those developments, Enzo Ferrari had announced that he was pulling out of racing – a ploy he had used before to attract financial support, and in which he was again successful on this occasion. Aurelio Lampredi had experimented with a 2-litre version of Ferrari's new Formula One car in the 1953 Italian Grand Prix. The Tipo 555 – nicknamed the 'Squalo' ('shark') from the menacing, bulbous shape housing fuel tanks on both sides – had performed badly at Monza, but Ferrari persisted, preparing it for the new season alongside the Tipo 625, a 2.5-litre version of the Tipo 500. It used the same basic four-cylinder engine, bored out to produce 230 bhp at 7,200 rpm.

Maserati developed the A6GCM into the 250F. The basic design had been laid down by the ex-Alfa, ex-Ferrari virtuoso Gioachino Colombo (>1948–49), who at this point moved on yet again, this time to Bugatti, where there were also plans for a return to Formula One racing. The 250F was taken over by another Maserati engineer, Giulio Alfieri.

BELOW: Phil Hill in a 4.5-litre Ferrari during the Carrera Panamericana road race in Mexico. Umberto Maglioli won the sports car class in a 4.9-litre Ferrari, beating Hill by 3 seconds after the 1,908-mile race; the saloon car class was won by Ray Crawford in a Lincoln. The race, inaugurated in 1950, was abandoned after 1954 because of the high number of casualties among spectators.

BELOW: The Rheims course was reputed to be one of the fastest in the world – and was the great circuit of the 1950s and 1960s. The 1954 race was the 33rd Grand Prix since 1906 but was advertised as the 41st, since the ACF counted eight of the pre-1906 inter-town races as Grands Prix. The track was re-routed to bypass the village of Gueux in 1954 (>1925, 1966).

PHOSCAO

41ème G° PRIX DE L'A.C.F.
REIMS
4 JUILLET 1954

LEFT: The stage-managed finish of the French Grand Prix. Juan Manuel Fangio (right) and Karl Kling cross the line together in Mercedes W196s — on the 40th anniversary of a similar occasion when Mercedes introduced a new car and trounced all opposition at the 1914 ACF GP. The W196 proved unstoppable: Fangio and Kling had a 100-yard lead at the first corner and won the race by a full lap from third-placed Robert Manzon's Ferrari 625.

British racing car makers, who had responded with enthusiasm to the Formula Two World Championship years, and had learned a great deal from them, lacked the resources to compete with the research departments of the great Italian companies. Tony Vandervell, one of the backers of BRM (>1950), commissioned John Cooper to build a new chassis to take a four-cylinder 2-litre engine built by Vandervell Products, based on the Norton motorcycle engine, which developed around 200 bhp. The chassis was based on the chassis of the Ferraris that Vandervell had raced as Thinwall Specials with De Dion rear suspension, and was fitted with Girling disc brakes and Ferrari-type steering. It was the first car to bear the name Vanwall, which Vandervell coined from his own name and his Thinwall bearing business.

The most widely anticipated new car of the new formula came from Germany. Mercedes-Benz had decided to return to racing in 1952, and after some success in sports car racing (>1952), chose the 2.5 formula to make its Grand Prix comeback. Once the decision had been taken, the board committed the full resources of its research department to it — and the result was the superb W196. The man in overall charge was new, Dr Fritz Nallinger, but there remained a direct link with the company's glorious past, especially with Mercedes' heyday in the 1930s: Alfred Neubauer, the team manager, and Rudolf Uhlenhaut, the chief engineer. The cars were a closely guarded secret until they made their debut (see pages 192–193). To drive them, Neubauer took on Juan Manuel Fangio and three German drivers, Karl Kling, Hans Herrmann

ABOVE: Karl Kling at speed in the streamlined Mercedes W196 during the French Grand Prix. After race-winners Fangio and Kling, only five cars finished the Grand Prix – the other drivers overworked their engines trying to match the Mercedes' majestic progress. Alberto Ascari dropped out on the first lap with engine trouble on his Maserati 250F.

The 250Fs were built principally for sale to private entrants, from whom Maserati received so many orders that they offered clients A6GCMs as an interim measure, re-engined with a new six-cylinder 240-bhp engine that had been destined for the 250F.

In great secret, Alfa-Romeo was also designing a new Formula One car, the Tipo 160. It was of revolutionary design, the driver's seat located behind the rear axle. The engine produced 300 bhp in tests, but the board abandoned the whole idea in order to concentrate instead on producing cars for sale to the public. Another Italian firm to tackle the new Formula One was Lancia. When he took over the company from his father, Gianni Lancia decided to re-enter the fray, employing the doyen of Italian designers, Vittorio Jano (>1923, 1932, 1937). Jano decided to use a V-8 engine in a completely new design (see box overleaf).

ABOVE: The engine of Alberto Ascari's Maserati blew up in front of the main stand on lap 40 of the British Grand Prix at Silverstone. It was the second engine failure Ascari had suffered in the race: his own Maserati developed valve problems on lap 21 and he took over teammate Luigi Villoresi's car (No. 32).

and Hermann Lang, the former European Champion (>1939).

Neither the Lancia D-50, nor the Mercedes W196 was ready for the first race under the new formula, the Argentinian Grand Prix in Buenos Aires on 17 January. Fangio was therefore free to drive the Maserati 250F in its debut race. Of the 17 cars lined up for it, eight were Maseratis – another 250F for Onofre Marimon, and the rest were privately entered A6GCMs. The Ferrari team was Froilan Gonzalez, Giuseppe Farina, Mike Hawthorn and Maurice Trintignant. Alberto Ascari and Luigi Villoresi had both quit Ferrari for Lancia, joining Eugenio Castellotti, but without cars they stayed away. Fangio thrilled his home crowd to win from three Ferraris, and giving Maserati a debut win for the 250F.

The Indianapolis 500 at the end of May was still a World Championship event, but few American drivers took part in Grands Prix and few Grand Prix drivers went to Indianapolis. Bill Vukovich (>1953) took the lead half-way through the race and won, gaining eight World Championship points for his second win in a row in the KK500A.

While the Mercedes W196 was still not finished, Fangio continued to build up the points: he won the third round of the Championship, the Belgian Grand Prix at Spa, in a Maserati 250F. A fortnight later Mercedes was ready to make its debut as forcefully as possible (>1914, 1934) in the French Grand Prix at Rheims. Motor racing fans arrived long before the race, camping out around the circuit to get a look at what promised to be a historic race. The four Mercedes caused a sensation when they were unveiled. They seemed to be taking the racing car into a new age, with their futuristic, streamlined, silver-painted bodies. Practice soon established that they did not only look good. Fangio took pole position with a lap at 124 mph, and Kling was just 1 second slower, joining Fangio on the front row of the grid next to Ascari who was driving a 250F; the inexperienced Herrmann was in the third row.

As the starter's flag fell, Fangio and Kling went into the lead as one. Ascari, still finding his way with the 250F, was slow to start, leaving a gap for Gonzalez to come through from the second row to chase the two silver cars. At the end of the first lap, spectators in the grand-

MILESTONES

On 21 February Lee Petty won the Daytona Beach and road race in a Chrysler; he also took the NASCAR championship (1959).

Christian Lautenschlager died; he had worked his way from Mercedes' shop floor to win the French Grand Prix for Germany in 1908 and 1914.

All 33 cars in the Indianapolis 500 used four-cylinder Offenhauser engines, the first time one manufacturer achieved such predominance.

Froilan Gonzalez and Maurice Trintignant won the 24-hour race at Le Mans for Ferrari, who also won the Sports Car World Championship.

On 29 May Stirling Moss won his first Formula One race at Aintree; his first World Championship points came for third place in the Belgian Grand Prix.

On 30 October Wilbur Shaw, President of the Indianapolis Speedway and three times winner of the race, died in a plane crash, aged 52.

Mille Miglia: Alberto Ascari in a six-cylinder, 3.3-litre Lancia D24 (No. 602) preparing to overtake a Cisitalia driven by Claes and Brandoli (No. 2341). The numbers on the cars record the starting times of the contestants on the 24-hour clock – Claes and Brandoli left at 11.41 pm while Ascari set off over six hours later at 6.02 am. Ascari won the race in 11 hours 26 minutes 10 seconds at an average 87.27 mph; Paolo Marzotto was second in a four-cylinder, 2-litre Ferrari. Ascari's lightweight D24 developed around 250 bhp and had a remarkable power-to-weight ratio of 1 bhp to 8.14 pounds. For this year's contest two changes were made in honour of the great Tazio Nuvolari, who had died the previous summer: the circuit was altered to pass through Nuvolari's hometown of Mantua and a Nuvolari prize was offered for the fastest time over the 82.5-mile stretch from Cremona to Mantua – Ascari won at 112 mph.

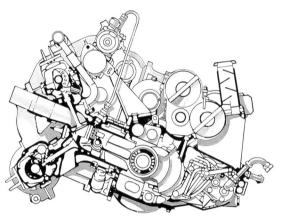

ABOVE: Mercedes improved the aerodynamics of the W196 by laying the engine on its side at an angle of 20 degrees to the horizontal. This made it possible to build a lower body with a smaller frontal area, which offered less wind resistance than a conventional vertical-engine car. The W196's 2.5-litre eight-cylinder in line unit developed 257 bhp at 8,200 rpm.

stand stood to see Kling just ahead of Fangio, with Gonzalez a good third. Lap after lap the Mercedes drivers gave a demonstration of superiority, driving wheel-to-wheel past the grandstands. Ascari retired after two laps. On lap 10 Hawthorn's brakes failed at the end of the straight; he aimed for the escape road, realized that he would hit the spectators, spun deliberately, and, by a miracle, avoided disaster. On lap 11 Herrmann managed to pass Gonzalez, then Gonzalez re-passed him a lap later. But the strain on the Ferrari showed, and as they came into the Thillois hairpin, Gonzalez's engine blew up and caught fire. At the same time he spun very close to Herrmann, who only just managed to avoid an accident. But Herrmann's car had also taken too much punishment, and with smoke pouring from the exhaust system he quickly retired also.

The two leaders continued serenely, Fangio occasionally waiting for Kling so that they could 'continue the show' together. As the end of the race approached, they arranged themselves for a close but stage-managed finish: Fangio, as team leader, just ahead of Kling. Mercedes had ended the long period of Italian dominance – and severely dented the pride of Ferrari and Maserati – at a stroke.

Two weeks later the Grand Prix circus moved to Silverstone for the British Grand Prix. Herrmann's car could not be repaired in time, so Kling and Fangio faced the Italians in just two cars. The opposition came from the Ferrari team – Gonzalez, Hawthorn and Trintignant in Tipo 625s – and from Ascari

ABOVE: The engine of the Lancia D50 was positioned diagonally in the chassis, so that the prop shaft could pass through the cockpit without going under the driver's seat. This enabled the car to be built closer to the ground for better cornering. The engine was also used as a load-bearing part of the frame, helping to reduce weight – at 620 kg, the D50 was one of the lightest racing cars on the circuit. Its 2.5-litre engine developed around 260 bhp.

and Marimon in Maserati 250Fs, with Stirling Moss in another bought for him by his father. Ken Wharton was driving another 250F bought by Sir Alfred Owen, who was now heading the BRM Trust, to give more British drivers experience of top-level racing. A single Vanwall was driven by Peter Collins among a horde of rather less competitive Coopers and Connaughts.

Fangio had broken all the Silverstone records in practice, but he found the circuit slippery, and Gonzalez, who loved Silverstone, was next to him on the grid only a second slower. Moss, one second slower still, was behind him. Gonzalez went into the lead followed by Hawthorn, Fangio and Moss. Fangio then passed Hawthorn and gradually closed the gap on Gonzalez, while Moss and Hawthorn disputed third place. Then it started

raining and the Mercedes slowed. Collins in eighth place in the Vanwall passed Kling at one point, then his engine failed and he was out. Fangio was also in trouble in the wet: he hit corner markers on several occasions, lost third gear, and try as he might, he could not catch Gonzalez. There were great cheers when Moss and Hawthorn, two British drivers – albeit in Italian cars – overtook Fangio. Then Moss's 250F broke a drive shaft and he was out. Gonzalez finally won; Hawthorn and Marimon were second and third for Ferrari, and Fangio, in the not-so-invincible Mercedes, came in fourth.

The pendulum swung back in the German Grand Prix. Mercedes were fielding four cars, including those driven by Herrmann and Lang. The opposition was missing Ascari, who was away at Monza testing the Lancia D-50,

RIGHT: The Mercedes W196. Bodies could be changed from 'open-wheelers' to 'streamliners': top speed was around 165 mph for the open-wheeler single-seater and 190 mph for the streamliner. In 1954 the W196 won the French, German, Swiss, Italian and Berlin Grands Prix.

and Marimon, who was killed in practice. In the race Fangio and Gonzalez again made the early running, but Gonzalez could not find the magic touch he had had at Silverstone. The death of his friend Marimon had also upset him greatly and he slowed, to be overtaken by Kling. On lap 16 he came into the pits, struggled out very close to physical collapse, and Hawthorn – whose Ferrari had broken – jumped in and raced off after the leaders. He passed Kling but could not catch Fangio, who duly won.

While the Lancia D-50 was still not ready, Ascari was free to drive for Ferrari in the Italian Grand Prix. He had never been comfortable in the Maserati 250F, but back in the Tipo 625 he led for the first 49 laps, fending off repeated challenges from Fangio in the Mercedes W196 and Moss in his 250F, until his gearbox failed. Moss took the lead and steadily widened the gap between himself and

LEFT: Juan Manuel Fangio in conference with Alfred Neubauer (>1922), Mercedes team manager since 1926. Neubauer was a ruthless promoter of Mercedes' interests and a great talent spotter, responsible for promoting Hermann Lang from mechanic to driver in 1935. He retired in 1955, when the company withdrew from competition, and for many years was racing adviser to the Mercedes Museum at Untertürkheim.

Fangio to 22 seconds. Then, 13 laps from the end, Moss's Maserati's oil pressure fell dramatically and he had to slow down. Fangio passed him to win again.

The last race of the season was the Spanish Grand Prix at Barcelona, where the Lancia D-50 finally made its debut. Ascari was fastest in practice in the new car, and there were high hopes that an Italian car could tackle the Germans. He set off in the lead, setting a lap record of 100.64 mph, and maintained it for 10 laps, but at that stage his clutch broke. The scramble for the lead between the American

driver Harry Schell in a Maserati, Trintignant and Hawthorn in Ferraris, and Fangio for Mercedes, took place with high winds blowing sand and litter all over the course and the cars. Hawthorn, in one of the Ferrari Tipo 555s, made the best of it to win.

Of the six Grands Prix that Mercedes entered, it had won four, the other two falling to Ferrari. Fangio took his second World Championship (>1951). It was a stunning debut for the W196 – but not quite the all-conquering debut Mercedes had recorded in 1914 and 1934.

The Mercedes W196 had a lightweight space-frame chassis and inboard hydraulic drum brakes on all four wheels. The engine used 'desmodromic' valves, which, instead of relying on springs to close them, were mechanically closed. It also had Bosch direct fuel injection and the five-speed gearbox was mounted on the rear axle.

The move to 'roadsters' in the Indianapolis 500 gathered pace. Bill Vukovich, who was looking for his third consecutive win in the race, drove the latest Kurtis creation, the KK500C, a car used by several other drivers. They included Jack McGrath who was fastest in qualifying, and who thereby set a new record of 142.58 mph.

The early stages of the race were spell-binding. McGrath took the lead, but Vukovich stuck with him wheel-to-wheel for three laps, then overtook him. The duel continued, McGrath taking the lead back on lap 15 and Vukovich retaliating a lap later. Vukovich managed to hold the lead until lap 57, when Rodger Ward's Kuzma-Offy broke an axle, hit the wall, turned over, and slewed back across the track. To avoid hitting it, Al Keller went on to the infield, rejoining down the track. In doing so, he hit Johnny Boyd, whose car then turned over several times. Coming through the debris, Vukovich's KK500C struck Boyd's car and somersaulted into a car park, hit two cars, then landed upside down and engulfed in flames. Vukovich was killed instantly.

Once the track had been cleared, Art Cross and Bob Sweikert, both in Kurtis KK500Cs, and Don Freeland in a Stevens-Offy, fought hard for the lead. Both Cross and Freeland's cars gave up under the strain, and Sweikert went on to win.

In Europe, Mercedes was keen to build on its success during the previous year by entering the Sports Car World Championship in addition to continuing Grand Prix racing. Their designers used the basis of the W196 to build a sports car, the 3-litre two-seater 300SLR, and Neubauer took on Stirling Moss to join Juan Manuel Fangio, Hans Herrmann and Karl Kling. A great deal of work had gone into developing the W196 in order to make it adaptable for the different circuits. The power output was raised to 280 bhp at 8,500 rpm, giving it a top speed close to 190 mph. The wheelbase had been shortened by 5½ inches, and there was a special even shorter-wheelbase version for particularly tight circuits such as Monaco. For most races the more conventional body – with open wheels – was used, although the 'Streamliners' as they became known, were retained for the very fast circuits such as Monza.

The three Italian challengers had all improved their cars. At Ferrari the development of the Tipos 555 and 625 continued, the engine now giving around 270 bhp at 7,500 rpm and a top speed of around 170 mph. The team was Froilan Gonzalez, Giuseppe Farina, Mike Hawthorn and Maurice Trintignant.

ABOVE: Close racing at the Indianapolis 500. Drivers from the left: Cal Niday (No. 22), who crashed after 425 miles; Jim Rathmann (No. 33), finished 14th; Jim Davies (No. 15), came third at an average 126.299 mph; Pat O'Conner (No. 29), finished eighth; Art Cross (No. 99), retired after 422 miles; Pat Flaherty (No. 89), came tenth. For the second consecutive year, every car in the 500 had a four-cylinder Offenhauser engine.

MILESTONES

Bob Sweikert's win at Indianapolis in the KK500C 'roadster' was the fifth for Kurtis in six years; it was also the last (>1950, 1956).

Giuseppe Farina's last Grand Prix drive was in Belgium; the first World Champion retired (>1966) after failing to qualify at Indianapolis.

When the AAA withdrew from racing after the Le Mans crash, the United States Auto Club (USAC) replaced it, at the behest of Tony Hulman (>1942–45).

The ban on motor racing in Switzerland following the Le Mans accident was made permanent. A Swiss Grand Prix was staged in 1982 – in France.

Aurelio Lampredi, the designer behind Ferrari racing cars and engines, left the company to work for Fiat on production cars.

Bob Sweikert won the AAA National Championship (>1909), the last driver to hold the title – which was then renamed after the USAC (>1979).

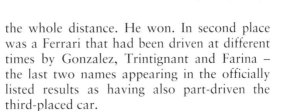

LEFT: Bob Sweikert, winner of the Indianapolis 500. The newspaper he is holding shows the crash in which Bill Vukovich (>1954, >1953) was killed. Sweikert died the following year from injuries sustained in an accident during a race on a half-mile track at Salem, Indianapolis.

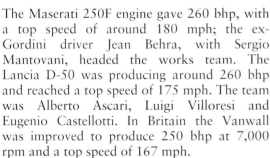

The Maserati 250F engine gave 260 bhp, with a top speed of around 180 mph; the ex-Gordini driver Jean Behra, with Sergio Mantovani, headed the works team. The Lancia D-50 was producing around 260 bhp and reached a top speed of 175 mph. The team was Alberto Ascari, Luigi Villoresi and Eugenio Castellotti. In Britain the Vanwall was improved to produce 250 bhp at 7,000 rpm and a top speed of 167 mph.

The Championship started, as was becoming traditional, with a journey from the European winter to Argentina and the January summer of the southern hemisphere. This time the drivers arrived in the middle of a heat wave amid temperatures of 130°F (54°C). Despite the heat, the grandstands were packed to see Fangio take the lead for Mercedes. Most of the drivers came in to allow a relief driver to take over. Moss dropped out in the middle of a lap, parking out on the circuit. Fangio – a quiet but utterly determined man – was one of only two drivers to stick it out for the whole distance. He won. In second place was a Ferrari that had been driven at different times by Gonzalez, Trintignant and Farina – the last two names appearing in the officially listed results as having also part-driven the third-placed car.

Before the Grand Prix season got under way in Europe, Mercedes tackled the Mille Miglia. There was an all-time record of 521 entries for the race, ranging from 350-cc bubble-cars to two 310-bhp Mercedes 300SLRs capable of 185 mph, driven by Fangio and Moss. Fangio chose to drive alone, but Moss decided to take a navigator, a British journal-

ABOVE: Juan Manuel Fangio (No. 2) and Stirling Moss (No. 6) leading shortly after the start of the Monaco Grand Prix in the ultra-short chassis Mercedes W196s. Moss and Fangio both retired; the race was won by Maurice Trintignant in a Ferrari 625. Alberto Ascari (Lancia D50, No. 26) ended the Grand Prix in the harbour after a crash.

ist, Denis Jenkinson. The pair went over the route minutely, making detailed pace notes for every gradient and corner, recording the information on a continuous roll of paper from which Jenkinson was later to read while indicating the appropriate speed and gear using a specially-devised system of hand signals. They broke all records for the race, finishing in 10 hours 7 minutes 48 seconds at an average speed of 98.3 mph – 10 mph faster than the previous record and 32 minutes ahead of Fangio. It was one of the classic road-race drives of all time.

On 22 May, came the Monaco Grand Prix. The Lancia D-50s had been successful in several minor races, and much was expected of them. Louis Chiron, a Monégasque aged 56, was given a place alongside the regular team of Ascari, Villoresi and Castellotti. Moss and Fangio took the lead, Ascari and Castellotti chasing them, but both Mercedes developed valve problems and dropped out. Ascari took the lead until a serious misjudgement landed him in the harbour; luckily he was uninjured. Trintignant in a Ferrari Tipo 625 then took on Castellotti and succeeded in beating him to the chequered flag.

Four days later, Ascari was testing a Ferrari sports car at Monza when he crashed and was killed. There was no explanation for the accident, making the death even more poignant for Italy. Villoresi, his great friend and mentor, was distraught, as was Gianni Lancia. Even after the initial shock had passed, Lancia decided he had had enough. He had been

spending far more than was justified on the D-50s, with little result, and the company's finances were in very poor shape. He sold Lancia and handed the D-50s over to Ferrari complete with spares, mechanics, an experimental streamliner body, the driver Eugenio Castellotti and the designer Vittorio Jano, and sponsorship to race them from the Agnelli family which owned Fiat.

Even such a great survivor as Enzo Ferrari, whose own cars were now becoming increasingly uncompetitive, must have wondered at this untoward turn of events.

Mercedes entered three 300SLRs for the 24-hour sports car race at Le Mans for Fangio, Moss and 'Levegh' (Pierre Velghe), challenging the reputation built up by Jaguar and Ferrari in what was the most prestigious sports car race.

Castellotti led from the start for Ferrari. Then a duel between Fangio and Hawthorn in a D-Type Jaguar developed into the feature of the race. At 6.30 pm Hawthorn headed for the pits, passing Lance Macklin in a much slower Austin Healey. Hawthorn touched the brakes and Macklin moved to avoid him, straight into the path of Levegh's 300SLR doing 150 mph. The Mercedes somersaulted into the crowd, caught fire, and broke into pieces that hurtled among the crowd, killing Levegh, 83 spectators, and injuring 100 more. It was motor racing's worst-ever crash, and coming so soon after the deaths of Vukovich, Ascari, and several spectators in the Mille Miglia (including a child), there were instant repercussions. Racing

Le Mans, Saturday 12 June, 6.30 pm: the smoking wreckage of Pierre Levegh's Mercedes 300SLR after it had collided with Lance Macklin's Austin Healey 100S at 150 mph during the 24-hour sports car race. Levegh and 83 spectators were killed and over 100 injured in what was motor racing's worst ever disaster, one of the few accidents to change the course of the sport's history (>1903, 1924, 1957, 1964). Macklin was uninjured but was thrown into deep shock. Incredibly, the race continued, and for a time another Mercedes 300SLR, driven by Juan Manuel Fangio and Stirling Moss, was in the lead. Then, at 2 am the following morning, the Mercedes were withdrawn on direct orders from the company's head office in Stuttgart. As a result of the Le Mans tragedy, the authorities became much more safety-conscious and racing in France was only permitted again after circuits had passed stringent safety checks. Mike Hawthorn and Ivor Bueb won the race in a Jaguar having covered 2,592.91 miles at an average 106.99 mph, but it was a hollow victory.

was banned in France – the ban including the imminent Grand Prix – in Switzerland, Spain and Mexico. The American Automobile Association (AAA) withdrew from the international governing body, FIA. Too late there was a general recognition that speeds had increased far beyond the capacity of any circuit to ensure safety without spending a considerable amount of money first.

Racing was not banned in Britain or Italy, and the British Grand Prix went ahead as planned on a new circuit at Aintree, near Liverpool (the site of the famous horse race, the Grand National). In view of the real possibility that a British driver might win a Grand Prix, a huge crowd – estimated at 150,000 – turned up to see Moss at the wheel of the Mercedes. There were four W196s in the race:

BELOW: Mercedes team manager Alfred Neubauer (centre) congratulating the victorious British team in the Mille Miglia – driver Stirling Moss (right) and navigator Denis Jenkinson. Their winning time was 10 hours 7 minutes 48 seconds, 32 minutes ahead of second-placed Juan Manuel Fangio, also in a Mercedes.

MILLE MIGLIA CIRCUIT

Start & finish
MILAN
Brescia
Verona
VENICE
Cremona
Mantua
Padua
Rovigo
Piacenza
Parma
Ferrara
Reggio Emilia
Bologna
Ravenna
Forli
Rimini
Florence
Pesaro
Ancona
Siena
ITALY
Pescara
CORSICA
L'Aquila
TYRRHENIAN SEA
ROME

LEFT: The tradition of racing on open roads took a long time to die in Italy. The Mercedes 300SLR driven to victory in the Mille Miglia by Stirling Moss with Denis Jenkinson as navigator was based on Mercedes' all-conquering Formula 1 cars and was capable of over 150 mph. Few concessions were made to the safety of spectators. Eager for a glimpse of the 300SLR at top speed, they lined the straight roads and then scattered to the verges as the car approached. By 1955, the Mille Miglia was living on borrowed time (>1957).

ABOVE LEFT: The 1,000-mile route followed by the Mille Miglia drivers.

for Fangio, Moss, Kling and Piero Taruffi. The Italian challenge was somewhat muted following the withdrawal of Lancia, whose cars were not yet in the hands of Ferrari; he therefore fielded Tipo 625s for Hawthorn, Trintignant and Castellotti. Luigi Villoresi had withdrawn from racing following the death of Ascari. Works Maseratis were driven by Jean Behra, Roberto Mieres and a young Italian, Luigi Musso. The number of British drivers was growing: Lance Macklin was driving Moss's 250F, Ken Wharton and Harry Schell were driving Vanwalls, and right at the back of the grid was an Australian, Jack Brabham, driving an experimental Cooper, the 'Formula One Special', a mid-engined sports car.

Moss was fastest in practice, followed by Fangio, Behra, Kling and Taruffi. Moss and Fangio, who had now earned themselves the nickname 'The Train', went into their custom-

ary lead, with Behra in third place. Wharton's Vanwall burst an oil pipe. Brabham was lapped on lap 5 and broke down on lap 41. Hawthorn was overcome by fumes and retired to the pits where Castellotti, whose own Ferrari had broken, took it over. Schell's Vanwall also broke, but he got back in the race in Wharton's car which he had by then persuaded the mechanics to repair. Towards the end, with Moss in the lead, Alfred Neubauer began orchestrating the finish from the pits. He slowed Fangio down, then encouraged Kling to catch up, and Taruffi to do the same, even though he was a lap behind. They finished in that order – Moss first, Fangio in second place, Kling third and Taruffi fourth.

It was the first time a British driver had won the national Grand Prix.

Monza had been extensively refurbished at a cost of £500,000, but the new concrete surface on the banked curves was very rough, and driving on it at up to 180 mph in practice took a heavy toll on tyres and suspension systems. Drivers strapped themselves into tight corsetry belts in order to minimise jarring, and mechanics hardened the cars' suspensions to stop the tails of the cars grounding after the bigger bumps. The Lancia D-50s were to make their debut for Ferrari, but they went through so many tyres in practice, often spin-

BELOW: Stirling Moss and Juan Manuel Fangio celebrating Moss's home win in the British Grand Prix at Aintree. The two drivers enjoyed a close relationship – each recognised the other's rare ability, but the older Fangio remained Moss's mentor.

RIGHT: Stirling Moss crossing the line just 0.1 second ahead of Juan Manuel Fangio in the British Grand Prix. Some suspected a stage-managed finish to allow Moss the victory on British soil, but afterwards Fangio said that Moss had won the race on merit. Fangio finished the season as World Champion, with Moss in second place.

ABOVE: Stirling Moss in a
Mercedes W196 leading
from team-mates Juan
Manuel Fangio and Piero
Taruffi in the Italian Grand
Prix on 11 September.
Moss retired on lap 27
with engine trouble; Fangio
and Taruffi were first and
second. It was Mercedes'
last race before the
company withdrew from
motor racing.

ning out of control, that they were withdrawn.
Moss and Fangio found that at very high
speeds the noses of their Streamliner bodies
lifted under aerodynamic forces. Mercedes
engineers quickly fashioned fairings which
used the airflow past the cars to hold the front
of the cars down.

The Mercedes started lapping in the first
four places at an average of 130 mph, giving a
wonderful display. Then Moss's car broke
down, as also did Kling's. Castellotti took
over third place in a Ferrari Tipo 555. The
surface continued to take a heavy toll: both
Vanwalls retired, followed by the retirements
of Hawthorn's Ferrari and Peter Collins' 250F.
Fangio won; Taruffi came in second.

Mercedes had thus been denied a final
flourish to its all-too-brief return to Grand
Prix racing. Only a few people knew that at
the end of the season – after Moss had added
the Targa Florio to the year's laurels – that
they would withdraw altogether. The official
reason given was that the resources of the
research department were needed for production cars, but a feeling has ever since persisted
that the Le Mans crash put the final seal on the
decision. Whatever the truth, after a sentimen-
tal ceremony the magnificent W196s and
300SLRs were stationed in pride of place in
the Mercedes museum.

ABOVE: Italian racing
brotherhood. Vittorio Jano
(left) with Alberto Ascari
(centre) and Luigi Villoresi.
Jano, Alfa-Romeo's chief
designer from 1923 to
1937, created the P2 car in
which Ascari's father,
Antonio, was killed in the
ACF Grand Prix at
Montlhéry in 1925.
Alberto Ascari and
Villoresi were very close
friends – when Ascari was
killed testing a Ferrari
sports car at Monza in
May, Villoresi was
devastated and
temporarily abandoned
racing.

Following Mercedes-Benz's decision to withdraw from motor racing, the two top drivers of the day, Juan Manuel Fangio and Stirling Moss, signed up for rival Italian teams. Fangio joined Ferrari, while Moss went to Maserati – and freed from Mercedes' team discipline, their duels became real.

Ferrari modified the Lancia D-50s. The distinctive pannier fuel tanks were fared into the main bodywork, but they were empty, the fuel transferred to the rear of the car; the V-8 engine no longer formed a stressed member of the chassis. In addition to Fangio, Ferrari took on Peter Collins, Eugenio Castellotti, Luigi Musso and Olivier Gendebien. Giulio Alfieri experimented with the Maserati 250F, trying disc brakes, fuel injection, and streamlined bodies. Later in the year he offset the engine and transmission, dropping the whole car by 8 inches (20.3 centimetres). In addition to Moss, Maserati put Jean Behra under contract.

The British challenge was growing. At Vanwall, Tony Vandervell commissioned a new chassis from Colin Chapman (>1982), whose Lotus company produced lightweight sports cars. The body was styled by an aerodynamicist, Frank Costin, and with a much improved four-cylinder engine that produced 285 bhp, the result was a much lighter, sleeker car for Maurice Trintignant and Harry Schell. Under the direction of Sir Alfred Owen, BRM (>1950) produced a new Formula One car, the P25. It was light and – with its four-cylinder engine producing 270 bhp at 8,000 rpm – fast, but quite unreliable. Owen took on Mike Hawthorn and another talented British driver, Tony Brooks.

Frank Kurtis's 'roadsters' had achieved a string of successes in America: this year, two out of every three cars on the Indianapolis 500 grid were variants of his KK500. Another designer took the 'roadster' theme even further in the form of the John Zink Special, designed by A. J. Watson. John Zink owned the KK500C in which Bob Sweikert had won in 1955. Watson had prepared it for the race, but for 1956 he designed the new Zink car. The 350-bhp Offenhauser ('Offy') engine was

RIGHT: Juan Manuel Fangio – winner of the World Drivers' Championship for the third successive year – with his wife Andrea. Fangio headed the Championship table with 30 points, ahead of Stirling Moss with 27.

RIGHT: Juan Manuel Fangio at speed in the Lancia-Ferrari D50 during the French Grand Prix at Rheims. He finished fourth, 1 minute 35 seconds behind race-winner Peter Collins in another D50. The V-8, 2.5-litre, 240-bhp D50 was the car of the year, winning the Argentine (Fangio), Belgian (Collins), French (Collins), British (Fangio) and German (Fangio) Grands Prix. Despite such success, Fangio did not like the D50 and was never really happy driving it.

still offset to the left, not lying down but upright, and in this car the body itself was offset too, putting even more weight on the left. The result was a rather taller but narrower car, with a smaller frontal area. Pat Flaherty broke all the Indianapolis Speedway's records in it, setting a new lap record of 145.596 mph while qualifying for the 500.

He won the race, after picking his way through the debris of the many accidents that left only nine cars still on the track to finish. One of those finishers, Dick Rathmann, also crashed after he had jubilantly taken the chequered flag in fifth place.

The Argentinian Grand Prix was a straight fight between the Ferrari-Lancia D-50s and Maserati. Carlos Menditeguy unexpectedly took the lead in his privately-entered Maserati 250F and held it for 43 laps, nearly lapping Fangio, before he retired with rear suspension

MILESTONES

The Type 251 marked the last racing car built by the company started by Ettore Bugatti before the First World War (>1911, 1947).

After struggling financially, and following the failure of his Type 32 F1 car, Amédée Gordini gave up making racing cars and joined Renault.

Archie Scott-Brown, who led two Ferraris before retiring in the British Grand Prix, had only one hand. He died in the 1958 Belgian Grand Prix.

The 40th Targa Florio was won by Umberto Maglioli in a 1.5-litre Porsche Spyder RS, the first major victory for the company.

The Italian-born American driver Ralph de Palma, AAA National Champion twice (>1912) and Indianapolis 500 winner, died aged 73.

The first driver to hold the National Championship under the jurisdiction of the United States Auto Club was Jimmy Bryan.

failure. But it was Fangio who won, the D-50's first Championship victory.

The Ferrari team came to Britain for a non-Championship race, the International Trophy at Silverstone on 6 May. Both Vanwall and BRM were on the grid, and with Maserati not in contention, Moss drove a Vanwall, taking pole position. Hawthorne shot into the lead in the BRM, and maintained it for ten laps against determined opposition from the Ferraris and Moss, until the BRM's engine failed and Moss took the lead. Fangio and Collins continued to challenge, breaking their D-50s in the process, and Moss duly went on to record another victory.

The Fangio-Moss duel continued at Monaco, where Moss – back in his Maserati – took pole position and led from the start. On lap 3 Fangio spun his D-50 and Schell crashed avoiding him. Fangio then took over Collins' car and set off after Moss again, but could not catch him, finishing second.

In the Belgian Grand Prix, both Fangio and

ABOVE: The six-cylinder 2.5-litre 270-bhp Maserati 250F, the only car to stand up to the superiority of the Lancia-Ferrari D50 in 1956. Stirling Moss drove the 250F to victories in the Monaco and Italian Grands Prix and came second in the German and third in the Belgian; his Maserati team-mate Jean Behra came third in both the German and French Grands Prix, also in a 250F.

Moss retired with mechanical problems, allowing the No.2 Ferrari driver Peter Collins to register his first Championship victory (>1958).

The Grand Prix organized by the Automobile Club de France (ACF) was held at Rheims again. Colin Chapman was a surprise addition to the Vanwall team, but in a practice session his brakes locked up and he rammed Hawthorn's Vanwall. The brakes could not be repaired, and he did not start. Fangio took pole position, with Collins and Castellotti alongside him on the grid; Moss was well back on row three, behind the Vanwall of Schell.

The Ferraris moved off together, giving a demonstration run for the first few laps, swapping the lead now and then to entertain the crowd. Schell had to go into the pits with fuel-injection problems, then Hawthorn retired unwell and Schell took over his car. He steadily gained on the Ferraris and by lap 23 was lying fourth, 24 seconds behind Fangio. The Ferrari pits had until then believed that Schell was a lap behind. When they realized that he was not, they signalled to their three drivers to speed up. Fangio took the lead on lap 30, but Collins and Castellotti could not shake off Schell, and a lap later he passed them both. Twice Schell managed to pull up alongside Fangio on the straight, and once got his nose in front, but the wily Fangio held him off each time, setting a new lap record of 127.37 mph.

Schell had overtaxed his engine in the fight for the lead, and he began to fall back, finally going into the pits on lap 38. Fangio's car also needed attention two laps later, letting Collins and Castellotti into the front, from which position Collins cruised on to win his second Championship race.

The British Grand Prix two weeks later culminated in another duel between Moss and Fangio, but not before the BRM had given the home crowd some thrilling laps.

Hawthorn was on the front row of the grid alongside Moss, Fangio and Collins, and he immediately shot into the lead with teammate Brooks second. The two BRM drivers extended their lead. Fangio, in third place, then managed to pass Brooks but could not catch Hawthorn who stayed a stubborn 5 seconds ahead. Under pressure, Fangio made one of his rare mistakes and spun off at Beckett's corner, rejoining the race in seventh place. Moss then challenged Hawthorn and eventually overtook him on lap 15. Hawthorn went in with transmission problems on lap 23, and Fangio took over second place, with Collins in third. Then Collins dropped out on lap 64 and Moss went in four laps later, rejoining again in second place – only for his transmission to fail. He was out, and Fangio was left to win the British Grand Prix for the first time.

The season ended on a note of mixed controversy and sportsmanship in the Italian

Grand Prix. Collins was leading the Drivers' Championship and needed only to finish third to clinch the title. Moss battled with the three D-50s until he ran out of fuel. As he was coasting along, he was given a gentle push by a Maserati colleague, helping him towards the pits where he refuelled, bringing protests but no disqualification. Then Fangio's car broke down and, in the tradition of the time, Peter Collins, currently lying third and within sight of the Championship, came in and handed over to the team's No.1 driver, Fangio, so giving up his own chances of the title. Fangio set off after Moss, who was in second place behind Musso for Ferrari. Three laps later the steering on Musso's D-50 failed: Moss took the lead and won.

Fangio was second, but his own points total meant that it was he who won his fourth World Championship.

It had been a Ferrari-Lancia year, but the theme underlying it had been the battles between Fangio and Moss. Underlying that was the steady improvement not only of British drivers but of British cars which had found the speed but still for the moment lacked the reliability.

LEFT: The Bugatti 251 in the pits at the French Grand Prix. The last racing car to bear the famous Bugatti name (>1912, 1924), it was designed by Gioachino Colombo – the creator of the Alfa-Romeo Tipo 158/9 (>1951). The 251's eight-cylinder 2.4-litre engine was mounted behind the driver in a transverse position (>1965).

BELOW: Maurice Trintignant driving the Bugatti 251 in the French Grand Prix. The car's handling proved to be poor – it had a tendency to weave at high speeds and was difficult to control over bumps – and Trintignant retired after 18 laps. The 251 was returned to the Bugatti factory – and never raced again.

Italian mastery of Grand Prix racing had reached its high water mark. Except for Mercedes-Benz's intervention in 1954 and 1955, Italian manufacturers had been at the top for a decade, but 1957 marked a sea change in their fortunes. The postwar drivers on which that success had been built – Jean-Pierre Wimille, Giuseppe Farina, Alberto Ascari, Froilan Gonzalez and Luigi Villoresi – were either dead or retired, and in their place were new names, British names, many of them associated with increasingly competitive British cars.

As if to underline Italy's relative decline in motor racing, one of its greatest races, the Mille Miglia, was banned in 1957 after a fearsome accident. Lying fourth, Alfonse de Portago's Ferrari burst a tyre at 170 mph. It left the road, cut down a telegraph pole, scythed through a group of spectators, hit a bank, and careered back on to the road, killing nine people, five of them children, together with de Portago and his co-driver. The barrage of protest – from the Roman Catholic Church among others – ensured that the Mille Miglia would never be run again.

For the Indianapolis 500, the United States Auto Club made a cosmetic change to the formula, reducing engine size from 270 cubic inches to 252 cubic inches – which had little or no effect on speed. Yet another designer came up with a variation on the 'roadster' theme. George Salih persuaded Leo Goosen at Offenhauser to build an engine that could lie almost horizontal in the chassis, making the car even lower. He moved the engine even further to the left, and put the sleekest of bodies around it, with a tail fin for stability. In the car, Sam Hanks won after leading for nearly three-quarters of the race.

RIGHT and *BELOW:* Juan Manuel Fangio's greatest drive, the German Grand Prix at the Nürburgring on 4 August. Driving a Maserati, one of his favourite cars, he slashed 23 seconds off the lap record, bringing it down to 9 minutes 17.4 seconds – an average 91.54 mph – and beat Mike Hawthorn's Ferrari by 3.6 seconds after a breathtaking chase.

MILESTONES

On 14 March Eugenio Castellotti, the promising 26-year-old Italian driver, was killed when he crashed testing a Ferrari at Modena.

The tradition of starting the Indianapolis 500 by giving the instruction to drivers, 'Gentlemen, start your engines', was first established.

On 29 June ten Indianapolis drivers brought their cars to Monza for the Race of Two Worlds. The idea was for them to compete with Grand Prix drivers.

No Grand Prix drivers took part in the Race of Two Worlds; Jimmy Bryan won, so taking the $35,000 prize.

The first Formula One victory for the BRM P25 was in the Caen Grand Prix in Normandy. It was driven by Jean Behra, the reigning French Champion.

For the first time in the history of the World Championship, the Ferrari team did not win a single championship race.

The reigning World Drivers' Champion, Juan Manuel Fangio (>1956), had been unhappy both with the cars and the management at Ferrari, and had moved back to his first home, Maserati. Ferrari's drivers for this season – Mike Hawthorn, Peter Collins, Maurice Trintignant and Luigi Musso – were driving the latest development of the Ferrari-Lancia D-50 (>1955), the Tipo 801, which now sported a Ferrari body.

Tony Vandervell had taken on a full-time team of Stirling Moss, Tony Brooks, and a newcomer to Formula One, Stuart Lewis-Evans. The year also marked the start of what became a legend in Grand Prix racing. Rob Walker, a wealthy Scottish team-owner, financed a 2-litre mid-engined Cooper with a Coventry Climax engine, based on experience with a similar Formula Two car. The T43 lacked the power of the 2.5-litre Formula One cars, but it was much lighter and nimbler, especially on twisting circuits such as Monaco – where it made its debut, driven by Jack Brabham, an Australian driver who had been working with Cooper and driving their cars in Formula Two races and in Australia.

Monaco was also the scene for the first clash between the Vanwalls and 'those bloody red cars', as Vandervell described the Ferraris and Maseratis. Moss took the lead, but crashed, as swiftly afterwards did Hawthorn and Collins in their Ferraris. Fangio managed to avoid the wreckage and take the lead, while Brabham – at home on the switchback circuit in the Cooper – was third. Fangio won; Tony Brooks was second. In the closing laps Brabham's fuel pump came loose, and he had physically to push the Cooper over the line into sixth place.

This year there was no Dutch or Belgian Grand Prix. Fangio put in a virtuoso performance in France, and had taken the lead in the World Championship table as the drivers gathered at Aintree for the British Grand Prix. Moss took pole position. Jean Behra's Maserati 250F was placed on the front row of the grid between him and Tony Brooks in the second Vanwall. (Brooks had overturned an Aston Martin at Le Mans two weeks earlier, and was still sore.) In the race, Behra led at the start, but Moss managed to catch him and take the lead on lap 1, steadily increasing it

LEFT: After the Argentine GP held in January, the Monaco Grand Prix was the second race of the season to count towards the World Championship. Fangio notched up his second victory of the year.

BELOW: Indianapolis-winner Sam Hanks. His triumph came 17 years after his first 500 appearance in 1940, when he finished 14th in a Duray-engined Wiel. He announced his retirement in Victory Lane immediately after the 1957 race. In later years, he returned to the 500 as a volunteer official.

over Behra, Hawthorn, Brooks, Musso, Lewis-Evans and Fangio in seventh place. Then came the Cooper-Climaxes of Brabham and Roy Salvadori. After 20 laps, Behra started gaining on Moss, and the Vanwall's engine started misfiring. Moss came in for hurried attention to an earth strap, but still the engine stuttered, so Brooks was called in to hand his car over to Moss. He rejoined in ninth place, and by lap 35 he had caught and passed Fangio. It took him another twelve laps to overhaul Musso and Collins, putting himself in fourth place, behind Stuart Lewis-Evans, Hawthorne and Behra. The crowd was at fever pitch. Fate intervened. Behra's flywheel assembly collapsed, and Hawthorn's Ferrari punctured a tyre on the debris. Moss took the lead and, with the pressure off, slackened the pace, coasting past the grandstands just ahead of Lewis-Evans to truly thunderous applause, Musso a lap behind. Then Lewis-Evans' throttle linkage jammed. The crowd waited with bated breath in case some malfunction might still rob them of a British driver's winning the British Grand Prix in a British car. But Moss's Vanwall lasted the distance, and as Moss took the chequered flag the torch passed from Italy to Britain.

In the German Grand Prix, the Vanwall drivers found the Nürburgring extremely rough and unsuitable for their cars. Fangio, who needed to win to clinch his fifth World Championship, took pole position. It was a race of mathematics: the Ferrari 801s carried enough fuel for the whole 312 miles, whereas Fangio in his Maserati would have to stop to refuel. Fangio decided to carry sufficient fuel only for 12 laps, hoping to build up enough of a lead while the car was light to enable him to rejoin from the pits without losing the lead. Hawthorn shot off the line, but his car was heavy with fuel and by lap 3 Fangio had passed him. As he went into the pits with a lead of 30 seconds, Fangio's plan seemed to be

working. Then it went wrong. One of the hub nuts was lost during the wheel change – and he rejoined 45 seconds behind the Ferraris. Hawthorn and Collins diced for the lead while Fangio, his own car now heavy with fuel, made little impression. But on lap 16 the timekeepers could hardly believe their stopwatches: the lead was suddenly down to 33 seconds, then 25.5 seconds . . . By lap 18 it was only 13 seconds. Whatever magic had taken hold of Fangio, it continued. He put on a demonstration of pure genius – and two laps later he was just 2 seconds behind Collins. On the last lap he got inside Collins on a corner and moments later slid almost effortlessly past Hawthorn to win by 3.6 seconds.

It was one of the most memorable drives in the history of the sport. At the age of 46, Fangio had broken his own lap record for the Nürburgring ten times in the race, and he had found new depths of skill and determination to beat the cream of Britain's younger drivers – something they immediately acknowledged by carrying him shoulder-high through the pits. It was his last victory in a World Championship race, clinching his fifth title, a record that stands to this day. He retired in 1958, having worked his way from humble origins to being one of Argentina's great national heroes, as much for his quiet dignity as his driving skill. His own comment after the race was, 'I don't ever want to have to drive like that again . . .'

RIGHT: Critical moment. Stirling Moss taking over Tony Brooks' Vanwall on lap 26 of the British Grand Prix after his own car had developed problems. Moss rejoined the race in ninth place. Brooks, who was still recovering from an accident at Le Mans three weeks before, continued in Moss's car but was forced to retire on lap 51 with fuel pump trouble.

AINTREE CIRCUIT

Beechers Bend

Valentines Way

Country Corner

Railway straight

Village Corner

Sefton Straight

Cottage Corner

Enclosure

Waterway Corner

Start & Finish

Pits

Stands

Paddock

ABOVE: The Aintree circuit, near Liverpool, was built on the site of the course used for one of Britain's top horse races, the Grand National. The motor racing circuit was opened in 1954 and was used for five Grands Prix – in 1955, 1957, 1959, 1961 and 1962. Racing on the 3-mile track initially ran anticlockwise but was quickly changed to run in the conventional clockwise direction. The final lap record was set by Jim Clark in a Lotus on his way to victory in the 1962 Grand Prix: 93.91 mph.

ABOVE: Triumphant moment. Tony Vandervell (centre) (>1967), the man behind the race-winning Vanwall car, savours victory in the British Grand Prix – with Tony Brooks (left) and Stirling Moss. The Grand Prix win generated tremendous enthusiasm for motor racing in Britain and was the foundation for the country's rise to a dominant position in the sport.

RIGHT: Historic moment. Stirling Moss in the Vanwall crossing the line to win the British Grand Prix – the first time a British car had won a major Grand Prix since 1923 and the first ever victory by British car and driver in the British Grand Prix. His winning time was 3 hours 6 minutes 37.8 seconds – 25.6 seconds ahead of Luigi Musso's Lancia-Ferrari D50 in second place.

The dominance of the Offenhauser engine, especially of the latest versions designed to work well lying on their side, continued at Indianapolis. Using the same engine, chassis designers went on in their search for any innovation that gave a little more speed on the straights or that shaved fractions of seconds off the 800 corners. Frank Kurtis – his cars filling 16 of the 33 places on the grid – tried independent front suspension on the D.A. Lubricant Special, the KK500H. A. J. Watson persisted with his upright engine design in the John Zink Specials (>1956), but lightened the cars by using a thinner gauge of aluminium sheet for the bodies and fibreglass for the tail sections. Luigi Lesovsky moved the oil tank outside the car on the left to increase the left-hand bias. George Salih entered the Belond AP Parts Special, the car in which Sam Hanks had won the race in 1957, this time driven by Jimmy Bryan.

In the race, Ed Elisian – who had started in pole position in a John Zink Special – spun on the third turn of the first lap. Dick Rathmann hit him, and the two cars virtually blocked the track. Eleven other cars either hit them or hit each other in by far the worst pile-up in the Speedway's history. Pat O'Connor was killed, two other drivers were seriously injured, and in all eight cars were eliminated. Once racing

'Monzanapolis' – an attempt to recreate the Indianapolis 500 style of racing on the high-speed Monza circuit. At the rolling start of the first heat of the 1958 race, Bob Veith (No. 9) in a Bowes Seal-Fast and Luigi Musso (No. 12) in a Ferrari lead the way. Jim Rathmann (No. 5), the winner of both heat (at 167.3 mph) and final (at 166.72 mph) in a John Zink Leader Card, is third behind Veith. Stirling Moss, fifth behind Musso, in an Eldorado Maserati, finished seventh. The race was an unlikely effort to reunite two racing traditions that had developed separately since the First World War: the spectator-led American tradition and the less commercialized, driver-oriented European tradition.

restarted, the lead changed 17 times between Tony Bettenhausen, George Amick, Johnny Boyd, Eddie Sachs and Jimmy Bryan. Bryan won, giving Salih and the Belond Special a second successive victory.

In Grand Prix racing the number of World Championship races was increased to ten, and a manufacturers' World Championship was introduced. Special fuels were banned, following pressure from the petrol companies, but although the intention behind this was to oblige the teams to use ordinary pump fuel, most entrants used 130-octane aviation fuel. Minimum race length was reduced from 500 kilometres to 300 or two hours – a change that favoured the smaller cars.

The theme of the year remained the battle between Italian and British cars, but the balance was reversed. Maserati had withdrawn its works team, leaving Ferrari alone to represent Italy. In Britain, Vanwall and BRM were joined in Formula One by Cooper and Lotus. The Vanwalls had changed little, still giving around 280 bhp on pump fuel. The Formula One Cooper T45 started the season using a 2-litre Climax engine in the mid-engined position which, at 195 bhp, was much less powerful than the engines of the bigger cars, but because the Coopers were much lighter too, the power-to-weight ratio was broadly the same. What they lacked was the top speed of the Ferraris and Vanwalls, putting them at a disadvantage on circuits like Rheims, which had long straights. Colin Chapman used the same Climax engine, but he put it in the front of the Lotus 12.

Enzo Ferrari introduced a new car, the Tipo 246, christened the Dino after his son Alfredo, known as Alfredino, who had died of muscular dystrophy in 1956 after working with Vittorio Jano on the new V-6 engine. The car had started life in Formula Two as the Tipo 156 and at that time had a 1.5-litre V-6 engine, which was now enlarged to 2.5 litres for Formula One. Ferrari continued to hold out against disc brakes.

The season started as usual in Argentina. The Grand Prix had been arranged at short notice, and neither Vanwall nor BRM made it. The grid was made up of ten Maserati 250Fs, one of them driven by Fangio; three Ferraris, driven by Mike Hawthorn, Peter Collins and Luigi Musso; and just a single blue-painted Cooper T45, entered by the Scottish private owner Rob Walker and driven by Stirling Moss. The Maseratis were unhappy on the lower grade of fuel, and the race was a battle between Hawthorn, Musso and Moss. The

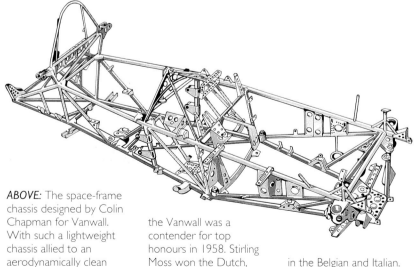

LEFT: Peter Collins in a Ferrari 246 on the way to victory in the British Grand Prix. Sadly, Collins' great promise was never fulfilled – he was killed in the next Championship race, the German Grand Prix.

ABOVE: The BBC's voice of motor racing – John Bolster. He began covering the sport for BBC radio in around 1950 and moved into television commentary for the sports magazine programme *Grandstand* in the mid-1950s.

ABOVE: The space-frame chassis designed by Colin Chapman for Vanwall. With such a lightweight chassis allied to an aerodynamically clean body and one of the most powerful engines in Formula One, the Vanwall was a contender for top honours in 1958. Stirling Moss won the Dutch, Portuguese and Moroccan Grands Prix in it and Tony Brooks drove it to victory in the Belgian and Italian. Tony Vandervell won the Constructors' World Championship.

209

ABOVE: Race-winner Jimmy Bryan (No.1) ahead of second-placed George Amick (No. 99) in the Indianapolis 500. For the second consecutive year, the winning car was a Belond Special designed by George Salih.

RIGHT: Mike Hawthorn congratulating Peter Collins on his victory in the British Grand Prix. Collins finished in 2 hours 9 minutes 4.2 seconds, 24.2 seconds ahead of Hawthorn.

Ferrari drivers were the first to go in for tyres, and when they rejoined they did not press Moss, whom they expected to go in for the same reason, having then to let them into the lead. Moss's pit crew prepared tyres for him, but he drove on carefully, preserving his rubber – which was nonetheless worn through to the canvas by the end of the race. The ruse worked, and he won a historic victory – the first World Championship race to be won by a mid-engined car, and the first also by a privately-entered car.

Moss was back in his Vanwall for Monaco. The race saw the debut of the front-engined Lotus 12s driven by Graham Hill (>1964, 1965) and Cliff Allison and which used the same 2.2-litre engine as the Cooper. But the Coopers were faster on the twisting circuit, and were among the fastest five in practice; one of them was a Rob Walker car, driven by Maurice Trintignant. The Vanwalls all retired with mechanical problems, and Trintignant won a well-deserved second victory in a row for Walker.

It was a stunning start to the season for Cooper, but the traditional cars reasserted themselves soon afterwards: Moss won the Dutch Grand Prix and then Tony Brooks the Belgian Grand Prix for Vanwall.

Juan Manuel Fangio appeared in the French Grand Prix at Rheims driving a Maserati, the name in which he had started his career in Europe in 1948. It was his last race. Two other 250Fs were driven by the former Indianapolis winner Troy Ruttman (>1952), and another

American, Phil Hill (>1961), who had started racing in sports cars in America. Fellow American Harry Schell took the lead at the start in a BRM, but by lap 2 Hawthorn had taken the lead. A lap later the Ferraris were lying first, second and third thanks to the power of the V-6 engine. Then Musso challenged Hawthorn, crashed, and was fatally injured, and Collins shot into an escape road when his brake pedal jammed. Brooks moved into second place for Vanwall, then dropped out after a terrific battle with Moss. But Moss could not catch Hawthorn, who won; Moss came in second. The German driver Wolfgang von Trips gave Ferrari third place too – but it was a bittersweet victory after the death of Musso, the last of the top-rank Italian drivers.

Ferrari's No.2 British driver, Peter Collins, won the British Grand Prix for Ferrari – then

MILESTONES

Juan Manuel Fangio drove the Frank Kurtis-designed D.A. Lubricant Special in a 1-mile speed trial at the Trenton N.J. paved speedway.

Paul Goldsmith, driving a Pontiac, won the last NASCAR 160-mile stock cars race on the beach and road circuit at Daytona Beach (>1959).

A.J. Foyt drove in the Indianapolis 500 for the first time in his long career in a Dean Van Lines Special. He retired after 148 laps (>1961, 1964, 1967, 1977).

The Connaught team, with financial problems, was bought by Bernard Ecclestone, who raced the cars in Australia and Europe (>1981).

Mike Costin and Keith Duckworth set up Cosworth Engineering to develop racing engines from Ford production engines (>1967, 1983).

Bruce McLaren won the first New Zealand Driver to Europe Award (>1970); he came fifth in the German Grand Prix in a Formula Two Cooper-Climax.

he too was killed in the very next event, the German Grand Prix. Brooks won that for Vanwall. Moss then won the Portuguese Grand Prix and Brooks the Italian Grand Prix, giving Vanwall a strong position in the Manufacturers' Championship.

The Drivers' Championship, however, was finely balanced between Hawthorn and Moss. Hawthorn had won only a single race, the French Grand Prix, to Moss's three – but Hawthorn had five second places, which put him just on top.

Everything depended on the last race of the year, the Moroccan Grand Prix at Casablanca. Moss took the lead and drove a faultless race, but his team-mate Stuart Lewis-Evans crashed and was fatally burned. Hawthorn left the circuit at one point and stalled. He pushed the car back on to the road and restarted without assistance, taking second place behind Moss, only to be disqualified for 'pushing his car against the traffic', which was not permitted. Given the points for another second place Hawthorn would be World Champion, but with his elimination Moss would win the Championship outright.

Then Moss intervened, pointing out that he had seen Hawthorn push his car backwards only on the pavement, which was not against the rules. Moss's word was at once accepted, Hawthorn's position was confirmed – and with it he took the title from Moss. Vanwall won the year's Manufacturers' Championship against determined opposition from Ferrari, giving Britain the double.

TOP: The result that stunned the motor racing establishment – Stirling Moss's victory in the Argentine Grand Prix in a mid-engined 1.9-litre 180-bhp Cooper-Climax. It was the first World Championship victory by a mid-engined car and a vindication of Charles and John Cooper's design, which followed Auto Union's pioneering work with mid-engined cars in the 1930s. It was also a triumphant moment for the burgeoning British motor racing industry. Moss finished in 2 hours 19 minutes 33.7 seconds, 2.7 seconds ahead of a Ferrari Dino 156 driven by Luigi Musso. Although its victory was dismissed by some critics as a freak at the time, the winning Cooper-Climax proved to be the forerunner of the modern racing car.

ABOVE: French driver Jean Behra (>1959) narrowly escaped death during the Glover Trophy race at Goodwood on Easter Monday. After coming into the chicane too fast, his BRM hit the wall and lost a wheel. Mike Hawthorn won the race in a V-6 Ferrari at 94.96 mph. Behra never won a Grand Prix: from 52 starts he amassed 51 points.

CHAPTER NINE
EVOLUTION, REVOLUTION &
ENGINES IN THE BACK

In America, the low, sleek, front-engined, Offenhauser-powered Indianapolis cars, with their left-handed bias, reached a peak of form and function in the late 1950s and early 1960s. Improvements in speed and handling were achieved with ingenious, but small, changes rather than by radical reappraisal. But in Europe, a revolution was taking place in Grand Prix racing, a sea change which, before it was over, would spread across the Atlantic and revolutionize the Indianapolis car as well.

The most obvious outward manifestation of that change was moving the engine from the front to the back. But it went further than that. Formula One racing was being hijacked from the major European manufacturers such as Alfa-Romeo, Talbot, Mercedes-Benz, Lancia and Maserati, who made the whole racing car themselves and saw racing as promoting their name. The hijackers were a new breed of entrepreneurs who bought the best engines and components off the shelf, then built their own cars. Once they started winning, the big companies pulled out.

In a curious circular way, those entrepreneurs – Tony Vandervell, Charles and John Cooper, and Colin Chapman – were closer to men like Eddie Kuzma, Frank Kurtis, and A. J. Watson and their predecessors at Indianapolis, who had been building cars around Leo Goosen's Offenhauser engines since before the war. It is no accident that the revolution took place in Britain, where the automobile industry was made up of thousands of small engineering companies who supplied British companies with everything from engines and gearboxes to steering arms and radiators.

The process was sustained, as it had been by Offenhauser in America, by people who built racing engines – first Coventry-Climax, then Cosworth, both from Britain's engineering heartland around Birmingham.

Enzo Ferrari, an entrepreneur who preferred to think of himself as one of the big companies, dismissed the new breed as mere *assemblatori* – but to survive, he had to adopt not only the back-to-front layout of their cars, but also their entrepreneurial ways.

Grand Prix invades Indianapolis: the American racing establishment received a nasty shock when Jim Clark won the 1965 500 in a Lotus – the first European driver since René Thomas (>1914) to win the race. European manufacturers were attracted to the 500 by its lavish prize money.

At Indianapolis, the brief era of the extreme 'laydown' Belond Specials came to an end. A. J. Watson refined his upright-engined cars, producing two new cars, the Leader Card and Simoniz Specials. A feature of them was pneumatic jacks under the cars. When a Special came into the pits, a compressed air hose was attached and the car sat up. Pit-stops in the Watson pit were reduced to between 21 and 25 seconds.

In this year's 500, Johnny Thompson took pole position in the Racing Associates car designed by Luigi Lesovsky. Jimmy Bryan, the previous year's winner, suffered the indignity of losing his clutch on the first lap and retiring. The early part of the race was fast and competitive. Rodger Ward took the lead in the Leader Card Special on the fifth lap. Then a lap later, Eddie Sachs challenged him but spun off in the effort, and the yellow flag came out. When racing restarted, Jim Rathmann in the Simoniz Special – the second Watson car – challenged and eventually found a way past on lap 13. While the two Watson drivers jousted for the lead, Pat Flaherty in a third Watson car – the John Zink Special – came up and took the lead on lap 28. The Watson-designed cars were lighter on their tyres than most of the cars. Rathmann and Flaherty held out until lap 44, but Ward retained contact with them to lap 48, when the yellow flags came out again for another accident, rejoining while the others were not racing. By lap 90 he was back in the lead again, and he never lost it – despite repeated challenges from Rathmann, who took second place by 23.5 seconds in a new record average speed for the race of 135.86 mph, notwithstanding the yellow flags that had slowed the race down.

In January British motor racing suffered a grievous loss when the first British World Champion, Mike Hawthorn, was killed in a crash on the public road near Guildford in Surrey. It was already reeling from the news that Tony Vandervell to all intents and purposes had finally withdrawn the Vanwalls from racing. He had been badly shaken by the death of Stuart Lewis-Evans, and his own health was not good (>1967).

Stirling Moss was in much demand as a driver by works teams, but he chose to drive for the Scottish-based team owned and run by Rob Walker alongside Maurice Trintignant, the last of the prewar Grand Prix drivers racing in World Championship events. Walker had a Cooper prepared specially for him with a BRM engine, but it proved unsatisfactory and they reverted to the Climax engine, which is what he raced with for the year.

ABOVE: Stirling Moss in a Cooper 51 entered by wealthy Scot Rob Walker in the Monaco Grand Prix. Bad luck cost Moss the race – his transmission failed while he was leading on lap 81 and Jack Brabham won in a works Cooper. Moss spent a large part of his career driving for Walker, the heir to the Johnny Walker Scotch whisky fortune.

LEFT: Rodger Ward (>1962), winner of the Indianapolis 500. He qualified sixth fastest at 144.035 mph; pole position went to Johnny Thomson in a Racing Associates Lesovsky at 145.908 mph. Ward took home $106,850 out of a total purse of $338,100.

LEFT: The old days at Daytona.

BELOW: The modern 2.5-mile 'tri-oval' stock-car circuit, opened in 1959, cost more than $3,000,000 to build. It was the same length as the speedway at Indianapolis – and consisted of one long straight, two equal end curves steeply banked at 31 degrees and a second side stretch taking in a fast curve. In pre-practice trials for an early April meeting, Jim Rathmann touched 173 mph in the Pontiac-engined Firestone Special during tyre tests.

The Daytona Speedway

After 20 years' experience of organizing races on Daytona's beach-road circuit, Bill France built the Daytona International Speedway as a challenge to the pre-eminence of Indianapolis in American racing. He constructed the track just off Highway 92, 12 miles from the Florida resort of Daytona Beach. The complex included a main grandstand to seat 13,000 fans and within the track there was room for 60,000 more. The first Daytona 500 was run on 22 February. It was won by Lee Petty in an Oldsmobile.

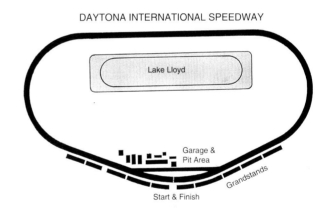

DAYTONA INTERNATIONAL SPEEDWAY

Lake Lloyd

Garage & Pit Area

Grandstands

Start & Finish

Coventry-Climax had produced a 2.5-litre engine, giving Coopers the full-sized engine for Formula One for the first time. Jack Brabham was not only a driver for the Cooper team, he was also technically gifted and worked closely with John Cooper to produce the new car for the season, the T51. In particular, strenuous efforts were made to improve the gearbox and to incorporate independent front suspension. The company still sold cars to private entrants, but the works team included Bruce McLaren and an American driver, Masten Gregory. A third team, the Italian Scuderia Centro-Sud ran Coopers with Maserati engines.

Even with Vanwall out, the British Formula One industry was growing. BRM fielded a team of Harry Schell and the Swedish driver Joakim Bonnier driving their front-engined P25s. Colin Chapman took the 2.5-litre Climax engine and created the Lotus Mk 16 round it for drivers Graham Hill and Innes Ireland. The sports car manufacturer, Aston Martin – who at this time was beating Ferrari in the sports car championship – entered Formula One with a front-engined DBR4/1.

Ferrari further improved the Tipo 246 Dino, retaining the disc brakes that had been fitted to Hawthorn's car for the Italian Grand Prix the previous year. The V-6 engine was giving 280 bhp at 8,500 rpm. There were no Italian drivers in the team of Tony Brooks, Phil Hill, Dan Gurney (a second American), Jean Behra, and a sports car driver, Olivier Gendebien.

At Monaco Behra took the lead, Moss right behind him, followed by Brabham. Behra led for 23 laps, as Moss stuck to him like glue. Then the Ferrari's engine exploded. Moss drew away from Brabham, extending the lead to nearly a lap, when his gearbox started making loud noises and he hurried into the pits. Brabham took the lead. Moss restarted, but drove only one more lap before retiring. So Brabham won, breaking the lap record in the process, and taking first blood for Cooper.

At the Dutch Grand Prix, Jo Bonnier took pole position for BRM alongside Moss and Brabham on the front row of the grid. Bonnier duly took the lead, and although Moss managed to pull ahead by lap 15, his gearbox failed again and he retired. Bonnier took the chequered flag to give BRM its first World Championship win after a decade of trying. In the French Grand Prix, Ferrari challenged the onward march of the mid-engined cars: Brooks won at Rheims, with Phil Hill second. Jean Behra, who had led the race for Ferrari for 30 laps, retired with a wrecked engine. After the race, he fell out with Enzo Ferrari

and his fellow drivers, and left. Ferrari also had a strike to contend with at his Maranello factory, so there were no cars to send to the British Grand Prix – which Brabham won.

In the days leading up to the German Grand Prix, which had been moved to the AVUS circuit near Berlin, Jean Behra was driving a Porsche in a sports car race when he

Many people in motor racing may be reluctant to admit it, but the possibility of spectacular crashes has always been one of the sport's attractions. In the German Grand Prix at AVUS on 2 August (**ABOVE**) German driver Hans Herrmann lost control of his BRM. He was thrown clear and survived almost unhurt, but the car was reduced to a tangle of battered metal. In the junior race which preceded the Italian Grand Prix at Monza on 13 September (**ABOVE RIGHT**) a horrific 100-mph collision between Alfredo Tinazzo and Antonio Criballeri shocked even the most hardened spectators. Both drivers were killed instantly.

MILESTONES

The FIA adopted Formula Junior: unsupercharged cars up to 1,100 cc/400 kg without double overhead camshaft engines, using pump fuel.

The Mercedes driver Rudolf Caracciola, the ex-European Champion (>1935, 1937, 1938), died of liver failure in Lugano, Switzerland, aged 58.

Edgar Barth and Wolfgang Seidel won the Targa Florio in a 1.5-litre Porsche RSK. It was the first time that Porsches took the first three places.

The first mid-engined BRM, the Type 48, made a debut at Monza in the Italian Grand Prix driven by Ron Flockhart, but retired after 67 laps.

Jim Clark, who started racing saloon cars in his native Scotland, drove a Gemini in a Formula Junior race. It was his first single-seater.

Aston Martin won the 24-hour Le Mans sports car race, and the Sports Car World Championship, ahead of Ferrari and Porsche.

lost control on the high-speed North Curve banking, crashed, and was killed, casting a shadow over the race in which Ferrari made use of the high-speed track to register a crushing first-, second- and third-place victory for Brooks, Gurney and Hill.

Moss then won the Portuguese and Italian Grands Prix – in the latter, by employing the same ruse he had used in the Argentinian Grand Prix in 1958. He had knock-off hubs fitted to the Cooper, suggesting he would be coming in for tyres, when he knew the Ferraris would be doing the whole race on one set; he took the lead, then – as the Ferraris waited for him to dive into the pits – forged ahead without changing to win.

The last race was a new one in the calendar: the US Grand Prix. It was held on a disused airfield, Hendrick Field, near Sebring in Florida. There were 19 cars in the race. Moss lined up in pole position; Brabham and Schell were alongside him on the front row, both in Coopers. Behind them were Trintignant, in the second Rob Walker Cooper, and Brooks in the fastest of the Ferraris. Brooks' team-mates Wolfgang von Trips, Cliff Allison and Phil Hill comprised the third row, behind whom were Innes Ireland for Lotus and Bruce McLaren in the other works Cooper. Right at the back was Rodger Ward, Indianapolis winner and US National Champion in a Kurtis-Offy Midget dirt track racer.

Moss led from the start, opening up a 2-second lead over Brabham that he extended to 10 seconds by lap 10 – when yet again his gearbox gave up, and he was out, losing a second chance to win the Championship in the last race of the season. If Brabham failed to get any points and Brooks won, the Championship would be a tie. Brabham continued well ahead of Trintignant and McLaren, who were fighting it out for second place, when on the final lap he ran out of fuel. Both shot past him, McLaren to win by half of one second. McLaren became the youngest man ever to win a World Championship event, at the age of 22.

Brooks was third, before Brabham pushed his car over the line for fourth place. He was World Champion, and Cooper had won the Manufacturers' Trophy.

The year 1960 was one of transition in Grand Prix racing, as manufacturers continued to run the 2.5-litre cars while preparing for the new formula in 1961: 1.5-litre engines using commercial fuel, with no supercharged equivalent, in cars weighing specifically no more than 450 kilograms (992 pounds, 0.443 ton). The British teams wanted to retain their 2.5-litre engines, and they fought the FIA to do so throughout the year.

Ferrari bowed to the inevitable and adopted the mid-engined layout. The front-engined Tipo 246 – something of a dinosaur among the smaller, mid-engined cars – remained their mainstay, but they were augmented by mid-engined prototypes, such as the Tipo 246P (which was really a Dino with the engine in the back), and by the first Tipo 156, a new Formula Two car with a 1.5-litre V-6 engine. Another front-engined car was the Scarab, the first American Formula One car, built by the Woolworth heir Lance Reventlow. It had a

BELOW: Stirling Moss leading at Monaco, on his way to giving Lotus its first victory in a World Championship race. Moss's four-cylinder in-line 2.5-litre Lotus 18 Climax produced 239 bhp at 6,750 rpm. It was owned and entered by Rob Walker (>1959). Behind Moss is Jack Brabham in a 'lowline' Cooper T53.

BELOW: Happy and glorious. Stirling Moss (right) beside Prince Rainier (centre) and Princess Grace of Monaco during the playing of the British National Anthem after Moss's win in the Monaco Grand Prix. Moss took pole position, a crucial factor on the twisting street circuit.

ABOVE: Tragedy at Indianapolis. A homemade grandstand collapsed during the pace lap, killing two people and injuring 40. Local architect and amateur photographer J.

Parke Randall, covering the race as a 'stringer' for the *Indianapolis News*, was taking shots of the race when the screams of spectators made him turn round to get this picture.

RIGHT: Phil Hill, winner of the Italian Grand Prix in a Ferrari 246 – the first American to win a European Grand Prix since Jimmy Murphy (>1921).

fuel-injected four-cylinder Offenhauser engine – designed by Leo Goosen and producing 230 bhp – which, like its Indianapolis cousins, was laid on its side.

Cooper was working on the sleeker, lower T53 with an improved gearbox for Jack Brabham and Bruce McLaren, but it was not ready for the beginning of the season. Graham Hill moved from Lotus to BRM to drive the mid-engined BRM Type 48. Colin Chapman unveiled his first mid-engined car, the Lotus 18. Not for the last time, Chapman was introducing a radical new idea that others eventually took up: the rear suspension used a light alloy hub to carry the wheel, attached to a lower wishbone, while the half-shaft acted as the upper wishbone. The car was really a more refined version of the Cooper, and had the same 2.5-litre Coventry-Climax engine which now produced 243 bhp. But it was even lighter, weighing only 390 kilograms to the Cooper T53's 435 kilograms, and there were some people who thought that it was too light – that Chapman had gone too far, and it would break.

Britain now had two names at the top of Formula One, Cooper and Lotus, and rivalry between them became a feature of 1961. The Lotus 18 had hardly been tested when it was

flown to Argentina for the first Grand Prix of the season, causing a sensation when Innes Ireland took pole position. He then led from the start, giving the Ferrari and Cooper drivers a shock, before spinning off on lap 2. Then one of the disc brakes disintegrated, and finally the steering started to malfunction, so that Ireland was unable to make any further impression on the race. Bruce McLaren won for Cooper, barely two months since his first victory at Sebring (>1959); Ireland was sixth.

Back in Britain, Ireland beat Stirling Moss twice in a day at Goodwood, once when Moss was driving a Cooper in a Formula Two race, and once when he was driving a Porsche in a Formula One race. Then Ireland won the Formula One International Trophy Race at Silverstone, again beating Moss. The implications were clear, and Rob Walker bought a Lotus 18 for Moss in time for the Monaco Grand Prix. At Monaco Moss tried both the Lotus and the Cooper, and although he found the Lotus trickier to handle, he took pole position in it and chose to drive it in the race.

Monaco saw the debut of two more cars: the mid-engined Ferrari driven by another American, Richie Ginther, and Scarabs driven by Reventlow and Chuck Daigh. Joakim Bonnier led at the start in a BRM, but Moss

overtook him on lap 17, then followed by Brabham. When it started to rain, Moss eased off and Brabham took the lead, only to crash. After a pit-stop for a new plug lead, Moss led to the end, but on the last few laps he heard an unusual vibration from the back. In the pits he discovered that the front engine mountings had broken, leaving the front of the engine supported only by the water hose – which did little to counter criticism of the Lotus 18's lightweight construction.

That reputation was endorsed in the run-up to the Belgian Grand Prix at Spa. The 'low-line' T53 Coopers were ready and they were faster, as Brabham demonstrated by breaking the lap record by 7 seconds in practice, taking pole position. Also during practice, Moss hit a bump on a corner at 140 mph in his Lotus. The half-shaft broke, the left rear wheel came off, and he careened into a bank backwards at 90 mph. He was badly injured, with several fractures, and was taken to hospital. In the same practice session, a steering weld broke on another Lotus 18 privately entered by Mike Taylor, who crashed and was killed. Then, in the race, the Lotus works driver Alan Stacey, also driving a Lotus 18, crashed and was killed, due reportedly to hitting a bird. Chris Bristow, a protege of Moss's, also died when he crashed in a Cooper. Brabham won

ABOVE: Robert 'Junior' Johnson, winner of the Daytona 500 in a Pontiac at 124.74 mph. Johnson picked up racing skills outpacing police cars while running bootleg whisky. He progressed to stock cars, but his racing career was interrupted when he was caught in a raid and sent to jail. Johnson was later made famous by American writer Tom Wolfe in *The Last American Hero* (1964).

MILESTONES

On 19 March Jim Clark won the Formula Junior race at Goodwood in Colin Chapman's Lotus 18, the first-ever victory for the type.

The first victory for Ferrari's first mid-engined car, the Tipo 156, was by Wolfgang von Trips in a Formula Two race at Stuttgart.

The American driver Harry Schell, who lived in Paris, was killed driving his own Cooper in practice in the wet at Silverstone.

The last appearance of the Maserati 250F (>1954) in a World Championship race was in the United States Grand Prix, in which one was driven by Robert Drake.

Louis Wagner – winner of the 1906 Vanderbilt Cup in a Darracq, and who drove in the first-ever Grand Prix at Le Mans – died aged 78.

Seven times World Motorcycle Champion, John Surtees came second in the British Grand Prix for Lotus, earning his first Championship points.

ABOVE: Jack Brabham's Cooper-Climax leading Phil Hill's Ferrari in the French Grand Prix. The race was a British triumph – Coopers came home

1-2-3-4: Brabham was first, Olivier Gendebien second, Bruce McLaren third and Henry Taylor fourth. Hill retired on lap 29 with a stripped transmission.

ABOVE: Rising star Jim Clark in a Ford-engined Lotus 18 on his way to victory in the John Davy Trophy for Formula Junior cars at Brands Hatch on 1 August. Clark drove the Type 18 in Formulas One, Two and Junior using different sizes of engine. He won his first World Championship points with a fifth place in the Belgian Grand Prix on 19 June, and later in the season was fifth in the French and third in the Portuguese Grands Prix, all in Lotus 18s.

the race with McLaren second – a great debut for the T53, but one overshadowed by what was the blackest weekend for British motor racing.

With Moss injured, and Brabham and McLaren in their new T53s, the steam went out of the Lotus-Cooper battle. At the French Grand Prix at Rheims the Italians were once again in contention. After a fierce battle with Phil Hill and Wolfgang von Trips, Brabham won – the first time the Grand Prix had been won by a mid-engined car in the World Championship. After a poor showing in the race, the Scarab team went back to the United States.

Still recovering from his accident at Spa, Stirling Moss had to be content with acting as the starter for the British Grand Prix at Silverstone. Brabham led, but on lap 37 Graham Hill challenged him in the BRM. After a long tussle Hill spun, just seven laps from the end, leaving Brabham to take his fourth suc-

cessive victory, a record not achieved since Alberto Ascari did it in 1952.

The Italian Grand Prix was a walkover for Ferrari. For the first time since 1956, the Milan automobile club had decided to use the banked oval as part of the circuit. It was notoriously rough and not suitable for the ultralight mid-engined British cars. The British drivers and teams all boycotted the race, and Ferrari entered Formula Two cars. It was the only Ferrari victory of the year: Phil Hill was first, Richie Ginther second, Willy Mairesse third, and Wolfgang von Trips fifth in a midengined Tipo 156. It was the last time a World Championship race was won by a frontengined car.

Brabham put the World Drivers' Championship beyond doubt by winning the Portuguese Grand Prix, with team-mate McLaren second, to present Cooper with the Manufacturers' World Championship, but he did not win the last race of the season, the United States Grand Prix at Riverside in California. Moss had returned to racing, and took pole position in the Lotus 18 from Brabham by 0.6 second. Brabham led at the start but, wary of running out of fuel again, he had overfilled his fuel tanks. Fuel gushed through a breather pipe on to the hot exhaust, causing a burst of fire that then extinguished itself. He called in at the pits to investigate and Moss took the lead – which he held to the end, thereby winning the last race of the 2.5-litre formula.

The Golden Jubilee of the Indianapolis 500 produced one of the finest races in the history of the Speedway. From pole position, Eddie Sachs took the lead in the Dean Van Lines Special, and the fight for the lead started from the first lap when Jim Hurtubise passed him. Jim Rathmann and Rodger Ward gained on Hurtubise in their A. J. Watson cars, and by lap 35 – when Hurtubise went into the pits for tyres – the average speed was a staggering 144.5 mph. Rathmann took the lead and, when he went in for tyres, Parnelli Jones took over, driving in his first race.

On lap 49 Don Davies' car leaked oil on to his tyres, and he spun right in front of the grandstands. As he got out of the car to run for safety, six cars piled into each other trying to avoid him. Once the debris was cleared, the race settled down into a battle between Eddie Sachs, Rodger Ward, Jim Rathmann, Troy Ruttmann and A.J. Foyt, resolving finally into a duel between Sachs and Foyt. They swapped the lead for 40 laps before lap 155, when they went into the pits together for their last scheduled pit-stop, coming out again neck-and-neck. Unknown to Foyt, the pressure fuel system in his pits had failed, and the crew had managed only to fill half his tank. On lap 184 they called him in for more fuel, and he rejoined 30 seconds behind Sachs. With three laps to go, Sachs noticed canvas showing on his tyres, and rather than risk a blow-out, he went in. Foyt took the lead just as Sachs was coming out again, and he won by 8.3 seconds.

As the FIA introduced the new Formula in 1961, so it had also deleted Indianapolis from the World Championship. So it was ironic to see in ninth place in the 500 a rear-engined Cooper driven by the reigning World Champion, Jack Brabham. Brabham and Cooper were not chasing Championship points – they were attracted by the $400,000 purse, the richest prize in motor sport. The Cooper was similar to the 1960 Grand Prix car, although the suspension had been modified to suit the left-handed circuit and the engine was offset to the left. At 2.7 litres and 255 bhp, the engine was far less powerful than the 252-cu.in. (4.2-litre) Offys which produced well over 400 bhp. On the straights it was 10 mph slower than the roadsters – 150 mph to 160 mph – but through the corners the little car was faster, at 145 mph compared with 140 mph. Brabham had qualified for the race on the first day at 145.144 mph, then flown to Monte Carlo, arriving at midday on race day for the Monaco Grand Prix.

As the first race of the new formula, Monaco was a showcase for the new cars. The British teams had fought the FIA over the 1.5-litre formula and lost, and both Climax and BRM were late in starting work on new engines. Neither was ready for Monaco, and their customers Cooper and Lotus had to use an interim version of the four-cylinder Formula Two Climax engine which produced

MILESTONES

The new formula required Grand Prix cars to have ignition cut-out switches, roll bars, dual braking, open wheels, and self-starters.

Ferrari's Sports Car World Championship win was aided by its first mid-engined sports car, a derivative of the Tipo 246 Formula One car.

To date, Giancarlo Baghetti's victory in the French Grand Prix at Rheims is the only time a driver has won his first World Championship race.

On 8 October Innes Ireland won the United States Grand Prix at Watkins Glen, the first World Championship win for the Lotus works team.

Innes Ireland was unexpectedly fired by Colin Chapman at the end of the year. Jim Clark took over as No.1 driver in the Lotus team.

In October, the last brick-paved parts of the Indianapolis track were asphalted, except for a narrow strip at the start-finish line.

ABOVE: The new 1.5-litre Coventry-Climax engine at the Italian Grand Prix on 10 September. The engine had made its debut at the German Grand Prix on 6 August, when Jack Brabham used it in a Cooper – but crashed on the first lap. At Monza, Stirling Moss tried out one of the new engines in a Lotus and Brabham used another in a Cooper; both drivers retired. The new Climax became the most successful engine of the 1.5-litre formula.

ABOVE: Dan Gurney in a Porsche (No. 46) and Stirling Moss in a Lotus-Climax (No. 28) neck-and-neck during the Italian Grand Prix at Monza. Moss retired on lap 36 with a broken front wheel bearing; Gurney finished second, 31.2 seconds behind Phil Hill's Ferrari. Bruce McLaren was third in a Cooper-Climax, almost 2 minutes further behind. Hill's victory clinched the World Drivers' Championship in sad circumstances.

around 150 bhp. Against this, Ferrari – who had been working on a 1.5-litre engine for some time – had two versions of the V-6 (one at a 65-degree V, the other at a 120-degree V) that produced around 185 bhp at 9,500 rpm. The team was Phil Hill, Richie Ginther and Wolfgang von Trips. Porsche, who had been successful in both Formula Two and sports car racing, chose Monaco to move into Formula One. They entered two ex-Formula-Two cars with air-cooled engines based on the 1.5-litre RSK unit which developed around 150 bhp. Their drivers were Jo Bonnier and the United States driver Dan Gurney. Lotus entered two Type 21s (using the interim Climax engine) for Jim Clark and Innes Ireland. Against all the new competition, Stirling Moss took pole position in his obsolete Lotus 18.

ABOVE: Panic at the Italian Grand Prix. A Monza official waves the danger flag after the 140-mph crash between Wolfgang von Trips' Ferrari and Jim Clark's Lotus in which von Trips was killed. Von Trips' body (left centre) and Clark (right centre) have been thrown out onto the ground. German-born von Trips died aged 33, just as his racing career was taking off: he was leading in the World Championship after two wins and a second place.

The race was a classic. Moss was giving away around 35 bhp to the Ferraris, but on lap 14 he took the lead from Ginther. Then Phil Hill moved up and started whittling away at Moss's lead, closing it to 3.5 seconds at the half-way point. Moss responded with a new burst of genius, pulling away as the other two Ferraris moved into third and fourth place. For the rest of the race the four cars were rarely more than 11 seconds apart, but despite repeated challenges, Moss achieved one of those rare victories in which sheer skill more than compensated for lower technical performance (>1935, 1957).

The Ferraris reasserted themselves in the next two Grands Prix. Von Trips won the Dutch and Hill the Belgian. For the French Grand Prix they were joined by a new Italian

BELOW: The Gasworks Hairpin, a few seconds after the start of the Monaco Grand Prix. Richie Ginther's V-6 Ferrari (No. 36) leads from Jim Clark's works Lotus-Climax (No. 28) and Stirling Moss's Rob Walker Lotus-Climax (No. 20, partly obscured by Clark). Moss won by 3.6 seconds from Ginther. Clark finished tenth.

RIGHT: Jo Bonnier's Porsche (No. 10) ahead of Giancarlo Baghetti's Ferrari (No. 50) and Dan Gurney's Porsche (No. 12) in the French Grand Prix at Rheims on 2 July. Baghetti won the race – his World Championship debut – in 2 hours 14 minutes 17.5 seconds, just 0.1 second ahead of Gurney. Bonnier dropped back to finish seventh.

driver, Giancarlo Baghetti, driving a Tipo 156 sponsored by a consortium of Italian automobile clubs bent on producing a new world-class Italian driver. Hill, Ginther and von Trips had Tipo 156s with newer 120-degree engines. The fast Rheims circuit favoured the Ferraris, and they swept into the lead with Moss in fourth place. When Moss's brakes started to fade, Baghetti passed him while himself being relentlessly harried by Clark and Ireland. Von Trips briefly took the lead from Hill, only to finish up in the pits with a wrecked engine. Baghetti was lying third, now under pressure from Bonnier and Gurney in their Porsches, but the young Italian drove a remarkably cool race considering the pressure he was under. Out in front, Hill came up behind Moss and the two had an unnecessary tussle that resulted in Hill's spinning off at the Thillois Hairpin. Then Ginther's oil pressure began to drop. He was unable to take on oil under the rules, so a couple of laps later he stopped out on the track rather than wreck his engine.

Suddenly all Ferrari's hopes rested on Baghetti in his first World Championship race. The two Porsche drivers were still mercilessly challenging him, and Gurney was leading on the last lap. As they came out of the last corner, Baghetti put his foot on the floor on the straight, swung out of Gurney's slipstream, using the final burst of speed to win by one tenth of a second, the first Italian driver to win a World Championship race since Alberto Ascari (>1953).

Von Trips was leading the Drivers' Championship table, with Phil Hill in second place, and Ferrari had already won enough points to be assured of the Manufacturers' Championship when the teams met again at Monza for the Italian Grand Prix. The three Ferraris took their accustomed position at the front – Hill, Ginther then von Trips – with Clark challenging von Trips from fourth place. Going into the Curva Parabolica, Clark and von Trips collided. Von Trips' car left the track and ploughed into the crowd, killing 14 spectators. Von Trips died too, and Enzo Ferrari withdrew the rest of the team, except for Hill – who won the race, and with it the World Championship.

Taking both Formula One titles and the 1961 Sports Car World Championship, 1961 was a great year for Ferrari. But with the sadness of von Trips' death, Ferrari withdrew for the rest of the season. The year ended with acrimony too. At his factory at Maranello there was dissension, and Carlo Chiti, the Chief Engineer, and Romolo Tavoli, the team manager, left at the end of the year to join a new Italian racing team, Automobili Turismo e Sport (ATS) in Bologna (>1962).

ABOVE: Ferrari's first rear-engined car, the Tipo 156. Its V-6 engine was the best prepared for the new formula, and the 156 won five out of eight World Championship Grands Prix – the Dutch (driven by Wolfgang von Trips), the Belgian (Phil Hill), the French (Giancarlo Baghetti), the British (von Trips) and the Italian (Hill). Ferrari won the Constructors' World Championship with 45 points, to Lotus's 35 and Porsche's 22 points.

RIGHT: Anthony Joseph Foyt, US National Champion for the second successive year and winner of the 500 in the year of Indianapolis Speedway's Golden Anniversary. He also won the Daytona 500 and the Le Mans 24-hour race.

With a successful year behind them, the new team at Ferrari left the Tipo 156 'Sharknose' largely unchanged but improved the engine to use four valves per cylinder instead of two, and a six-speed gearbox. The World Champion, Phil Hill, was retained alongside Giancarlo Baghetti and a new driver from Mexico, Ricardo Rodriguez.

Having been soundly beaten by Ferrari, the British teams – BRM, Lotus and Cooper, and now including two new names, Lola and Brabham – responded vigorously. At Lola, Eric Broadley, who had been busy building Formula Junior cars for some years, based his Formula One car on the new Coventry-Climax V-8 engine. The team was sponsored by the Bowmaker finance house and included drivers John Surtees and Roy Salvadori. Jack Brabham had left Cooper to found Motor Racing Developments. He persuaded a long-time friend, the designer Ron Tauranac, to join him from Australia and together they planned a Formula One car under the designation BT3 (B for Brabham, T for Tauranac) that would be capable of using either the Climax or the BRM engine. For use until it was ready for racing, he bought a Lotus 24 from Colin Chapman.

Lotus and Cooper both used the new Climax V-8 engine which incorporated two major advances: transistorized ignition and fuel injection. The advantage of fuel injection was that by using a measured amount of fuel at specified rpm, the engine gave better acceleration, was more efficient, and made combustion cooler. The Climax engine produced 185 bhp at 8,500 rpm. Coopers put it in their new T66, which had a tubular space-frame, together with a six-speed gearbox. Their drivers were Bruce McLaren and the South African driver Tony Maggs.

ABOVE: First-lap accident at the Monaco Grand Prix. Richie Ginther's BRM (No. 8, right) collided with Maurice Trintignant's Lotus-Climax (No. 30, background) and Innes Ireland's Lotus-Climax (left). Ireland drove to the pits for repairs and continued; Ginther and Trintignant retired.

LEFT: High speeds on the banked curves of the Daytona International Speedway often resulted in dramatic pile-ups. In the second qualifying heat for the fourth annual 500, four cars spun and crashed. From left: Speedy Thompson (No. 15), Marvin Finch (No. 90, background), Darel Dieringer (No. 39) and Bobby Johns (No. 72). The fifth car, driven by Rick White (right background, obscured by smoke), stayed in the heat to finish third. The 500 was won by Marvin Panch in a Pontiac at 149.601 mph.

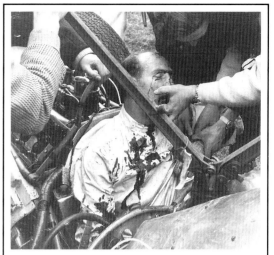

The end of a great career. Stirling Moss is cut from the wreckage of his Lotus after the crash that led to his retirement. Moss was chasing race-leader Graham Hill's BRM after a pit-stop had put him behind during the 100-mile Glover Trophy race in the Easter meeting at Goodwood. He was gaining on Hill and set a new Formula One record – 105.37 mph – before crashing on lap 26. Moss was the most talented driver never to win the World Championship – and one of the best-liked on the Grand Prix circuit, a superb sportsman and a man of total integrity.

ABOVE: Graham Hill in a works BRM P578 winning the German Grand Prix at the Nürburgring on 5 August. His time was 2 hours 38 minutes 45.3 seconds: 80.35 mph. The new BRM made its debut at the Brussels Grand Prix, when Hill won the first heat in it. The 1.5-litre, 90-degree V-8 engine produced 184 bhp at 10,000 rpm using Lucas fuel injection.

Colin Chapman had sold Lotus 24s both to Brabham and to a second team sponsored by another finance house, UDT-Laysall, whose driver was Innes Ireland. But for his works drivers – Jim Clark and Trevor Taylor – he came up with a revolutionary car, the Lotus 25: the first modern racing car to be built with a monocoque chassis. The monocoque principle had been used in aircraft for many years. The stiffness of the body was achieved by giving the body shell the inherent strength needed to support itself, the engine and the suspension, rather than by using triangulated steel tubing. The 25 was made up of four 'boxes' enclosed in a wrap-around aluminium skin. The two at the side and one at the back contained the fuel tanks, and the one at the front doubled up as the oil tank. Suspension was attached to the front and rear boxes, and the engine was itself used to add stiffness by attaching it to the chassis on rigid mounts.

Chapman preferred carburettors to Climax's Lucas fuel injection.

BRM had reached rock bottom in 1961. Graham Hill had managed a fifth and a sixth place, and Tony Brooks – who retired at the end of the season and was replaced by the American driver Richie Ginther – a fifth. Sir Alfred Owen made it plain that unless the team won something in 1962, he would halt the inflow of money that kept it alive. Peter Berthon, who had been part of BRM since the start, was sidelined and the development of the Type 578 was taken over by Tony Rudd. The BRM V-8 engine, which also used Lucas fuel injection and transistorized ignition, developed 190 bhp. The changes brought an immediate effect in non-championship races: Hill won the first heat in the Brussels Grand Prix in the car's debut race, and went on to win the Richmond Trophy at Goodwood and the International Trophy at Silverstone, beating Clark in a Lotus 24.

Porsche introduced a new car, the Type 804, for Dan Gurney and Joakim Bonnier. The air-cooled 753 engine used carburettors rather than fuel injection, and its eight cylinders, in two banks of four, were opposite each other in the 'flat-8' configuration.

When the teams gathered for their new cars' joint debuts at Zandvoort for the Dutch

Grand Prix, one driver was sadly missing – Stirling Moss, who had crashed very badly at Goodwood at the Easter meeting (see box). In practice, Graham Hill managed a lap in 1 minute 32.6 seconds (101.311 mph), compared with the 1 minute 33.3 seconds set by Moss the previous year. Phil Hill, on the other hand, could not even equal his own practice times from the previous year. Surtees took pole position in the Bowmaker Lotus with the new record of 1 minute 32.5 seconds. He was followed on the grid by four more British cars: Clark for Lotus, Brabham in his own Lotus 24, Graham Hill for BRM, and McLaren for Cooper. Behind them were Gurney for Porsche and Phil Hill for Ferrari.

Clark led the armada of new machinery at the start, from Graham Hill, Gurney and Surtees. By lap 3 he had stretched the lead to 3 seconds. Rodriguez then spun in the Ferrari, taking Brabham off with him – after which the teething troubles started. Clark clearly had problems selecting his gears, and Graham Hill started to gain on him. Surtees' Lola broke a wishbone and he crashed; he was unhurt, but Reg Parnell – the team manager – called in the other Lola driven by Salvadori. Gurney was also having gearbox problems. By lap 11 Clark had lost several gears and Graham Hill had passed him. By lap 20 Hill had a 20-second lead in front of McLaren and Phil Hill. McLaren lost his gears, and he was out. Innes Ireland's car's brakes locked up and he crashed. Graham Hill won by 30 seconds, taking his first World Championship race and BRM's second.

It was a fiercely contested season. Bruce McLaren won at Monaco after Clark, who had taken pole position, once again suffered gearbox problems. Two weeks later, the Lotus 25's gearbox had been sorted out and Clark took the lead in the Belgian Grand Prix on lap

8 to win his first World Championship race and the first for the monocoque Lotus 25. Then Gurney took the chequered flag at the French Grand Prix for his and for Porsche's first World Championship victory.

The keenly anticipated British Grand Prix was held at Aintree for the last time. Clark made a superb start and established a good lead over Surtees on the first lap. By lap 34 he had lapped Phil Hill in the only Ferrari, and he went on to lap both Gurney and Brabham on the way to winning his second World Championship race of the year, and giving a hint of a very special talent.

The battle for the Championship was between Clark and Graham Hill. The BRM 578 was slightly more powerful than the Lotus 25, and slightly heavier. Hill took the German and Italian Grands Prix, only for

LEFT: Double first. American Dan Gurney's win in a Porsche in the French Grand Prix at Rouen on 8 July was his first World Championship victory. It was also the first – and only – victory in the World Championship for Porsche (>1983). Gurney came from the third row of the starting grid to beat the field in a total of 2 hours 7 minutes 35.5 seconds: equivalent to a 101.89 mph average. His car's air-cooled flat-8 engine developed 185 bhp at 9,200 rpm.

LEFT: Rodger Ward (>1959), winner of the Indianapolis 500. Ward's average speed – 140.293 mph – was the first winner's average above 140 mph. He also won the first 500 drivers' golf championship, held this year. His winning car, the Leader Card 500, was designed by A. J. Watson – the most successful designer of the roadster era.

Clark to fight back at the US Grand Prix at Watkins Glen. He took pole position and won, after a tussle with Hill, by 8.2 seconds. In the Championship, Hill had 31 points to Clark's 30, and the result rested on the South African Grand Prix at East London on 29 December. Clark again took pole position, led magnificently – and just as it seemed that he must win the title, he lost his oil through a faulty plug. Hill won the race and the Championship, more than meeting Sir Alfred Owen's dictum that it was success or the end of BRM.

At the end of the season, Phil Hill left Ferrari to join the other ex-Ferrari men who had a promising car in their ATS Type 100. John Surtees moved from Bowmaker-Lola to Ferrari. Grand Prix racing also lost its German entrant when Porsche announced its decision to leave Formula One and concentrate its efforts on sports car racing, in which it was having success.

ABOVE: Jim Clark (left) and Graham Hill, the best of the second generation of British drivers who came to prominence in the early 1960s. Clark, born in March 1936, grew up at Duns in the Scottish borders and began racing regularly aged 22. He joined Lotus in 1960 and made his World Championship debut that same season. Hill was born in Hampstead, London, in February 1929. He joined Lotus as a mechanic in 1955; his World Championship debut was at Monaco in a Lotus in 1958, when he came fourth.

MILESTONES

The points for a win in a World Championship race were raised from 8 to 9, with 6 points for second place, and 4-3-2-1 points down to sixth.

Parnelli Jones qualified for Indianapolis at 150.370 in an A. J. Watson car, the first qualifying speed above 150 mph. In the race he finished seventh.

The first American mid-engined car at Indianapolis since the war was a Mickey Thompson-Buick Special in which Dan Gurney was 20th.

Rodger Ward won his second 500 (>1959), the first driver to complete six consecutive races, finishing in the top four in each race.

The Brabham BT3 made its debut in the German Grand Prix. Its first Championship points came with Jack Brabham's fourth in the US Grand Prix.

Ferrari's promising new Mexican driver, Ricardo Rodriguez, aged 20, was killed during practice for the Mexican Grand Prix.

RIGHT: A legend in the making. Jim Clark in a Lotus 25 in the Belgian Grand Prix at Spa-Francorchamps, one of the fastest circuits in the World Championship. He won at 114.1 mph, the second of four consecutive victories in the Belgian Grand Prix.

If the 1962 season had been a struggle between several British drivers driving for the main British teams, the next season was dominated by just one driver and one car: Jim Clark and the Lotus 25. And for the first time in decades, the British – Clark, Lotus and Colin Chapman – took their expertise across the Atlantic to Indianapolis. Chapman had been taken by Dan Gurney to watch the 500 in 1962 and had been astonished at how far behind Grand Prix technology the Indy cars had lapsed. He had been stirred by the challenge of beating them – and stirred too by the huge prize money at stake. Rodger Ward won $125,015: many times the value of a Grand Prix win.

As Chapman was looking at Indianapolis, so too was the huge Ford company looking to challenge the dominance of the Offenhauser engine, in particular to produce a competitor for the Offy by developing the side-valve engine from the Ford Falcon. In this connection Ford talked to a number of American designers, including A. J. Watson, whose cars had won the last four 500s. Then when Clark won the US Grand Prix in 1962, they started talking to Lotus too. Ford and Lotus agreed to take on the Indianapolis establishment together. Chapman would develop a monocoque car

based on the Lotus 25 with a Colotti gearbox, to be known as the Lotus 29, while Ford would produce a lightweight 4.2-litre V-8 with alloy crankcase, block and head. Clark took the car to Ford's test track in Arizona in March, and from there to the Indianapolis Speedway, at which the current lap record had been set by Parnelli Jones at 150.729 mph.

ABOVE: The first bend of the Belgian Grand Prix on 9 June. Jim Clark, the race-winner, started on the third row of the grid after mechanical problems. He and Graham Hill (BRM) made superb starts to establish an early lead.

First time out, Clark managed 146 mph. The following day, Gurney raised it to 150.501. The cars were tiny by comparison with the traditional roadsters, and the Indy specialists had not expected such results. They were also troubled to learn that the Lotus drivers Clark and Gurney intended to complete the race with only two pit-stops, whereas they would need three.

Parnelli Jones was fastest in qualifying, taking pole position with the fastest practice time of 151.153 mph; Clark was fifth fastest qualifier at 149.75 mph. After briefly losing the lead to Jim Hurtubise in his V-8 supercharged Novi on the first lap, Jones stayed at the front for the first 66 laps, at which point he went into the pits for fuel. Roger McCluskey briefly led until he too had to go into the pits, then Clark took over, with Gurney second. Gurney went in on lap 92 and, after a bad pit-stop lasting 42 seconds, rejoined in seventh place. Clark followed him in and was out again in 23 seconds, but Jones had regained the lead, lapping at 150 mph and

trying to build up a cushion of time against his third pit-stop. Clark quickly re-established himself in second place behind, but Jones began to pull away steadily by 1 second a lap as his fuel load lightened. Some way behind them came Eddie Sachs, A.J. Foyt and Roger McCluskey, all in Offy-powered roadsters. When Jones went in for his second pit-stop he led by 45 seconds and rejoined in the lead. But Jones's car was now heavy with fuel, and Clark's was getting lighter. Then Duane Carter's engine spewed oil all over the track and the yellow flags came out. Jones saw his opportunity and took his third pit-stop while the flags were out, rejoining 12 seconds ahead of Clark. Clark closed the gap to 5 seconds as Jones's car started leaking oil. Both Sachs and McCluskey spun on the oil. Clark held back for the moment.

In the pits, Chapman protested vigorously that Jones should be 'black-flagged' – that he should be compulsorily brought in for leaking oil, and the black flag was brought out by the Clerk of the Course, Harlan Fengler. J. C. Agajanian argued equally vigorously that the oil was no longer leaking, and that Jones should therefore be allowed to race on. Fengler trained binoculars on Jones and decided it was water that was leaking; he left Jones to race. Then Sachs spun again – and this time he crashed, bringing out the yellow flags once more. Clark was in amongst a group of cars, while Jones was out in front. With seven laps

LEFT: The long straight approaching the pits at the Nürburgring – John Surtees in a Ferrari 156 leads from Jim Clark in a Lotus 25 on lap 7 of the German Grand Prix. Surtees won, 1 minute 17.5 seconds ahead.

ABOVE: Lotus triumph. Jim Clark, Colin Chapman and team driver Mike Spence celebrate victory in both the Drivers' and Constructors' World Championships after the Italian Grand Prix.

to go, the green lights came on again. But Clark could not close the gap, and Jones won by 19 seconds.

Controversy about the decision not to eliminate Jones reigned long after the race, not only within the Lotus team. Eddie Sachs expressed his views on the matter a little too vigorously to Jones at the victory luncheon the following day – and Jones punched him in the face. Clark, Gurney and Chapman had rattled the Indianapolis traditionalists. Lotus had shown them where the engine in a racing car should be, in the same way that Cooper had shown Maserati and Ferrari a few years earlier. Even more directly, with Clark's second place they had also relieved the American competitors of a substantial amount of money – $55,000 from a total purse of $494,030.

During qualifying for Indianapolis, Clark had returned to Europe for the Monaco Grand Prix. Once again the gearbox on the Lotus 25 let him down, and it was Graham Hill in a BRM who won the inaugural race of the World Championship.

The Grand Prix constructors had all improved their cars. The BRM V-8 was producing around 205 bhp – slightly more powerful than Clark's Lotus, which had been fitted with fuel injection and produced 200 bhp. Ferrari also had fuel injection and was experimenting with a semi-monocoque chassis: the main body of the car was monocoque, but the engine and rear suspension were mounted on a tubular frame. In addition, Ferrari gave up the traditional wire-spoked wheels in favour of lightweight alloy wheels. The Ferrari drivers were John Surtees and the Belgian Willy Mairesse.

The Monaco result was an abberation. Clark won the Dutch Grand Prix; he took pole position and then won the Belgian and French Grands Prix, and after them the British Grand Prix, so joining only Ascari among

RIGHT: The poster for the German Grand Prix, held at the Nürburgring, one of motor racing's most famous venues. The mountainous, twisting circuit was frequently wet in patches, making the track liable to change from one part of the circuit to another. Drivers never knew what to expect around the next corner.

MILESTONES

After more than half a century of making luxury and racing cars, the Bugatti company was taken over by Hispano-Suiza (>1912, 1924, 1946–47, 1956).

The first time a driver won a Formula One race in a car with his own name came when Jack Brabham won a non-Championship race at Stuttgart.

Graham Hill and Richie Ginther drove a gas-turbine-powered (jet) Rover-BRM in the Le Mans 24-hour race to finish at an average 107.8 mph.

The Tyrrell Racing Organization was founded by Ken Tyrrell to compete in Formula Three. He signed a young Scottish driver, Jackie Stewart.

After a disastrous season, the Italian team ATS folded. Phil Hill failed to win any points in the World Championship in the Type 100.

The FIA's Commission Sportive Internationale (CSI) announced that Formula One would be 3 litres or 1.5 litres supercharged from 1966.

Parnelli Jones, winner of the Indianapolis 500 in the 252-cu. in. Offy-engined Agajanian Willard Battery Special. Jones (>1976) was one of the great names at

Indianapolis in the 1960s. Born in 1933, he first entered the 500 in 1961 after a long stint in stock-car and sprint-car racing. He announced his retirement from National

Championship races in 1968 and went on to become a team owner at Indianapolis. In the 1970s he ventured into Formula One with th VPJ4 car.

LEFT: Graham Hill in a BRM, winner of the US Grand Prix at Watkins Glen, New York State, on 6 October. His time was 2 hours 19 minutes 22.1 seconds, 34.2 seconds ahead of team-mate Richie Ginther. Jim Clark, the World Champion and Hill's great rival, finished third.

drivers who by that time had won four World Championship races in a row. John Surtees had always been among Clark's strongest challengers, and at the German Grand Prix he wrested victory from Clark, whose car's engine was not running well. It was Surtees' first World Championship win, and the first for Ferrari since the Italian Grand Prix two years before, in 1961. Mairesse crashed badly in the race and was replaced at Ferrari by Lorenzo Bandini.

In relation to Clark there was an echo of the days of Fangio. Other drivers could win only when he had a problem with his car; when he had no mechanical problems he was unbeatable. The Lotus was on top form at Monza, where Clark finally clinched the Championship by winning the Italian Grand Prix, taking the Constructors' title for Lotus at the same time.

In the US Grand Prix he was left on the line with a flat battery, but even though he started a lap down on everybody else, he finished third, behind Richie Ginther and Graham Hill for BRM. In Mexico – the first time the Mexican Grand Prix was part of the World Championship – he took pole position, led the race all the way, and won again.

The 9 points for the win at Mexico were not added to Clark's score in the World Championship because only the best six results counted – he had won seven of the ten races. Graham Hill was second with 29 points. Clark was only 26 years old, but he was already regarded alongside drivers like Stirling Moss, Juan Manuel Fangio, Alberto Ascari and Tazio Nuvolari as one of those with an aura of invincibility about them. It was not only Grands Prix he won: he was just as much at home in minor races. In his first Championship year (>1965) he drove in 22 other races, winning 13 of them, ranging from saloon car events in a Lotus Cortina to the Milwaukee 200 Indy Car race.

The Monaco Grand Prix was the first of the World Championship season and the grid showed the changes since the previous year. Lola had abandoned Formula One and ATS had folded, so the competition was between the established teams of Ferrari, Lotus, BRM and Cooper, and that of the relative new-comer, Brabham.

Cooper's racing had declined following Jack Brabham's departure. Its last victory had been exactly two years previously at Monaco, when Bruce McLaren had triumphed, and although McLaren had consistently driven into the points, the cars were simply not competitive. Phil Hill had joined Cooper after ATS folded, but he was no longer as fast as he was, and he and McLaren were back on the fifth row of the Monaco grid. Brabham was second fastest in practice, and his team-mate Dan Gurney was on the third row of the grid. Their BT7s had the very latest V-8 Climax engine, and Brabham had retained a space-frame chassis

ABOVE: Jim Clark in a Lotus 25 at the Monaco Grand Prix on 10 May. Clark retired on lap 90 with engine failure. Fourteen of the 16 starters had V-8 engines – the odd ones out were the two V-6 Ferraris. Just six engines were still running at the finish – four BRM and two Coventry-Climax.

LEFT: Graham Hill in a BRM at the Monaco Grand Prix – the distinctive markings on his helmet are those of the London Rowing Club, of which he was a member. Hill is associated with the Monaco Grand Prix more than any other race. He won it five times (>1963, 1964, 1965, 1968, 1969).

rather than a monocoque. BRM had followed Colin Chapman's lead, experimenting first in 1963 with a semi-monocoque – the Type 61, which had a frame at the rear to support the engine – but the Type 261 had a full monocoque for Graham Hill and Richie Ginther, who revelled in the handling of the new car and in the 210 bhp of the BRM V-8. Hill was on the second row of the grid and Ginther on the fourth.

Ferrari announced that they were going to concentrate on sports car racing, like their great rivals, Porsche. Porsche had altogether quit Formula One, but Ferrari still fielded six cars – two with the old V-6 engine, two Tipo 158 'Aeros' with a semi-monocoque chassis and a 210-bhp V-8 engine, and they were developing two 512 V-12 cars, which had a new 220-bhp engine designed by Mauro Forghieri. Forghieri had formed a close working relationship with John Surtees, and morale

in the team was high as a result. Surtees was on the second row of the grid, and Lorenzo Bandini on the fourth.

In pole position was the reigning World Champion, Jim Clark, who had returned from the four-weeks-long qualifying period at Indianapolis to drive a Lotus 25 (the new Lotus 33 was not ready). He went flat out from the start and established a lead of 3 seconds over Brabham on the first lap. Behind them came Graham Hill for BRM, Gurney in a Brabham, and Surtees for Ferrari. Clark led for the first 30 laps, during which both Surtees and Brabham retired. Then he started experiencing handling problems. His roll bar had worked loose, and when it came off he went into the pits for a safety check. Gurney took the lead, Graham Hill just behind. Clark rejoined and challenged them, the three having a great battle, just 2 seconds covering all three cars. Hill in turn began to challenge Gurney, and on lap 53 he took the lead, breaking the lap record in the process. Gurney finally retired with gearbox problems. But even from second place Clark could not catch Hill before his own engine failed. Hill won, his second victory in a row at Monaco; Ginther was second – a great result for BRM.

Brabham, Gurney and Clark all then flew to Indianapolis – Clark and Gurney to drive their new Lotus-Fords, and Brabham to drive the Zink-Urschel Trackburner, a rear-engined Offenhauser-powered special designed by Ron Tauranac. Of the 33 cars on the grid, 21 were front-engined, 18 of them with the traditional four-cylinder 4.2-litre Offy engines, and three with supercharged 2.8-litre V-8 Novis. After Clark's performance the previous year, the emphasis had been on making the roadsters lighter. A. J. Watson had designed both front- and mid-engined cars. A.J. Foyt was driving his front-engined Sheraton-Thompson Special, and Rodger Ward his mid-engined Kaiser Aluminum Leader Card Special, which was powered by a Ford V-8.

Of the twelve mid-engined cars, five used Offys and seven the new Ford V-8. The fuel-injected 4.2-litre Ford in the Lotus 34 gave Clark pole position, his fastest pratice lap 158.828 mph. With such a strong challenger, the race had aroused more than usual interest, and a crowd of 300,000 had gathered to watch as around 13,000 bhp was unleashed through open exhausts.

Clark went into the lead, last year's winner Parnelli Jones a close second in a Watson-Offy Agajanian Special. But on lap 2, Bobby Marsham – driving one of the previous year's Lotus 29s – overtook him, as did Ward in the

BELOW: A narrow escape. Parnelli Jones leaps from his Agajanian Bowes Seal-Fast Special in the pit lane at Indianapolis after the fuel tank caught fire as he rejoined the race following a pit-stop.

MILESTONES

Louie Meyer went to work for Ford, selling his share in Meyer-Drake – the Offenhauser engine business – to his partner Dale Drake.

For the first time in the Indianapolis 500's history, the total purse money exceeded half a million dollars – at $506,575 (>1911, 1993).

Charles Cooper, the Surrey garage-owner, died. His tiny, cheap, 500-cc racing cars ultimately revolutionized the sport worldwide.

The first Formula One Honda, the RA271, made its debut at the German Grand Prix driven by Ronnie Bucknum; he was 11th out of 22.

On 17 July Donald Campbell broke the world land speed record with 403.135 mph in 'Bluebird', a 4,100-hp gas-turbine-powered (jet) car.

Coventry-Climax announced they would not be making engines for the 3-litre Formula One that would come into force in the 1966 season.

ABOVE: Grand Prix newcomer. The monocoque Honda RA271 made its first appearance in August at the German Grand Prix – driven by Ronnie Bucknum. Bucknum, who had never driven a single-seater before, retired with four laps remaining while in eleventh place. The following month, he drove the car again in the Italian Grand Prix and held fifth place for a time, before being forced out with an overheated engine.

RIGHT: The Honda RA271's 60-degree V-12 engine was mounted transversely in the rear of the chassis (>1956). It was the most powerful engine of the 1.5-litre formula - Honda claimed an output of 240 bhp at 11,000 rpm. The engine had four valves per cylinder, together with six twin-choke carburettors and indirect fuel-injection designed by the Japanese Keihin company. Chief designer on the RA271 was Yoshio Nakamura.

Ford-powered Watson. On the same lap Dave MacDonald spun, hitting the wall on Turn 4 and rebounding into Eddie Sachs (>1963). Both cars burst into flames and another five cars hit the wreckage. MacDonald died in the flames, and Sachs died later from burns. The race was stopped. When it restarted, Clark took the lead, followed by Marsham and Gurney, with Jones and Foyt fighting for fourth place. Marsham then passed Clark and established a 20-second lead before an oil pipe broke. Gurney's mixture control jammed. Then Clark's rear left tyre lost its tread, and the wheel collapsed as he headed in towards the infield.

The Lotuses were out, and the fight was now between Jones, Foyt and Ward – all former winners. Jones stopped for fuel, but as he rejoined his car caught fire. Foyt in the front-engined Watson led Ward in the rear-engined Watson, and it was Foyt who won – the last time a front-engined car won the 500. Only five cars finished the 200 laps.

Back on the Grand Prix circuit, Clark won the Dutch and Belgian Grands Prix to take the lead in the World Championship. Then came the French Grand Prix at Rouen – a town resonant in motor racing history since the first-ever race had finished there 70 years previously (>1894). (According to the Automobile Club de France, the Rouen Grand Prix was also the 50th Grand Prix – but it was the 50th only if

BELOW: John Surtees, World Champion. Driving a Ferrari 158, he won the German and Italian Grands Prix, was second in the Dutch, United States and Mexican, and third in the British. Surtees was born in 1934, and started his racing career on British Vincent motorcycles in the early 1950s. He began racing cars in 1960, driving a Formula Junior Cooper-Austin for the Tyrrell team, his privately-owned Cooper-Climax in Formula Two and a works Lotus in Formula One. He joined Ferrari in 1963.

eight of the inter-town races of the first decade of the sport are included; reckoning otherwise, it was the 42nd.)

Clark took the lead, followed by Gurney and Brabham, both of them in Brabhams. Clark retired on lap 30, leaving Gurney in the lead. Then Graham Hill overtook Brabham and chased Gurney – but failed to catch him by just 0.8 second, giving Gurney the first victory for Brabham in a World Championship race. France's historic Grand Prix was an auspicious one for Jack Brabham, who thus became the first man to have his name entered both as winning driver in the race (>1960), and as manufacturer (>1966) – even if the winning driver was Dan Gurney.

Clark in his Lotus never found the form of the previous year. He won the British Grand Prix, but it was John Surtees who won the German and Italian races, and Ferrari's No.2 driver Bandini who won the Austrian Grand Prix – the first time that it had been included in the Championship. Graham Hill won the US Grand Prix for the third time running, putting him in the lead for the Championship, with 39 points to Surtees' 34 and Clark's 30. Any one of them could theoretically win it, so everything depended on the final race in Mexico. Clark started in the lead. Hill was barged by Bandini in one of the new flat-12 Ferraris. With four laps to go, Clark started slowing: he was losing oil pressure. He kept going, but Gurney passed him on the penultimate lap to win. Surtees came in in second place – enough to give him the title when Clark finished fifth.

Surtees' victory was another landmark: the first time anybody had ever been World Champion on both motorcycles and motor cars (albeit at different times).

RIGHT: One of the worst accidents in the history of Indianapolis. Rookie driver Dave MacDonald burned to death in the flaming wreckage of his car after colliding with Eddie Sachs. Sachs also died from burns and a third driver, Ronnie Duman was seriously injured. The race was stopped for 1 hour 43 minutes.

The last year of the 1.5-litre formula did not produce many new ideas as the major constructors prepared for the 3-litre formula the following year. It was Coventry-Climax's last year in the sport, but they produced a new engine for their regular customers: a 32-valve V-8 with eight camshafts, driven by a gear train instead of a chain drive. It produced 213 bhp, as against the 16-valve version's 205 bhp, but it was complicated and proved unreliable. Jim Clark preferred to use the more trusty, older engine.

Tyres were becoming wider but with a smaller perpendicular diameter – 'doughnut-shaped' in cross-section – as designers tried to find ways to convert more of the engine's power into traction. The tyre companies, now paying more attention to racing, produced special compounds to improve performance. Dunlop had been the traditional supplier in Grand Prix racing; Goodyear joined the fray.

Honda had increased its effort, improving the V-12 transverse engine in the RA272 and shedding some of its weight. To increase their cars' competitiveness they signed up Richie Ginther to join Ronnie Bucknum. BRM signed the Scottish driver Jackie Stewart, although he continued to race for Ken Tyrrell in the lower formulas (>1963). Bruce McLaren stayed with Cooper, but he was already planning his own team and had set up a factory at Colnbrook. Cooper signed the Austrian driver Jochen Rindt as No.2. Jack Brabham retained Dan Gurney and also signed up a quiet New

RIGHT: Joy for Colin Chapman as Jim Clark triumphs in the Lotus 38 at Indianapolis – the first win by a European car in the 500 since Howdy Wilcox's Peugeot in 1919. Chapman was renowned for explosive reactions to Lotus victories. He was often photographed throwing his hat high in the air as one of his cars took the chequered flag.

ABOVE: Jim Clark, winner of the Indianapolis 500. Victory came at the third attempt – he had finished second in 1963 and 24th in 1964, after dropping out on lap 47 with a mangled suspension. The winner's share of the $628,399 total purse was $166,621, a huge amount by Grand Prix standards. Clark's total time was 3 hours 19 minutes 5.34 seconds: 150.686 mph.

RIGHT: Pit-stop for A. J. Foyt's 255-cu. in. Ford-engined Lotus 34, the Sheraton-Thompson, during the Indianapolis 500. Foyt was classified 15th after retiring on lap 115. Indianapolis pit crews are famous for their efficiency. Many of the hazards of refuelling were reduced by the new rules requiring alcohol-based fuels rather than petrol.

Zealander, Denny Hulme (>1967). Ferrari continued with John Surtees and Lorenzo Bandini.

Clark won the first race in the World Championship on New Year's Day in South Africa, but neither he nor Dan Gurney were entered for the second, at Monaco, because it clashed with the Indianapolis 500 – which Lotus was now dedicated to winning. During preparation for the new formula there had been an attempt to draw the top level of American motor racing into a common formula, but it had been resisted, partly for the very reason that American racing – with its lucrative prizes – was reluctant to see money drain away to Europe.

Following the MacDonald crash in 1964, safety had been tightened up at Indianapolis. Two pit-stops were made mandatory. Pressure refuelling was banned in favour of gravity tanks, and petrol was banned altogether, the cars being required to run on alcohol-based fuels that were less volatile. On alcohol, cars were less efficient, managing only about 2.5 miles to the (US) gallon, whereas on petrol they had managed around 6.5 miles to the (US) gallon.

Of all the 33 starters, 28 were by now mid-engined, and 17 of them were powered by Ford V-8s which produced just over 500 bhp on alcohol fuel. The two Lotus 34s that had appeared in 1964 were now owned by two of Jim Clark's chief rivals, Parnelli Jones and A.J. Foyt. Colin Chapman had produced a new car for Clark, the Lotus 38, and Dan Gurney was driving the same car under the colours of his All-American Racing Team. Keen competition between the rival Lotus drivers started during qualifying. Clark put in a lap at a record 160.729 mph, only for Foyt to go out and raise it to 161.958 mph – the only two drivers to break the 160 mph barrier.

In the race, Clark and Foyt crossed the start line together, but it was Clark who came out of the first turn in front, with Gurney and Jones in third and fourth – so Lotuses held the first four places. On lap 2 Foyt managed to pass Clark, but Clark fought back and retook the lead on lap 3, each driver fighting for the psychological advantage. Jones then moved up to pass Foyt, and was 11 seconds behind Clark when Foyt retired on lap 116. This time Clark managed to hold on to his advantage, steadily drawing away from Jones to win by two laps – the first time that the Indianapolis 500 had been won by a mid-engined car, and the first time in 48 years that it had been won by a European driver.

While Clark had been at Indianapolis, Graham Hill had won at Monaco for the third time in a row. Once he was back in Europe, Clark showed all his old form and won the next five Grands Prix: the Belgian, French, British, Dutch and German events. By 1 August Clark had an unbeatable 54 points in the World Championship, and Lotus an equally unbeatable aggregate in the Constructors' Championship.

Not since the days of Juan Manuel Fangio had there been such a convincing and consistent driver. All the others could hope for was

MILESTONES

The legendary Alfa-Romeo designer Vittorio Jano (>1923, 1932), who conceived the first single-seater racing car in Europe, died in Italy.

Jules Goux, one of the great Peugeot drivers from before the First World War (>1909) and 1913 Indianapolis 500 winner, died in France.

Mario Andretti won the 'Rookie of the Year' award for third place in a Dean Van Lines Special in his debut at Indianapolis (>1969, 1978).

In 18th place in the 500, Bobby Unser's 2.8-litre 775-bhp Novi was the most powerful racing car since the Mercedes W125 (>1937).

Gordon Johncock was another rookie driver in the Indianapolis 500 (>1973, 1982); he was fifth in a Watson-designed Offy-powered car.

The French company Matra inherited a Formula Three project in a take-over. Jean-Pierre Beltoise won its first victory at Rheims (>1968).

to come second to him, or to profit from some untoward mechanical problem on his car. In the Italian Grand Prix a fuel pump failed, and Jackie Stewart duly won his first World Championship event. In the US Grand Prix a piston broke and Graham Hill won, placing him second in the World Championship.

The last race of the season was in Mexico City on 24 October. John Surtees had crashed in a sports car race in America and was out for the rest of the season. Ferrari tried out its new flat-12 engine with Bandini and Surtees' replacement, Ludovico Scarfiotti. Other than that, the teams were unchanged: Clark for Lotus – who took pole position using the 32-valve Climax engine – Graham Hill and Dan Gurney for BRM, McLaren and Rindt for Cooper, and Ginther and Bucknum for Honda.

With the Championship decided and the formula about to change, there was an end-of-term feel to the pre-race atmosphere. As part of the preparations, all the drivers were to take part in a publicity parade around the circuit driving Renault 8s. The organizers had sadly misjudged them. Instead of parading, they charged off around the circuit doing hand-brake turns, racing each other, some of them even going against the flow of the rest of the parade. Only Clark behaved with anything like proper decorum.

In the race, the British teams were given a shock. Honda's RA272 had been meticulously prepared, its 32-valve engine perfectly tuned to the conditions at 7,500 feet (2,286 metres) above sea level. From the second row of the grid Ginther shot into the lead, and by the first corner he was 50 yards in front of the pack, with Stewart in second place. Clark's engine failed and he retired on lap 8. At the half-way mark, Ginther was leading Dan Gurney for Brabham, and the two Americans had a tremendous battle – Gurney gaining and the lap record falling several times – before Ginther managed to take the chequered flag by just 3 seconds. It was Ginther's first World Championship win, and Honda's first, and it was the first time a World Championship race had been won on Goodyear tyres, throwing down the gauntlet to Dunlop's hitherto pre-eminent position.

So ended the 1.5-litre formula which, like so many changes before it, had inspired considerable progress, affirming the mid-engined design as the only way to build racing cars and

BELOW: The Flying Scotsman. Jackie Stewart in a BRM, heading for victory in the Italian Grand Prix at Monza on 12 September. His first World Championship victory came in the same season as his debut in the competition – in South Africa on 1 January, where he finished sixth.

LEFT: Graham Hill (BRM, No. 30) and Jim Clark (Lotus-Climax, No. 24) ahead of race-winner Jackie Stewart (BRM, No. 32) in the Italian Grand Prix. Clark was the fastest in practice at 1 minute 35.9 seconds (134.123 mph); second and third on the grid were John Surtees in a Ferrari (1 minute 36.1 seconds) and Stewart (1 minute 36.6 seconds). Clark retired on lap 63; Surtees retired on lap 35; Hill finished second.

ABOVE: Mario Andretti, US National Champion. Born in Italy in 1940, Andretti's childhood hero was Alberto Ascari. He was trained as a racing driver in the Italian government's Formula Junior programme. In 1959, the Andretti family moved to Nazareth, Pa., and shortly afterwards he began racing stock-cars and sprint-cars on local tracks. He made his debut in USAC events in 1964.

LEFT: The Lotus-Climax Type 33 was a stronger and lighter version of the Type 25. It had wider wheels than its predecessor and used the latest 13-inch diameter broad-tread Dunlop tyres. The 90-degree V-8 engine had four valves per cylinder and developed 210 bhp at 10,500 rpm. The Type 33 made its debut at the Aintree 200, when Jim Clark crashed it. He won the South African, Belgian, British, Dutch and German Grands Prix in the 33 – and the French in a 25.

consolidating the position of the British kit-car manufacturers. Of the 47 races run in five years, 34 were won using Climax engines, and their support at the top level of racing in Britain was going to be a hard act to follow. Lotus had become a force in the business, winning 22 of those races, and Indianapolis; Jim Clark had won 19 of them and Indianapolis, a record unmatched before in the sport.

To appreciate the measure of the dominance of the British teams and drivers, the record shows that BRM had come good in the period, winning eleven races to Ferrari's nine and Brabham's two; Cooper, in decline, won just the one. Porsche and Honda, both backed by giant companies with huge resources, won one race each.

1966

The first year of the 3-litre formula was one of transition. Few of the teams had made full preparation for the change to 3 litres, and the departure of Coventry-Climax from Formula One left a gaping hole in the British teams' supply of engines. They turned instead to a wide variety of engines. Some went back to the previous formula, using their old 2.5-litre Climaxes; others bored out their more recent 1.5-litre engines; and some linered down American engines, including the Ford V-8 that was gradually taking over from the Offenhauser at Indianapolis.

The first race of the new season was at Monaco. In pole position was Jim Clark, the reigning World Champion, in a Lotus 43 powered by a 1.5-litre V-8 Climax engine enlarged to 2 litres. The car had been designed to take a new engine, the BRM H-16 – a complicated piece of engineering combining two 1.5-litre V-8 engines, which BRM was then still in the process of developing. Next to Clark on the front row was John Surtees in the new flat-12 semi-monocoque Ferrari 312. Ferrari was the best prepared for the new formula, its engine derived from a successful sports car design with fuel injection.

On the second row were Graham Hill and Jackie Stewart in BRMs. They were also waiting for the BRM H-16, and in the meantime they were likewise using bored-out 1.5-litre Climaxes. Behind them was Lorenzo Bandini in a Ferrari with a pre-1961 246 engine, and next to him was Denny Hulme in a Brabham sporting another 2.5-litre vintage engine, a

BELOW: Graham Hill in the American Red Ball Lola-Ford, winner of the Indianapolis 500 at an average 144.317 mph. He qualified 15th fastest with 159.243 mph – and was the first rookie to win since 1927, when George Souders was victorious in a Duesenberg.

ABOVE: The poster for the French Grand Prix, held on the 60th anniversary of the first Grand Prix. It was the last Formula One Grand Prix to be held at Rheims – after 1966 the circuit hosted Formula Two, Three and sports car events. Jack Brabham's winning average for the whole race – 136.9 mph – was an all-time record at Rheims. Lorenzo Bandini in a Ferrari drove the fastest lap in the same race – 141.44 mph – which has stood as the lap record for the circuit to the present day.

sion of the Ford V-8, which proved unsatisfactory, Herd and McLaren turned to an Italian sports car engine, the Serenissima.

Behind McLaren came Jack Brabham in the BT19. Brabham's car still retained a spaceframe and was powered by an engine developed by the Australian spare parts distributor, Repco, who had started with an alloy V-8 Oldsmobile block and added alloy heads, overhead camshafts and fuel injection.

When the race started, Clark stayed stranded and immobile on the grid with a faulty gearbox. Surtees took the lead for Ferrari, Stewart close behind him in the BRM. The pair pulled away from the rest of the field and duelled for 13 laps before the Ferrari's differential broke, leaving Stewart in the lead. Hulme, Brabham and McLaren all retired, and although Bandini managed to pass Graham Hill – denying BRM occupancy of the first two places – Stewart won in record time.

At Indianapolis, the design revolution was nearly complete. There was only one front-engined car in the race, a Watson-Offy driven by Bobby Grim – who was the slowest qualifier at 158.367 mph. In pole position was Mario Andretti in a Brawner-Ford, who had qualified at 165.899 mph. Next to him was Jim Clark in a Lotus, this time painted red rather than British Racing Green: the colour of its sponsor, Scientifically Treated Petroleum (STP), a fuel additive company. There were 24 Ford V-8-engined cars and nine Offenhausers. Among the Ford-powered cars were five from a new and ambitious American team, Eagle, founded by Dan Gurney, the man who had triggered the design revolution with Colin Chapman (>1963). Eagle had grown out of his All-American Racers team of the previous year, and he was no longer only developing cars for Indianapolis: he had additionally established a factory in Britain to build cars for Formula

ABOVE: Jack Brabham (>1979) in a Repco-Brabham taking the chequered flag in the British Grand Prix at Brands Hatch on 16 July. He finished 9.6 seconds ahead of team-mate Denny Hulme.

LEFT: Brabham on the podium after his victory in the Dutch Grand Prix at Zandvoort on 24 July – his third successive Grand Prix win. He went on to claim both the World Drivers' and Constructors' Championships in 1966 –the only time a driver has won the Championship in a car bearing his own name as constructor.

Climax. Then came Jochen Rindt in a T81 Cooper-Maserati.

Cooper had been taken over by the Chipstead Motor Group, a British company with strong links to Maserati. The car had a monocoque chassis with a 2.5-litre engine derived from the Maserati 250F, updated with fuel injection by Giulio Alfieri (>1956).

Behind Rindt on the Monaco grid was Richie Ginther in another Cooper-Maserati, and next to him was Bruce McLaren in the first Formula One car under his own name, the M2B. It had been designed by Robin Herd and had a chassis made of Mallite – a 'sandwich' of two layers of aluminium bonded to balsa wood, which was both light and rigid. Sadly, the M2B did not have a suitable engine. Having experimented with a scaled-down ver-

MILESTONES

Wankel rotary engines and gas-turbine (jet) engines were included in Formula One; capacity specifications were issued subsequently.

BMC Mini Coopers took the first three places in the Monte Carlo Rally – but were disqualified on a technicality over their lights.

Dr Giuseppe Farina, the first World Champion in 1950, died in a car crash on a public road on his way to watch the French Grand Prix.

Ford GT40s took the first three places in the Le Mans 24-hours race. The winners were the New Zealanders Bruce McLaren and Chris Amon.

Road racing in North America expanded with the staging of the first races in the Canadian-American Challenge Cup (Can-Am) series for sports cars.

Robin Herd, an aircraft engineer from the Royal Aircraft Establishment at Farnborough, joined McLaren as a designer.

One. Lloyd Ruby was the team's fastest qualifier on the second row of the grid; Gurney was
back on the seventh row.

Another team with its roots in Formula One
was Lola, whose cars were sponsored by John
Mecom. Three of them had Ford engines – for
Graham Hill, Jackie Stewart and Larry
Dickson – and one had an Offy, for Rodger
Ward. Parnelli Jones drove an Agajanian
Special with a 2.8-litre supercharged Offy.

The race started with a spectacular accident,
and it ended close to farce. Going into Turn 1,
Billy Foster and Gordon Johncock collided,
and 16 cars promptly piled into the wreckage.
Wheels ripped off and flew in all directions.
The race was stopped but, incredibly, nobody
was injured. When it restarted, Clark led the
much-depleted field; Andretti was in second
place until he was black-flagged with smoke
pouring from his car. On lap 62 Clark spun on
Turn 4, finishing up in the infield. The mishap
cost him 25 seconds, and in the meanwhile
Lloyd Ruby had taken over for Eagle. A Lotus-
Eagle battle ensued. Clark led when Ruby
went into the pits, but then spun yet again and
Ruby took the lead once more; Jackie Stewart
inherited second place.

With 350 miles gone, it looked like a win
for Gurney's man. Then smoke started trailing
from his car, becoming thicker and thicker
until he was black-flagged, leaving the lead to
Stewart. Stewart himself retired with ten laps
to go, and Clark thought he was in second
place. According to the Indianapolis timers,
however, Graham Hill had passed him in the
Lola-Ford, so Hill was now officially leading.
The Lotus team were convinced that Clark was
ahead. Both pits signalled their drivers accordingly. Hill finished first, and headed for the

New engines for the 3-litre
formula. Honda's 90-
degree 400-bhp V12 unit
was unveiled in the RA273
at the Italian Grand Prix
(**ABOVE**). Richie Ginther
crashed the car on lap 17.
The lightweight 315-bhp
V-8 Repco (**RIGHT**) which
powered Jack Brabham to
the World Championship
was developed from a
General Motors Olds-
mobile F85 all-aluminium
block. It weighed just 340
pounds.

LEFT: The V-12 engine developed by the Sussex-based Weslake company for American driver Dan Gurney's Eagle car. The light, compact unit – designed by ex-BRM engineer Aubrey Woods – had four valves per cylinder and produced 370 bhp at 9,500 rpm. The new engine first ran on 17 August 1966 and made its racing debut at the Italian Grand Prix. Gurney retired on lap eight after the oil filter collapsed.

LEFT: The H-16 BRM making its debut at Monza in the Italian Grand Prix. The engine had two flat-8 banks of cylinders laid one above the other developing 400 bhp. It was a complicated engine, prone to breakdowns: Graham Hill and Jackie Stewart in H-16 BRMS and Jim Clark in an H-16-engined Lotus were all forced to retire.

Victory Lane, acknowledging the cheers from the grandstand. Then Clark came round and did the same. Chapman protested loudly – but the official result stood, and a second British name went up on the winners list.

John Surtees won the Belgian Grand Prix for Ferrari, then left the team after disagreements with the team manager over the allocation of cars. The next race was the French Grand Prix at Rheims, on the sixtieth anniversary of the first-ever Grand Prix (>1906). Surtees was on the front row of the grid, now in a works Cooper-Maserati, and there was a Ferrari on both sides of him: Bandini in pole position, and Mike Parkes, who had replaced him in the Ferrari team. Surtees roared away from the grid, only to be left stranded when his

fuel pump drive immediately sheared. Bandini took the lead, followed by Brabham in the Brabham-Repco. The Ferraris were faster than the Brabham-Repco, and Brabham had to slip-stream Bandini to keep up, only losing the tow when they started to lap back-markers. Suddenly Bandini's accelerator snapped, and Brabham was leading – although Parkes was gaining on him. Brabham judged the race perfectly, allowing Parkes to gain but keeping just enough in hand, without breaking the car, to win.

The sixtieth anniversary of the first Grand Prix thus represented another landmark in motor racing: the first victory by a driver in a car that also carried his name as constructor. The quiet, dignified Australian went on to win the next three Grands Prix, also taking the World Championship (his third) and the Constructors' Championship (his first) – still a unique double.

RIGHT: Graham Hill in a Lotus 33 powered by a V-8 BRM engine during the Monaco Grand Prix. Lotus decided after the South African Grand Prix that running their BRM H-16-engined cars was too costly – so for Monaco they used the V-8 instead. Hill drove a superb race despite faulty brakes and clutch, finishing second behind Denny Hulme's Brabham-Repco.

The transitional period between the old and the new formulas continued into the early part of the second year of the 3-litre era. Each race took on its own character, with its own distinctive elements. Some harked back to past glories; others saw the decline of apparent certainties. Still more signposted the future.

The most futuristic idea came in the Indianapolis 500, where the first gas-turbine car not only made its debut, but came within a whisker of winning. It was the brainchild of Andy Grantanelli, an entrant at Indianapolis since 1946, and a great publicist. One of his businesses was the fuel additive STP, and the 'jet' car was painted in STP red. Grantanelli commissioned Ken Wallis to build the car around a lightweight Pratt & Whitney jet helicopter engine which produced 550 hp, using the power to drive all four wheels.

Indianapolis' racing establishment had risen to the challenge of the British invasion. The Lotuses of Jim Clark and Graham Hill were well down the list of qualifiers. For the first time, all 33 cars qualified at over 160 mph, Parnelli Jones sixth fastest in the STP Special, christened the 'Whooshmobile' by the press. In the race, Jones went into the lead in dramatic style, passing four cars on the outside of Turn 1 and taking the lead from Mario Andretti after Turn 2. He then led for most of the race, looking a certain winner. With three laps to go, however, a bearing failed and he retired. On the last lap there was a five-car pile-up just in front of the grandstands, and it was A.J. Foyt who picked his way through the smoke and debris at 50 mph to win – the fourth three-time 500 winner (>1936, 1940, 1948).

MILESTONES

Phil Hill, the first American World Champion, retired to pursue his career as a classic car restorer, journalist and race commentator.

Tony Vandervell died. His Vanwall team had given British motor racing a model of organization and excellence in the 1950s.

After a brief career as a driver, Frank Williams started business in his Harrow flat, dealing in and racing Brabham cars (>1980, 1993).

Maserati (>1932) finally departed from Grand Prix racing when their contract to supply engines to Cooper expired.

The land speed record driver Donald Campbell was killed on Coniston Water attempting to break the world water speed record (>1964).

The International Grand Prix Medical Service was established to provide specialist trackside facilities and to assist local doctors.

The World Championship had kicked off with the South African Grand Prix. Enzo Ferrari did not enter his cars. He was engaged in a long-standing duel with Ford, which had produced the GT40 to challenge Ferrari's domination of sports car racing, and Ferrari was concentrating on winning at Le Mans. Dan Gurney's Eagle team of beautiful Formula One cars was at Kyalami – another element in the American counter-offensive against the European invasion at Indianapolis. But their Weslake engines, built near Rye in Sussex, England, were not ready, and Gurney was using a four-cylinder 2.5-litre Climax. The Lotus drivers, Clark and Hill (who had joined from BRM), were driving Lotus 43s

with the unreliable BRM H-16 engine. In the race, Denny Hulme led, in a Brabham-Repco BT19, until he had to stop for attention to his brakes. Jim Clark's car overheated and Hill crashed, and the race was won by Pedro Rodriguez in a Cooper-Maserati – Cooper's last Grand Prix victory (>1958).

The new Brabham-Repco BT24 was unveiled at Monaco. Ron Tauranac had persisted with the space-frame chassis, using the unspectacular (but reliable) Repco V-8 engine which produced 330 bhp, compared with around 400 bhp from the opposition. Ferrari entered three V-12 312s for Lorenzo Bandini, Chris Amon (a young New Zealander) and Ludovico Scarfiotti. Richie Ginther, who was driving for Eagle, was too slow in practice to secure a place on the grid, and having failed also to qualify for Indianapolis he retired from racing. In the Monaco Grand Prix, Bandini held the lead while the field thinned out behind him through retirements. At the half-way mark Hulme managed to pass him. Then Bandini's car overturned and caught fire; he was trapped inside and burned. Hulme won, but Bandini died four days later.

Colin Chapman chose the Dutch Grand Prix at Zandvoort for the debut of his latest creation, the Lotus 49. It was not Chapman's own design: he had taken on Maurice Phillippe, another car designer who had started in the aviation industry. The idea behind it was to use a monocoque chassis, but instead of siting the engine in it, bolting it straight on to the back of it, right behind the driver, complete with gearbox, drive shafts and rear sus-

LEFT: Rounding the chicane between the tunnel and the Tabac corner in the Monaco Grand Prix. Bruce McLaren's McLaren-BRM leads from Dan Gurney's Eagle-Weslake, John Surtees' Honda and Jack Brabham's Brabham-Repco. McLaren came fourth; Gurney, Surtees and Brabham retired.

RIGHT: The start of the British Grand Prix at Silverstone. Jochen Rindt's Cooper-Maserati (No. 11) and Chris Amon's Ferrari (No. 8) trail Dan Gurney's Eagle-Weslake (No. 9), Jack Brabham's Brabham-Repco (No. 1) and Denny Hulme's Brabham-Repco (No. 2). Hulme finished second, Amon came third, Brabham was fourth; Rindt and Gurney retired.

pension. And the engine itself was completely new, the Cosworth V-8 DFV, giving about 400 bhp. It was the product of Chapman's successfully persuading Ford to back Keith Duckworth to produce a new unit from their four-cylinder four-valve Formula Two engine, the Four-Valve A (FVA). They put two FVAs together – hence the name 'Double Four-Valve' (DFV). Hill took pole position, breaking the lap record, then he led the race until a camshaft drive broke, and he retired. Clark then gave the new car a debut win.

The Eagle team arrived for the Belgian Grand Prix fresh from Dan Gurney's victory in the Le Mans 24-hour race in the Ford GT40. He won at Spa, the first 'all-American' victory in a Grand Prix for 46 years (>1921). The French Grand Prix started out as a duel between the reliable, if perhaps rather dated Brabhams, and the new, brasher Lotuses. Reliability triumphed over novelty – both Lotuses dropped out. Brabham won the race, with Hulme second.

It had been a bad year for Enzo Ferrari, who fielded only the one car for Amon at Silverstone for the British Grand Prix. Mike Parkes had crashed badly at Spa; his promising career was over before it had really started. The race was between the two Lotuses, the two Brabhams, and Amon's Ferrari. Clark (Lotus) led at a furious pace, and the five front-runners lapped the rest of the field. Then Hill's engine broke. But Clark's held out – and he won his fifth British Grand Prix. The Brabhams triumphed in the next two Grands

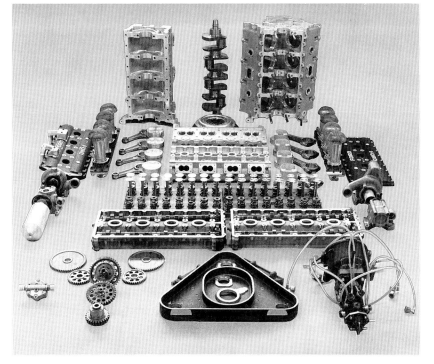

Prix: Hulme won in Germany with Brabham second, then those positions were reversed at the Canadian Grand Prix. It was that Grand Prix – the first in Canada to count towards the Championship – that Bruce McLaren chose for the debut of his new car, the M5A, powered by the new BRM V-12 engine. He had abandoned Mallite and returned to aluminium for the chassis. In the race, he came seventh after his engine started misfiring badly because of a flat battery.

ABOVE: The Ford Double Four Valve (DFV) engine was built for Lotus by Cosworth Engineering. The engine made a triumphant debut at the Dutch Grand Prix on 4 June, when Jim Clark won at 104.44 mph. DFV-engined cars took pole position for the following eleven Grands Prix.

LEFT: Sports-car racing used 'wings' before Formula One. The Chaparral 2E (No. 66, far left, in the Riverside leg of the Can-Am Challenge Cup series) was the latest in a successful string of sports cars built by Texans Jim Hall and James 'Hap' Sharp. The 2E's aerofoil (or wing) was attached to the rear suspension, not the chassis – and its angle could be changed by the driver. A sister car, the 2F – also with a wing – was driven to victory in the 1967 Brands Hatch 500 Miles Race by Phil Hill and Mike Spence.

Honda then unveiled its new car, the V-12 RA3000, at the Italian Grand Prix. It had been built by John Surtees at Slough, near London, close to the Lola factory. The press christened it the 'Hondola'.

The race was the high point of an exciting season. Gurney led until his engine failed. Clark took over, but then suffered a puncture which cost him a complete lap. He rejoined well behind the leaders, and started on the seemingly impossible task of passing the leaders twice to take the lead. He used Hill's slipstream to pass them the first time – but Hill's engine then packed up and Brabham took the lead. As the end of the race approached, Clark had made up the deficit. He passed Brabham and went into the lead – only to run out of fuel on the final lap. Brabham and Surtees then raced wheel-to-wheel to the flag without asking for, or giving, any quarter. Surtees won, giving Honda its first European Grand Prix victory.

Jim Clark finished the season on a high note, winning the United States Grand Prix (which he finished with one wheel hanging loose) and the Mexican race, raising his tally to four, against two each for Brabham and Hulme in their Brabham-Repcos. But the Brabham team took the honours in the Championships because of their cars' reliability, having finished most races in the points. Denny Hulme took the World Drivers' Championship, with Brabham in second place and Clark third; Brabham took his second Constructors' Championship.

ABOVE: Denny Hulme won the 1967 World Championship driving for Brabham-Repco. Hulme won the Monaco and German Grands Prix, was second in the French, British and Canadian and third in the Mexican, US and Dutch Grands Prix. He also drove a McLaren-Chevrolet as half of Bruce McLaren's winning team in the Can-Am Challenge series in the United States. New Zealand-born Hulme drove for the Brabham Formula Junior team in 1962–3, and had occasional races in Formula One in 1964–5 before joining the Brabham Formula One team in 1966.

CHAPTER TEN
COSWORTH, WINGS &
FREEDOM FOR ALL

The 1960s were years of change in the Western World. In music, fashion, business and morality, the old, hierarchical order gave way to a new, individual, freer age. Ideas were tested for viability rather than for acceptability.

Motor racing was no exception. The combination of social, economic and technical forces that produced Bob Dylan, Carnaby Street and *That Was the Week That Was* also produced the Cosworth racing engine and shapely racing cars smothered in advertising: the seeds of teams like McLaren and Williams, which dominate the sport today. Overt commercialism – advertising on cars – was banned in Grands Prix until 1968, when the older men on the governing bodies succumbed to the demands of younger people who wanted change so that they could make money. Talent had become a commodity – and supreme talent, in a competitive world, commanded huge attention and made millionaires of people overnight.

Into this new fluid world, opened up by young, can-do people, came the Cosworth DFV engine, the single most important factor in reinforcing the new entrepreneurial spirit in motor racing. Colin Chapman, Bruce McLaren, Ken Tyrrell, Frank Williams, John Surtees, the founders of March, and Graham Hill built their livelihoods around it. With that common factor they then struggled to beat each other through their own engineering inspiration and excellence in chassis design, particularly in aerodynamics.

Getting it right brought success. Winning attracted sponsorship, which produced the money for more ingenious engineering and more success – a virtuous circle for those who could make it work. Some succeeded beyond their wildest dreams; others failed to combine the necessary range of talents. Some died attempting it – and all saw others die pushing cars through new frontiers of design and technology, as the racing car went through a period of evolution as swift and far-reaching as any in its history.

Legendary power. The Cosworth DFV engine (>1983) was used by the World Champion driver every year from 1968 to 1976 – with the exception of 1975, when Niki Lauda won the Championship in a Ferrari. To the present day, the DFV has won more Grands Prix than any other engine.

1968

It was a watershed year for the British teams in Grand Prix. The gaping hole left by the departure of Coventry-Climax from racing had been filled by Cosworth. Lotus had had exclusive use of the DFV engine for 1967, but in 1968 any team that could afford £7,500 could buy one. A new era was about to begin.

The first race of the season was in South Africa, where the Lotus Team appeared in British Racing Green for the last time. Colin Chapman had negotiated a deal with Imperial Tobacco for the works team to be known as Gold Leaf Team Lotus, and the cars would henceforward be painted red and white, the colours of the cigarette packet. Lotus' star driver, Jim Clark, took pole position and won; Graham Hill – the team's No.2 – came in in second place.

It was Clark's 25th Championship victory, putting him one ahead of Juan Manuel Fangio's record (>1958). On 7 April he was driving one of the new Gold Leaf-liveried cars in a Formula Two race at Hockenheim in Germany. The track was wet, there were no safety barriers, and trees lined the circuit. Nobody witnessed Clark crash into the trees at speed; he died before reaching hospital. His death was a huge blow to Lotus, and was felt keenly throughout a sport that had lost its most talented driver.

Lotus was at the top, and Clark had been central to Colin Chapman's plans on both sides of the Atlantic. Sports car sales were buoyant and profitable, much of it on the back of publicity gained from success in Formula One. With a full commitment to Grand Prix, Chapman was also tackling Indianapolis again (>1963), this time with the Lotus 56, a gas-turbine-powered car backed by Andy Grantanelli (>1967).

First the Ford V-8 engine, and now jet engines, had shaken Dale Drake and Leo Goosen (>1919) at Offenhauser, destroying their virtual monopoly on supplying engines for the Indianapolis 500, the top race in America. They suffered financially, and in determined response produced a 168-cu.in. (2.75-litre) turbocharged four-cylinder engine. Turbochargers were another way of forcing fuel and air into the engine under pressure. The compressor was powered by a small turbine driven by the exhaust gases as they were expelled through the exhaust pipe, rather than through gears direct from the engine (a supercharger; >1923). It had the advantage of being 'free', rather than taking power from the engine, and had been used on aircraft and truck engines for many years. Drake and Goosen managed to boost the power of the

MILESTONES

The Automobile Club de France was renamed the Fédération Française du Sport Automobile; the ACF Grand Prix officially became the French Grand Prix (>1895, 1906).

Jo Siffert's victory in the British Grand Prix in a Lotus 49B for the Rob Walker team was the last Grand Prix victory for a private entrant (>1958).

The Italian driver Ludovico Scarfiotti (>1965) lost his life driving a Porsche Spyder in practice for the Rossfeld Hill Climb in Germany.

Mario Andretti took pole position in a Lotus 49B in his first Grand Prix, the United States race; he retired with clutch failure (>1969, 1978).

Honda withdrew from Formula One at the end of the season having won two Grands Prix and come fourth in the Constructors' Championship once, in 1967.

Dan Gurney withdrew the Eagle team (>1967) from Formula One after one Grand Prix victory in order to concentrate its efforts on racing in America.

RIGHT: It's the money that counts. Huge costs were incurred running a Grand Prix team – most of all in moving the cars, drivers and a large technical crew to races around the world. Lotus clinched a lucrative sponsorship deal with Imperial Tobacco – manufacturers of Gold Leaf cigarettes – and became known as Gold Leaf Team Lotus.

LEFT: Defending World Champion Denny Hulme in the McLaren-Ford M7A (No. 1). The M7A used the engine as a load-bearing member of the chassis – as in the Lotus 49. Hulme won two Grands Prix and finished third in the World Championship table. It was his first season with Bruce McLaren after leaving Jack Brabham's team.

BELOW: Mario Andretti in a Lotus-Ford at Monza – where he planned to make his Formula One debut in the Italian Grand Prix. After practice, he flew to the United States to take part in the Hoosier 100. He then returned to Monza, but was barred for taking part in another race in the 24 hours before a World Championship event.

new Offy right up to 650 bhp at 8,000 rpm.

Thirteen of the cars on the grid for the 500 chose the new Offy, although Dan Gurney and his All-American Racers chose to stick with the Ford. Bobby Unser was driving an Offy-powered Eagle.

There was resistance to gas-turbine engines at Indianapolis. The racing establishment had been shaken by the first onslaught of new technology from Britain, and the name of Lotus linked to jet engines worried teams' owners and drivers, and they lobbied the USAC hard to restrict gas-turbine power output. The limit for the area of the air intake had previously been set at 23.99 square inches, but for 1968 – following the performance of Grantanelli's jet car in 1967 – the USAC reduced it to 15.99 square inches, forcing Lotus to reduce the size of the compressor in the engine, limiting power to around 430 bhp.

The Lotus 56 had the engine in the back, driving all four wheels. But its most striking feature was its overall shape – it looked like a wedge of cheese, the nose very close to the ground at the front, sloping uniformly to the rear. The idea was to use the whole body to create an aerodynamic downforce, increasing traction, making better use of the power and improving cornering. Four cars were produced: one for Clark, one for Hill, one for an American driver to be nominated by

Grantanelli, and one spare. Clark's place in the team was taken by Mike Spence who, during practice, drove the second fastest lap ever at the Speedway, at 169.55 mph. During a later practice session he hit the wall: a front wheel came off, hit him, and killed him. Coming just a month after the death of Clark, it was too much for Chapman. He went back to Europe, leaving the team to Grantanelli, who in turn was having a running battle with the authorities over safety and conformity with the regulations.

The three remaining turbine cars were driven by Graham Hill and two Indianapolis veterans, Joe Leonard and Art Pollard. Leonard took pole position with 171.599 mph; Hill took second spot at 171.208 mph, and Bobby Unser's turbocharged Eagle-Offy was third on the grid at 169.507 mph.

Leonard led at the start, but Unser passed him on lap 7 before Lloyd Ruby in another turbo-Offy car passed him too. Leonard was under orders to let them lead, then use his extra speed at the end when they thought he was not in contention. So Unser and Ruby swapped the lead while Leonard kept in contact in third place. Hill was fourth, but on lap 112 hit the wall. Chapman – back from Europe and in the pits – reportedly turned

ashen as the public address system announced Hill had crashed – but Hill was in fact unhurt.

Leonard made his bid on lap 175, and took the lead as Ruby dropped back with magneto problems. Then on lap 182 the yellow flags came out for an accident, and everybody had to slow down. The jet-powered cars were unhappy running slowly: their air-intake pressure and jet-pipe temperature increased and the engine began overheating. They also had slower acceleration, so when the green lights came on again, Leonard put his foot on the floor and the engine responded by 'flaming out' – that is, by stopping. The same thing happened to Pollard. Unser shot by, to win a great victory for the Offy engine. But coming so close for a second time was the last straw for gas-turbine cars, which have never raced at the Speedway since.

Two deaths in a month, followed by failure at Indianapolis, might have caused Lotus to fall apart. That it didn't was largely due to the courage and determination of Graham Hill. Taking the pressure on his shoulders, he won two Grands Prix – in Spain and at Monaco – even while qualifying for Indianapolis.

The design experience of the wedge-shaped Lotus 56 was incorporated into the Lotus 49, now called the 49B, with a rising extension at

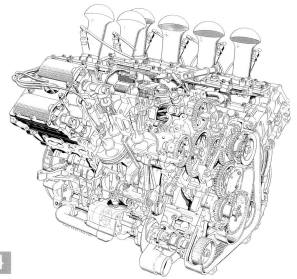

BELOW: The four-camshaft V-8 Ford Cosworth DFV engine which took Graham Hill to the World Drivers' Championship and gave Lotus the Constructors' title. It had Lucas ignition and fuel injection, developing 410 bhp at 9,000 rpm. Lotus's Colin Chapman played a crucial role in the engine's development: he was responsible for introducing Mike Costin and Keith Duckworth – partners in Cosworth Engineering, which manufactured the DFV -and also for persuading Ford to pay the engine's £100,000 research and development costs.

ABOVE: The new Honda RA302 had a 120-degree 32-valve V-8 air-cooled engine. Large ducts led the air to crankcase and cylinder heads. Using fuel injection, it developed 390 bhp at 10,500 rpm. Following Jo Schlesser's fatal crash in the car on its debut in the French Grand Prix on 7 July, a second RA302 was tried in practice for the Italian Grand Prix two months later – but did not race because of handling problems.

RIGHT: Downforce. In the US Grand Prix, the pressure exerted by the front wing broke the nose cone on Mario Andretti's Lotus. He soldiered on, retiring on lap 33 for a different reason – a faulty clutch.

LEFT: The racing car sprouts wings (>1969). Every car in the Canadian Grand Prix at St-Jovite on 22 September used some kind of aerofoil. The effect of the aerofoil was to push the car down, increasing traction. One of the main reasons for its popularity was that it enabled designers to make effective use of the extra power available from the Ford Cosworth DFV engine.

the rear, over the engine. The wedge shape pointed to the increasing importance of aerodynamics in racing car design. To make full use of the extra power of the DFV engine, designers looked for ways to increase traction. The effect of the wedge was to increase the downforce on the tyres, which were also becoming wider, providing a greater area of rubber in contact with the road. Then designers found a way to go a stage further, using the airflow more directly to push the car down on the road and improve traction. Brabham and Ferrari appeared at the Belgian Grand Prix with aerofoils, or 'wings', mounted on struts above the rear of their cars. The aerofoil was a small, inverted aircraft wing which, in technical terms, exerted its lift downwards, increasing traction. To compensate, small winglets were added on both sides of the nose cone to produce a downforce on the front wheels as well. There was little benefit at speed on the straights, where they produced additional frontal area which slowed the cars down. Their real advantage came on the corners, enabling higher speeds through increased traction. Chris Amon, in his winged Ferrari, was fastest in practice at Spa. Both the Lotuses retired with drive shaft failures. Bruce McLaren won the race in his new M7A.

RIGHT: Death of a hero – the wreckage of Jim Clark's Lotus after the crash at Hockenheim in which he was killed. Sudden and violent death was an ever-present risk in motor racing. From the late 1960s on, the top drivers – led by Jackie Stewart – campaigned vigorously and successfully for improved safety measures in the design of tracks and for emergency medical aid.

The Dutch Grand Prix saw a new name in the World Championship winners' records: Matra. Ken Tyrrell, whose team had been successful in the lower formulas, ordered DFVs as soon as he heard that they would be available to everybody. He also had one of the top drivers, in Jackie Stewart, and he had financial backing from the Dunlop Tyre company. All he lacked was a chassis to put them in. For some years he had used Matra chassis in his Formula Two cars, and he now turned to them. Matra, who had also been a successful in Formula Two, was also planning to move to Formula One – in which France had not been represented since 1957. They were sponsored by the Elf oil company and by the French government, which had stepped in with a grant of 6 million francs (£800,000). Matra had a V-12 engine under development for Formula One racing, and when Tyrrell approached them with some of the best engines in racing, they were happy to supply chassis. Elf even provided financial assistance to Tyrrell, whose team became known as Matra International, while the Matra works team was called Elf-Matra. Tyrrell's DFV-engined car was the MS10, driven by Jackie Stewart, and the Elf-Matra V-12 car, the MS11, was driven by Jean-Pierre Beltoise. Both teams were represented at the Dutch Grand Prix, which Stewart won; Beltoise came in second – a Matra double that left their backers jubilant . . . although some might have preferred the result the other way round.

Colin Chapman embraced aerofoils enthusiastically, going a stage further still. At the French Grand Prix the Lotus 49Bs appeared with wings mounted directly on to the suspension struts, bringing the downforce to bear more effectively on the wheels. It was a brave move: at 150 mph the additional downforce was around 400 pounds (181 kilograms), putting more stress on many parts of the car, especially the suspension. There were other dangers. When Jackie Oliver – the new Lotus driver – crossed the slipstream of another car

ABOVE: Jacky Ickx's Ferrari passing the blazing remains of Jo Schlesser's air-cooled Honda RA302 in the French Grand Prix at Rouen. Schlesser was burned alive in the crash – on his Formula One debut.

in practice, the sudden change in airflow over it abruptly robbed the car of its traction and it slid off the track, hitting a concrete gatepost. Fortunately, the monocoque protected Oliver, who escaped unscathed.

The French Grand Prix saw the debut of another new car, the Honda RA302, built entirely by Honda, which had a V-8 air-cooled engine. At Rouen its engine was misfiring, it was tricky to handle, and the circuit was wet: John Surtees declined to drive it. He stuck to his older RA301. Honda took on a French driver, Jo Schlesser. In the race, Schlesser lost control, crashed, and was killed. Jacky Ickx won for Ferrari, with Surtees in second place.

Monza, with its mixture of very fast straights and corners, was a challenge for the 'winged' cars. Several teams experimented with movable aerofoils, reducing the angle of incidence – and thereby the frontal area – on the straights, minimising the adverse effect, then increasing the angle on the corners to give maximum downforce. After a hard-fought race during which Surtees, McLaren, Stewart and Jo Siffert all led at various points, Denny Hulme won for McLaren.

The World Championship table was close: Hill, Stewart and Hulme were all capable of winning, depending on the result of the last race in Mexico. Hill rose to the occasion, taking the Drivers' title himself and securing the year's Constructors' Championship for Colin Chapman and Lotus. In eighth place was Vic Elford in a Cooper. Cooper had lost its sponsorship from the petrol giant BP, and the company that had brought about the revolution in racing car design declined steadily through the year. Mexico was the venue for its last works entry (>1959, 1969).

LEFT: Bobby Unser, winner of the Indianapolis 500 and US National Champion. He won four of the first five races on the USAC schedule – at Las Vegas; Phoenix, Arizona; Trenton, New Jersey; and Indianapolis – and finished the season 11 points ahead of Mario Andretti in the Championship.

LEFT: Front row for the Indianapolis 500: Bobby Unser in the Offy-engined Eagle (No. 3); Graham Hill's turbine-engined Lotus (No. 70); and Joe Leonard in pole position in another turbine Lotus (No. 60). Unser won; Hill crashed; Leonard retired. Unser's victory was the first for a supercharged car since 1946, when George Robson won in a Thorne Engineering Sparks.

In Grand Prix racing, the quest to make better use of the power of the DFV engine continued. Movable aerofoils were developed further, most teams adding a second wing over the front wheels as well. Lotus, Matra and McLaren also started experimenting with four-wheel-drive, to produce the Lotus 63, the Matra MS84 and the McLaren M9A respectively.

In the pre-season jostling for the best cars, Jochen Rindt moved from Brabham to Lotus, while Jacky Ickx joined Brabham from Ferrari which, with no new car, continued with only Chris Amon. John Surtees moved to BRM following the departure of Honda, where he was joined by Jackie Oliver from Lotus. Bruce McLaren and Denny Hulme continued at McLaren.

The two Matra teams merged. Jean-Pierre Beltoise joined Jackie Stewart in Ken Tyrrell's Elf-International team, while Elf-Matra concentrated on sports car racing. The V-12 Matra engine proved uncompetitive against the DFV: whereas the Tyrrell-run team, with Cosworth engines, had finished the previous season in third place in the Constructors' Championship with 45 points, Elf-Matra had only scored 8. The new Matra car, the MS80, had a monocoque chassis that was 15 kilograms (33 pounds) lighter than the MS10, even with larger fuel tanks for the new, thirstier DFV. Stewart gave the team a good start to the season, winning the South African Grand Prix in his MS10, before he gave the MS80 its debut at a non-Championship race at Brands Hatch – and won.

Then came the Spanish Grand Prix at Barcelona. Aerofoils had grown and multiplied, most teams running with wider wings front and aft, and mounted higher to get them out of the car's turbulence and the slipstreams of other cars. The Lotus 49B had a fourth pedal next to the clutch that enabled the driver to alter the incidence of the wing – to optimise the downforce either for speed on the straights or for adhesion on the corners. At one point in the Barcelona circuit there was a dip in the road. As the cars went into it at speed, they sank on the suspension then lifted as they came out. The Lotus aerofoils had been stressed to take the effect of the extra download – but not the upload that followed. On the third lap Graham Hill's wing snapped just as he came out of the dip, and he crashed into the barriers, unhurt. He quickly realized that the failure had been caused by the continuous flexing of the aerofoil by repeatedly going through the dip during practice and the race. He tried to get a message to the Lotus pits to warn Rindt, but he was too late. On the next lap Rindt's wing gave way at exactly the same spot, and he crashed within yards of Hill's car. Rindt was badly hurt. Later in the race, the wing on Ickx's Ferrari bent in the middle, and he retired.

It was a brush with death that the authorities could not ignore. Concerns had been expressed about aerofoils already, and when the teams gathered for the Monaco Grand Prix two weeks later, the CSI met in emergency session. During practice aerofoils were banned. The drivers and the teams protested, and for a time the decision was reversed, then it was reversed again with a promise to publish rules governing wing size in time for the

BELOW: To make the fullest use of the power of the Cosworth DFV engine, designers turned to aerodynamics to produce a downforce – which pushed the car more firmly against the track, increasing traction between the tyres and the road surface. The device used was an aeroplane wing, but instead of producing lift the wing was turned upside down to provide the downforce.

MILESTONES

March Engineering was formed in April with a factory at Bicester, Oxfordshire, to make and race cars in Formulas One, Two and Three (>1970, 1983).

The remaining assets of the Cooper racing team (>1955) were auctioned off on 11 June. John Cooper bought a garage business in Sussex.

The CSI amended the rules for Formula One to make it obligatory for all cars to be fitted with an on-board fire extinguisher.

To relieve the financial difficulties brought about by Ferrari's protracted sports car duel with Ford, Fiat bought a 50% share in the company.

Nobody invested in gas-turbine-powered cars at Indianapolis once the rules were changed to limit air-intake size to 11.99 square inches.

Full-face 'Bell Star' helmets, with a bridge around the lower jaw and a visor, were used for the first time in the Indianapolis 500.

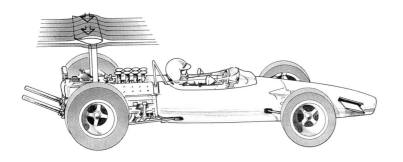

next race, the Dutch Grand Prix.

In the Monaco race, Stewart took pole position in the MS80 and led from Amon and Hill for nine laps, until a drive shaft broke. Hill then passed Amon to win his fifth Monaco Grand Prix – his last World Championship victory. The CSI then announced that aerofoils would have to be mounted no higher than 80 centimetres (31½ inches) above the underside of the car, and could be no wider than 110 centimetres (43½ inches).

At Indianapolis the USAC had also

BELOW: Experimenting with aerofoils during practice for the Monaco Grand Prix – Pedro Rodriguez removed the front wings on his V12 BRM. He was 14th on the grid; in the race he retired on lap 16.

ABOVE: John Surtees' V12 BRM – with wings – during the first day's practice for the Monaco Grand Prix. Because of the authorities' ban on the use of aerofoils, practice times from the first day were ruled out. Surtees took sixth place on the starting grid – his best practice time 1.4 seconds slower than pole-winner Jackie Stewart.

LEFT: John Surtees' BRM between practice sessions at the Monaco Grand Prix. Monaco was an odd place for a controversy over aerofoils – wings made little difference on the twisting, low-speed circuit. In the race, Surtees retired following a dramatic accident with Jack Brabham's V8 Brabham-Cosworth just before the tunnel on lap 10.

rewritten its rules. The advent of high-mounted aerofoils in Formula One had caused alarm, and fearing another invasion from Europe the USAC limited the overall height of the body to achieve broadly the same result. They also reduced the area of the intake for gas-turbine-powered cars still further, to 11.99 square inches – making them hopelessly uncompetitive; so nobody built them. Turbocharged engines were also limited to 162 cubic inches (2.65 litres), rather than the 171 (2.8) of previous years. Ford also produced turbocharged engines and in this year's 500 – with the exception of Dan Gurney's 319-cu.in. (5.23-litre) Weslake and two Brabham-Repcos – all the engines were turbocharged Fords or Offys.

Having failed to establish the gas-turbine engine at Indianapolis, Andy Grantanelli turned again to Lotus to build a four-wheel-drive conventionally-engined car, the Lotus 64, to be driven by Mario Andretti, Graham Hill and Jochen Rindt. In early practice Andretti drove a lap at 171.657 mph – then the right rear hub broke: he crashed and was badly burned. Once the fault was discovered, the Lotus 64s were withdrawn and Andretti hired a Ford-powered Hawk.

A.J. Foyt took pole position in his Offy-powered Coyote at 170.568 mph, compared with Andretti's 169.851 in second place. Bobby Unser was in third place on the grid alongside a rookie driver, Mark Donohue (>1972), driving for Roger Penske's team (>1978). The race was a taut contest between Foyt and Andretti, until Foyt dropped out on lap 181. Mario Andretti won, giving Andy Grantanelli his first victory in the 500.

In Grand Prix racing there was no competition for the Ford-Cosworth. In the Monaco Grand Prix DFV-powered cars had taken the first six places, and in the French race they took the first nine. Stewart was the dominant driver – he won the French Grand Prix, with Beltoise second in a Matra-Ford – and, having

LEFT: Jacques-Bernard ('Jacky') Ickx in a Brabham BT26 at the Spanish Grand Prix. He retired six laps from the end with a broken rear wishbone on the Brabham, but qualified as a finisher having covered more than 90 per cent of the distance. He ended the season second in the World Championship with 37 points, behind Jackie Stewart with 63.

ABOVE: The 430-bhp four-wheel-drive Lotus 63 first appeared at the Dutch Grand Prix on 21 June, but did not race. John Miles drove it in its racing debut in the French Grand Prix at Clermont-Ferrand on 6 July. He retired after just one lap with fuel pump trouble. The car retired from every World Championship Grand Prix it entered in 1969.

won four out of five races, already had a good lead in the World Championship when the teams arrived at Silverstone for the British Grand Prix. During the two-hour official practice session there were 100 prizes for the fastest lap within each of the half-hour stages. Stewart crashed during practice, and then qualified in Beltoise's car while Beltoise took over the four-wheel-drive MS84.

The British Grand Prix confirmed that Rindt represented the best hope for Lotus against the rapidly-rising Tyrrell-Matra star. Stewart and Rindt were great friends, but there

was no quarter asked or given, especially that day at Silverstone. Neither Hill nor Rindt was happy with the new four-wheel-drive Lotus 63, preferring the rather long-in-the-tooth 49Bs. Chapman had already sold one of the 49Bs to the private entrant Jo Bonnier, but persuaded him to lend it back to the team for Hill to drive. Bonnier agreed to drive the 63 instead. Rindt took pole position for Lotus by 0.4 second, and in the race, he led Stewart by a fraction into the first corner. Stewart regained the lead on lap 6, with the rest of the field far behind. On Lap 14, Rindt was back in front. Then two laps later they lapped Beltoise in the MS84, passing one each side of him. For the rest of the race the two were rarely more than 3 seconds apart, Rindt demonstrating that he was a force to be reckoned with.

Stewart then noticed that one of the side plates on Rindt's new lower wing had come loose and was fouling the tyre. He pulled alongside to indicate the problem, and Rindt went into the pits for the side plate to be wrenched off, rejoining 20 seconds behind Stewart. Then Stewart's engine started spluttering when one of the fuel pumps failed, and Rindt started gaining. With just 6 laps to go, Rindt's engine started spluttering too, as he ran low on fuel, and he had to go in again, this time rejoining in fourth place. Stewart won, taking his record for the season to five out of six races – but he knew that in Rindt he had a serious challenger. Chapman had also met a match for his fiery temperament, as he found out after the race when Rindt took him to task over the Lotus team's shortcomings. The first ten cars home in the British Grand Prix were all powered by Cosworth DFVs.

Of the three four-wheel-drive cars in the race, Derek Bell retired on lap 5 with suspension problems on the McLaren M9A, Jo

Bonnier retired a lap later when the Lotus 63's engine packed up, and Beltoise finished ninth in the Matra MS84. The theory that four-wheel drive was another way of applying more engine power to forward speed and acceleration and, for drivers, gave improved handling in the wet, came under scrutiny. Compared with the advantage gained from good aerodynamics and better tyres, four-wheel-drive cars were discerned to be complicated and overweight. Ford withdrew its support for the Lotus project, and other projects – including an experimental car built by Cosworth but never raced – were abandoned when designers realized they represented a rather expensive blind alley (>1982).

The Italian Grand Prix was another high-speed duel between Rindt and Stewart, which Stewart won by 0.5 second. Beltoise came in only half a length behind Rindt in a second Matra-Ford. With six out of the eight World Championship events won, Stewart's lead was now unassailable. Jacky Ickx took the Canadian race for Brabham. The US Grand Prix at Watkins Glen had a prize of $50,000 for the winner out of a purse of $200,000 – far above the earnings in European Grands Prix. Rindt took pole position and streaked into the lead, Stewart close behind, as the two once again left the rest of the field well behind. Under pressure from Stewart, Rindt slid wide on a corner, letting Stewart into the lead. Rindt took it back on lap 21, then Stewart retired, having lost oil pressure. The serious

opposition out of the way, Rindt took his foot off the throttle, conserving his car to win his first World Championship race – to great applause. He used the prize money to build a luxury home by Lake Geneva, not far from where Jackie Stewart lived.

Rindt's Lotus team-mate Graham Hill had a far less happy race. He spun off and stalled, and after pushing his 49B downhill, jumped in on the move and bump-started it. In doing so, he was unable to do up his safety harness, and so drove without it. Then he noticed a tyre was losing pressure. On his way to the pits it burst, and he crashed. Hurled out of the cockpit, he broke both legs.

Denny Hulme won the last race of the season in Mexico, but Matra finished the clear victor in the Constructors' Championship with 66 points to Brabham's 48. There was no Championship for engines, but if there had been it would have gone to Cosworth. DFV-powered cars won all the eleven World Championship races, and took second place in them all as well. Seen another way: of the overall 66 possible places that counted for points, DFVs filled 62 of them. With much the same power available to everybody, designers found other ways to try to stay ahead – aerodynamics, tyres, and four-wheel drive. But the single most important difference remained the drivers' own abilities, and when they were closely matched – as were Stewart's and Rindt's – the spectators got the kind of racing they paid for.

BELOW: Mario Andretti in the STP Oil Treatment Special entering Victory Circle after winning the Indianapolis 500 at a record speed of 156.867 mph. He led for 116 of the race's 200 laps and finished almost three laps ahead of second-placed Dan Gurney's Olsonite Eagle (155.337 mph average). In the 1968 500, Andretti had come last.

LEFT: Parnelli Jones cornering hard in a Ford Mustang (No. 15) during the '24 Hours of Daytona' sports car race on 2-3 February. The race was won by Mark Donohue and Chuck Parsons in a Sunoco Lola-Chevrolet. They covered 2,386.31 miles: an average 99.26 mph.

It was a year for arrivals – new names, new cars and new teams emerged into the spotlight. It was also a year for departures, some of them voluntary and graceful, others sad and violent.

The newest team was March, founded by four young men whose initials made up the name: Max Mosley, a lawyer and former Formula Two driver; Alan Rees, another former Formula Two driver; Graham Coaker, from the aircraft industry; and Robin Herd, the ex-McLaren designer. They set up in business both to build cars and to race them – for which they needed sponsorship. They found it from Andy Grantanelli's STP company, running a two-driver Grand Prix team with an extra car for Mario Andretti. Like most contemporary teams they wanted to sign Jochen Rindt, but Rindt – despite a difficult relationship with Colin Chapman at Lotus – stayed there. Lotus had the edge, and Chapman was building a new car, to be known as the Lotus 72.

Herd's first design for March was the 701, built around the Cosworth engine, and for the works team they eventually signed Chris Amon and Jo Siffert, in addition to Mario Andretti. But March had another Formula One customer, Ken Tyrrell. His deal with Matra to supply chassis ended when Matra was taken over by Simca, which was in turn

ABOVE: The French Grand Prix at Clermont-Ferrand on 5 July. Jack Brabham in Brabham BT33 (No. 23) leads from Jochen Rindt's Lotus 72 (No. 6) and Henri Pescarolo in a Matra-Simca MS120 (No. 20). Rindt won; Brabham finished third, 37.22 seconds behind second-placed Chris Amon's March 701; Pescarolo was fifth.

owned by Chrysler, whose board would not contemplate allowing one of its subsidiaries to use Ford engines. Matra offered Tyrrell its V-12, but he declined, preferring to stick with the DFV, which was now producing around 450 bhp. March supplied Tyrrell with three 701 chassis, and the March-Ford Tyrrells made their debut at the South African Grand Prix. At the same time, Tyrrell had decided he should start building his own cars, and took on Derek Gardner who had worked on the abortive Matra MS84 four-wheel-drive project. The French oil giant Elf continued to back Tyrrell, with the provision that the second driver in his team must be French, so Johnny Servoz-Gavin joined Jackie Stewart from

ABOVE: Jochen Rindt, the only driver to be named World Champion after his death. He won the Monaco, Dutch, French, British and German Grands Prix before being killed in a 170-mph smash during practice for the Italian Grand Prix. He joined Lotus in 1969 after driving for Cooper in 1965–67 and Brabham in 1968. A temperamental man, he never formed the close relationship with Colin Chapman that Jim Clark had enjoyed.

Formula Two. Matra continued to race its V-12, with Jean-Pierre Beltoise as the driver.

Frank Williams had started in much the same way as Ken Tyrrell. He had a talented driver in Piers Courage, and lacked a Formula One chassis for his DFVs. He turned to the Italian sports car maker de Tomaso, and the Williams-de Tomaso was another to make its debut in the South African Grand Prix.

John Surtees also turned constructor. His TS7 would not be ready until later in the year: in the meantime he drove a McLaren M7A.

The established teams brought out new cars too. Ferrari's 312B used a semi-monocoque chassis with 'horns' at the rear from which the flat-12 460-bhp engine hung. Ferrari took on Jacky Ickx and a new name from Switzerland, Gianclaudio 'Clay' Regazzoni. BRM also had a new car, the P153, which had a V-12 engine; its drivers were Pedro Gonzalez and Jackie Oliver, and it had financial backing from the perfume manufacturer Yardley. Brabham built his first monocoque, the BT33, using the Cosworth engine, for Repco had pulled out of racing. Jack Brabham took on a young German driver named Rolf Stommelen. Bruce McLaren improved the M7A into the M14A, retaining Denny Hulme as his No.2.

At Lotus, Colin Chapman and Maurice Phillippe amalgamated aspects of the Lotus 56 gas-turbine, Lotus 63 Grand Prix and Lotus 64 four-wheel-drive Indianapolis cars into the Lotus 72. Its wedge shape was strongly reminiscent of the 56 (>1968), and to maximise it, the radiator had been moved from the front to just behind the driver, with air scoops on both sides – an innovation that was followed by most designers – which also reduced the heat around the driver's feet. As much weight as possible had been concentrated at the back.

ABOVE: Al Unser in a Ford-engined Colt, the Johnny Lightning Special, during time trials for the Indianapolis 500. Unser was fastest qualifier at 170.221 mph, and won the race at an average 155.749 mph. His car was prepared by renowned Indianapolis mechanic George Bignotti.

LEFT: Al Unser. He won $271,697.72 for first place in the 500, out of a total of $1,000,002.22 – the first million-dollar purse at Indianapolis. He also won the US National Championship.

265

ABOVE: First of March. The first March car, the aluminium monocoque Type 701, made its debut at the South African Grand Prix at Kyalami. Chris Amon in a works car (No. 15) retired on lap 14 with an overheated engine; Jackie Stewart, driving a 701 for the Tyrrell team, finished third.

ABOVE: Clay Regazzoni in the 460-bhp Ferrari 312B during the Italian Grand Prix on 6 September. He was third on the grid behind Pedro Rodriguez's BRM and Ferrari team-mate Jacky Ickx in pole position. Regazzoni won the race in 1 hour 39 minutes 6.88 seconds: an average 147.08 mph.

The aerofoil was three-tiered and could be adjusted to suit the conditions at each circuit. But it was not ready for South Africa.

After his crash at Watkins Glen, many thought Graham Hill would not race again – but he was at Kyalami, South Africa, in a Rob Walker Lotus 49B even though he had to be lifted in and out of the cockpit to drive. There were four March cars on the grid, representing both March and Elf-Tyrrell, and Jackie Stewart took pole position in one of them, Chris Amon next to him in a works car. Stewart took the lead at the start, only to be passed by Jack Brabham. Piers Courage in the Williams-de Tomaso then hit a kerb too hard and retired. Brabham held on to the lead and won.

The Spanish Grand Prix saw the debut of the Lotus 72 and the first outing for the Ferrari 312Bs – but neither made any impression. Stewart took pole position, led the race, and duly won March's first victory. Mario Andretti's third, in a works March, brought him his first Championship points. Stewart looked as if he would take the Monaco Grand Prix too, for he took the lead, followed by Amon in the works March. Then his engine failed and Amon's suspension collapsed, leaving Brabham in the lead. Rindt was just behind: unhappy with the Lotus 72, he had reverted to a Lotus 49B. With victory almost in sight, Brabham spun off – and Rindt passed him to win.

A sad absence from the grid at Spa for the Belgian Grand Prix was that of Bruce

McLaren. Just days before, he had been testing a sports car at Goodwood for the American Can-Am series. The hood flew up, obscured his view, and he crashed and was killed. Dan Gurney stepped into the breach alongside Hulme. Pedro Rodriguez then won the race – the first BRM victory for four years. By the time of the Dutch Grand Prix at Zandvoort, Rindt was happy with the Lotus 72. In the race, he had a fierce duel with Jacky Ickx in the new Ferrari, who snatched the lead on the first corner. One lap later, Rindt was in front; and he was 10 seconds ahead by lap 10. Meanwhile, a battle was developing for sixth place between Regazzoni's Ferrari, John Miles in the Lotus 72, Piers Courage in the Williams-de Tomaso, and Beltoise in the Matra. On lap 23 Courage spun off and rolled over several times, spewing petrol, which then caught fire. Courage died in the flames.

Rindt won the race, and with the Lotus 72 now sorted out, he looked unbeatable. He went on to win the French, British and German Grands Prix, achieving a total of five victories and 45 points in the Championship. For the Italian Grand Prix he was joined in the Lotus team by a young Brazilian, Emerson Fittipaldi (>1972, 1974, 1989). During practice Rindt experimented, driving without winglets on the front of his car. He was just approaching the right-handed Curva Parabolica, under maximum braking, when the brake shaft broke. The car hit the safety barrier, which gave way. He hit one of the

MILESTONES

François Szisz (>1903, 1906), who won the first-ever Grand Prix at Le Mans in a 90-hp Renault, died aged 97 in Tiszaszentimre, Hungary.

Formula One was amended to make rubber fuel tanks mandatory. To house them, monocoque construction also became virtually obligatory.

For the first time in the history of the Indianapolis 500, the total purse exceeded $1 million: $1,000,002. The winner's share was $271,697.

Increased traction was achieved using tyres known as 'slicks'; with no tread, they were fine in dry conditions, but lethal in the wet.

Rob Walker's private team of blue-painted cars (>1958) – the blue represented Scotland – pulled out of racing at the end of the season.

Jack Brabham, three times World Champion driver and twice champion contructor, retired at the end of the season, aged 44 (>1959, 1966, 1979).

uprights and was killed instantly, ending one of the most promising careers of the period. Miles left the team.

Clay Regazzoni won the race for Ferrari. Ickx then took the Canadian Grand Prix, having also won in Austria. In the final race of the season, the United States Grand Prix, it was possible for Ickx to overtake Rindt's points total and win the Drivers' Championship. But for the US race, Lotus – who had missed the previous two races – returned. In their team a young Swedish driver, Reine Wissell, joined Fittipaldi – who won. Wissell came in in third, giving Lotus the Constructors' title, and, by denying points to others, giving Rindt the Drivers' title, for the first time awarded posthumously.

LEFT: Jean-Pierre Beltoise in a Matra Simca (No. 4) passing the scene of the crash between Jacky Ickx's Ferrari and Jackie Oliver's BRM in the Spanish Grand Prix. Oliver collided with Ickx when the BRM's brakes failed on the first lap. Both drivers survived, although Ickx suffered severe burns.

The cross-fertilization between Grand Prix and Indianapolis bore new fruit in 1971. It also produced higher speeds. The four fastest qualifiers for the 500 all drove cars that had their roots in both traditions – three of them wedge-shaped turbocharged M16 McLarens with 152-cubic-inch Offenhauser engines. Fastest of all was Peter Revson – at 178.696 mph, an increase of more than 8 mph on the previous year. Second was Mark Donohue in the same type of car, entered by Roger Penske (>1978, 1988), at 177.087 mph. Then came Bobby Unser in an Eagle with the same Offenhauser engine. Fourth was Denny Hulme in another McLaren. In fifth place was Al Unser, the previous year's winner, in his Ford V-8 Johnny Lightning Special.

Mark Donohue led for the first 66 laps, then his transmission failed and Al Unser took over. A fierce fight ensued between Unser and Joe Leonard in a similar car, the lead swapping back and forth until Leonard's turbocharger failed. Bobby Unser then moved into second place behind his brother, with Revson in third and A.J. Foyt fourth. A good pit-stop then put Revson ahead of Bobby Unser. On lap 165, a tyre burst on Mike Mosley's Eagle and he collided with Bobby Unser: the yellow flags came out while Gary Bettenhausen stopped and rescued Mosley. Al Unser won the race, but the competitiveness of the Eagle and McLaren cars was evident, and they were to dominate racing at the Speedway for several years thereafter.

In Grand Prix racing there were few new cars: most teams just improved their existing designs. McLaren introduced the M19A – which was at once unofficially christened the Coke Bottle when it was first unveiled and the press saw the huge bulges on each side where the fuel tanks ran alongside the driver's cockpit. The Brabham BT34 was similarly nicknamed the Lobster Claw, after the protruding radiators on both sides at the front. Frank Costin, whose work on the aerodynamics of racing cars had started in the 1950s with Vanwall, was responsible for the look of the new, more streamlined March 711. Its most distinctive feature was the front aerofoil which protruded from a central pylon on the nose cone. The 711's brakes were mounted inboard, linked to the wheels via shafts after the fashion of the Lotus 72.

The most exciting newcomer was the first Tyrrell, which was known not by type but by its chassis number: 001. Jackie Stewart had taken pole position in it in the Canadian Grand Prix the previous year, and no expense had been spared in preparing it for the new season. Tyrrell's March 701s had cost £9,000; the first of the new Tyrrell cars cost well over £30,000 complete, with its new Cosworth engine and Hewland gearbox. Derek Gardner had spent many hours testing the shape in a wind-tunnel at Surrey University to perfect the distinctive, spade-like front aerofoil and the shapely, bulging monocoque. The fuel tanks were on each side of the driver, to help concentrate weight within the wheelbase and close to the centre of the car, making it highly manoeuvrable. The latest Cosworth engine was bolted straight on to the back of the 'tub' in the manner pioneered by Colin Chapman in the Lotus 49. One of the most innovative features of the car was the first use of double discs in the brakes, to help cooling.

Jackie Stewart had been approached by Ferrari, but he stayed with Ken Tyrrell out of

BELOW: Tyrrell-Ford leading the US Grand Prix. Jackie Stewart (No. 8) ahead of team-mate François Cevert (No. 9), with Clay Regazzoni's Ferrari (No. 5) giving chase. Cevert won; Stewart had tyre problems, and finished fifth; Regazzoni came sixth.

MILESTONES

Jack Brabham's company Motor Racing Developments, after passing first to Ron Tauranac, was bought by Bernard Ecclestone (>1958, 1981).

Emerson Fittipaldi finished second in a minor Formula One race at Hockenheim in the Lotus 56B, the only gas-turbine Formula One car.

Al Unser was the first driver to use two-way radio to talk to his pits during the Indianapolis 500, using a system developed by RCA.

BRM's two top drivers both died in crashes: Pedro Rodriguez in a sports car race in July, and Jo Siffert at Brands Hatch in October.

The Mexican Grand Prix was disqualified from the World Championship for poor standards of safety; in 1970 spectators had reached the side of the track.

The first 'slick' tyres, without tread, based on the type used in drag racing, were introduced by Goodyear for the South African Grand Prix.

RIGHT: A fruitful relationship – World Champion Jackie Stewart with team-owner Ken Tyrrell. Born in 1924, Tyrrell was a driver in Formula Two and Three during the 1950s, but retired in 1960 to run Cooper's Formula Junior team. He gave Stewart his first big break – signing him for the Cooper-BMC Formula Three team in 1964; the pair stayed together, moving to Matra, first in Formula Two and then in 1968 in Formula One. Tyrrell formed his own team in 1970.

BELOW: Jackie Stewart led from start to finish in the Monaco Grand Prix.

ABOVE: Fruits of victory. The year 1971 was a triumphant one for Ken Tyrrell. Tyrrell-Ford took the World Constructors' Championship with 73 points – the team winning seven Grands Prix: Jackie Stewart, six; François Cevert, one.

loyalty, and to drive the new car. His team-mate was François Cevert, a tall Frenchman, whose new car – 002 – was 4 inches (10 centimetres) longer in the wheelbase than Stewart's in order to accommodate his lanky frame. The Elf-Tyrrell team set new standards of preparation. Tyrrell, Stewart and Cevert spent weeks in January, testing the cars and hundreds of Goodyear tyres.

Having failed to secure Stewart, Ferrari signed the former Indianapolis winner Mario Andretti, who had been born in Italy and whose boyhood hero had been Alberto Ascari. Andretti gave Ferrari a great boost at the start of the season by winning the South African Grand Prix, his first victory, continuing Ferrari's climb back out of the doldrums with the 312B (>1970).

Then Stewart and Tyrrell took hold of the World Championship in a way not seen since the days of Jim Clark (>1965). Stewart took the Spanish Grand Prix from Jacky Ickx in a Ferrari, and Chris Amon who had left March for Matra-Simca.

The President of the Auto Club de Monaco, Louis Chiron (>1927), started the fortieth Monaco Grand Prix in unsettled weather. Stewart took the lead, opening up an immediate gap from the rest of the pack. Because most of the cars were powered by the same Cosworth engine, the skill of the driver played an increasingly important part in winning. Stewart drove a near-perfect race, setting a new lap record in the process, to finish comfortably ahead of Ronnie Peterson for March.

At Zandvoort, Stewart was involved in a collision in wet conditions. The Ferraris were

ABOVE: Nanni Galli (No. 22, March-Ford), Helmut Marko (No. 21, BRM) and Mike Hailwood (No. 9, Surtees-Ford) during the Italian Grand Prix. Although talented enough to survive in the rarefied atmosphere of Formula One, a large number of drivers fail to make a lasting mark at the highest level. In this race, Hailwood (>1974, 1981) finished fourth; Marko and Galli retired.

ABOVE: Ronnie Peterson in a March-Ford 711 in the Rothmans World Championship Victory Race at Brands Hatch on 24 October. The race was abandoned on lap 14 after the fatal crash of Jo Siffert's BRM.

fitted with Firestone tyres, which proved much better in the wet, and after Stewart's untimely exit the Dutch race was dominated by Jacky Ickx.

Stewart went on to win the French Grand Prix – the first to be held on the new purpose-built *autodrome* constructed at Le Castellet near Marseilles by the industrialist Paul Ricard and bearing his name. Cevert was second in the other Tyrrell. Then Stewart really got into his stride. At Silverstone, practice for the British Grand Prix was fiercely competitive. Clay Regazzoni and Stewart qualified in exactly the same time, Regazzoni taking pole position: just 3 seconds covered the entire grid except for the two slowest cars. Jo Siffert in a BRM P160 lined up in third position.

Regazzoni and Ickx – through from the second row – took the lead for Ferrari, before Stewart braked that fraction of a second later going into Stowe Corner on lap 2 to take the lead, at that point followed by Siffert in the BRM. Stewart then gave another virtuoso performance, pulling away steadily until he had over half a minute's lead, which he held for the rest of the race.

Stewart and Cevert produced another first-and-second for Tyrrell in the German Grand Prix at the Nürburgring, Cevert this time setting a new lap record. Then the new BRM gave the all-conquering Tyrrells a nasty shock in the Austrian Grand Prix. Jo Siffert took pole position and in the race proceeded to lead from flag to flag. Stewart experienced an even nastier personal shock when a wheel came off, sending him spinning off the track. At Monza the leading bunch of drivers – Stewart, Regazzoni, Amon, Siffert and his BRM team-mate Peter Gethin – all took part in a thrilling display of slipstreaming, every one of them leading at different stages in the race. Gethin took the flag by less than a car's length, having snatched the lead back from Peterson in the March with a marvellous piece of late braking on the very last corner.

In the last two races of the season, the Tyrrells reasserted themselves. Stewart won at Mosport in Canada in pouring rain, and he led the United States Grand Prix until his engine faltered and Cevert took over to win his first Grand Prix – indeed, the first time a French driver had won a World Championship event since 1958, when Maurice Trintignant won at Monaco in a Cooper.

Tyrrell had crushed the opposition in both World Championships. Stewart and Cevert won seven of the eleven races between them, Stewart taking his second Drivers' title with 62 points to Peterson's 33, and Tyrrell taking the Constructors' title by 73 points to 36 – all in the team's first year with the new car.

ABOVE: Ronnie Peterson at Silverstone for the GKN-*Daily Express* International Trophy in May. Driving a March 711 with 430-bhp Alfa-Romeo engine, he crashed in the first of two heats when the car's throttle stuck open and was taken to hospital. Aggregate winner of the two heats was Graham Hill in a Brabham-Ford, at an average 128.53 mph.

BELOW: Number One at Indianapolis – Al Unser, winner of the 500 in a Ford-engined Colt, the Johnny Lightning Special, at an average 157.735 mph. In pre-qualification practice, Mark Donohue in an Offy-engined McLaren was the first man to lap the Speedway in less than 50 seconds – 180.9 mph. In the race, Donohue was classified 25th after retiring on lap 66.

The effect of turbocharging on speeds in the Indianapolis 500 was spectacular. In 1971 Peter Revson had taken pole position with the fastest practice lap of 178.696 mph. In 1972 Bobby Unser qualified for the favoured spot in his Offy-powered Eagle at 195.940 mph – an increase of more than 17 mph – the greatest increase in speed from one year to the next in the Speedway's history.

In third and fourth place on the grid were two McLaren M16s entered by Roger Penske and driven by Mark Donohue and Gary Bettenhausen. McLaren's designer, Gordon Coppuck, had been influenced by the shape of the Lotus 56 and 72 – continuing the interaction between Indianapolis racing and Grand Prix – and its wedge shape, coupled with around 900 bhp from the Offy engine, set a trend for the future. Its great opponents were Dan Gurney's Eagles, which used the same engine. Bettenhausen led for 181 laps before Jerry Grant took over in an Eagle-Offy. Then Donohue passed him during the final pit-stop, to take McLaren's first Indianapolis victory.

From the late 1960s, the advertising of cigarettes was restricted in public places and altogether banned on television. One of the side-effects was to provide a boost to the finance available to Grand Prix motor racing, which expanded steadily as tobacco companies saw racing cars as ideal alternative billboards, and poured in sponsorship money. John Player changed brands: Gold Leaf cars gave way to John Player Specials, the new season's cars painted black with a thin gold line, identical to the packet. In reality the John Player Specials were Lotus 72s – although the name Lotus did not appear on the car at all. The Player company went even further. It sponsored the British Grand Prix (which thus became the John Player Grand Prix instead) – a move that upset many British fans. BRM changed its sponsor from Yardley cosmetics to Marlboro cigarettes and embarked on an ambitious programme, aiming to run five cars, even after the deaths of two of their top drivers the previous year.

The new commercialism spread beyond the tobacco companies: Goodyear and Firestone tyres publicized their contributions, Shell Oil continued its support – even Brooke Bond Tea tested the market by backing Surtees. Yardley shifted its allegiance to McLaren, and Frank Williams was backed by the Politoy toy company. Elf continued to support Tyrrell, while Matra and STP continued to support March. Ferrari went on racing in Italian red, but decals for fuel, tyre and brake companies multiplied on their cars. A new Italian team, Tecno

ABOVE: Emerson Fittipaldi in the John Player Special Lotus 72 during the Spanish Grand Prix at Jarama on 1 May. The 72's wedge shape was derived from the Lotus 56 Indianapolis car. The shape was made possible by moving the radiator from the front of the car to the waist (centre, beside driver), another of Colin Chapman's radical ideas.

– the brainchild of the Pederzani brothers, Luciano and Gianfranco – was born on the back of support from the drinks company Martini & Rossi.

In all there were eleven teams to contest the 1972 season. Most ran two cars plus a spare, but with their new resources some expanded to three; BRM's five was the most ambitious. The increased number of cars created a new demand for drivers, giving lesser-known names – many from Formula Two – an opportunity to move up. At Brabham, Wilson Fittipaldi (older brother of Lotus's Emerson) joined Carlos Reutemann, from Argentina. The Brazilian Carlos Pace joined Williams. Niki Lauda, from Austria, joined March. The Indianapolis veteran Peter Revson joined McLaren, while the young South African Jody Scheckter also drove occasionally for the

ABOVE: Emerson Fittipaldi winning the British Grand Prix at Brands Hatch on 17 July. Brazilian-born Fittipaldi (>1993) was the greatest of the second generation of South American drivers, who followed in the footsteps of Juan Manuel Fangio and Froilan Gonzalez.

LEFT: The start of the British Grand Prix. Jacky Ickx (No. 5, Ferrari) beat Emerson Fittipaldi (No. 8, Lotus-Ford) into the first bend, while Jean-Pierre Beltoise (No. 11, BRM) came from the third row of the grid to take third place at this stage. Fittipaldi won; Ickx retired on lap 48; Beltoise finished 11th.

McLaren team. The former Motorcycle World Champion Mike Hailwood – who had joined Surtees in 1971 – moved up to No.1 driver as John Surtees retired from active racing to manage the team. Ferrari continued with Clay Regazzoni, Jacky Ickx and Mario Andretti; Jackie Stewart and François Cevert likewise stayed with Tyrrell. But Chris Amon went to Matra, and Graham Hill went to Brabham.

The number of races also increased by one:

the Argentinian Grand Prix returned after an absence of 12 years, reflecting the growth in interest which followed the influx of South American drivers. There was wild enthusiasm in Buenos Aires when the local driver, Carlos Reutemann, was fastest in practice – although an older hand, the reigning World Champion Jackie Stewart, reasserted himself in the race, leading from flag to flag.

More cars meant fuller grids. The Monaco Grand Prix, previously restricted to 16 cars, suddenly found room for 25. Race day in Monte Carlo was one of the wettest on

ABOVE: Emerson Fittipaldi with his wife Marie Helena after clinching the World Drivers' Championship with victory in the Italian Grand Prix on 10 September. A driver of tremendous natural talent, he won his first World Championship race – at Watkins Glen in a Lotus-Ford in October 1970 – only months after first driving a Formula One car.

273

record, and as the swollen pack surged off in a huge burst of spray, only those at the front were really able to see where they were going. Jean-Pierre Beltoise (BRM) took the lead, and while those behind him spun and collided in a series of minor accidents, he hung on to his place in front to win his first World Championship race, to the great joy of BRM's new sponsors.

The season settled down into a duel between Emerson Fittipaldi and Stewart. Fittipaldi won the Spanish and Belgian Grands Prix; Stewart won the French Grand Prix at Clermont-Ferrand, putting them at two victories apiece as they lined up for the British Grand Prix.

There were 26 cars on the grid at Brands Hatch, including five from March, three Brabhams, three BRMs and three Lotuses. Jacky Ickx took pole position, Emerson Fittipaldi alongside him, and Stewart immediately behind. Ickx took the lead, with Fittipaldi second, followed by Beltoise and Stewart. The Ferraris were faster on the straights, and Ickx stayed at the front – but Stewart moved up to third place. All three front-runners bunched up at the corners, looking for a chance advantage. When Fittipaldi

slid wide at Druids Corner, Stewart slipped into second place for a few laps. Then Fittipaldi repassed him on the straight and began to gain on Ickx as the Ferrari started leaking oil. Eventually the oil leak caused Ickx to retire. Fittipaldi led by a whisker from Stewart, the pair giving the crowd a thrilling race, but the John Player Special (JPS) Lotus

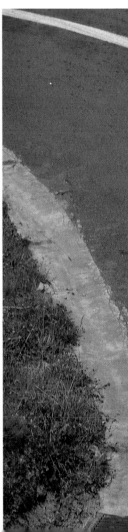

ABOVE: Denny Hulme in a McLaren-Ford M19A, winner of the South African Grand Prix. He finished in 1 hour 45 minutes 49.1 seconds, 14.1 seconds ahead of Emerson Fittipaldi's Lotus-Ford – Hulme's only Grand Prix win of the year. Hulme's strong leadership played a vital role in holding the McLaren team together after Bruce McLaren's death (>1970).

BELOW: Frenchman Jean-Pierre Beltoise in a BRM P160 storming to victory in terrible conditions at Monaco. He drove a fearless race to clinch what was his only World Championship win from 85 starts.

just had the edge, and Fittipaldi won. The Player company could not have wished for a better result – its own car winning its own race!

Ickx won the German Grand Prix at the Nürburgring – Ferrari's only victory of the season – then Emerson Fittipaldi took the Austrian Grand Prix, making the victory tally four to two in his favour over Stewart. He had only to win the Italian Grand Prix to take the Championship at the tender age of 25.

Monza was celebrating its fiftieth birthday, but for many fans it was doing it the wrong way. Drivers had always disliked the extremely fast circuit which encouraged flat-out racing and slipstreaming. Spectators loved the close finishes which had become a feature of the circuit. But the drivers won the day, and two sets of chicanes were marked out on two straights by a series of rubber cones. Instead of his customary battle with Stewart, who retired on the first lap, Fittipaldi found himself fighting Ferrari on its home ground as Ickx and Regazzoni roared off into the lead together. On lap 14 Pace spun in the middle of one of the chicanes, and Regazzoni hit the spinning Brabham, putting Fittipaldi in second place. But the Lotus simply could not match the

speed of Ickx's Ferrari. Suddenly, on lap 46, the Ferrari's engine died as the car came out of the Curva Parabolica: it was the result of an electrical fault, and Ickx was out – Fittipaldi could ease up. He won the race and the Championship – the youngest driver ever to do so – also thereby giving Lotus its fifth Constructors' title.

Stewart won the last two races of the season, the Canadian and US Grands Prix, finishing with 45 points to Emerson Fittipaldi's 61 – but the Flying Scotsman had met his match. There were great celebrations in Brazil, where Fittipaldi was hailed as a national hero (much as Juan Manuel Fangio had been in Argentina 20 years previously), generating new enthusiasm for motor racing within South America (>1973).

MILESTONES

Jean-Pierre Beltoise's win in Monaco was BRM's last. Jo Bonnier, who gave BRM its first victory (>1959), was killed at Le Mans.

Graham Hill won at Le Mans in a Matra-Simca, achieving a unique triple: World Champion, Indianapolis 500 winner, and Le Mans 24-hour classic winner.

After another disappointing season, Matra-Simca gave up Formula One at the end of the year to concentrate on sports car racing.

After an absence of 66 years, the French company Renault (>1903, 1906) decided to return to motor racing; it started with sports car races (>1977).

The founder and president since 1948 of NASCAR, Bill France (>1936), stepped down in favour of his son, Bill France Jr.

A.J. Foyt won the Daytona 500 – the first driver to win the stock car and Indy Car classics, and the 24-hour sports car race at Le Mans.

LEFT: Jackie Stewart made a victorious comeback in the French Grand Prix following a six-week illness. His Tyrrell-Ford was third on the grid behind Denny Hulme's McLaren-Ford (second) and Chris Amon's Matra-Simca in pole position. Stewart finished in 1 hour 52 minutes 21.5 seconds: 101.57 mph average.

The theme at Indianapolis remained power and speed. For the 1973 500 race, all 33 starters were turbocharged, 22 of them with Offy engines which peaked at 1,000 bhp. Johnny Rutherford set a new record qualifying time of 198.413 mph driving a McLaren M16, his single-lap record of 199.071 mph tantalizingly close to the 200 mph barrier (>1977). The battle lines were increasingly between McLaren and Eagle, who between them filled 26 of the 33 places on the grid, including the five fastest qualifiers.

But while the technical progress of the cars was swift and sure, increased speed was partly responsible for one of most tragic races in the history of the Speedway. In practice, Art Pollard hit the wall on Turn 1 with enough momentum for the wreck to travel along the wall, finishing up at Turn 2 upside down; Pollard was killed. Race day dawned – and it started raining. Although the rain lifted for the parade, the track was soaked. As the grid accelerated into the first lap drivers jostling for any advantage in the spray, one collision set off a chain reaction that in all wrecked twelve cars. Salt Walther hit the wall on the first turn. His car was heavy with fuel: the tanks ruptured, spraying the crowd with flaming petrol and scattering them with debris. Thirteen spectators were injured; Walther survived, though with severe injuries.

The race was stopped for the track to be cleared; then the rain began to fall again, and it was postponed. On Tuesday it was postponed again due to rain, after just the pace lap.

MILESTONES

Richard Petty won the Daytona 500 for the fifth time in a Dodge at 157.205 mph after a fierce duel with his STP team-mate, Buddy Baker.

Mike Hailwood was awarded the George Medal for risking his life to save Clay Regazzoni, who crashed on fire in the South African Grand Prix.

On 23 July Eddie Rickenbacker died, aged 83. He started racing in 1910, and owned Indianapolis Speedway from 1927 to 1944.

Ferrari went through a lean spell, gaining only 12 points in the Drivers' Championship – only 3 points ahead of Shadow in its first season.

The most powerful circuit-racing car ever built was the 5.4-litre turbocharged 1,100-hp Can-Am Porsche Spyder driven by Mark Donohue.

The last-ever Targa Florio was staged in Sicily – the 57th race in 67 years, it was won by Herbert Müller and Gijs van Lennep in a Porsche.

On Wednesday the race actually got under way – third time lucky. Among the early leaders was Swede Savage in an Eagle, until he hit the wall on Turn 4, spraying the track with burning fuel. The car disintegrated and he was fatally injured. To compound the tragedy, an emergency truck set off up the pit lane the wrong way, and ran over a pit mechanic, Armando Teran, killing him. The race was red-flagged – and while the drivers waited, the rain began falling again. Then it was restarted, then stopped again for rain on lap 133. The race officials and drivers had had enough: it was called off. Gordon Johncock, who was leading at that point in an Eagle-Offy, was proclaimed the winner – not with a chequered flag, but by an official in the pits.

During the winter, there had been the usual ebb and flow of talent within the Grand Prix teams. The Swedish driver Ronnie Peterson joined Emerson Fittipaldi at Lotus, but designer Maurice Phillippe left to build a Formula One car for Parnelli Jones in

ABOVE: Carlos Reutemann (Brabham, No. 10), Denny Hulme (McLaren, No. 7) and Emerson Fittipaldi (Lotus, No. 1) during the German Grand Prix at the Nürburgring. Reutemann retired; Hulme was 12th; Fittipaldi came sixth.

RIGHT: Emerson Fittipaldi taking shelter. He finished the season second in the World Drivers' Championship with 55 points – behind Jackie Stewart's 71 – despite a persistent ankle injury following a crash in practice for the Dutch Grand Prix.

LEFT: Carlos Reutemann in a Brabham BT37 in the Brazilian Grand Prix. He finished 11th. Argentine-born Reutemann – another of an astonishing crop of talented South American drivers - stayed with the Brabham team throughout his career. He finished seventh in the 1973 Drivers' Championship with 16 points; his best placing was third in the French and US Grands Prix.

California. The vacancy caused by his going was filled by Ralph Bellamy from McLaren.

Gordon Coppuck took over development of McLaren's M23, the only completely new car of the season, built from scratch to conform to the new Formula One requirement for 'deformable structures' around the fuel tanks, to cushion impact and help prevent fire. The M23 drew heavily on Coppuck's experience with its American cousin, the M16 Indianapolis car.

Jackie Stewart and François Cevert stayed with Tyrrell. Derek Gardner's new 006 was beautiful and simple, with as much weight as possible concentrated within the wheelbase, making it highly manoeuvrable. Gordon Murray stayed with Brabham, as did Carlos Reutemann and Wilson Fittipaldi. Robin Herd stayed at March, where he concentrated on developing other aspects of the business.

The two oldest surviving teams, Ferrari and BRM, were both at a low ebb. BRM was in fact in terminal decline. Tony Southgate had left to join Shadow, a new American Formula One team that was sponsored by Universal Oil Products and run by Alan Rees, who had left March with team drivers Jean-Pierre Beltoise and Niki Lauda. At Ferrari, Mauro Forghieri (>1964) was moved to long-term development, while his assistant Sandro Colombo took over the Formula One management, although Forghieri returned later in the season (>1984, 1987).

There were three other new names: Ensign, a German team based on driver Rikky von Opel, using an adapted March chassis; Embassy cigarettes, a new Formula One sponsor for Graham Hill using Shadow cars; and Lord Alexander Hesketh's Hesketh team, with driver James Hunt (>1976).

The number of races expanded again, to fifteen, including two new Grands Prix – in Brazil and Sweden. Emerson Fittipaldi won the South American round of the Championship, taking the Argentinian and Brazilian Grands Prix. Then Stewart won the South African and Belgian races, taking his total of Grand Prix victories to 24, just one fewer than Jim Clark's record of 25.

After the first few laps at Monaco, the Stewart-Fittipaldi duel continued – Stewart leading, with Niki Lauda in third place until the BRM's gearbox failed. The duel continued right to the end: Stewart won by just over 1 second, equalling Clark's record in style.

Denny Hulme broke the Lotus-Tyrrell run by taking the flag at the first Swedish Grand Prix, at Anderstorp, giving McLaren's new M23 its first victory (>1976). In the French Grand Prix, two No.2 drivers – Peterson and Cevert – took over the reins in the Lotus-Tyrrell battle. Peterson (JPS Lotus) won; Cevert (Tyrrell) was second. Then Peterson took pole position for the British Grand Prix,

RIGHT: Graham Hill (left) and Jackie Stewart. Driving a Shadow, Hill (>1962, 1968) had a poor year, dropping out of five Grands Prix with mechanical trouble. Stewart retired at the end of the season – at the very top of the sport. He was World Champion for the third time (>1969, 1971) and had amassed 27 Grand Prix wins, more than any other driver since the World Championship was inaugurated (>1950).

RIGHT: 'Super Swede'. Ronnie Peterson (>1978) in a Lotus 72D, heading for victory in the United States Grand Prix on 7 October. He finished just 0.688 second ahead of James Hunt in a March. Peterson had moved to Lotus from March earlier in the year.

staged at Silverstone.

It was a race many drivers later wanted to forget. Lauda's BRM broke a drive shaft on the grid and he was hit from behind by Jackie Oliver in a Shadow, taking a wheel off. As the race got under way, Peterson took the lead in front of Stewart, but Stewart passed him on the first lap and pulled away from the rest of the field. As Jody Scheckter, lying fourth, completed his first lap, his McLaren M23

skidded on an oil patch. He drifted on to the grass, bounced back on to the track, right into the path of the crowded field led by his teammate Denny Hulme. Scheckter hit the pit wall sideways; Hulme hit him; and the rest of the field piled into each other, damaging twelve cars. Only one driver, Andrea de Adamich was injured, with a broken ankle. Stewart only just managed to avoid ploughing into the wreckage at the end of his second lap. Three

cars were repaired, but nine were eliminated.

Peterson led the restarted race, Lauda – his car repaired – in hot pursuit, followed by Stewart, until Stewart spun after selecting the wrong gear at a corner. Finally the newcomers, Peterson and James Hunt, and the veterans, Peter Revson and Denny Hulme, were left to chase the points, although Stewart's main rival for the World Championship, Emerson Fittipaldi, stayed with them until his drive shaft broke. Revson took the race for McLaren – his first Grand Prix victory.

Having missed beating Clark's record, Stewart made up for it by taking the Dutch and German Grands Prix, giving him 27 Grand Prix wins – more than enough to take his third World Drivers' title.

The last race of the season was the United States Grand Prix. Stewart had planned to retire after the race, his 100th Grand Prix, but his team-mate François Cevert was killed in an accident and Ken Tyrrell withdrew the team. The occasion was overshadowed by Cevert's death, but the newcomers were as competitive as ever. Lauda was in front at one point – the first time that he had ever led a World Championship event – before Peterson and Hunt came to the front, fighting a close battle which Peterson finally won. His victory, with Emerson Fittipaldi's points, gave Lotus its sixth Constructors' title.

Monaco

The famous 'round the houses' circuit in Monte Carlo was modified in 1973. The new route bypassed the old Tabac by curling around the swimming pool with two chicanes. It remained a gruelling drive for drivers – and engines. Of 25 starters in the 1973 race, 16 broke down – but the Ford engines of race-winner Jackie Stewart and second-placed Emerson Fittipaldi performed faultlessly.

RIGHT: Jackie Stewart in a Tyrrell-Ford took pole position and chequered flag in the 1973 Monaco Grand Prix. Stewart enjoyed the demanding Monaco circuit more than any other in the World Championship.

BELOW: The new circuit.

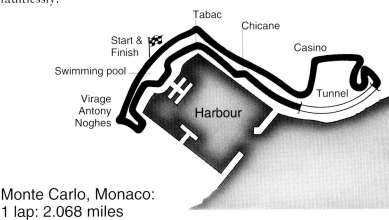

Monte Carlo, Monaco:
1 lap: 2.068 miles

The traumatic events during the 1973 Indianapolis 500 prompted changes to the rules. The limit on fuel consumption was reduced from 340 to 280 (US) gallons, and the fuel tank had to be positioned on the left of the car – on the infield side, away from the spectators. Tank capacity was restricted to 40 gallons – which meant at least six pit-stops – but because it was possible to change a set of tyres in the time it took to put in 40 gallons, each set of tyres would now not have to last as long. That in turn meant they could be made of softer compounds, making them stickier.

The USAC rule-makers were also alarmed at the progress of the turbocharger. Foyt engines – the Ford V-8s that A.J. Foyt had taken over when Henry Ford II decided to pull out of racing – produced around 825 bhp. The four-cylinder Offys were producing around 1,000 bhp. To restrict power, the USAC introduced 'pop-off valves', which teams had to fit to the inlet manifold. Once boost reached a pressure of 39 pounds per square inch, the valve opened, acting as a limiter on the boost. They were highly unpopular with most drivers, and it was generally agreed that they gave an advantage to the Foyt-engined cars because they came into operation closer to the Foyt's maximum power output.

A.J. Foyt himself took pole position following a fastest qualifying lap at 191.632 mph – down 7 mph on the previous year – but Wally

RIGHT: James Hunt (>1993) took third place in a Hesketh-Ford in the Swedish Grand Prix. Following Jackie Stewart's retirement (>1973), British hopes for Grand Prix success rested on the shoulders of this 27-year-old Englishman. The Hesketh team – owned by Lord Alexander Hesketh (>1973) – was notorious for its loud parties, but it fielded excellent cars and was a solid base for Hunt's bid for stardom.

MILESTONES

The effectiveness of the rear aerofoil on Formula One cars was reduced by fixing its position 1 metre (39.37 inches) from the axle.

Hans-Joachim Stuck, son of the Auto Union driver Hans Stuck (>1934), made his Formula One debut in Argentina driving a March 741.

The American driver Peter Revson (>1971) was killed when the suspension broke in the Shadow DN3 he was testing at Kyalami in South Africa.

Mike Hailwood retired after a bad accident in the German Grand Prix in the Yardley-McLaren. He was killed in a road accident in 1981.

Denny Hulme retired from Formula One after ten seasons that included 112 Grand Prix starts, eight victories and one World Championship (>1967).

Goodyear won the 'tyre war' with Firestone, equipping every winning car in the 15 races in the World Championship (>1977).

Dallenbach, second fastest in his Eagle-Offy, beat Foyt into the first turn. The most surprising start came from Johnny Rutherford, who started in 25th place on the grid in his McLaren-Offy, and passed nine cars before he reached Turn 2. By lap 11 he was in third place. Foyt was now leading, and a fierce battle followed between him, Bobby Unser for Eagle, and Rutherford, who took the lead on lap 65. The battle continued until lap 142, when Foyt's scavenger pump failed, and although Unser closed to within 11 seconds of Rutherford, he had to reduce turbocharger boost to conserve fuel – and Rutherford won.

It was a year of changing fortunes in the Formula One Championship. The new drivers

the current Constructors' Champions and with six Constructors' titles and five Drivers' titles behind them, was also now in a trough. Their new car, the Lotus 76, was launched at the London Theatre with a great fanfare – the first John Player Special to start from scratch under the tobacco giant's sponsorship. It was lighter, and had a new, sleeker monocoque, or 'tub', although the Cosworth engine, brakes and suspension were arranged in much the same way as before. The most novel feature was an electromagnetic clutch, operated by a button on the top of the gear lever. The idea was to free the driver's left foot to depress only the brake: he could brake with the left while keeping the revs up with the right when going into corners. The clutch caused a lot of problems, and the handling was not as good as the Lotus 72's, so Ronnie Peterson persuaded Colin Chapman to revert to the older cars for the Monaco Grand Prix – and promptly won it.

Emerson Fittipaldi had left Lotus for McLaren, to drive the M23 alongside Denny Hulme. They had arguably the best car, and they were well financed – their success in America bringing the backing of the American oil giant Texaco, in addition to sponsorship by Marlboro cigarettes. A third M23 was

ABOVE: Clay Regazzoni (No. 11, Ferrari) ahead of Jean-Pierre Jarier (Shadow), Jacky Ickx (No. 2, Lotus) and Ronnie Peterson (No. 1, Lotus) in the US Grand Prix. Regazzoni finished 11th; Jarier was 10th; Ickx retired; Peterson was 13th.

RIGHT: Regazzoni (centre) on the podium after victory in a Ferrari in the German Grand Prix on 4 August. South African driver Jody Scheckter (left) came second in a Tyrrell-Ford, and Carlos Reutemann (right) third in a Brabham-Ford.

brought into Formula One by the expansion of the previous two years either fell by the wayside or made their mark. Three who rapidly made their presence felt were Niki Lauda at Ferrari, Carlos Reutemann at Brabham, and South African Jody Scheckter at Tyrrell. François Cevert's death and Jackie Stewart's retirement had left Ken Tyrrell with a big hole to fill, but he had a talent for picking new drivers, and duly brought the young Frenchman Patrick Depailler into the team.

BRM was all but a spent force. Its V-12 engine was uncompetitive, and in the previous year the team gained only 10 Championship points.

Lotus, pre-eminent for more than a decade,

RIGHT: Emerson Fittipaldi in a McLaren M23 at the German Grand Prix. He retired after two laps because of damage sustained when his car was shunted on the starting grid by another M23, driven by Denny Hulme.

sponsored by Yardley Cosmetics for Mike Hailwood. Hulme started the season well, winning the Argentinian Grand Prix, before Fittipaldi added the Brazilian, Belgian and Canadian races to the M23's crown.

From its low point in 1973, Ferrari was on the way back up. A test track was built at Fiorano, near the Maranello factory, where aerodynamics, tyres and engines could be tested for hours on end close to the factory. The emphasis was once again on Formula One rather than on sports car racing, and Mauro Forghieri was given winning as his priority. Forghieri became technical director, while the team management was put under Luca di Montezemolo. Forghieri's new 312B3s were the fastest cars of the season. Lauda took nine pole positions, and Clay Regazzoni one more – but for reasons of bad luck and poor reliability, the promise in fact yielded only two Championship wins: Lauda won in Holland and Regazzoni in Germany.

Nonetheless, Niki Lauda was leading the Championship at the time of the British Grand Prix, for which he had a practice time identical to Peterson's in the Lotus 72. In the race, he led from Scheckter and Regazzoni, steadily pulling away from them until lap 55, when he sustained a slow puncture. The Ferrari started handling badly, but he stuck with it, eager for the points, despite signals from the pits that they had a new tyre ready. With five laps to go, Scheckter's Tyrrell passed him. The tyre

ABOVE: Emerson Fittipaldi, World Champion for the second time (>1972). He was born in Brazil in 1946, the son of a journalist, Wilson Fittipaldi, who had covered Juan Manuel Fangio's European successes in 1950. He came to Europe in 1969.

finally burst on the last lap but one, and he rumbled into the pits on the flat. The pit crew changed it in 20 seconds – but by then the pit lane was choked with people watching Scheckter take the chequered flag. Fearing an accident, a marshal showed him the red flag, placing him ninth. He was furious and appealed to the FIA, who raised his position to fifth because the red flag, which signified the end of the race, had been shown incorrectly.

Reutemann won the Austrian Grand Prix for Brabham, and Peterson the Italian Grand Prix for Lotus, and as the end of the season – in the form of the United States Grand Prix – approached, both Championship titles were undecided. McLaren was leading in the Constructors' race, but any one from Fittipaldi and Regazzoni, both with 52 points,

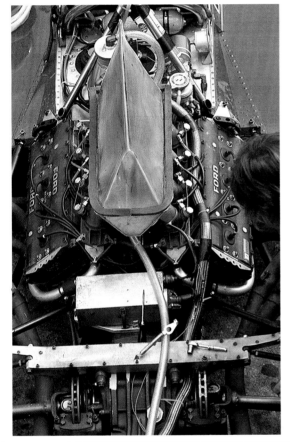

and Scheckter with 45 points, could still become World Champion, although Scheckter only if the other two failed to finish.

Practice produced some surprises. None of the potential World Champions lined up at the front of the grid. Reutemann took pole position, James Hunt in the Hesketh alongside him. Behind them were Mario Andretti in the Parnelli Jones VPJ4, designed by Maurice Phillippe, and Carlos Pace. Then came the contenders for the title and another American team, Penske, its Cosworth-powered car driven by Indianapolis winner Mark Donohue.

Reutemann and Hunt pulled away, with Pace in third; behind came Lauda, Scheckter and Fittipaldi. Regazzoni was in ninth place and experiencing suspension problems, and as long as he was out of contention, Fittipaldi drove a tactical race, needing only the certainty of more points than the Ferrari driver to take the title. When Scheckter dropped out with a broken fuel pipe, Fittipaldi's position improved to fourth place. Hunt lost second place to Pace, after the Hesketh developed an intermittent fuel problem – and that is how they finished. Reutemann and Pace brought in the Brabhams in the first two places.

There was jubilation all round – at the McLaren pit, for taking both Championship titles, their first; and at the Brabham pit for a victory that pointed to their team's becoming a force again.

LEFT: The power behind McLaren's victory in the Constructors' Championship – the 365-lb 460-bhp Ford Cosworth DFV engine. The engine had a small frontal area which enabled designers to keep down the width of the car, thus making it more efficient aerodynamically.

British team-owner Frank Williams' first Formula One success was in 1969, with Brabhams. During the early 1970s, his team ran de Tomaso and March cars. The first Williams car, the FX3 – sponsored by the toy company Politoys – renamed Iso-Marlboros – competed in 1973–74. Williams had difficulty keeping his team together in these years; his first real success came in 1978 with the FW06 (*LEFT*) (>1979).

Having made Formula One its priority, Ferrari produced a much-modified 312 for 1975, the 312T. The wheelbase was lengthened, and the flat-12 engine tuned to produce 500 bhp. Mauro Forghieri followed Derek Gardner's lead with the Tyrrell 006 (>1973), striving for a 'low polar moment of inertia' by putting as much of the weight of the car within the wheelbase. To achieve it, Forghieri moved the gearbox through 90 degrees, using bevel gears to enable him to lay it sideways, bringing the weight closer to the centre, and giving it the T suffix that stood for *trasversale*. The car was highly manoeuvrable, and at first tricky to handle, but once Niki Lauda found its full potential he loved it.

The ebb and flow of ingenuity and effort in top-level racing, which had lifted Ferrari from its low point, saw Lotus head in the opposite direction. The Lotus 76 had been a complete failure: Ronnie Peterson and Jacky Ickx had no option but to continue with the ageing 72s. Colin Chapman, who had come up with radical ideas three times before – the monocoque, the engine bolted to the 'tub', the wedge shape – had a long, hard think and decided he needed a completely new idea to put Lotus back on top. What he came up with was as far-sighted

as ever – the 'wing car'. The idea was very simple to conceive, but much harder to deliver: using the whole car as an aerodynamic device to give it downforce on the track, rather than relying on inverted wings at the back and front. He wrote a long document that he then issued to Lotus's technical director, Tony Rudd, and told him to set up a special team to make it work (>1977).

In the opening rounds of the World Championship in South America, the Ferrari drivers Lauda and Clay Regazzoni were using the older 312Bs until the *trasversale* was ready. Emerson Fittipaldi won the Argentinian Grand Prix for McLaren, and Carlos Pace won the Brazilian for Brabham. The 312Ts made their racing debut at Kyalami in the South African Grand Prix, but they were still finding their full potential, and Jody Scheckter won on home territory for Tyrrell.

The Spanish Grand Prix was nearly cancelled when the drivers found that safety precautions were very poor. Noticing that there were bolts missing from the Armco barriers, at first they refused to drive – until the organizers threatened to have the cars impounded, and they raced under duress. The two new Ferraris were involved in a collision with

BELOW: Carlos Reutemann in a Brabham-Ford, winner of the German Grand Prix at the Nürburgring on 3 August. He finished 1 minute 37.7 seconds ahead of Jaques Laffite in a Williams FW04 – winning Frank Williams' first World Championship points as a constructor.

RIGHT: The start of the French Grand Prix. From the left: Jody Scheckter (No. 3, Tyrrell-Ford), Niki Lauda (No. 12, Ferrari), Carlos Pace (No. 8, Brabham-Ford), Clay Regazzoni (No. 11, Ferrari) and Carlos Reutemann (No. 7, Brabham-Ford). Lauda won; Scheckter came ninth; Reutemann was 14th; Pace and Regazzoni retired.

ABOVE: Ferrari renaissance. Niki Lauda at speed in the 312 *trasversale* during the French Grand Prix at the Paul Ricard circuit, near Marseilles. The 312T's twelve-cylinder 180-degree engine developed around 500 bhp at 12,200 rpm. Lauda and the new car gave Ferrari the first of three World Constructors' Championships (>1976, 1977).

ABOVE: Niki Lauda, 1975 World Champion (>1977). He took pole position in nine out of 14 World Championship events and won five – in Monaco, Belgium, Sweden, France and the USA. He finished with 64½ points, ahead of Emerson Fittipaldi with 45.

ing at the time, he was announced the winner.

Lauda took pole position for the next race, at Monaco, which started in rain. His Ferrari was in the lead by the end of the first lap, followed by Peterson in the Lotus 72, Tom Pryce for Shadow, then Scheckter, Fittipaldi and Pace. The weather changed, and they all went in for dry-weather tyres. A superb 20-second pit-stop put Fittipaldi in second place, but nothing he could do could catch Lauda, who won a landmark victory for Ferrari – the first for the *trasversale*, their first at Monaco since 1955, and Lauda's own first in the race.

Fittipaldi was still leading the World Championship, but Lauda managed to pull back by winning the Belgian and Swedish races. Then the Ferraris were forced into sec-

Mario Andretti's Parnelli VPJ4, putting them both out. Fittipaldi drove only a few laps at a desultory pace, then retired to sit the rest of the race out in sullen protest. He did not have to wait long. The wing on Rolf Stommelen's Hill-Cosworth came off, and he spun into the barrier, killing nine people. The organizers then stopped the race, and because Jochen Mass – the new No.2 at McLaren – was lead-

laurels went to Ferrari: Regazzoni won, and Lauda came in in third place, clinching both titles, Ferrari's first since 1964. To cap it all, Lauda went on to win the richest prize on the Grand Prix circuit, the US Grand Prix.

Indianapolis was another struggle between the great names of the day in American racing. Dan Gurney, who had been trying to win the 500 for 14 years as both driver and team owner with Eagle and All-American Racers, had his hopes pinned on Bobby Unser. Eagle's great opponent, McLaren, was represented by the previous year's winning driver, Johnny Rutherford. Some of the greatest names in the Speedway's history were represented in a new form. Wally Dallenbach was driving a Wildcat car sponsored by STP, which had a new engine, the SGD. It was in fact an Offy, heavily modified, the initials standing for Sparks

ABOVE: Home win for Ferrari – Clay Regazzoni in the 312T, winner of the Italian Grand Prix ahead of Emerson Fittipaldi (McLaren-Ford) and Ferrari team-mate Niki Lauda.

ond and third places in the Dutch Grand Prix, beaten on tyre changes by James Hunt, who thereby gave Hesketh its first victory (>1976). Lauda won the French Grand Prix, putting him ahead in the title race – but Fittipaldi then won the British Grand Prix.

Lauda could clinch the title by finishing in the points in the Italian Grand Prix. The two Ferraris led from the start, Regazzoni in front. There was a huge pile-up in the chicane, which put five cars out of the running. Then Lauda's car started handling badly due to a faulty shock absorber. Fittipaldi gained steadily, passing Lauda with six laps to go – but the

ABOVE: Mary Hulman, wife of Speedway owner Tony Hulman (>1977), took on from her husband the responsibility of getting the 500 under way by pronouncing the traditional opening line: 'Gentlemen, start your engines.'

MILESTONES

With little success as a driver, Wilson Fittipaldi turned team owner, backed by Brazil's huge sugar company, Copersucar (>1976).

After 17 seasons, Graham Hill retired after failing to qualify for Monaco. He drove in 176 Grands Prix, achieving 14 wins and two World Drivers' titles.

The state-owned French car giant Renault decided to enter Formula One with a turbocharged 1.5-litre version of its V-6 sports car unit.

Roger Penske's No.1 driver, the Indy winner Mark Donohue, died in a crash during practice for the Austrian Grand Prix at Zeltweg.

On 28 November Graham Hill, his driver Tom Brise, and five members of his team were killed when the aircraft Hill was piloting crashed.

A.J. Foyt became United States Auto Club National Champion for a record sixth time. He won previously in 1960, 1961, 1963, 1964 and 1967.

Goosen Drake. Art Sparks had worked with Leo Goosen on modifications to his engines in the 1930s (>1937), and he was still in touch. Goosen had been working with Offenhausers, and before them Millers, for more than 50 years (>1919). Sparks suggested using a narrower valve layout to improve fuel-air breathing, similar to the Ford Cosworth's; Dale Drake, who owned the company, agreed. Goosen drew up the modifications, but before the project was complete, both Goosen and Drake died, and Drake's son completed it, naming it after the trio of veterans who had built it.

The other great name in contention was another folk legend at Indianapolis – A.J. Foyt, a man ambitious to become the first driver ever to win the 500 four times. He was in pole position in a Foyt-powered Coyote. Next to him was Gordon Johncock (>1982), and on the outside of the front row was Bobby Unser. Johncock was first into Turn 1, taking the lead from Foyt; then Foyt moved to the front under pressure from both Unser and Rutherford. On lap 60 they were joined by Dallenbach, and a great battle between the four ensued. The yellow flags came out on lap 133, after Tom Sneva had a spectacular accident, right in front of the VIP stand, which wrecked his car although he was virtually uninjured. The duel thereafter resumed until Dallenbach retired with a burnt-out piston on lap 162.

With 30 laps to go, a heavy rainstorm approached the Speedway, starting its downpour on Turns 3 and 4. Dan Gurney could be heard on the radio imploring Unser to slow down before he entered the wet zone, but Unser barely eased off, went into the wall of water, nearly lost it, recovered, nearly lost it again, then regained complete control in time to see another car spinning around in a cloud of spray in front of him. He slowed right down, to 35 mph, as he crossed the line. The Chief Steward, seeing the severity of the rain, cancelled the rest of the race, so Unser won – giving Gurney his place among the winning team owners at Indianapolis.

BELOW: James Hunt in the Cosworth-engined Hesketh 308C during the British Grand Prix at Silverstone on 19 July. He was involved in a major accident on lap 56 – with Tony Brise, Jody Scheckter, Carlos Pace, David Morgan, Brian Henton, Wilson Fittipaldi and John Nicholson. The race was stopped: Hunt was classified fourth. Earlier in the season, Hunt had scored his first World Championship win – in the Dutch Grand Prix.

RIGHT: One of the most courageous comebacks in the history of motor racing. Niki Lauda finished fourth in the Italian Grand Prix on 12 September – less than six weeks after a horrific accident in the German Grand Prix.

BELOW: Head to head. The 1976 World Championship was a thrilling confrontation between Niki Lauda (left) and James Hunt. The ruthless competition was restricted to the track, however; when not locked in the struggle for points, they treated each other politely and with respect.

Having dominated Grand Prix racing for a decade with their DFV engine, Cosworth entered the lucrative business of supplying engines to Indianapolis teams, and the engine they supplied was a turbocharged cousin of the DFV, the DFX. It was Parnelli Jones who, when he gave up his Formula One project, the Cosworth-powered VPJ4, at the end of 1975 to concentrate on Indianapolis, realized that the DFV had potential at Indianapolis. He reduced its cubic capacity to 162 cubic inches (2.65 litres), added a turbocharger, and managed to get 880 bhp out of it at 9,200 rpm. Eager to open up a new and highly lucrative market, Cosworth produced the new engine for Indianapolis: the DFX was born.

For its first appearance at the Speedway, Al Unser qualified fourth fastest in the Parnelli car; Johnny Rutherford took pole position for McLaren again. In the race, Rutherford had a fierce tussle with his fellow Texan A.J. Foyt for 255 miles, until rain once again brought the race to a premature end, with Rutherford in the lead. Unser and the Cosworth-powered Parnelli were seventh (>1977, 1978).

This year the World Championship was run over 16 races – the latest entries were races in Japan and a second United States Grand Prix, at Long Beach, California. In another attempt to limit the designers' scope to increase speed, the formula was changed: the high air-scoops above the drivers' heads were banned; the rear wing was moved forward 20 centimetres (8 inches); overall width was limited to 215 centimetres (7 feet ½ inch); height was restricted to 85 centimetres (2 feet 9½ inches) above the lowest unsprung part of the car; tyre width was limited to 21 inches (533 millimetres); and wheel diameter limited to 13 inches (330 millimetres).

Emerson Fittipaldi had left McLaren to join his brother Wilson's Copersucar-Fittipaldi team – a surprising move in relation to his level of expertise and his brother's lack of experience. Lord Hesketh then decided that Formula One racing at the top level was too expensive and pulled out, leaving James Hunt with no car. Hunt was quickly snapped up by McLaren, with Jochen Mass as second driver. Mario Andretti joined Ronnie Peterson at Lotus to drive the Lotus 77, an interim car, pending the completion of the 'wing car' (>1974). Unhappy with the arrangement, however, Peterson left to join March early in the season.

It was a season dominated by the reigning World Champion, Niki Lauda, who stayed with Ferrari, and James Hunt, now with McLaren. Ferrari made a strong start: Lauda won the first two races – the Brazilian and South African Grands Prix – although he had to battle all the way with Hunt, who finished just half a second behind at Kyalami. Lauda's team-mate Clay Regazzoni then won the Long Beach Grand Prix.

It was a season also bedevilled by controversy. The new regulations came into force at the Spanish Grand Prix, in which the McLaren drivers found their form, lying in first and second places for much of the race – pushing Lauda into third place – until Mass's engine blew up. Hunt won, but in their eagerness to enforce the new regulations, officials carried out spot checks on the cars and Hunt's M23D was found to be 1.8 centimetres (seven tenths of an inch) over the maximum width and he was disqualified. McLaren protested to the FIA – but Lauda was awarded the race, giving Ferrari four races out of four and a 27-point lead in the Championship.

Lauda won the next two Grands Prix. Then Jody Scheckter and Patrick Depailler came first and second in the Swedish Grand Prix in the six-wheeled Tyrrell; Lauda was third, taking his lead to a massive 47 points. Lauda retired from the French Grand Prix with a mechanical fault and Hunt won the race, narrowing the lead. On the very next day, the result of the appeal over the Spanish Grand Prix was announced – in Hunt's favour, cutting Lauda's lead to 26 points: Lauda was

RIGHT: British triumph. James Hunt's McLaren-Ford (No. 11) in the Japanese Grand Prix, aiming for third place in the race – and victory in the World Championship. Because the visibility was so bad, he was not sure that he had come third until reassured at the finish by delighted McLaren pit-crew.

MILESTONES

The Argentinian Grand Prix was cancelled because of political unrest which finally led to a bloodless coup against President Isabel Peron in March.

John Watson's win in Austria was Penske's only Grand Prix victory. Roger Penske then concentrated on Indy Car racing.

Guy Ligier's Vichy-based team moved into Formula One with backing from Gitanes cigarettes and using a Matra V-12 engine in its JS5 car.

The German Grand Prix was moved from the Nürburgring (>1927) to Hockenheim following Lauda's accident. It was moved back in 1985.

Lella Lombardi, the only woman ever to gain World Championship points – in Spain in 1975 – failed to qualify for the British Grand Prix.

Alfa-Romeo returned to Formula One after an absence of 25 years; the Italian firm supplied a flat-12 engine for the Brabham-Alfa BT45.

abruptly 21 points down in the course of a single weekend.

The new situation heightened tension between the teams for the British Grand Prix. Hunt was fastest in practice on the first day, then Lauda just beat him to pole position on the second day. The two were alongside each other on the front row of the grid, Regazzoni just behind. Lauda made a good start, but Hunt was slow and Regazzoni shot through, reaching the first corner just behind Lauda. The two Ferraris collided. Lauda pulled clear, but Regazzoni went broadside to the approaching pack and Hunt hit him. Trying to avoid the crash, the French driver Jacques Laffite, in a Ligier, hit the bank. The race was stopped for the debris to be cleared. For the restart Regazzoni, Hunt and Laffite all appeared in their spare cars, but officials decided that under the rules they could not be allowed to compete, and they were ordered from the grid. There were howls of disapproval from the crowd – and further discussions ensued. Meanwhile, McLaren mechanics repaired Hunt's car. The officials changed their minds and allowed all three to race.

Lauda led for the first 45 laps before his gearbox started mis-selecting gears and he fell back. Hunt won. Now it was Ferrari's turn to appeal to the FIA on the grounds that Hunt's car had been worked on when the race was not in progress, putting the Championship lead in limbo once again.

The two men were side by side on the grid again for the German Grand Prix at the Nürburgring. The circuit was wet in patches, and Lauda had wet-weather tyres. On the first lap he fell back a long way, and stopped to change for dry-weather tyres. Coming into the Bergwerk corner at 150 mph on a damp surface, he lost control and ploughed into a bank, ricocheted into the path of the oncoming cars, two of which hit him, then hit the opposite bank, already on fire. Four other drivers stopped and dragged him from the flames, but his face had been severely burned and he had inhaled noxious fumes from the burning car.

BELOW: Wally Dallenbach (Sinmast, No. 40) ahead of Al Loquasto (Frostie Root Beer, No. 86) in the Indianapolis 500. Dallenbach came fourth; Loquasto was 25th. Janet Guthrie, the first woman to enter the 500, passed the rookie test but failed to qualify for the race (>1978).

RIGHT: The Long Beach Grand Prix. Patrick Depailler's Tyrrell (No. 4), Niki Lauda's Ferrari (No. 1), Tom Pryce's Shadow (No. 16) and Ronnie Peterson's March (No. 10). Lauda finished second; Depailler was third; Peterson was 10th; Pryce retired.

ABOVE: The six-wheeler Tyrrell P34. Designer Derek Gardner said he used smaller, 10-inch-diameter front wheels to reduce aerodynamic uplift at the nose and to increase cornering speeds. The P34 had quite a successful debut season in 1976 – the high point being first (Jody Scheckter) and second (Patrick Depailler) in the Swedish Grand Prix on 13 June.

ABOVE: One for the rule book. The first-lap shunt at the British Grand Prix, from left: Clay Regazzoni's Ferrari (No. 2), Carlos Pace's Brabham (No. 8), James Hunt's McLaren (No. 11), Jochen Mass' McLaren (No. 12), Chris Amon's Ensign (No. 22). Subsequent controversy centred on whether Hunt was still moving when the red flags stopped the race.

Lauda was taken to hospital. The race was restarted, and Hunt won again, closing on Lauda by yet another 9 points in the Championship.

Lauda was in intensive care, and the doctors gave him little hope of survival, even arranging for a priest to administer the last rites. But Lauda was a fighter. He refused to die, and made a painful recovery. While Lauda was in hospital, Hunt won the Dutch Grand Prix, to lie only 2 points behind him in the World Championship at the Italian Grand Prix – where Lauda arrived, horribly scarred, to continue the battle: an extraordinary testi-mony to his courage and indomitable forti-tude. This time Hunt retired and Lauda came fourth, widening the gap again. It was widened still further when the FIA announced that it had upheld Ferrari's appeal over the British Grand Prix, which was now officially awarded to Lauda.

Spurred on by the perversity of the decision, Hunt went out with a vengeance, winning the Canadian and United States Grands Prix – races from which Lauda gained only 3 points, putting them neck-and-neck again. With only one race to go – the first-ever Japanese Grand Prix – Lauda was just 3 points ahead of Hunt.

The Fuji circuit was shrouded in mist and rain, which delayed the start. When the cars did get away, Lauda did two laps then retired. Later, Ferrari announced that it was because of a technical failure, but Lauda himself insisted on the truth – he had retired because he regarded the conditions as too dangerous. The race continued: Mario Andretti gave Lotus their only victory of the season. But Hunt's third place was enough to give him the Championship by 1 point after the closest battle in its 26-year history.

CHAPTER ELEVEN
TURBOS, TELEVISION &
PLASTIC ROLLER SKATES

Over the course of more than 80 years, the racing car had evolved into a highly specialized, temperamental vehicle. Like a thoroughbred horse it needed constant care and attention.

In the late 1970s, the process accelerated: 'ground effects' – wings and other devices that literally stuck the car to the ground with forces up to three times that of gravity – were introduced. In theory, if the track were turned upside down, a car with ground effects would continue on, glued to the surface by suction. Designers increasingly took the lead from the aircraft industry, and used exotic materials – notably carbon fibre – to make stronger monocoques. Hence arose the derisory term 'plastic roller skate', coined by those who preferred their cars made of traditional aluminium.

Engines also went through a revolution. Absent from Grand Prix racing since 1907, Renault introduced turbocharging to Formula One in 1977, producing 520 bhp by 1980. By 1985 BMW was getting 1,300 bhp out of the same cubic capacity. As the turbo engine developed, so did the electronic systems to manage it – microchips to give precision fuel efficiency and perfect ignition timing, computers to record performance during practice – so that cars could be set up perfectly for each circuit, then monitored during the race via a data link.

In addition came exotic fuels, new compounds for tyres . . .

Progress has always had a high price, but in the 1980s it soared. A Formula One team of two cars cost more than £20 million a year. Sponsorship to provide the cars and drivers became the powerbase in the sport, and the teams recognized it. Led by Roger Penske in the United States, they wrested power from the traditional governing bodies, principally by earning the right to negotiate television coverage. At the end of the 1980s, the Grand Prix World Championship and the Indy Car World Series (with races across the States, in Canada and Australia) were being watched by a worldwide television audience exceeded only by audiences for the Olympic Games and World Cup soccer.

Motor racing was barely a sport – it was a high-tech multi-million-pound global industry.

Turbos and television: Alain Prost demonstrating the Renault RE30 for the cameras prior to the French Grand Prix in 1981.

It was a year of surprises in Formula One racing – of debuts and departures, of new relationships made and old ones broken. Clay Regazzoni left Ferrari at the beginning of the season to join Ensign, his place being taken by Carlos Reutemann, from Brabham. The six-wheeled P34 failed to live up to expectations, so Jody Scheckter left Tyrrell to drive for a completely new name: Wolf. Walter Wolf, a Canadian oil plant manufacturer, had bought the Hesketh cars and equipment and taken on the designer, Harvey Postlethwaite, when it folded. He merged the new assets with those of Williams, in which he had taken a controlling interest in 1976 when it was in financial difficulties. They had a disastrous season in 1976 and Frank Williams left, to be replaced by Peter Warr, the ex-Lotus team manager. For 1977 they had a completely new car – the WR1 – in which Scheckter won the first race of the season in Argentina. He went on to win both the Monaco and Canadian Grands Prix, putting him second in the World Drivers' Championship and Wolf fourth in the Constructors' in its opening season, suggesting great promise.

During the year, a close working relationship developed between Colin Chapman and Mario Andretti, just as Lotus needed a good driver to develop the Lotus 78 'wing car' for which Andretti had great enthusiasm. It was the kind of relationship that Chapman had enjoyed with Jim Clark but since failed to find with other drivers. The Lotus 78 was unveiled in December 1976, the result of a great deal of research, including some 400 hours of wind-tunnel tests alone. The monocoque was made of Cellite, an aluminium honeycomb sandwiched between two layers of Duralumin, a very strong and stiff material used in aircraft. On each side were pods with an air intake at the front, which contained the radiators, and 'upside-down wings', which provided the downforce. The wings were hollow, and doubled as fuel tanks. The crucial point was that they were enclosed within the pods, creating inside a low-pressure area, or partial vacuum, which literally sucked the whole car towards the track, giving 15 per cent more downforce than 'conventional' wings, which it also retained at front and back. Goodyear had to develop special tyres with much stiffer walls that could take the extra force. Andretti was later to refer to driving the car as if it was 'painted to the road'.

Andretti gave the Lotus 78 its first World Championship win at the United States West Grand Prix at Long Beach, and went on to add victories at the Spanish, French and Italian races, while team-mate Gunnar Nilsson took

BELOW: Super Mario. Mario Andretti in a Lotus 78 during the French Grand Prix. He took pole position and drove the fastest lap (115.26 mph), but trailed John Watson's Brabham-Alfa for most of the race – until Watson ran out of fuel just before the finish. Andretti won in 1 hour 39 minutes 40.13 seconds, just 1.55 seconds ahead of Watson.

British Racing Motors' career in top-level racing (>1950) ended in disarray in 1977. A new car, the P207, was launched – but did not compete in a single World Championship event. Australian driver Larry Perkins was signed up: he missed the first race, in Argentina, because the car was stranded in England – and the second, in Brazil, because it broke down in practice. The last appearance by a BRM car in the World Championship was at the third race, the South African Grand Prix on 5 March (left). Perkins drove a 1976 car – the P201B/204 – because the P207 was still not ready. He finished 15th; later in the season he left the team. When the P207 was available, drivers Conny Andersson and Teddy Pilette failed to qualify in a succession of races, and BRM's sponsorship deal with Rotary Watches fell apart.

the Belgian. Like all Chapman's innovations, the 'wing car' concept set the standard and was followed by other designers.

The debut of a technical development that was to have as far-reaching an effect on Grand Prix racing as wings, but which had a less auspicious beginning, took place at the British Grand Prix. The huge French car company Renault had noticed that Formula One allowed for a 1.5-litre supercharged engine, even though nobody had used the option. They decided to take on the British 'kit-car' teams, adapting their 90-degree V-6 sports car engine – using a turbocharger to give 500 bhp at 11,000 rpm – and building their own chassis. In 21st place on the Silverstone grid was the

first Renault to enter a Grand Prix since 1907: the RS01, driven by Jean-Pierre Jabouille. He retired early on with a manifold fracture, and failed to finish four other races in 1977, but the car marked the beginning of a new chapter in Formula One (>1979).

After two years at the top, Ferrari's fortunes came under pressure. Niki Lauda's retirement from the Japanese Grand Prix in 1976 had brought him heavy criticism in the Italian press, and there had been implicit criticism too from Ferrari, who excluded him from the winter testing programme at Fiorano. In the Brazilian Grand Prix, Reutemann had been given a new wing for his 312T – and he won the race – but the wing was not offered to

LEFT: Emerson Fittipaldi in the Copersucar-Fittipaldi-Ford F5 during the British Grand Prix. He retired with engine trouble. Fittipaldi had a very disappointing season in the F5 – not even a driver of his talent could win in a car that was not remotely a threat to the established teams.

RIGHT: The engine that changed the face of Formula One. Renault's EF1 Turbo was the first turbocharged engine in Grand Prix racing when it made its debut in the RS01 at the British Grand Prix. Jean-Pierre Jabouille was 21st on the grid and retired after 16 laps when the turbocharger developed problems.

Two people were killed and seven injured in a spectacular accident during the Japanese Grand Prix – but both drivers walked away. Gilles Villeneuve's Ferrari caught the back of Ronnie Peterson's Tyrrell at the end of the main straight. The Ferrari was catapulted into the air (**LEFT**) and came down on its nose (**BELOW**), before bouncing into a prohibited area which was packed with fans and photographers. The two people who died were a spectator and a track official who had been attempting to move the fans to a safer place.

Lauda. After that, the Ferrari team and the management felt the full force of Lauda's considerable personality as he demanded the best, and pressed for more testing and preparation.

Lauda won the South African Grand Prix, and came a very close second to Andretti in the Lotus 78 at Long Beach. He and Reutemann built up the points, putting Ferrari well ahead in both Championships. Lauda won the German and Dutch Grands Prix, immediately after which – the very next day after the Dutch race – he announced that he would leave Ferrari at the end of the season. The announcement caused uproar among Italian spectators, and Lauda was so concerned for his personal safety that he hired bodyguards for the Italian Grand Prix.

In the race, Lauda had to settle for second place behind Andretti, but with the better overall record of finishing, he was still ahead in the Championship. During practice for the US Grand Prix, the war of nerves between Lauda and Ferrari was made even more tense when his personal mechanic Ermanno Cuoghi was sacked. Lauda did enough to clinch the title by coming fourth. Next, in Canada, he refused to drive. He also missed the Japanese Grand Prix, ending his time with Ferrari on the sourest of notes. Ferrari took on the French-Canadian Gilles Villeneuve, who had shown great promise in his debut in the British Grand Prix, but he was unable to repeat his success that year. Ferrari took the Constructors' title for the third successive year – an extraordinary first – thanks mainly to Lauda.

Nevertheless, the high point of the year was A.J. Foyt's continuing quest to be the first driver to win the Indianapolis 500 four times. Tom Sneva took pole position, Foyt behind him on the second row. Gordon Johncock took the lead, and Foyt had to be content with second place until the first pit-stop, when an excellent turnround put him just ahead. There followed a classic wheel-to-wheel duel until Foyt ran out of fuel, coasting nearly a whole lap round to the pits. At the half-way point, Johncock was half a lap ahead, then Foyt gave one of those rare demonstrations of determination which raised even his high level of skill. Fifty laps later, he was just 2 seconds behind Johncock. Then he went in for fuel just before the yellow flags came out. Johncock took full advantage of the flags to refuel, and was 15 seconds ahead when the green flags came out. Once again, Foyt settled down again to claw

ABOVE: Historic triumph. A.J. Foyt in Victory Circle – the first man to win the 500 four times. He qualified fourth fastest at 194.563 mph; his winning time was 3 hours 5 minutes 57.16 seconds – 161.331 mph.

back the lead, halving it by the last fuel stop. With sixteen laps to go, the crankshaft on Johncock's Offy broke, and he was out. Foyt's car lasted to the end, making him the first man to win four 500s in the 66-year history of the race. His comment afterwards was, 'That's the finest day of my life!'

After the race, Foyt did a lap of honour in the back of an open car, his arm resting on the shoulders of a frail-looking Tony Hulman, the man who had made racing at Indianapolis what it was (>1942–45). Hulman died in October, but by then – thanks to his wise investment of the profits from the Speedway – its finances were in a very good state, and its status as a national institution assured.

MILESTONES

The first driver to exceed 200 mph qualifying for the Indianapolis 500 (>1925) was Tom Sneva, at 200.535 mph in a McLaren-Cosworth.

The first woman to qualify for Indianapolis was Janet Guthrie. She was 26th on the grid having qualified at 188.403 mph, and finished 29th (>1978).

The Brazilian driver Carlos Pace, who started the season well for Brabham, was killed in a light aircraft crash at the age of 33.

Tom Pryce died at Kyalami when he hit and killed a marshal crossing the track with a fire extinguisher to help another driver.

The season saw the last appearance of the BRM team (>1950), which was then disbanded. The remaining cars were sold at auction in 1981.

Jody Scheckter's victory for Wolf-Ford at Monaco was the one-hundredth time a Grand Prix had been won by a Cosworth-engined car (>1967).

The words on almost everybody's lips were 'ground effects'. The term had replaced 'wing car' to describe the new Lotus 79, a refined version of the 78. The sides of the pods had 'sliding skirts' on the outside, to seal the area of low pressure underneath. The fuel was contained in a single fuel cell behind the driver, so that the wings in the pods could be extended, moving the driver's position forward, making him more exposed to danger. On the plus side, it also meant that the fuel tank was in the middle of the car, at less risk of being punctured in a crash. The new cars were not ready at first, and Mario Andretti and Ronnie Peterson (who had rejoined the team from Tyrrell) drove 78s for the early part of the season: Andretti won in Argentina and Peterson in South Africa. Carlos Reutemann made sure the Lotuses did not have it all their own way, winning for Ferrari in Brazil and in the United States Grand Prix at Long Beach.

The designer merry-go-round continued. Colin Chapman lost some of his key people: Ralph Bellamy went to Copersucar-Fittipaldi

and Tony Southgate returned to Shadow. At McLaren, Gordon Coppuck was developing a ground effects car – the M28 – with a honeycomb monocoque chassis, but it was not yet ready for 1978, and James Hunt and Patrick Tambay continued with the M26, a refined version of the venerable M23.

Having shown great promise in the early part of 1977, Wolf had been eclipsed by Lotus and Ferrari. Harvey Postlethwaite brought out a wing car for 1978 – the WR5 – in which Jody Scheckter managed some good place results but no victories. Frank Williams set up Williams Grand Prix Engineering, backed by the Saudi Arabian airline, Saudia. He took Patrick Head with him from Wolf, and signed on the Australian driver Alan Jones. Their first

BELOW: Lotus supremo. Mario Andretti in a Lotus 79 on the way to victory in the Spanish Grand Prix on 4 June. He finished just over 7 seconds ahead of team-mate Ronnie Peterson in second place;

Jacques Laffite was third in a Ligier-Matra. At this stage of the season, Andretti and Peterson filled the first two places in the World Championship, ahead of Patrick Depailler.

RIGHT: The Lotus pits at the German Grand Prix. Team sponsors John Player were furious that journalists and fans continued to refer to the cars as Lotuses rather than as 'John Player Specials'.

LEFT: The Lotus team in 1977 – Mario Andretti (left), Colin Chapman (centre) and Gunnar Nilsson. In 1978, Andretti won the World Drivers' Championship and Chapman celebrated the Constructors' Championship for Lotus-Ford. Nilsson was to have been team leader for Arrows after leaving Lotus at the end of 1977, but he developed cancer and was too ill to race. He died in London's Charing Cross Hospital on 20 October 1978.

car – the FW06, which had no ground effects – was outclassed during the season while Head worked hard on a full ground effects car for 1979.

Maurice Phillippe replaced Derek Gardner at Tyrrell. Peterson now back at Lotus, Ken Tyrrell signed Patrick Depailler and Didier Pironi to drive a four-wheeled derivative of the P34. It was not a ground effects car, but Depailler revived the team's fortunes with a win at Monaco – after which it was thoroughly outclassed by the Lotus.

Shadow had a wing car – the DN9 – which had been designed by Tony Southgate before he and Alan Rees departed to set up their own new team: Arrows. Shadow's drivers, Clay Regazzoni and Hans-Joachim Stuck, shorn of much of their back-up and in the face of the advance of Lotus, had a very poor season. They had more success in the High Court. The first Arrows car – the FA1, a ground effects car – was built in record time; in it Riccardo Patrese came sixth at Long Beach and Monaco, and second in Sweden. But it had so many similarities to the DN9 that Shadow took Arrows to court, where they were judged to be in breach of copyright and banned from using the car. They had another new car ready for Patrese in record time.

The Lotus 79 made its debut at Zolder for the Belgian Grand Prix. Andretti was a full second faster than the rest of the field in practice and led from flag to flag, announcing Lotus's return to dominance in some style. Peterson

was second in a 78. For the Spanish Grand Prix, both drivers were in 79s. They were first and second fastest in practice, and in the race, Andretti won, with Peterson second. Chapman's idea, which had taken three years to grow, had blossomed.

There was a hiccough to Lotus's progress in Sweden. Niki Lauda had joined Brabham, where Gordon Murray had come up with a very different way of achieving ground effects. The BT46B had a huge fan at the rear, driven

MILESTONES

Hans Stuck, the Auto Union driver (>1934), died in February aged 78, having seen his son Hans-Joachim compete in Grands Prix.

Janet Guthrie, the first woman to qualify for the Indianapolis 500 in 1977, finished in ninth place overall in a Wildcat-Offy.

The first victory for Michelin radial tyres came with Carlos Reutemann's victory in the Brazilian Grand Prix in a Ferrari 312T3.

Championship Auto Racing Teams (CART) Inc. was founded by Indy Car teams to run a series of Indy Car races in defiance of the USAC.

For 1979 the CSI banned sliding skirts in ground effects cars. The Formula One Constructors' Association (FOCA) teams ignored the ban (>1981).

Mario Andretti's World Drivers' Championship gave him a unique triple with the Indianapolis 500 (>1969) and Daytona 500.

by the engine, which sucked air from under the car's skirts, giving much the same effect. It caused some controversy, for 'movable aerodynamic devices' had been banned since 1969, but it was allowed to race. Andretti retired and Lauda won – but just as other designers were reaching for what looked like a short cut to downforce, the 'fan car' was banned.

Murray stripped the car down to the monocoque and rebuilt it without the fan. Its Alfa-Romeo engine gave it a slight power advantage over Lotus's Cosworth, and at the French Grand Prix at the Paul Ricard circuit Lauda and John Watson were very fast in practice. Andretti's Lotus hit a kerb in practice, and Watson took pole position by .05 second from him. As the race started, they both charged for the first corner, the Brabham just ahead – but although it was faster on the straights, the Lotus was quicker through the corners, and Andretti finished the first lap ahead. It became a Lotus-Brabham duel, as Lauda and Peterson moved up to third and fourth place. Watson stayed wide on a corner to let Lauda through, but Peterson also saw the gap and charged through too, right on Lauda's tail. Peterson and Lauda touched several times as they fought for second place, but Lauda's engine was failing and he dropped back, leaving the two Lotuses in front. James Hunt then moved up to challenge them for McLaren, and was on Peterson's tail on the last lap when he suddenly spun and fell back; he had been sick from the violent manoeuvring. It was Lotus's third first-and-second in four races.

Reutemann won the British Grand Prix for Ferrari after both of the Lotuses retired. Then Andretti won the German Grand Prix, in which Peterson retired. Peterson won in Austria, where Andretti crashed, and Andretti won in Holland, with Peterson second. Andretti led the World Championship, and the only driver who could seriously challenge him was team-mate Peterson. Andretti could clinch it at the Italian Grand Prix. He took pole position, but there was a multiple collision at the start, in which Peterson was pushed under a barrier. The Lotus caught fire, but he was dragged clear by other drivers and rushed to hospital with both legs broken. At the restart of the race, Andretti and Gilles Villeneuve jumped the starter's flag and were penalized one minute. Andretti achieved the fastest lap and was first over the line, but was placed sixth, the 1 point enough to give him the title. That night Peterson died in hospital, taking all the joy out of victory. The race was credited to Brabham: Lauda was given first and Watson second.

ABOVE: Reminder of the more genteel days of motor racing. The German Automobile Club held an international two-day meeting for historic cars at Germany's celebrated Nürburgring, in mid-August. Winner of the main event was Briton John Harper, who won a 15-lap race for the weekend's 23 quickest cars in a Lister-Jaguar, by 4.0 seconds from David Ham in a similar car.

At Indianapolis, three top teams – Penske, McLaren and Parnelli – had switched to the Cosworth DFX, together with a new team, Chaparral, and the five fastest qualifiers were all powered by Cosworths. Tom Sneva was fastest, at 202.156 mph – the first time the qualifying speed was over 200 mph – then came Danny Ongais for Parnelli, Rick Mears for Penske, Johnny Rutherford for McLaren, and Al Unser in the Chaparral.

In the race, Ongais took the lead in a close fight with Sneva, then Unser came up to take on the challenge after Sneva fell back to conserve fuel. Unser took the lead when the Chaparral team managed an 11.6-second pit-stop to the Parnellis' 17 seconds, rejoining 5 seconds ahead and going on to win by 8 seconds. Cosworth had arrived.

LEFT: Niki Lauda in the controversial Brabham BT46B Fan Car in the Swedish Grand Prix. Other drivers complained that the fan picked up dirt from the track and blew it at the car behind. Emerson Fittipaldi and Mario Andretti said that their visors were covered with dirt after following the BT42 during practice.

ABOVE: The thrilling spectacle of the Indianapolis 500 continued to draw huge crowds. In the first moments of the race, Danny Ongais (Interscope Racing, No. 25) pulls away from Rick Mears (CAM2 Motor Oil, No. 71; >1979), Johnny Rutherford (1st National City/McLaren, No.4) and Al Unser (1st National City, No. 2). Pole-winner Tom Sneva (Norton Spirit) is in the lead ahead of Ongais, but out of the picture. Only race-winner Unser and runner-up Sneva went the full 200-lap distance; Rutherford completed 180 laps, Ongais 145, and Mears 103.

RIGHT: The turbocharged engine comes of age. Jean-Pierre Jabouille drove the Renault RS11 to a famous victory in the French Grand Prix on 1 July. His team-mate René Arnoux in another RS11 was second-fastest qualifier alongside Jabouille on the front row of the grid and drove the fastest lap: 122.91 mph.

BELOW RIGHT: Clay Regazzoni in a Williams FW07 in the Spanish Grand Prix. The FW07 – designed by Patrick Head – successfully developed the 'ground effects' aerodynamics pioneered by Colin Chapman with the Lotus 78 and 79.

The idea of 'ground effects' did not take long to spread across the Atlantic. Two teams, Penske and Chaparral, followed Colin Chapman's lead. But the topic buzzing in the pits during the month-long qualifying fiesta at Indianapolis in May was not technical, it was legal. Championship Auto Racing Teams (CART) was determined to wrest control of the sport from the USAC, which it regarded as out of touch with the needs of the teams and drivers. They had started their own series of races for Indy Cars, and when the time came for qualifying in the 500, drivers who were members of CART were banned for not being 'in good standing with the United States Auto Club'. Gordon Johncock, Al and Bobby Unser, Danny Ongais, Wally Dallenbach and Steve Krisiloff – who were directors of CART and known as the CART Six – went to court to plead that the Speedway was denying them the freedom to earn their livelihood – and the court found in their favour.

After that, the race was an anticlimax. The Unser brothers led for most of the race. Al dominated the first half until his transmission failed, then Bobby took over until 18 laps from the end, when he lost fourth gear. Rick Mears took the lead and won for Penske.

In Grand Prix racing, the relationship between drivers and the governing bodies was going through a similar power struggle. The teams served notice that having invested so much in their ground effects and skirt technology, they would ignore the ruling from FIA to

MILESTONES

Louis Chiron died in Monte Carlo. One of the top drivers between the wars (>1927), he was later President of the Auto Club de Monaco.

Jack Brabham – the first man to win both the Drivers' and the Constructors' Championship (>1959, 1966) – was knighted and so became Sir Jack Brabham.

A.J. Foyt achieved a unique double, becoming USAC National Champion and USAC National Stock Car Champion in the same year.

CART began its 15-race PPG Industries/Indy Car World Series. The first Champion was Rick Mears; Bobby Unser was runner-up.

Former World Champions Niki Lauda (>1975, 1977, 1984) and James Hunt (>1976) both retired, Lauda to develop his airline business.

The FIA replaces the Commission Sportive with the Fédération Internationale du Sport Automobile (FISA) to control motor racing's World Championships.

seconds, just under 30 seconds ahead of Ferrari team-mate Jody Scheckter. He also drove a record fastest lap: 89.56 mph. Patrese retired after the Arrows' brakes developed problems.

remove them. Their firm stand succeeded – the FIA backed down – although it was clear it was not the end of the battle.

Colin Chapman at Lotus and Gordon Murray at Brabham were already looking to the next development in ground effects with the Lotus 80 and BT48 respectively. To this end, Alfa-Romeo had built a V-12 engine (as opposed to the flat-12 that Brabham was using) to enable the ground effects pods to run the full length of the car. They wanted to increase the efficiency of the system – to reduce the drag caused by the wings by making them shallower and longer, while at the same time increasing the downforce.

The idea was not successful. The new shape of wing did not produce enough downforce – and there was another problem. Under acceler-

ation and without the front wing, the front of the car lifted. The front of the pods rose high enough to allow air to creep in under the skirts, reducing the area of low pressure underneath. When the acceleration was reduced, the skirts became effective again, sucking the front down – and setting up an oscillation on the suspension that the driver was powerless to control. They called it 'porpoising', and one way to lessen it was to stiffen the suspension. The suspension on ground effects cars was already stiffer, and this extra rigidity in turn made the ride very hard for the driver. With cornering speeds already higher because of the ground effects – applying more than 2g of side-force to the driver – driving racing cars was becoming something of a physical endurance test. Lotus persevered with the Lotus 80, but eventually Chapman gave up, and Mario Andretti and Carlos Reutemann reverted to the 79s, which were uncompetitive. They did not win a single race all season: an abrupt U-turn in fortunes.

Ferrari persisted with its flat-12 engine in the 312T4, making the ground effects fit around it and using the top surface of the body to create as much downforce as possible.

At Williams, Patrick Head went for a full ground effects car, the FW07. It was a small car with an ingenious spring-loaded system for the sliding skirts, and it produced good downforce. Clay Regazzoni and Alan Jones gave the car its debut at the Spanish Grand Prix.

The renaissance of French racing at the top

level continued. Renault had moved on from the experimental phase and produced two cars – the RS10 and RS11 – running a two-car team of turbocharged cars driven by Jean-Pierre Jabouille and René Arnoux. The engine now had two KKK turbochargers, one for each bank of cylinders, and produced around 520 bhp. During testing, other teams had to take notice as the new Renaults were clearly some 15 to 20 mph faster than all the rest. Nonetheless, it was Ligier's new ground effects JS11 that revived French fortunes at the start of the season. Matra had withdrawn and Ligier was using the Cosworth engine. While the other teams were still sorting out their new cars, Jacques Laffite took the first two Grands Prix of the season, in Argentina and Brazil,

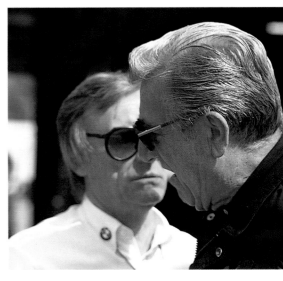

RIGHT: Niki Lauda in a Brabham BT48 during the Monaco Grand Prix. He retired on lap 22 after an accident with Didier Pironi's Tyrrell-Ford. Lauda, World Champion in 1975 and 1977, took the motor-racing world by surprise when he announced his retirement from the sport on 28 September, during practice for the Canadian Grand Prix. He said he had lost interest (>1981, 1984).

with Patrick Depailler second at Interlagos (Brazil) in a second Ligier.

The new 312T4 Ferrari then made its debut at Kyalami for the South African Grand Prix. Gilles Villeneuve and Jody Scheckter took a firm grip for Ferrari again: Villeneuve won, and Scheckter was second. Depailler managed to regain Ligier's initiative by winning at Jarama in Spain, before Scheckter climbed back on top of the Championship table, taking the races in Belgium and at Monaco.

The Ligier's consistent performances and the presence of the new Renaults prompted great expectations at Dijon for the French Grand Prix. Jabouille and Arnoux did not disappoint the capacity crowd, occupying the

front row of the grid after the two fastest times in practice. But what was thrilling to the crowd was worrying for the kit-car teams who had dominated racing for more than a decade. They eyed the turbocharged engine warily, knowing that it was financed by a huge motoring conglomerate together with state funding. The main challengers were Ferrari – also supported by a huge company, Fiat – and Brabham, the fastest of the small teams.

Jabouille made a good start, but Arnoux nearly stalled on the grid, and Villeneuve needed no second bidding to surge into the gap and lead into the first corner. At the end of the first lap the order was Villeneuve, Jabouille, Scheckter, Nelson Piquet (Brabham), Jean-

LEFT: Between 1979 and 1981, motor racing was dominated by the power struggle between Jean-Marie Balestre (right) of the Fédération Internationale de l'Automobile (FIA), and Bernie Ecclestone of the Formula One Constructors Association (FOCA).

BELOW: Racing car or low-flying aircraft? 'Ground effects' was the use of airflow underneath the car as well as over the wings mounted on top to create downforce and to 'stick' the car more firmly to the track. It was the principal tool of the kit-car teams in their struggle with the large manufacturers such as Renault, Ferrari and Alfa-Romeo – with their turbocharged engines and huge resources. The different approaches of small and large teams was at the heart of the power struggle that nearly tore the sport apart in the early 1980s.

Pierre Jarier (Ligier), Niki Lauda (Brabham), Laffite, Jones, then Arnoux. A lap later, Villeneuve was pulling away and Jabouille was making little evident attempt to catch him. Arnoux, on the other hand, was storming through the field: he forced his way into third place by lap 14. Jabouille now bent to the task and pulled back, and by lap 30 was right on Villeneuve's tail.

Scheckter had fallen back, so Villeneuve had no support against the two Renaults. Jabouille then passed the Ferrari on the pit straight and drew out a three-second lead. Villeneuve's tyres were worn and he slowed. Arnoux closed on him, and for the last five laps the two gave one of the most thrilling battles seen in Grand Prix racing for many years, sliding into corners together. With five laps to go, Arnoux outbraked Villeneuve and went into the lead – but Villeneuve did not give up, and on the last lap he left his braking a crucial split-second later, took the inside with all four tyres smoking, and went back in front. It was just less than a perfect result for the French crowd, who knew they had seen the beginning of a new era: the turbo era.

The first half of the season had been dominated by the duel between Ferrari and the French Ligier and then Renault, but during the second half the challenge came from Williams and their FW07. Clay Regazzoni won the British Grand Prix – Williams' first victory, two weeks after the French race – with Arnoux second. Then Alan Jones took the next three Grands Prix: the German, Austrian and Dutch. But Ferrari's Scheckter and Villeneuve were out by themselves at the top of the World Championship table, and the Italian Grand Prix was the clincher between them. Scheckter and Villeneuve finished virtually together, to finish 1-2 in the race and in the Championship.

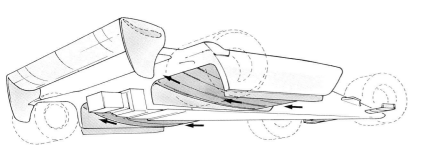

LEFT: Al Unser in a Cosworth-engined Chaparral during the Indianapolis 500. He qualified third fastest at 192.503 mph, but retired from the race on lap 104 with transmission problems. He finished fifth in the US Championship with 2085 points. Youthful winner Rick Mears had 4060.

The effort and competitiveness at the top in Formula One takes a heavy toll on the fortunes of teams and individual drivers, which can rise and fall with cruel suddenness. After failing to find success on the track, making sponsorship difficult to obtain, Shadow gave up the struggle. Despite Emerson Fittipaldi's driving, Copersucar-Fittipaldi also failed to find much success, so when Walter Wolf lost interest in Formula One, Wolf merged with Fittipaldi. McLaren and Tyrrell were both in poor shape, lacking both money and results, and Lotus, having enjoyed considerable success with the Lotus 79, was in the doldrums again with the 80 and 81. Even Ferrari – the only team to win the Constructors' title three times in a row (>1975, 1976, 1977), and again in 1979 – sank down the league table while the 126, their first turbo car, was being developed.

Alfa-Romeo made a comeback (>1951), not just as an engine supplier but with a new car, the Tipo 179, designed by Carlo Chiti. Renault, which had poured resources into the turbocharged engine, adopted sliding skirts as well, making a purposeful bid for the Championship with two new cars, the RE21 and RE22 (in which the RE stood for Renault-Elf). Spurred on by its first victory in Canada the previous year, Williams produced the FW07B with a stiffer, composite monocoque, and wings extended right back through the

rear suspension. Brabham switched engines from Alfa to Cosworth in their BT49.

Competition on the track was overshadowed by conflicts off it. At the end of 1979 Jean-Marie Balestre, the president of FISA, decreed that sliding skirts were to be banned from 1981, and the minimum weight limit would be increased to 585 kilograms (1,290 pounds) – both moves favouring the larger companies in that heavier cars needed more power, and more power was available only by using turbos. The Renault victory in the French Grand Prix at Dijon had thrilled the crowd, but it had worried the 'kit-car' teams. They had dominated Grand Prix racing for

ABOVE: The Monaco Grand Prix. Derek Daly in a Tyrrell-Ford (No. 4) cartwheeled after hitting Bruno Giacomelli's Alfa-Romeo on the first lap. Jacques Laffite in a Ligier (No. 26), Patrick Depailler in an Alfa-Romeo (No. 22) and Nelson Piquet in a Brabham (No. 5) steered clear. The race was won by Carlos Reutemann in a Williams; Laffite was second; Piquet came third; Depailler retired on lap 55.

MILESTONES

The Indianapolis 500 included Offy-powered cars for the last time (>1935); the best-placed was Gary Bettenhausen's Wildcat II.

Alfred Neubauer (>1922) – the great Mercedes-Benz team manager in their two bouts of success in the 1930s and 1950s – died aged 89.

Raymond Mays died, aged 81 (>1936); it was he who founded English Racing Automobiles (ERA) and British Racing Motors (BRM).

Clay Regazzoni crashed driving for Ensign in the Long Beach Grand Prix; he was paralysed from the waist down (>1970, 1979).

On 1 August Patrick Depailler, whose career started on motor cycles in 1963, was killed testing an Alfa-Romeo at Hockenheim.

After five poor seasons with his brother's Copersucar-Fittipaldi team, Emerson Fittipaldi retired from Formula One racing (>1976, 1989, 1993).

RIGHT: Johnny Rutherford, winner of the Indianapolis 500 for the third time (>1974, 1976). Born in Texas in 1938, Rutherford began racing in 1959. His first appearance at Indianapolis was in 1963, when he lasted just 43 laps.

LEFT: The Cosworth-engined Pennzoil Chaparral in which Rutherford won the 500. Twenty-four of the 33 starters were powered by the Cosworth engine. He took pole position with 192.526 mph – ahead of Mario Andretti in a Penske (191.012 mph) – and led for 118 of the race's 200 laps. He finished in 3 hours 29 minutes 59.56 seconds, 18 seconds ahead of second-placed Tom Sneva's McLaren.

more than a decade and they eyed the turbo-charger warily, in the knowledge that it was expensive. Renault, with state funding and backed by the huge Elf oil company, Ferrari, backed by one of Italy's largest companies, Fiat, and now Alfa-Romeo, could afford turbos, while they would find it difficult.

Balestre was additionally determined to re-establish FISA's control over the sport and to limit the rising power of the Formula One Constructors' Association (FOCA) which, under the leadership of Bernard Ecclestone, had negotiated lucrative contracts for the tele-vision coverage of races. Banning skirts hit the kit-car teams where it hurt. They would find it difficult to afford turbocharged engines and

relied on their ingenuity in ground effects tech-nology to stay competitive.

In America, the United States Auto Club (USAC) and Championship Auto Racing Teams (CART) mended their fences, forming the Championship Racing League (CRL) to sanction races – including the Indianapolis 500 – under their joint auspices. The two lead-ing teams in Indy Car racing, Penske and Chaparral, used full ground effects. The designer at Chaparral was John Barnard, from Britain, and the driver was the two-time win-ner, Johnny Rutherford. Penske's drivers were Bobby Unser, Gordon Johncock, Rick Mears and Mario Andretti. In the race, Rutherford took pole position and after a brief duel with

Andretti and Unser, led for 124 out of the 200 laps, to win by 28 seconds – his third Indianapolis victory. The concord between the USAC and CART broke down just a month after the race, but by then CART had the upper hand and continued to run its own Indy Car World Series.

The Grand Prix season reflected the seesaw of the political battle. The first result was a boost to the kit-car teams, when Alan Jones won the Argentinian Grand Prix for Williams and Nelson Piquet was second for Brabham. Then Renault took the limelight: René Arnoux won in Brazil after Jean-Pierre Jabouille retired. Arnoux also won in South Africa, where Jacques Laffite and Didier Pironi came in in second and third places in their Ligiers, raising French hopes of real championship success. There was an unpleasant incident at Kyalami when Balestre was barred from joining the first three on the rostrum.

The kit cars fought back, and brought Renault's run of success to a halt with a win for Piquet and Brabham at Long Beach, for Pironi and Ligier in Belgium, and for Carlos Reutemann and Williams at Monaco.

Then came the Spanish Grand Prix – and the FOCA-FISA row, which had been smouldering in the background, flared up again. FISA had introduced compulsory briefings for drivers before each race, imposing hefty fines on those who failed to appear. As part of the struggle, some drivers had not attended the briefings prior to the Belgium and Monaco

Grands Prix – and they had not paid the fines either. Both sides stood firm in Spain, FISA backed by Renault, Ferrari and Alfa, FOCA backed by the other teams. Hours of discussion brought no result, so FISA declared the race void. FOCA promptly sanctioned it, and although Renault, Ferrari and Alfa pulled out, the race went ahead. Alan Jones won, but his points did not count towards either World Championship.

Waiting game: the Spanish Grand Prix was delayed while FOCA and FISA were locked in confrontation over who ran the sport. To while away the time, mechanics from the Brabham and Williams teams organized a game of football in the pits at Jarama. Williams driver Alan Jones won the race; whether his mechanics achieved a unique double by winning the football game is not known.

RIGHT: Australian driver Alan Jones in a Williams FW07, winner of the Argentine Grand Prix on 13 January. The FW07 used a Ford-Cosworth DFV, now in its 14th year of Formula One racing. Jones finished just over 24 seconds ahead of Nelson Piquet in a Brabham. He won more four more Grands Prix – the French, British, Canadian and US – to take the World Championship with 67 points. Piquet was second with 54.

As the French Grand Prix approached, the Championships were in crisis. Goodyear threatened to withdraw from the sport altogether unless the internal differences were settled. They called a meeting with the other sponsors, FISA and FOCA at Lausanne, where a compromise was reached. It was later rejected by Balestre, after which Ecclestone and FOCA stated that unless the compromise arrangements were held to, the kit car teams would break away and start their own Championship. Five days before the date set for the French Grand Prix there was another meeting, this time at Heathrow Airport. It lasted twelve hours, after which another compromise was reached, all the outstanding fines were paid, and the race went ahead.

There was an atmosphere of heightened rivalry between the turbocharged teams and the others at the Paul Ricard circuit. Laffite was fastest in practice, then Arnoux, putting Ligier and Renault alongside each other on the front row of the grid. Behind them came Pironi in the other Ligier, then Jones and Reutemann for Williams, in front of Jabouille and a new French driver, Alain Prost, for McLaren (>1985). French confidence swelled even more

when Laffite took the lead, followed by Arnoux and Pironi ahead of Jones, Reutemann and Piquet. The only blot on the start – from a French point of view – was that Jabouille was left on the line with a broken drive shaft.

Arnoux fell back and Jones moved up to challenge first Pironi then Laffite. By lap 35 he had closed to within 2 seconds – and Laffite's tyres were worn. Jones outbraked him on a corner to take the lead, and held it to the end. Grabbing a huge Union Jack, he waved it throughout his lap of honour.

Jones took the British Grand Prix at Brands Hatch for Williams, Laffite the German Grand Prix for Ligier, and Jabouille won in Austria for Renault. Piquet won at Zandvoort (Holland) and Monza (Italy), putting him 1 point ahead of Jones in the Championship table. Piquet's Brabham and Jones' Williams were on the front row of the grid for the last race of the season. They collided going into the first corner. Piquet restarted in a spare car but the engine failed – and Jones held off the opposition to clinch the Drivers' title, giving Williams the Constructors' title by a massive 120 points to Ligier's 66. Renault was fourth with 34 points – a sad ending to a year that had started with such high hopes.

ABOVE: Waiting for the sky to clear at the Canadian Grand Prix. Rain is the one element that regularly brings motor racing to a halt. The only thing worse than rain is changeable weather – when drivers have to gamble on whether to start with wet or dry tyres; or – worse still – whether to stop in mid-race simply to change them.

The power struggle between the teams and FISA remained the year's theme in Grand Prix. In Indy Car racing, in which Championship Auto Racing Teams (CART) had established itself, the controversy moved from the boardroom to the track. Mario Andretti and Gordon Johncock drove Wildcat-Cosworths for the Patrick Indy Car team; Bobby Unser drove for Penske. During the 500 the three had a fierce battle, until Johncock dropped out. Unser and Andretti then raced for the flag. Unser won and was given the full Victory Lane treatment. Then the stewards penalized him 1 lap for passing while the yellow flags were out – and the race was awarded to Andretti, making him a two-time winner. But Unser appealed, and in October he was awarded the race . . . after paying a fine of $40,000.

In Grand Prix racing, FISA and the Formula One Constructors' Association (FOCA) squared up to each other for yet another round in settling their differences. In November 1980 Bernard Ecclestone had announced that FOCA would run its own World Professional Championship sanctioned by a new organization, the World Federation of Motor Sport. But the race organizers lined up behind FISA, as did the sponsors. Goodyear – utterly fed up with the wrangling – went as far as to say it would withdraw from racing altogether. Neither side would back down, and the first casualty of the row was the Argentinian Grand Prix, which was postponed. Grand Prix racing

then held a summit meeting on 19 January at Maranello, the home of the man with the longest memory in motor racing, Enzo Ferrari (>1919). What became known as the Concorde agreement emerged. FOCA agreed to acknowledge FISA's supremacy as rule-maker in the sport, and FOCA won the right to continue negotiating the financial details of racing with race organizers and television companies, subject to the rubber-stamp approval of FISA. On the issue of skirts, the ban on the sliding variety stood, but fixed skirts – with a clearance of 60 millimetres (2.4 inches) – were permitted.

The agreement came too late to save the South African Grand Prix for the Championship: only teams loyal to FOCA took part. Alan Jones won, but gained no points for it. The kit-car teams continued their run of successes: Jones and Carlos Reutemann

MILESTONES

Mike Hailwood – the former Motorcycle World Champion, who drove in 50 Championship races – was killed in a road crash, aged 41 (>1974).

A new entry to the World Championships was Toleman, financed by one of Britain's largest haulage contractors, Ted Toleman (>1985).

As part of its general tightening up of Formula One rules, FISA banned four-wheel-drive and six-wheeled cars from the Championship.

Bobby Unser retired. The three-time Indianapolis winner, with 35 Indy Car Series victories to his credit, became a TV race commentator.

The British driver Nigel Mansell signed a test contract with Lotus after a successful career in Formula Ford and Formula Three (>1992).

The first World Championship victory for a car with a carbon-fibre monocoque was John Watson's McLaren MP4 in the British Grand Prix.

won at Long Beach and in Brazil respectively for Williams, before Nelson Piquet won the deferred Argentinian and the San Marino races for Brabham. Reutemann took the Belgian race for Williams. Gilles Villeneuve then put Ferrari back on the map by winning the next two Grands Prix, in Monaco and Spain, in the new turbocharged Ferrari 126. Its V-6 engine, with twin KKK turbochargers, was very powerful, but the car was tricky to handle. Only 1.2 seconds covered the first five cars home at Jarama.

In third place in Spain was John Watson in another new car, the McLaren MP4. It was the work of John Barnard, who had joined McLaren from Chaparral when the team was taken over by Ron Dennis. A new company, McLaren International, was formed largely at the behest of McLaren's sponsor Marlboro, who funded development of the MP4. It had full ground effects and a carbon-fibre monocoque; its first victory came in the British Grand Prix, Watson its driver (>1988).

Jacques Laffite then took the Austrian and Canadian Grands Prix for Talbot-Matra-Ligier, and Alain Prost – quickly establishing himself among the top drivers – won the Dutch and Italian races for Renault. But the late French surge was not enough to win the titles. Alan Jones won the final race on a tight street circuit in Las Vegas – a race in which any one from Piquet, Reutemann and Laffite might secure enough points to win the Drivers' Championship – but Piquet's fifth place was sufficient to give him the title by 1 point from Reutemann. Had Jones' victory in the South African race counted, he would have been World Champion again.

ABOVE LEFT: Danny Ongais broke both his legs when he crashed his Interscope on lap 65 of the Indianapolis 500. An unconnected fire (beyond Ongais) broke out in Rick Mears' pit area. Mears was hurt, but bounced back to win the CART/PPG Indy Car World Series.

LEFT: Elio de Angelis in a Lotus 81 during the Long Beach Grand Prix. De Angelis had been due to drive the Lotus 88 – which used two chassis, one inside the other, enabling the outer one to be lowered to increase ground effect. But this design was ruled illegal before the race.

The forward march of the turbo continued and gathered pace. The dominant position of the Cosworth DFV engine was under threat: whereas it produced around 500 bhp, the Renault turbo was getting up to 560. During the year Ferrari introduced water-injection – Renault followed suit – and power rose to close on 600 bhp. The kit-car teams had seen the way things were going. Those who could afford to were looking for turbocharged engines themselves. Brabham negotiated an exclusive contract with BMW. McLaren flirted with a small supplier, then settled on an exclusive deal with Porsche, with finance from a Franco-Arabian consortium, Téchniques d'Avant-Garde (TAG). Lotus was in negotiation with Renault to buy their turbo engine. For 1982, however, they had to continue with their Cosworth engines.

If the Cosworth was under threat 'at home' in Europe, then it was quite the reverse in America. Of the 33 starters in the Indianapolis 500, no fewer than 29 had DFX engines. But the British invasion had gone further than that: 17 of the chassis had been built by March, including A.J. Foyt's, and all the Penske cars had been built in Roger Penske's own factory in Dorset. In the race, a first lap accident took out Foyt and Kevin Cogan. The race was between Gordon Johncock in one of Patrick Racing's then remaining Cosworth-powered Wildcats, and Rick Mears in a Penske PC10. Racing hard with 12 laps to go, the veteran Johncock was ahead by 11.8 seconds. Mears then bent to the task and gained steadily in the closing laps, to be just 4 seconds behind with 4 laps to go. Johncock had a tyre problem: a front tyre had overheated and become swollen, and he was forced to ease off slightly. Mears was gaining – Johncock knew it, but he husbanded his tyres and judged his speed perfectly, never giving the younger man quite enough leeway to overtake. As they went into the last lap, the gap was less than 1 second. Mears challenged, but Johncock had just enough in reserve to make it to the flag by 0.16 second – the closest result in the Speedway's history. It was the last time an American-built chassis won the race.

The struggle between the larger and smaller teams in Grand Prix racing went on unabated. Without the sliding skirts, keeping the side pods consistently close to the ground was crucial, and the only way to do so within the rules was to make the suspension harder, so there was little or no bounce in the car. Any lift off the road surface would release the low pressure area under the pods, with potentially disastrous results. It was a matter of genuine con-

cern to FISA that there would one day be a fatal accident caused simply by a car's going over a kerb, losing its suction, and leaving the circuit.

The cars now went round corners with very little drift, as if on rails, creating side-forces on the driver of between 3g and 4g while at the same time shaking and buffeting the driver vigorously on the rock-hard suspension. Many a driver found that his neck muscles were not strong enough to hold his head vertical with the added weight of the helmet, and fitted a medically approved support to help him keep it upright.

Another change in the rules reduced the minimum weight limit by 5 kilograms (11 pounds) – a move in favour of the smaller teams, if rather a small one. To finish up with the lightest car possible, the teams resorted to all kinds of ingenious ploys at the weigh-in, from overfilling the engine and gearboxes with

ABOVE: Motor town. Detroit – the capital of America's car industry and home of Motown music – hosted the United States Grand Prix (East) for the first time on 6 June. British driver John Watson came from 17th place on the grid to win in a McLaren-Cosworth. The drivers complained about the surface – Watson said it was like a washboard.

oil, to Brabham's and Williams' ruse of fitting water tanks to their cars, ostensibly to provide a cooling system for the brakes but effectively using them as temporary ballast, releasing the water during the race to lighten the car, then topping up again after the race before the cars were weighed once more.

There were also some changes among the drivers. Alan Jones retired and went back to Australia. Carlos Reutemann continued to drive for Williams but announced he was retiring at the end of the season. The biggest surprise of all was that Niki Lauda came out of retirement to drive for McLaren. John Watson also moved to McLaren, while Riccardo Patrese joined Nelson Piquet at Brabham.

BELOW: The closest finish in the history of the Indianapolis 500. Gordon Johncock's STP Oil Treatment Special took the chequered flag 0.16 second ahead of Rick Mears' Gould Charge. The winning time was 3 hours 5 minutes 9.14 seconds.

BELOW: Veteran winner. Johncock was born in Michigan in August 1936. He made his first appearance in the Indianapolis 500 in 1965, finishing fifth (>1973). He retired in 1985, but made a comeback in the 1987 500, retiring after 76 laps.

MILESTONES

Colin Chapman died suddenly of a heart attack, aged 54. The founder of Lotus, he was the genius behind many innovations in Formula One.

The purse in the Indianapolis 500 first exceeded $2 million. Out of a total of $2,067,475, the winner's share was $290,606 (>1911, 1985).

The Brabham BT49C was fitted with hydraulic suspension which allowed the car to be lowered during racing to improve downforce.

Johncock's victory at Indianapolis in Patrick's Wildcat-Cosworth was the last time an American-built chassis won the Indianapolis 500.

The Porsche 956 racing sports car started its career by taking the first three places at Le Mans; it was to win four years in a row.

Of the 16 Grands Prix in the World Championship, seven were won by turbocharged cars and nine by normally-aspirated cars.

Keijo 'Keke' Rosberg, a driver from Finland, filled the gap at Williams. René Arnoux and Alain Prost stayed at Renault, and Didier Pironi joined Gilles Villeneuve at Ferrari.

The full advantage of the turbo cars at altitude was felt in the South African Grand Prix at Kyalami, 4,000 feet (1,220 metres) above sea level. Ferrari and Renault brought their turbo cars, and for this race Brabham also had its four-cylinder BMW turbo engine. The three teams dominated the race. Prost won, from Reutemann, who was fastest of the non-turbo cars. The turbo drivers suffered numerous mechanical problems, especially the new BMW engine in the Brabham, and Nelson Piquet reverted to the normally-aspirated engine for the Brazilian Grand Prix – which he won. Second was Rosberg in the Williams – both cars fitted with the water tanks. Ferrari and Renault protested, and the first and second drivers were both disqualified, moving Prost up from third place in the Renault to first, giving him two wins in a row in the World Championship.

Niki Lauda won the Long Beach Grand Prix for McLaren, demonstrating that his considerable skills had not deserted him, and everybody started preparing for the San Marino Grand Prix at Imola. Then the row between the Formula One Constructors' Association (FOCA) and FISA erupted again. The FOCA teams boycotted the race in protest at the disqualification of Piquet and Rosberg in Brazil. Only 14 cars took part: the two Ferraris finished first and second after trouncing the Renaults in front of their home crowd. Even then, not all the competition was between the two teams – there was rivalry within them. Villeneuve, the leader of the two Ferraris out

in front, assumed that his team-mate would follow convention and not contest the race. He was wrong. On the last lap, Pironi pulled off a very risky manoeuvre on one of the last corners to take the lead and win from a disgusted Villeneuve.

There were glum faces on the victory rostrum, and lasting bitterness between the two Ferrari drivers: Villeneuve for a time refused to speak to Pironi (>1987).

FOCA then backed down and accepted the ban on water-cooled brakes, but the animosity between the two factions in the sport had barely subsided when they met again for the Belgian Grand Prix two weeks later. Even less had the atmosphere improved between the two Ferrari drivers. When Pironi put up some very fast times in practice, Villeneuve went out to

beat them. Coming over a rise, at top speed, he suddenly came across Jochen Mass slowing down, and hit him. Mass was unhurt, but Villeneuve was fatally injured. Ferrari packed their bags and went home before the race. Watson won for McLaren.

Cars were now so evenly matched that the way in which victories were won depended on the particular car and driver on the particular day on the particular track. Patrese and Brabham found the right combination of all these factors at Monaco to record his first Grand Prix win. Watson won again for McLaren in Detroit. Piquet gave the Brabham turbo its first victory in Canada, and Pironi won at Zandvoort in Holland for Ferrari. Lauda then took the British Grand Prix for McLaren. Finally, Arnoux and Prost gave the

BOTTOM: World Champion Nelson Piquet in a Brabham-BMW during practice for the Detroit Grand Prix. The car suffered engine troubles and Piquet failed to qualify for the race. He finished the season eleventh in the Championship with 20 points – after winning just once, in the Canadian Grand Prix on 13 June.

ABOVE: Keke Rosberg in a Williams-Cosworth in the Monaco Grand Prix. He crashed at the old chicane on lap 65, and retired. Rosberg won the World Championship with 44 points, ahead of Britain's John Watson and France's Didier Pironi with 39 points.

ABOVE: Keke Rosberg (with cap) celebrating victory in the Swiss Grand Prix, held at Dijon-Prenois in France. Rosberg was rare among Finnish drivers in reaching the top in Formula One – though many of his countrymen excelled in rally driving.

ABOVE RIGHT: The Renault RS01 – the first turbocharged Formula One car – at the Royal Automobile Club in Pall Mall, central London, for display. The club's library houses a distinguished collection of journals and books on motor racing.

French crowd at the Paul Ricard circuit the result they had been waiting for, putting the Renaults first and second. The sixteen races in the Championship were won by eleven different drivers. Keke Rosberg took the Drivers' title having scored only one victory, in the Swiss Grand Prix – which was held at Dijon in France because racing was banned in Switzerland (>1955) – and Ferrari took the Constructors' title: an unexpectedly equitable sharing of the honours between the large and small teams.

Top-level motor racing had been plagued by internal squabbles over money, power and status for four years. In 1983 a new, more stable order emerged. Turbocharging finally triumphed over ground effects in Grand Prix racing, eclipsing the Cosworth engine in the Formula One Championship. Meanwhile, at Indianapolis the new teams bought their cars off the shelf rather than design and build them themselves – and that generally meant buying British. Of the 33 starters in the 500, 32 were powered by Cosworth DFX engines, 20 of the chassis were built by March, the four Penskes were British-built, and two were Lolas.

In the World Championship, FISA's role was predominantly to write the rules. For 1983, in a gesture towards the lighter carbon-fibre materials used to make Formula One monocoques, the minimum weight limit was lowered to 540 kilograms (1,191 pounds). But the shattering news for the non-turbo, predominantly British-based teams, was that they would also have to have flat undersides – eliminating at a stroke the ground effects that had always been their advantage.

While the smaller teams looked for turbo power, the season reflected the period of transition: there were wins for the turbo teams and last hurrahs for the normally-aspirated cars. Then the turbo took over. Brabham was the only small team with a turbocharged engine, and Nelson Piquet opened the season with a victory for them in the Brazilian Grand Prix. John Watson won the Long Beach Grand Prix

MILESTONES

March Engineering's 1,000th racing car was a Cosworth-powered 83C Indy Car produced for A.J. Foyt; in the 500, he retired on lap 24.

With very little to show for a decade of racing, Copersucar-Fittipaldi ceased trading and closed its headquarters in Reading.

Keke Rosberg's victory at Monaco for Tyrrell was the last victory for the Cosworth DFV engine, after an unparalleled record (>1967, 1985).

The sons of two Indianapolis entrants took part in the 500: Geoff Brabham (>1961), who was fourth, and Al Unser Jr (>1970), who was tenth.

A Lotus with 'active suspension' – a computer-controlled system to keep the car's underside at the optimum angle – was tested (>1987).

Richard Noble broke the world land speed record at 633 mph in 'Thrust II', which was powered by a Rolls-Royce Avon jet engine.

ABOVE: Al Unser Snr (Hertz-Penske, No. 7), Al Unser Jr (Coors Light Silver Bullet, No. 10) and Tom Sneva (Texaco Star, No. 5) in the Indianapolis 500. There was a storm of controversy after the race because Al Jr – who was several laps down – did all he could to block Sneva and stop him catching Al Snr. But Sneva got through to beat Al Snr into second place and win the 500.

RIGHT: Tom Sneva in Victory Circle after his first victory in the 500.

for McLaren, with team-mate Niki Lauda second, forcing René Arnoux – this season in a Ferrari – into third place.

Alain Prost then put Renault in front for the second successive time in the French Grand Prix – and the turbo teams had a field day at San Marino, where Patrick Tambay won for Ferrari followed home by Prost and Arnoux. Keke Rosberg won at Monaco in a Williams-Ford, beating the turbos on the twisting road circuit, before Prost won in Belgium. Michele Alboreto won in Detroit in a Tyrrell that used a Cosworth DFY engine – a derivative of the DFV with a shorter stroke – the last victory for six years by a normally-aspirated engine (>1989).

The second half of the season was all turbo. Lotus, where former Matra and Ligier designer Gérard Ducarouge had taken over following Colin Chapman's death (>1982), now had its Renault turbos for the 93T. McLaren continued with the Cosworth engine in the MP4/1E, an interim version of the car, but also raced it with the Porsche-TAG turbo engine. Williams had arranged to use a V-6 Honda engine.

The teams with the turbo experience dominated the second half of the season: Arnoux won in Canada, Germany and Holland; Prost added the British and Austrian Grands Prix to Renault's battle honours; and Piquet took the Italian, the European (at Brands Hatch) and the South African Grands Prix for Brabham-BMW – and the Drivers' Championship.

It was a great disappointment to Renault – the pioneers of turbocharging – that one of the kit-car teams' drivers had won the first turbocharged title, and little better that the Constructors' title went to Ferrari.

But it was a watershed year. The FISA-FOCA rows had largely been settled, both sides getting much of what they wanted. The patience of the paying public and of the sponsors had been sorely tried by the power struggle, but turbocharging had arrived, and the smaller teams had staved off the banning of ground effects just long enough to equip themselves with turbos. The inheritors of the turbo revolution would be not only those who had brought it about but also those who had initially resisted it.

LEFT: World Champion Nelson Piquet on the podium after taking third place in a Brabham-BMW in the last race of the season, the South African Grand Prix at Kyalami. Born in Brazil in 1952, he began racing in karts and saloon cars. He came to Europe in 1977 and won the European Formula Three championship the following year (>1981, 1987).

ABOVE: Jacques Laffite in a Williams-Cosworth in the Brazilian Grand Prix on 13 March. He finished fourth, but was officially third following the disqualification of his team-mate Keke Rosberg for receiving a push-start. It was Laffite's best position in a disappointing season – he came eleventh in the World Championship with 11 points.

Turbocharging the World Championship had been expensive. But the paymasters of the sport – the sponsors – had coughed up so as to keep their teams competitive. McLaren brought out the MP4/2 with the Porsche-TAG engine, Brabham the BT52 powered by BMW, and Williams the FW09 with the Honda engine. Lotus had the Renault engine, as did Ligier. Toleman had a new engine designed by Brian Hart in England. Of the smaller teams, only Ken Tyrrell was without turbo power, so he was forced to get every last ounce of power out of the Cosworth DFV. Ferrari had an improved turbo, the 126C4, and Renault had a new lighter engine with a lighter, alloy block.

The advance of the turbo meant the advance of power, and FISA was concerned to restrict that increase. Turbocharged engines were thirsty: FISA limited fuel to 220 litres (48.4 UK gallons, 58.1 US gallons) and banned refuelling stops. Drivers would have to be careful in their use of the turbo boost or they would run out of fuel, and the electronic management systems began to play an ever more important part in winning.

Renault had not found the success it had anticipated in the World Championship, although its position had been improving year by year. In 1983 the team had looked likely to win the Championship – only to be overtaken

LEFT: A star is born. Nigel Mansell in a Lotus 95T in the rain-soaked Monaco Grand Prix. He was superb in practice and led the race for 5 laps before crashing on lap 16. Mansell was born in 1954 in Birmingham, and began racing karts before moving to Formula Ford and Formula Three in 1976–77. He won his first Lotus test contract in 1981.

ABOVE: Niki Lauda in a McLaren-TAG MP4 during the United States (Dallas) Grand Prix. He crashed and retired on lap 60, just four laps after team-mate Alain Prost had dropped out after hitting the wall. The McLaren MP4 was the finest Formula One racing car of the 1980s. Its V-6 TAG Turbo P01 engine developed 750 bhp at 11,500 rpm at race boost.

by Ferrari in the Constructors' Championship and by Nelson Piquet (for Brabham) in the Drivers' title. In the post mortem that followed, the blame fell on Alain Prost, and he was fired. Signed on to replace him were Derek Warwick and Patrick Tambay.

Prost was quickly picked up by McLaren, where he joined Niki Lauda, giving Ron Dennis just the right combination of factors to win – a generous sponsor in Marlboro, a good car in John Barnard's MP4, the Porsche-TAG engine that was fitted with by far the best fuel management system made by Bosch, and the best tyres from Michelin.

McLaren kept its own counsel in the run-up to the first race of the season, in Brazil. Elio de Angelis took pole position for Lotus, Michele Alboreto alongside him on the front row for Ferrari. On the second row was Warwick's

Renault and Prost's McLaren, behind them Lauda in the other McLaren and Nigel Mansell in the other Lotus. Alboreto led for the first twelve laps, then a brake calliper broke and he spun off. Lauda then had a minor bump with Warwick, which damaged the Renault's suspension. Lauda took the lead, only to have to retire with an electrical fault, leaving the lead to Warwick. The damaged suspension slowed him, and Prost got past into the lead and went on to win.

In the South African Grand Prix, Niki Lauda came home in first place, Prost was second, and Warwick third.

Renault put a huge effort into trying to win the French Grand Prix at Dijon. Practice was a three-cornered battle between Renault, Lotus and McLaren. Patrick Tambay took pole position, alongside de Angelis in the Renault-powered Lotus. Then came Piquet for Brabham, Keke Rosberg for Williams, Prost, and Nigel Mansell in the second Lotus.

Tambay led for the first half of the race, chased remorselessly by the two Lotuses. In the second half, Lauda and Prost in their McLarens forced their way through to challenge the Renault, Prost taking on his old team first. Suddenly his car started to suffer from a

BELOW: Alain Prost (right) and Niki Lauda rounded off a triumphant season for McLaren by finishing first and second in the Portuguese Grand Prix on 21 October. Between them, they won 12 out of 16 races. McLaren won the Constructors' Championship by 86 points from Ferrari. Lauda pipped Prost to the drivers' title by half a point.

MILESTONES

Richard Petty won the Firecracker 200 at Daytona on 4 July, becoming the first driver in NASCAR's history to win 200 races.

Enzo Ferrari's illegitimate son, Piero Lardi, took over Ferrari's Formula One team following the departure of Mauro Forghieri (>1964).

Carlo Chiti retired. He started his career with Alfa-Romeo in the early 1950s, and it was he who brought them back to Grand Prix racing.

Alfa-Romeos appeared in the multicoloured livery of the Italian fashion house Benetton as part of a sponsorship deal (>1985, 1986).

The Austrian Grand Prix was the first Grand Prix in which every entrant was turbocharged – Tyrrell, the only DFV-user, failed to qualify.

Emerson Fittipaldi came out of retirement to drive in the Indianapolis 500. He was placed 32nd in a March-Cosworth (>1989, 1993).

severe vibration. A front wheel had come loose and he had to go into the pits to have it fixed. Lauda took over the job as Tambay's brakes started to fade. When he took the Renault wide on a corner, Lauda was through on the inside. But both had to stop for tyres. Tambay went in first; Lauda went in ten laps later and joined behind him, but managed to get ahead again without difficulty. Lauda won – making it four out of five for McLaren – a bitter disappointment to Renault on its home turf, and, with no victories at all, a further symptom of their relative decline.

The Monaco Grand Prix two weeks later was held in pouring rain. Prost put his McLaren on pole position. Alongside him this time was Nigel Mansell for Lotus – his first time on the front row of the grid. Way back in 13th place on the grid was a young Brazilian, Ayrton Senna, in a Toleman. Prost took the lead, followed by Mansell, great plumes of spray shrouding the rest of the field. Behind them there was a series of crashes. On the first corner Warwick hit the barrier attempting to find a way through the pack, then his team-mate Tambay hit him, putting both Renaults out. French hopes were further dashed when the two Ligiers – driven by Andrea de Cesaris and François Hesnault – collided. At the end of the first lap Prost was leading, still followed by Mansell. Senna was giving an extraordinary display of driving in the wet by coming up into seventh place.

Prost suddenly came upon Teo Fabi's Brabham in the middle of the circuit. He aimed for the gap between the car and the barrier and just made it, striking a track marshal a glancing blow as he did so. But he had slowed down enough to let Mansell through – and once in front, Mansell stormed ahead, driving too quickly for the conditions. Six laps later he spun into the barrier, putting Prost back in the lead. The rain was falling even more heavily, but through it all Senna was driving brilliantly, now in second place and gaining on Prost. Just as it seemed he must pass the McLaren, the red flags came out. Prost slowed down, letting Senna through, but it was too late and the race went to Prost – albeit with only half points for everybody. The Clerk of the Course, Jacky Ickx – no stranger to rain at Monaco himself (>1972) – had decided it was too dangerous: a decision that immediately brought accusations of favouring a Frenchman's winning. Later FISA fined Ickx $6,000 and suspended his Clerk of the Course licence for not consulting his stewards before making the decision.

The Championship was between the two McLaren drivers, Prost and Lauda. Prost was ahead by 10½ points as the Championship moved across to North America, where the McLarens were given a nasty shock. Piquet (Brabham) took the Detroit Grand Prix and Rosberg (Williams) the Dallas Grand Prix. In Detroit, second over the finishing line was Martin Brundle in a Cosworth-powered Tyrrell. After the race the scrutineers discovered traces of lead in the reservoir for the water injection, evidently the result of its being topped up not only with water but with lead shot as ballast. The Tyrrell team was disqualified, not only from the race but for the rest of the year's Championship. Ken Tyrrell appealed, and was granted an injunction to let him race on until it was heard – but it failed, and he missed the last four races of the season.

Back in Europe, the McLarens found their form again – and after a great battle with Piquet, Lauda won the British Grand Prix. It was the first of seven wins for McLaren, alternating between the two drivers, which left Lauda with 66 points to Prost's 62½in the Championship as they formed up on the grid at Estoril in Portugal for the decider. Prost led for much of the race, Mansell in second and Lauda in third – a line-up that would give Prost the title. Then Mansell spun off, putting Lauda into second place – enough to give him the title by just half a point from Prost. McLaren took the Constructors' title by a massive 143½ points to Ferrari's 57½. Renault was back in fifth place.

Italian fashion company Benetton's multi-coloured design first appeared on race tracks around the world in the 1984 season, adorning Alfa-Romeo 184Ts. In the Detroit Grand Prix on 24 June, Riccardo Patrese in a 184T (**ABOVE**) performed indifferently in practice and spun and retired on lap 21. Benetton was not impressed with Alfa-Romeo's performances in 1984 and switched to British team Toleman for 1985.

LEFT: Young British driver Martin Brundle in a Tyrrell-Cosworth drove superbly to finish second in the Detroit Grand Prix – but was later disqualified in the controversy over the lead shot in Tyrrell's water reservoir for the fuel-injection system. Born in 1959, Brundle started racing saloon cars aged 17. He was second to Ayrton Senna in the British Formula Three Championship in 1983, driving a Ralt RT3.

ABOVE: The start of the German Grand Prix at Hockenheim on 5 August. Alain Prost in a McLaren took pole position and went on to win – the first time he had won the German Grand Prix. He finished in 1 hour 24 minutes 43.210 seconds – an average 131.61 mph – just over 3 seconds ahead of McLaren team-mate Niki Lauda in second place. British driver Derek Warwick was third in a V-6 Renault.

LEFT: Victory at last. Nigel Mansell celebrating his first World Championship win – for Williams-Honda in the European Grand Prix at Brands Hatch. He finished in 1 hour 32 minutes 58.109 seconds, 21.396 seconds ahead of Ayrton Senna in a Lotus-Renault. Mansell was third on the grid, behind Nelson Piquet (Brabham) and pole-winner Senna.

ABOVE: Nigel Mansell in a Williams-Honda in the British Grand Prix. He retired on lap 18 with clutch problems. Mansell was fifth on the grid, 1.084 second slower than team-mate Keke Rosberg in pole. Once speeds of 160 mph were routinely being achieved in practice, serious questions began to be asked about the safety implications of the tubocharged engine.

Now that Formula One was turbocharged, a large number of great names in high-performance motoring had been drawn into the World Championship – Renault, BMW, Ferrari, Porsche, Honda, Goodyear and Bosch. They put their reputations at stake for the sake of winning, and with their huge resources the power output of the engines rose dramatically, despite FISA's attempts to curb it by imposing fuel limits. At the beginning of the year, Ferrari announced that its latest engine produced 1,000 bhp in qualifying trim, and around 900 in racing trim. BMW's was higher, at around 1,100 bhp for qualifying. Competition in the companies' laboratories had produced ways around the restrictions, mainly through better fuel management systems and greater fuel efficiency. Drivers could adjust the amount of turbo boost to suit the occasion – maximum for qualifying, the right balance between wrecking the engine, reliability, and fuel economy for the race. Tyre companies produced ultra-soft tyres for qualifying which were dis-

carded after two or three laps.

There was a nasty shock for the Formula One teams when Michelin pulled out. Goodyear and Pirelli stayed in, but tolerances in the set-up between car and tyres were so crucial, and the ex-Michelin teams' cars designed so specifically around the tyres, that they had to redesign the cars for optimum performance. McLaren signed up with Goodyear, and John Barnard spent hours testing in the wind-tunnel and on the track after fitting new hubs, making small adjustments to the suspension to get it right. The Bosch fuel system was honed to perfection, enabling the McLarens to start each race with exactly the right amount of fuel, rather than taking on a bit more for safety, adding a little more weight. McLaren retained the same team: their World Champion, Niki Lauda, and Alain Prost.

Brabham turned to Pirelli for tyres for the BT54 after Bernard Ecclestone clinched a very advantageous deal for their backing. It was the last car with an aluminium outer skin com-

ABOVE: Champion driver, champion car. Alain Prost in a McLaren MP4 in the British Grand Prix. He won in 1 hour 18 minutes 10.436 seconds: 146.28 mph.

LEFT: Alain Prost (centre), winner of the World Drivers' Championship in a McLaren with 73 points – 20 points ahead of Italian driver Michele Alboreto, who finished second. Prost won five Grands Prix – the Brazilian, Monaco, Austrian and Italian, as well as the British. McLaren-TAG won the Constructors' title with 90 points, ahead of Ferrari with 82.

MILESTONES

The first tests of a new turbocharged Formula One engine developed by Cosworth and Ford were made in Britain and America (>1989).

The last normally-aspirated car of the 3-litre era to enter the World Championship was Martin Brundle's Tyrrell in Germany (>1989).

The first all-German Formula One car since 1962 was the Zakspeed 841, designed by Paul Brian and driven by Jonathan Palmer.

The reigning World Champion driver, Niki Lauda, announced his second retirement at his home Grand Prix in Austria (>1977, 1981).

Between 1981 and 1985, the purse at Indianapolis more than doubled from $1,605,375 to $3,217,025, due to the efforts of CART (>1978).

Having pioneered turbocharging, Renault pulled out with no Championships to show for it.

bined with carbon-fibre. The team did 12,000 miles in testing the new combination at Kyalami, South Africa, during December and January to get the relationship between the tyres and the cars right. At the same time, the reliability of the BMW engine was improved. The Brabham drivers were Nelson Piquet and Marc Surer.

For its 1985 car – the FW10 – Williams combined the new Honda V-6 turbo engine with a new moulded carbon-composite monocoque. Honda put enormous resources into the engine, which produced around 1,100 bhp in qualifying trim and 800-850 bhp for racing. Jacques Laffite returned to Ligier after one season with Williams, and Nigel Mansell (who had not been truly happy at Lotus since Colin Chapman's death) moved to fill the gap – the start of a long relationship with Williams.

On Mansell's departure, Ayrton Senna moved from Toleman to Lotus. Gérard

Ducarouge's 97T was equipped with Goodyear tyres, and retained the Renault engine. Tyrrell secured the use of the Renault too, so that, with Ligier, four teams were using it. Toleman was in deep financial problems. They had switched from Pirelli to Michelin tyres in the previous season; Goodyear was by now supporting too many teams to add them to their list, so they were without tyre sponsorship. Spirit – another small team – had a contract with Pirelli, however, and after long negotiations in the early part of the season, the two teams were merged, under Benetton's sponsorship, using Pirelli tyres (>1986), their driver Teo Fabi.

The three large company teams were all in different stages of relative decline. Alfa-Romeo had been eighth in the Constructors' Championship in 1984, and its cars were clearly uncompetitive. Renault, bedevilled by cutbacks brought on by heavy trading losses in the touring car market and industrial trouble following lay-offs, was only three places higher – not a happy state of affairs for the company that had brought about the turbo revolution. Team manager Gérard Larousse and chief engineer Michel Tetu were sidelined by the management, and they left to join Ligier, further hastening Renault's decline. Ferrari, second in the Constructors' table, suffered disruption when Mauro Forghieri was moved from Formula One.

The story of the year was the coming to prominence of three drivers whose names – together with that of Nelson Piquet – would dominate the Championship for the next eight years: Alain Prost, Nigel Mansell and Ayrton Senna. Prost took a grip on the Championship at the start of the season, winning in Brazil: McLaren's eighth successive victory. Ayrton Senna then spoilt their record by taking the

Portuguese Grand Prix at Estoril in pouring rain, reinforcing his reputation for driving in the wet after Monaco the previous year, and winning his first Grand Prix for Lotus. It was also the first time a Renault engine had won a Grand Prix in other than a Renault car.

At Imola, Senna led the San Marino Grand Prix but used too much boost and ran out of fuel. Stefan Johansson then took the lead for Ferrari, and the same thing happened. Prost roared to the front and won. At the weigh-in after the race, his McLaren was found to be 2 kilograms (4 pounds 6 ounces) under the minimum weight limit, and he was disqualified.

Nürburgring

The 1985 German Grand Prix was held on a new 2.82-mile circuit at the historic Nürburgring in the Eifel mountains. It was the first time that the race had been run at the Nürburgring since Niki Lauda's horrific accident in 1976 on the original circuit. Between 1977 and 1984 the Grand Prix was at Hockenheim. The new circuit lacked the appeal of the old Nürburgring – its designers had been more concerned with safety than spectators – and from 1986, the German Grand Prix was once again held at Hockenheim.

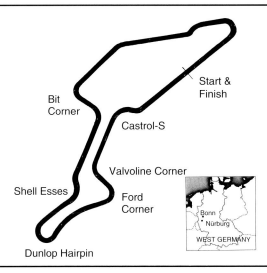

The Nürburgring's new circuit. Facilities were modern, but fans complained that the large concrete grandstands were situated too far from the track.

Bit Corner

Start & Finish

Castrol-S

Valvoline Corner

Shell Esses

Ford Corner

Bonn
Nürburg
WEST GERMANY

Dunlop Hairpin

Nürburgring:
1 lap: 2.82 miles

ABOVE: Danny 'Spin-and-Win' Sullivan (March-Cosworth, No. 5) out of control ahead of Mario Andretti (Lola-Cosworth, No. 3) in the Indianapolis 500. Sullivan was the first man to win the 500 after spinning in the race.

RIGHT: Sullivan the day after his famous 500 victory. Born in March 1950 in Louisville, Kentucky, he began racing in Formula Ford and Formula Three races in England. His first race at Indianapolis was in 1982 when he was classified 14th after crashing.

ABOVE RIGHT: America's First Family of racing. Al Unser Snr (right) congratulates his son Al Jr on victory in the Meadowlands Grand Prix in New York on 30 June. It was Al Jr's first win in the CART/PPG Indy Car World Series in 1985. He finished the season second in the series with 136 points, just three points behind his father.

next five races, three going to Prost and one to Lauda. But Alboreto won the German Grand Prix and Senna the Belgian.

The European Grand Prix, at Brands Hatch, was a landmark race. Senna was fastest in practice, but in the race Mansell passed him to win – his first-ever Grand Prix win, and the first by a British driver since 1977 (>1987, 1992). Prost was fourth, for him a low placing that nonetheless gave him the title – the first Frenchman to win the World Championship since it was inaugurated 35 years previously (>1986, 1989).

The 1985 Indianapolis 500 was something of a landmark too, if in a very different way. The prize money had risen steadily since CART had taken more control of the commercial aspects of the business, more than doubling from $1,605,375 in 1981 to $3,217,025. The grid was once again dominated by British-built cars – 24 March chassis and 29 Cosworth engines – but the fastest were a pair of Buick-powered Marches driven by Scott Brayton and Pancho Carter. Brayton set a new qualifying record of 212.583 mph.

In the race, Mario Andretti in a Lola T900 took the lead after a couple of laps, and held it for 118 more against determined challenges from Danny Sullivan in a Penske-March 85C. Sullivan made it past Andretti by taking a line through a turn which involved crossing the rumble strip that marked the edge of the track. As he recrossed it coming out of the corner, the car was unbalanced and he spun, right in front of Andretti, at around 200 mph. Andretti managed to avoid hitting him, and re-took the lead. With only 12 laps to go, Sullivan made the same move and again took the lead, to deny Andretti his second Indy win by 2.5 seconds.

The race was awarded to Elio de Angelis who had come in second in a Lotus. Later it was explained that the weight loss in Prost's car was due to greater than expected use of oil, brake pads and tyre rubber. The extremely tight tolerances and fine margins that drivers were working to was amply demonstrated in the next race, at Monaco, which Prost won, only to run out of fuel on his lap of honour.

The McLarens faltered again in North America. Michele Alboreto won in Canada for Ferrari, Keke Rosberg in Detroit for Williams. Then Piquet took the French Grand Prix for Brabham. Thereafter the McLarens reasserted themselves completely, winning four of the

The Indianapolis 500 was 75 years old. As if in celebration of the idea of its founding fathers – that it should centre on the richest prize in motor racing – the total prize money this year topped $4 million for the first time, at $4,001,050 (>1911). It was also the year in which the two lines of garages which formed the famous 'Gasoline Alley' – where generations of racing drivers and mechanics had prepared their cars – was demolished and new ones built.

The race was delayed for two days due to rain, and when the cars did finally line up on the grid, a subtle change in the pecking order was evident. All the cars were built in Britain, by either March, Lola or Penske, and Lola was beginning to erode March's dominant position. Most were still powered by the V-8 Cosworth turbocharged engine, but two American engines also featured: Chevrolet with a racing V-8, also built in Britain, and Buick with a V-6 stock block-based engine. Rick Mears was fastest qualifier in a March-Cosworth entered by Penske.

The race was a tight battle between four drivers – Mears, and Bobby Rahal, Kevin Cogan and Michael Andretti – all in March-Cosworths. Andretti led for 45 laps, then fell back as the other three fought for the flag right to the end. Rahal won by 1.44 seconds from Cogan, who was 1.88 seconds ahead of Mears.

Rahal's share of the purse was $581,062, taking his personal winnings in the Indy Car World Series to more than $1 million for the year. His earnings – which would double with commercial endorsements – showed the increase in the most successful drivers' income. It was the same in Grand Prix racing, where the select few drivers who won most of the races commanded multi-million pound contracts. As drivers became international

RIGHT: Bobby Rahal, winner of the Indianapolis 500.

BELOW: Bobby Rahal (No. 3) leading Kevin Cogan (No. 7) and Rick Mears (No. 4) in the Indianapolis 500. All three were driving March-Cosworths. It was a classic race, the three drivers scrapping for the big prize right to the flag.

BELOW: Pit-stop for Nigel Mansell in the British Grand Prix on 13 July. He was driving the latest Williams-Honda – the FW11, equipped with car-to-pit telemetry. He won in 1 hour 30 minutes 38.471 seconds – 5.574 seconds ahead of team-mate Nelson Piquet.

sporting superstars, so the relationship between them and their team, and between drivers in the same team, changed. Individual success brought power, and the convention that the No.2 driver in a team would give way to the No.1 driver began to break down – nowhere more spectacularly or with more significant consequences than at Williams.

Nelson Piquet left Brabham to join Williams, where the financial package was more attractive and the car more competitive. As a former World Champion, he expected Nigel Mansell to play second fiddle to him, and expected the team to support him first and foremost – but Mansell was out to win, against

his team-mate as well as the rest of the field. Elio de Angelis joined Brabham from Lotus, where he felt that Ayrton Senna had been getting preferential treatment; Senna was then powerful enough to block the appointment of Derek Warwick as de Angelis' replacement in favour of Johnny Dumfries, just promoted from Formula Three, whom he saw as less of a threat.

Rewards were rising, but so were costs. Brabham was the only team to bring out a completely new car, the BT55. Gordon Murray used a variation on the idea used with great success in the 1950s at Indianapolis – laying the engine on its side to reduce frontal area. The long-wheelbase low-slung car cost Brabham's sponsors, Olivetti, £6.8 million. Brabham tried to lure Niki Lauda back to drive it but was unsuccessful, so in addition to de Angelis, Brabham took on Riccardo Patrese. The car was an expensive mistake. During the entire season Patrese managed just two sixth places – 2 points in the Championship – and de Angelis crashed at 180 mph while testing it at the Paul Ricard circuit and died in hospital two days later.

At McLaren, the 'dream ticket' of Ron Dennis and John Barnard had run its course. Their fortunes at a low ebb again, Ferrari made overtures to Barnard, and he was able not only to command a very substantial fee but to insist that he wanted to work in Britain, so Enzo Ferrari – the doyen of Italian motor racing – agreed to his advanced design depart-

LEFT: Last-gasp victory. Alain Prost triumphant after clinching his second World Championship with first place in the Australian Grand Prix. His rival for the title, Nigel Mansell, crashed on lap 64. Prost's win depended on a desperate gamble. For the last 15 laps, the fuel readout in his cockpit showed that he was 5 litres short. But instead of slowing to conserve what he had, he banked on the in-car computer having malfunctioned and continued at full speed. His hunch was right – the computer was wrong.

RIGHT: The Hungarian Grand Prix on 10 August revealed a huge appetite for motor racing in the countries of eastern Europe. A crowd of 200,000 watched the race – and a further 180,000 attended over the practice days. The race itself was business as usual: Nelson Piquet won in a Williams-Honda, 17.673 seconds ahead of Ayrton Senna in a Lotus-Renault.

ment's being set up in Guildford, just to the south of London.

On 8 March the Williams team suffered a shattering blow. Frank Williams crashed a hired car on the way back from the Paul Ricard circuit, at which he had been supervising testing. He was severely injured and remained in hospital for months, emerging in a wheelchair, paralysed from the waist down. The new FW11 Williams was nonetheless the favourite for the season, benefiting from Honda's huge investment in its V-6 engine.

New regulations from FISA stipulated that only turbocharged engines were to be used, and the fuel allowance was reduced further, to 195 litres (42.9 UK gallons, 51.5 US gallons). Cars were fitted with a computer which measured not only fuel consumption but other performance parameters, including the level of boost the driver was using. The computer was connected to a data link on the car, which downloaded the information to the pits each lap, so the team manager could radio back instructions to the driver. Honda took electronic monitoring a stage further: the information received was relayed back to Tokyo by satellite during the race so it could be analysed there too, and suggestions made on how to improve performance.

Piquet justified Frank Williams' faith in him by winning the first race of the season, the Brazilian Grand Prix. Ayrton Senna then took pole position in Spain and led the race. Behind

him, the two Williams drivers had a battle in which Mansell showed that he was on a level with Piquet. When Piquet's engine gave out and he retired, Mansell charged after Senna, failing by only one hundredth of a second to take the flag.

The fine margins to which the drivers operated were again evident at San Marino, where Alain Prost won for McLaren: his fuel ran out just as he crossed the line. Prost stayed on form, winning at Monaco – his team-mate Keke Rosberg second – but he crashed in spectacular fashion in the Belgian Grand Prix, in which Mansell then beat Senna into second

ABOVE: Jacques Laffite's Ligier-Renault JS27 in the pits at Imola during the San Marino Grand Prix. He retired after 14 laps when the car developed transmission problems. Laffite had a quiet season, finishing in the top three just twice – third in the Brazilian Grand Prix on 23 March and second in the Detroit Grand Prix on 22 June.

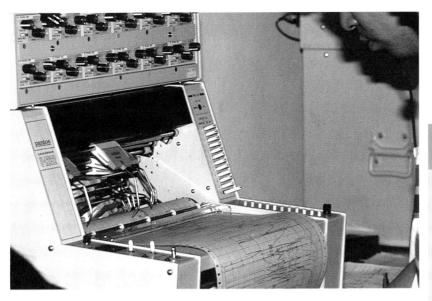

MILESTONES

The Italian fashion house Benetton bought the Toleman team (>1981) it had sponsored since 1985; the cars were then renamed Benettons.

The Chevrolet Corvette pace car at Indianapolis was driven by the test pilot 'Chuck' Yeager, the first man to fly faster than sound.

The French Grand Prix was veteran Enzo Ferrari's 400th World Championship event; neither of his drivers finished in the points.

The Hungarian Grand Prix at the new Hungaroring, near Budapest, on 10 August, was the first Grand Prix held behind the Iron Curtain.

Bill Elliot received a special $1 million prize for winning three of the four classic NASCAR races: the Daytona, Winston and Southern 500s.

Hans-Joachim Stuck and Derek Bell won the Le Mans 24-hour sports car race in a Porsche 956, the company's sixth successive victory.

LEFT: Cleaning a tyre before the San Marino Grand Prix. Italian firm Pirelli came into Formula One racing in 1981, with radial-ply tyres. The development of new tyre designs and materials is one area in which racing continues to benefit the ordinary driver, by improving road safety.

place. Senna was showing superb form, taking nine pole positions over the season, but the Lotus was not equal to the Williams and he won only two races. Gerhard Berger won in Mexico, giving Benetton its first victory – but the season belonged to Williams. Piquet won four races in all, and Mansell five.

There were high hopes of a British World Champion at the start of the Australian Grand Prix on the streets of Adelaide. Prost and Piquet both had 63 points, and Mansell had

70. Mansell had just to finish fourth to take the title, whereas Piquet and Prost both had to win. Rosberg, who announced his retirement at the race, led at the start, and at the half-way mark was still ahead of Piquet, Mansell and Prost. As long as Rosberg was ahead, Mansell would be Champion. Then one of Rosberg's tyres burst. Even with Piquet in the lead, Mansell in second place would still win the Championship. Suddenly, with less than a quarter of the race to go, a rear tyre exploded on Mansell's Williams. He just managed to bring the car to a safe halt, then walked back to the pits, bitterness and disappointment all over his face.

The Williams team called Piquet into the pits for a precautionary tyre change, which turned out to be unnecessary. He rejoined in second place, behind Prost, who made no mistakes and won the race. Having looked invincible, neither of the Williams drivers achieved the greatest goal. Prost's 25th Grand Prix victory earned him a second successive World title, and he joined that elite band of Alberto Ascari (>1953), Juan Manuel Fangio (>1955) and Jack Brabham (>1960) to win the title twice in a row. Williams had to be satisfied with the Constructors' Championship.

The Cosworth V-8 engine's long reign at Indianapolis was over at last. Two great American names had now entered the fray – Chevrolet, with a V-8 720-bhp aluminium turbo racing engine built by Ilmor Engineering in Britain, and Buick, with an equally powerful V-6. A third challenger was the V-8 Judd-Honda, a Japanese design using British expertise to prepare it for racing. In chassis development, March's dominant position was under similar challenge from Lola and Penske.

Mario Andretti put the Newman-Haas team on pole position in his Lola-Chevy by qualifying at 215.37 mph. In second place on the grid was another Lola-Chevy driven by the previous year's winner, Bobby Rahal. The Penske team had also turned from Cosworth to Chevy, but they found their new PC-16 uncompetitive, and after Danny Ongais crashed one in qualifying, Roger Penske returned to the previous year's March-Cosworths, replacing Ongais with the 48-year-old veteran and three-times winner, Al Unser (Senior). Rick Mears put his March in third place on the grid, while Unser qualified in 21st place.

In the race, Andretti took the lead and by lap 13 was passing the tailenders, lapping Unser on lap 17. At the half-way mark he had a comfortable 5-second lead over Robert Guerrero in another March-Cosworth. By that stage most of the rest of the serious opposition was out through mechanical failure. At three-quarters distance, Unser had moved up to third place and Andretti was a lap ahead of Guerrero, who had been forced into the pits after losing a nose cone. Then the fuel system on Andretti's car failed on lap 178, and he was out. Guerrero made a final pit-stop, looking as if he had the race sewn up, but stalled coming out of the pits. Unser was suddenly in the lead. The yellow flags came out as Andretti's car was towed away, and the cars bunched up, Guerrero in sixth place with four laps to go. He passed three, including Al Unser Junior, but could not catch his father, who won. It was Unser Snr's fourth victory, equalling A.J. Foyt's record. It was also the fifth March victory in a row, Penske's sixth, and the tenth successive win for the Cosworth engine (>1988).

Thanks to the turbo revolution, Formula One cars were now capable of well over 200 mph. But such progress had come at a price few were any longer prepared to pay. The top teams used special engines for qualifying, boosted to 1,200-1,300 bhp for a few laps, after which they were wrecked. It kept them on top, but it was extremely costly. Renault –

MILESTONES

On 6 April March Engineering (>1969) went public – the first racing car manufacturer to do so – its shares quoted on the Stock Exchange.

After retiring from Formula One racing, Didier Pironi took up powerboat racing. He was killed in an accident off the Isle of Wight.

Alain Prost's victory in the Portuguese Grand Prix at Estoril was his 28th, breaking Jackie Stewart's record total that was set in 1973.

The Colin Chapman Trophy for normally-aspirated cars went to Tyrrell-Cosworth; the Jim Clark Trophy for drivers went to Jonathan Palmer.

Satoru Nakajima, first Japanese driver in Formula One, finished 11th in the Drivers' Championship; his best result was fourth in the British Grand Prix.

After the costly failure of the BT55, Bernard Ecclestone withdrew Brabham from World Championship racing at the end of the season.

ABOVE: The Indianapolis 500. Pancho Carter in a March-Cosworth (No. 29), Rick Mears in a March-Chevrolet (No. 8), Davy Jones in another March-Cosworth (No. 44) and Mario Andretti in a Lola-Chevrolet (No. 5). Andretti was ninth; Mears was 23rd; Jones was 28th; Carter was 29th. Carter had survived a hair-raising practice crash in which he flipped his car right over.

who had started the turbo revolution – pulled out. Lotus had moved to Honda. BMW, after completely redesigning its engine for the failed Brabham BT55, wanted to pull out but was restrained by contractual obligations to Brabham for the 1987 season.

Everybody in the sport knew that the only way to curb the high speeds and costs was to abandon the turbocharger. They agreed to phase it out over two years. In 1987, normally-aspirated engines would be permitted again, the size increased to 3.5 litres from 3 litres. Those cars using them were allowed a lower weight limit of 500 kilograms (1,102.3 pounds). The power of the turbo was limited to around 600 bhp using pop-off valves set at 4 times atmospheric pressure. For 1988, the valves would act at 2.5 times atmospheric pressure and the fuel limit would be lowered to

150 litres (33 UK gallons, 39.6 US gallons) for the turbos (whereas there would be no limit for the normally-aspirated cars). From 1989, turbos would be banned completely, the formula based on 3.5-litre normally-aspirated engines. It was agreed that there would be no changes after that until at least 1991. If any further incentive to drop the turbo was needed, a trophy was introduced for the non-turbo entries – the Colin Chapman Cup for the Constructors and the Jim Clark Cup for the drivers. The only disgruntled elements were engine makers, such as Honda, whose huge investment in turbo technology now had a limited shelf-life.

The new rules gave a new lease of life to the Cosworth V-8 in Grand Prix racing just as its star was beginning to wane at Indianapolis. The new DFZ produced 575 bhp at 10,000

BELOW: Nigel Mansell going for broke in a Williams-Honda at the Belgian Grand Prix. Sparks flew after a first lap collision between pole-winner Mansell and Ayrton Senna's Lotus-Honda. Mansell had to be escorted from Senna's pit after a confrontation.

rpm, so the turbos still had a power advantage, but they were also heavier. In the first year of the transition they were expected still to be well on top. Tyrrell, March and Lola all went for the non-turbo option in 1987.

The mood of change in the sport was enhanced by another spin of the merry-go-round among the designers. Brabham's fortunes were down following the failure of the BT55, and they reverted to an updated version of the 1985 car. John Barnard's departure to Ferrari left a hole at McLaren, where the MP4/3 was completed by Steve Nicholls. After 17 years with Brabham, Gordon Murray joined McLaren. The Ferrari 187 had a new V-6 turbo engine, but Barnard's task was to look ahead beyond the turbo era to the new formula. The Ferrari team drivers were

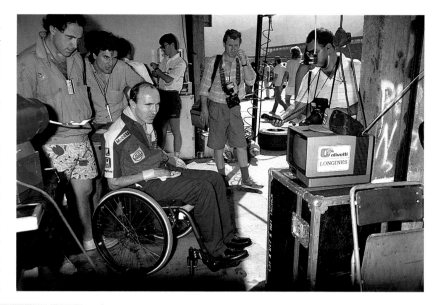

ABOVE RIGHT: Back in action. Frank Williams returned to the pits in a wheelchair after sustaining serious injuries in a road accident. He was renowned for his dedication to detail (>1986).

RIGHT: Nelson Piquet and his pit crew reviewing lap times on a Longines monitor during practice for the Japanese Grand Prix, held at Suzuka on 1 November. He failed to gain any points in the race, but won the World Drivers' Championship with 73 points, 12 ahead of team-mate Nigel Mansell. Williams won the Constructors' Championship from McLaren by a margin of 61 points.

Michele Alboreto and Gerhard Berger, who had moved from Benetton. Benetton secured the Ford V-6 turbo engine for its B187; driving for them were the Belgian Thierry Boutsen and Teo Fabi.

On Lotus's change to Honda engines, Stefan Johansson left them to be replaced by Satoru Nakajima, the first Japanese driver to graduate to Formula One. The Lotus 99T was fitted with 'active suspension'. A computer, fed by sensors that monitored speed and acceleration, adjusted the suspension through electromagnetic valves on damper units, giving the optimum ride. Another change at Lotus was

colour: the black and gold of the John Player Specials was replaced by the yellow and blue of R. J. Reynolds' Camel cigarettes.

With the Honda engine and Ayrton Senna as driver, Lotus looked highly competitive for 1987 – but the 99T proved less than equal to the latest Williams-Honda FW11 and the McLaren-TAG MP4/3. Senna was nonetheless one of the four top drivers of the year, together with Alain Prost of McLaren and the Williams drivers Nigel Mansell and Nelson Piquet.

The reigning World Champion, Alain Prost, took the first race of the season in Brazil; Piquet was second. Mansell failed to finish

LEFT: Williams domination. Nigel Mansell in a Williams-Honda (No. 5) leading team-mate Nelson Piquet (No. 6) in the French Grand Prix. Mansell had pole position; Piquet drove the fastest lap (122.64 mph). They finished first and second, Mansell besting his rival by 7.711 seconds.

ABOVE: Warming tyres before the Brazilian Grand Prix. Warm tyres are more adhesive than cold ones, and provide a better grip at the start of the race. Goodyear had a monopoly on supply in 1987. They furnished all the teams with the same type.

because of a tyre failure. In practice for the San Marino Grand Prix, Piquet crashed, putting him out of the race – which Mansell won from Senna. At Spa for the Belgian Grand Prix, Mansell took pole position but in the race collided with Senna, putting them both out and making a gift of the race to Prost and his McLaren team-mate Johansson. Mansell confronted Senna in the pits over the collision, and the incident ended in an unseemly scuffle.

Mansell looked set for victory at Monaco – he took pole position again, and led – until his exhaust split, and he was out. Senna gave the Lotus 99T its first victory. The active suspension was working, but it was very complicated for the advantage it gave. In fifth place was Jonathan Palmer in a Tyrrell-Cosworth, who thereby gained the first points for a non-turbo engine under the new regulations.

Mansell was in pole position at Detroit, and led, but had to drop out with leg cramps. The Lotus was more competitive on street circuits, such as Detroit and Monaco, and Senna took the lead to win, going one point clear of Prost at the top of the table. Piquet was back on form for the French Grand Prix at the fast Paul Ricard circuit, on which the two Williams-Hondas were unbeatable. Piquet led for most of the race before Mansell overtook him in a particularly daring way, and won, putting an utterly furious Nelson Piquet in second place.

The rivalry between team-mates Piquet and Mansell reached a peak in the British Grand Prix at Silverstone – another fast circuit on which the Williams cars had the advantage. Piquet was still smarting from Mansell's victory in France, having said in public that he thought Mansell's driving there had been dangerous. Now that Mansell was driving in front of his home crowd and Piquet was suggesting pointedly that Mansell should be reined in by the Williams management, the atmosphere between them was more than merely competitive. The rivalry started in practice: Piquet took pole position by one tenth of a second after a furious session in which both drivers spun off in their eagerness to beat the other. Senna and Prost, on the second row of the grid, were more than a second slower.

The start was spectacular, both Williams going for the line into the first corner, driving very closely together, leaving the outside free. Prost made the coolest of moves: he took the outside, then cut them both off, to go into the lead. But it was only for a moment – Piquet and Mansell passed him seconds later. After that, the two Williams left the rest of the field behind – a mixture of rivalry and the Honda engine taking them out of sight of the rest. Only seconds behind Piquet on lap 35, Mansell felt a vibration and went in for tyres, only to find he had lost a wheel-balancing weight. He was back on new tyres after a 9.2-second pit-stop, assuming Piquet would also have to go in for tyres. But it was soon evident that Piquet was going to hold on to his lead and had no intention of stopping. Mansell then applied the determination for which he was renowned to the seemingly hopeless task of catching Piquet. With 17 laps to go, there was 16.8 seconds between them. Mansell gained by more than a

second a lap, and with five laps to go the gap was down to 1.6 seconds – an extraordinary performance. With two laps to go, he nipped inside Piquet at Stowe Corner. Mansell was very low on fuel, but throwing caution to the winds he never let up until he crossed the line to win by 1.9 seconds. On his lap of honour, in front of a delirious crowd, Mansell stopped at Stowe and kissed the track.

The victory was to have lasting repercussions which unfolded during the rest of the season. Piquet was furious, and started looking for a new team. His search began a series of moves which together greatly altered the make-up of the teams for 1988. Ayrton Senna was also looking for a move and began negotiations with McLaren. Piquet, who had a strong relationship with Honda, agreed to move to Lotus. In the meantime Honda was in negotiation with McLaren to make them the second customer for their engine, in place of Williams. Partly because of Piquet's move, Honda eventually switched to McLaren. The new arrangements were announced at the Italian Grand Prix – and in this way Ron Dennis, Senna, Prost and McLaren effectively became the final beneficiaries of the rivalry between Mansell and Piquet.

BELOW: The Coca-Cola 600 at the Charlotte Motor Speedway, North Carolina, on 24 May. Bill Elliott (Ford, No. 9) was fastest qualifier at a record 170.901 mph. He retired in the race, which was won by Kyle Petty in a Ford at 131.483 mph. Elliott finished the season second in the NASCAR Winston Cup standings with 4,207 points, 489 behind winner Dale Earnhardt (Chevrolet).

BELOW: Toughing it out – the first of the two 125-mile qualifying races for the Daytona 500. There were several crashes – one of which left A.J. Foyt in hospital with a badly injured right shoulder. Ken Schrader in the Red Baron Frozen Pizza Ford Thunderbird won the qualifier – by just 4 inches, from Bill Elliott in another Thunderbird. Elliott then won the 500; Schrader came seventh.

RIGHT: Nigel Mansell's hopes of winning the 1987 World Championship ended in a spectacular crash in qualifying for the Japanese Grand Prix. He lost control of his Williams FW11B after clipping a kerb – and it was thrown into the air. Badly bruised, he was forbidden to drive in the race, and, after a night in the Nagoya University Clinic, he flew back to Europe – his season in tatters.

The struggle for the Championship continued, but Mansell's chances disappeared when he crashed at Suzuka in the battle for pole position with Piquet for the Japanese Grand Prix. He went to hospital with back injuries, and was out for the rest of the season. Piquet's engine failed in Japan, but he took his third World Championship because, with Mansell out, nobody else could catch him. Despite the engine failure, the result marked the high point of Williams-Honda, who took both Championships. Gerhard Berger took the last two races of the season for Ferrari.

RIGHT: Death of the turbo. FISA's decision to introduce pop-off valves – which limited the pressure at which fuel was forced into the engine – effectively neutralized the increased power of the turbocharged unit.

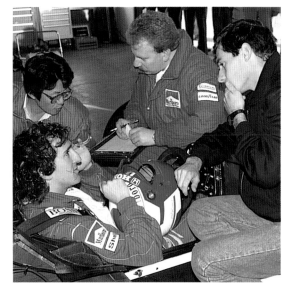

The Indianapolis 500 records are among the most meticulously kept of any race. Those for 1988 show a minor landmark: it was the first time that all three cars on the front row of the grid came from the same team. In pole position was Rick Mears, and beside him were Danny Sullivan and Al Unser Snr. All three men were driving for one of the most influential men in American racing — Roger Penske.

Penske had virtually transformed racing at Indianapolis by breaking with the United States Auto Club (USAC) in order to form Championship Auto Racing Teams (>1979). By 1988 CART had changed the power structure of motor racing in America: the new force was the racing team, a business built around an entrepreneur who could put together enough money through sponsorship to compete at the top level. To win, team bosses like Penske had to have the best — and by 1988 Penske's cars were built in Britain, where the most advanced racing industry in the world was thriving.

To attract such sponsorship, teams had to win. Those same record books show that, as he started the 1988 race, Rick Mears was the third highest money-earner in the 500's history, at a total of $1,663,919; he had been in pole position three times, and he had won the race twice (>1979, 1982). By the end of the race, he and Penske would be nearly a million dollars richer still.

The record books also show the race was chaotic. Seconds after the start Scott Brayton spun, taking Roberto Guerrero into the wall with him. Tony Bettenhausen braked to avoid them, spun, and followed them into the wall. When accidents happen at Indianapolis, yellow lights tell the drivers to hold their positions: no overtaking is permitted until the debris has been cleared. In 1988 they were switched on no fewer than 14 times; the race was processional for 68 of the 200 laps. Teo Fabi lost a wheel on lap 30; Tom Sneva went into the wall two laps later; A.J. Foyt crashed on lap 52; Arie Luyendyk hit Ludwig Heimrath on the straight; and Steve Chassey, Danny Sullivan and Rich Volger all came to grief. The race finished with the yellow lights on again. Rick Mears was first and Emerson Fittipaldi second, the only two drivers to complete 500 miles.

BELOW: Same cars, different sponsors: Rick Mears (Penzoil), Danny Sullivan (Miller) and Al Unser Snr (Hertz) at the

FAR LEFT, BOTTOM:
Rick Mears, a modern hero of Indianapolis, was born in Wichita, Kansas, in 1951; he now lives in Jupiter, Florida, with his wife Chris and two sons, Clint and Cole. His racing career began in 1970 driving sprint buggies at Ascot Park, California.

FAR LEFT, TOP: Champions Ayrton Senna and Alain Prost (far left, top) were team-mates at Marlboro McLaren, especially in front of the cameras, but they have always been personal rivals on and off the track (>1989).

LEFT: In the Monaco Grand Prix at Monte Carlo, Prost beat Senna; the speed and acceleration of Formula One cars have made the twisting road circuit obsolete, but the venue's prestige has kept it in the World Championship calendar.

Indianapolis 500. The PC-17's fuel system is managed by computer to maximize engine efficiency at 700-720 bhp.

The team structure had also transformed the Formula One World Championship, for which Ron Dennis of McLaren, backed by the Marlboro tobacco company, had put together the best possible car-and-driver combination. In 1988 he negotiated exclusive use of Honda turbocharged engines (>1978) to go in the McLaren-Honda MP4/4B. He also hired two of the best drivers: the young Brazilian Ayrton Senna (>1986), and the Frenchman and two-times former World Champion, Alain Prost (>1985, 1986).

The MP4 was indisputably the fastest car in Formula One; the only competition Prost and Senna had was each other. McLaren's superiority is best seen through statistics. Of the 16 races in the World Championship, Senna won 13 pole positions and 8 races, another record. He also won his first World Championship. Prost won seven races, and was runner-up in the championship. In ten races the pair finished first and second.

McLaren nearly made it a clean sweep, but two laps from the end of the Italian Grand Prix at Monza, Senna, who was leading, had a misunderstanding with Jean-Louis Schlesser in a Williams, and spun off into a sand-trap. Prost was already out, so the race was a gift for Gerhard Berger and Michele Alboreto, who came first and second for Ferrari.

In an ironic twist of fate, the one and only victory for Ferrari that year came just a month after Enzo Ferrari — who had been at the heart of motor racing for 70 years — died, aged 90 (>1919). One of the last links with a less commercial age had finally been severed.

MILESTONES

From 1988 the footpedals on Grand Prix cars had to be located behind the front axle, giving more protection to drivers' legs in an accident.

On 10 April Mario Andretti won his 50th Indy Car race at Phoenix — the first event in the Indy Car World Series. His son Michael was third.

In practice for the Indy 500, Danny Sullivan set a new lap record of 216.214 mph. It was broken the same day by Rick Mears at 219.198 mph.

On 13 November Alain Prost won the Australian Grand Prix, the last World Championship race where turbocharged engines were used (>1977).

LEFT: Spectator bonanza. The official attendance figure for the 30th Daytona 500 on 14 February was 135,000. The new 4,000-capacity grandstand overlooking the start-finish line was packed to the rafters.

One of the most commercial forms of motor racing is NASCAR's Winston Cup series of stock car races, of which the Daytona 500 remains the premier event (>1959). The cars carry the great names of the American automobile industry – cars that people can buy in the showrooms – re-inventing in a brash, populist style the original idea behind motor racing (>1894): to promote motor cars that people can buy for themselves. But under the bodywork the racing cars are different: for 1988 the V-8 5.8-litre engines produced around 450 bhp (down from 600 bhp the previous year) without turbochargers, and the driver's compartment was surrounded by a steel cage. They were heavily sponsored, many of them garishly – such as Darrell Waltrip's Chevrolet Monte Carlo in 1988 painted in the livery of Tide washing powder. Everything about stock car racing is audience-friendly, and it has grown in popularity and stature in America, mainly in the southern states. By the late 1980s it was challenging Indianapolis and other great sporting events for television audiences with its particular brand of close, fast, exciting and spectacular racing.

The 30th Daytona 500 was no exception. This was despite NASCAR's insistence on one-inch restrictor plates over the carburettor ports, which reduced power by 150 bhp. Ken Schrader's 193.8 mph put him in pole position in his Chevrolet Monte Carlo – but it was down 15 mph on the previous year because of the restrictor plates.

ABOVE: In the pits during the Daytona 500. Dale Earnhardt in the Childress/Mr Goodwrench Chevrolet Monte Carlo (No. 3, bottom) finished tenth; Richard Petty in the Petty Enterprises/STP Pontiac Grand (No. 43, centre) crashed dramatically on lap 105; Davey Allison in the Ranier/Havoline Ford Thunderbird (No. 28, top right) was runner-up.

His Chevy team-mate Waltrip started from fourth place on the grid of 42 cars, but led for the first 10 laps, with Rusty Wallace in second place in a Pontiac. Close behind Wallace was Bobby Allison, a 50-year-old NASCAR veteran, in a Buick Regal, followed by his son Davey Allison, aged 26, in a Ford Thunderbird. On lap 11 Bobby Allison 'drafted' into the lead. Drafting is a technique perfected by stock car drivers to use each other's slipstreams to build up speed, especially on the turns, then pull out using the tow like a slingshot, to gain and pass down the straight.

On lap 13 Waltrip drafted back into the lead, followed by Davey Allison. On lap 22 Mark Martin's Ford blew its engine, bringing out the yellow flags. The drivers headed for the pits and when racing restarted, Rusty Wallace took the lead. Although Waltrip and the Allisons were then well down the field, they worked their way up by lap 42 – only for the yellow flags to come out again when Connie Saylor crashed, and again when Cale Yarborough followed suit a few laps later.

By lap 53 Bobby Allison was leading, and he drew away from the field a little while Waltrip was busy working his way up through it. But after pit-stops, Waltrip regained the lead. On lap 103 Richard Petty lost control of his Pontiac coming out of a turn. He was shunted by Phil Barkdoll's Ford Thunderbird, then collided with A.J. Foyt's Oldsmobile Delta. Petty's car lifted off the track, rolling over in the air and bouncing off the safety fencing, pieces of the car flying off in all directions. What was left finished up in the middle of the track. Apart from a damaged ankle, Petty, a NASCAR legend, was unhurt (>1992).

Waltrip was once more down the field after pit-stops, but with another masterly display of driving he worked his way patiently through the tightly-packed field, to lead again by lap 153. Davey Allison was currently second and his father third. Another crash brought a final round of pit-stops before Davey Allison led the trio back into the fray, the two Allisons sandwiching Waltrip in the middle. Waltrip then fell back with a blown cylinder and the whole field tightened up into a long procession as drivers protected their positions. Bobby Allison passed his son, giving the Allisons père et fils first and second, a fairy-tale ending to a great race.

ABOVE: Bobby Allison in the Stavola Bros/Miller High Life Buick Regal, winner of the Daytona 500 in 3 hours 38 minutes 8 seconds: 137.531 mph. It was his third victory in the Daytona 500 – ten years after his first. He also won one of the two 125-mile qualifying races, ahead of Rusty Wallace's Blue Max/Kodak Pontiac Grand Prix. Wallace finished 7th in the 500, but went on to win the 1988 NASCAR Winston Cup.

RIGHT: Old-timer. At 50 years old, Bobby Allison was the oldest-ever winner of the Daytona 500. His wife Judy joked after the race: 'He'll probably be here till he's 95!' Later in the season, Allison came close to death in a smash at Pocono, Pa. He was in hospital for three months with fractured bones and internal injuries. One side effect was memory loss – he had no recollection of his Daytona 500 victory.

CHAPTER TWELVE
SAFETY, SPONSORSHIP &
THE PRICE OF VICTORY

'The more things change, the more they stay the same.'

Motor racing has seen many changes in a hundred years, yet its essential ingredients are what they were in 1894: state-of-the-art cars, competitive drivers, demanding circuits, people who want to watch – and money.

The thread of common experience for those who race, and those who watch, remains unchanged: the thrill of speed, the closeness to danger, and the possibility – however remote these days – of death. What has changed is that racing has become safer. Death is a rare visitor to the track today. When Derek Warwick crashed in the 1991 Italian Grand Prix, millions watched his Lotus apparently disintegrate around him as it somersaulted several times in the middle of the track. When it came to rest, they breathed again as he lifted himself out of the intact driver's compartment, ran back to the pits, and raced on in a spare car. After a century of motor racing the price of winning is exactly what it always was – whatever it takes. If it takes a million pounds to develop a gearbox that will shave one tenth of a second off every gearchange, and your driver changes gear 20 times a lap, that's 2 seconds a lap saved. Whole races have been won by smaller margins – so you pay.

The one new issue is the environment. As we question the way we use the motor car, so the sport built around it has to move with the times. The price of keeping the sport in a recognizable form will be to reconcile the need to be fast, thrilling, and a symbol of the potency of the motor car, with helping to put more efficient, 'greener' cars on the roads. Remaining the industry's laboratory in this respect is the challenge that faces motor racing as it starts its second century.

Motor racing today is a sport and a business – but, above all, it is theatre. Its survival depends on the continuing appeal of men and machines locked in individual competition.

RIGHT: On parade. The starting grid for the Indianapolis 500: in pole, Rick Mears (Penske-Chevy, No. 4), fastest qualifier at 223.885 mph; alongside, Al Unser (Lola-Chevy, No. 25) and Emerson Fittipaldi (Penske-Chevy, No. 20). Fittipaldi won; Unser was second; Mears retired after 113 laps, with engine trouble. On the second row, from right: Jim Crawford (Lola-Buick, No. 15), Mario Andretti (Lola-Chevy, No. 5) and Scott Brayton (Lola-Buick, No. 22). Andretti was fourth; Brayton sixth; Crawford retired after 135 laps.

Twenty teams entered Formula One in the first year of the new formula. But money had changed the Championship and the teams were split, a clear gap emerging between those at the top who had the lion's share of the sponsorship, and a second division who could afford neither the technology nor the drivers to be truly competitive.

At the top was McLaren. Ron Dennis retained the two best drivers, Ayrton Senna and Alain Prost, and he continued his fruitful relationship with Honda. Frank Williams had had a poor season in 1988 with the Judd engine, and now he teamed up with Renault who had come back to Formula One as an engine supplier, though not as an entrant. Nigel Mansell had left, so Williams signed on Riccardo Patrese and Thierry Boutsen. Honda and Renault both went for a rather unusual V-10 configuration.

Ferrari opted for a V-12 engine for John Barnard's F1-89 project, known as the Ferrari 640 (>1986). It was a superb, clean-looking car, with functional lines, but its most innovative feature was a seven-speed semi-automatic gearbox which allowed the driver to change up or down with a flick of either end of a bar across the back of the steering wheel. Mansell gave Ferrari a tremendous boost by winning his first race for them, and the first of the season, in Brazil, despite problems with the gearbox in the early part of the season.

The fourth top team was Benetton, which used the more traditional Ford V-8 engine. Its drivers were the Italian Alessandro Nannini and a young Englishman, Johnny Herbert. Lotus, with Nelson Piquet, and Brabham – great names of the last quarter-century – were in sad decline. Both used the Judd engine, as did March, Tyrrell, Arrows and Ligier, while other smaller teams used the Ford.

As if to emphasize the division in the sport, the McLaren drivers won ten of the 16 races between them. Six went to Senna, and four to Prost. Senna was the faster driver, and he was temperamentally unprepared to give an inch. Prost, who had been with McLaren for six sea-

ABOVE: Rolling for the start of the Daytona 500. Race-winner Darrell Waltrip is on the front row in the Hendrick/Tide Chevrolet Monte Carlo (No. 17, left); runner-up Ken Schrader is in pole in another Monte Carlo.

MILESTONES

With 20 teams in Formula One, elimination trials reduced the field to 30 before official practice, from which 26 qualified for the grid.

The first win by a Porsche-engined car in the PPG/Indy Car World Series came in Ohio with Teo Fabi's victory in a March 89 chassis.

Lamborghini entered Formula One for the first time, supplying engines to Lola. They were not successful, and withdrew after one season.

Having designed the F1-89, John Barnard did not renew his three-year contract with Ferrari and left in October to join the Benetton team.

After a year off, Brabham returned with the Judd-powered BT58; Bernard Ecclestone had sold it to Fiat, then to a Swiss financier.

Yamaha, the Japanese motorcycle company, entered Formula One with a V-8 engine for the German team, Zakspeed; it was underpowered.

LEFT: Ex-Formula One World Champion Emerson Fittipaldi added the Indianapolis 500 to his crown – winning in 2 hours 59 minutes 1.040 seconds: 167.581 mph. He was the first foreign-born driver to win the 500 since Mario Andretti (>1969). He won $1,001,604 – the first time the winner's purse had topped $1 million (>1993).

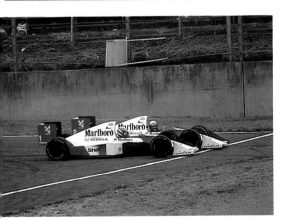

LEFT: Team spirit? Ayrton Senna and Alain Prost leaving the track locked together after their collision in the Japanese Grand Prix. For the second year running, the two fastest drivers in the World Championship effectively only had each other to race against. Their super-competitiveness – so much part of the job – was a hazard to the team when taken too far.

Grands Prix – in Spain, Japan and Australia – but Prost had only to win one of them to secure the title.

Senna won in Spain. In Japan, Prost took the lead with Senna right behind him. As they approached the chicane, Senna tried to out-brake Prost, and neither gave way. They slid off the circuit, locked together. Prost was Champion, or so he thought. But Senna got the marshals to push-start him and, after stopping for a new nose cone, flew off after Nannini who had taken the lead – and just beat him to the line. Confusion reigned for a time, then Senna was disqualified for missing out part of the circuit when he restarted. Senna protested loudly, and McLaren appealed, but the decision stood. Moreover, Senna was fined $100,000 and a ban imposed on his racing licence, suspended for six months. Nannini was awarded the race.

The gulf between rich and poor in the Championship was evident in the points for the Constructors' title. McLaren won, with 141 points – more than one third of all the points available – and the top four teams took 316 points between them. The other 16 teams' total was 66.

sons, was equally competitive, and the personal rivalry between the pair increased during the season. So personal was it that it was widely reported that the two did not exchange a word for months.

Mansell was the only driver able to stand up to them; he won in Hungary after a great battle with Senna. But generally the McLarens had it all their own way. After thirteen races, Prost was ahead in the Championship. Senna could still win if he took all three remaining

Throughout its long history, the men at the Indianapolis Speedway have regarded their 500-mile race as the greatest in the world. In 80 years, it had seen many changes, the most recent being an increasingly international flavour. It is the centrepiece of a series of races in the United States, Canada and Australia. The cars are largely built in Britain, and drivers from outside the United States take part. But at heart, the event remains what it has always been – a robust piece of real Americana.

It is the fastest race in the world. In 1990 Al Unser Jr set a new one-lap qualifying record of 228.502 mph – down the short straights he must therefore have been travelling at well over 240 mph. It is the richest prize in motor sport. In 1990 the total purse was $6.3 million; more than $1 million went to the winner, and even the last of the 33 starters took away with more than $100,000. It is the biggest seated sports event in the world, accommodating more than 400,000 people in the grandstands, another 100,000 standing. The month-long festival of practice and qualification is a pilgrimage for many fans. The rituals come to a climax as the start approaches: bands march and pretty girls wave batons, thousands of multicoloured balloons float skywards, a celebrity leads half a million people in singing Back Home in Indiana, the Archbishop of Indianapolis blesses the cars – then the waver-

ing voice of Mary Hulman crackles over the public address system: 'Gentlemen, start your engines.'

The previous year's winner – the Brazilian driver and former double Formula One World Champion Emerson Fittipaldi – led for 128 of the first 135 laps. He then had to make an unscheduled pit-stop to change his tyres, which

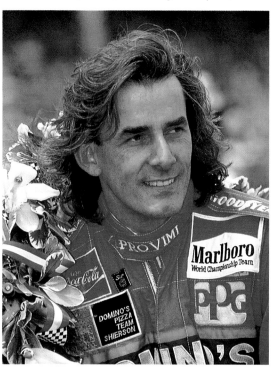

FAR RIGHT: Dutchman Arie Luyendyk averaged a record 185.984 mph to win the Indianapolis 500. He was third fastest qualifier at 223.304 mph behind Rick Mears (224.215 mph; finished fifth) and pole-winner Emerson Fittipaldi (225.301 mph; finished third). Luyendyk came to the USA in 1980 to compete in Formula Super Vee, and began in Indy cars in 1985 driving for Art Groenevelt, owner of Provimi Veal.

RIGHT: Bobby Rahal's Lola-Chevrolet in the pits during the Indianapolis 500. Rahal was born in January 1953, in Medina, Ohio. His 500 debut was in 1982, when he finished eleventh. In 1990 he was fourth fastest qualifier at 222.694 mph, and came second – 11.034 seconds behind Arie Luyendyk.

were blistering. Bobby Rahal took over and in turn led until lap 167 when he experienced handling problems, allowing the Dutch driver Arie Luyendyk into the lead. He held it to the end, setting a new record speed for the race of 185.981 mph. The following day the Speedway staff started preparing for next year.

While Indianapolis becomes more international, so America's other great race – the Daytona 500 – has spawned the most popular form of motor racing in the United States (>1959). NASCAR's 29-race Winston Cup series, of which the 500 is the jewel in the crown, is younger than Indianapolis, but now much larger in its reach. NASCAR stock car

races have spread as far as Watkins Glen in New York, although most of them are still concentrated in the southern states. Stock car racing is rooted very firmly in America's automobile culture: NASCAR-sanctioned races take place on around 600 local circuits around the country.

The 1990 Daytona 500 was dominated by a veteran, Dale Earnhardt in a Chevrolet Lumina, until on the last lap but one he drove over a piece of wreckage left from an earlier crash and sustained a puncture. Going into the third turn the Chevy drifted up the banking, leaving room below for five cars to pass, the leader a 32-year-old unknown driver from Washington State, Derrike Cope, who hung on to win his first Daytona 500.

The Grand Prix season started under a familiar black cloud of controversy, dispute and ill-feeling. Ayrton Senna was still smarting over FISA's ruling that he should forfeit the previous year's Japanese Grand Prix and with it the World Championship – not to mention the small matter of a $100,000 fine. Both sides were adamant, and they would not back down: FISA stood firm by not renewing Senna's racing licence until he accepted its rulings. FISA won the argument as the first race of the season – on the street circuit in Phoenix, Arizona – approached. Senna settled with FISA

The men behind the winners. Indy Car team owner Roger Penske (**ABOVE**) and Ron Dennis (**RIGHT**), chief of McLaren's World Championship team – the two most successful managers in the world at the beginning of the 1990s. The Penske team had five winners in the Indianapolis 500 in the 1980s – Bobby Unser (1981), Rick Mears (1984), Danny Sullivan (1985), Al Unser (1987) – and Mears again (1988).

Penske is also a manufacturer, producing racing cars at a factory in Dorset, England, which are used by other Indy Car teams. McLaren's victory in the Constructors' Championship in 1990 was their sixth – and the third in succession, matching Ferrari's renowned hat-trick in the mid-1970s. McLaren drivers won the Drivers' Championship six times between 1984 and 1990 (>1984, 1985, 1986, 1988, 1989, 1991).

and promptly went out and won, showing that despite his sulky behaviour he was the best driver around.

Senna's great rivalry with Alain Prost inside the McLaren team, which had dominated proceedings in 1989, was at an end. Prost had swapped places with Gerhard Berger, going to Ferrari, while Berger joined Senna at McLaren. The atmosphere at McLaren improved – but the exchange made little difference on the track where the two drivers were even more free to pursue their vendetta, now from different teams. Feelings were still running high when the Grand Prix circus arrived in Rio for the Brazilian Grand Prix. Senna supporters wore T-shirts which indicated, in fairly crude terms, where they felt Jean-Marie Balestre should go. The President of FISA took no chances, and arrived to watch the race surrounded by bodyguards.

Senna took pole position in front of his home crowd, and they cheered to the echo when he led the race in typical aggressive fashion. As he was passing a back-marker, however, the two cars touched and Senna had to make an unscheduled pit-stop to change a nose cone. The much-reviled Prost swept into the lead and won, taking his first victory for his new masters at Ferrari and striking a wounding blow to Brazilian pride at the same time.

Senna and Prost continued neck-and-neck in

the Championship, on three Grand Prix victories each when they met again for the British Grand Prix at Silverstone. Nigel Mansell was looking for his third win in the race, and was unhappy with his Ferrari during practice, but that did not stop him taking pole position. Senna got away from him at the start, then Mansell took the lead at Stowe Corner. The crowd erupted with pleasure, and Mansell – driving flat out – was able to raise an arm to acknowledge the cheers. They were not to

LEFT: One for the cameras. A friendly greeting between fierce rivals Ayrton Senna (left) and reigning World Champion Alain Prost was stage-managed for the press at Monza. Behind the smiles, the competition between the two men was one of the most bitter, personal and long-running in motor racing history.

know that in fact he was having problems with the Ferrari gearbox. It would suddenly start changing gear, up or down, without his touching the lever. At one point it went from seventh to first, revving the engine to more than 16,000 rpm. Berger passed him, then he clawed back the lead, but he was forced retire. Prost won again, the victory taking him ahead of Senna in the Championship. Furious at the failure of his car, Mansell decided to announce what had been on his mind for some time – that he had decided to retire from racing with effect from the end of the season. Prost's victory was swept from the headlines.

Ayrton Senna took back the lead in the Championship by winning the German Grand Prix, then moved steadily ahead, taking the Belgian and Italian races too. As the Japanese Grand Prix approached, and the season drew to a climax, the tense situation at the top of the table was the same as in 1989 – except in reverse. Senna was ahead on points and Prost had to win to stop him from lifting the title. Senna was on top form, taking the 51st pole position of his career. Prost was second fastest, and the pair left the line together for what both knew would be the decider. And it was decided, just 15 seconds later. Prost was on the outside as they went into the first corner, a fast right-hander, Senna on the inside. Both men held their positions without wavering as the cars closed on each other. They knew what was coming was inevitable, unless one of them gave way, but neither would, so they touched, locked together, and – just as they had the previous year – spun off into a sand-trap from which there was no escape. Nelson Piquet won the race for Benetton, but his victory was overshadowed by the row that followed when Senna was confirmed as World Champion.

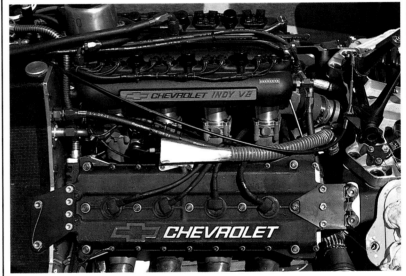

The Chevy Indy V-8 took over from the Cosworth as the top Indy-Car engine in the late 1980s. It first appeared at the Indianapolis 500 in Al Unser's Penske in 1986; by 1990 the Ilmor-Chevy – as it is also known – was powering the first six finishers. It is manufactured in England by Ilmor Engineering, founded by ex-Cosworth engineers Mario Ilien and Paul Morgan in 1983.

MILESTONES

Riccardo Patrese's victory at Imola was his first for seven years. He became the first driver to enter 200 Grands Prix at the British event.

Random drug tests were introduced at the British Grand Prix for all taking part in the World Drivers' Championship.

Derek Warwick overturned his Lotus several times in the Italian Grand Prix, smashing it to pieces. He ran to the pits and raced on in a spare car.

Alain Prost's win in the French Grand Prix was the 100th World Championship victory for Ferrari and Prost's 42nd (>1981).

The competition for the Indy Car World Series was between Al Unser Jr and Michael Andretti, both sons of former winners; Unser won.

Lotus came eighth in the Constructors' table, so R. J. Reynolds switched Camel cigarettes' sponsorship to Williams-Renault.

It is difficult to talk about a modern racing car – with its sticky tyres and composite monocoque chassis, smothered in advertising – as a classic car, in the way that a 1914 Mercedes, a Miller 122, or a Maserati 250F so easily fit the description. But if ever a car of the 1980s and 1990s deserved the description, that car is the McLaren MP4. With five Constructors' titles and also three Drivers' Championships to its credit, it is truly the modern classic. For its eleventh Formula One season, Honda produced a V-12 engine – the RA121E – which, after teething troubles, was able to produce 780 bhp at 14,800 rpm, or 223 bhp per litre capacity, without any super-charging (>1981).

The season started with four straight wins for the MP4/6 – in the US, Brazilian, San Marino and Monaco Grands Prix – giving Senna and McLaren maximum points. Alain Prost was second for Ferrari at Phoenix, Riccardo Patrese for Williams-Renault was runner-up at Interlagos (Brazil), team-mate Gerhard Berger was less than 2 seconds behind at Imola (San Marino), and Mansell was second at Monte Carlo. There were even worries expressed that with such dominance, motor racing fans might stay away if the results became too predictable. Then, with just a quarter of the season gone, the MP4/6 faltered. Senna retired from the Canadian Grand Prix with an electrical fault – the race went to Nelson Piquet for Benetton – and for much of the middle part of the season he was plagued by computer problems, just as the Williams team got the FW14 right. In the German Grand Prix Senna ran out of fuel because of a faulty readout.

Nigel Mansell had been guaranteed full No.1 status at Williams, with Patrese as No.2. The FW14 had problems with its six-speed semi-automatic gearbox in the early part of the season, but they were largely sorted out in time for the Mexican Grand Prix, where it was clearly a match for the MP4 with its new RS3 V-10 engine. It fell to Patrese to produce the first win for Williams, Mansell in second place. Then Mansell took off, winning the French, British and German Grands Prix in quick-fire succession and so turning the Championship into a close battle again.

But Senna won in Hungary, after a close fight with Mansell, and then again at Spa (Belgium), where it was Mansell's turn to retire with an electrical fault. Mansell won the Italian Grand Prix, closing the gap yet again. Then at Estoril, a wheel on Mansell's car was not replaced properly and came off as he was leaving the pit lane. Patrese showed the

FW14's prowess by winning, but Senna was second, stretching his Championship points lead still further. Mansell clawed his way back into the running by winning in Spain a week later – and the Championship looked settled for its usual denouement at Suzuka, in Japan.

The crowds who were expecting to see it all happen on the first corner (>1990) were disappointed. Berger took the lead, followed by Senna, who held Mansell at bay in third place. Mansell pressed hard, but on the tenth lap he made a small slip and spun into a sand-trap from which he could not extricate himself.

ABOVE: Back to the beach! As Indy Car racing has grown, it has become international – with races in Canada and Australia. The first event of the season was the Gold Coast Indy Car Grand Prix, held at the Surfers Paradise Circuit in Queensland, Australia. John Andretti won in a Lola-Chevy at an average 81.953 mph.

MILESTONES

Having announced his retirement from Formula One racing, Nigel Mansell was persuaded by Frank Williams to join his team (>1992).

Jean-Marie Balestre was ousted as President of FISA by the election of the British lawyer, and founder of March, Max Mosley (>1970).

Rick Mears' victory at Indianapolis made him the third man to win the Indianapolis 500 four times, after Al Unser Snr and A.J. Foyt.

A.J. Foyt took part in his 34th Indianapolis 500, more than any other driver in the history of the race (>1958, 1961, 1964, 1967, 1977).

Nelson Piquet, whose Formula One debut was in 1978, became the second man ever to drive in 200 Grands Prix (>1981, 1982, 1987).

Total prize money for the 17 races in the PPG Indy Car World Series was $20 million. One third of the total was the purse for the Indianapolis 500.

Senna was now World Champion, but he set off after Berger: winning – that was all that counted. He failed by less than one second, nonetheless giving McLaren first and second places. In Australia, Senna beat Mansell by less than two seconds to round off a season of close and competitive racing that was without the personal element which had characterized the struggles between Senna and Prost.

It was the fourth successive victory in both Championships for the MP4 and for Honda – something that had never before been achieved. Senna's points margin over Mansell was 96 to 72, and McLaren's over Williams was 139 to 125, suggesting that Ron Dennis's bright and shining star could be eclipsed.

TOP: Fast-rising NASCAR star Ernie Irvan won the Daytona 500 in the Morgan-McClure/Kodak Chevrolet Lumina in 3 hours 22 minutes 30 seconds: an average 148.148 mph. He was second on the starting grid behind Davey Allison in the Robert Yates/Havoline Ford Thunderbird. Allison crashed three laps from the end.

ABOVE: Ernie Irvan, 32, was raised in California and began racing stock cars in 1976. He finished fifth in the NASCAR Winston Cup in 1991 – his fourth full season in the competition – with 3,925 points; winner was Dale Earnhardt with 4,287.

RIGHT: Ayrton Senna in a McLaren-Honda, winner of the Monaco Grand Prix at an average 85.28 mph. It was his third successive victory at Monaco – and his fourth overall. He took pole position ahead of Stefano Modena in a Tyrrell-Honda and finished in 1 hour 53 minutes 2.334 seconds, 18.348 seconds in front of second-placed Nigel Mansell in a Williams-Renault. Jean Alesi was third in a Ferrari, almost 30 seconds further back. In the 1980s and 1990s, Senna's name has become associated with Monaco in the way that Graham Hill's was in the 1960s (>1993).

RIGHT: All-American pageant. Al Unser Jr in a Galmer G92-Chevrolet won the Indianapolis 500 in 3 hours 43 minutes 4.991 seconds. His father Al Snr was third.

RIGHT: Farewell to 'The King'. Stock-car legend Richard Petty drove his final Daytona 500 in 1992 – and was appointed Grand Marshal for the day. He gave the order to start engines and headed the field through the parade lap before dropping back to his position on the 16th row for the rolling start. The son of Lee Petty – winner of the first Daytona 500 (>1959) – he won the race seven times. In 1992 he finished 16th.

In the United States, it was a year for the racing dynasties. Davey Allison followed in his father's footsteps by winning the Daytona 500 (>1988), and in the Indianapolis 500 the two most renowned Indy Car dynasties – the Andrettis and the Unsers – fielded six drivers between them. Mario Andretti was racing alongside his two sons, Michael and Jeff, and his nephew John; the two Unsers were Al, and his son Al Jr.

Michael and Mario, both driving Lola-Fords for the Newman-Haas team, swept into first and second place, Michael ahead of his father. Mario's engine started misfiring and he went into the pits, but by the end of lap 4 Michael had stretched his lead to 8 seconds over Arie Luyendyk and Eddie Cheever. Roberto Guerrero, who had taken pole position, had crashed on the parade lap, trying to warm up his tyres in the cold weather by swerving from side to side. On lap 74 Jim Crawford crashed trying to overtake John Andretti; he hit both members of the Penske team, Rick Mears and Emerson Fittipaldi, and took them both out. Mario Andretti then went head-on into the wall, breaking his toes and finishing up in hospital – where he was shortly joined by his son Jeff suffering from concussion and badly injured legs. Jim Vasser crashed and broke his leg, while Gary Bettenhausen, Arie Luyendyk and Brian Bonner all came to grief. There were injuries, but nobody was killed.

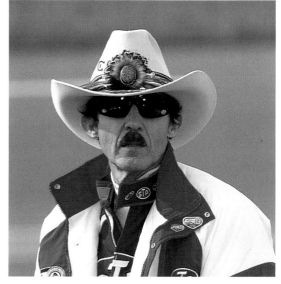

The Canadian driver Scott Goodyear was now second, 22 seconds behind Michael Andretti. With 11 laps to go, Andretti's fuel pump failed and he coasted to a halt. Seven laps from home, Al Unser Jr started racing Goodyear for the flag and took a very slender lead. Coming out of the last turn he tried 'to make the race car as wide as I could' – and just won by 0.043 second, the narrowest-ever margin, from Goodyear. His father was third.

While three generations of one racing family celebrated in Victory Lane, Michael Andretti went to see his father and brother in hospital.

BELOW: Four out of four. Nigel Mansell in a Williams-Renault at the Spanish Grand Prix on 3 May. His victory meant that he had won every race of the season so far. He finished in 1 hour 56 minutes 10.674 seconds, 23.9 seconds ahead of second-placed Michael Schumacher in a Benetton-Ford.

In Grand Prix racing, it was one man's year. Nigel Mansell arrived at Williams at just the right time. Frank Williams and Renault had moved ahead of their rivals McLaren and Honda. The FW14B was more powerful than the MP4/7A – which was in any case not ready for the first two races of the season, both of which Mansell won. It was ready for Brazil, but even with Ayrton Senna at the wheel the McLaren-Honda was 2 seconds behind Mansell on the grid. Mansell won again.

Mansell set an all-time record by winning in Spain and San Marino – the first driver to win the first five races of the season. Senna checked his progress in Monaco and Canada, but the British driver won in France, Britain and Germany, taking his total to eight out of ten. He could win the Drivers' Championship in Hungary if he got four points more than his team-mate Riccardo Patrese. Going into the lead, Patrese cut across Mansell, letting both the McLarens through. Mansell passed Berger, but Senna held him up as Patrese went off into the distance. Patrese then spun off. Now, provided Mansell could finish better than fourth, he would be certain of the Championship. Suddenly, with 16 laps to go, he sustained a puncture. He rejoined the race in sixth place, and charged to the finish. Senna took the chequered flag, but Mansell was second – and he had won the title.

Mansell won again in Portugal, beating Senna's record of eight races over a single season – but by then he was on his way out of Formula One. In the ensuing negotiations for 1993, Mansell parted company with Williams and opened negotiations with Newman-Haas to drive in the Indy Car World Series. Meanwhile, Senna offered to drive for Williams for nothing.

MILESTONES

Ferrari's 500th Grand Prix entry was in Hungary. The occasion was marked by a procession of veteran cars that were driven by veteran drivers.

Ayrton Senna was banned from driving in Britain for 28 days after being caught speeding on the M25 in July at 121 mph in a Porsche.

After being taken over by a Japanese conglomerate and renamed Leyton House, March reverted to its old name for Formula One (>1969).

After finding illegal additives in some teams' fuel in the French Grand Prix, FISA announced that in future the rules would be fully enforced.

Clifford Allison, second son of Bobby Allison and brother of Davey Allison – both Daytona 500 winners – was killed in practice in Michigan.

Nigel Mansell ended his Formula One career with a total of 176 Grands Prix starts and 30 World Championship victories (>1980).

ABOVE: World Champion at last – Nigel Mansell with his wife Rosanne. He took the title with nine victories and a total of 108 points – almost twice as many as his Williams team-mate Riccardo Patrese in second place. His determined driving – and the superb Williams-Renault FW14B – gave Williams the Constructors' title by a margin of 65 points from McLaren. Mansell and his wife were childhood sweethearts and have been together since the beginning of his career. He has always given her much of the credit for his success.

Throughout its history, motor racing has had to face periodic bouts of restructuring brought about either by war or by the unseen hand of economics. At a gala evening attended by most of the powerful men of the sport, Walter Thoma, the European President of Philip Morris cigarettes, whose Marlboro brand had sponsored many of the high-tech developments of the 1980s, observed icily: "The message about world recession seems to have taken a great deal of time to penetrate the world of Formula 1."

The potent mixture of economics and sporting politics had already seen the loss of one of Formula 1's other great sponsors, Honda, while the departure of its reigning World Champion, Nigel Mansell, for Indy Car racing in America was unprecedented. Mansell left following Williams's decision, heavily backed by its French sponsors Renault and Elf, to take on Alain Prost.

Alain Prost and Ayrton Senna had both been vying for the Williams seat. Both had been World Champion three times, and both wanted to be the first to reach four and Prost not only won the battle for the top seat, he did so just as Honda's departure had weakened McLaren. Senna's 1993 car had a Ford engine leaving him well behind Prost on power. The World Championship started predictably, with Prost winning the first race in South Africa with Senna second. Then Senna moved ahead in his native Brazil when Prost spun off in rain.

Prost versus Senna made the headlines, but behind them the next generation of top drivers was showing its form: Damon Hill in the No.2 slot at Williams was second in Brazil and Michael Schumacher, from Germany, was third for Benetton.

The third round in the Championship took place in pouring rain at Donington where Senna upset the form book even further with one of the most memorable drives of his career. He started in fifth place, then took the whole field on lap one, winning from Hill with Prost third.

MILESTONES

Tom Wheatcroft, owner of Donington, secured the return of Grand Prix racing to Britain's first-ever road racing circuit (>1938).

The second woman to drive in the Indianapolis 500 was Lyn St James in a Lola-Ford; she retired on lap 176, finishing 25th (>1977).

On 15 June James Hunt – Britain's former World Champion turned BBC TV commentator – died suddenly of a heart attack, aged 45 (>1976).

In a debate at Britain's National Motor Museum, Tazio Nuvolari was voted the greatest racing driver in the history of the sport (>1953).

TOP: Damon Hill in a Williams-Renault during the European Grand Prix at Donington. He finished second, 1 minute 23.199 seconds behind Ayrton Senna's McLaren-Ford. In the wake of Nigel Mansell's departure to Indy Car racing, British hopes for Formula One success rest largely with Hill, the son of the great Graham Hill (>1975).

ABOVE: Senna's race. Ayrton Senna in a McLaren-Ford won the Monaco Grand Prix for a fifth successive year. His time was 1 hour 52 minutes 10.947 seconds.

Senna retired from the San Marino Grand Prix and Prost won, closing the gap between them to two points. Prost took the lead back in Spain, then took pole position in Monaco but he jumped the start and was penalised. Schumacher took the lead until his hydraulics failed, leaving Senna to take back the lead in the title race with his sixth victory at Monaco.

It is the mark of a truly great driver to win in an underpowered car (>1935/58) and Senna showed how great he was, but Prost then reasserted himself, winning in Canada, France, Britain and Germany, becoming the first driver in the history of the sport to win over 50 Grands Prix.

The title looked Prost's for the taking, but in Hungary, Damon Hill won his first Grand Prix, followed by an extraordinary run of form for a newcomer, winning also in Belgium and Italy. Then Schumacher took his second victory (>1992) in Portugal. But Prost was second, enough to give him his fourth World title.

Prost immediately announced his retirement and Ayrton Senna won the last two races, in Japan and Australia, ending his six years with McLaren on a high note marred only by punching Eddie Irvine in the pits after a disagreement approaching a corner as to which of them should take precedence.

In America, Nigel Mansell won the first Indy Car race of the season in Adelaide, Australia and rapidly established the same rapport with the fans which he had enjoyed on the Grand Prix circuit. Emerson Fittipaldi won the Indianapolis 500, but though Mansell failed to win that ultimate prize in motor racing, he achieved a unique double by clinching the PPK Indy Car Championship, the first Formula 1 World Champion to do so.

ABOVE: Emerson Fittipaldi (centre), winner of the Indianapolis 500. Fittipaldi's record – twice World Champion (>1972, 1974) and twice winner of the 500 – is a formidable achievement and one that is unique in the history of motor racing. He is still doing the business – almost a quarter of a century after winning his first Grand Prix (>1970).

LEFT: Nigel Mansell in a Lola-Ford during the Indianapolis 500. He qualified eighth fastest at 220.255 mph and did extremely well to finish third in his 500 debut. As this book goes to press, Mansell is leading on points in the Indy Car World Series.

Throughout 1993, a battle had raged between the Formula 1 teams and the FIA over the rules for 1994, in particular the use of electronic driver aids such as active suspension and traction control systems. The FIA won and they were banned, along with anti-lock brakes, continuously variable transmission and electronic throttle controls. The idea was to put more emphasis on driver skill than technology, making the racing more exciting to watch, especially on television; in the same spirit refuelling during races was reintroduced. Benetton adapted to the changes most effectively, and Michael Schumacher won the first two Grands Prix, in Brazil and Japan, giving him maximum points.

Ayrton Senna, having secured his Williams place at last, failed to finish either race. At Imola, Formula 1 entered one of the most troubled periods of its modern history. Roland Ratzenberger, driving for Simtek in only his second Grand Prix, was killed in qualifying, the first death on a race weekend for 12 years. Then Ayrton Senna died in the race when his Williams left the track at Tamburello corner and smashed into the wall. A shock wave went through the sport: two deaths, and Senna was one of the best drivers in the history of motor racing. If it could happen to him it could happen to anybody.

The FIA and the teams confronted each other once again. The result was another round of changes, this time designed to slow the cars down. When Karl Wendlinger crashed his Sauber-Mercedes in practice for Monaco, and was rushed to hospital in a coma, the already brittle nerves of the sport were tested even

further, but the race restored some confidence; Schumacher won, inheriting the crown of 'the man to beat' from Senna.

Schumacher came second in the next race in Spain, but even in defeat he stamped his authority on Formula 1 by driving most of the race with his gearbox jammed in fifth gear. Damon Hill won, restoring confidence at Williams too. But even though Williams's test driver, David Coulthard, had done well driving the second car, then coming fifth in Canada, Williams brought Nigel Mansell back from America for a 'guest appearance' in the French Grand Prix; he had to retire with engine problems and Schumacher won again.

For the rest of the season Formula 1 sank into bitter controversy surrounding the Benetton team. When Hill took pole position by .03 of a second from Schumacher at the British Grand Prix, Schumacher overtook him on the warm up lap, breaking the rules. In the race, Hill took the lead and Schumacher was ordered to stop for a five second penalty. He stayed out, then he was shown the black flag, which he also ignored for several laps. Hill won and Schumacher was disqualified.

Schumacher won on home ground at Hockenheim, then in Hungary and Belgium, but the 35 point lead it gave him over Hill was short-lived: Benetton was stripped of victory for breaching the rules on the design of its undertray and banned for the next two races for ignoring the black flag at Silverstone. Schumacher's lead was cut to 21 points.

Hill won the next two races, at Monza and Estoril, closing the gap to 1 point. Schumacher won in Spain with Hill second, then Hill won

ABOVE: Tragic moment: three-times World Champion Ayrton Senna being lifted out of his wrecked Williams following his 140 mph crash at Tamburello corner at Imola in the San Marino GP; he died in hospital.

MILESTONES

In September, Team Lotus went into administration owing around £7m; at the end of the season it was sold to an American businessman.

Al Unser Snr, four times Indianapolis 500 winner, announces his retirement, aged 55; his son took pole position and won the race (>1970/71/78/87).

Mario Andretti, aged 53 and one of the greatest competitors in Grands Prix and Indy Car racing, retired after 31 years (>1965/9/78).

Goodyear Tyres, one of the most consistent supporters of Formula 1, took its 300th Grand Prix when Damon Hill won in Spain for Williams.

Richard Noble, the 'Fastest Man on Earth', reveals plans for an 850 mph twin-jet car, Thrust 3, to attempt a new land speed record (>1983).

In October, McLaren announced plans for a new Formula 1 engine financed by Mercedes but built by the British firm Ilmor Engineering.

in Japan with Schumacher second, putting him just 1 point behind again. The decider was in Australia: Schumacher led, with Hill right on his exhaust when Schumacher, under pressure from Hill, hit a wall. Hill tried to go through on the inside of the next corner, but Schumacher closed in, pushing Hill on to the kerb. The cars touched and the Benetton spun off. Hill went on, but his suspension had been damaged and he was also out. The title went to Schumacher, the first German ever to win the World Championship.

BELOW: Terrifying moment: Jos Verstappen's Benetton engulfed in flames during the German GP at Hockenheim; a fuel valve stayed open after the pressure refuelling hose was removed, spraying fuel on to the hot engine; neither Verstappen, nor any members of the pit crew was seriously injured.

LEFT: Controversial moment: Michael Schumacher's Benetton and Damon Hill's Williams collide in the Australian GP putting both out of the last race of 1994; the incident gave Schumacher the World Championship.

ABOVE: Triumphant moment: scion of America's greatest racing family, Al Unser Jr won the richest prize in motor racing, the Indianapolis 500, for Penske-Mercedes-Benz; he also took the PPK Indy Car Championship.

After the disasters of 1994, Formula One started the year seeking to re-establish its credibility. The cars had less down force and safety was improved at many circuits, particularly at Imola where new chicanes were introduced at the Tamburello and Villeneuve corners where Ayrton Senna and Roland Ratzenberger had been killed. But safety had to compete with the demands of a TV dependant sport, and refuelling stops, introduced to provide more excitement, but which had caused dramatic fires in the pits, remained.

The battle between Williams and Benetton dominated the season, the FW17 faster than the BW195 though less reliable. The V10 Renault RS7 engine which powered both separated the two top teams from the rest. The Ferrari was powerful but unreliable, Mercedes was in its first year with McLaren and the Peugeot which powered Jordans was not in the same league. Benetton's pitwork was better due in no small measure to Michael Schumacher's ability to inspire good teamwork and because his ability to adapt his skills to each circuit gave them the flexibility to plan the race and judge the refuelling stops to maximise any advantage.

McLaren signed Nigel Mansell (>1992/3) but in pre-season testing, he found he could not fit in the car, so McLaren started to build a special car for him.

At Interlagos, Sao Paulo, Brazil, it seemed that controversy would continue to rule. Under new rules the minimum weight of the car and driver was 595kg, so the heavier the driver the better, if the weight could be shed before the race. Schumacher weighed in 9kg more than the previous year so the race started amid allegations of cheating. Damon Hill's suspension failed and Schumacher won, with Coulthard second for Williams, but both teams were then disqualified after samples of their Elf race fuel did not match a sample taken earlier. Gerhard Berger was awarded the race for Ferrari while Benetton and Williams appealed. At Buenos Aires Coulthard took pole position for the first Argentinean GP for 14 years. Damon Hill won and when the fuel appeal was upheld Schumacher took the lead in the Championship with 14 points to Hill's 10.

At Imola the drivers held a minute's silence for Ayrton Senna. Mansell's car was ready but though he was eighth fastest on the grid, during practice he forgot where the clutch was (on the steering wheel) and spun off. Damon Hill won a symbolic victory for Williams, exorcising some of the ghosts of 1994; Mansell finished tenth, two laps behind Hill. Benetton was on form in Spain where Schumacher took pole, led from start to finish, with Johnnie Herbert second.

Mansell gave up during the race and he and McLaren agreed to part company shortly afterwards.

In Monaco Bennetton could afford a one-stop strategy because, even with a heavier car, Schumacher was quicker than Hill, and though Hill took pole and led for 23 laps, when he went in for fuel Schumacher stayed out until lap 36 and won by 35 secs. The rivalry between Hill and Schumacher became public following an incident in the French Grand Prix when Hill, in the lead, came up on a back marker and eased off sharply and Schumacher nearly rammed him from behind; Schumacher clearly thought the move was deliberate and confronted Hill after the race.

The rivalry continued at Silverstone: Hill was on a two-stop strategy to Schumacher's one and when he stopped for the second time, on lap 41,

MILESTONES

Juan Manuel Fangio, the great Argentinean racing driver and the only man to win the Drivers' World Championship five times (>1951/4567), died aged 84.

Jean Alesi won his first Grand Prix in Canada after Damon Hill and Michael Schumacher retired giving Ferrari its first win since Alain Prost at Estoril, 1989.

The Simtek team, having survived Roland Ratzenberger's tragic death (>1994), failed to appear at the Canadian GP and went into receivership owing $6m.

When the Sunday Times published a list of the 500 richest people in Britain it put Bernie Ecclestone 196th with a reported income of £45m a year.

McLaren F1 GTR sports cars took four of the first five places in the Le Mans 24 hour race; the winners were JJ Lehto/Yannick Dalmas/Masonori Sekiya.

Dick Scammel, Racing Director at Cosworth, whose career started as a mechanic with Lotus, was awarded the MBE in the birthday honours list (>1967).

RIGHT: Pacific Podium: Michael Schumacher in ebullient mood having just won his second consecutive Drivers' World Championship at Aida, Japan. Schumacher and Hill finished the season on 102 and 69 points respectively, with Hill's team mate, David Coulthard, next, on 49 points, and a third British driver, Johnny Herbert, fourth on 45 points. Schumacher led 40% of all the laps driven in the season, to Hill's 30% and in career terms, Schumacher finished with 19 wins from 69 races (27.5%) to Damon Hill's 13 out of 51 (25.5%).

Schumacher took the lead. By lap 44 Hill was right on Schumacher's tail and tried to overtake at Priory corner, but they collided to give Herbert his first Grand Prix victory.

The battle continued: Schumacher had a convincing win at Hockenheim, then Hill had an equally convincing win at the Hungaroring, but Schumacher's victory in the Belgian GP after qualifying only 16 on the grid, then storming through to lead by lap 16 marked him out as the man to beat. Hill then shunted Schumacher at Monza and Hill was given a suspended one race ban; Bernie Ecclestone told both drivers to cut out the rough behaviour. Schumacher's victory in the European GP at the Nurburgring put him within three points of the Championship which he duly took at the Pacific GP at Aida in Japan, giving him his second consecutive title, the youngest driver ever

to achieve it. At Suzuka, he won the Japanese GP giving Benetton the Constructors title, the first time they had won it.

Schumacher's position as the man to beat was enhanced because he won when the opposition had the edge. The FW17 was the best car of the season, but Hill and Coulthard could only turn 5 of their 12 pole positions into victories while Schumacher and Herbert won 9 races from 4 pole positions. Ferrari was a distant third to Benetton and Williams, so the Italian company decided to make an investment by signing Schumacher for 1996. Williams signed Hill again, but Coulthard went to McLaren and he was joined by Jacques Villeneuve, the son of Gilles Villeneuve, the great Canadian driver (>1982). Jacques Villeneuve had not only won the Indianapolis 500, but the PPG Indy Car Championship as well.

BELOW: Monaco Mayhem:Damon Hill leads Michael Schumacher into Ste Devote as David Coulthard's Williams is launched into the air when his rear wheel rode up over Jean Alesi's front wheel; Coulthard landed on Gerhard Berger, stopping the race; Coulthard, Alesi and Berger all re-started in spare cars and Berger, whose re-mount had a much less powerful engine, did well to finish third.

BELOW: Chips off the Old Block: the Canadian driver Jacques Villeneuve, son of the late Gilles Villeneuve (>1982), about to win the 79th Indianapolis 500 in only his second Indy Car season (>1996/7). Having collected an early two-lap penalty for passing the pace car, he drove magnificently to win from another second generation driver, Christian Fittipaldi (>1989), completing the season by taking the PPG Indy Car Championship from yet another Champion (>1990), and son of a former Champion (>1970/83), Al Unser Jnr, by 171 points to 161.

RIGHT: Mood Change: Jacques Villeneuve's magnificent drive in the European GP at the Nurburgring, only his fourth in Formula 1 which he led from start to finish giving him his first Grand Prix victory and second place behind Schumacher in the Drivers' Championship, did much to convince the sport and the Williams' team that he was the challenger to the German Champion (>1995/7)

The Concorde Agreement, which set out the commercial relationship between FOCA and the Formula 1 teams, expired at the end of 1996 and negotiations for a new agreement to divide up the revenues from global television sales dominated behind the scenes discussions. The sport's reliance on tobacco sponsorship was under threat in Europe where tobacco advertising on television was clearly going to be banned. Systems to get round the problem by enabling broadcasters to change the track side hoardings to acceptable ads electronically as the signal was beamed to certain countries were in development, and Bernie Ecclestone was setting up his own coverage of the sport in preparation for the day when digital television would again revolutionise the sport with a pay per view channel with the feature that viewers could select their own camera position: on-board, track side, helicopter or data.

Michael Schumacher arrived at Ferrari where he did his best to damp down the very high expectations raised by his reported $25m fee for the season. His presence dominated at Ferrari where John Barnard had come up with a new car, the F310, powered by a new V10 Ferrari engine. Benetton, which had lost the services of Schumacher after the best year in its history, had hired Ferrari's drivers, Gerhard Berger and Jean Alesi. At Williams, Damon Hill's new teammate, Jacques Villeneuve, was not going to play second fiddle.

The season started on a new circuit at Melbourne, Australia, where Jacques Villeneuve took everybody by surprise by taking pole position from Damon Hill for an all-Williams front row, then leading for most of the race. When Hill did get ahead after refuelling, Villeneuve came back and overtook him, leading until five laps from the end when, on the verge of winning his first Grand Prix from pole, he had oil pressure problems following a brief excursion

off the track under pressure from Hill and had to slow down, letting Hill into the lead and then coming second. In Brazil, Hill reasserted himself by taking a commanding lead after changing from wet tyres to slicks before anybody else, then winning again in Argentina giving him maximum points from three races with Villeneuve second in the Championship.

At the European GP at the Nurburgring, it was the other way round. Villeneuve had found his form and did what he had been threatening to do all season, won his first Grand Prix in some style, leading from start to finish. At Williams the mood began to change as Villeneuve was increasingly seen as a serious challenger to Schumacher. At Imola, Villeneuve

ABOVE: Team Mates: Jacques Villeneuve winning his second GP in Hungary from Damon Hill by less than a second, giving him 62 points to Hill's 79 in the Drivers' Championship with four races to go. The hard-fought 1-2 victory also gave Frank William's team its fifth consecutive Constructors' title (>1992/7).

MILESTONES

LEFT: Great Briton: Damon Hill's victory in the Japanese GP at Suzuka, his 21st in 69 races, gave him the title he had wanted ever since he went to races with his father. It was a great moment for him, for his family, his team and his country, but the story had a bittersweet ending when Williams announced a few days later that it was not signing the new World Champion for the following season. Undaunted, Hill, widely respected as a sportsman and gentleman, signed up for a brand new British team, Arrows-Yamaha..

Following a track invasion by fans immediately after the end of the San Marino GP at Imola, the FIA World Council fined the organisers $1m.

In Britain, TV coverage of the World Championship moved from the BBC to ITV for a reported £70m, retaining commentator Murray Walker.

After an association lasting 23 years, Ron Denis's McLaren team switched its main sponsor from Marlboro cigarettes to the German brand, West.

A delegation from China visited the Spanish GP adding substance to rumours that the Communists may sanction a Chinese Grand Prix.

Former World and Indy Car Champion, Emerson Fittipaldi, crashed in CART's Michigan 500 seriously injuring his back (>1972/4 &1989).

Scott Brayton, who took pole position for the Indianapolis 500, then crashed in practice and was killed, the first Indy Car death for seven years.

ABOVE: Indy Car Split: Jimmy Vasser on his way to victory on the street circuit at Surfers Paradise in Australia; he went on to win four of the sixteen races in the PPG Indy Car World Series, which were held in the US, Brazil and Canada, and take the Championship; for the first time, the Indianapolis 500 was not part of the series; it was won by Buddy Lazier.

France, then took pole at Silverstone only to spin off leaving Villeneuve to win. Hill won his 20th Grand Prix in front of Schumacher's home crowd at Hockenheim but even though Villeneuve just managed to beat Hill in Hungary by 0.7sec, Hill looked unassailable. A bad patch then closed the gap when Schumacher took the Belgian and Italian GPs and Villeneuve the Portuguese leaving Hill with everything to do at Suzuka. Villeneuve took pole, then lost a wheel and Hill did it, by 97 points to Villeneuve's 78. Damon Hill had realised a personal and a family dream, the first of the second generation of drivers to become World Champion after his father Graham (>1968). The Williams car gave Hill and Villeneuve a huge advantage: between them, they won 12 of the 16 Grands Prix and gave Williams the Constructors title by a massive 175 points from Ferrari with 70.

Schumacher's departure from the Benetton team was keenly felt: Jean Alesi and Gerhard Berger failed to win a single race in the 1996 season.

It was all change at Indianapolis for its 80th 500 mile race. Politics intervened and the new owner of the circuit separated from the CART and the PPG Indy Car Championship which took over many of the races in the calendar while the Indianapolis Racing League could only manage three races, culminating with the 500 and producing joint champions in Scott Sharp and Buzz Calkins, neither of whom won a race. The best drivers and teams went with the PPG and held a 500 mile race on the same day at another circuit, splitting the fans.

dropped out through suspension problems and Hill took the race from Schumacher giving him 46 championship points to Villeneuve's 22. It looked as if Hill would open up an even greater lead at Monaco, but an oil pressure problem forced him out and the race went to Panis for Ligier.

In Spain, in the wet, the sternest test of drivers, Schumacher showed that, despite his poor showing in the rankings, he was still the best natural driver. Hill took pole then spun off on lap 10 but Schumacher drove on as if there were no rain in a manner which many compared with Senna's famous wet victories in Portugal and at Donington (>1985,1993).

Hill won the next two races, in Canada and

After fourteen years, the holder of the Land Speed Record, Richard Noble, went back to the Black Rock Desert with a new car, Thrust SSC. His aim was not just to beat the old record (>1983), but to establish a supersonic LSR. He was not going to drive the new car himself, but employed an RAF fighter pilot, Sqn Ldr Andy Green, instead. Green succeeded on 25th September with a double run averaging 714.144 mph then on 15 October, he put it beyond doubt with a supersonic double run of 763.035 mph, just above Mach 1, almost a hundred years since the first LSR of 39.245 mph (>1898).

In Formula 1, the reigning World Champion, Damon Hill, moved to Arrows and started the first race of the season, the Australian GP at a new circuit in Melbourne, in an unaccustomed 13th place on the grid. David Coulthard won for McLaren, its first victory in 49 races (>1993). After that, in Brazil, the season settled down into the familiar battle between the top teams and the top drivers: Ferrari with Michael Schumacher and Eddie Irvine and Williams with Jacques Villeneuve and Harald-Heinz Frentzen, and that rivalry came to the fore at Interlagos where Schumacher took the lead, until Villeneuve slipstreamed past him on the first lap to win.

Villeneuve won again in Argentina, opening up a gap of 14 points in the Drivers' Championship after Schumacher was involved in an accident at the start. Villeneuve retired at Imola and Monaco and Schumacher took the lead by 24 points to 20. In Spain, the positions were reversed to 30/27 following a peerless drive by Villeneuve with Schumacher in fourth place, then reversed again in Canada when Schumacher won a rather lucky victory. Villeneuve challenged strongly from the start then spun off at the last corner of the first lap. The gap widened to Schumacher 47 to Villeneuve 33 in France, then narrowed again at Silverstone where Villeneuve won and

MILESTONES

To give France a top Formula 1 team, Alain Prost bought Ligier, renaming it Prost-Mugen Honda with drivers Olivier Panis and Shinji Nakano.

Jackie Stewart formed Stewart-Ford with his son Paul as manager and drivers Rubens Barrichello and Jan Magnussen and no tobacco sponsorship.

Jacques Villeneuve's victory in the British Grand Prix at Silverstone gave Frank William's team its 100th Grand Prix victory.

Gerhard Berger, aged 38, announced his retirement at the end of the season after competing in 210 Grands Prix and winning 10 of them.

Olivier Panis' third place in the Brazilian GP at Interlagos, gave Prost-Mugen Honda its first place on the podium in only its second race.

Brazilian driver Rubens Barrichello's second place in Monaco gave Stewart-Ford its first place on the podium after five races.

ABOVE: Blonde Bombshell: Jacques Villeneuve on the podium after snatching the Formula 1 Drivers' World Championship from Michael Schumacher in a bitterly fought last race of the season in Spain; his dyed hair prompted his pit crew and fans to wear blond wigs to celebrate his victory.

LEFT: Brit Abroad: Mark Blundell (No 18, left) winning the Budweiser/GI Joe 200 Indy Car race at Portland International Raceway, Oregon in the PPG World Series by 0.027th of a second from Gil de Ferran.

ABOVE: Comeback: Damon Hill returned briefly to the spotlight when he out-braked Michael Schumacher to take the lead in the Hungarian GP then used the power of his Arrows-Yamaha to lead for much of the race until one lap from the end when hydraulic failure caused him to slow down and he was passed by Villeneuve.

Schumacher retired with a faulty wheel bearing.

Gerhard Berger won at Hockenheim with Schumacher second after Villeneuve spun off in a duel with Trulli, then the Canadian pulled back to 53 points to Schumacher's 56 by winning in Hungary. Schumacher won in Belgium with Villeneuve in sixth place after an unscheduled early pit stop dashed his chances, putting him on 54 to Schumacher's 66.

In what turned out to be a bad day for the tifosi and the Ferrari revival, Coulthard drove a careful race at Monza to win the Italian GP from Alesi with Frentzen third, Hakkinen fourth, Villeneuve fifth, then Schumacher, with Irvine 8th. Italian gloom deepened when Villeneuve won in Austria and Schumacher could only manage sixth after a 10 second penalty for ignoring a yellow flag, narrowing his lead over Villeneuve to 68 to 67. Two weeks later, Schumacher had to retire at the Nurburgring after a collision with his brother Ralf and Villeneuve went on to win and overtake Schumacher by 77 points to 68.

At Suzuka, Villeneuve came close to loosing any chance of the Championship. He was under a two-race suspended ban for ignoring a yellow flag at Monza. He did the same thing during the warm up lap for the Japanese GP and was banned from the race, though Williams immediately appealed and he was allowed to race, knowing that he was unlikely to be allowed to keep any points he gained. He started on pole position and fought a bitter race, managing only fifth with Schumacher winning, to put him on 78 points to Villeneuve's 79. Frentzen's second place gave Williams its sixth consecutive Constructor's title. The FIA duly took away Villeneuve's two points, reversing the lead in the Drivers' Championship, and putting Schumacher a single point ahead.

The build up to the last race, the European GP at Jerez, was dark. All Schumacher had to do to win the Championship was take Villeneuve out. Schumacher led much of the race with Villeneuve second. They refuelled on laps 43 and 44 and by lap 47 Villeneuve was all over the back of Schumacher's Ferrari and as they came up to the slow Dry Sack corner at the end of the long, fast straight, Villeneuve braked late and slipped inside Schumacher who then turned in on him, hitting the Williams hard before going off into a sand trap and finishing in wheel spinning impotence.

Villeneuve's car had been damaged and was handling oddly but he nursed it through the 19 remaining laps, giving way to the two McLaren's of Hakkinen and Coulthard on the last lap rather than fight them. His third place was enough to give him the Drivers' Championship and by winning against the odds in only his second season, Villeneuve was the hero of the hour, only the fourth driver to win the US PPG World Series and the World Championship, after Mario Andretti, Nigel Mansell and Emerson Fittipaldi.

For Ferrari and the tifosi, the mood turned to despair; they had expected Ferrari's first Championship since Jody Scheckter took the title at Monza in 1979, narrowly beating his Ferrari team mate, Gilles Villeneuve, Jacques' father, for the title (>1979/82).

In the continuing search for a balance between spectacle and safety the formula for 1998 was changed making the next generation of F1 cars slower: tyres will have grooves in them, making them less sticky, the aerodynamics which will reduce downforce further, less efficient brakes which will lengthen braking distances. These changes, and the withdrawal of Renault Sport from Formula 1 after revolutionising the sport with its turbocharged engine (>1977) will open up the field in 1998 and if the mandarins of the sport have got it right, make it more exciting.

CHAPTER THIRTEEN

PERSONALITIES & PROMOTION WITH A GLOBAL REACH

In an age of digital communication, economic growth and commercial globalisation, motor racing has been re-engineered for the needs of the twenty-first century.

In 1997, the Grand Prix was a test bed for the development of the motor car paid for as a promotional tool for tobacco. By 2007, it was part of an integrated business, a marketing toolbox, not only for cars but a much wider range of luxury goods and global brands. In the process, the focus had shifted from the cars to the drivers and their gilded, celebrity, lives: executive jets, security guards and multiple homes. The decade that produced history's most successful racing driver, Michael Schumacher, also made him 'the world's first billionaire athlete.'

Grand Prix racing's global reach also appealed to the promotional needs of national governments. Guided by Bernie Ecclestone's political and economic instincts, it put down roots in the world's new economies at the expense of its European heartland. In 1998, eleven of sixteen Grands Prix – nearly three-quarters – were in Europe; the remainder in South America, Australia, Canada and Japan. In 2007, nine of the seventeen races were in North and South America and Australia, the Far East, including Malaysia and China, and the Middle East, including Bahrain and Turkey; many of the new races run on new, state-of-the-art circuits financed by government investment, literally a world away from Silverstone, Britain's disused airfield with its car parks in the slippery mud of adjoining farmers' fields.

In 1998, eight of the eleven teams on the starting grid had the names of the entrepreneurs who had created the 'kit car revolution,' and their natural heirs: Williams, Tyrell, Stewart, McLaren, Jordan, Prost, Sauber, and Minardi. In 2007, the position had been almost reversed: nearly all the teams carried the names of their engine suppliers and part owners, particularly the German, French and Japanese car makers: Mercedes, BMW, Renault, Honda and Toyota.

It was the decade the manufacturers reversed the individualism of the *scuderia*, or team. But just as one new era became established, so another appeared on the horizon: in 1997, the environment was the preserve of tree-hugging activists; in 2007, global warming and carbon emissions were centre stage. Greening the motorcar business has set new challenges: how to balance the new realities with the spectacle of high-technology gladiatorial combat?

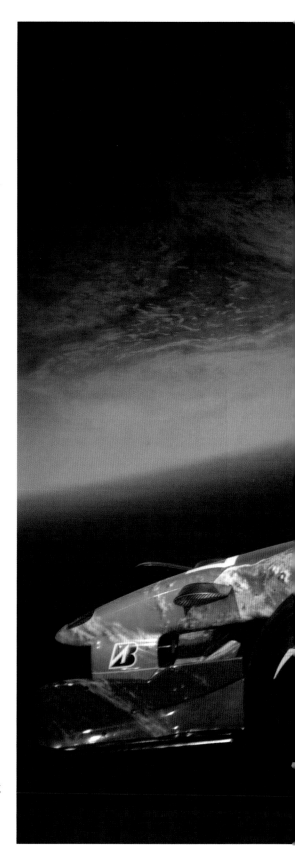

The Future is Green: in 2007, Honda led the way towards transforming the image of Formula 1 with its logo-free 'earth car' and softer appearance of its drivers, Rubens Barrichello and Jenson Button.

A new Concorde Agreement between Bernie Ecclestone, the undisputed boss of the sport, the FIA, the governing body, and the team owners, was signed in Monte Carlo. The terms were secret, but it was widely reported that the teams would share over $20 million from the TV rights, while Ecclestone was reported to be using those rights to raise around $1.5 billion through a bond issue to finance a subscriber digital TV channel.

To make Grands Prix more entertaining for TV audiences, there was also agreement on new regulations designed in part to slow the cars down: tyres had to have three grooves in them to reduce cornering speeds and encourage more overtaking, while the cars were reduced by 200 millimetres, making them 10% slimmer. Agreement on the regulations triggered the traditional battle of wits between the governing body, designers and technically minded drivers to find ways to minimise their effect, as had happened ever since racing cars were first built to a formula (>1901).

Just as traditionally, the Championship started in controversy. The new McLarens were supreme in qualifying for the Australian GP in Melbourne: Mika Hakinnen and David Coulthard occupied the front row of the grid ahead of Ferrari's great hope for the season,

Michael Schumacher. However, the new Ferrari developed engine problems and Schumacher's failed on lap 5, while the two McLarens scampered away in first and second place. However, on lap 35 there was a mix up in pit signals which brought the McLarens in simultaneously and it was Coulthard who emerged in the lead. With three laps to go, Coulthard rather obviously let Hakinnen pass him, honouring a pre-race agreement that whichever of them was first into the first corner would be left in the lead, following the tradition that Grands Prix are team races and such arrangements are acceptable.

Hakinnen won because Coulthard honoured the agreement, but it looked like a fix and the race promoters complained to the FIA that it was not what people came to see – they had paid to see competition. The FIA duly genuflected in the direction of the paying customer by issuing a directive that marshals would in future report 'any acts prejudicial to the interests of any competition should be penalised severely under the terms of the international sporting code.'

The team orders controversy simmered on for several seasons but at Interlagos for the Brazil GP two weeks later, another controversy flared up when several teams lodged complaints

BELOW: First corner melee: reigning World Champion Jacques Villeneuve just in the lead at the Gilles Villeneuve street circuit in Montreal. Moments later, the race was stopped following an accident.

that Williams, Jordan and McLaren had dual braking systems which infringed the rules because potentially they made all four wheels steerable. They were banned during race weekend, but the result was a McLaren 1-2 again, Hakinnen first and Coulthard second, giving McLaren maximum points in both Championships. However, Ferrari was improving: Schumacher was third and at Buenos Aires, for the Argentinean GP, though Coulthard was on pole, Schumacher was second, Hakinnen third and Ferrari's second driver, Eddie Irvine, fourth.

Schumacher won by over twenty seconds. By the time the championship reached Silverstone for the British GP, Hakinnen was leading Schumacher by just 6 points, and there was the prospect of a real competition between McLaren and Ferrari. It was competitive both on and off the track: it rained heavily, great plumes of spray following all the cars making overtaking even more difficult than usual. The conditions favoured Schumacher; but, even though he was exceptional in the wet, he was on the wrong tyres and Hakinnen led for the first 50 laps, building up a huge lead despite slithering off the circuit during the wettest part of the race and damaging a front wing. It was so wet that the safety car was deployed, slowing the pack down and bringing Schumacher right up behind him.

However, while under the safety car, Schumacher passed Alexander Wurz, breaching the rules. Then, on lap 51, Hakinnen eased off because his car was performing oddly, and

LEFT: Master class: Michael Schumacher's skill in the wet was crucial to victory in the British GP; he won by 22 seconds after a controversial 10 second stop-go penalty after the chequered flag (1999).

Schumacher took the lead. Shortly afterwards, the stewards handed the Ferrari team a note giving Schumacher a ten-second penalty for overtaking Wurz. Under the rules, if a penalty is imposed within twelve laps of the flag it can be added to the lapsed time after the race rather than coming into the pits to serve it, but it had happened seventeen laps before the end. Schumacher stayed out and took the chequered flag, with Hakinnen second, then came into the pits to serve his penalty after the race had finished.

McLaren was furious. Serving the penalty during the race could have given Hakinnen victory, and since it had taken a long time for the notice to be served on Ferrari, it appeared they had been given some kind of special treatment. Later, an inquiry decided that because of the late serving the penalty did not stand, so the result did, and Schumacher moved to 54 points,

LEFT: Open door: Alexander Wurz left enough room for Michael Schumacher to try and squeeze past at Monaco's Loews hairpin. The pair collided again, damaging Schumacher's car and putting Wurz out of the race.

just two behind Hakinnen. Hakinnen then punished Ferrari by winning the next two races, putting him on 76 points to Schumacher's 60.

At Spa, the Belgian GP was wet, with a lot of accidents. At the start, four cars collided and retired, including Barrichello's Stewart. At the re-start, Hakinnen collided with Johnnie Herbert, putting two more out. Once the race got going, Wurz retired after a collision with Coulthard, who was able to continue only to collide with Schumacher later, putting them both out. Jacques Villeneuve and Toranosuke Tagaki retired after accidents; a collision with Shinje Nakano put Giancarlo Fisichella out; Eddie Irvine spun off. With both McLarens and both Ferraris out of the race, Damon Hill and Ralf Schumacher picked their way through the debris to take Jordan's first ever Grand Prix victory.

Normal service was resumed for the Italian GP at Monza where Schumacher and Irvine gave the *tifosi* what they wanted, a Ferrari 1-2 which put the Championship on a knife edge with Schumacher and Hakinnen on 80 points each with two races to go.

In a great fight at the Nürburgring in the Luxembourg GP, Schumacher went into the lead but Hakinnen managed to get ahead in a pit stop and, despite everything Schumacher tried, held on to win by just over 2 seconds, taking the championship down to the wire at the Japanese GP with Hakinnen on 90 points and Schumacher on 86, which meant either could win the title. Schumacher took pole by $\frac{2}{10}$ths of a second, but stalled on the grid. He had to start from the back of the grid; he fought his way up to third before retiring with a puncture.

Hakinnen led from start to finish and became World Champion, but it was an anticlimactic end to a climactic championship. McLaren took the Constructors' title by 156 points to Ferrari's 133, while the rest of the field clocked up 127 points between them; evidence if it was needed that McLaren and Ferrari were in a class of their own.

The strength of the World Championship owed a great deal to the single-minded perseverance of Bernie Ecclestone. His powerful position was in contrast to the equivalent form of open wheel racing in America run by CART, a federation of the team owners. They had broken away from the authority of the US Automobile Club and the Indianapolis Speedway (>1978). By 1998, their own series rivalled Formula 1 in many respects: there were nineteen international races across the US, Canada, South America, Australia and Japan; with plans to bring their style of racing to Europe, they had a new sponsor in FedEx, and an Italian star driver, Alessandro Zanardi, who took the title in 1998.

However, the split with Indianapolis had weakened US open wheel racing. The Indianapolis 500, once America's most prestigious race by far, had become the jewel in the crown of a second rate series: the Indy Car League established in 1995 by Tony George, the speedway's owner who had invested millions of dollars in the IRL. On top of that, he had also invited NASCAR to hold stock car races at Indianapolis and was having discussions with Bernie Ecclestone about re-instituting the US GP on a road circuit within the speedway.

There had been a relationship between the World Championship and Indianapolis since the 1950s, when the 500 had been part of it

and there had been cross-fertilisation between the drivers and teams since Jim Clark and Lotus won the race in a rear-engined car, dragging Indy racing away from its comfort zone of front-engined 'Offys' who all used the same engine (>1963/1965). The relationship had never really gone away, and the 1998 500 winner was Eddie Cheever, a 40 year-old American veteran who had started out in Formula 1 in 1978 before moving to Indy car racing in 1990.

The winds of change were once again blowing through US motor racing. Both open wheel series were in relative decline to America's most colourful and richest form of domestic motor sport, NASCAR, which was celebrating 50 years of stock car racing (>1948). The drivers in NASCAR's year-round, 35-race, Winston Cup series were household names in America: men like the series' winner, Jeff Gordon, driving for Rick Hendrick's Chevrolet team, and NASCAR's legendary Dale Earnhardt Snr., seven times champion, still racing in his 50s, 1998 winner of the stock car classic, the Daytona 500, and whose son, Dale Earnhardt Jnr. won the 1998 NASCAR junior series and would move up to the Winston Cup in 1999 (>2002).

LEFT: In his first year with Champ Car, the British driver Dario Franchitti took 5 pole positions, won three races, and came third in the Fed Ex championship (>2007).

BELOW LEFT: Three times a Champion: Jeff Gordon took his third NASCAR Winston Cup Championship, winning 13 races to equal the record set by NASCAR legend Richard Petty (>1973/1992).

MILESTONES

Bernie Ecclestone returns a £1m donation to the Labour Party following a row about a meeting with Tony Blair to discuss prolonging tobacco advertising in Formula 1.

Frank Williams, Adrian Newey and Patrick Head of Williams are formally acquitted of charges in an Italian court relating to Ayrton Senna's death at Imola (>1994).

The Swedish driver, Kenny Brack, won the IRL series with three victories and 6th place in the Indianapolis 500 in his second year for A.J. Foyt's team (>1958).

Indianapolis 500 winner and CART stalwart Bobby Rahal retires from driving to concentrate on being a team owner; he came tenth in the FedEx Championship (>1986, 1990).

Ferrari celebrates its 600th Grand Prix start at Spa with many of its former drivers including Phil Hill (>1961) John Surtees (>1964) and Niki Lauda (>1975/1977).

The CEO of Benetton, Dave Richards, resigned after only 1 year, after replacing Flavio Briatore following reported disagreements with the Benetton family (>2002).

The financial markets of a booming world economy saw consolidation within Formula 1, the disappearance of some historic names, and the emergence of new alliances. McLaren sold 40% of the company to its long standing partner, Daimler-Chrysler, while Jackie Stewart sold his whole team to Ford, which also bought Cosworth Engineering for a reported $60 million–$90 million to bid for the World Championship using another Ford-owned British brand: Jaguar (>1955).

The fusing of Ford, Cosworth and Stewart coincided with the departure of the man who had brought them together in the first place, Ken Tyrell (>1963), who sold his team for a reported $90 million to British American Racing, a new team built around the 1997 World Champion, Jacques Villeneuve, by his manager and mentor, Craig Pollock. British American Tobacco was backed with a budget of £250 million over five years.

As tobacco sponsorship increasingly came under bans in Europe and with huge interest in Formula 1 in Far Eastern markets, where tobacco advertising rules were less strict, BAR divided the livery of its cars between two brands: 555 and Luckies, attracting huge publicity. But, as long anticipated by Ecclestone, Formula 1 would follow the money east, and that became evident when the World Championship was unveiled including the first Malaysian GP at a purpose built, and by European standards, futuristic circuit at Sepang, near Kuala Lumpur.

The season started, as ever, in Australia. It was Michael Schumacher's fourth season with Ferrari and much was expected of the combination, but it was McLaren who filled the front of the grid and shot off into the lead as Schumacher's car stalled on the grid and he

RIGHT: President of the FIA, Max Mosely, who ultimately has to deal with Formula 1's annual crop of controversies, has been with FIA since 1986, having started his career with March (>1970).

had to start from the back. Both McLarens retired with mechanical failures, handing the lead to Eddie Irvine, which he turned into his first Grand Prix victory.

Mechanical problems and crashes characterised the early races. In Canada, Schumacher crashed mightily, but sideways, into a wall from which he escaped unhurt. He won at San Marino and Monaco, while Hakinnen won at Canada and Brazil, giving him an 8 point lead as they lined up for the British GP. Neither of them finished the race: the McLarens shot away from the start as usual, but while Schumacher was challenging Irvine as they approached Stowe corner for the first time, the Ferrari's hydraulics failed on braking and Schumacher collided headlong into the tyre wall which split apart on impact. Schumacher struggled to get out of the car only to slump back in again. Both his legs were broken.

As he was airlifted to hospital, Hakinnen lost a wheel following a pit stop. Coulthard won, but Irvine's second place brought him equal with Schumacher in the Championship on 32 points to Hakinnen's 40. Schumacher was temporarily replaced by Mika Salo, leaving Irvine to lead the Ferrari challenge. He won the Austrian GP, with Hakinnen third, to narrow the gap to 2 points. Then, in the German GP, Hakinnen crashed spectacularly into the barrier after a tyre failure. Irvine won, to give him an 8 point lead in the championship.

By the time Schumacher was back for the first Malaysian GP, where he took pole position, Hakinnen was 2 points ahead of Irvine who could still win the Championship for Ferrari, so it was the German's turn to play second fiddle (which he did superbly) and with Irvine the winner and Hakinnen third, Irvine was 4 points ahead. However, after a stewards' inspection, both Ferraris were disqualified over the size of their bargeboards. Either way, Irvine could still win the Championship, but when the

BELOW: Alessandro Zanardi won two CART championships before replacing Jacques Villeneuve at Williams; he scored no World Championship points while his team mate, Ralf Schumacher, scored 35 for sixth place (>1998/2001).

MILESTONES

Johnny Herbert's victory in the European GP at the Nürbergring was the first for Jackie Stewart's team in only its third season; Rubens Barrichello was third in another Stewart.

Bernie Ecclestone, having raised a reported $850m for his family trust through a Eurobond issue, has a successful heart bypass operation in London (>1997).

The 1996 World Champion, Damon Hill, the son of double World Champion Graham Hill (>1962/1968), retired from Formula 1 after nine seasons (>1992).

Pierluigi Martini, Yannick Dalmas, and Jo Winkelhok won the Le Mans 24-Hour sports car race for BMW from Ukyo Katayama, Toshio Suzuki and Keichi Tsuchia for Toyota (>1906).

When Ferrari's Eddie Irvine signed up for Jaguar in 2000, he swapped places with the Brazilian driver Rubens Barrichello from Stewart (>1994).

IRL 1997 Champion Tony Stewart was named 1999 NASCAR 'Rookie of the Year' following his move to stock car racing and fourth place in the Winston Cup (>2002).

ABOVE: Michael Schumacher took the lead in the World Championship by winning at San Marino only to have his and Ferrari's 1999 hopes dashed when he broke his legs in a major accident at Silverstone.

BELOW: Veteran: Dale Earnhardt Snr, known as 'The Intimidator', ranked second in NASCAR 50 Greatest Drivers, was seven times NASCAR champion, equal with another legend, Richard Petty (>1992/2001).

FIA enquiry reinstated Ferrari's first and second places, which reignited the feeling that Ferrari led a charmed life, a Ferrari Championship was possible for the first time in twenty years.

In Japan, Hakinnen drove a faultless race and won with Schumacher second and Irvine third, clinching his second title by 2 points. Schumacher was still fifth having missed seven races, and Ferrari took the Constructors' title by 4 points; their only one since 1979.

Formula 1 saw crashes but no fatalities. In America, it was different: in CART races, Gonzalo Rodriguez hit the barrier at the California Speedway and died, and Greg Moore was killed in the California 500; in IRL's race at Charlotte, North Carolina, three spectators were killed when a racing accident sent debris into the grandstand.

ABOVE: Jacques Villeneuve's huge crash in qualifying at Eau Rouge on the famous Spa road circuit in Belgium; his BAR team mate, Ricardo Zonta, crashed at the same spot minutes later.

The year of the millennium, ushered in with fireworks and all night parties around the world, was also the fiftieth anniversary of the Formula 1 World Championship. Motor racing had changed beyond recognition in the fifty years since the first race had been staged at Silverstone, just as the world was still getting back to normal after the privations of the Second World War (>1950). Silverstone was still recognizably a wartime airfield and the cars, around which the formula had been set rather than the other way round, were mostly pre-war Italian voiturettes: the iconic Alfa Romeo 150s and Maserati 4CLTs. With a few notable exceptions, such as the gifted ex-mechanic Juan Manuel Fangio, the drivers were playboys, such as the aristocratic Giuseppe Farina, Prince Bira of Thailand and Emmanuel de Graffenried, who raced his pre-war Maserati at his own expense.

The only living link across the half a century was Ferrari, who were not ready for Silverstone but made it to Monaco for the second World Championship race, where Alberto Ascari came second. He went on to give Ferrari its first Championship in 1952 before dying whilst testing a Ferrari sports car in 1955. All Italy wept: Ascari was to Ferrari and Italy in the early 1950s what Michael Schumacher was to Ferrari, Italy and Germany in 2000 – a champion. In forty-nine years, Ferrari had won eight Drivers' Championships and nine Constructors' Championships, one of them since 1979, and that is what Michael Schumacher was being paid a reported $25 million a year to change (>1996).

In 1950, there had been seven Grands Prix in the World Championship, which included the Indianapolis 500 until 1961 when the first US GP at the Watkins Glen road racing circuit replaced it. In 2000, there were seventeen races, including the first US Grand Prix for a decade which, in an ironic twist of history, would take place at the Indianapolis Speedway on a road racing circuit built in the infield and using part of the banked oval.

The Formula 1 season started in muscular style with two McLarens filling the front row of the grid at Albert Park in Melbourne and two Ferraris behind them. The McLarens took the lead, and then first Coulthard, then Hakinnen retired with engine failure, as did

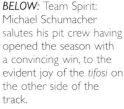

BELOW: Team Spirit: Michael Schumacher salutes his pit crew having opened the season with a convincing win, to the evident joy of the *tifosi* on the other side of the track.

LEFT: Loyalty to the Prancing Horse: Ferrari fans demonstrate their consistent passion over the twenty years since their team had last won the Drivers' World Championship.

Jordan's Heinz-Harald Frentzen who was challenging from third position, leaving Schumacher and Barrichello to open the season with a Ferrari 1-2 and maximum points in the Championship, while McLaren had no points.

At Interlagos in Sao Paulo, Hakinnen and Coulthard were back on the front of the grid, ahead of the two Ferraris again, but Schumacher took the lead and held it until the pit stops when Hakinnen got out in front. McLaren's race then fell apart: Hakinnen's oil pressure failed and he retired and while Coulthard raced Schumacher and finished second, in post-race scrutineering, his car was deemed to be seven millimetres too low and he was disqualified. Unlike the Ferrari disqualifications in Malaysia the previous year over millimetres on their bargeboards, Coulthard's disqualification was upheld on appeal, rather to the surprise of many in the sport, which re-fuelled the rumours that Ferrari was being given a gilded passage in the Championship.

At Imola, Hakinnen took his third successive pole position, but alongside him was Michael Schumacher, not Coulthard. Hakinnen, who was on a one-stop strategy, led for over half the race before going in to refuel, but Schumacher stayed out four laps longer on light fuel and came out of the pits in the lead where he stayed for the rest of the race. Hakinnen was second, breaking his duck, but Schumacher had maximum points and a commanding lead over all comers.

The British GP at Silverstone, where it had all stared fifty years earlier, was held in April in 2000, two months earlier than usual. On the track, McLaren showed that they were back on terms with Ferrari, and there was great joy for the British fans when David Coulthard won with Hakinnen second and Schumacher third. However, it rained heavily and the story promptly moved from the track to the sur-

rounding fields which were used as temporary public car parks which quickly turned into mud flats. TV images of tractors towing Jaguars on to terra firma moved the story into the headlines but for the wrong reasons: as Bernie Ecclestone had been pointing out for some time, Silverstone, still owned by the gentlemanly British Racing Drivers' Club and with all its historic connections, was no longer up to even European standards, let alone those of the new purpose-built racing complexes planned for the Middle and Far East.

ABOVE: Eddie Jordan, one of the great independent characters in Formula 1; his team struggled against the growing financial muscle of industry-backed competitors as winds of change blew through the World Championship (>2005).

LEFT: Decision Makers: Bernie Ecclestone confers with Charlie Whiting, FIA Safety Delegate and Race Director. Their relationship started when Ecclestone owned Brabham where Whiting was Chief Mechanic and the team won two World Championships (>1981/1983).

ABOVE: Celebration: Ferrari Team Principal Jean Todt holds Michael Schumacher aloft following the Japanese GP where he clinched Ferrari's first Drivers' World Championship for twenty years and the first of five consecutive championships in the new century (>2004).

RIGHT: Gladiatorial Spectacle: the Food City 500, Round 6 of NASCARs 35-race Winston Cup held at the half-mile, state of the art Bristol Speedway in Tennessee; the winner was Rusty Wallace (USA) in 3 hours 1 minute 40 seconds, an average speed of 88.018 mph.

For the rest of the season, both McLaren drivers suffered with engineering problems but both fought for points, both drivers winning and coming second until Hakinnen finally overtook Schumacher by two points in the Hungarian GP, setting the championship up well for the huge crowds at Indianapolis for the first US GP.

Ferrari concentrated on Schumacher, who took pole position with Coulthard alongside him, then Hakinnen, then Barrichello. Coulthard managed to jump the start and take an early lead but had to take a ten-second penalty by driving through the pits leaving him well down the field. Hakinnen steadily eroded the eleven-second lead which Schumacher had established until his engine caught fire. With just two races to go, Ferrari had overturned McLaren's resurgence and a Ferrari Driver's Championship was in sight again. The Japanese Grand Prix followed the script: Hakinnen took an early lead, Schumacher got ahead in the pit stops, and once in the lead he kept it to the chequered flag with Hakinnen second.

Schumacher had done it. He had broken Ferrari's long barren period and they both deserved to: he had won nine of the seventeen races in a highly reliable car, while McLaren, often slightly quicker, broke down too often. Coulthard's third place in the Championship provided the evidence that Ferrari also had the right strategy: McLaren's points were split between drivers, while Ferrari concentrated on supporting Schumacher. What

was beyond doubt was that Ferrari and McLaren were dominant. Ferrari won the Constructors' title with 156 points to McLaren's 143, but the other nine teams could only muster 107 points between them.

Schumacher, already something of a legend, had moved up a gear in the Ferrari firmament, in Formula 1 and internationally. The feeling that Ferrari had been lucky in its treatment at the hands of the rule makers persisted, but nothing could take away the sense that the victory was deserved and that as a consequence, Formula 1 was a healthier sport with Ferrari back with the silverware and laurels.

American open wheel racing was not in such good shape. The split between the owner of the Indianapolis Speedway, Tony George, and CART continued to sap the energy which should have gone into improving the overall brand. Signs of strain in the running of CART surfaced when the CEO, Andrew Craig, resigned, his place being filled temporarily by the team owner and one-time Indianapolis 500 winner, Bobby Rahal (>2001).

The 500 remained the jewel in the crown, but like many of the IRL races it failed to fill the grandstands and the 2000 winner was the 1999 CART Champion, Juan Pablo Montoya, whose name was already being linked to Formula 1 for 2001. Buddy Lazier was second in the 500 and took the nine-race IRL championship.

Unlike IRL, the FedEx CART Championship was an international series. The winner was the Brazilian driver, Gil de Farran, which emphasised

MILESTONES

The Chairman of the McLaren Group, Ron Dennis, was made a CBE in the Queen's birthday honours list (>1981)

NASCAR veteran Darrell Waltrip, 53, who had won the Winston Cup three times in the early 1980s, retired after 28 years and 84 victories in stock car racing.

The most successful woman driver was Sarah Fisher, 19, who led nine laps in the IRL race at Sparta, Kentucky where she finished third in her rookie year (>2006).

The Benetton family agreed to sell its F1 team to Renault for a reported £75m, a move which saw the return of Flavio Briatore to Formula 1 (>1984).

David Coulthard escaped unharmed when the executive jet flying him to Monaco crashed during an emergency landing at Lyon airport in France, killing both pilots.

Bernie Ecclestone appeared in 6th = place the *Sunday Times* Rich List as worth £2 billion, and in 1st place in the same newspaper's list of high earners, on £617m.

LEFT: Tradition: Juan Pablo Montoya, drinking milk and garlanded with laurels having just won the 84th Indianapolis 500, poses with the Borg Warner Trophy, awarded to winners since 1936 (>2001).

ABOVE: NASCAR Champion Bobby Labonte on the podium with IRL boss Tony George at Indianapolis where he won the Brickyard 400, a stock car race run on

America's most hallowed open wheel circuit; Indianapolis also staged the 2000 United States Grand Prix, the first for a decade.

BELOW: Trouble Shooter: former CART CEO, team owner and driver Bobby Rahal joined Jaguar at the end of their first, lacklustre season to revitalise their prospects; he was replaced by Niki Lauda in 2001 (>2005).

how, in America, being international was part of the problem. To succeed in the American media meant having American drivers as heroes, and of the top ten in 2000, only two were American: Jimmy Vasser and Michael Andretti, who between them had won just three of the nineteen races in the series. Gil de Farran, Roberto Mareno, Helio Castroneves and Christian da Matta, were Brazilian. The second placed driver in the Championship, Adrian Fernandez, was Mexican, and a Canadian, Paul Tracy, a Swede, Kenny Brack, and the Columbian, Juan Pablo Montoya, completed the list. There were no American drivers in the two top teams run by Pat Patrick and Roger Penske who built his cars in England and used Honda engines.

In America's great motor racing success story, NASCAR, the driver line up was 100% American. However, a vain attempt to attract a higher-spending fan base backfired and attendances went down as fast as ticket prices went up. Stock car racing is first and foremost a spectator sport, designed to appeal to the widest possible American audience who identify with the drivers and the cars which carry the names and weight of long-standing American manufacturers like Ford, Chevrolet, and Pontiac; whose driver, Bobby Labonte, won the Winston Cup. CART racing is for enthusiasts, but as such, it struggled to get the media attention and hence the sponsorship money on which all motor racing depends.

The year of global celebration was followed by unsettling, global sadness following the tragic events of 11th September 2001. The World Championship, with its commercial, extrovert, hedonistic culture, which emphasised western values and had to move cars, people and technical systems from one country to another every fortnight, suddenly had to exist in a world in the grip of security problems which bordered on war, even as it planned to include races in the Middle and Far East.

ABOVE: Luca de Montezemolo started work as an assistant to Enzo Ferrari. He was the architect of Ferrari's successful return to World Championship form; he was also the driving force behind the organisation of the 1990 Football World Cup in Italy.

The first signs of falling economic growth appeared on the horizon just as CART planned two oval races in Europe, in Germany and England, in response to the World Championship expanding into its domestic market. In America, NASCAR and the Indy Racing League were cooperating to boost trackside attendances and TV coverage: NASCAR did a deal with NBC and FOX for $400 million.

In Formula 1, Bernie Ecclestone sold a majority share in his TV business to the German media company Kirch; a deal that upset the new paymasters of the World Championship, the motor manufacturers, who were looking for a greater share of the commercial pie in exchange for their investment. They threatened to start a rival World Championship series; echoing Ecclestone's own threat to create a new contest, which was the means by which he had established his position as the rights holder in the first place (>1978/1981).

It was a serious threat. The manufacturers had considerable influence over the teams, but they lacked one crucial ingredient: Bernie Ecclestone himself, the benign and self-interested dictator who made the whole operation work. Men who can achieve the difficult balance between the aspirations of paying fans who see motor racing as a sport with business attached, and those who see it as a commercial slice of popular culture based on sport, are rare. NASCAR had a whole family of them; the family of tough-minded Bill France who had made stock car racing a nationwide phenomenon, and the kind of figure CART lacked.

As economies slowed, the FIA was determined to keep the costs of the World Championship down, while the drivers and the teams chafed at anything which got in the way of winning. The compromises needed were expressed in the multiple names and in the liveries of their cars. Of eleven teams, nine contained the name of their main sponsor or engine supplier, or both: Benson & Hedges Jordan Honda, Red Bull Sauber Petronas and West McLaren Mercedes. The other two were among the oldest names in motor sport: Jaguar and Ferrari.

Michael Schumacher and Rubens Barrichello filled the first row of the grid with Ferraris at Albert Park for the Australian GP. Coulthard managed to split the two Ferraris at the chequered flag, with Schumacher first, but at Sepang they came first and second. In Brazil, Coulthard made a firm overtaking manoeuvre on Barrichello to spoil the Ferrari parade and narrow the gap slightly, but as the teams left the southern hemisphere for Europe, Ferrari had made a good start in retaining both championships.

Their plans suffered a setback at Imola, where Schumacher had to retire with brake failure in front of Ferrari's home supporters and Ralf Schumacher won for Williams-BMW ahead of their new signing, Juan Pablo Montoya, following his Indianapolis 500 and CART Championship victories (>1999/2000).

Normal Ferrari service was resumed through the summer: of the next seven races, Schumacher won four and came second in three, winning his second title in Hungary with four races still to go.

One of them was the Italian GP at Monza, but the weekend was completely overshadowed by the terrorist attacks of the World Trade Centre in New York, which also coincided with the first CART race at the Eurospeedway in Germany. What should have been a sporting weekend for the trans-Atlantic racing fraternity in Europe turned into a test of character as drivers, teams, sponsors and promoters made sure the show went on. At Monza, Juan Pablo Montoya took pole and won in a straight fight

MILESTONES

NASCAR's hero Dale Earnhardt Snr was killed in an accident while leading the Daytona 500; his son, Dale Earnhardt Jnr was third in the same race (>1999).

Ken Tyrell, who started racing driving F2 Coopers in the 1950s then became one of the pioneers of the British 'kit car' revolution of the 1960s, died of cancer (>1999).

John Cooper, who started a motor racing revolution with his father Charles in their Surrey garage by building rear-engined cars at affordable prices, died aged 77 (>1952).

As part of cutting costs, IRL confirmed it would move to a 3.5 litre non-superchargd engine formula from 2003; CART was indecisive as to whether to follow suit.

CART cancelled its race at the Texas Motor Speedway due to very high G forces experienced by drivers, prompting a lawsuit with the circuit's owners.

Murray Walker, ex-racing motor cyclist, veteran BBC and ITV motor racing commentator, and inventor of the catchphrase 'Unless I'm very much mistaken,' retired, aged 78.

ABOVE LEFT: Alessandro Zanardi's car (66) is hit by Alex Tagliani's at around 185 mph at CART's American Memorial race at the Eurospeedway at Lausitz. Zanardi was leading, and rejoining after a pit stop, when he spun in front of Tagliani who hit him just behind the front wheels; the impact split the monococque.

LEFT: Raining on Italy's Parade: Juan Pablo Montoya's BMW Williams leading the Michael Schumacher and Rubens Barrichello's Ferraris at Monza; Montoya won his first Grand Prix victory, finishing 6th in the World Championship (>2000).

BELOW: CART comes to Northamptonshire: Massimiliano 'Max' Papis, one of the drivers who came to Europe for the Rockingham 500, one of two rounds in the FedEx Championship in the fateful month of September 2001.

with Schumacher and Barrichello; at the Eurospeedway, Alex Zanardi, who had returned to CART fold after a poor 1999 season with Williams, crashed and had to have both legs amputated.

The US GP at Indianapolis went ahead as scheduled. Schumacher took pole position with Mika Hakinnen second, but the Finn was penalised for ignoring a red light in the morning practice and had to start in fourth place. It was his penultimate appearance in a Grand Prix which he won in a strongly contested race against both Schumacher brothers and Montoya.

Schumacher took his tally of pole positions to eleven, with seven victories, and completed the season with 123 points; Coulthard was second with 65 points. Schumacher's fourth championship equalled Alan Prost's tally (>1985), making Juan Manuel Fangio's record five world titles the next target for Ferrari.

The economic downturn of 2001 continued into 2002. Global advertising expenditure, the ultimate lifeblood of top level motor racing on both sides of the Atlantic, slumped for the second year in succession after two decades of growth. TV audiences were down, Bernie Ecclestone's digital TV subscription operation was unprofitable, and even Kirch, the huge German media business to whom he had sold a majority stake in Formula 1 TV rights, was struggling.

Economic pressure brought a shake up in the rankings of the Formula 1 teams, dividing them into three groups. At the top were those owned by major motor manufacturers or linked to them in long-term relationships, such as Ferrari with Fiat, McLaren with Mercedes and Williams with BMW. Next came a group whose aim was to be fourth in the championships, staying in touch with the top teams at best: Sauber, Jordan and BAR. The rest struggled in the prevailing financial climate, falling back as the difference in budgets tended to widen the gap between the top and the bottom of the rankings.

The key to success was a mixture of momentum and continuity, both of which were expensive. Ferrari benefited from continuity in its

MILESTONES

Rob Walker, for whom Stirling Moss drove a Cooper-Climax to win the Argentinean GP in 1958, the first rear-engined victory in Formula 1, died aged 84 (>1957).

CART appointed a new Chief Executive, Chris Pook, who announced that as a cost cutting measure, all its teams in future will use the same Cosworth V-8 engine (>2003).

Tom Kristensen, Frank Biela and Emanuele Pirro won the 24-Hour sports car race at Le Mans in an Audi, a record third successive victory for the team.

The FIA changed the World Championship scoring structure to include the first eight rather than six finishers, with 10 for first place, 8 for second, then 6-5-4-3-2-1.

Bernie Ecclestone and his wife Slavica moved to 5th place in the Sunday Times Rich List with a family fortune valued at £2.9 billion (>2001).

Helio Castroneves won his second Indianapolis 500 running after Paul Tracy, a CART driver who crossed the line first, was relegated to second place for overtaking under a yellow flag.

core senior team: Michael Schumacher, Jean Todt, Team Principal, Ross Brawn, Technical Director and race tactician, and Rory Byrne, Chief Designer, all of whom extended their contracts. By comparison, at BAR, Dave Richards, one-time CEO at Benetton, who arrived to cut costs, a change in style which was bound to cause disruption to established relationships, replaced Craig Pollock. There were also budget cuts at Jordan, and at the bottom it was an open secret that Prost and Arrows were struggling to survive.

At the same time, there were signs of positive investment. In Bahrain, the government commissioned Herman Tilke, the German architect who had designed the Sepang complex in Malaysia, to design a road racing circuit, a major statement of confidence in the international appeal of the sport. From Japan,

LEFT: Double First: Rubens Barrichello and Michael Schumacher looking sheepish together on top of the podium in Austria after Barrichello, under team orders, controversially handed Schumacher victory on the last lap.

Toyota saw motor racing as a prime source of exposure and supported both the World Championship and US open wheel racing. It had its own Formula 1 works team in 2002, with $80 million start up costs including the development of its own V-10 engine from scratch, and was supported by another giant Japanese corporation, Panasonic. Its weakness was its drivers, Mika Salo and Alan McNish, neither of whom had a strong track record.

In America, Toyota transferred its allegiance from CART to IRL; a major political move within US open wheel racing with far reaching implications. The key element was the Indianapolis 500 race – the primary open-wheel race, which Tony George used to commercial advantage. Roger Penske, one of the founders of CART, switched from CART to IRL in 2002. A new star was born in the IRL firmament, Sam Hornish, an American driver, who took the title at the age of twenty-three from Penske's Brazilian drivers, though Helio Castroneves won the Indianapolis 500.

NASCAR's strategy of keeping costs down through a tight formula ensured the close racing which appealed to American fans. Stock car racing continued to benefit from its well-established fan base, its year-round, thirty-race series, claiming it was America's second largest sport after the National Football League, and produced a crop of popular heroes from its drivers who enriched US popular culture; such as Tony Stewart who won the Winston Cup.

In Formula 1, it was Ferrari's year again: Michael Schumacher was even more dominant, winning eleven of the seventeen Grands Prix. They included the British GP at Silverstone, his sixtieth victory, and the French GP where he clinched the World Championship with six races still to go, matching Juan Manuel Fangio's record of five championships which had stood for nearly half a century (>1957).

Ferrari's domination of the first part of the season troubled some people as the races lost their unpredictability and the championship its excitement. However, Ferrari surpassed themselves in the remaining six races: both Schumacher and Barrichello won three, and in five of the races they were second to each other. Another record fell when they finished the season with 221 points in the Constructors' title; exactly the same as the whole of the rest of the field, including McLaren and Williams, put together. Ferrari was truly in a class of its own.

In the rankings, Renault leapfrogged BAR, Jordan and Sauber, to take the coveted fourth position in the Constructors' title, all of them scoring fewer points than the previous year, while Jaguar stood still. Prost disintegrated during the season and disappeared.

LEFT: Sarah Fisher, voted Most Popular Driver 2002 by the IRL Crew, qualified ninth for the Indianapolis 500 at 229 mph, finished 24th and took pole at the Indy 300 at Kentucky, leading for 26 laps and finishing 8th, heralding women's place as professional racing drivers.

Michael Schumacher was a global star and a huge asset to Formula 1. However, his three dominant years had created predictability for race goers and television audiences and they wanted more competition. There had been a five times World Champion before, but when Juan Manuel Fangio achieved it (>1957), he was forty-six years old and retired after two more races; Schumacher was thirty-four and showed no inclination to stop racing.

In the quest for greater competition, Max Mosely of the FIA proposed rule changes intended to make races less predictable, including phasing out expensive launch and traction control systems and scheduling qualifying over two days, culminating with individual flying laps on the Saturday. After qualifying the cars had to stay in a *parc fermé* overnight and start the race without any changes to fuel of tyres.

RIGHT: Fernando Alonso takes a podium bow following his first Grand Prix victory, at the Hungaroring. He finished sixth in the World Championship, ahead of his team mate Jarno Trulli, heralding Renault's renaissance and his own talent.

ABOVE: German GP: Ralf Schumacher set off a chain reaction when he collided with Rubens Barrichello, who hit Mika Hakkinen in the first corner, resulting in five cars retiring while Juan Pablo Montoya took the lead which he held to the end.

onship as new faces made their mark: Coulthard won in Australia, with Juan-Pablo Montoya second and Kimi Raikonnen third; Raikonnen won in Malaysia with Barrichello second and Alonso third – his first podium finish and three places ahead of Michael Schumacher. Giancarlo Fisichella won in Brazil for Jordan, with Raikinnen second and Alonso third again, while Schumacher retired after uncharacteristically spinning off on the wet surface.

After three races, the championship looked very open: Coulthard and Raikonnen were equal in the lead, Jarno Trulli and Alonso tied for third place, with Barrichello, Fisichella, Montoya, and Schumacher, in equal fifth place. Schumacher reasserted himself on top of the podium at Imola, then won three of the next four grands prix in the new Ferrari F2003, to lead Raikonnen by 3 points. Alonso's second place in Spain and third place in the championship sent a surge of delight through his home country.

Many commentators tipped Alonso as a future World Champion and, as if to prove them right, he took pole in Hungary, led the race from start to finish and became the youngest driver to win a Grand Prix; three months younger than Bruce McLaren (>1959). Schumacher's eighth place reduced his lead to 1 point over Montoya and Ferrari lagged by 8 points in the Constructors' title with three races to go.

Seven points covered the top three drivers at Monza: Raikonnen Montoya and Schumacher, who won, with Raikonnen second, setting up the last two races as the kind of battle for the crown which attracted worldwide interest. Schumacher widened the gap, winning at Indianapolis to put him on 92 points with Raikonnen second, on 83.

Greater competition could also come from personnel changes. The three top teams, Ferrari, Williams and McLaren, tended not to change stable, winning combinations, but further down the rankings, changing talent was often seen as a way forward. Jaguar dropped its principal, Niki Lauda, and Eddie Irvine and Pedro de la Rosa, replacing them with Tony Parnell, Mark Webber, and Antonio Pizzonia. When Jenson Button signed for BAR, Flavio Briatore promoted Renault's twenty-two-year-old test driver, Fernando Alonso, making him the youngest on the grid.

Schumacher was noticeably absent from the podium in the opening rounds of the champi-

At Suzuka, Schumacher looked set to win a record sixth title and even in the event of a draw, he would win because he had a greater number of race victories. However, he only qualified fourteenth on the grid and had to stop for a new nosecone after a coming together with Sato, finishing eighth for just 1 point. It was just enough, but Barrichello kept Raikonnen in second place for Schumacher to take the title by 2 points.

Michael Schumacher's sixth championship had broken Fangio's record, but possibly more importantly, he did it the way everybody wanted: a close finish that went down to the wire. A total of eight drivers had won Grands Prix, representing Germany, Brazil, Colombia, Britain, Finland, Italy and Spain, and Alonso's sixth place in the championship made him a highly visible challenger.

If Formula 1 was on the up, American open wheel racing continued to decline. CART renamed their international series the ChampCar World Series Powered by Ford with all the cars using the Ford-Cosworth XFE V-8 engine. However, a number of drivers, teams and sponsors defected to IRL and some drivers to NASCAR, marking the low point in CART's twenty-five-year history. At the end of the season, CART went into bankruptcy.

At NASCAR Bill France Jnr, who had taken over from his father Bill Snr in 1972, retired, handing the NASCAR chair to his son, Brian, whose qualifications were business and mar-

keting rather than racing. The last winner of the Winston Cup was Matt Kenseth: from 2004, it became the Nexel Cup after the mobile phone company, another sign of telecommunications interest in motor racing as a promotional tool.

MILESTONES

Tom Kristensen, Rinaldo Capello and Guy Smith won the Le Mans 24-Hour sports car race in a Bentley EXP, with another Bentley second (>1929).

Bernie Ecclestone invested a reported £4m in Minardi to stabilise its finances when negotiations with Gazprom, Russian's giant energy company, failed.

After competing in the Indianapolis 500, Michael Andretti, announced his retirement from driving to concentrate on building his racing team (>1986).

Tom Walkinshaw's Arrows team was placed in administration before the World Championship, started, leaving only ten teams in the competition (>1978).

Gil de Farran won the Indianapolis 500 and came second in the IRL Championship, following which the Brazilian announced his retirement from racing (>2005).

Takuma Sato replaced Jacques Villeneuve at BAR-Honda when the 1997 World Champion decided to withdraw from the Japanese GP; Sato finished sixth.

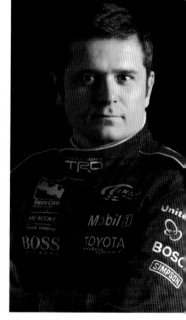

BELOW: CART Down Under: Ryan Hunter-Ray (USA), Darren Manning (GB) and Jimmy Vasser (USA) share the podium at the Surfers Paradise Street Circuit in Australia.

RIGHT: Gil de Ferran, the all-round American open wheel racer, was Champ Car Champion in 2001 and 2002 and winner of the Indianapolis 500 in 2003, all for Roger Penske's team.

The world economy was growing again by 2004, with global brands looking to use the top echelons of motor racing's appeal in popular culture as a marketing tool. Racing drivers were not only national icons, as Schumacher had shown in Germany and Alonso was already showing in Spain, but they also led iconic lives which depended on internationally recognized luxury goods, from mobile phones and sunglasses to watches to executive jets. Their racing cars were not only sumptuous billboards, they reflected singularly international motoring brands: Ferrari, Mercedes, BMW, Renault, Honda and Toyota.

But behind the glossy façade lay the hard economic realities and men who manipulated them to corporate advantage. In 2004, they were preoccupied with the revenues generated by the World Championship's commercial rights variously put at between £600 million and £800 million. The creditor banks of the Kirch media empire, which controlled the 75% stake in Bernie Ecclestone's company that owned them, wanted the highest price; the motor manufacturers wanted a slice of their value in return for their investment, and pressurised Ecclestone by threatening to start a rival global series.

Demand for more national Grands Prix was buoyant and 2004 saw a record eighteen Championship races, the extra venues being new, purpose-built, government-backed circuits in Bahrain and Shanghai, designed by the German architect Hermann Tilke, with long straights and hairpins to encourage overtaking. In the interests of greater competition, the FIA continued to refine the regulations, focusing on qualifying: drivers did their flying laps in the order they finished the previous race, then the order was reversed in the final qualifying round, keeping the contenders for pole position right to the end.

Unlike the competitive 2003, in 2004, though records tumbled during the year, they did so to one team: Ferrari. In Australia, Schumacher and Barrichello filled the front row of the grid, led the race as a pair, and finished with maximum points. At Sepang, Barrichello slipped to sixth but at Sakhir, in the first Bahrain Grand Prix, they managed another Ferrari 1-2, then again in Spain, and it was not until Monaco that Jarno Trulli edged Schumacher off the top position on the podium.

However, it was a temporary blip: Schumacher won the next seven Grands Prix taking his total to twelve victories out of thirteen races and after Hungary, he had 120 points to Barrichello's 82 and Button's 65, with Trulli on 46 and Alonso on 45.

BELOW: Sporting Billionaires: the owner of Chelsea Footbal Club, Roman Abramovich, gets a personal tour of the Monaco pit lane with Bernie Ecclestone.

BELOW: New Era: the start of the first ever Chinese GP at the Shanghai International Circuit; Rubens Barrichello won for Ferrari.

The headline was Ferrari: the only driver who could catch Schumacher was his team mate, Barrichello, and in the Constructors' title, Ferrari had 202 points to Renault's 91 and BAR's 83. But the story was the rankings: Williams and McLaren had been eclipsed by BAR and Renault. McLaren fought back at the Belgian Grand Prix: the race was variously led by Trulli, Alonso, Schumacher and Raikonnen, but it resolved into a fight between Schumacher and Raikinnen, who took the chequered flag, beating Schumacher by 3.1 seconds, but Schumacher's 128 points was enough to put his seventh championship beyond doubt.

In the last four races, Schumacher and Barrichello amassed a record 262 points, took the first two places in the drivers' championship and won a record fourteenth Constructors' title for Ferrari. Below them, the wind of

MILESTONES

The Austrian Red Bull drinks company bought Jaguar Racing from Ford, signing David Coulthard and the Austrian Christian Klien as drivers for 2005.

Gianni Agnelli, the boss of Fiat, which owned Ferrari, died aged 82, having seen the company's competitiveness and position in motor sport restored (>1969).

Ferrari records: 6 successive Constructors' titles, total 14; 5 successive drivers' titles, total 14; 704 Grand Prix starts, 195 wins and 190 pole positions.

Schumacher records: 7 Drivers' titles, 213 GPs; 83 victories; 36 second places; 18 third places, 63 pole positions; 66 fastest laps and 1186 Championship points (>2006).

After a big accident at Silverstone, finishing behind BAR drivers Jenson Button and Takuma Sato in several races, Jarno Trulli left Renault for Toyota.

HM Queen Elizabeth opens the McLaren Technology Centre at Woking, Surrey.

change was blowing: Button, Sato, Alonso and Trulli kept BAR and Renault above Williams and McLaren, a sign of things to come.

In America, the headlines were that Dale Earnhardt Jnr, the face of US motor racing, won the Daytona 500 and five other races and was fifth in the first Nexel Cup, won by Kurt Busch. There was also the beginning of a renaissance in American open wheel racing: Sebastien Bourdais, a Frenchman, won IRL's IndyCar series, and the Brazilian Tony Kanaan and Britain's Dan Wheldon took the first two places in the ChampCar series for Michael Andretti's team, and came second and third in the Indianapolis 500 behind the American winner, Buddy Rice.

However, the story in America was the emergence of a new generation of movers and shakers at the top of the sport. NASCAR's new figurehead, Brian France, brought in new sponsors and created a knockout competition for the top ten drivers, to coincide with the National Football League finals in naked competition for TV audiences. ChampCar's

ABOVE: Touching Moment: Michael Schumacher's Ferrari came off worst following his coming together with Juan Pablo Montoya's Williams at Monaco; it broke his suspension and he retired, breaking a run of five successive victories.

BELOW: Ferrari Dominance: with both championships in the bag, Rubens Barrichello and Michael Schumacher put on a display of force in the Italian GP at Monza, much to the delight of the *tifosi*.

new figurehead, Kevin Kalkhoven, not only renamed and expanded the series but bought its engine supplier, Cosworth, from Ford. IRL's figurehead for a decade, Tony George, saw his IRL series attract more attention, and he had brought the US Grand Prix to Indianapolis.

Formula 1's figurehead, the almost legendary Bernie Ecclestone, was still in control of the World Championship after nearly three decades. The whispered question for manufacturers, sponsors, drivers, team principals, race promoters and other figureheads was: what happens after Bernie?

International motor racing was booming. The 2005 World Championship was extended to nineteen races to accommodate the Turkish Grand Prix at another new circuit designed by Hermann Tilke. Formula 1 was a $4-billion-a-year-business making investors willing, despite what seemed like the perpetual row over control of the commercial rights and threats of a breakaway series.

Behind the purely commercial arguments there was also a split over the formula of the cars between the FIA, which wanted to move towards more homogenised cars to cut costs, and some of the teams who saw themselves as the guardians of Formula 1's heritage of perpetual technological development. The phenomenal rise of stock car racing in America

was an example of how motor racing could be made hugely profitable, but with almost identical cars. American open wheel racing also showed that splits could kill the golden goose, so while the rows went on, so did balancing the money with image and technology.

There was also a new ingredient: nationalism. National TV channels found that audiences peaked when their nationals were doing well; the most recent example being Spain, up by 50% on the back of Fernando Alonso's championship prospects. Nationalism was behind a new international series which one investor believed represented a gap in the market: Sheik Hasher Maktoum al Maktoum of Dubai. He created what he called 'The World Cup of Motorsport,' eleven races during the Formula 1 off season using a fleet of identical Lola cars with V-8 Zytec engines driven as part of a national team.

Formula 1 attracted very wealthy individuals. The Austrian high energy drinks magnate, Dietrich Mateschitz, who had bought the Jaguar team and renamed it Red Bull, then bought Minardi as well. The Canadian steel billionaire, Alex Schnaider, bought Jordan,

ABOVE: Enthusiastic: Renault fans follow their team round the world as part the growing identification of spectators with individual teams, a phenomenon traditionally the preserve of Ferrari's dedicated *tifosi.*

LEFT: Majestic: the control tower at the Sakhir circuit in Bahrain built at a cost of $150m to attract motor racing of all kinds to the Gulf.

BELOW: Politic: Bernie Ecclestone with Sheik Fawaz bin Mohammed al Khalifa, the boss of the Sakhir circuit in Bahrain. Ecclestone showed great diplomatic skill in promoting Formula 1 as a global sport and the World Championship as a global business.

MILESTONES

Alex Schnaider sold Midland to Michiel Mol, renaming it Spyker, after the sports car maker and changing engine suppliers from Ferrari to Cosworth.

The Brazilian Gil de Farran became Sporting Director of BAR as Honda bought the whole team as the basis of a Honda Formula 1 team for 2006.

McLaren's Technical Director, Adrian Newey, moved to Red Bull Racing as Chief Technical Officer for 2006.

Maurice Trintignant, who raced in Bugattis in the 1930s, won the 24-Hour Le Mans sports car race and the Monaco Grand Prix twice, died aged 87.

McLaren protégé Lewis Hamilton wins 15 of the 20 races in the Formula 3 Euro Series, taking the series by 172 points to 94 for his nearest rival.

In an FIA survey of fans, there were large majorities for more overtaking, more teams, greater driver skill and technical excellence based on high technology.

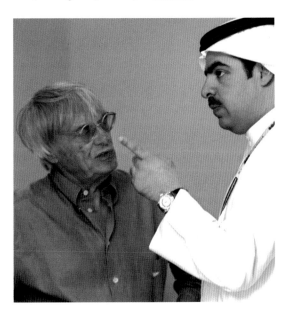

renamed it Midland, and hired two unknown drivers, Tiago Monteiro, from Portugal and Narian Kathikayan, from India.

The first half of the season showed that Renault had adapted to the technical changes best. Alonso was dominant, winning four of the first seven Grands Prix with a second, third and fourth place. However, it was McLaren which improved its position with Raikonnen winning two of those races. At the halfway mark Alonso led the championship with 59 points from Raikonnen and Trulli on 27 each and Michael Schumacher was eighth with 16 points.

At Indianapolis, the World Championship faltered badly. During the Friday session, Ralf Schumacher's Toyota shed its left-rear tyre at the banked Turn 13, hitting the wall badly though he was unhurt. The loading on his Michelin tyres was too high at top speed and the company advised its seven customers that their tyres were unsafe on that turn unless speeds were reduced. To avoid disappointing the crowd, suggestions included putting a chicane in the turn or simply limiting the speed, but the FIA would not agree.

Saturday qualifying took place without incident. However, on the Sunday, the Michelin teams, stuck between loyalty to the fans and risking people's lives, let alone the legal implications, ordered their drivers not to race. The three Bridgestone teams, Ferrari, Jordan and Minardi lined up to jeers from the crowd and a race of sorts took place, with Schumacher and Barrichello circling for 72 laps, undoing all the work selling Formula 1 to US racing fans who demanded, and got, compensation. The post mortem went on for months: the FIA called the non-participating teams before the World Motor Sports Council but the threat of disciplinary action was dropped in July, and in September Tony George confirmed the US Grand Prix for 2006.

In the midst of controversy, the World Championship was settled. It soon became clear that Schumacher was not in contention. Alonso won two of the next seven races and Raikonnen three, but Alonso's four second places kept him on top with 111 to Raikonnen's 86. In Brazil, he only needed third place to become Champion. He won, ending Ferrari's unbroken five-year run and confirming himself and Renault as the new top team.

In America, where open wheel racing had been afflicted by controversy for twenty-five years, there were signs of recovery under Kevin Kalkhoven, Jerry Forsythe, and their ChampCar brand. Unlike its Formula 1 cousin, ChampCar had embraced the homogenised or 'dumbed down' car, all teams racing the Panoz with a

LEFT: Euphoric: Fernando Alonso's explosive reaction in the *parc fermé* at Interlagos on becoming the youngest ever World Champion, the beginning of the end of five years of Ferrari dominance.

Cosworth XFE engine. Its rival, IRL's IndyCar series, still used Honda and Toyota engines, but for 2006, they would move to a single car, the Dallara IR4-Honda.

A British driver, Dan Wheldon, won the IRL title and the Indianapolis 500, but in a sign of the times, America's classic race was led for the first time by a woman, Danica Patrick, who finished twelfth.

BELOW: Dynastic: America's First Family of motor racing, Grandfather Mario Andretti and his son Michael congratulate his grandson Marco on winning the Sonoma 100 in the IRL Menard's Infiniti Pro series; Marco won 2 races and came 10th in the Championship (>2007).

In a twist of history, Renault, the winners of the first ever Grand Prix, held both World Championships in 2006, Grand Prix racing's centenary year (>1906), the same year that oval racing celebrated the ninetieth Indianapolis 500, a link with the past broken only by war (>1908).

A distinct sense of momentum pervaded the World Championship. There were eleven teams again, including a new entrant from Japan, Super Aguri, competing in eighteen Grands Prix. The new, 2.4 litre V-8, engine formula came into force, encouraging the top teams to supply engines to those lower down the grid, spreading development costs. Ferrari supplied Red Bull, Toyota supplied Spyker, BMW supplied Sauber and Honda supplied Super Aguri. The threat of a split over the commercial rights negotiations was lifted: 50% of the revenues, which some reports put at $1 billion, would go to the teams with immediate effect.

The qualifying process was changed again to a knockout format over three sessions of fifteen minutes each, the first two whittling the twenty-two cars down to ten, who then fought it out for pole, intended as a spectacle and christened the 'shoot out'.

Fernando Alonso dominated the first nine races, winning six of them to Schumacher's two, putting him ahead by 84 points to 59. Alonso then faltered and Schumacher won five of the next seven races to the Spaniard's three second places and no wins. Schumacher won in China, drawing level with Alonso on points with 116 each, but Schumacher's one extra victory made him the leader; Renault was one point ahead in the Constructors' championship.

The penultimate Grand Prix, in Japan, was full of competing emotions. It was the last to

RIGHT: Renault Moment: Flavio Briatore embraces Fernando Alonso and Giancarlo Fisichella following their 1-2 in the Malaysian GP; Renault won both championships, 100 years after winning the first ever Grand Prix at Le Mans (>1906).

be held at Suzuka, the scene of many decisive moments in the Championship in the previous twenty years, to go to the Toyota-owned Fuji circuit in 2007. There was a sea of red flags, not for Ferrari but for Takuma Sato and Super Aguri, an all-Japanese combination named after Aguri Suzuki, the only Japanese driver to stand on the podium at Suzuka where he came third in 1990.

With sixteen seasons and seven Drivers' titles to his name, Schumacher had already announced his retirement at the end of the season, raising anticipation that he could win a final, eighth title. He started second on the grid, alongside his team mate Felipe Massa, with two Toyotas separating the Ferraris from the Renaults where Alonso was in fifth place. By lap 3 Schumacher was leading and by lap 14 Alonso had overtaken Massa and was on Schumacher's case, never more than five to six seconds behind. Under the pressure, on lap 37, the Ferrari engine blew up. Alonso had turned the tables with one race to go.

The atmosphere at Interlagos was even more charged than Suzuka. It was Massa's national Grand Prix and the whole country was willing him to become the first Brazilian driver to win it since Ayrton Senna (>1991). However, whether Schumacher could bring off a near miracle by winning the last race of his career and taking the Championship again, an outcome which would require Alonso not to score, was the question that preoccupied the rest of the world.

Schumacher's bad fortune persisted when his engine faltered in qualifying and he missed the final shoot out for pole, starting tenth on the grid with Alonso fourth; Massa was on pole. Alonso moved steadily up to second place while Schumacher had to fight his way up to fifth, but he touched Fisichella's Renault with

BELOW: Great Start: Fernando Alonso takes the chequered flag in the first GP of the season, beating Michael Schumacher by just over a second. Schumacher started on pole with Alonso fifth on the grid, but the Renault R26 was superior to the Ferrari 248.

his left rear tyre while overtaking, causing a puncture and an unscheduled pit stop and had to rejoin at the back on lap 9.

Sixty laps later, he was in fourth place with only Jenson Button's Honda between him and Alonso. Two laps later, that is how the race finished: Massa won his home GP, to a great emotional outburst from the Brazilian fans, Alonso second, to huge acclaim for a second, successive World Championship and Michael Schumacher to retirement, without the hoped-for blaze of glory.

Schumacher's magnificent drive had shown he was still at the peak of his powers, and there were those who were saddened by the fact and the manner of his departure. However, there were many who did not mourn his passing. It was not just his dominance, which was respected as a massive talent, it was the ethics of Schumacher's approach to racing. He seemed prepared to use any opportunity to his advantage, most recently at Monaco where, having set the fastest time in qualifying, he 'parked' his car against the barrier at Rascasse so other drivers could not beat it; he was sent to the back of the grid by way of a penalty.

Schumacher was a great talent but whether he was a great Champion, in the rounded sense and sporting tradition of men like Alberto Ascari, Juan Manuel Fangio, Jackie Stewart, John Surtees, Mario Andretti and Emmerson Fittipaldi, remains a question for history to judge.

For 2007, Ferrari replaced Schumacher with Kimi Raikonnen, whose McLaren seat was filled by Fernando Alonso. But alongside the World Champion was a twenty-two year-old rookie: Lewis Hamilton, the first black driver in Formula 1. Hamilton started his career on the podium in Australia, coming third. Two weeks later, at Sepang, he came second, the first driver to score points in his first two GPs in forty-three years. In Bahrain, he was second again, the first driver ever to finish his first three GPs on the podium. Second again in Spain, he beat Alonso to become the youngest driver ever to lead the Championship.

Headlines multiplied: Alonso won at Monaco but Hamilton was second, putting them level on points. At Montreal, Hamilton took his first pole position and won his first Grand Prix, demonstrating great skill under pressure in a race dogged by accidents and safety cars. American fans were waiting, and Hamilton did not disappoint at Indianapolis, snatching pole position from Alonso and fighting all the way to the chequered flag to lead the Championship by 10 points.

In seven races, Hamilton had grabbed head-lines as well as points and by featuring on the cover of *Autosport*, he stirred emotions too. Appearing on *The David Letterman Show*, Dario Franchitti, the Indianapolis 500 winner, was not impressed: 'A Scot wins the Indy 500 and doesn't make the cover?'

In a triumph of the application of talent over experience, Lewis Hamilton had re-shaped perceptions of Formula 1: history was in the making again.

ABOVE: Moving Out: 15 years after winning his first Grand Prix and over decade after joining Ferrari, Michael Schumacher leaves the stage as one of the all time greats of Formula 1 and a hard act to follow.

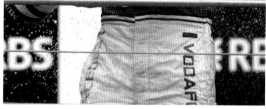

LEFT: Moving Up: Lewis Hamilton celebrates winning the US Grand Prix at Indianapolis, his seventh podium finish in the first seven rounds of the World Championship, an unprecedented record for any driver in his rookie year and extending his lead in the title race over his team mate, the reigning, double World Champion: Fernando Alonso.

MILESTONES

Lewis Hamilton won five races in Formula 1's support series, GP2, in 2006, taking the title and moving to McLaren's F1 team for 2007 alongside Fernando Alonso.

The French team won the 2005-2006 A1GP title followed by Switzerland and Great Britain; all drivers used the same Lola-Zytek cars.

An Audi team won the Le Mans 24-Hour sports car race in a diesel car, the RD10 TDI, the first time a diesel had won in the 74 year history of the race.

Sam Hornish was IndyCar champion and won the 90th Indianapolis 500 by 0.063 of a second from Marco Andretti, the third generation of Andrettis to race there.

Keith Duckworth, one of the founders of Cosworth and designer of the famous DFV racing engines which revolutionised top level racing in the 1960s, died aged 75 (>1968).

Michael Schumacher's records: 7 World Championships, 91 Grand Prix victories, 13 in one season, 158 podium finishes, 68 pole positions and 76 fastest laps.

These race results are not exhaustive, but instead reflect motor racing at the top level. Contestants' names are followed by their nationality – see key below – and car, team or sponsor as appropriate. The winner's average speed (after the driver's name) and the fastest lap are also given, wherever this information is available or appropriate. Although contestants' full names are usually given, this is not always the case in the earlier years, owing to the incomplete nature of the sources. Place-names refer to the site of a circuit or the starting point of a road race. From 1898 we include under each year the driver of the fastest motor vehicle, designated for convenience the 'Fastest Man on Earth'. This is, unless otherwise stated, the official world record (the unofficial is sometimes included in the main text of the book among the 'Milestones). A speed followed by (US record) means that the record was not accepted by European authorities. For the earliest period the phrase 'Fastest Man on Earth' is not to be taken literally because, of course, steam trains were then faster than motor cars. Finally, 'US National Champion' refers, from 1909–55, to the winner of the AAA National Championship; from 1956–78 to the winner of the USAC National Championship; and from 1979 to the present to the winner of the PPG Indy Car World Series.

KEY TO ABBREVIATIONS OF NATIONALITY

Alg : Algeria
Arg : Argentina
Aus : Austria
Austral : Australia
Bel : Belgium
Bra : Brazil
Can : Canada
Col : Colombia
Fin : Finland
Fr : France
GB : Great Britain
Ger : Germany
Hol : Holland
Hun : Hungary
It : Italy
Jap : Japan
Mex : Mexico
Mon : Monaco
NZ : New Zealand
Por : Portugal
SA : South Africa
SM : San Marino
Sp : Spain
Swe : Sweden
Switz : Switzerland
USA : United States of America
Zim : Zimbabwe

1894

PARIS–ROUEN TRIAL 22 July
1st Count Jules de Dion [Fr] *De Dion 11.6 mph*
2nd Georges Lemaître [Fr] *Peugeot*
3rd Doriot [Fr] *Peugeot*

1895

PARIS–BORDEAUX–PARIS 11–13 June
1st A. Koechlin [Fr] *Peugeot 12.2 mph*
2nd Émile Levassor [Fr] *Panhard-Levassor*
3rd Rigoulot [Fr] *Peugeot*
Levassor was first to arrive but was placed second for infringing a competition rule

'TIMES-HERALD' EXHIBITION RUN Chicago 2 Nov
1st Oscar Mueller [USA] *Mueller-Benz 9.8 mph*
2nd J. Frank Duryea [USA] *Duryea Motor Wagon*
Only two contestants took part

'TIMES-HERALD' CONTEST Chicago 18 Nov
1st J. Frank Duryea [USA] *Duryea 5.1 mph*
2nd Oscar Mueller [USA] *Mueller-Benz*
No third place listed

1896

'COSMOPOLITAN' ROAD RACE New York City 30 May
1st J. Frank Duryea [USA] *Duryea*
2nd Charles E. Duryea [USA] *Duryea*
No third place listed

PROVIDENCE RACE Rhode Island 7. 8. 11 Sept
1st A. L. Riker [USA]/C. H. Whiting [USA] *Riker Electric 25 mph*
2nd Henry B. Morris [USA]/Adams [USA] *Electric Carriage*
3rd J. Frank Duryea [USA] *Duryea*
Aggregate result based on three heats

PARIS–MARSEILLES–PARIS 24 Sept–3 Oct
1st Mayade [Fr] *Panhard 15.7 mph*
2nd Merkel [Fr] *Panhard*
3rd Viet [Fr] *De Dion Tricycle*

EMANCIPATION DAY RUN LONDON–BRIGHTON 14 Nov
1st Léon Bollée [Fr] *Bollée Tricycle*
2nd Camille Bollée [Fr] *Bollée Tricycle*
3rd Earl of Winchilsea [GB] *Panhard Wagonette*

1897

MARSEILLES–NICE–LA TURBIE 29–31 Jan
1st Count Gaston de Chasseloup-Laubat [Fr] *De Dion 19.2 mph*
2nd Georges Lemaître [Fr] *Peugeot*
3rd Charles Prévost [Fr] *Panhard*

PARIS–DIEPPE 24 July
TWO-SEATER CARS:
1st Gilles Hourgières [Fr] *Panhard 23.1 mph*
2nd Fernand Charron [Fr] *Panhard*
3rd Charles Prévost [Fr] *Peugeot*
FOUR-SEATER CARS:
1st Count Jules de Dion [Fr] *De Dion 24.6 mph*
2nd François Giraud [Fr] *Panhard*
3rd Ernest Archdeacon [GB] *Delahaye*
SIX-SEATER CARS:
1st Daniel Courtois [Fr] *Delahaye 17.8 mph*
2nd Doriot [Fr] *Peugeot*
Only two contestants listed
VOITURETTES:
1st Jamin [Fr] *Bollée 25.2 mph*
2nd Pellier [Fr] *Bollée*
3rd De Nanteuil [Fr] *Bollée*

PARIS–TROUVILLE 14 Aug
1st Gilles Hourgières [Fr] *Panhard 25.2 mph*
2nd Georges Lemaître [Fr] *Peugeot*
3rd Count Jules de Dion [Fr] *De Dion*

1898

Fastest Man on Earth: Count Gaston de Chasseloup-Laubat [Fr] *Jeantaud 39.245 mph*

MARSEILLES–NICE 6–7 March
CLASS I RESULTS:
1st Fernand Charron [Fr] *Panhard 20.4 mph*
2nd Gilles Hourgières [Fr] *Panhard*
3rd René de Knyff [Fr] *Panhard*
CLASS 2 RESULTS:
1st Georges Richard [Fr] *G. Richard 12.7 mph*
2nd Labouré [Fr] *Parisienne*
No third place listed
CLASS 3 RESULTS:
1st Viscount de Soulier [Fr] *Bollée 13.4 mph*
2nd Manet [Fr] *Bollée*
3rd Catzigras [Fr] *Bollée*
CLASS 4 RESULTS:
1st Osmont [Fr] *De Dion 15.3 mph*
2nd Guyennet [Fr] *De Dion*
3rd G. de Meaulne [Fr] *De Dion*

CRITERIUM DES ENTRAINEURS Paris 11–12 May
1st René de Knyff [Fr] *Panhard 22.1 mph*
2nd Fernand Charron [Fr] *Panhard*
3rd Breuil [Fr] *Panhard*

PARIS–AMSTERDAM–PARIS 7–13 July
1st Fernand Charron [Fr] *Panhard 26.9 mph*
2nd Léonce Girardot [Fr] *Panhard*
3rd François Giraud [Fr] *Bollée*

BORDEAUX–BIARRITZ 21 Aug
1st Loysel [Fr] *Bollée 26.7 mph*
2nd A. Koechlin [Fr] *Peugeot*
3rd Georges Lemaître [Fr] *Peugeot*

1899

Fastest Man on Earth: Camille Jenatzy [Bel] *Jenatzy 65.792 mph*

NICE–CASTELLANE–NICE 21 March
1st Georges Lemaître [Fr] *Peugeot 26 mph*
2nd Léonce Girardot [Fr] *Panhard*
3rd A. Koechlin [Fr] *Peugeot*

PARIS–BORDEAUX 24 May
1st Fernand Charron [Fr] *Panhard 29.9 mph*
2nd René de Knyff [Fr] *Panhard*
3rd Léonce Girardot [Fr] *Panhard*

TOUR DE FRANCE Paris 16–24 July
1st René de Knyff [Fr] *Panhard 30.2 mph*
2nd Léonce Girardot [Fr] *Panhard*
3rd Count Gaston de Chasseloup-Laubat [Fr] *Panhard*

BORDEAUX–BIARRITZ 1 Oct
CARS:
1st 'Levegh' (Pierre Velghe) [Fr] *Mors 37 mph*
2nd Antony [Fr] *Mors*
3rd Petit [Fr] *Peugeot*
VOITURETTES:
Ravenez [Fr] *Decauville 25.5 mph*
No other places listed

1900

Fastest Man on Earth: Camille Jenatzy (>1899)

CIRCUIT DU SUD–OUEST Pau 25 Feb
1st René de Knyff [Fr] *Panhard 43.8 mph*
2nd Count Bozon de Périgord [Fr] *Panhard*
3rd Gilles Hourgières [Fr] *Panhard*

NICE–MARSEILLES 26 March
1st René de Knyff [Fr] *Panhard 36.7 mph*
2nd Gilles Hourgières [Fr] *Panhard*
3rd Fernand Charron [Fr] *Panhard*

GORDON BENNETT TROPHY Paris 14 June
1st Fernand Charron [Fr] *Panhard 38.6 mph*
2nd Léonce Girardot [Fr] *Panhard*
No third place listed

PARIS–TOULOUSE–PARIS 25.27.28 July
HEAVY CARS:
1st 'Levegh' [Fr] *Mors 40.2 mph*
2nd Pinson [Fr] *Panhard*
3rd Carl Voigt [Fr] *Panhard*
VOITURETTES:
1st Louis Renault [Fr] *Renault 18.8 mph*
2nd Schrader [Fr] *Aster*
3rd Grus [Fr] *Renault*

Fastest Man on Earth: Camille Jenatzy (>1899)

GRAND PRIX DE PAU 17 Feb
HEAVY CARS:
1st Maurice Farman [Fr] *Panhard 46.1 mph*
2nd Léonce Girardot [Fr] *Panhard*
No third place listed
LIGHT CARS:
1st Henri Farman [Fr] *Darracq 38.1 mph*
2nd J. Edmond [Fr] *Darracq*
No third place listed
VOITURETTES:
1st Louis Renault [Fr] *Renault 32.1 mph*
2nd Oury [Fr] *Renault*
No third place listed

NICE–SALON–NICE 25 March
CARS:
1st Christian Werner [Ger] *Mercedes 36 mph*
2nd Degrais [Fr] *Rochet-Schneider*
3rd Baron Pierre de Caters [Fr] *Mors*
VOITURETTES:
1st Henri Farman [Fr] *Darracq 29.9 mph*
2nd J. Edmond [Fr] *Darracq*
3rd Marcellin [Fr] *Darracq*

PARIS–BORDEAUX 29 May (including the second Gordon Bennett Trophy)
HEAVY CARS:
1st Henri Fournier [Fr] *Mors 53 mph*
2nd Maurice Farman [Fr] *Panhard*
3rd Carl Voigt [Fr] *Panhard*
LIGHT CARS:
1st François Giraud [Fr] *Panhard 40.2 mph*
2nd Paul Baras [Fr] *Darracq*
3rd J. Edmond [Fr] *Darracq*
VOITURETTES:
1st Louis Renault [Fr] *Renault 34.3 mph*
2nd Marcel Renault [Fr] *Renault*
3rd Oury [Fr] *Renault*

GORDON BENNETT TROPHY Paris 29 May
1st Léonce Girardot [Fr] *Panhard 37.2 mph*
Only one contestant finished

PARIS–BERLIN 27–29 June
HEAVY CARS:
1st Henri Fournier [Fr] *Mors 44.1 mph*
2nd Léonce Girardot [Fr] *Panhard*
3rd René de Knyff [Fr] *Panhard*
LIGHT CARS:
1st François Giraud [Fr] *Panhard 35.5 mph*
2nd G. Berteaux [Fr] *Panhard*
3rd Georges Teste [Fr] *Panhard*
VOITURETTES:
1st Louis Renault [Fr] *Renault 36.9 mph*
2nd Grus [Fr] *Renault*
3rd Morin [Fr] *Corre*

Fastest Man on Earth: Augieres [Bel] *Mors 77.136 mph*

CIRCUIT DU NORD, ALCOHOL RACE Paris 15–16 May
HEAVY CARS:
1st Maurice Farman [Fr] *Panhard 44.8 mph*
2nd Charles Jarrott [GB] *Panhard*
3rd Rutishauser [Fr] *Serpollet*
LIGHT CARS:
1st Marcellin [Fr] *Darracq 41.2 mph*
2nd Henri Farman [Fr] *Panhard*
3rd Louis-Émile Rigolly [Fr] *GobronBrillié*
VOITURETTES:
1st Grus [Fr] *Renault 33.6 mph*
2nd Oury [Fr] *Renault*
3rd Cormier [Fr] *Renault*

PARIS–VIENNA 26–29 June (including the third Gordon Bennett Trophy)
HEAVY CARS:
1st Henri Farman [Fr] *Panhard 38.4 mph*
2nd Count Louis Zborowski [GB] *Mercedes*
3rd Maurice Farman [Fr] *Panhard*
LIGHT CARS:
1st Marcel Renault [Fr] *Renault 38.9 mph*
2nd J. Edmond [Fr] *Darracq*
3rd Paul Baras [Fr] *Darracq*
VOITURETTES:
1st Guillaume [Fr] *Darracq 30.6 mph*
2nd Grus [Fr] *Renault*
3rd Cormier [Fr] *Renault*

GORDON BENNETT TROPHY Paris 26–28 June
Selwyn Edge [Austral] *Napier 31.8 mph*
Only one contestant finished

CIRCUIT DES ARDENNES Bastogne 31 July
HEAVY CARS:
1st Charles Jarrott [GB] *Panhard 53.98 mph*
2nd Fernand Gabriel [Fr] *Mors*
3rd William K. Vanderbilt [USA] *Mors*
Fastest lap: Baron Pierre de Crawhez [Bel] *Panhard 57.1mph*
LIGHT CARS:
1st Louis-Émile Rigolly [Fr] *Gobron-Brillié 46.3 mph*
2nd Jacques Guders [Fr] *Panhard*
3rd J. Edmond [Fr] *Darracq*

CIRCUIT DES ARDENNES DES VOITURETTES Bastogne 31 July
1st Jean Corre [Fr] *Corre 33.22 mph*
2nd Paul Vonlatum [Fr] *Clément*
3rd Lura [Fr] *Prunel*
Fastest lap: Vonlatum *40.31 mph*

Fastest Man on Earth: Arthur Duray [Fr] *Gobron-Brillié 84.732 mph*

PARIS–MADRID 24 May
HEAVY CARS:
1st Fernand Gabriel [Fr] *Mors 65.3 mph*
2nd Joseph Salleron [Fr] *Mors*
3rd Charles Jarrott [GB] *De Dietrich*
LIGHT CARS:
1st Louis Renault [Fr] *Renault 62.3 mph*
2nd Paul Baras [Fr] *Darracq*
3rd Page [Fr] *Decauville*
VOITURETTES:
1st Masson [Fr] *Clément 47.2 mph*
2nd Barillier [Fr] *Richard-Brasier*
3rd Louis Wagner [Fr] *Darracq*

CIRCUIT DES ARDENNES Bastogne 23 June
HEAVY CARS:
1st Baron Pierre de Crawhez [Bel] *Panhard 54.3 mph*
2nd Léonce Girardot [Fr] *CGV*
3rd de Brou [Fr] *De Dietrich*
Fastest lap: de Crawhez *56.55 mph*

LIGHT CARS:
1st Paul Baras [Fr] *Darracq 48.9 mph*
2nd Philippe Tavernaux [Fr] *Gobron-Brillié*
3rd Alessandro Cagno [It] *Fiat*
Fastest lap: Baras *53.63 mph*

CIRCUIT DES ARDENNES DES VOITURETTES Arlon 23 June
1st Louis Wagner [Fr] *Darracq 43.07 mph*
2nd A. Villemain [Fr] *Darracq*
3rd Denis [Fr] *De Boisse*
Fastest lap: Wagner *46.89 mph*

GORDON BENNETT TROPHY Athy 2 July
1st Camille Jenatzy [Bel] *Mercedes 49.2 mph*
2nd René de Knyff [Fr] *Panhard*
3rd Henri Farman [Fr] *Panhard*
Fastest lap: (Circuit A) Foxhall Keene [USA] *Mercedes 52.2 mph*; (Circuit B) Fernand Gabriel [Fr] *Mors 51.7 mph*

Fastest Man on Earth: Paul Baras [Fr] *Darracq 104.530 mph*; William K. Vanderbilt [USA] *Mercedes 92.308 mph* (US record)

GORDON BENNETT TROPHY Homburg 17 June
1st Léon Théry [Fr] *Richard-Brasier 54.49 mph*
2nd Camille Jenatzy [Bel] *Mercedes*
3rd Henri Rougier [Fr] *Turcat-Méry*
Fastest lap: Théry *55.3 mph*

CIRCUIT DES ARDENNES DES VOITURETTES Bastogne 24 July
Albert Clément [Fr] *Clément-Bayard 33.5 mph*
Only one contestant finished
Fastest lap: Clément *39.7 mph*

CIRCUIT DES ARDENNES Bastogne 25 July
HEAVY CARS:
1st George Heath [USA] *Panhard 56.4 mph*
2nd Georges Teste [Fr] *Panhard*
3rd Albert Clément [Fr] *Clément-Bayard*
Fastest lap: Hubert le Blon [Fr] *Hotchkiss 63.3 mph*
LIGHT CARS:
1st de la Touloubre [Fr] *Darracq 47 mph*
2nd Victor Hémery [Fr] *Darracq*
3rd J. Edmond [Fr] *Darracq*

'COPPA FLORIO'* Brescia 4 Sept
1st Vincenzo Lancia [It] *Fiat 71.92 mph*
2nd Georges Teste [Fr] *Panhard*
3rd Count Vincenzo Florio [It] *Mercedes*
LIGHT CARS:
1st Victor Hémery [Fr] *Darracq 64.7 mph*
2nd Carlo Raggio [It] *Itala*
No third place listed
*Although this was called the 'Coppa Florio', the first true Coppa Florio took Place in 1905

VANDERBILT CUP Long Island 8 Oct
1st George Heath [USA] *Panhard 52.2 mph*
2nd Albert Clément [Fr] *Clément-Bayard*
No third place listed
Fastest lap: Georges Teste [Fr] *Panhard 70.8 mph*

Fastest Man on Earth: Victor Hémery [Fr] *Darracq 109.65mph*; Herbert Bowden [USA] *Mercedes 109.75 mph* (US record)

GORDON BENNETT TROPHY Auvergne 5 July
1st Léon Théry [Fr] *Richard-Brasier 48.46 mph*
2nd Felice Nazzaro [It] *Fiat*
3rd Alessandro Cagno [It] *Fiat*
Fastest lap: Vincenzo Lancia [It] *Fiat 52.6 mph*

CIRCUIT DES ARDENNES DES VOITURETTES Bastogne 6 Aug
1st Louis Wagner [Fr] *Darracq 39.88 mph*
2nd Philippe Tavernaux [Fr] *Grégoire*
No third place listed
Fastest lap: Wagner *48.28 mph*

CIRCUIT DES ARDENNES Bastogne 7 Aug
HEAVY CARS:
    1st Victor Hémery [Fr] *Darracq 61.6 mph*
    2nd Henri Tart [Fr] *Panhard*
    3rd Hubert le Blon [Fr] *Panhard*
    Fastest lap: Henri Rougier [Fr] *De Dietrich 68.51 mph*
LIGHT CARS:
    Edward Montjoie [Fr] *Darracq 46.7 mph*
    Only one contestant listed

COPPA FLORIO Brescia 10 Sept
    1st Carlo Raggio [It] *Itala 65.13 mph*
    2nd Arthur Duray [Fr] *De Dietrich*
    3rd Vincenzo Lancia [It] *Fiat*

VANDERBILT CUP Long Island 14 Oct
    1st Victor Hémery [Fr] *Darracq 61.5 mph*
    2nd George Heath [USA] *Panhard*
    3rd Joe Tracy [USA] *Locomobile*
    Fastest lap: Vincenzo Lancia [It] *Fiat 72.8 mph*

1906

Fastest Man on Earth: Victor Hémery (>1905); Fred H. Marriott [USA] Stanley Steamer *127.659 mph* (US record)

TARGA FLORIO Grande Circuito Madonie 6 May
    1st Alessandro Cagno [It] *Itala 29.08 mph*
    2nd Ettore Graziani [It] *Itala*
    3rd Paul Bablot [Fr] *Berliet*
    Fastest lap: Cagno *32.53 mph*

GRAND PRIX DE L'AUTOMOBILE CLUB DE FRANCE Le Mans 26–27 June
    1st François Szisz [Fr] *Renault 62.88 mph*
    2nd Felice Nazzaro [It] *Fiat*
    3rd Albert Clément [Fr] *Clément-Bayard*
    Fastest lap: Paul Baras [Fr] *Brasier 73.3 mph*

CIRCUIT DES ARDENNES Bastogne 13 Aug
HEAVY CARS:
    1st Arthur Duray [Fr] *De Dietrich 65.8 mph*
    2nd Rene Hanriot [Fr] *Darracq*
    3rd Henri Rougier [Fr] *De Dietrich*
    Fastest lap: Louis Wagner [Fr] *Darracq 70 mph*
LIGHT CARS:
    Demogeot [Fr] *Darracq 40.9 mph*
    Only one contestant listed

VANDERBILT CUP Long Island 6 Oct
    1st Louis Wagner [Fr] *Darracq 61.4 mph*
    2nd Vincenzo Lancia [It] *Fiat*
    3rd Arthur Duray [Fr] *De Dietrich*
    Fastest lap: Joe Tracy [USA] *Locomobile 67.6 mph*

COUPE DE L'AUTO Rambouillet 12 Nov
    1st Georges Sizaire [Fr] *Sizaire-Naudin 34.98 mph*
    2nd Ménart Lucas [Fr] *Delage*
    3rd Giosue Giuppone [It] *Lion-Peugeot*
    Fastest lap: Sizaire *38.28 mph*

1907

Fastest Man on Earth: Victor Hémery (>1905)

COPPA DELLE VETTURETTE Madonie 18 April
    1st Louis Naudin [Fr] *Sizaire-Naudin 23.75 mph*
    2nd Count Vincenzo Florio [It] *De Dion-Bouton*
    3rd Giovanni Stabile [It] *De Dion-Bouton*
    Fastest lap: Naudin *24.01 mph*

TARGA FLORIO Grande Circuito Madonie 22 April
    1st Felice Nazzaro [It] *Fiat 33.6 mph*
    2nd Vincenzo Lancia [It] *Fiat*
    3rd Maurice Fabry [Fr] *Itala*
    Fastest lap: Nazzaro *34.38 mph*

KAISERPREIS [KAISER PRIZE] Taunus 14 June
    1st Felice Nazzaro [It] *Fiat 52.5 mph*
    2nd Lucien Hautvast [Fr] *Pipe*
    3rd Carl Jams [Ger] *Opel*
    Fastest lap: Vincenzo Lancia [It] *Fiat 53.5 mph*

GRAND PRIX DE L'AUTOMOBILE CLUB DE FRANCE Dieppe 2 July
    1st Felice Nazzara [It] *Fiat 70.5 mph*
    2nd François Szisz [Fr] *Renault*
    3rd Paul Baras [Fr] *Brasier*
    Fastest lap: Arthur Duray [Fr] *De Dietrich 75.4 mph*

CIRCUIT DES ARDENNES Bastogne 27 July
    1st Baron Pierre de Caters [Fr] *Mercedes 57.3 mph*
    2nd Kenelm Lee Guinness [GB] *Darracq*
    3rd Camille Jenatzy [Bel] *Mercedes*
    Fastest lap: Jenatzy *66.6 mph*

COPPA FLORIO Brescia 1 Sept
    1st Ferdinando Minoia [It] *Isotta-Fraschini 64.7 mph*
    2nd Victor Hémery [Fr] *Benz*
    3rd René Hanriot [Fr] *Benz*
    Fastest lap: Minoia *66.5 mph*

CORSA SICILIANA VETTURETTE Palermo 13 Aug
    1st Count Vincenzo Florio [Ft] *De Dion-Bouton 22.63 mph*
    2nd Giovanni Stabile [It] *De Dion-Bouton*
    3rd Paolo Tasca [It] *De Dion-Bouton*
    Fastest lap: as race time

COUPE DE L'AUTO Rambouillet 28 Oct
    1st Louis Naudin [Fr] *Sizaire-Naudin 40.69 mph*
    2nd Georges Sizaire [Fr] *Sizaire-Naudin*
    3rd Jules Goux [Fr] *Lion-Peugeot*
    Fastest lap: Sizaire *45.03 mph*

1908

Fastest Man on Earth: Victor Hémery (>1905)

TARGA FLORIO Grande Circuito Madonie 18 May
    1st Vincenzo Trucco [It] *Isotta-Fraschini 37.25 mph*
    2nd Vincenzo Lancia [It] *Fiat*
    3rd Ernesto Ceirano [It] *SPA*
    Fastest lap: Felice Nazzara [It] *Fiat 36.17 mph*

GRAND PRIX DES VOITURETTES Dieppe 6 July
    1st Albert Guyot [Fr] *Delage 49.74 mph*
    2nd Louis Naudin [Fr] *Sizaire-Naudin*
    3rd Jules Goux [Fr] *Lion-Peugeot*
    Fastest lap: Naudin *53.31 mph*

GRAND PRIX DE L'AUTOMOBILE CLUB DE FRANCE Dieppe 7 July
    1st Christian Lautenschlager [Ger] *Mercedes 69.05 mph*
    2nd Victor Hémery [Fr] *Benz*
    3rd Rene Hanriot [Fr] *Benz*
    Fastest lap: Otto Salzer [Ger] *Mercedes 78.45 mph*

COPPA FLORIO Bologna 6 Sept
    1st Felice Nazzara [It] *Fiat 74.1 mph*
    2nd Vincenzo Trucco [It] *De Dietrich*
    3rd Alessandro Cagno [It] *Itala*
    Fastest lap: Vincenzo Lancia [It] *Fiat 82.44 mph*

COUPE DES VOITURETTES Compiegne 27 Sept
    1st Louis Naudin [Fr] *Sizaire-Naudin 47.8 mph*
    2nd Georges Sizaire [Fr] *SizaireNaudin*
    3rd Jules Goux [Fr] *Lion-Peugeot*
    Fastest lap: Sizaire *48.37 mph*

AMERICAN GRAND PRIZE Savannah 26 Nov
    1st Louis Wagner [Fr] *Fiat 65.11 mph*
    2nd Victor Hémery [Fr] *Benz*
    3rd Felice Nazzara [It] *Fiat*
    Fastest lap: Ralph de Palma [USA] *Fiat 69.8 mph*

1909

US National Champion: George Robertson
Fastest Man on Earth: Victor Hémery [Fr] *Benz 125.95 mph*

TARGA FLORIO Grande Circuito Madonie 2 May
    1st Francesco Ciuppa [It] *SPA 34.04 mph*
    2nd Count Vincenzo Florio [It] *Fiat*
    3rd Guido Airoldi [It] *Lancia*
    Fastest lap: as race time

COPA DE CATALUÑA Sitges 26 May
    1st Jules Goux [Fr] *Lion-Peugeot 36.1 mph*
    2nd Georges Sizaire [Fr] *Sizaire-Naudin*
    3rd Soyez [Fr] *Werner*
    Fastest lap: not available

COUPE DES VOITURETTES Boulogne 20 June
    1st Giosue Giuppone [It] *Lion-Peugeot 47.46 mph*
    2nd Jules Goux [Fr] *Lion-Peugeot*
    3rd René Thomas [Fr] *Le Gui*
    Fastest lap: Georges Boillot [Fr] *Lion-Peugeot 52.78 mph*

COUPE DE NORMANDIE Caen 29 Aug
    1st Georges Boillot [Fr] *Lion-Peugeot 65.41 mph*
    2nd René Thomas [Fr] *Le Gui*
    3rd Giosue Giuppone [It] *Lion-Peugeot*
    Fastest lap: Boillot *68.97 mph*

COUPE D'OSTENDE Ostend 14 Sept
    1st Giosue Giuppone [It] *Lion-Peugeot 54.52 mph*
    2nd René Thomas [Fr] *Le Gui*
    No third place listed
    Fastest lap: Joseph Collomb [Fr] *Corre-La Licorne* [actual
        speed not available]

1910

US National Champion: Ray Harroun
Fastest Man on Earth: Victor Hémery (>1909); Barney Oldfield [USA] *Benz 131.724 mph* (US record)

TARGA FLORIO Grande Circuito Madonie 15 May
    1st Tullio Cariolato [It] *Franco 29.19 mph*
    2nd L. de Prosperis [It] Sigma
    Only two contestants finished
    Fastest lap: Cariolato *30.76 mph*

COPA DE CATALUÑA Sitges 30 May
    1st Jules Goux [Fr] *Lion-Peugeot 48.74 mph*
    2nd Giosue Giuppone [It] *Lion-Peugeot*
    3rd Alfonso Carreras [Sp] *Hispano-Suiza*
    Fastest lap: not available

COUPE D'OSTENDE Ostend 4 Sept
    1st Paolo Zuccarelli [It] *Hispano-Suiza 52.38 mph*
    2nd Georges Boillot [Fr] *Lion-Peugeot*
    3rd Louis Pilleverdier [Fr] *Hispano-Suiza*
    Fastest lap: not available

COUPE DE NORMANDIE Caen 9 Sept
    1st Jules Goux [Fr] *Lion-Peugeot 67.85 mph*
    2nd Georges Boillot [Fr] *Lion-Peugeot*
    No third place listed
    Fastest lap: Boillot *71.9 mph*

AMERICAN GRAND PRIZE Savannah 12 Nov
    1st David Bruce-Brown [USA] *Benz 70.55 mph*
    2nd Victor Hémery [Fr] *Benz*
    3rd Bob Burman [USA] *Marquette*
    Fastest lap: Felice Nazzara [It] *Fiat 75.7 mph*

1911

US National Champion: Ralph Mulford
Fastest Man on Earth: Victor Hémery (>1909); Bob Burman [USA] *Blitzen Benz 141.732 mph* (US record)

TARGA FLORIO Grande Circuito Madonie 14 May
    1st Ernesto Ceirano [It] *SCAT 29.13 mph*
    2nd Mario Cortese [It] *Lancia*
    3rd B. Soldatenkoff Mercedes
    Fastest lap: Cortese *31.58 mph*

INDIANAPOLIS 500 30 May
    1st Ray Harroun [USA] *Nordyke & Marmon 74.602 mph*
    2nd Ralph Mulford [USA] Lozier Motor
    3rd David Bruce-Brown [USA] *Fiat*
    Fastest qualifier: not available

COUPE DES VOITURETTES Boulogne 25 June
1st Paul Bablot [Fr] *Delage 55.2 mph*
2nd Georges Boillot [Fr] *Lion-Peugeot*
3rd René Thomas [Fr] *Delage*
Fastest lap: Boillot *57.11 mph*

AMERICAN GRAND PRIZE Savannah 30 Nov
1st David Bruce-Brown [USA] *Fiat 74.45 mph*
2nd Eddie Hearne [USA] *Benz*
3rd Ralph de Palma [USA] *Mercedes*
Fastest lap: Victor Hémery [Fr] *Benz 81.6 mph*

1912

US National Champion: Ralph de Palma
Fastest Man on Earth: Victor Hémery (>1909)

TARGA FLORIO One circuit of Sicily 25–26 May
1st Cyril Snipe [GB]/Padrini [It] *SCAT 26.5 mph*
2nd Garetto [It]/Guglielminetti [It] *Lancia*
3rd G. Giordano [It]/Ascone [It] *Fiat*

INDIANAPOLIS 500 30 May
1st Joe Dawson [USA] *National Motor Vehicle 78.72 mph*
2nd Teddy Tetzlaff [USA] *Fiat*
3rd Hughie Hughes [GB] *Mercer Motors*
Fastest qualifier: David Bruce-Brown [USA] *National Motor Vehicle 88.45 mph*

GRAND PRIX DE L'AUTOMOBILE CLUB DE FRANCE (Voiturettes) Dieppe 25–26 June
1st Victor Rigal [Fr] *Sunbeam 65.3 mph*
2nd Dario Resta [GB] *Sunbeam*
3rd Émile Médinger [Fr] *Sunbeam*
Fastest lap: Rigal *74.8 mph*

GRAND PRIX DE L'AUTOMOBILE CLUB DE FRANCE Dieppe 25–26 June
1st Georges Boillot [Fr] *Peugeot 68.45 mph*
2nd Louis Wagner [Fr] *Fiat*
3rd Victor Rigal [Fr] *Sunbeam*
Fastest lap: David Bruce-Brown [USA] *Fiat 78.02 mph*

COUPE DE LA SARTHE Le Mans 9 Sept
1st Jules Goux [Fr] *Peugeot 74.13 mph*
2nd Paolo Zuccarelli [It] *Lion-Peugeot*
3rd René Champoiseau [Fr] *Th. Schneider*
Fastest lap: Georges Boillot [Fr] *Peugeot L-76 80 mph*

GRAND PRIX DE FRANCE (Voiturettes) Le Mans 9 Sept
1st Paolo Zuccarelli [It] *Lion-Peugeot 66.4 mph*
2nd René Champoiseau [Fr] *Th. Schneider*
3rd Léon Molon [Fr] *Vinot-Deguignand*
Fastest lap: Zuccarelli *71.35 mph*

AMERICAN GRAND PRIZE Wauwatosa 5 Oct
1st Caleb Bragg [USA] *Fiat 68.4 mph*
2nd Erwin Bergdoll [USA] *Benz*
3rd Gil Anderson [USA] *Stutz*
Fastest lap: Teddy Tetzlaff [USA] *Fiat 77.3 mph*

1913

US National Champion: Earl Cooper
Fastest Man on Earth: Victor Hémery (>1909)

TARGA FLORIO One circuit of Sicily 11–12 May
1st Felice Nazzara [It] *Nazzara 33.78 mph*
2nd Giovanni Marsaglia [It] *Aquila-Italiana*
3rd A. Mariani [It] *De Vecchi*

INDIANAPOLIS 500 30 May
1st Jules Goux [Fr] *Peugeot 75.93 mph*
2nd Spencer Wishart [USA] *Mercer Motors*
3rd Charlie Merz [USA] *Stutz*
Fastest qualifier: Jack Tower [USA] Mason Motor *88.23 mph*

GRAND PRIX DE L'AUTOMOBILE CLUB DE FRANCE Amiens 12 July
1st Georges Boillot [Fr] *Peugeot 72.12 mph*
2nd Jules Goux [Fr] *Peugeot*
3rd Jean Chassagne [Fr] *Sunbeam*
Fastest lap: Paul Bablot [Fr] *Delage 76.72 mph*

GRAND PRIX DE FRANCE Le Mans 5 Aug
1st Paul Bablot [Fr] *Delage 76.89 mph*
2nd Albert Guyot [Fr] *Delage*
3rd Theodore Pilette [Bel] *Mercedes*
Fastest lap: Bablot *82.52 mph*

COUPE DES VOITURETTES Boulogne 21 Sept
1st Georges Boillot [Fr] *Peugeot 63.32 mph*
2nd Jules Goux [Fr] *Peugeot*
3rd Kenelm Lee Guinness [GB] *Sunbeam*
Fastest lap: Goux *66.25 mph*

GUADARRAMA GRAND PRIX Date not available
1st C. de Salamanca [Sp] *Rolls-Royce 54 mph*
2nd Marquis de Aulencia [Sp] *De Dietrich*
3rd E. Platford [GB] *Rolls-Royce*
Fastest lap: not available

1914

US National Champion: Ralph de Palma
Fastest Man on Earth: L. G. Hornsted [GB] *Benz 124.1 mph*

VANDERBILT CUP Santa Monica 26 Feb
1st Ralph de Palma [USA] *Mercedes 75.49 mph*
2nd Barney Oldfield [USA] Mercer
3rd Billy Carlson [USA] Mason
Fastest lap: not available

AMERICAN GRAND PRIZE Santa Monica 28 Feb
1st Eddie Pullen [USA] *Mercer 77.2 mph*
2nd G. Ball [USA] *Marmon*
3rd Billie Taylor [USA] *Alco*
Fastest lap: Teddy Tetzlaff [USA] *Fiat 86.6 mph*

TARGA FLORIO One circuit of Sicily 24–25 May
1st Ernesto Ceirano [It] *SCAT 38.7 mph*
2nd A. Mariani [It] *De Vecchi*
3rd Luigi Lopez [It] *Fiat*

INDIANAPOLIS 500 30 May
1st René Thomas [Fr] *L Delage 82.47 mph*
2nd Arthur Duray [Fr] *Peugeot*
3rd Albert Guyot [Fr] *Delage*
Fastest qualifier: Georges Boillot [Fr] *Peugeot 99.86 mph*

GRAND PRIX DE L'AUTOMOBILE CLUB DE FRANCE Lyons 4 July
1st Christian Lautenschlager [Ger] *Mercedes 65.66 mph*
2nd Louis Wagner [Fr] *Mercedes*
3rd Otto Salzer [Ger] *Mercedes*
Fastest lap: Max Sailer [Ger] *Mercedes 69.8 mph*

1915

US National Champion: Earl Cooper
Fastest Man on Earth: L. G. Hornsted (>1914)

AMERICAN GRAND PRIZE San Francisco 27 Feb
1st Dario Resta [GB] *Peugeot 56.13 mph*
2nd Howdy Wilcox [USA] *Stutz*
3rd Hughie Hughes [GB] *Ono*
Fastest lap: not available

VANDERBILT CUP San Francisco 6 March
1st Dario Resta [GB] *Peugeot 66.45 mph*
2nd Howdy Wilcox [USA] *Stutz*
3rd Eddie Pullen [USA] *Mercer*
Fastest lap: not available

INDIANAPOLIS 500 31 May
1st Ralph de Palma [USA] *Mercedes 89.84 mph*
2nd Dario Resta [GB] *Peugeot Auto Import*
3rd Gil Anderson [USA] *Stutz Motor Car*
Fastest qualifier: Howdy Wilcox [USA] *Stutz Motor Car 98.9 mph*

1916

US National Champion: Dario Resta [GB]
Fastest Man on Earth: L. G. Hornsted (>1914)

INDIANAPOLIS 300* 30 May
1st Dario Resta [GB] *Peugeot Auto Racing 84 mph*
2nd Wilbur d'Alene [USA] *Duesenberg*
3rd Ralph Mulford [USA] *Peugeot*
Fastest qualifier: Johnny Aitken [USA] *Peugeot 96.69 mph*
*Race shortened to 300 from usual 500 miles out of respect for the war being waged in Europe

VANDERBILT CUP Santa Monica 16 Nov
1st Dario Resta [GB] *Peugeot 86.98 mph*
2nd Earl Cooper [USA] *Stutz*
3rd William Weightman [USA] *Duesenberg*
Fastest lap: not available

AMERICAN GRAND PRIZE Santa Monica 18 Nov
1st Howdy Wilcox [USA]/Johnny Aitken [USA] *Peugeot 85.59mph*
2nd Earl Cooper [USA] *Stutz*
3rd A. Patterson [USA] *Hudson*
Fastest lap: not available

1919

US National Champion: Howdy Wilcox
Fastest Man on Earth: L. G. Hornsted (>1914); Ralph de Palma [USA] *Packard 149.875 mph (US record)*

INDIANAPOLIS 500 30 May
1st Howdy Wilcox [USA] *Peugeot 88.05 mph*
2nd Eddie Hearne [USA] *Durant*
3rd Jules Goux [Fr] *Peugeot*
Fastest qualifier: René Thomas [Fr] *Ernest Ballot 104.7 mph*

TARGA FLORIO Medio Circuito Madonie 23 Nov
1st Andre Boillot [Fr] *Peugeot 34.19 mph*
2nd Antonio Moriondo [It] *Itala*
3rd Domenico Gamboni [It] *Diatto*
Fastest lap: Boillot *35.1 mph*

1920

US National Champion: Tommy Milton
Fastest Man on Earth: L. G. Hornsted (>1914); Tommy Milton [USA] *Duesenberg 156.03 mph (US record)*

INDIANAPOLIS 500 30 May
1st Gaston Chevrolet [USA] *Monroe 88.62 mph*
2nd René Thomas [Fr] *Ernest Ballot*
3rd Tommy Milton [USA] *Duesenberg*
Fastest qualifier: Ralph de Palma [USA] *Ballot 99.15 mph*

CIRCUITO DI MUGELLO 13 June
1st Giuseppe Campari [It] *Alfa-Romeo 37.8 mph*
2nd Augusto Tarabusi [It] *Diatto*
3rd Edoardo Weber [It] *Fiat*
Fastest lap: Carlo Masetti [It] *Fiat 42.09 mph*

TARGA FLORIO Medio Circuito Madonie 24 Oct
1st Guido Meregalli [It] *Nazzara 35.99 mph*
2nd Enzo *Ferrari* [It] *Alfa-Romeo*
3rd Luigi Lopez [It] *Darracq*
Fastest lap: Ferrari *31.97 mph*

1921

US National Champion: Tommy Milton
Fastest Man on Earth: L. G. Hornsted (>1914)

TARGA FLORIO Medio Circuito Madonie 29 May
1st Count Giulio Masetti [It] *Fiat 36.19 mph*
2nd Max Sailer [Ger] *Mercedes*
3rd Giuseppe Campari [It] *Alfa-Romeo*
Fastest lap: Sailer *37.43 mph*

INDIANAPOLIS 500 30 May
1st Tommy Milton [USA] *Frontenac* 89.62 mph
2nd Roscoe Sarles [USA] *Duesenberg*
3rd Percy Ford [USA]/Jules Ellingboe [USA] *Frontenac*
Fastest qualifier Ralph de Palma [USA] *Ballot* 100.75 mph

CIRCUITO DI MUGELLO 24 July
1st Giuseppe Campari [It] *Alfa-Romeo* 38.88 mph
2nd Enzo *Ferrari* [It] *Alfa-Romeo*
3rd Ugo Sivocci [It] *Alfa-Romeo*
Fastest lap: Sivocci *41.56 mph*

FRENCH GRAND PRIX Le Mans 26 July
1st Jimmy Murphy [USA] *Duesenberg* 78.1 mph
2nd Ralph de Palma [USA] *Ballot*
3rd Jules Goux [Fr] *Ballot*
Fastest lap: Murphy *83.4 mph*

ITALIAN GRAND PRIX Brescia 4 Sept
1st Jules Goux [Fr] *Ballot* 89.94 mph
2nd Jean Chassagne [Fr] *Ballot*
3rd Louis Wagner [Fr] *Fiat*
Fastest lap: Pietro Bordino [It] *Fiat* 93.43 mph

PENYA RHIN GRAND PRIX Villafranca 16 Oct
1st Pierre de Vizcaya [Sp] *Bugatti* 54.29 mph
2nd Jacques Mones-Maury [Fr] *Bugatti*
3rd Louis Revaux [Fr] *Bignan*
Fastest lap: not available

JUNIOR CAR CLUB 200 Brooklands 22 Oct
1st Henry Segrave [GB] *Talbot-Darracq* 88.82 mph
2nd Kenelm Lee Guinness [GB] *Talbot-Darracq*
3rd Malcolm Campbell [GB] *Talbot-Darracq*
Fastest lap: not available

US National Champion: Jimmy Murphy
Fastest Man on Earth: Kenelm Lee Guinness [GB] *Sunbeam* 133.75 mph

TARGA FLORIO Medio Circuito Madonie 2 April
1st Count Giulio Masetti [It] *Mercedes* 39.2 mph
2nd Jules Goux [Fr] *Ballot*
3rd Giulio Forest [Fr] *Ballot*
Fastest lap: Masetti *41.15 mph*

INDIANAPOLIS 500 30 May
1st Jimmy Murphy [USA] *Jimmy Murphy* 94.48 mph
2nd Harry Hartz [USA] *Duesenberg Straight-8*
3rd Eddie Hearne [USA] *Ballot*
Fastest qualifier: Murphy *100.5 mph*

TOURIST TROPHY Isle of Man 22 June
1st Jean Chassagne [Fr] *Sunbeam* 55.78 mph
2nd Frank Clément [GB] *Bentley*
3rd O. Payne [GB] *Vauxhall*
Fastest lap:Henry Segrave [GB] *Sunbeam* 577 mph

INTERNATIONAL 1500 TROPHY Isle of Man 22 June
1st Algernon Lee Guinness [GB] *Talbot-Darracq* 53.31 mph
2nd Albert Divo [Fr] *Talbot-Darracq*
3rd Jacques Mones-Maury *Bugatti*
Fastest lap: Guinness *55.15 mph*

FRENCH GRAND PRIX Strasbourg 16 July
1st Felice Nazzaro [It] *Fiat* 79.33 mph
2nd Pierre de Vizcaya [Sp] *Bugatti*
3rd Piero Marco [It] *Bugatti*
Fastest lap: Pietro Bordino [It] *Fiat* 87.75 mph

JUNIOR CAR CLUB 200 Brooklands 19 Aug
1st Kenelm Lee Guinness [GB] *Aston-Martin* 88.06 mph
2nd G. Stead [GB] *Aston-Martin*
3rd Henry Segrave [GB] *Talbot-Darracq*
Fastest lap: Guinness *95.78 mph*

ITALIAN GRAND PRIX Monza 3 Sept
1st Pietro Bordino [It] *Fiat* 86.9 mph
2nd Felice Nazzaro [It] *Fiat*
3rd Pierre de Vizcaya [Sp] *Bugatti*
Fastest lap: Bordino *91.03 mph*

GRAN PREMIO [GRAND PRIX] DELLE VETTURETTE Monza 3 Sept
1st Pietro Bordino [It] *Fiat* 83.27 mph
2nd Enrico Giaccone [It] *Fiat*
3rd Evasio Lampiano [It] *Fiat*
Fastest lap: Bordino *90.2 mph*

US National Champion: Eddie Hearne
Fastest Man on Earth: Kenelm Lee Guinness (> 1922)

TARGA FLORIO Medio Circuito Madonie 15 April
1st Ugo Sivocci [It] *Alfa-Romeo* 36.77 mph
2nd Antonio Ascari [It] *Alfa-Romeo*
3rd Ferdinando Minoia [It] *Steyr*
Fastest lap: Ascari *39.67 mph*

INDIANAPOLIS 500 30 May
1st Tommy Milton [USA] *H. C. S. Motor* 90.95 mph
2nd Harry Hartz [USA] *R. Cliff Durant*
3rd Jimmy Murphy [USA] *R. Cliff Durant*
Fastest qualifier: Milton *108.17 mph*

FRENCH GRAND PRIX Tours 2 June
1st Henry Segrave [GB] *Sunbeam* 75.3 mph
2nd Albert Divo [Fr] *Sunbeam*
3rd Ernest Friderich [Fr] *Bugatti*
Fastest lap: Pietro Bordino [It] *Fiat* 88.05 mph

SAN SEBASTIAN GRAND PRIX 8 July
1st Albert Guyot [Fr] *Rolland-Pilain* 58.06 mph
2nd Gaston Delalande [Fr] *Rolland-Pilain*
3rd Jean Haimovici [Fr] *Ballot*
Fastest lap: not available

ITALIAN (EUROPEAN) GRAND PRIX Monza 9 Sept
1st Carlo Salamano [It] *Fiat* 91.03 mph
2nd Felice Nazzaro [It] *Fiat*
3rd Jimmy Murphy [USA] *Miller*
Fastest lap: Pietro Bordino [It] *Fiat* 99.86 mph

JUNIOR CAR CLUB 200 Brooklands 13 Oct
1st Maurice Harvey [GB] *Alvis* 93.29 mph
2nd Léon Cushman [GB] *Bugatti*
3rd John Joyce [GB] AC
Fastest lap: Carlo Salamano [It] *Fiat*/Malcolm Campbell [GB] *Fiat* 101.64 mph

SPANISH GRAND PRIX Sitges-Terramar 23 Oct
1st Albert Divo [Fr] *Sunbeam* 96.87 mph
2nd Count Louis Zborowski [GB] *Miller*
3rd Alfonso Carreras [Sp] *Elizalde*
Fastest lap: Zborowski *97.49 mph*

US National Champion: Jimmy Murphy
Fastest Man on Earth: Malcolm Campbell [GB] *Sunbeam* 146.16 mph

TARGA FLORIO Medio Circuito Madonie 27 April
1st Christian Werner [Ger] *Mercedes* 41.02 mph
2nd Count Giulio Masetti [It] *Alfa-Romeo*
3rd Pietro Bordino [It] *Fiat*
Fastest lap: Werner *42.29 mph*

INDIANAPOLIS 500 30 May
1st Lora Corum [USA]/Joe Boyer [USA] *Duesenberg* 98.23 mph
2nd Earl Cooper [USA] Studebaker
3rd Jimmy Murphy [USA] Miller
Fastest qualifier; Murphy *108.037 mph*

FRENCH (EUROPEAN) GRAND PRIX Lyons 3 Aug
1st Giuseppe Campari [It] *Alfa-Romeo* 70.97 mph
2nd Albert Divo [Fr] *Delage*
3rd Robert Benoist [Fr] *Delage*
Fastest lap: Henry Segrave [GB] *Sunbeam* 76.25 mph

SAN SEBASTIAN GRAND PRIX 25 Sept
1st Henry Segrave [GB] *Sunbeam* 64.09 mph
2nd Bartolomeo Costantini [It] *Bugatti*
3rd Andre Morel [Fr] *Delage*
Fastest lap: Costantini *71.7 mph*

ITALIAN GRAND PRIX Monza 19 Oct
1st Antonio Ascari [It] *Alfa-Romeo* 98.79 mph
2nd Louis Wagner [Fr] *Alfa-Romeo*
3rd Giuseppe Campari [It]/E. Presenti [It] *Alfa-Romeo*
Fastest lap: Ascar1104.38 mph

US National Champion: Peter de Paolo
Fastest Man on Earth: Malcolm Campbell [GB] *Sunbeam* 150.87 mph

TARGA FLORIO Medio Circuito Madonie 3 May
1st Bartolomeo Costantini [It] *Bugatti* 44.5 mph
2nd Louis Wagner [Fr] *Peugeot*
3rd Andre Boillot [Fr] *Peugeot*
Fastest lap: Costantini *45.34 mph*

INDIANAPOLIS 500 30 May
1st Peter de Paolo [USA] *Duesenberg* 101.13 mph
2nd Dave Lewis [USA] *Junior 8*
3rd Phil Shafer [USA] *Duesenberg*
Fastest qualifier: 'Leon Duray' (George Stewart) [USA] Miller *113.196 mph*

BELGIAN (EUROPEAN) GRAND PRIX Spa 29 June
1st Antonio Ascari [It] *Alfa-Romeo* 74.56 mph
2nd Giuseppe Campari [It] *Alfa-Romeo*
Fastest lap: Ascari *81.5 mph*
Only two contestants finished

FRENCH GRAND PRIX Montlhéry 26 July
1st Robert Benoist [Fr]/Albert Divo [Fr] *Delage* 69.7 mph
2nd Louis Wagner [Fr]/Paul Torchy [Fr] *Delage*
3rd Count Giulio Masetti [It] *Sunbeam*
Fastest lap: Divo *80.3 mph*

ITALIAN GRAND PRIX Monza 6 Sept
1st Count Gastone Brilli-Peri [It] *Alfa-Romeo* 94.82 mph
2nd Giuseppe Campari [It]/Giovanni Minozzi [It] *Alfa-Romeo*
3rd Bartolomeo Costantini [It] *Bugatti*
Fastest lap: Peter Kreis [USA] *Duesenberg* 103.21 mph

SAN SEBASTIAN GRAND PRIX 19 Sept
1st Albert Divo [Fr]/Andre Morel [Fr] *Delage* 76.73 mph
2nd Robert Benoist [Fr] *Delage*
3rd Rene Thomas [Fr] *Delage*
Fastest lap: Bartolomeo Costantini [It] *Bugatti* 82.75 mph

US National Champion: Harry Hartz
Fastest Man on Earth: J. G. Parry Thomas [GB] *Higham Special 'Babs'* 171.02 mph

TARGA FLORIO Medio Circuito Madonie 25 April
1st Bartolomeo Costantini [It] *Bugatti* 45.68 mph
2nd Ferdinando Minoia [It] *Bugatti*
3rd Jules Goux [Fr] *Bugatti*
Fastest lap: Costantini *46.72 mph*

INDIANAPOLIS 500 31 May
1st Frank Lockhart [USA] *Miller* 95.904 mph
2nd Harry Hartz [USA] *Miller*
3rd Cliff Woodbury [USA] *Boyle*
Fastest qualifier: Earl Cooper [USA] *Front Drive Miller* 111.735 mph

FRENCH GRAND PRIX Miramas 27 June
1st Jules Goux [Fr] *Bugatti* 68.2 mph
2nd Bartolomeo Costantini [It] *Bugatti*
Only two contestants finished
Fastest lap: Goux *79.4 mph*

GERMAN GRAND PRIX Avus II July
1st Rudi Caracciola [Ger] *Mercedes 83.89 mph*
2nd Christian Rieken [Ger] *NAG*
3rd W. Cleer [Ger] *Alfa-Romeo*
Fastest lap: Ferdinando Minoia [It] *OM 100.16 mph*

SPANISH (EUROPEAN) GRAND PRIX Lasarte 18 July
1st Jules Goux [Fr] *Bugatti 70.4 mph*
2nd Edmond Bourlier [Fr]/Robert Sénéchal [Fr] *Delage*
3rd Bartolomeo Costantini [It] *Bugatti*
Fastest lap: Goux *81.5 mph*

BRITISH (RAC) GRAND PRIX Brooklands 7 Aug
1st Robert Sénéchal [Fr]/Louis Wagner [Fr] *Delage 71.61 mph*
2nd Malcolm Campbell [GB] *Bugatti*
3rd Robert Benoist [Fr]/Andre Dubonnet [Fr] *Delage*
Fastest lap: Henry Segrave [GB] *Talbot 85 mph*

ITALIAN GRAND PRIX Monza 11 Sept
1st 'Sabipa' (Louis Charaval) [Fr] *Bugatti 85.87 mph*
2nd Bartolomeo Costantini [It] *Bugatti*
Fastest lap: Costantini *98.3 mph*
Only two contestants finished

US National Champion: Peter de Paolo
Fastest Man on Earth: Henry Segrave [GB] *Sunbeam 203.79 mph*

MILLE MIGLIA Brescia 26–27 March
1st Ferdinando Minoia [It]/Giuseppe Morandi [It] *OM 48.27 mph*
2nd T. Danieli [It]/Renato Balestrero [It] *OM*
3rd Mario Danieli [1t]/Archimede Rosa [It] *OM*

TARGA FLORIO Medio Circuito Madonie 24 April
1st Emilio Materassi [It] *Bugatti 44.16 mph*
2nd Count Carlo Alberto Conelli [It] *Bugatti*
3rd Alfieri Maserati [It] *Maserati*
Fastest lap: Materassi *46.82 mph*

INDIANAPOLIS 500 30 May
1st George Souders [USA] *Duesenberg 97.545 mph*
2nd Earl DeVore [USA] *Miller*
3rd Anthony Gulotta [USA] *Miller*
Fastest qualifier: Frank Lockhart [USA] *Perfect Circle Miller 120.1 mph*

FRENCH GRAND PRIX Montlhéry 3 July
1st Robert Benoist [Fr] *Delage 77.24 mph*
2nd Edmond Bourlier [Fr] *Delage*
3rd Andre Morel [Fr] *Delage*
Fastest lap: Benoist *81.43 mph*

GERMAN GRAND PRIX Nürburging 17 July
1st Otto Merz [Ger] *Mercedes-Benz 63.39 mph*
2nd Christian Werner [Ger] *Mercedes-Benz*
3rd Willy Walb [Ger] *Mercedes-Benz*
Fastest lap: Werner *66.49 mph*

SPANISH GRAND PRIX Lasarte 31 July
1st Robert Benoist [Fr] *Delage 80.52 mph*
2nd Count Carlo Alberto Conelli [It] *Bugatti*
3rd Edmond Bourlier [Fr] *Delage*
Fastest lap: Benoist *85.41 mph*

BRITISH (RAC) GRAND PRIX Brooklands 7 Aug
1st Robert Benoist [Fr] *Delage 85.59 mph*
2nd Edmond Bourlier [Fr] *Delage*
3rd Albert Divo [Fr] *Delage*
Fastest lap: not available

ITALIAN (EUROPEAN) GRAND PRIX Monza 4 Sept
1st Robert Benoist [Fr] *Delage 90.04 mph*
2nd Giuseppe Morandi [It] *OM*
3rd Peter Kreis [USA]/Earl Cooper [USA] *Miller*
Fastest lap: Benoist *94.31 mph*

MILAN GRAND PRIX 4 Sept
1st Pietro Bordino [It] *Fiat 94.57 mph*
2nd Giuseppe Campari [It] *Alfa-Romeo*
3rd Count Aymo Maggi [It] *Bugatti*
Fastest lap: Bordino *96.59 mph*

US National Champion: Louie Meyer
Fastest Man on Earth: Ray Keech [USA] *Triplex Special 207.55 mph*

MILLE MIGLIA Brescia 31 March–1 April
1st Giuseppe Campari [It]/Giulio Ramponi [It] *Alfa-Romeo 52.58 mph*
2nd Franco Mazotti [It]/Archimede Rosa [It] *OM*
3rd Gildo Strazza [It]/Varallo [It] *Lancia*

BORDINO PRIZE Alessandria 22 April
1st Tazio Nuvolari [It] *Bugatti 63.45 mph*
2nd Achille Varzi [It] *Bugatti*
3rd Federico Valpreda [It] *Delage*
Fastest lap: Emilio Materassi [It] *Talbot 64.3 mph*

TARGA FLORIO Medio Circuito Madonie 6 May
1st Albert Divo [Fr] *Bugatti 45.66 mph*
2nd Giuseppe Campari [It] *Alfa-Romeo*
3rd Count Carlo Alberto Conelli [It] *Bugatti*
Fastest lap: Louis Chiron [Mon] *Bugatti 46.48 mph*

INDIANAPOLIS 500 30 May
1st Louie Meyer [USA] *Miller 99.482 mph*
2nd Lou Moore [USA] *Miller*
3rd George Souders [USA] *State Auto Insurance*
Fastest qualifier: Léon Duray [Fr] *Miller 122.391 mph*

ROME GRAND PRIX Trefontana 10 June
1st Louis Chiron [Mon] *Bugatti 78.55 mph*
2nd Count Gastone Brilli-Peri [It] *Bugatti*
3rd Emilio Materassi [It] *Talbot*
Fastest lap: Chiron *80.4 mph*

CREMONA CIRCUIT 24 June
1st Luigi Arcangeli [It] *Talbot 101.36 mph*
2nd Tazio Nuvolari [It] *Bugatti*
3rd Emilio Materassi [It] *Talbot*
Fastest lap: Giuseppe Campari [It] *Alfa-Romeo 108.6 mph*

FRENCH GRAND PRIX Comminges I July
1st 'W. Williams' (William Grover-Williams) [GB] *Bugatti 84.86 mph*
2nd Rousseau [Fr] *Salmson*
3rd Edouard Brisson [Fr] *Stutz*
Fastest lap: 'Williams' *86.15 mph*

MARNE GRAND PRIX Rheims 5 July
1st Louis Chiron [Mon] *Bugatti 82.5 mph*
2nd Robert Gauthier [Fr] *Bugatti*
3rd Philippe Auber [Fr] *Bugatti*
Fastest lap: Chiron *91.4 mph*

GERMAN GRAND PRIX Nürburging 5 July
1st Rudi Caracciola [Ger]/Christian Werner [Ger] *Mercedes-Benz 64.56 mph*
2nd Otto Merz [Ger] *Mercedes-Benz*
3rd Christian Werner [Ger]/Willy Walb [Ger] *Mercedes-Benz*
Fastest lap: Caracciola *69.34 mph*

SAN SEBASTIAN GRAND PRIX 25 July
1st Louis Chiron [Mon] *Bugatti 80.58 mph*
2nd Robert Benoist [Fr] *Bugatti*
3rd Marcel Lehoux [Fr] *Bugatti*
Fastest lap: Chiron *88.25 mph*

MONTENERO GRAND PRIX 19 Aug
1st Emilio Materassi [It] *Talbot 52.77 mph*
2nd Tazio Nuvolari [It] *Bugatti*
3rd Giuseppe Campari [It] *Alfa-Romeo*
Fastest lap: Nuvolari *53.8 mph*

ITALIAN (EUROPEAN) GRAND PRIX Monza 9 Sept
1st Louis Chiron [Mon] *Bugatti 99.36 mph*
2nd Giuseppe Campari [It]/Achille Varzi [It] *Alfa-Romeo*
3rd Tazio Nuvolari [It] *Bugatti*
Fastest lap: Luigi Arcangeli [It] *Talbot 103.2 mph*

US National Champion: Louie Meyer
Fastest Man on Earth: Henry Segrave [GB] *Irving Napier 'Golden Arrow' 231.446 mph*

MILLE MIGLIA Brescia 13–14 April
1st Giuseppe Campari [It]/Giulio Ramponi [It] *Alfa-Romeo 56.05 mph*
2nd Giuseppe Morandi [It]/Archimede Rosa [It] *OM*
3rd Achille Varzi [It]/G. Colombo [It] *Alfa-Romeo*

MONACO GRAND PRIX Monte Carlo 14 April
1st W. Williams' [GB] *Bugatti 50.23 mph*
2nd Georges Bouriano [Bel] *Bugatti*
3rd Rudi Caracciola [Ger] *Mercedes-Benz*
Fastest lap: 'Williams' *52.7 mph*

BORDINO PRIZE Alessandria 21 April
1st Achille Varzi [It] *Alfa-Romeo 68.24 mph*
2nd Baconin Borzacchini [It] *Maserati*
3rd Ernesto Maserati [It] *Maserati*
Fastest lap: Varzi *68.6 mph*

TARGA FLORIO Medio Circuito Madonie 5 May
1st Albert Divo [Fr] *Bugatti 46.21 mph*
2nd Ferdinando Minoia [It] *Bugatti*
3rd Count Gastone Brilli-Peri [It] *Alfa-Romeo*
Fastest lap: Minoia *47.07 mph*

ROME GRAND PRIX Trefontana 26 May
1st Achille Varzi [It] *Alfa-Romeo 80.2 mph*
2nd Count Gastone Brilli-Peri [It] *Alfa-Romeo*
3rd Albert Divo [Fr] *Bugatti*
Fastest lap: Brilli-Peri *83.12 mph*

INDIANAPOLIS 500 30 May
1st Ray Keech [USA] *Simplex Piston Ring 97.585 mph*
2nd Louie Meyer [USA] *Miller*
3rd Jimmy Gleason [USA] *A. S. Duesenberg*
Fastest qualifier: Cliff Woodbury [USA] *Boyle Valve 120.599 mph*

FRENCH GRAND PRIX Le Mans 30 June
1st 'W. Williams' [GB] *Bugatti 82.66 mph*
2nd Andre Boillot [Fr] *Peugeot*
3rd Count Carlo Alberto Conelli [It] *Bugatti*
Fastest lap: 'Williams' *86.93 mph*

CREMONA CIRCUIT 1 July
1st Count Gastone Brilli-Peri [It] *Alfa-Romeo 14.41 mph*
2nd Achille Varzi [It] *Alfa-Romeo*
3rd Ernesto Maserati [It] *Maserati*
Fastest lap: Alfieri Maserati [It] *Maserati 124.4 mph*

GERMAN GRAND PRIX Nürburging 14 July
1st Louis Chiron [Mon] *Bugatti 66.79 mph*
2nd Georges Philippe [Fr] *Bugatti*
3rd August Momberger [Ger] *Mercedes-Benz*
Fastest lap: Chiron *69.97 mph*

MARNE GRAND PRIX Rheims 14 July
1st Philippe Etancelin [Fr] *Bugatti 85.5 mph*
3rd Juan Zanelli [Chile] *Bugatti*
3rd Marcel Lehoux [Fr] *Bugatti*
Fastest lap: Etancelin *88.6 mph*

MONTENERO GRAND PRIX 21 July
1st Achille Varzi [It] *Alfa-Romeo 54.17 mph*
2nd Tazio Nuvolari [It] *Alfa-Romeo*
3rd Giuseppe Campari [It] *Alfa-Romeo*
Fastest lap: Nuvolari *55.3 mph*

SPANISH GRAND PRIX Lasarte 25 July
1st Louis Chiron [Mon] *Bugatti 72.4 mph*
2nd Georges Philippe [Fr]/Guy Bouriat [Fr] *Bugatti*
3rd Marcel Lehoux [Fr] *Bugatti*
Fastest lap: Chiron *86.84 mph*

MONZA GRAND PRIX 15 September
1st Achille Varzi [It] *Alfa-Romeo 116.83 mph*
2nd Tazio Nuvolari [It] *Alfa-Romeo*
3rd August Momberger [Ger] *Mercedes-Benz*
Fastest lap: Alfieri Maserati [It] *Maserati 124.2 mph*

US National Champion: Billy Arnold
Fastest Man on Earth: Henry Segrave (>1929)

MONACO GRAND PRIX Monte Carlo 6 April
1st Rene Dreyfus [Fr] *Bugatti 53.63 mph*
2nd Louis Chiron [Mon] *Bugatti*
3rd Guy Bouriat [Fr] *Bugatti*
Fastest lap: Dreyfus *56.01 mph*

MILLE MIGLIA Brescia 16–17 April
1st Tazio Nuvolari [It]/Giovanni Guidotti [It] *Alfa-Romeo 62.78 mph*
2nd Achille Varzi DWG. Canavesi [It] *Alfa-Romeo*
3rd Giuseppe Campari [It]/Attilio Marinoni [It] *Alfa-Romeo*

TARGA FLORIO Medio Circuito Madonie 4 May
1st Achille Varzi [It] *Alfa-Romeo 48.52 mph*
2nd Louis Chiron [Mon] *Bugatti*
3rd Count Carlo Alberto Conelli [It] *Bugatti*
Fastest lap: Varzi *49.38 mph*

ROME GRAND PRIX Trefontana 25 May
1st Luigi Arcangeli [It] *Maserati 83.6 mph*
2nd Guy Bouriat [Fr] *Bugatti*
3rd Heinrich-Joachim von Morgen [Ger] *Bugatti*
Fastest lap: Bouriat *86.6 mph*

INDIANAPOLIS 500 30 May
1st Billy Arnold [USA] *Miller-Hartz 100.448 mph*
2nd Shorty Canton [USA] *Miller Schofield*
3rd Louis Schneider [USA] *Bowes Seal Fast*
Fastest qualifier: Arnold *113.263 mph*

MARNE GRAND PRIX Rheims 29 June
1st Rene Dreyfus [Fr] *Bugatti 88.5 mph*
2nd Marcel Lehoux [Fr] *Bugatti*
3rd Michel Dore [Fr] *Bugatti*
Fastest lap: Dreyfus *91 mph*

BELGIAN (EUROPEAN) GRAND PRIX Spa 20 July
1st Louis Chiron [Mon] *Bugatti 72.1 mph*
2nd Guy Bouriat [Fr] *Bugatti*
3rd Albert Divo [Fr] *Bugatti*
Fastest lap: Bouriat *78.5 mph*

COPPA CIANO Montenero 3 Aug
1st Luigi Fagioli [It] *Maserati 54.47 mph*
2nd Giuseppe Campari [It] *Alfa-Romeo*
3rd Count Aymo Maggi [It] *Bugatti*
Fastest lap: Tazio Nuvolari [It] *Alfa-Romeo 57.2 mph*

COPPA ACERBO Pescara 17 Aug
1st Achille Varzi [It] *Maserati 75.35 mph*
2nd Ernesto Maserati [It] *Maserati*
3rd Baconin Borzacchini [It] *Alfa-Romeo*
Fastest lap: Tazio Nuvolari [It] *Alfa-Romeo 78.3 mph*

MONZA GRAND PRIX 7 Sept
1st Achille Varzi [It] *Maserati 93.55 mph*
2nd Luigi Arcangeli [It] *Maserati*
3rd Ernesto Maserati [It] *Maserati*
Fastest lap: Varzi *100.6 mph*

FRENCH GRAND PRIX Pau 21 Sept
1st Philippe Etancelin [Fr] *Bugatti 90.4 mph*
2nd Henry Birkin [GB] *Bentley*
3rd Juan Zanelli [Chile] *Bugatti*
Fastest lap: W. Williams' [GB] *Bugatti 96.73 mph*

SPANISH GRAND PRIX Lasarte 4 Oct
1st Achille Varzi [It] *Maserati 86.82 mph*
2nd Count Aymo Maggi [It] *Maserati*
3rd Henri Stoffel [Fr] *Peugeot*
Fastest lap: Varzi *91.09 mph*

US National Champion: Louis Schneider
Fastest Man on Earth: Malcolm Campbell [GB] *Napier-Campbell Bluebird 246.09 mph*

MILLE MIGLIA Brescia 11-12 April
1st Rudi Caracciola [Ger]/Wilhelm Sebastian [Ger] *Mercedes-Benz 63.21 mph*
2nd Giuseppe Campari [It]/Attilio Marinoni [It] *Alfa-Romeo*
3rd Giuseppe Morandi [It]/Archimede Rosa [It] *OM*

MONACO GRAND PRIX Monte Carlo 19 April
1st Louis Chiron [Mon] *Bugatti 54.09 mph*
2nd Luigi Fagioli [It] *Maserati*
3rd Achille Varzi [It] *Bugatti*
Fastest lap: Chiron *56.01 mph*

TARGA FLORIO Grande Circuito Madonie 10 May
1st Tazio Nuvolari [It] *Alfa-Romeo 40.29 mph*
2nd Baconin Borzacchini [It] *Alfa-Romeo*
3rd Achille Varzi [It] *Bugatti*
Fastest lap: Varzi *43.83 mph*

ITALIAN (EUROPEAN) GRAND PRIX Monza 24 May
1st Giuseppe Campari [It]/Tazio Nuvolari [It] *Alfa-Romeo 96.17 mph*
2nd Ferdinando Minoia [It]/Baconin Borzacchini [It] *Alfa-Romeo*
3rd Albert Divo [Fr]/Guy Bouriat [Fr] *Bugatti*
Fastest lap: Nuvolan *105 mph*

INDIANAPOLIS 500 30 May
1st Louis Schneider [USA] *Bowes Seal Fast 96.629 mph*
2nd Fred Frame [USA] *Duesenberg*
3rd Ralph Hepburn [USA] *Miller*
Fastest qualifier: Billy Arnold [USA] *Miller-Hartz 116.08 mph*

FRENCH GRAND PRIX Montlhery 21 June
1st Achille Varzi [It]/Louis Chiron [Mon] *Bugatti 78.21 mph*
2nd Giuseppe Campari [It]/Baconin Borzacchini [It] *Alfa-Romeo*
3rd Clémente Biondetti [It]/G. Parenti [It] *Maserati*
Fastest lap: Luigi Fagioli [It] *Maserati 85.6 mph*

BELGIAN GRAND PRIX Spa 12 July
1st 'W. Williams' [CB]/Count Carlo Alberto Conelli [It] *Bugatti 82.04 mph*
2nd Tazio Nuvolari [It]/Baconin Borzacchini [It] *Alfa-Romeo*
3rd Ferdinando Minoia [It]/E. Minozzi [It] *Alfa-Romeo*
Fastest lap: Louis Chiron [Mon] *Bugatti 88 mph*

GERMAN GRAND PRIX Nürburging 19 July
1st Rudi Caracciola [Ger] *Mercedes 67.4 mph*
2nd Louis Chiron [Mon] *Bugatti*
3rd Achille Varzi [It] *Bugatti*
Fastest lap: Varzi *72.6 mph*

MONZA GRAND PRIX 6 Sept
1st Luigi Fagioli [It] *Maserati 96.6 mph*
2nd Baconin Borzacchini [It] *Alfa-Romeo*
3rd Achille Varzi [It] *Bugatti*
Fastest lap: Tazio Nuvolari [It] *Alfa-Romeo 101.23 mph*

CZECHOSLOVAKIAN GRAND PRIX Brno 27 Sept
1st Louis Chiron [Mon] *Bugatti 73.26 mph*
2nd Hans Stuck [Ger] *Mercedes*
3rd Heinrich-Joachim von Morgen [Ger] *Bugatti*
Fastest lap: Chiron *75.36 mph*

US National Champion: Bob Carey
Fastest Man on Earth: Malcolm Campbell [GB] *Napier-Campbell Bluebird 253.97 mph*

MILLE MIGLIA Brescia 9-10 April
1st Baconin Borzacchini [It]/A. Bignami [It] *Alfa-Romeo 68.67 mph*
2nd Marquis Antonio Brivio [It]/Count Felice Trossi [It] *Alfa-Romeo*
3rd Luigi Scarfiotti [It]/Guido d'Ippolito [It] *Alfa-Romeo*

MONACO GRAND PRIX Monte Carlo 17 April
1st Tazio Nuvolari [It] *Alfa-Romeo 55.81 mph*
2nd Rudi Caracciola [Ger] *Alfa-Romeo*
3rd Luigi Fagioli [It] *Maserati*
Fastest lap: Achille Varzi [It] *Bugatti 58.3 mph*

TARGA FLORIO Piccolo Circuito Madonie 8 May
1st Tazio Nuvolari [It] *Alfa-Romeo 49.31 mph*
2nd Baconin Borzacchini [It] *Alfa-Romeo*
3rd Louis Chiron [Mon] *Bugatti.*
Fastest lap: Nuvolari *50.59 mph*

AVUSRENNEN [AVUS RACES] Berlin 22 May
1st Manfred von Brauchitsch [Ger] *Mercedes 120.07 mph*
2nd Rudi Caracciola [Ger] *Alfa-Romeo*
3rd Hans Stuber [Ger] *Bugatti*
Fastest lap: Rene Dreyfus [Fr] *Maserati 130.39 mph*

EIFELRENNEN [EIFEL RACES] Nürburging 29 May
1st Rudi Caracciola [Ger] *Alfa-Romeo 70.7 mph*
2nd Rene Dreyfus [Fr] *Bugatti*
3rd Manfred von Brauchitsch [Ger] *Mercedes*
Fastest lap: Caracciola *72.8 mph*

INDIANAPOLIS 500 30 May
1st Fred Frame [USA] *Miller-Harry Hartz 104.144 mph*
2nd Howdy Wilcox [USA] *Lion Head*
3rd Cliff Bergere [USA] *Studebaker*
Fastest qualifier: Lou Moore [USA] *Boyle Valve 117.363 mph*

ITALIAN GRAND PRIX Monza 5 June
1st Tazio Nuvolari [It]/Giuseppe Campari [It] *Alfa-Romeo 104.13 mph*
2nd Luigi Fagioli [It]/Ernesto Maserati [It] *Maserati*
3rd Baconin Borzacchini [It]/Attilio Marinoni [It]/Rudi Caracciola [Ger] *Alfa-Romeo*
Fastest lap: Fagioi *112.22 mph*

FRENCH GRAND PRIX Rheims 3 July
1st Tazio Nuvolari [It] *Alfa-Romeo 92.26 mph*
2nd Baconin Borzacchini [It] *Alfa-Romeo*
3rd Rudi Caracciola [Ger] *Alfa-Romeo*
Fastest lap: Nuvolari *99.5 mph*

GERMAN GRAND PRIX Nürburging 7 July
1st Rudi Caracciola [Ger] *Alfa-Romeo 74.13 mph*
2nd Tazio Nuvolari [It] *Alfa-Romeo*
3rd Baconin Borzacchini [It] *Alfa-Romeo*
Fastest lap: Nuvolari *77.55 mph*

COPPA CIANO Montenero 31 July
1st Tazio Nuvolari [It] *Alfa-Romeo 53.91 mph*
2nd Baconin Borzacchini [It] *Alfa-Romeo*
3rd Giuseppe Campari [It] *Alfa-Romeo*
Fastest lap: Nuvolari *54.5 mph*

COPPA ACERBO Pescara 14 Aug
1st Tazio Nuvolari [It] *Alfa-Romeo 86.89 mph*
2nd Rudi Caracciola [Ger] *Alfa-Romeo*
3rd Louis Chiron [Mon] *Bugatti*
Fastest lap: Nuvolari *90.3 mph*

CZECHOSLOVAKIAN GRAND PRIX Brno 4 Sept
1st Louis Chiron [Mon] *Bugatti 67.67 mph*
2nd Luigi Fagioli [It] *Maserati*
3rd Tazio Nuvolari [It] *Alfa-Romeo*
Fastest lap: Chiron *73.73 mph*

MONZA GRAND PRIX 11 Sept
1st Rudi Caracciola [Ger] *Alfa-Romeo 110.8 mph*
2nd Luigi Fagioli [It] *Maserati*
3rd Tazio Nuvolari [It] *Alfa-Romeo*
Fastest lap: Nuvolari *113.7 mph*

MARSEILLES GRAND PRIX 25 Sept
1st Raymond Sommer [Fr] *Alfa-Romeo 109.14 mph*
2nd Tazio Nuvolari [It] *Alfa-Romeo*
3rd Guy Moll [Fr] *Bugatti*
Fastest lap: Nuvolari *124.11 mph*

1933

US National Champion: Louie Meyer
Fastest Man on Earth: Malcolm Campbell [GB] *Campbell-Special Bluebird 272.46 mph*

PAU GRAND PRIX 19 Feb
1st Marcel Lehoux [Fr] *Bugatti 45.38 mph*
2nd Guy Moll [Fr] *Bugatti*
3rd Philippe Etancelin [Fr] *Alfa-Romeo*
Fastest lap: Etancelin *47.79 mph*

TUNIS GRAND PRIX Carthage 29 March
1st Tazio Nuvolari [It] *Alfa-Romeo 83.81 mph*
2nd Baconin Borzacchini [It] *Alfa-Romeo*
3rd Goffredo Zehender [It] *Maserati*
Fastest lap: Nuvolari *92.58 mph*

MILLE MIGLIA Brescia 9-10 April
1st Tazio Nuvolari [It]/Compagnoni [It] *Alfa-Romeo 67.85 mph*
2nd Luigi Castelbarco [It]/Franco Cortese [It] *Alfa-Romeo*
3rd Piero Taruffi [It]/Lelio Pellegrini [It] *Alfa-Romeo*

MONACO GRAND PRIX Monte Carlo 23 April
1st Achille Varzi [It] *Bugatti 57.04 mph*
2nd Baconin Borzacchini [It] *Alfa-Romeo*
3rd Rene Dreyfus [Fr] *Bugatti*
Fastest lap: Varzi *59.77 mph*

TRIPOLI GRAND PRIX Mellaha 7 May
1st Achille Varzi [It] *Bugatti 104.76 mph*
2nd Tazio Nuvolari [It] *Alfa-Romeo*
3rd Henry Birkin [GB] *Maserati*
Fastest lap: Varzi *109.35 mph*

AVUSRENNEN [AVUS RACES] Berlin 21 May
1st Achille Varzi [It] *Bugatti 128.48 mph*
2nd Count Stanislas Czaykowski [Pol] *Bugatti*
3rd Tazio Nuvolari [It]/Baconin Borzacchini [It] *Alfa-Romeo*
Fastest lap: Czaykowsi *137.77 mph*

EIFELRENNEN [EIFEL RACES] Nürburging 28 May
1st Tazio Nuvolari [It] *Alfa-Romeo 70.48 mph*
2nd Manfred von Brauchitsch [Ger] *Mercedes*
3rd Piero Taruffi [It] *Alfa-Romeo*
Fastest lap: not available

TARGA FLORIO Piccolo Circuito Madonie 28 May
1st Marquis Antonio Brivio [It] *Alfa-Romeo 47.56 mph*
2nd Renato Balestrero [It] *Alfa-Romeo*
3rd Guglielmo Carraroli [It] *Alfa-Romeo*
Fastest lap: Baconin Borzacchini [It] *Alfa-Romeo 49.43 mph*

INDIANAPOLIS 500 30 May
1st Louie Meyer [USA] *Tydol 104.162 mph*
2nd Wilbur Shaw [USA] *Mallory*
3rd Lou Moore [USA] *Foreman Axle*
Fastest qualifier: Bill Cummings [USA] *Boyle Products 118.521 mph*

FRENCH GRAND PRIX Montlhéry 11 June
1st Giuseppe Campari [It] *Maserati 81.52 mph*
2nd Philippe Etancelin [Fr] *Alfa-Romeo*
3rd George Eyston [GB] *Alfa-Romeo*
Fastest lap: Campari *86.6 mph*

MARNE GRAND PRIX Rheims 2 July
1st Philippe Etancelin [Fr] *Alfa-Romeo 90.59 mph*
2nd Jean-Pierre Wimille [Fr] *Alfa-Romeo*
3rd Raymond Sommer [Fr] *Alfa-Romeo*
Fastest lap: Giuseppe Campari [It] *Maserati 96 mph*

BELGIAN GRAND PRIX Spa 9 July
1st Tazio Nuvolari [It] *Maserati 89.23 mph*
2nd Achille Varzi [It] *Bugatti*
3rd Rene Dreyfus [Fr] *Bugatti*
Fastest lap: Nuvolari *92.33 mph*

COPPA CIANO Montenero 30 July
1st Tazio Nuvolari [It] *Maserati 54.18 mph*
2nd Marquis Antonio Brivio [It] *Alfa-Romeo*
3rd Giuseppe Campari [It] *Alfa-Romeo*
Fastest lap: Nuvolari *55.38 mph*

NICE GRAND PRIX 6 Aug
1st Tazio Nuvolari [It] *Maserati 64.56 mph*
2nd Rene Dreyfus [Fr] *Bugatti*
3rd Guy Moll [Fr] *Alfa-Romeo*
Fastest lap: Nuvolari *67.19 mph*

COPPA ACERBO Pescara 13 Aug
1st Luigi Fagioli [It] *Alfa-Romeo 88.03 mph*
2nd Tazio Nuvolari [It] *Maserati*
3rd Piero Taruffi [It] *Maserati*
Fastest lap: Nuvolari *90.4 mph*

COMMINGES GRAND PRIX 20 Aug
1st Luigi Fagioli [It] *Alfa-Romeo 89.08 mph*
2nd Jean-Pierre Wimille [Fr] *Alfa-Romeo*
3rd Guy Moll [Fr] *Alfa-Romeo*
Fastest lap: Fagioli *91.51 mph*

MARSEILLES GRAND PRIX 27 Aug
1st Louis Chiron [Mon] *Alfa-Romeo 111.22 mph*
2nd Luigi Fagioli [It] *Alfa-Romeo*
3rd Guy Moll [Fr] *Alfa-Romeo*
Fastest lap: Chiron *121.57 mph*

ITALIAN GRAND PRIX Monza 10 Sept
1st Luigi Fagioli [It] *Alfa-Romeo 108.58 mph*
2nd Tazio Nuvolari [It] *Maserati*
3rd Goffredo Zehender [It] *Maserati*
Fastest lap: Fagioli *115.82 mph*

MONZA GRAND PRIX 10 Sept
1st Marcel Lehoux [Fr] *Bugatti 108.99 mph*
2nd Guy Moll [Fr] *Alfa-Romeo*
3rd Felice Bonetto [It] *Alfa-Romeo*
Fastest lap: Count Stanislas Czaykowski [Pol] *Bugatti 116.81 mph*

CZECHOSLOVAKIAN GRAND PRIX Brno 17 Sept
1st Louis Chiron [Mon] *Alfa-Romeo 63.57 mph*
2nd Luigi Fagioli [It] *Alfa-Romeo*
3rd Jean-Pierre Wimille [Fr] *Alfa-Romeo*
Fastest lap: Chiron *70.8 mph*

SPANISH GRAND PRIX Lasarte 24 Sept
1st Louis Chiron [Mon] *Alfa-Romeo 83.32 mph*
2nd Luigi Fagioli [It] *Alfa-Romeo*
3rd Marcel Lehoux [Fr] *Bugatti*
Fastest lap: Tazio Nuvolari [It] *Maserati 96.59 mph*

1934

US National Champion: Bill Cummings
Fastest Man on Earth: Malcolm Campbell (>1933)

MONACO GRAND PRIX Monte Carlo 2 April
1st Guy Moll [Fr] *Alfa-Romeo 55.86 mph*
2nd Louis Chiron [Mon] *Alfa-Romeo*
3rd Rene Dreyfus [Fr] *Bugatti*
Fastest lap: Count Felice Trossi [It] *Alfa-Romeo 59.7 mph*

MILLE MIGLIA Brescia 8 April
1st Achille Varzi [It]/A. Bignami [It] *Alfa-Romeo 71.44 mph*
2nd Tazio Nuvolari [It]/Eugenio Siena [It] *Alfa-Romeo*
3rd Louis Chiron [Mon]/Archimede Rosa [It] *Alfa-Romeo*

TARGA FLORIO Piccolo Circuito Madonie 20 May
1st Achille Varzi [It] *Alfa-Romeo 43.01 mph*
2nd Nando Barbieri [It] *Alfa-Romeo*
3rd Costantino Magistri [It] *Alfa-Romeo*
Fastest lap: Pietro Ghersi [It] *Alfa-Romeo 45.65 mph*

AVUSRENNEN [AVUS RACES] Berlin 27 May
1st Guy Moll [Fr] *Alfa-Romeo 127.5 mph*
2nd Achille Varzi [It] *Alfa-Romeo*
3rd August Momberger [Ger] *Auto Union*
Fastest lap: Momberger *140.33 mph*

INDIANAPOLIS 500 30 May
1st Bill Cummings [USA] *Boyle Products 104.863 mph*
2nd Mauri Rose [USA] *Leon Duray*
3rd Lou Moore [USA] *Foreman Axle*
Fastest qualifier Kelly Petillo [USA] *Red Lion 119.329 mph*

EIFELRENNEN [EIFEL RACES] Nürburging 3 June
1st Manfred von Brauchitsch [Ger] *Mercedes-Benz 76.12 mph*
2nd Hans Stuck [Ger] *Auto Union*
3rd Louis Chiron [Mon] *Alfa-Romeo*
Fastest lap: von Brauchitsch *79 mph*

FRENCH GRAND PRIX Montlhéry 1 July
1st Louis Chiron [Mon] *Alfa-Romeo 85.55 mph*
2nd Achille Varzi [It] *Alfa-Romeo*
3rd Count Felice Trossi [It]/Guy Moll [Fr] *Alfa-Romeo*
Fastest lap: Chiron *91.44 mph*

GERMAN GRAND PRIX Nürburging 20 July
1st Hans Stuck [Ger] *Auto Union 76.39 mph*
2nd Luigi Fagioli [It] *Mercedes-Benz*
3rd Louis Chiron [Mon] *Alfa-Romeo*
Fastest lap: Stuck *79.29 mph*

BELGIAN GRAND PRIX Spa 29 July
1st Rene Dreyfus [Fr] *Bugatti 86.91 mph*
2nd Marquis Antonio Brivio [It] *Bugatti*
3rd Raymond Sommer [Fr] *Maserati*
Fastest lap: Brivio *96.38 mph*

COPPA ACERBO Pescara 15 Aug
1st Luigi Fagioli [It] *Mercedes-Benz 80.26 mph*
2nd Tazio Nuvolari [It] *Maserati*
3rd Marquis Antonio Brivio [It] *Bugatti*
Fastest lap: Guy Moll [Fr] *Alfa-Romeo 90.5 mph*

SWISS GRAND PRIX Bremgarten 26 Aug
1st Hans Stuck [Ger] *Auto Union 87.21 mph*
2nd August Momberger [Ger] *Auto Union*
3rd Rene Dreyfus [Fr] *Bugatti*
Fastest lap: Momberger *94.42 mph*

ITALIAN GRAND PRIX Monza 9 Sept
1st Rudi Caracciola [Ger]/Luigi Fagioli [It] *Mercedes-Benz 65.37 mph*
2nd Hans Stuck [Ger]/Prince Hermann zu Leiningen [Ger] *Auto Union*
3rd Count Felice Trossi [It]/Gianfranco Comotti [It] *Alfa-Romeo*
Fastest lap: Stuck *72.59 mph*

SPANISH GRAND PRIX Lasarte 23 Sept
1st Luigi Fagioli [It] *Mercedes-Benz 97.13 mph*
2nd Rudi Caracciola [Ger] *Mercedes-Benz*
3rd Tazio Nuvolari [It] *Bugatti*
Fastest lap: Hans Stuck [Ger] *Auto Union 101.96 mph*

CZECHOSLOVAKIAN GRAND PRIX Brno 30 Sept
1st Hans Stuck [Ger] *Auto Union 79.21 mph*
2nd Luigi Fagioli [It] *Mercedes-Benz*
3rd Tazio Nuvolari [It] *Maserati*
Fastest lap: Fagioli *81.23 mph*

1935

US National Champion: Kelly Petillo
Fastest Man on Earth: Malcolm Campbell [GB] *Campbell-Special Bluebird 301.13 mph*

MILLE MIGLIA Brescia 14 April
1st Carlo Pintacuda [It]/Marquis della Stufa *Alfa-Romeo 71.72 mph*
2nd Mario Tadini Chiari [It] *Alfa-Romeo*
3rd Giovanni Battaglia [It]/B. Tuffanelli [It] *Alfa-Romeo*

MONACO GRAND PRIX Monte Carlo 22 April
1st Luigi Fagioli [It] *Mercedes-Benz 58.17 mph*
2nd Rene Dreyfus [Fr] *Alfa-Romeo*
3rd Marquis Antonio Brivio [It] *Alfa-Romeo*
Fastest lap: Fagioli *60.08 mph*

TARGA FLORIO Piccolo Circuito Madonie 28 April
1st Marquis Antonio Brivio [It] *Alfa-Romeo 49.18 mph*
2nd Louis Chiron [Mon] *Alfa-Romeo*
3rd Nando Barbieri [It] *Maserati*
Fastest lap: Brivio *49.6 mph*

TUNIS GRAND PRIX Carthage 5 May
1st Achille Varzi [It] *Auto Union 101.2 mph*
2nd Jean-Pierre Wimille [Fr] *Bugatti*
3rd Philippe Etancelin [Fr] *Maserati*
Fastest lap: Varzi *105.15 mph*

TRIPOLI GRAND PRIX Mellaha 12 May
1st Rudi Caracciola [Ger] *Mercedes-Benz 123.03 mph*
2nd Achille Varzi [It] *Auto Union*
3rd Luigi Fagioli [It] *Mercedes-Benz*
Fastest lap: Caracciola *136.81 mph*

AVUSRENNEN [AVUS RACES] Berlin 26 May
1st Luigi Fagioli [It] *Mercedes-Benz 148.83 mph*
2nd Louis Chiron [Mon] *Alfa-Romeo*
3rd Achille Varzi [It] *Auto Union*
Fastest lap: Hans Stuck [Ger] *Auto Union 161.88 mph*

INDIANAPOLIS 500 30 May
1st Kelly Petillo [USA] *Gilmore Speedway 106.24 mph*
2nd Wilbur Shaw [USA] *Gil Pirrung*
3rd Bill Cummings [USA] *Boyle Products*
Fastest qualifier: Rex Mays [USA] *Gilmore 120.736 mph*

EIFELRENNEN [EIFEL RACES] Nürburging 3 June
1st Rudi Caracciola [Ger] *Mercedes-Benz 72.8 mph*
2nd Bernd Rosemeyer [Ger] *Auto Union*
3rd Louis Chiron [Mon] *Alfa-Romeo*
Fastest lap: Caracciola *75.6 mph*

PENYA RHIN GRAND PRIX Montjuich Park 17 June
1st Luigi Fagioli [It] *Mercedes-Benz 66.99 mph*
2nd Rudi Caracciola [Ger] *Mercedes-Benz*
3rd Tazio Nuvolari [It] *Alfa-Romeo*
Fastest lap: Caracciola *68.94 mph*

FRENCH GRAND PRIX Montlhéry 23 June
1st Rudi Caracciola [Ger] *Mercedes-Benz 77.39 mph*
2nd Manfred von Brauchitsch [Ger] *Mercedes-Benz*
3rd Goffredo Zehender [It] *Maserati*
Fastest lap: Tazio Nuvolari [It] *Alfa-Romeo 85 mph*

BELGIAN GRAND PRIX Spa 14 July
1st Rudi Caracciola [Ger] *Mercedes-Benz 97.8 mph*
2nd Manfred von Brauchitsch [Ger]/Luigi Fagioli [It]
Mercedes-Benz
3rd Louis Chiron [Mon] *Alfa-Romeo*
Fastest lap: von Brauchitsch *103.7 mph*

GERMAN GRAND PRIX Nürburging 28 July
1st Tazio Nuvolari [It] *Alfa-Romeo 75.43 mph*
2nd Hans Stuck [Ger] *Auto Union*
3rd Rudi Caracciola [Ger] *Mercedes-Benz*
Fastest lap: Manfred von Brauchitsch [Ger] *Mercedes-Benz 80.73 mph*

COPPA ACERBO Pescara 15 Aug
1st Achille Varzi [It] *Auto Union 86.6 mph*
2nd Bernd Rosemeyer [Ger] *Auto Union*
3rd Marquis Antonio Brivio [It] *Alfa-Romeo*
Fastest lap: Varzi *90.9 mph*

SWISS GRAND PRIX Bremgarten 25 Aug
1st Rudi Caracciola [Ger] *Mercedes-Benz 89.95 mph*
2nd Luigi Fagioli [It] *Mercedes-Benz*
3rd Bernd Rosemeyer [Ger] *Auto Union*
Fastest lap: Fagioli *99.5 mph*

ITALIAN GRAND PRIX Monza 8 Sept
1st Hans Stuck [Ger] *Auto Union 85.17 mph*
2nd Rene Dreyfus [Fr]/Tazio Nuvolari [It] *Alfa-Romeo*
3rd Paul Pietsch [Ger]/Bernd Rosemeyer [Ger] *Auto Union*
Fastest lap: Nuvolari *90.77 mph*

SPANISH GRAND PRIX Lasarte 22 Sept
1st Rudi Caracciola [Ger] *Mercedes-Benz 101.92 mph*
2nd Luigi Fagioli [It] *Mercedes-Benz*
3rd Manfred von Brauchitsch [Ger] *Mercedes-Benz*
Fastest lap: Achille Varzi [It] *Auto Union 108.11 mph*

CZECHOSLOVAKIAN GRAND PRIX Brno 29 Sept
1st Bernd Rosemeyer [Ger] *Auto Union 82.39 mph*
2nd Tazio Nuvolari [It] *Alfa-Romeo*
3rd Louis Chiron [Mon] *Alfa-Romeo*
Fastest lap: Achille Varzi [It] *Auto Union 85.21 mph*

BRITISH (DONINGTON) GRAND PRIX 6 Oct
1st Richard Shuttleworth [GB] *Alfa-Romeo 63.97 mph*
2nd Earl Howe [GB] *Bugatti*
3rd Charlie Martin [GB] *Bugatti*
Fastest lap: not available

1936

US National Champion: Mauri Rose
Fastest Man on Earth: Malcolm Campbell (>1935)

MILLE MIGLIA Brescia 5 April
1st Marquis Antonio Brivio [It]/Ongaro [It] *Alfa-Romeo 76.01 mph*
2nd Giuseppe Farina [It]/Meazza [It] *Alfa-Romeo*
3rd Carlo Pintacuda [It]/Stefani [It] *Alfa-Romeo*

MONACO GRAND PRIX Monte Carlo 13 April
1st Rudi Caracciola [Ger] *Mercedes-Benz 51.69 mph*
2nd Achille Varzi [It] *Auto Union*
3rd Hans Stuck [Ger] *Auto Union*
Fastest lap: Stuck *56.01 mph*

TRIPOLI GRAND PRIX Mellaha 10 May
1st Achille Varzi [It] *Auto Union 129.01 mph*
2nd Hans Stuck [Ger] *Auto Union*
3rd Luigi Fagioli [It] *Mercedes-Benz*
Fastest lap: Varzi *141.29 mph*

TUNIS GRAND PRIX Carthage 17 May
1st Rudi Caracciola [Ger] *Mercedes-Benz 99.62 mph*
2nd Carlo Pintacuda [It] *Alfa-Romeo*
3rd Jean-Pierre Wimille [Fr] *Bugatti*
Fastest lap: Bernd Rosemeyer [Ger] *Auto Union 103.79 mph*

INDIANAPOLIS 500 30 May
1st Louie Meyer [USA] *Ring Free 109.069 mph*
2nd Ted Horn [USA] *Miller-Hartz*
3rd Doc MacKenzie [USA] *Gilmore Speedway*
Fastest qualifier: Rex Mays [USA] *Gilmore 119.644 mph*

PENYA RHIN GRAND PRIX Montjuich Park 7 June
1st Tazio Nuvolari [It] *Alfa-Romeo 69.21 mph*
2nd Rudi Caracciola [Ger] *Mercedes-Benz*
3rd Giuseppe Farina [It] *Alfa-Romeo*
Fastest lap: Nuvolari *71.85 mph*

EIFELRENNEN [EIFEL RACES] Nürburging 14 June
1st Bernd Rosemeyer [Ger] *Auto Union 72.71 mph*
2nd Tazio Nuvolari [It] *Alfa-Romeo*
3rd Marquis Antonio Brivio [It] *Alfa-Romeo*
Fastest lap: Rosemeyer *74.46 mph*

HUNGARIAN GRAND PRIX Budapest 21 June
1st Tazio Nuvolari [It] *Alfa-Romeo 69.1 mph*
2nd Bernd Rosemeyer [Ger] *Auto Union*
3rd Achille Varzi [It] *Auto Union*
Fastest lap: Nuvolari *71.84 mph*

FRENCH GRAND PRIX Montlhéry 28 June
1st Jean-Pierre Wimille [Fr]/Raymond Sommer [Fr] *Bugatti 77.85 mph*
2nd M. Paris [Fr]/Marcel Mongin [Fr] *Delahaye*
3rd Robert Brunet [Fr]/Goffredo Zehender [It] *Delahaye*
Fastest lap: Rene Dreyfus [Fr] *Talbot 83.19 mph*

MILAN CIRCUIT 28 June
1st Tazio Nuvolari [It] *Alfa-Romeo 60.02 mph*
2nd Achille Varzi [It] *Auto Union*
3rd Giuseppe Farina [It] *Alfa-Romeo*
Fastest lap: Varzi *62.26 mph*

GERMAN GRAND PRIX Nürburging 26 July
1st Bernd Rosemeyer [Ger] *Auto Union 81.8 mph*
2nd Hans Stuck [Ger] *Auto Union*
3rd Marquis Antonio Brivio [It] *Alfa-Romeo*
Fastest lap: Rosemeyer *85.52 mph*

COPPA CIANO Livorno 2 Aug
1st Tazio Nuvolari [It] *Alfa-Romeo 74.8 mph*
2nd Marquis Antonio Brivio [It] *Alfa-Romeo*
3rd Rene Dreyfus [Fr] *Alfa-Romeo*
Fastest lap: Nuvolari *77.05 mph*

COPPA ACERBO Pescara 15 Aug
1st Bernd Rosemeyer [Ger] *Auto Union 86.48 mph*
2nd Ernst von Delius [Ger] *Auto Union*
3rd Achille Varzi [It] *Auto Union*
Fastest lap: Varzi *89.04 mph*

SWISS GRAND PRIX Bremgarten 23 Aug
1st Bernd Rosemeyer [Ger] *Auto Union 100.45 mph*
2nd Achille Varzi [It] *Auto Union*
3rd Hans Stuck [Ger] *Auto Union*
Fastest lap: Rosemeyer *105.42 mph*

ITALIAN GRAND PRIX Monza 13 Sept
1st Bernd Rosemeyer [Ger] *Auto Union 84.59 mph*
2nd Tazio Nuvolari [It] *Alfa-Romeo*
3rd Ernst von Delius [Ger] *Auto Union*
Fastest lap: Rosemeyer *87.18 mph*

BRITISH (DONINGTON) GRAND PRIX 3 Oct
1st Hans Rusch [Switz]/Richard Seaman [GB] *Alfa-Romeo 69.23 mph*
2nd Charlie Martin [GB] *Alfa-Romeo*
3rd Peter Whitehead [GB]/Peter Walker [GB] *ERA*
Fastest lap: not available

TARGA FLORIO Piccolo Circuito Madonie 20 Dec
1st Costantino Magistri [It] *Lancia Augusta 42.12 mph*
2nd Salvatore di Pietro [It] *Lancia Augusta*
3rd Gladio [It] *Lancia Augusta*
Fastest lap: Magistri *41.66 mph*

1937

US National Champion: Wilbur Shaw
Fastest Man on Earth: George Eyston [GB] *Thunderbolt 312 mph*

MILLE MIGLIA Brescia 4–5 April
1st Carlo Pintacuda [It]/Mambelli [It] *Alfa-Romeo 7 1.71 mph*
2nd Giuseppe Farina [It]/Meazza [It] *Alfa-Romeo*
3rd Laury Schell [Fr]/Rene Carriere [Fr] *Delahaye*

TRIPOLI GRAND PRIX Mellaha 9 May
1st Hermann Lang [Ger] *Mercedes-Benz 134.25 mph*
2nd Bernd Rosemeyer [Ger] *Auto Union*
3rd Ernst von Delius [Ger] *Auto Union*
Fastest lap: Hans Stuck [Ger] *Auto Union 142.44 mph*

TARGA FLORIO Palermo 23 May
1st Francesco Severi [It] *Maserati 66.86 mph*
2nd Giovanni Lurani [It] *Maserati*
3rd Ettore Bianco [It] *Maserati*
Fastest lap: Giovanni Rocco [It] *Maserati 75.45 mph*

AVUSRENNEN [AVUS RACES] Berlin 30 May
1st Hermann Lang [Ger] *Mercedes-Benz 162.61 mph*
2nd Ernst von Delius [Ger] *Auto Union*
3rd Rudi Hasse [Ger] *Auto Union*
Fastest lap: Bernd Rosemeyer [Ger] *Auto Union 172.75 mph*

INDIANAPOLIS 500 31 May
1st Wilbur Shaw [USA] *Shaw-Gilmore 113.58 mph*
2nd Ralph Hepburn [USA] *Hamilton-Harris*
3rd Ted Horn [USA] *Miller-Harry Hartz*
Fastest qualifier: Jimmy Snyder [USA] *Sparks 125.287 mph*

EIFELRENNEN [EIFEL RACES] Nürburging 13 June
1st Bernd Rosemeyer [Ger] *Auto Union 82.95 mph*
2nd Rudi Caracciola [Ger] *Mercedes-Benz*
3rd Manfred von Brauchitsch [Ger] *Mercedes-Benz*
Fastest lap: Rosemeyer *85.13 mph*

VANDERBILT CUP Long Island 3 July
1st Bernd Rosemeyer [Ger] *Auto Union 82.56 mph*
2nd Richard Seaman [GB] *Mercedes-Benz*
3rd Rex Mays [USA] *Alfa-Romeo*
Fastest lap: Rudi Caracciola [Ger] *Mercedes-Benz 84.5 mph*

FRENCH GRAND PRIX Montlhéry 4 July
1st Louis Chiron [Mon] *Lago-Talbot 82.47 mph*
2nd Gianfranco Comotti [It] *Lago-Talbot*
3rd Albert Divo [Fr] *Lago-Talbot*
Fastest lap: Chiron *83.64 mph*

BELGIAN GRAND PRIX Spa 11 July
1st Rudi Hasse [Ger] *Auto Union 104.07 mph*
2nd Hans Stuck [Ger] *Auto Union*
3rd Hermann Lang [Ger] *Mercedes-Benz*
Fastest lap: Lang *108.8 mph*

GERMAN GRAND PRIX Nürburging 25 July
1st Rudi Caracciola [Ger] *Mercedes-Benz 82.77 mph*
2nd Manfred von Brauchitsch [Ger] *Mercedes-Benz*
3rd Bernd Rosemeyer [Ger] *Auto Union*
Fastest lap: Rosemeyer *85.57 mph*

MONACO GRAND PRIX Monte Carlo 8 Aug
1st Manfred von Brauchitsch [Ger] *Mercedes-Benz 62.35 mph*
2nd Rudi Caracciola [Ger] *Mercedes-Benz*
3rd Christian Kautz [Switz] *Mercedes-Benz*
Fastest lap: Caracciola *66.99 mph*

COPPA ACERBO Pescara 15 Aug
1st Bernd Rosemeyer [Ger] *Auto Union 87.61 mph*
2nd Manfred von Brauchitsch [Ger] *Mercedes-Benz*
3rd Hermann Muller [Ger] *Auto Union*
Fastest lap: Rosemeyer *92 mph*

SWISS GRAND PRIX Bremgarten 22 Aug
1st Rudi Caracciola [Ger] *Mercedes-Benz 98.61 mph*
2nd Hermann Lang [Ger] *Mercedes-Benz*
3rd Manfred von Brauchitsch [Ger] *Mercedes-Benz*
Fastest lap: Caracciola *107.14 (P)*

ITALIAN GRAND PRIX Livorno 12 Sept
1st Rudi Caracciola [Ger] *Mercedes-Benz 81.59 mph*
2nd Hermann Lang [Ger] *Mercedes-Benz*
3rd Bernd Rosemeyer [Ger] *Auto Union*
Fastest lap: Caracciola *84.5 mph*

CZECHOSLOVAKIAN GRAND PRIX Brno 26 Sept
1st Rudi Caracciola [Ger] *Mercedes-Benz 85.97 mph*
2nd Manfred von Brauchitsch [Ger] *Mercedes-Benz*
3rd Hermann Muller [Ger]/Bernd Rosemeyer [Ger] *Auto Union*
Fastest lap: Caracciola *94.89 mph*

BRITISH (DONINGTON) GRAND PRIX 2 Oct
1st Bernd Rosemeyer [Ger] *Auto Union 82.86 mph*
2nd Manfred von Brauchitsch [Ger] *Mercedes-Benz*
3rd Rudi Caracciola [Ger] *Mercedes-Benz*
Fastest lap: Rosemeyer/von Brauchitsch *85.52 mph*

1938

US National Champion: Floyd Roberts
Fastest Man on Earth: George Eyston [GB] *Thunderbolt 357.5 mph*

MILLE MIGLIA Brescia 3–4 April
1st Clémente Biondetti [It]/Stefani [It] *Alfa-Romeo 84.61 mph*
2nd Carlo Pintacuda [It]/Mambelli [It] *Alfa-Romeo*
3rd Piero Dusio [It]/Boninsegni [It] *Alfa-Romeo*

PAU GRAND PRIX 10 April
1st Rene Dreyfus [Fr] *Delahaye 54.64 mph*
2nd Rudi Caracciola [Ger]/Hermann Lang [Ger] *Mercedes-Benz*
3rd Gianfranco Comotti [It] *Delahaye*
Fastest lap: Caracciola *57.86 mph*

TARGA FLORIO Palermo 22 May
1st Giovanni Rocco [It] *Maserati 71.03 mph*
2nd 'Ralph' *Maserati*
3rd Luigi Villoresi [It] *Maserati*
Fastest lap: Marazza [It] *Maserati 74.23 mph*

INDIANAPOLIS 500 30 May
1st Floyd Roberts [USA] *Burd Piston Ring 117.2 mph*
2nd Wilbur Shaw [USA] *Wilbur Shaw*
3rd Chet Miller [USA] *I.B.E.W.*
Fastest qualifier: Ronney Householder [USA] *Thorne-Sparks 125.769 mph*

FRENCH GRAND PRIX Rheims 3 July
1st Manfred von Brauchitsch [Ger] *Mercedes-Benz 101.3 mph*
2nd Rudi Caracciola [Ger] *Mercedes-Benz*
3rd Hermann Lang [Ger] *Mercedes-Benz*
Fastest lap: Lang *105.87 mph*

GERMAN GRAND PRIX Nürburging 24 July
1st Richard Seaman [GB] *Mercedes-Benz 80.75 mph*
2nd Hermann Lang [Ger]/Rudi Caracciola [Ger] *Mercedes-Benz*
3rd Hans Stuck [Ger] *Auto Union*
Fastest lap: Seaman *83.76 mph*

COPPA CIANO Livorno 7 Aug
1st Hermann Lang [Ger] *Mercedes-Benz 85.94 mph*
2nd Giuseppe Farina [It] *Alfa-Romeo*
3rd Jean-pierre Wimille [Fr]/Clémente Biondetti [It] *Alfa-Romeo*
Fastest lap: Lang/Manfred von Brauchitsch [Ger] *Mercedes-Benz 89.17 mph*

COPPA ACERBO Pescara 14 Aug
1st Rudi Caracciola [Ger] *Mercedes-Benz 83.69 mph*
2nd Giuseppe Farina [It] *Alfa-Romeo*
3rd C. Belmondo [It] *Alfa-Romeo*
Fastest lap: Luigi Villoresi [It] *Maserati 87.79 mph*

SWISS GRAND PRIX Bremgarten 21 Aug
1st Rudi Caracciola [Ger] *Mercedes-Benz 89.44 mph*
2nd Richard Seaman [GB] *Mercedes-Benz*
3rd Manfred von Brauchitsch [Ger] *Mercedes-Benz*
Fastest lap: Seaman *95.35 mph*

ITALIAN GRAND PRIX Monza 11 Sept
1st Tazio Nuvolari [It] *Auto Union 96.7 mph*
2nd Giuseppe Farina [It] *Alfa-Romeo*
3rd Rudi Caracciola [Ger]/Manfred von Brauchitsch [Ger] *Mercedes-Benz*
Fastest lap: Hermann Lang [Ger] *Mercedes-Benz 101.38 mph*

BRITISH (DONINGTON) GRAND PRIX 22 Oct
1st Tazio Nuvolari [It] *Auto Union 80.49 mph*
2nd Hermann Lang [Ger] *Mercedes-Benz*
3rd Richard Seaman [GB] *Mercedes-Benz*
Fastest lap: Nuvolari *83.71 mph*

1939

US National Champion: Wilbur Shaw
Fastest Man on Earth: John Cobb [GB] *Railton Mobil Special 369.74 mph*

PAU GRAND PRIX 2 April
1st Hermann Lang [Ger] *Mercedes-Benz 56.09 mph*
2nd Manfred von Brauchitsch [Ger] *Mercedes-Benz*
3rd Philippe Etancelin [Fr] *Talbot*
Fastest lap: von Brauchitsch *57.83 mph*

TRIPOLI GRAND PRIX Mellaha 7 May
1st Hermann Lang [Ger] *Mercedes-Benz 122.91 mph*
2nd Rudi Caracciola [Ger] *Mercedes-Benz*
3rd Emilio Villoresi [It] *Alfa-Romeo*
Fastest lap: Lang *33.5 mph*

TARGA FLORIO Palermo 14 May
1st Luigi Villoresi [It] *Maserati 84.79 mph*
2nd Piero Taruffi [It] *Maserati*
3rd Guido Barbieri [It] *Maserati*
Fastest lap: Villoresi *87.92 mph*

EIFELRENNEN [EIFEL RACES] Nürburging 21 May
1st Hermann Lang [Ger] *Mercedes-Benz 84.14 mph*
2nd Tazio Nuvolari [It] *Auto Union*
3rd Rudi Caracciola [Ger] *Mercedes-Benz*
Fastest lap: Lang *86 mph*

INDIANAPOLIS 500 30 May
1st Wilbur Shaw [USA] *Boyle Racing Headquarters 115.035 mph*
2nd Jimmy Snyder [USA] *Thorne Engineering*
3rd Cliff Bergere [USA] *Offenhauser*
Fastest qualifier: Snyder *130.138 mph*

BELGIAN GRAND PRIX Spa 26 June
1st Hermann Lang [Ger] *Mercedes-Benz 94.39 mph*
2nd Rudi Hasse [Ger] *Auto Union*
3rd Manfred von Brauchitsch [Ger] *Mercedes-Benz*
Fastest lap: Lang *109.12 mph*

FRENCH GRAND PRIX Rheims 9 July
1st Hermann Muller [Ger] *Auto Union 105.25 mph*
2nd Georg Meier [Ger] *Auto Union*
3rd R. le Begue [Fr] *Talbot*
Fastest lap: Hermann Lang [Ger] *Mercedes-Benz 114.87 mph*

GERMAN GRAND PRIX Nürburging 23 July
1st Rudi Caracciola [Ger] *Mercedes-Benz 75.12 mph*
2nd Hermann Muller [Ger] *Auto Union*
3rd Paul Pietsch [It] *Maserati*
Fastest lap: Caracciola *81.66 mph*

SWISS GRAND PRIX Bremgarten 20 Aug
1st Hermann Lang [Ger] *Mercedes-Benz 96.02 mph*
2nd Rudi Caracciola [Ger] *Mercedes-Benz*
3rd Manfred von Brauchitsch [Ger] *Mercedes-Benz*
Fastest lap: Caracciola *104.32 mph*

YUGOSLAV GRAND PRIX Belgrade 3 Sept
1st Tazio Nuvolari [It] *Auto Union 81.21 mph*
2nd Manfred von Brauchitsch [Ger] *Mercedes-Benz*
3rd Hermann Muller [Ger] *Auto Union*
Fastest lap: Nuvolari/von Brauchitsch *83.9 mph*
Although the official Mille Miglia was not run this year, an unofficial race did take place, from Tobruk to Tripoli.

1940

US National Champion: Rex Mays
Fastest Man on Earth: John Cobb (>1939)

MILLE MIGLIA (GRAN PREMIO [GRAND PRIX] DELLA MILLE MIGLIA) Brescia 28 April
1st Huschke von Hanstein [Ger]/Walter Baumer [Ger] *BMW 104.2 mph*
2nd Giuseppe Farina [It]/Mambelli [It] *Alfa-Romeo*
3rd Brudes [Ger]/Roese [Ger] *BMW*

TRIPOLI GRAND PRIX Mellaha 12 May
1st Giuseppe Farina [It] *Alfa-Romeo 128.22 mph*
2nd Clémente Biondetti [It] *Alfa-Romeo*
3rd Count Felice Trossi [It] *Alfa-Romeo*
Fastest lap: not available

TARGA FLORIO Palermo 23 May
1st Luigi Villoresi [It] *Maserati 88.42 mph*
2nd Franco Cortese [It] *Maserati*
3rd Giovanni Rocco [It] *Maserati*
Fastest lap: Villoresi *91.7 mph*

INDIANAPOLIS 500 30 May
1st Wilbur Shaw [USA] *Boyle Racing Headquarters* 114.277 mph
2nd Rex Mays [USA] *Bowes Seal Fast*
3rd Mauri Rose [USA] *Elgin Piston Pin*
Fastest qualifier: Mays *127.85 mph*

US National Champion: Rex Mays
Fastest Man on Earth: John Cobb (>1939)

INDIANAPOLIS 500 30 May
1st Floyd Davis [USA]/Mauri Rose [USA] *Noc-Out Hose Clamp 115.117 mph*
2nd Rex Mays [USA] *Bowes Seal Fast*
3rd Ted Horn [USA] *T.E.C.*
Fastest qualifier Mauri Rose [USA] *Elgin Piston Pin 128.691 mph*

Fastest Man on Earth: John Cobb (>1939)

COUPE ROBERT BENOIST Paris 9 Sept
1st Amédée Gordini [Fr] *Simca 58.85 mph*
2nd Brunot [Fr] *Riley*
3rd Boucard [Fr] *Salmson*
Fastest lap: Gordini *60.5 mph*

COUPE DE LA LIBERATION Paris 9 Sept
1st Henri Louveau [Fr] *Maserati 60.99 mph*
2nd Veuillet [Fr] *MG*
3rd Lescaud [Fr] *Amilcar*
Fastest lap: Louveau *66.2 mph*

COUPE DES PRISONNIERS Paris 9 Sept
1st Jean-Pierre Wimille [Fr] *Bugatti 70.1 mph*
2nd Raymond Sommer [Fr] *Talbot*
3rd Chabaud [Fr] *Delahaye*
Fastest lap: Wimille *72 mph*

US National Champion: Ted Horn
Fastest Man on Earth: John Cobb (>1939)

INDIANAPOLIS 500 30 May
1st George Robson [USA] *Thorne Engineering 114.82 mph*
2nd Jimmy Jackson [USA] *Jimmy Jackson*
3rd Ted Horn [USA] *Boyle Maserati*
Fastest qualifier Ralph Hepburn [USA] *Novi Governor 133.944 mph*

GRAND PRIX DES NATIONS Geneva 21 July
1st Giuseppe Farina [It] *Alfa-Romeo 64.1 mph*
2nd Count Felice Trossi [It] *Alfa-Romeo*
3rd Jean-Pierre Wimille [Fr] *Alfa-Romeo*
Fastest lap: Wimille *68.76 mph*

CIRCUIT OF TURIN 4 Sept
1st Achille Varzi [It] *Alfa-Romeo 64.62 mph*
2nd Jean-Pierre Wimille [Fr] *Alfa-Romeo*
3rd Raymond Sommer [Fr] *Maserati*
Fastest lap: Wimille *73.58 mph*

CIRCUIT OF MILAN 29 Sept
1st Count Felice Trossi [It] *Alfa-Romeo 55.59 mph*
2nd Achille Varzi [It] *Alfa-Romeo*
3rd Consalvo Sanesi [It] *Alfa-Romeo*
Fastest lap: Varzi/Giuseppe Farina [It] *Alfa-Romeo 56.7 mph*

US National Champion: Ted Horn
Fastest Man on Earth: John Cobb [GB] *Railton Mobil Special 394.19 mph*

INDIANAPOLIS 500 30 May
1st Mauri Rose [USA] *Blue Crown Spark Plug 116.338 mph*
2nd Bill Holland [USA] *Blue Crown Spark Plug*
3rd Ted Horn [USA] *Bennett*
Fastest qualifier: Holland *128.756 mph*

SWISS GRAND PRIX Bremgarten 8 June
1st Jean-Pierre Wimille [Fr] *Alfa-Romeo 95.42 mph*
2nd Achille Varzi [It] *Alfa-Romeo*
3rd Count Felice Trossi [It] *Alfa-Romeo*
Fastest lap: Raymond Sommer [Fr] *Maserati 97.03 mph*

MILLE MIGLIA Brescia 21–22 June
1st Clémente Biondetti [It]/Emilio Romano [It] *Alfa-Romeo 70.14 mph*
2nd Tazio Nuvolari [It]/Carena [It] *Cisitalia*
3rd Inigo Bernabei [It]/Pacini [It] *Cistalia*

BELGIAN (EUROPEAN) GRAND PRIX Spa 29 June
1st Jean-Pierre Wimille [Fr] *Alfa-Romeo 95.28 mph*
2nd Achille Varzi [It] *Alfa-Romeo*
3rd Count Felice Trossi [It] *Alfa-Romeo*
Fastest lap: Wimille *101.94 mph*

BARI GRAND PRIX 13 July
1st Achille Varzi [It] *Alfa-Romeo 65.1 mph*
2nd Consalvo Sanesi [It] *Alfa-Romeo*
3rd N. Grieco [It] *Maserati*
Fastest lap: Varzi *70.68 mph*

ITALIAN GRAND PRIX Milan 7 Sept
1st Count Felice Trossi [It] *Alfa-Romeo 70.29 mph*
2nd Achille Varzi [It] *Alfa-Romeo*
3rd Consalvo Sanesi [It] *Alfa-Romeo*
Fastest lap: Trossi *74.16 mph*

FRENCH GRAND PRIX Lyons 21 Sept
1st Louis Chiron [Mon] Talbot *78.09 mph*
2nd Henri Louveau [Fr] *Maserati*
3rd E. Chaboud [Fr] *Lago-Talbot*
Fastest lap: Luigi Villoresi [It] *Maserati*/Alberto Ascari [It] *Maserati*/Baron Emanuel de Graffenried [Switz] *Maserati 82.4 mph*

US National Champion: Ted Horn
Fastest Man on Earth: John Cobb (>1947)

TARGA FLORIO One circuit of Sicily 4 April
1st Clémente Biondetti [It]/Prince Igor Troubetzkoi [It] *Ferrari 55.16 mph*
2nd Piero Taruffi [It]/Rabbia [It] *Cisitalia*
3rd Adolfo Macchieraldo [It]/Antonio Savio [It] *Cisitalia*

MILLE MIGLIA Brescia 1–2 May
1st Clémente Biondetti [It]/Navone [It] *Ferrari 75.76 mph*
2nd Comirato [It]/Dumas *Fiat*
3rd F. Apruzzi [It]/A. Apruzzi [It] *Fiat*

MONACO GRAND PRIX Monte Carlo 16 May
1st Giuseppe Farina [It] *Maserati 59.61 mph*
2nd Louis Chiron [Mon] *Talbot*
3rd Baron Emanuel de Graffenried [Switz] *Maserati*
Fastest lap: Farina *62.32 mph*

INDIANAPOLIS 500 31 May
1st Mauri Rose [USA] *Blue Crown Spark Plug 119.814 mph*
2nd Bill Holland [USA] *Blue Crown Spark Plug*
3rd Duke Nalon [USA] *Novi Grooved Piston*
Fastest qualifier: Nalon *131.603 mph*

SWISS (EUROPEAN) GRAND PRIX Bremgarten 4 July
1st Count Felice Trossi [It] *Alfa-Romeo 90.81 mph*
2nd Jean-Pierre Wimille [Fr] *Alfa-Romeo*
3rd Luigi Villoresi [It] *Maserati*
Fastest lap: Wimille *95.05 mph*

FRENCH GRAND PRIX Rheims 18 July
1st Jean-Pierre Wimille [Fr] *Alfa-Romeo 102.1 mph*
2nd Consalvo Sanesi [It] *Alfa-Romeo*
3rd Alberto Ascari [It] *Alfa-Romeo*
Fastest lap: Wimille *108.14 mph*

ITALIAN GRAND PRIX Turin 5 Sept
1st Jean-Pierre Wimille [Fr] *Alfa-Romeo 70.38 mph*
2nd Luigi Villoresi [It] *Maserati*
3rd Raymond Sommer [Fr] *Ferrari*
Fastest lap: Wimille *78.61 mph (P)*

BRITISH GRAND PRIX Silverstone 2 Oct
1st Luigi Villoresi [It] *Maserati 72.28 mph*
2nd Alberto Ascari [It] *Maserati*
3rd Bob Gerard [GB] *ERA*
Fastest lap: Villoresi *76.82 mph*

MONZA GRAND PRIX 17 Oct
1st Jean-Pierre Wimille [Fr] *Alfa-Romeo 109.98 mph*
2nd Count Felice Trossi [It] *Alfa-Romeo*
3rd Consalvo Sanesi [It] *Alfa-Romeo*
Fastest lap: Sanesi *116.95 mph*

US National Champion: Johnnie Parsons
Fastest Man on Earth: John Cobb (1947)

TARGA FLORIO One circuit of Sicily 20 March
1st Clémente Biondetti [It]/Benedetti [It] *Ferrari 50.64 mph*
2nd Franco Rol [It]/Richiero [It] *Alfa-Romeo*
3rd Giovanni Rocco [It]/Prete [It] *AMP*

SAN REMO GRAND PRIX 3 April
1st Juan Manuel Fangio [Arg] *Maserati 62.87 mph*
2nd 'B. Bira' (Prince Birabongse Bhanudej Bhanubandth) [Siam] *Maserati*
3rd Baron Emanuel de Graffenried [Switz] *Maserati*
Fastest lap: 'Bira' *64.66 mph*

PAU GRAND PRIX 18 April
1st Juan Manuel Fangio [Arg] *Maserati 52.7 mph*
2nd Baron Emanuel de Graffenried [Switz] *Maserati*
3rd B. Campos [Arg] *Maserati*
Fastest lap: Fangio *56.85 mph*

MILLE MIGLIA Brescia 24–25 April
1st Clémente Biondetti [It]/Salani [It] *Ferrari*
2nd Felice Bonetto [It]/Carpani [It] *Ferrari*
3rd Franco Rol [It]/Richiero [It] *Alfa-Romeo*

BRITISH GRAND PRIX Silverstone 14 May
1st Baron Emanuel de Graffenried [Switz] *Maserati 77.31 mph*
2nd Bob Gerard [GB] *ERA*
3rd Louis Rosier [Fr] *Lago-Talbot*
Fastest lap: 'B. Bira' [Siam] *Maserati 82.82 mph*

INDIANAPOLIS 500 30 May
1st Bill Holland [USA] *Blue Crown Spark Plug 121.327 mph*
2nd Johnny Parsons [USA] *Kurtis-Kraft*
3rd George Connor [USA] *Blue Crown Spark Plug*
Fastest qualifier: Parsons *132.9 mph*

BELGIAN GRAND PRIX Spa 9 June
1st Louis Rosier [Fr] *Talbot 96.95 mph*
2nd Luigi Villoresi [It] *Ferrari*
3rd Alberto Ascari [It] *Ferrari*
Fastest lap: Giuseppe Farina [It] *Maserati 101.64 mph*

SWISS GRAND PRIX Bremgarten 3 July
1st Alberto Ascari [It] *Ferrari 90.76 mph*
2nd Luigi Villoresi [It] *Ferrari*
3rd Raymond Sommer [Fr] *Lago-Talbot*
Fastest lap: Giuseppe Farina [It] *Maserati 95.1 mph*

FRENCH GRAND PRIX Rheims 17 July
1st Louis Chiron [Mon] *Talbot 99.98 mph*
2nd 'B. Bira' [Siam] *Maserati*
3rd Peter Whitehead [GB] *Ferran*
Fastest lap: Whitehead *105.1 mph*

DUTCH GRAND PRIX Zandvoort 31 July
1st Luigi Villoresi [It] *Ferrari 77.12 mph*
2nd Baron Emanuel de Graffenried [Switz] *Maserati*
3rd 'B. Bira' [Siam] *Maserati*
Fastest lap: 'B. Bira' *79.49 mph*

INTERNATIONAL TROPHY Silverstone 20 Aug
1st Alberto Ascari [It] *Ferrari 89.58 mph*
2nd Giuseppe Farina [It] *Maserati*
3rd Luigi Villoresi [It] *Ferrari*
Fastest lap: Ascari *93.35 mph*

ITALIAN (EUROPEAN) GRAND PRIX Monza 11 Sept
1st Alberto Ascari [It] *Ferrari 105.04 mph*
2nd Philippe Etancelin [Fr] *Talbot*
3rd Bira' [Siam] *Maserati*
Fastest lap: Ascari *111.14 mph*

CZECHOSLOVAKIAN GRAND PRIX Brno 25 Sept
1st Peter Whitehead [GB] *Ferrari 78.72 mph*
2nd Philippe Etancelin [Fr] *Talbot*
3rd Franco Cortese [It] *Maserati*
Fastest lap: 'B. Bira' [Siam] *Maserati 82.29 mph*

World Champion: Giuseppe Farina [It]
US National Champion: Henry Banks
Fastest Man on Earth: John Cobb (>1947)

GRANDS PRIX

BRITISH Silverstone 13 May
1st Giuseppe Farina [It] *Alfa-Romeo 90.95 mph*
2nd Luigi Fagioli [It] *Alfa-Romeo*
3rd Reg Parnell [GB] *Alfa-Romeo*
Fastest lap: Farina *94.02 mph*

MONACO Monte Carlo 21 May
1st Juan Manuel Fangio [Arg] *Alfa-Romeo 61.33 mph*
2nd Alberto Ascari [It] *Ferrari*
3rd Louis Chiron [Mon] *Maserati*
Fastest lap: Fangio *64.09 mph*

INDIANAPOLIS 500 30 May
1st Johnny Parsons [USA] *Wynn's Friction 124.002 mph*
2nd Bill Holland [USA] *Blue Crown Spark Plug*
3rd Mauri Rose [USA] *Offenhauser*
Fastest qualifier: Walt Faulkner [USA] *Grant Piston Ring 134.343 mph*

SWISS Bremgarten 4 June
1st Giuseppe Farina [It] *Alfa-Romeo 92.76 mph*
2nd Luigi Fagioli [It] *Alfa-Romeo*
3rd Louis Rosier [Fr] *Lago-Talbot*
Fastest lap: Farina *100.78 mph*

BELGIAN Spa 18 June
1st Juan Manuel Fangio [Arg] *Alfa-Romeo 110.05 mph*
2nd Luigi Fagioli [It] *Alfa-Romeo*
3rd Louis Rosier [Fr] *Lago-Talbot*
Fastest lap: Giuseppe Farina [It] *Alfa-Romeo 115.15 mph*

FRENCH Rheims 2 July
1st Juan Manuel Fangio [Arg] *Alfa-Romeo 104.83 mph*
2nd Luigi Fagioli [It] *Alfa-Romeo*
3rd Peter Whitehead [GB] *Ferrari*
Fastest lap: Fangio *112.35 mph*

ITALIAN Monza 3 Sept
1st Giuseppe Farina [It] *Alfa-Romeo 109.63 mph*
2nd Dorino Serafini [It] *Alberto Ascari [It] Ferrari*
3rd Luigi Fagioli [It] *Alfa-Romeo*
Fastest lap: Juan Manuel Fangio [Arg] *Alfa-Romeo 117.44 mph*

TARGA FLORIO One circuit of Sicily 2 April
1st Franco Bornigia [It]/Mario Bornigia [It] *Alfa-Romeo 54.01 mph*
2nd Inigo Bernabei [It]/Pacini [It] *Ferrari*
3rd Stefano La Motta [It]/Gennaro Alterio [It] *Ferrari*

MILLE MIGLIA Brescia 23–24 April
1st Giannino Marzotto [It]/Crosara [It] *Ferrari 77 mph*
2nd Donna Serafini [It]/Salani [It] *Ferrari*
3rd Juan Manuel Fangio [Arg]/Zanardi [It] *Alfa-Romeo*

World Champion: Juan Manuel Fangio [Arg]
US National Champion: Tony Bettenhausen, Sr
Fastest Man on Earth: John Cobb (>1947)

GRANDS PRIX

SWISS Bremgarten 27 May
1st Juan Manuel Fangio [Arg] *Alfa-Romeo 89.05 mph*
2nd Piero Taruffi [It] *Ferrari*
3rd Giuseppe Farina [It] *Alfa-Romeo*
Fastest lap: Fangio *95.18 mph*

INDIANAPOLIS 500 30 May
1st Lee Wallard [USA] *Murrell Belanger 126.244 mph*
2nd Mike Nazaruk [USA] *Jim Robbins*
3rd Jack McGrath [USA] *Jack Hinkle*
Fastest qualifier: Walt Faulkner [USA] *Agajanian Grant Piston Ring 136.872 mph*

BELGIAN Spa 17 June
1st Giuseppe Farina [It] *Alfa-Romeo 114.26 mph*
2nd Alberto Ascari [It] *Ferrari*
3rd Luigi Villoresi [It] *Ferrari*
Fastest lap: Juan Manuel Fangio [Arg] *Alfa-Romeo 120.51 mph*

FRENCH Rheims 1 July
1st Juan Manuel Fangio [Arg]/Luigi Fagioli [It] *Alfa-Romeo 110.97 mph*
2nd Alberto Ascari [It]/Froilan Gonzalez [Arg] *Ferrari*
3rd Luigi Villoresi [It] *Ferrari*
Fastest lap: Fangio *118.29 mph*

BRITISH Silverstone 14 July
1st Froilan Gonzalez [Arg] *Ferrari 96.11 mph*
2nd Juan Manuel Fangio [Arg] *Alfa-Romeo*
3rd Luigi Villoresi [It] *Ferrari*
Fastest lap: Giuseppe Farina [It] *Alfa-Romeo 99.99 mph*

GERMAN Nürburging 29 July
1st Alberto Ascari [It] *Ferrari 83.76 mph*
2nd Juan Manuel Fangio [Arg] *Alfa-Romeo*
3rd Froilan Gonzalez [Arg] *Ferrari*
Fastest lap: Fangio *85.69 mph*

ITALIAN Monza 16 Sept
1st Alberto Ascari [It] *Ferrari 115.53 mph*
2nd Froilan Gonzalez [Arg] *Ferrari*
3rd Giuseppe Farina [It]/Felice Bonetto [It] *Alfa-Romeo*
Fastest lap: Farina *120.97 mph*

SPANISH Pedralbes 28 Oct
1st Juan Manuel Fangio [Arg] *Alfa-Romeo 98.76 mph*
2nd Froilan Gonzalez [Arg] *Ferrari*
3rd Giuseppe Farina [It] *Alfa-Romeo*
Fastest lap: Fangio *105.2 mph*

MILLE MIGLIA Brescia 28–29 April
1st Luigi Villoresi [It]/Cassani [It] *Ferrari 76.13 mph*
2nd Giovanni Bracco [It]/Umberto Maglioli [It] *Lancia Aurelia*
3rd Piero Scotti [It]/Ruspaggiari [It] *Ferrari*

TARGA FLORIO Piccolo Circuito Madonie 9 Sept
1st Franco Cortese [It] *Frazer Nash 47.62 mph*
2nd F. Cornacchia [It]/Giovanni Bracco [It] *Ferrari*
3rd Inigo Bernabei [It]/Pacini [It] *Maserati*
Fastest lap: Bracco *51.11 mph*

World Champion: Alberto Ascari [It]
US National Champion: Chuck Stevenson
Fastest Man on Earth: John Cobb (>1947)

GRANDS PRIX

SWISS Bremgarten 18 May
1st Piero Taruffi [It] *Ferrari 92.78 mph*
2nd Rudi Fischer [Switz] *Ferrari*
3rd Jean Behra [Fr] *Gordini*
Fastest lap: Taruffi *96.25 mph*

INDIANAPOLIS 500 30 May
1st Troy Ruttman [USA] *J. C. Agajanian 128.922 mph*
2nd Jim Rathmann [USA] *Grancor-Wynn's Oil*
3rd Sam Hanks [USA] *Bardahl*
Fastest qualifier: Chet Miller [USA] *Novi Pure Oil 139.034 mph*

BELGIAN Spa 22 June
1st Alberto Ascari [It] *Ferrari 103.13 mph*
2nd Giuseppe Farina [It] *Ferrari*
3rd Robert Manzon [Fr] *Gordini*
Fastest lap: Ascari *107.44 mph*

FRENCH Rouen-Les-Essarts 6 July
1st Alberto Ascari [It] *Ferrari 80.14 mph*
2nd Giuseppe Farina [It] *Ferrari*
3rd Piero Taruffi [It] *Ferrari*
Fastest lap: Farina *83.1 mph*

BRITISH Silverstone 19 July
1st Alberto Ascari [It] *Ferrari 90.92 mph*
2nd Piero Taruffi [It] *Ferrari*
3rd Mike Hawthorn [GB] *Cooper-Bristol*
Fastest lap: Ascari *94.08 mph*

GERMAN Nürburging 3 Aug
1st Alberto Ascari [It] *Ferrari 82.2 mph*
2nd Giuseppe Farina [It] *Ferrari*
3rd Rudi Fischer [Switz] *Ferrari*
Fastest lap: Ascari *84.33 mph*

DUTCH Zandvoort 17 Aug
1st Alberto Ascari [It] *Ferrari 81.15 mph*
2nd Giuseppe Farina [It] *Ferrari*
3rd Luigi Villoresi [It] *Ferrari*
Fastest lap: Ascari *85.43 mph*

ITALIAN Monza 7 Sept
1st Alberto Ascari [It] *Ferrari 109.8 mph*
2nd Froilan Gonzalez [Arg] *Maserati*
3rd Luigi Villoresi [It] *Ferrari*
Fastest lap: Ascari/Gonzalez *111.76 mph*

MILLE MIGLIA Brescia 4–5 May
1st Giovanni Bracco [It]/Rolfo [It] *Ferrari 80.36 mph*
2nd Karl Kling [Ger]/Hans Klenk [Ger] *Mercedes-Benz*
3rd Luigi Fagioli [It]/Borghi [It] *Lancia Aurelia*

TARGA FLORIO Piccolo Circuito Madonie 29 June
1st Felice Bonetto [It] *Lancia Aurelia 49.73 mph*
2nd Luigi Valenzano [It] *Lancia Aurelia*
3rd Enrico Anselmi [It] *Lancia Aurelia*
Fastest lap: G. Cabianca [It] *Osca 52.22 mph*

World Champion: Alberto Ascari [It]
US National Champion: Sam Hanks
Fastest Man on Earth: John Cobb (>1947)

GRANDS PRIX

ARGENTINE Buenos Aires 18 Jan
1st Alberto Ascari [It] *Ferrari 78.14 mph*
2nd Luigi Villoresi [It] *Ferrari*
3rd Froilan Gonzalez [Arg] *Maserati*
Fastest lap: Ascari *80.74 mph*

INDIANAPOLIS 500 30 May
1st Bill Vukovich [USA] *Fuel Injection 128.74 mph*
2nd Art Cross [USA] *Springfield Welding*
3rd Sam Hanks [USA] *Bardahl*
Fastest qualifier: Vukovich *138.392 mph*

DUTCH Zandvoort 7 June
1st Alberto Ascari [It] *Ferrari 81.04 mph*
2nd Giuseppe Farina [It] *Ferrari*
3rd Felice Bonetto [It]/Froilan Gonzalez [Arg] *Maserati*
Fastest lap: Luigi Villoresi [It] *Ferrari 83.15 mph*

BELGIAN Spa 21 June
1st Alberto Ascari [It] *Ferrari 112.47 mph*
2nd Luigi Villoresi [It] *Ferrari*
3rd Onofre Marimon [Arg] *Maserati*
Fastest lap: Froilan Gonzalez [Arg] *Maserati 115.27 mph*

FRENCH Rheims 5 July
1st Mike Hawthorn [GB] *Ferrari 113.65 mph*
2nd Juan Manuel Fangio [Arg] *Maserati*
3rd Froilan Gonzalez [Arg] *Maserati*
Fastest lap: Fangio *115.91 mph*

BRITISH Silverstone 18 July
1st Alberto Ascari [It] *Ferrari 92.97 mph*
2nd Juan Manuel Fangio [Arg] *Maserati*
3rd Giuseppe Farina [It] *Ferrari*
Fastest lap: Gonzalez/Ascari *95.79 mph*

GERMAN Nürburging 2 Aug
1st Giuseppe Farina [It] *Ferrari 83.89 mph*
2nd Juan Manuel Fangio [Arg] *Maserati*
3rd Mike Hawthorn [GB] *Ferrari*
Fastest lap: Alberto Ascari [It] *Ferrari 85.62 mph*

SWISS Bremgarten 23 Aug
1st Alberto Ascari [It] *Ferrari 97.17 mph*
2nd Giuseppe Farina [It] *Ferrari*
3rd Mike Hawthorn [GB] *Ferrari*
Fastest lap: Ascari *100.96 mph*

ITALIAN Monza 13 Sept
1st Juan Manuel Fangio [Arg] *Maserati 110.69 mph*
2nd Giuseppe Farina [It] *Ferrari*
3rd Luigi Villoresi [It] *Ferrari*
Fastest lap: Fangio *113.2 mph*

MILLE MIGLIA Brescia 25–26 April
1st Gannino Marzotto [It]/Crosara [It] *Ferrari 88.96 mph*
2nd Juan Manuel Fangio [Arg]/Giancarlo Sala [It] *Alfa-Romeo*
3rd Felice Bonetto [It]/Peruzzi [It] *Lancia*

TARGA FLORIO Piccolo Circuito Madonie 14 May
1st Umberto Maglioli [It] *Lancia 50.11 mph*
2nd Emilio Giletti [It] *Maserati*
3rd Sergio Mantovani [It]/Juan Manuel Fangio [Arg] *Maserati*
Fastest lap: Piero Taruffi [It] *Lancia 53.98 mph*

1954

World Champion: Juan Manuel Fangio [Arg]
US National Champion: Jimmy Bryan
Fastest Man on Earth: John Cobb (>1947)

GRANDS PRIX

ARGENTINE Buenos Aires 17 Jan
1st Juan Manuel Fangio [Arg] *Maserati 70.13 mph*
2nd Giuseppe Farina [It] *Ferrari*
3rd Froilan Gonzalez [Arg] *Ferrari*
Fastest lap: Gonzalez *80.76 mph*

INDIANAPOLIS 500 31 May
1st Bill Vukovich [USA] *Fuel Injection 130.84 mph*
2nd Jimmy Bryan [USA] *Dean Van Lines*
3rd Jack McGrath [USA] *Jack Hinkle*
Fastest qualifier: McGrath *141.033 mph*

BELGIAN Spa 20 June
1st Juan Manuel Fangio [Arg] *Maserati 115.08 mph*
2nd Maurice Trintignant [Fr] *Ferrari*
3rd Stirling Moss [GB] *Maserati*
Fastest lap: Fangio *118.97 mph*

FRENCH Rheims 4 July
1st Juan Manuel Fangio [Arg] *Mercedes-Benz 115.97 mph*
2nd Karl Kling [Ger] *Mercedes-Benz*
3rd Robert Manzon [Fr] *Ferrari*
Fastest lap: Hans Herrmann [Ger] *Mercedes-Benz 121.46 mph*

BRITISH Silverstone 17 July
1st Froilan Gonzalez [Arg] *Ferrari 89.69 mph*
2nd Mike Hawthorn [GB] *Ferrari*
3rd Onofre Marimon [Arg] *Maserati*
Fastest lap: Gonzalez/Hawthorn/Marimon /Juan Manuel Fangio [Arg] *Mercedes-Benz*/Stirling Moss [GB] *Maserati*/Alberto Ascari [It] *Maserati*/Jean Behra [Fr] *Gordini 95.79 mph*

GERMAN Nürburging 1 Aug
1st Juan Manuel Fangio [Arg] *Mercedes-Benz 82.87mph*
2nd Froilan Gonzalez [Arg]/Mike Hawthorn [GB] *Ferrari*
3rd Maurice Trintignant [Fr] *Ferrari*
Fastest lap: Karl Kling [Ger] *Mercedes-Benz 85.75 mph*

SWISS Bremgarten 22 Aug
1st Juan Manuel Fangio [Arg] *Mercedes-Benz 99.17 mph*
2nd Froilan Gonzalez [Arg] *Ferrari*
3rd Hans Herrmann [Ger] *Mercedes-Benz*
Fastest lap: Fangio *101.97 mph*

ITALIAN Monza 5 Sept
1st Juan Manuel Fangio [Arg] *Mercedes-Benz 111.98 mph*
2nd Mike Hawthorn [GB] *Ferrari*
3rd Froilan Gonzalez [Arg]/Umberto Maglioli [It] *Ferrari*
Fastest lap: Gonzalez *116.66 mph*

SPANISH Pedralbes 24 Oct
1st Mike Hawthorn [GB] *Ferrari 97.16 mph*
2nd Luigi Musso [It] *Maserati*
3rd Juan Manuel Fangio [Arg] *Mercedes-Benz*
Fastest lap: Alberto Ascari [It] *Lancia 100.64 mph*

MILLE MIGLIA Brescia 1–2 May
1st Alberto Ascari [It] *Lancia 87.27 mph*
2nd Paolo Marzotto [It] *Ferrari*
3rd Luigi Musso [It]/Zocca [It] *Maserati*

TARGA FLORIO Piccolo Circuito Madonie 30 May
1st Piero Taruffi [It] *Lancia 55.88 mph*
2nd Luigi Musso [It] *Maserati 3rd Roberto Piodi* [It] *Lancia*
Fastest lap: Eugenio Castellotti [It] *Ferrari 57.73 mph*

1955

World Champion: Juan Manuel Fangio [Arg]
US National Champion: Bob Sweikert
Fastest Man on Earth: John Cobb (>1947)

GRANDS PRIX

ARGENTINE Buenos Aires 16 Jan
1st Juan Manuel Fangio [Arg] *Mercedes-Benz 77.51 mph*
2nd Froilan Gonzalez [Arg]/Giuseppe Farina [It]/Maurice Trintignant [Fr] *Ferrari*
3rd Farina/Umberto Maglioli [It]/Trintignant [Fr] *Ferrari*
Fastest lap: Fangio *80.81 mph*

MONACO Monte Carlo 22 May
1st Maurice Trintignant [Fr] *Ferrari 65.81 mph*
2nd Eugenio Castellotti [It] *Lancia*
3rd Jean Behra [Fr]/Cesare Perdisa [It] *Maserati*
Fastest lap: Juan Manuel Fangio [Arg] *Mercedes-Benz 68.7 mph*

INDIANAPOLIS 500 30 May
1st Bob Sweikert [USA] *John Zink 128.209 mph*
2nd Tony Bettenhausen [USA] *H. A. Chapman*
3rd Jim Davies [USA] *Bardahl*
Fastest qualifier: Jack McGrath [USA] *Jack Hinkle 142.58 mph*

BELGIAN Spa 5 June
1st Juan Manuel Fangio [Arg] *Mercedes-Benz 118.83 mph*
2nd Stirling Moss [GB] *MercedesBenz*
3rd Giuseppe Farina [It] *Ferrari*
Fastest lap: Fangio *121.21 mph*

DUTCH Zandvoort 19 June
1st Juan Manuel Fangio [Arg] *Mercedes-Benz 89.6 mph*
2nd Stirling Moss [GB] *MercedesBenz*
3rd Luigi Musso [It] *Maserati*
Fastest lap: Roberto Mieres [Arg] *Maserati 92.96 mph*

BRITISH Aintree 16 July
1st Stirling Moss [GB] *Mercedes-Benz 86.47 mph*
2nd Juan Manuel Fangio [Arg] *Mercedes-Benz*
3rd Karl Kling [Ger] *Mercedes-Benz*
Fastest lap: Moss *89.7 mph*

ITALIAN Monza 11 Sept
1st Juan Manuel Fangio [Arg] *Mercedes-Benz 128.49 mph*
2nd Piero Taruffi [It] *Mercedes-Benz*
3rd Eugenio Castellotti [It] *Ferrari*
Fastest lap: Stirling Moss [GB] *Mercedes-Benz 134.03 mph*

MILLE MIGLIA Brescia 1–2 May
1st Stirling Moss [GB]/Denis Jenkinson [GB] *Mercedes-Benz 98.53 mph*
2nd Juan Manuel Fangio [Arg] *Mercedes-Benz*
3rd Umberto Maglioli [It] *Ferrari*

TARGA FLORIO Piccolo Circuito Madonie 16 Oct
1st Stirling Moss [GB]/Peter Collins [GB] *Mercedes-Benz 59.83 mph*
2nd Juan Manuel Fangio [Arg]/Karl Kling [Ger] *Mercedes-Benz*
3rd Eugenio Castellotti [It]/Robert Manzon [Fr] *Ferrari*
Fastest lap: Moss *62.26 mph*

1956

World Champion: Juan Manuel Fangio [Arg]
US National Champion: Jimmy Bryan
Fastest Man on Earth: John Cobb (>1947)

GRANDS PRIX

ARGENTINE Buenos Aires 22 Jan
1st Luigi Musso [It]/Juan Manuel Fangio [Arg] *Lancia-Ferrari 79.39 mph*
2nd Jean Behra [Fr] *Maserati*
3rd Mike Hawthorn [GB] *Maserati*
Fastest lap: Fangio *83.11 mph*

MONACO Monte Carlo 13 May
1st Stirling Moss [GB] *Maserati 64.94 mph*
2nd Peter Collins [CB]/Juan Manuel Fangio [Arg] *Lancia-Ferrari*
3rd Jean Behra [Fr] *Maserati*
Fastest lap: Fangio *67.39 mph*

INDIANAPOLIS 500 30 May
1st Pat Flaherty [USA] *John Zink 128.49 mph*
2nd Sam Hanks [USA] *Jones & Maley*
3rd Don Freeland [USA] *Bob Estes*
Fastest qualifier: Flaherty *145.596 mph*

BELGIAN Spa 3 June
1st Peter Collins [GB] *Lancia-Ferrari 118.44 mph*
2nd Paul Frère [Bel] *Lancia-Ferrari*
3rd Cesare Perdisa [It]/Stirling Moss [GB] *Maserati*
Fastest lap: Moss *124.01 mph*

FRENCH Rheims 1 July
1st Peter Collins [GB] *Lancia-Ferrari 122.29 mph*
2nd Eugenio Castellotti [It] *LanciaFerrari*
3rd Jean Behra [Fr] *Maserati*
Fastest lap: Juan Manuel Fangio [Arg] *Lancia-Ferrari 127.37 mph*

BRITISH Silverstone 14 July
1st Juan Manuel Fangio [Arg] *Lancia-Ferrari 98.65 mph*
2nd Marquis Alfonso de Portago [Sp]/Peter Collins [GB] *Lancia-Ferrari*
3rd Jean Behra [Fr] *Maserati*
Fastest lap: Stirling Moss [GB] *Maserati 102.1 mph*

GERMAN Nürburging 5 Aug
1st Juan Manuel Fangio [Arg] *Lancia-Ferrari 85.54 mph*
2nd Stirling Moss [GB] *Maserati*
3rd Jean Behra [Fr] *Maserati*
Fastest lap: Fangio *87.73 mph*

ITALIAN Monza 2 Sept
1st Stirling Moss [GB] *Maserati 129.73 mph*
2nd Peter Collins [GB]/Juan Manuel Fangio [Arg] *Lancia-Ferrari*
3rd Ron Flockhart [GB] *Connaught*
Fastest lap: Moss *135.41 mph*

MILLE MIGLIA Brescia 29–30 April
1st Eugenio Castellotti [It] *Ferrari 85.9 mph*
2nd Peter Collins [GB]/Louis Klementaski *Ferrari*
3rd Luigi Musso [It] *Ferrari*

TARGA FLORIO Piccolo Circuito Madonie 10 June
1st Umberto Maglioli [It] *Porsche 56.4 mph*
2nd Piero Taruffi [It] *Maserati*
3rd Olivier Gendebien-[Bel]/Hans Herrmann [Ger] *Ferrari*
Fastest lap: Eugenio Castellotti [It] *Ferrari 59.65 mph*

World Champion: Juan Manuel Fangio [Arg]
US National Champion: Jimmy Bryan
Fastest Man on Earth: John Cobb (>1947)

GRANDS PRIX

ARGENTINE Buenos Aires 13 Jan
1st Juan Manuel Fangio [Arg] *Maserati 80.61 mph*
2nd Jean Behra [Fr] *Maserati*
3rd Carlos Menditeguy [Arg] *Maserati*
Fastest lap: Stirling Moss [GB] *Maserati 83.58 mph*

MONACO Monte Carlo 19 May
1st Juan Manuel Fangio [Arg] *Maserati 64.72 mph*
2nd Tony Brooks [GB] *Vanwall*
3rd Masten Gregory [USA] *Maserati*
Fastest lap: Fangio *66.62 mph*

INDIANAPOLIS 500 30 May
1st Sam Hanks [USA] *Belond Exhaust 135.601 mph*
2nd Jim Rathmann [USA] *Chiropractic*
3rd Jimmy Bryan [USA] *Dean Van Lines*
Fastest qualifier: Paul Russo [USA] *Novi Auto 144.817 mph*

FRENCH Rouen 7 July
1st Juan Manuel Fangio [Arg] *Maserati 100.02 mph*
2nd Luigi Musso [It] *Lancia-Ferrari*
3rd Peter Collins [GB] *Lancia-Ferrari*
Fastest lap: Musso *102.87 mph*

BRITISH Aintree 20 July
1st Tony Brooks [GB]/Stirling Moss [GB] *Vanwall 86.79 mph*
2nd Luigi Musso [It] *Lancia-Ferrari*
3rd Mike Hawthorn [GB] *Lancia-Ferrari*
Fastest lap: Moss *90.6 mph*

GERMAN Nürburging 4 Aug
1st Juan Manuel Fangio [Arg] *Maserati 88.82 mph*
2nd Mike Hawthorn [GB] *Lancia-Ferrari*
3rd Peter Collins [GB] *Lancia-Ferrari*
Fastest lap: Fangio *91.54 mph*

PESCARA 18 Aug
1st Stirling Moss [GB] *Vanwall 95.7 mph*
2nd Juan Manuel Fangio [Arg] *Maserati*
3rd Harry Schell [USA] *Maserati*
Fastest lap: Moss *97.88 mph*

ITALIAN Monza 8 Sept
1st Stirling Moss [GB] *Vanwall 120.27 mph*
2nd Juan Manuel Fangio [Arg] *Maserati*
3rd Wolfgang von Trips [Ger] *Lancia-Ferrari*
Fastest lap: Tony Brooks [GB] *Vanwall 124.03 mph*

TARGA FLORIO Official race not held

MILLE MIGLIA Brescia 12-13 May
1st Piero Taruffi [It] *Ferrari 95.39 mph*
2nd Wolfgang von Trips [Ger] *Ferrari*
3rd Olivier Gendebien [Bel]/Philip Washer [Bel] *Ferrari*

World Champion: Mike Hawthorn [GB]
US National Champion: Tony Bettenhausen, Sr
Fastest Man on Earth: John Cobb (>1947)

GRANDS PRIX

ARGENTINE Buenos Aires 18 Jan
1st Stirling Moss [GB] *Cooper-Climax 83.61 mph*
2nd Luigi Musso [It] *Ferrari*
3rd Mike Hawthorn [GB] *Ferrari*
Fastest lap: Juan Manuel Fangio [Arg] *Maserati 85.96 mph*

MONACO Monte Carlo 18 May
1st Maurice Trintignant [Fr] *Cooper-Climax 67.99 mph*
2nd Luigi Musso [It] *Ferrari*
3rd Peter Collins [GB] *Ferrari*
Fastest lap: Mike Hawthorn [GB] *Ferrari 69.93 mph*

DUTCH Zandvoort 25 May
1st Stirling Moss [GB] *Vanwall 93.95 mph*
2nd Harry Schell [USA] *BRM*
3rd Jean Behra [Fr] *BRM*
Fastest lap: Moss *96.1 mph*

INDIANAPOLIS 500 30 May
1st Jimmy Bryan [USA] *Belond AP 133.791 mph*
2nd George Amick [USA] *Norman Demler*
3rd Johnny Boyd [USA] *Bowes Seal Fast*
Fastest qualifier: Dick Rathmann [USA] *McNamara 145.974 mph*

BELGIAN Spa 15 June
1st Tony Brooks [GB] *Vanwall 129.92 mph*
2nd Mike Hawthorn [GB] *Ferrari*
3rd Stuart Lewis-Evans [GB] *Vanwall*
Fastest lap: Hawthorn *132.36 mph*

FRENCH Rheims 6 July
1st Mike Hawthorn [GB] *Ferrari 125.45 mph*
2nd Stirling Moss [GB] *Vanwall*
3rd Wolfgang von Trips [Ger] *Ferrari*
Fastest lap: Hawthorn *128.16 mph*

BRITISH Silverstone 19 July
1st Peter Collins [GB] *Ferrari 102.05 mph*
2nd Mike Hawthorn [GB] *Ferrari*
3rd Roy Salvadori [GB] *Cooper-Climax*
Fastest lap: Hawthorn *104.53 mph*

GERMAN Nürburging 3 Aug
1st Tony Brooks [GB] *Vanwall 90.31 mph*
2nd Roy Salvadori [GB] *Cooper-Climax*
3rd Maurice Trintignant [Fr] *Cooper-Climax*
Fastest lap: Stirling Moss [GB] *Vanwall 92.91 mph*

PORTUGUESE Oporto 24 Aug
1st Stirling Moss [GB] *Vanwall 105.03 mph*
2nd Mike Hawthorn [GB] *Ferrari*
3rd Stuart Lewis-Evans [GB] *Vanwall*
Fastest lap: Hawthorn *107.5 mph*

ITALIAN Monza 7 Sept
1st Tony Brooks [GB] *Vanwall 121.22 mph*
2nd Mike Hawthorn [GB] *Ferrari*
3rd Phil Hill [USA] *Ferrari*
Fastest lap: Hill *125 mph*

MOROCCAN Casablanca 19 Oct
1st Stirling Moss [GB] *Vanwall 116.46 mph*
2nd Mike Hawthorn [GB] *Ferrari*
3rd Phil Hill [USA] *Ferrari*
Fastest lap: Moss *119.59 mph*

TARGA FLORIO Piccolo Circuito Madonie 11 May
1st Luigi Musso [It]/Olivier Gendebien [Bel] *Ferrari 58.7 mph*
2nd Jean Behra [Fr]/Giorgio Scarlatti [It] *Porsche*
3rd Wolfgang von Trips [Ger]/Mike Hawthorn [GB] *Ferrari*
Fastest lap: Stirling Moss [GB] *Aston Martin 63.33 mph*

World Champion: Jack Brabham [Austral]
US National Champion: Rodger Ward
Fastest Man on Earth: John Cobb (>1947)

GRANDS PRIX

MONACO Monte Carlo 10 May
1st Jack Brabham [Austral] *Cooper-Climax 66.71 mph*
2nd Tony Brooks [GB] *Ferrari*
3rd Maurice Trintignant [Fr] *Cooper-Climax*
Fastest lap: Brabham *70.07 mph*

INDIANAPOLIS 500 30 May
1st Rodger Ward [USA] *Leader Card 500 Roadster 135.857 mph*
2nd Jim Rathmann [USA] *Simoniz*
3rd Johnny Thomson [USA] *Racing Associates*
Fastest qualifier: Thomson *145.908 mph*

DUTCH Zandvoort 31 May
1st Jo Bonnier [Swe] *BRM 93.46 mph*
2nd Jack Brabham [Austral] *Cooper-Climax*
3rd Masten Gregory [USA] *Cooper-Climax*
Fastest lap: Stirling Moss [GB] *Cooper-Climax 96.99 mph*

FRENCH Rheims 5 July
1st Tony Brooks [GB] *Ferrari 127.43 mph*
2nd Phil Hill [USA] *Ferrari*
3rd Jack Brabham [Austral] *Cooper-Climax*
Fastest lap: Stirling Moss [GB] *BRM 130.05 mph*

BRITISH Aintree 18 July
1st Jack Brabham [Austral] *89.88 mph*
2nd Stirling Moss [GB] *BRM*
3rd Bruce McLaren [NZ] *Cooper-Climax*
Fastest lap: Moss/McLaren *92.31 mph*

GERMAN AVUS 2 Aug
1st Tony Brooks [GB] *Ferrari 143.35 mph*
2nd Dan Gurney [USA] *Ferrari*
3rd Phil Hill [USA] *Ferrari*
Fastest lap: Brooks *149.14 mph*

PORTUGUESE Monsanto 23 Aug
1st Stirling Moss [GB] *Cooper-Climax 95.32 mph*
2nd Masten Gregory [USA] *Cooper-Climax*
3rd Dan Gurney [USA] *Ferrari*
Fastest lap: Moss *97.3 mph*

ITALIAN Monza 13 Sept
1st Stirling Moss [GB] *Cooper-Climax 124.38 mph*
2nd Phil Hill [USA] *Ferrari*
3rd Jack Brabham [Austral] *Cooper-Climax*
Fastest lap: Hill *128.11 mph*

UNITED STATES Sebring 12 Dec
1st Bruce McLaren [NZ] *Cooper-Climax 98.83 mph*
2nd Maurice Trintignant [Fr] *Cooper-Climax*
3rd Tony Brooks [GB] *Ferrari*
Fastest lap: Trintignant *101.19 mph*

TARGA FLORIO Piccolo Circuito Madonie 24 May
1st Edgar Barth [Ger]/Wolfgang Seidel [Ger] *Porsche 56.61 mph*
2nd H. Linge [Ger]/Scagliarini [It] *Porsche*
3rd Baron Antonio Pucci [It]/Huschke von Hanstein [Ger] *Porsche*
Fastest lap: Jo Bonnier [Swe] *Porsche 62 mph*

1960

World Champion: Jack Brabham [Austral]
US National Champion: A.J. Foyt
Fastest Man on Earth: John Cobb (>1947)

GRANDS PRIX

ARGENTINE Buenos Aires 7 Feb
1st Bruce McLaren [NZ] *Cooper-Climax 82.77 mph*
2nd Cliff Allison [GB] *Ferrari*
3rd Maurice Trintignant [Fr]/Stirling Moss [GB] *Cooper-Climax*
Fastest lap: Moss *88.48 mph*

MONACO Monte Carlo 29 May
1st Stirling Moss [GB] *Lotus-Climax 67.48 mph*
2nd Bruce McLaren [NZ] *Cooper-Climax*
3rd Phil Hill [USA] *Ferrari*
Fastest lap: McLaren *73.13 mph*

INDIANAPOLIS 500 30 May
1st Jim Rathmann [USA] *Ken-Paul 138.767 mph*
2nd Rodger Ward [USA] *Leader Card 500 Roadster*
3rd Paul Goldsmith [USA] *Norman Demler*
Fastest qualifier: Jim Hurtubise [USA] *Travelon Trailer 149.056 mph*

DUTCH Zandvoort 6 June
1st Jack Brabham [Austral] *Cooper-Climax 96.27 mph*
2nd Innes Ireland [GB] *Lotus-Climax*
3rd Graham Hill [GB] *BRM*
Fastest lap: Stirling Moss [GB] *Lotus-Climax 99.99 mph*

BELGIAN Spa 19 June
1st Jack Brabham [Austral] *Cooper-Climax 133.63 mph*
2nd Bruce McLaren [NZ] *Cooper-Climax*
3rd Olivier Gendebien [Bel] *Cooper-Climax*
Fastest lap: Brabham/Phil Hill [USA] *Ferrari*/Innes Ireland [GB] *Lotus-Climax 136.01 mph*

FRENCH Rheims 3 July
1st Jack Brabham [Austral] *Cooper-Climax 132.19 mph*
2nd Olivier Gendebien [Bel] *Cooper-Climax*
3rd Bruce McLaren [NZ] *Cooper-Climax*
Fastest lap: Brabham *135.06 mph*

BRITISH Silverstone 16 July
1st Jack Brabham [Austral] *Cooper-Climax 108.69 mph*
2nd John Surtees [GB] *Lotus-Climax*
3rd Innes Ireland [GB] *Lotus-Climax*
Fastest lap: Graham Hill [GB] *BRM 111.62 mph*

PORTUGUESE Oporto 14 Aug
1st Jack Brabham [Austral] *Cooper-Climax 109.27 mph*
2nd Bruce McLaren [NZ] *Cooper-Climax*
3rd Jim Clark [GB] *Lotus-Climax*
Fastest lap: John Surtees [GB] *Lotus-Climax 112.31 mph*

ITALIAN Monza 4 Sept
1st Phil Hill [USA] *Ferrari 132.06 mph*
2nd Richie Ginther [USA] *Ferrari*
3rd Willy Mairesse [Bel] *Ferrari*
Fastest lap: Hill *136.73 mph*

UNITED STATES Riverside 20 Nov
1st Stirling Moss [GB] *Lotus-Climax 99 mph*
2nd Innes Ireland [GB] *Lotus-Climax*
3rd Bruce McLaren [NZ] *Cooper-Climax*
Fastest lap: jack Brabham [Austral] *Cooper-Climax 101.38 mph*

TARGA FLORIO Piccolo Circuito Madonie 8 May
1st Jo Bonnier [Swe]/Graham Hill [GB] *Porsche 59.11 mph*
2nd Wolfgang von Trips [Ger]/Phil Hill [USA] *Ferrari*
3rd Olivier Gendebien [Bel]/Hans Herrmann [Ger] *Porsche*
Fastest lap: Bonnier *63.12 mph*

1961

World Champion: Phil Hill [USA]
US National Champion: A.J. Foyt
Fastest Man on Earth: John Cobb (>1947)

GRANDS PRIX

MONACO Monte Carlo 14 May
1st Stirling Moss [GB] *Lotus-Climax 70.7 mph*
2nd Richie Ginther [USA] *Ferrari*
3rd Phil Hill [USA] *Ferrari*
Fastest lap: Ginther/Moss *72.05 mph*

DUTCH Zandvoort 22 May
1st Wolfgang von Trips [Ger] *Ferrari 96.21 mph*
2nd Phil Hill [USA] *Ferrari*
3rd Jim Clark [GB] *Lotus-Climax*
Fastest lap: Clark *98.21 mph*

BELGIAN Spa 18 June
1st Phil Hill [USA] *Ferrari 128.15 mph*
2nd Wolfgang von Trips [Ger] *Ferrari*
3rd Richie Ginther [USA] *Ferrari*
Fastest lap: Ginther *31.53 mph*

FRENCH Rheims 2 July
1st Giancarlo Baghetti [It] *Ferrari 119.85 mph*
2nd Dan Gurney [USA] *Porsche*
3rd Jim Clark [GB] *Lotus-Climax*
Fastest lap: Phil Hill [USA] *Ferrari 126.25 mph*

BRITISH Aintree 15 July
1st Wolfgang von Trips [Ger] *Ferrari 83.91 mph*
2nd Phil Hill [USA] *Ferron*
3rd Richie Ginther [USA] *Ferrari*
Fastest lap: Tony Brooks [GB] *BRM-Climax 91.68 mph*

GERMAN Nürburging 6 Aug
1st Stirling Moss [GB] *Lotus-Climax 92.3 mph*
2nd Wolfgang von Trips [Ger] *Ferrari*
3rd Phil Hill [USA] *Ferrari*
Fastest lap: Hill *94.88 mph*

ITALIAN Monza 10 Sept
1st Phil Hill [USA] *Ferrari 130.11 mph*
2nd Dan Gurney [USA] *Porsche*
3rd Bruce McLaren [NZ] *Cooper-Climax*
Fastest lap: Giancarlo Baghetti [It] *Ferrari 132.83 mph*

UNITED STATES Watkins Glen 8 Oct
1st Innes Ireland [GB] *Lotus-Climax 103.17 mph*
2nd Dan Gurney [USA] *Porsche*
3rd Tony Brooks [GB] *BRM-Climax*
Fastest lap: Stirling Moss [GB] *Lotus-Climax 105.8 mph*

TARGA FLORIO Piccolo Circuito Madonie 30 April
1st Wolfgang von Trips [Gel/Olivier Gendebien [Bel] *Ferrari 64.27 mph*
2nd Dan Gurney [USA]/Jo Bonnier [Swe] *Porsche*
3rd Edgar Barth [Ger]/Hans Herrmann [Ger] *Porsche*
Fastest lap: Gendebien *66.87 mph*

INDIANAPOLIS 500 30 May
1st A.J. Foyt [USA] *Bowes Seal Fast 139.13 mph*
2nd Eddie Sachs [USA] *Dean Van Lines*
3rd Rodger Ward [USA] *Webb's Sun City*
Fastest qualifier: Sachs *147.481 mph*

1962

World Champion: Graham Hill [GB]
US National Champion: Rodger Ward
Fastest Man on Earth: John Cobb (>1947)

GRANDS PRIX

DUTCH Zandvoort 20 May
1st Graham Hill [GB] *BRM 95.44 mph*
2nd Trevor Taylor [GB] *Lotus-Climax*
3rd Phil Hill [USA] *Ferrari*
Fastest lap: Bruce McLaren [NZ] *Cooper-Climax 99.36 mph*

MONACO Monte Carlo 3 June
1st Bruce McLaren [NZ] *Cooper-Climax 70.46 mph*
2nd Phil Hill [USA] *Ferrari*
3rd Lorenzo Bandini [It] *Ferrari*
Fastest lap: Jim Clark [GB] *Lotus-Climax 73.67 mph*

BELGIAN Spa 17 June
1st Jim Clark [GB] *Lotus-Climax 131.9 mph*
2nd Graham Hill [GB] *BRM*
3rd Phil Hill [USA] *Ferrari*
Fastest lap: Clark *133.98 mph*

FRENCH Rouen 8 July
1st Dan Gurney [USA] *Porsche 101.89 mph*
2nd Tony Maggs [SA] *Cooper-Climax*
3rd Richie Ginther [USA] *BRM*
Fastest lap: Graham Hill [GB] *BRM 106.9 mph*

BRITISH Aintree 21 July
1st Jim Clark [GB] *Lotus-Climax 92.25 mph*
2nd John Surtees [GB] *Lola-Climax*
3rd Bruce McLaren [NZ] *Cooper-Climax*
Fastest lap: Clark *93.91 mph*

GERMAN Nürburging 5 Aug
1st Graham Hill [GB] *BRM 80.35 mph*
2nd John Surtees [GB] *Lola-Climax*
3rd Dan Gurney [USA] *Porsche*
Fastest lap: Hill *83.35 mph*

ITALIAN Monza 16 Sept
1st Graham Hill [GB] *BRM 123.62 mph*
2nd Richie Ginther [USA] *BRM*
3rd Bruce McLaren [NZ] *Cooper-Climax*
Fastest lap: Hill *125.73 mph*

UNITED STATES Watkins Glen 7 Oct
1st Jim Clark [GB] *Lotus-Climax 108.48 mph*
2nd Graham Hill [GB] *BRM*
3rd Bruce McLaren [NZ] *Cooper-Climax*
Fastest lap: Clark *110.4 mph*

SOUTH AFRICAN East London 29 Dec
1st Graham Hill [GB] *BRM 93.57 mph*
2nd Bruce McLaren [NZ] *Cooper-Climax*
3rd Tony Maggs [SA] *Cooper-Climax*
Fastest lap: Jim Clark [GB] *Lotus-Climax 96.35 mph*

TARGA FLORIO Piccolo Circuito Madonie 6 May
1st Willy Mairesse [Bel]/Ricardo Rodriguez [Mex]/Olivier Gendebien [Bel] *Ferrari 63.33 mph*
2nd Giancarlo Baghetti [It]/Lorenzo Bandini [It] *Ferrari*
3rd Nino Vaccarella [It]/Jo Bonnier [Swe] *Porsche*
Fastest lap: Mairesse *66.94 mph*

INDIANAPOLIS 500 30 May
1st Rodger Ward [USA] *Leader Card 500 Roadster 140.293 mph*
2nd Len Sutton [USA] *Leader Card 500 Roadster*
3rd Eddie Sachs [USA] *Dean-Autolite*
Fastest qualifier: Parnelli Jones [USA] *Agajanian Willar Battery 150.37 mph*

World Champion: Jim Clark [GB]
US National Champion: A.J. Foyt
Fastest Man on Earth: Craig Breedlove [USA] *Spirit ofAmerica 407.45 mph (US record)*

GRANDS PRIX

MONACO Monte Carlo 26 May
1st Graham Hill [GB] *BRM 72.42 mph*
2nd Richie Ginther [USA] *BRM*
3rd Bruce McLaren [NZ] *Cooper-Climax*
Fastest lap: John Surtees [GB] *Ferrari 74.45 mph*

BELGIAN Spa 9 June
1st Jim Clark [GB] *Lotus-Climax 114.1 mph*
2nd Bruce McLaren [NZ] *Cooper-Climax*
3rd Dan Gurney [USA] *Brabham-Climax*
Fastest lap: Clark *132.47 mph*

DUTCH Zandvoort 23 June
1st Jim Clark [GB] *Lotus-Climax 97.53 mph*
2nd Dan Gurney [USA] *Brabham-Climax*
3rd John Surtees [GB] *Ferrari*
Fastest lap: Clark *100.1 mph*

FRENCH Rheims 30 June
1st Jim Clark [GB] *Lotus-Climax 125.31 mph*
2nd Tony Maggs [SA] *Cooper-Climax*
3rd Graham Hill [GB] *BRM*
Fastest lap: Clark *131.15 mph*

BRITISH Silverstone 20 July
1st Jim Clark [GB] *Lotus-Climax 107.35 mph*
2nd John Surtees [GB] *Ferrari*
3rd Graham Hill [GB] *BRM*
Fastest lap: Surtees *109.76 mph*

GERMAN Nürburging 4 Aug
1st John Surtees [GB] *Ferrari 95.83 mph*
2nd Jim Clark [GB] *Lotus-Climax*
3rd Richie Ginther [USA] *BRM*
Fastest lap: Surtees *96.82 mph*

ITALIAN Monza 8 Sept
1st Jim Clark [GB] *Lotus-Climax 127.74 mph*
2nd Richie Ginther [USA] *BRM*
3rd Bruce McLaren [NZ] *Cooper-Climax*
Fastest lap: Clark *130.05 mph*

UNITED STATES Watkins Glen 6 Oct
1st Graham Hill [GB] *BRM 108.92 mph*
2nd Richie Ginther [USA] *BRM*
3rd Jim Clark [GB] *Lotus-Climax*
Fastest lap: Clark *111.14 mph*

MEXICAN Mexico City 27 Oct
1st Jim Clark [GB] *Lotus-Climax 93.3 mph*
2nd Jack Brabham [Austral] *Brabham-Climax*
3rd Richie Ginther [USA] *BRM*
Fastest lap: Clark *94.71 mph*

SOUTH AFRICAN East London 28 Dec
1st Jim Clark [GB] *Lotus-Climax 95.1 mph*
2nd Dan Gurney [USA] *Brabham-Climax*
3rd Graham Hill [GB] *BRM*
Fastest lap: Gurney *98.41 mph*

TARGA FLORIO Piccolo Circuito Madonie 5 May
1st Jo Bonnier [Swe]/C. M. Abate *Porsche 64.57 mph*
2nd Lorenzo Bandini [It]/Ludovico Scarfiotti [It]/Willy Mairesse [Bel] *Ferrari*
3rd H. Linge [Ger]/Edgar Barth [Ger] *Porsche*
Fastest lap: Mike Parkes [GB] *Ferrari 66.83 mph*

INDIANAPOLIS 500 30 May
1st Parnelli Jones[USA] *J. C. Agajanian 143.137 mph*
2nd Jim Clark [GB] *Lotus-Ford*
3rd Foyt [USA] *Sheraton-Thompson*
Fastest qualifier: Jones *151.153 mph*

World Champion: John Surtees [GB]
US National Champion: A.J. Foyt
Fastest Man on Earth: Art Arfons [USA] *Green Monster 536.71 mph*

GRANDS PRIX

MONACO Monte Carlo 10 May
1st Graham Hill [GB] *BRM 72.64 mph*
2nd Richie Ginther [USA] *BRM*
3rd Peter Arundell [GB] *Lotus-Climax*
Fastest lap: Hill *74.92 mph*

DUTCH Zandvoort 24 May
1st Jim Clark [GB] *Lotus-Climax 98.02 mph*
2nd John Surtees [GB] *Ferrari*
3rd Peter Arundell [GB] *Lotus-Climax*
Fastest lap: Clark *101.07 mph*

BELGIAN Spa 14 June
1st Jim Clark [GB] *Lotus-Climax 132.79 mph*
2nd Bruce McLaren [NZ] *Cooper-Climax*
3rd Jack Brabham [Austral] *Brabham-Climax*
Fastest lap: Dan Gurney [USA] *Brabham-Climax 137.61 mph*

FRENCH Rouen 28 June
1st Dan Gurney [USA] *Brabham-Climax 108.77 mph*
2nd Graham Hill [GB] *BRM*
3rd Jack Brabham [Austral] *Brabham-Climax*
Fastest lap: Brabham *111.37 mph*

BRITISH Brands Hatch 11 July
1st Jim Clark [GB] *Lotus-Climax 94.14 mph*
2nd Graham Hill [GB] *BRM*
3rd John Surtees [GB] *Ferrari*
Fastest lap: Clark *96.56 mph*

GERMAN Nürburging 2 Aug
1st John Surtees [GB] *Ferrari 96.58 mph*
2nd Graham Hill [GB] *BRM*
3rd Lorenzo Bandini [It] *Ferrari*
Fastest lap: Surtees *98.31 mph*

AUSTRIAN Zeltweg 23 Aug
1st Lorenzo Bandini [It] *Ferrari 99.2 mph*
2nd Richie Ginther [USA] *BRM*
3rd Bob Anderson [GB] *Brabham-Climax*
Fastest lap: Dan Gurney [USA] *Brabham-Climax 101.57 mph*

ITALIAN Monza 6 Sept
1st John Surtees [GB] *Ferrari 127.78 mph*
2nd Bruce McLaren [NZ] *Cooper-Climax*
3rd Lorenzo Bandini [It] *Ferrari*
Fastest lap: Surtees *130.19 mph*

UNITED STATES Watkins Glen 4 Oct
1st Graham Hill [GB] *BRM 111.1 mph*
2nd John Surtees [GB] *Ferrari*
3rd Jo Siffert [Switz] *Brabham-BRM*
Fastest lap: Jim Clark [GB] *Lotus-Climax 113.89 mph*

MEXICAN Mexico City 25 Oct
1st Dan Gurney [USA] *Brabham-Climax 93.32 mph*
2nd John Surtees [GB] *Ferrari*
3rd Lorenzo Bandini [It] *Ferrari*
Fastest lap: Jim Clark [GB] *Lotus-Climax 94.49 mph*

TARGA FLORIO Piccolo Circuito Madonie 26 April
1st Colin Davis [GB]/Baron Antonio Pucci [It] *Porsche 62.16 mph*
2nd H. Linge [Ger]/G. Balzarini [It] *Porsche*
3rd Roberto Bussinello [It]/N. Todaro [It] *Alfa-Romeo*
Fastest lap: Davis *65.05 mph*

INDIANAPOLIS 500 30 May
1st A.J. Foyt [USA] *Sheraton-Thompson 147.35 mph*
2nd Rodger Ward [USA] *Kaiser Aluminum*
3rd Lloyd Ruby [USA] *Bill Forbes Racing Team*
Fastest qualifier: Jim Clark [GB] *Lotus-Ford 158.828 mph*

World Champion: Jim Clark [GB]
US National Champion: Mario Andretti
Fastest Man on Earth: Craig Breedlove [USA] *Spirit of America-Sonic 1 600.601 mph*

GRANDS PRIX

SOUTH AFRICAN East London 1 Jan
1st Jim Clark [GB] *Lotus-Climax 97.97 mph*
2nd John Surtees [GB] *Ferrari*
3rd Graham Hill [GB] *BRM*
Fastest lap: Clark *100.1 mph*

MONACO Monte Carlo 30 May
1st Graham Hill [GB] *BRM 74.34 mph*
2nd Lorenzo Bandini [It] *Ferrari*
3rd Jackie Stewart [GB] *BRM*
Fastest lap: Hill *76.72 mph*

BELGIAN Spa 13 June
1st Jim Clark [GB] *Lotus-Climax 117.16 mph*
2nd Jackie Stewart [GB] *BRM*
3rd Bruce McLaren [NZ] *Cooper-Climax*
Fastest lap: Clark *124.72 mph*

FRENCH Clermont-Ferrand 27 June
1st Jim Clark [GB] *Lotus-Climax 89.22 mph*
2nd Jackie Stewart [GB] *BRM*
3rd John Surtees [GB] *Ferrari*
Fastest lap: Clark *90.59 mph*

BRITISH Silverstone 10 July
1st Jim Clark [GB] *Lotus-Climax 112.02 mph*
2nd Graham Hill [GB] *BRM*
3rd John Surtees [GB] *Ferrari*
Fastest lap: Hill *114.29 mph*

DUTCH Zandvoort 18 July
1st Jim Clark [GB] *Lotus-Climax 100.87 mph*
2nd Jackie Stewart [GB] *BRM*
3rd Dan Gurney [USA] *Brabham-Climax*
Fastest lap: Clark *103.53 mph*

GERMAN Nürburging 1 Aug
1st Jim Clark [GB] *Lotus-Climax 99.76 mph*
2nd Graham Hill [GB] *BRM*
3rd Dan Gurney [USA] *Brabham-Climax*
Fastest lap: Clark *101.22 mph*

ITALIAN Monza 12 Sept
1st Jackie Stewart [GB] *BRM 130.46 mph*
2nd Graham Hill [GB] *BRM*
3rd Dan Gurney [USA] *Brabham-Climax*
Fastest lap: Jim Clark [GB] *Lotus-Climax 133.43 mph*

UNITED STATES Watkins Glen 3 Oct
1st Graham Hill [GB] *BRM 107.98 mph*
2nd Dan Gurney [USA] *Brabham-Climax*
3rd Jack Brabham [Austral] *Brabham-Climax*
Fastest lap: Hill *115.16 mph*

MEXICAN Mexico City 24 Oct
1st Richie Ginther [USA] *Honda 94.26 mph*
2nd Dan Gurney [USA] *Brabham-Climax*
3rd Mike Spence [GB] *Lotus-Climax*
Fastest lap: Gurney *96.55 mph*

TARGA FLORIO Piccolo Circuito Madonie 9 May
1st Nino Vaccarella [It]/Lorenzo Bandini [It] *Ferrari 63.59 mph*
2nd Colin Davis [GB]/Gerhard Miter [Ger] *Porsche*
3rd Umberto Maglioli [It]/H. Linge [Ger] *Porsche*
Fastest lap: Vaccarella *68.12 mph*

INDIANAPOLIS 500 31 May
1st Jim Clark [GB] *Lotus-Ford 150.686 mph*
2nd Parnelli Jones [USA] *Agajanian*
3rd Mario Andretti [USA] *Dean Van Lines*
Fastest qualifier: A.J. Foyt [USA] *Sheraton-Thompson 161.233 mph*

World Champion: Jack Brabham [Austral]
US National Champion: Mario Andretti
Fastest Man on Earth: Craig Breedlove (>1965)

GRANDS PRIX

MONACO Monte Carlo 22 May
  1st Jackie Stewart [GB] *BRM 76.52 mph*
  2nd Lorenzo Bandini [It] *Ferrari*
  3rd Graham Hill [GB] *BRM*
  Fastest lap: Bandini *78.34 mph*

BELGIAN Spa 12 June
  1st John Surtees [GB] *Ferrari 113.93 mph*
  2nd Jochen Rindt [Aus] *Cooper-Maserati*
  3rd Lorenzo Bandini [It] *Ferrari*
  Fastest lap: Surtees *121.92 mph*

FRENCH Rheims 3 July
  1st Jack Brabham [Austral] *Brabham-Repco 136.9 mph*
  2nd Mike Parkes [GB] *Ferrari*
  3rd Denny Hulme [NZ] *Brabham-Repco*
  Fastest lap: Lorenzo Bandini [It] *Ferrari 141.44 mph*

BRITISH Brands Hatch 16 July
  1st Jack Brabham [Austral] *Brabham-Repco 95.48 mph*
  2nd Denny Hulme [NZ] *Brabham-Repco*
  3rd Graham Hill [GB] *BRM*
  Fastest lap: Brabham *98.35 mph*

DUTCH Zandvoort 24 July
  1st Jack Brabham [Austral] *Brabham-Repco 100.11 mph*
  2nd Graham Hill [GB] *BRM*
  3rd Jim Clark [GB] *Lotus-Climax*
  Fastest lap: Denny Hulme [NZ] *Brabham-Repco
    103.53 mph*

GERMAN Nürburging 7 Aug
  1st Jack Brabham [Austral] *Brabham-Repco 86.75 mph*
  2nd John Surtees [GB] *Cooper-Maserati*
  3rd Jochen Rindt [Aus] *Cooper-Maserati*
  Fastest lap: Surtees *96.45 mph*

ITALIAN Monza 4 Sept
  1st Ludovico Scarfiotti [It] *Ferrari 135.92 mph*
  2nd Mike Parkes [GB] *Ferrari*
  3rd Denny Hulme [NZ] *Brabham-Repco*
  Fastest lap: Scarfiotti *139.2 mph*

UNITED STATES Watkins Glen 2 Oct
  1st Jim Clark [GB] Lotus-*BRM 114.94 mph*
  2nd Jochen Rindt [Aus] *Cooper-Maserati*
  3rd John Surtees [GB] *Cooper-Maserati*
  Fastest lap: Surtees *118.85 mph*

MEXICAN Mexico City 3 Oct
  1st John Surtees [GB] *Cooper-Maserati 95.72 mph*
  2nd Jack Brabham [Austral] *Brabham-Repco*
  3rd Denny Hulme [NZ] *Brabham-Repco*
  Fastest lap: Richie Ginther [USA] *Honda 98.33 mph*

TARGA FLORIO Piccolo Circuito Madonie 8 May
  1st Willy Mairesse [Bel]/Herbert Muller [Switz] *Porsche
    61.36 mph*
  2nd Giancarlo Baghetti [It]/J. Guichet [Fr] *Ferrari*
  3rd Baron Antonio Pucci [It]/V. Arena [It] *Porsche*
  Fastest lap: Nino Vaccarella [It] *Ferrari 63.99 mph*

INDIANAPOLIS 500 31 May
  1st Graham Hill [GB] *American Red Ball 144.317 mph*
  2nd Jim Clark [GB] *STP Gas Treatment*
  3rd Jim McElreath [USA] *Zink-UrschelSlick*
  Fastest qualifier: Mario Andretti [USA] *Dean Van Lines
    165.849 mph*

World Champion: Denny Hulme [NZ]
US National Champion: A.J. Foyt
Fastest Man on Earth: Craig Breedlove (>1965)

GRANDS PRIX

SOUTH AFRICAN Kyalami 2 Jan
  1st Pedro Rodriguez [Mex] *Cooper-Maserati 97.09 mph*
  2nd John Love [Zim] *Cooper-Climax*
  3rd John Surtees [GB] *Honda*
  Fastest lap: Denny Hulme [NZ] *Brabham-Repco
    101.87 mph*

MONACO Monte Carlo 7 May
  1st Denny Hulme [NZ] *Brabham-Repco 75.9 mph*
  2nd Graham Hill [GB] *Lotus-BRM*
  3rd Chris Amon [NZ] *Ferrari*
  Fastest lap: Jim Clark [GB] *Lotus-Climax 78.61 mph*

DUTCH Zandvoort 4 June
  1st Jim Clark [GB] *Lotus-Ford 104.44 mph*
  2nd Jack Brabham [Austral] *Brabham-Repco*
  3rd Denny Hulme [NZ] *Brabham-Repco*
  Fastest lap: Clark *106.49 mph*

BELGIAN Spa 18 June
  1st Dan Gurney [USA] *Eagle-Weslake 145.99 mph*
  2nd Jackie Stewart [GB] *BRM*
  3rd Chris Amon [NZ] *Ferrari*
  Fastest lap: Gurney *148.85 mph*

FRENCH Le Mans 2 July
  1st Jack Brabham [Austral] *Brabham-Repco 98.9 mph*
  2nd Denny Hulme [NZ] *Brabham-Repco*
  3rd Jackie Stewart [GB] *BRM*
  Fastest lap: Graham Hill [GB] *Lotus-Ford 102.29 mph*

BRITISH Silverstone 15 July
  1st Jim Clark [GB] *Lotus-Ford 117.64 mph*
  2nd Denny Hulme [NZ] *Brabham-Repco*
  3rd Chris Amon [NZ] *Ferrari*
  Fastest lap: Hulme *121.12 mph*

GERMAN Nürburging 6 Aug
  1st Denny Hulme [NZ] *Brabham-Repco 101.41 mph*
  2nd Jack Brabham [Austral] *Brabham-Repco*
  3rd Chris Amon [NZ] *Ferrari*
  Fastest lap: Dan Gurney [USA] *Eagle-Weslake
    103.17 mph*

CANADIAN Mosport 27 Aug
  1st Jack Brabham [Austral] *Brabham-Repco 82.65 mph*
  2nd Denny Hulme [NZ] *Brabham-Repco*
  3rd Dan Gurney [USA] *Eagle-Weslake*
  Fastest lap: Jim Clark [GB] *Lotus-Ford 106.54 mph*

ITALIAN Monza 10 Sept
  1st John Surtees [GB] *Honda 140.5 mph*
  2nd Jack Brabham [Austral] *Brabham-Repco*
  3rd Jim Clark [GB] *Lotus-Ford*
  Fastest lap: Clark *145.34 mph*

UNITED STATES Watkins Glen 1 Oct
  1st Jim Clark [GB] *Lotus-Ford 120.95 mph*
  2nd Graham Hill [GB] *Lotus-Ford*
  3rd Denny Hulme [NZ] *Brabham-Repco*
  Fastest lap: Hill *125.46 mph*

MEXICAN Mexico City 22 Oct
  1st Jim Clark [GB] *Lotus-Ford 101.42 mph*
  2nd Jack Brabham [Austral] *Brabham-Repco*
  3rd Denny Hulme [NZ] *Brabham-Repco*
  Fastest lap: Clark *103.44 mph*

TARGA FLORIO Piccolo Circuito Madonie 14 May
  1st Paul Hawkins [Austral]/Rolf Stommelen [Ger] *Porsche
    67.61 mph*
  2nd L. Cella [It]/G. Biscaldi [It] *Porsche*
  3rd Jochen Neerpasch/Vic Elford [GB] *Porsche*
  Fastest lap: Herbert Muller [Switz] *Ferrari 72.1 mph*

INDIANAPOLIS 500 30–31 May
  1st A.J. Foyt [USA] *Sheraton-Thompson 151.207 mph*
  2nd Al Unser [USA] *Retzloff Chemical*
  3rd Joe Leonard [USA] *Sheraton-Thompson*
  Fastest qualifier: Dan Gurney [USA] *Wagner Lockheed
    167.224 mph*

World Champion: Graham Hill [GB]
US National Champion: Bobby Unser
Fastest Man on Earth: Craig Breedlove (1965)

GRANDS PRIX

SOUTH AFRICAN Kyalami I Jan
  1st Jim Clark [GB] *Lotus-Ford 107.42 mph*
  2nd Graham Hill [GB] *Lotus-Ford*
  3rd Jochen Rindt [Aus] *Brabham-Repco*
  Fastest lap: Clark *109.68 mph*

SPANISH Jarama 12 May
  1st Graham Hill [GB] *Lotus-Ford 84.4 mph*
  2nd Denny Hulme [NZ] *McLaren-Ford*
  3rd Brian Redman [GB] *Cooper-BRM*
  Fastest lap: Jean-Pierre Beltoise [Fr] *Matra-Ford
    86.24 mph*

MONACO Monte Carlo 26 May
  1st Graham Hill [GB] *Lotus-Ford 77.82 mph*
  2nd Dickie Attwood [GB] *BRM*
  3rd Lucien Bianchi [Bel] *Cooper-BRM*
  Fastest lap: Attwood *79.85 mph*

BELGIAN Spa 9 June
  1st Bruce McLaren [NZ] *McLaren-Ford 147.14 mph*
  2nd Pedro Rodriguez [Mex] *BRM*
  3rd Jacky Ickx [Bel] *Ferrari*
  Fastest lap: John Surtees [GB] *Honda 149.84 mph*

DUTCH Zandvoort 23 June
  1st Jackie Stewart [GB] *Matra-Ford 84.66 mph*
  2nd Jean-Pierre Beltoise [Fr] *Matra*
  3rd Pedro Rodriguez [Mex] *BRM*
  Fastest lap: Beltoise *88.56 mph*

FRENCH Rouen 7 July
  1st Jacky Ickx [Bel] *Ferrari 100.45 mph*
  2nd John Surtees [GB] *Honda*
  3rd Jackie Stewart [GB] *Matra-Ford*
  Fastest lap: Pedro Rodriguez [Mex] *BRM 111.29 mph*

BRITISH Brands Hatch 20 July
  1st Jo Siffert [Switz] *Lotus-Ford 104.83 mph*
  2nd Chris Amon [NZ] *Ferrari*
  3rd Jacky Ickx [Bel] *Ferrari*
  Fastest lap: Siffert *106.35 mph*

GERMAN Nürburging 4 Aug
  1st Jackie Stewart [GB] *Matra-Ford 85.71 mph*
  2nd Graham Hill [GB] *Lotus-Ford*
  3rd Jochen Rindt [Aus] *Brabham-Repco*
  Fastest lap: Stewart *88.68 mph*

ITALIAN Monza 8 Sept
  1st Denny Hulme [NZ] *McLaren-Ford 145.41 mph*
  2nd Johnny Servoz-Gavin [Fr] *Matra-Ford*
  3rd Jacky Ickx [Bel] *Ferrari*
  Fastest lap: Jackie Oliver [GB] *Lotus-Ford 148.7 mph*

CANADIAN St Jovite 22 Sept
  1st Denny Hulme [NZ] *McLaren-Ford 97.22 mph*
  2nd Bruce McLaren [NZ] *McLaren-Ford*
  3rd Pedro Rodriguez [Mex] *BRM*
  Fastest lap: Jo Siffert [Switz] *Lotus-Ford 100.31 mph*

UNITED STATES Watkins Glen 6 Oct
  1st Jackie Stewart [GB] *Matra-Ford 124.9 mph*
  2nd Graham Hill [GB] *Lotus-Ford*
  3rd John Surtees [GB] *Honda*
  Fastest lap: Stewart *126.96 mph*

MEXICAN Mexico City 3 Nov
1st Graham Hill [GB] *Lotus-Ford 103.8 mph*
2nd Bruce McLaren [NZ] *McLaren-Ford*
3rd Jackie Oliver [GB] *Lotus-Ford*
Fastest lap: Jo Siffert [Switz] *Lotus-Ford 107.31 mph*

TARGA FLORIO Piccolo Circuito Madonie 5 May
1st Vic Elford [GB]/Umberto Maglioli [It] *Porsche 68.9 mph*
2nd Nanni Galli [It]/Ignazio Giunti [It] *Alfa-Romeo*
3rd Mario Casoni [It]/Lucien Bianchi [Bel] *Alfa-Romeo*
Fastest lap: Elford *74.49 mph*

INDIANAPOLIS 500 30 May
1st Bobby Unser [USA] *Rislone 152.882 mph*
2nd Dan Gurney [USA] *Olsonite*
3rd Mel Kenyon [USA] *City of Lebanon*
Fastest qualifier: Joe Leonard [USA] *STP Oil Treatment 171.599 mph*

1969

World Champion: Jackie Stewart [GB]
US National Champion: Mario Andretti
Fastest Man on Earth: Craig Breedlove (>1965)

GRANDS PRIX

SOUTH AFRICAN Kyalami 2 Jan
1st Jackie Stewart [GB] *Matra-Ford 110.62 mph*
2nd Graham Hill [GB] *Lotus-Ford*
3rd Denny Hulme [NZ] *McLaren-Ford*
Fastest lap: Stewart *12.5 mph*

SPANISH Montjuich Park 4 May
1st Jackie Stewart [GB] *Matra-Ford 92.91 mph*
2nd Bruce McLaren [NZ] *McLaren-Ford*
3rd Jean-Pierre Beltoise [Fr] *Matra-Ford*
Fastest lap: Jochen Rindt [Aus] *Lotus-Ford 96.02 mph*

MONACO Monte Carlo 18 May
1st Graham Hill [GB] *Lotus-Ford 80.18 mph*
2nd Piers Courage [GB] *Brabham-Ford*
3rd Jo Siffert [Switz] *Lotus-Ford*
Fastest lap: Jackie Stewart [GB] *Matra-Ford 82.67 mph*

DUTCH Zandvoort 21 June
1st Jackie Stewart [GB] *Matra-Ford 111.04 mph*
2nd Jo Siffert [Switz] *Lotus-Ford*
3rd Chris Amon [NZ] *Ferrari*
Fastest lap: Stewart *113.09 mph*

FRENCH Clermont-Ferrand 6 July
1st Jackie Stewart [GB] *Matra-Ford 97.71 mph*
2nd Jean-Pierre Beltoise [Fr] *Matra-Ford*
3rd Jacky Ickx [Bel] *Brabham-Ford*
Fastest lap: Stewart *98.62 mph*

BRITISH Silverstone 19 July
1st Jackie Stewart [GB] *Matra-Ford 127.25 mph*
2nd Jacky Ickx [Bel] *Brabham-Ford*
3rd Bruce McLaren [NZ] *McLaren-Ford*
Fastest lap: Stewart *129.61 mph*

GERMAN Nürburging 3 Aug
1st Jacky Ickx [Bel] *Brabham-Ford 108.43 mph*
2nd Jackie Stewart [GB] *Matra-Ford*
3rd Bruce McLaren [NZ] *McLaren-Ford*
Fastest lap: Ickx *110.13 mph*

ITALIAN Monza 7 Sept
1st Jackie Stewart [GB] *Matra-Ford 146.97 mph*
2nd Jochen Rindt [Aus] *Lotus-Ford*
3rd Jean-Pierre Beltoise [Fr] *Matra-Ford*
Fastest lap: Beltoise *150.97 mph*

CANADIAN Mosport 20 Sept
1st Jacky Ickx [Bel] *Brabham-Ford 111.18 mph*
2nd Jack Brabham [Austral] *Brabham-Ford*
3rd Jochen Rindt [Aus] *Lotus-Ford*
Fastest lap: Ickx/Brabham *113.39 mph*

UNITED STATES Watkins Glen 5 Oct
1st Jochen Rindt [Aus] *Lotus-Ford 126.36 mph*
2nd Piers Courage [GB] *Brabham-Ford*
3rd John Surtees [GB] *BRM*
Fastest lap: Rindt *128.7 mph*

MEXICAN Mexico City 19 Oct
1st Denny Hulme [NZ] *McLaren-Ford 106.15 mph*
2nd Jacky Ickx [Bel] *Brabham-Ford*
3rd Jack Brabham [Austral] *Brabham-Ford*
Fastest lap: Ickx *108.54 mph*

TARGA FLORIO Piccolo Circuito Madonie 5 May
1st Gerhard Miter [Ger]/Udo Schutz [Ger] *Porsche 72.99 mph*
2nd Vic Elford [GB]/Umberto Maglioli [It] *Porsche*
3rd Hans Herrmann [Ger]/Rolf Stommelen [Ger] *Porsche*
Fastest lap: Elford-Maglioli *76.39 mph*

INDIANAPOLIS 500 30 May
1st Mario Andretti [USA] *STP Oil Treatment 156.867 mph*
2nd Dan Gurney [USA] *Olsonite*
3rd Bobby Unser [USA] *Bardahl*
Fastest qualifier: A.J. Foyt [USA] *Sheraton-Thompson 170.568 mph*

1970

World Champion: Jochen Rindt [Aus]
US National Champion: Al Unser
Fastest Man on Earth: Gary Gabelich [USA] *The Blue Flame* 622.407 mph

GRANDS PRIX

SOUTH AFRICAN Kyalami 7 March
1st Jack Brabham [NZ] *Brabham-Ford 111.7 mph*
2nd Denny Hulme [NZ] *McLaren-Ford*
3rd Jackie Stewart [GB] *Matra-Ford*
Fastest lap: Brabham/John Surtees [GB] *McLaren-Ford 113.61 mph*

SPANISH Jarama 19 April
1st Jackie Stewart [GB] *March-Ford 87.22 mph*
2nd Bruce McLaren [NZ] *McLaren-Ford*
3rd Mario Andretti [USA] *March-Ford*
Fastest lap: Jack Brabham [Austral] *Brabham-Ford 90.34 mph*

MONACO Monte Carlo 10 May
1st Jochen Rindt [Aus] *Lotus-Ford 81.85 mph*
2nd Jack Brabham [Austral] *Brabham-Ford*
3rd Henri Pescarolo [Fr] *Matra-Simca*
Fastest lap: Rindt *84.56 mph*

BELGIAN Spa 7 June
1st Pedro Rodriguez [Mex] *BRM 149.94 mph*
2nd Chris Amon [NZ] *March-Ford*
3rd Jean-Pierre Beltoise [Fr] *Matra-Simca*
Fastest lap: Amon *152.08 mph*

DUTCH Zandvoort 21 June
1st Jochen Rindt [Aus] *Lotus-Ford 112.95 mph*
2nd Jackie Stewart [GB] *March-Ford*
3rd Jacky Ickx [Bel] *Ferrari*
Fastest lap: Ickx *118.38 mph*

FRENCH Clermont-Ferrand 5 July
1st Jochen Rindt [Aus] *Lotus-Ford 98.42 mph*
2nd Chris Amon [NZ] *March-Ford*
3rd Jack Brabham [Austral] *Brabham-Ford*
Fastest lap: Brabham *99.69 mph*

BRITISH Brands Hatch 18 July
1st Jochen Rindt [Aus] *Lotus-Ford 108.69 mph*
2nd Jack Brabham [Austral] *Brabham*
3rd Denny Hulme [NZ] *McLaren-Ford*
Fastest lap: Brabham *111.06 mph*

GERMAN Hockenheim 2 Aug
1st Jochen Rindt [Aus] *Lotus-Ford 124.07 mph*
2nd Jacky Ickx [Bel] *Ferrari*
3rd Denny Hulme [NZ] *McLaren-Ford*
Fastest lap: Ickx *126.03 mph*

AUSTRIAN Österreichring 16 Aug
1st Jacky Ickx [Bel] *Ferrari 129.2 mph*
2nd Clay Regazzoni [Switz] *Ferrari*
3rd Rolf Stommelen [Ger] *Brabham-Ford*
Fastest lap: Ickx/Regazzoni *131.7 mph*

ITALIAN Monza 6 Sept
1st Clay Regazzoni [Switz] *Ferrari 147.08 mph*
2nd Jackie Stewart [GB] *March-Ford*
3rd Jean-Pierre Beltoise [Fr] *Matra-Simca*
Fastest lap: Regazzoni *150.97 mph*

CANADIAN St Jovite 20 Sept
1st Jacky Ickx [Bel] *Ferrari 101.27 mph*
2nd Clay Regazzoni [Switz] *Ferrari*
3rd Chris Amon [NZ] *March-Ford*
Fastest lap: Regazzoni *103.47 mph*

UNITED STATES Watkins Glen 4 Oct
1st Emerson Fittipaldi [Bra] *Lotus-Ford 126.79 mph*
2nd Pedro Rodriguez [Mex] *BRM*
3rd Reine Wissell [Swe] *Lotus-Ford*
Fastest lap: Jacky Ickx [Bel] *Ferrari 131.97 mph*

MEXICAN Mexico City 25 Oct
1st Jacky Ickx [Bel] *Ferrari 106.78 mph*
2nd Clay Regazzoni [Switz] *Ferrari*
3rd Denny Hulme [NZ] *McLaren-Ford*
Fastest lap: Ickx *108.47 mph*

TARGA FLORIO Piccolo Circuito Madonie 3 May
1st Jo Siffert [Switz]/Brian Redman *Porsche 74.66 mph*
2nd Pedro Rodriguez [Mex]/Leo Kinnunen [Fin] *Porsche*
3rd Nino Vaccarella [It]/Ignazio Giunti [It] *Ferrari*
Fastest lap: Kinnunen *77.55 mph*

INDIANAPOLIS 500 30 May
1st Al Unser [USA] *Johnny Lightning 155.749 mph*
2nd Mark Donahue [USA] *Sunoco*
3rd Dan Gurney [USA] *Olsonite Eagle*
Fastest qualifier: Unser *170.221 mph*

1971

World Champion: Jackie Stewart [GB]
US National Champion: Joe Leonard
Fastest Man on Earth: Gary Gabelich (>1970)

GRANDS PRIX

SOUTH AFRICAN Kyalami 6 March
1st Mario Andretti [USA] *Ferrari 112.35 mph*
2nd Jackie Stewart [GB] *Tyrrell-Ford*
3rd Clay Regazzoni [Switz] *Ferrari*
Fastest lap: Andretti *114.33 mph*

SPANISH Montjuich Park 18 April
1st Jackie Stewart [GB] *Tyrrell-Ford 97.19 mph*
2nd Jacky Ickx [Bel] *Ferrari*
3rd Chris Amon [NZ] *Matra-Simca*
Fastest lap: Ickx *99.64 mph*

MONACO Monte Carlo 23 May
1st Jackie Stewart [GB] *Tyrrell-Ford 83.49 mph*
2nd Ronnie Peterson [Swe] *March-Ford*
3rd Jacky Ickx [Bel] *Ferrari*
Fastest lap: Stewart *85.59 mph*

DUTCH Zandvoort 20 June
1st Jacky Ickx [Bel] *Ferrari 94.06 mph*
2nd Pedro Rodriguez [Mex] *BRM*
3rd Clay Regazzoni [Switz] *Ferrari*
Fastest lap: Ickx *98.78 mph*

FRENCH Paul Ricard 4 July
1st Jackie Stewart [GB] *Tyrrell-Ford 111.66 mph*
2nd François Cevert [Fr] *Tyrrell-Ford*
3rd Emerson Fittipaldi [Bra] *Lotus-Ford*
Fastest lap: Stewart *113.92 mph*

BRITISH Silverstone 17 July
1st Jackie Stewart [GB] *Tyrrell-Ford 130.48 mph*
2nd Ronnie Peterson [Swe] *March-Ford*
3rd Emerson Fittipaldi [Bra] *Lotus-Ford*
Fastest lap: Stewart *131.88 mph*

GERMAN Nürburging 1Aug
1st Jackie Stewart [GB] *Tyrrell-Ford 114.45 mph*
2nd François Cevert [Fr] *Tyrrell-Ford*
3rd Clay Regazzoni [Switz] *Ferrari*
Fastest lap: Cevert *116.07 mph*

AUSTRIAN Österreichring 15 Aug
1st Jo Siffert [Switz] *BRM 131.64 mph*
2nd Emerson Fittipaldi [Bra] *Lotus-Ford*
3rd Tim Schenken [Austral] *Brabham-Ford*
Fastest lap: Siffert *134.28 mph*

ITALIAN Monza 5 Sept
1st Peter Gethin [GB] *BRM 150.75 mph*
2nd Ronnie Peterson [Swe] *March-Ford*
3rd François Cevert [Frj] *Tyrrell-Ford*
Fastest lap: Henri Pescarolo [Fr] *March-Ford 153.49 mph*

CANADIAN Mosport 19 Sept
1st Jackie Stewart [GB] *Tyrrell-Ford 81.95 mph*
2nd Ronnie Peterson [Swe] *March-Ford*
3rd Mark Donahue [USA] *McLaren-Ford*
Fastest lap: Denny Hulme [NZ] *McLaren-Ford 85.52 mph*

UNITED STATES Watkins Glen 3 Oct
1st François Cevert [Fr] *Tyrrell-Ford 115.1 mph*
2nd Jo Siffert [Switz] *BRM*
3rd Ronnie Peterson [Swe] *March-Ford*
Fastest lap: Jacky Ickx [Bel] *Ferrari 117.5 mph*

TARGA FLORIO Piccolo Circuito Madonie 16 May
1st Nino Vaccarella [It]/Theo Hezemans [Aus] *Alfa-Romeo 74.59 mph*
2nd Andrea de Adamich [It]/Gijs van Lennep [Hal] *Alfa-Romeo*
3rd Jo Bonnier [Swe]/Dickie Atwood [GB] *Lola*
Fastest lap: Vic Elford [GB] *Porsche 79.51 mph*

INDIANAPOLIS 500 29 May
1st Al Unser [USA] *Johnny Lightning 157.735 mph*
2nd Peter Revson [USA] *McLaren Cars*
3rd A.J. Foyt [USA] *ITT*
Fastest qualifier: *Revson 178.696 mph*

1972

World Champion: Emerson Fittipaldi [Bra]
US National Champion: Joe Leonard
Fastest Man on Earth: Gary Gabelich (>1970)

GRANDS PRIX

ARGENTINE Buenos Aires 23 Jan
1st Jackie Stewart [GB] *Tyrrell-Ford 100.42 mph*
2nd Denny Hulme [NZ] *McLaren-Ford*
3rd Jacky Ickx [Bel] *Ferrari*
Fastest lap: Stewart *101.58 mph*

SOUTH AFRICAN Kyalami 4 March
1st Denny Hulme [NZ] *McLaren-Ford 114.23 mph*
2nd Emerson Fittipaldi [Bra] *Lotus-Ford*
3rd Peter Revson [USA] *McLaren-Ford*
Fastest lap: Mike Hailwood [GB] *SurteesFord 116.35 mph*

SPANISH Jarama 1 May
1st Emerson Fittipaldi [Bra] *Lotus-Ford 92.35 mph*
2nd Jacky Ickx [Bel] *Ferrari*
3rd Clay Regazzoni [Switz] *Ferrari*
Fastest lap: Ickx *94 mph*

MONACO Monte Carlo 14 May
1st Jean-Pierre Beltoise [Fr] *BRM 63.85 mph*
2nd Jacky ickx [Bel] *Ferrari*
3rd Emerson Fittipaldi [Bra] *Lotus-Ford*
Fastest lap: Beltoise *70.35 mph*

BELGIAN Nivelles 4 June
1st Emerson Fittipaldi [Bra] *Lotus-Ford 113.35 mph*
2nd François Cevert [Fr] *Lotus-Ford*
3rd Denny Hulme [NZ] *McLaren-Ford*
Fastest lap: Chris Amon [NZ] *Matra-Simca 115.51 mph*

FRENCH Clermont-Ferrand 2 July
1st Jackie Stewart [GB] *Tyrrell-Ford 101.57 mph*
2nd Emerson Fittipaldi [Bra] *Lotus-Ford*
3rd Chris Amon [NZ] *Matra-Simca*
Fastest lap: Amon *103.61 mph*

BRITISH Brands Hatch 15 July
1st Emerson Fittipaldi [Bra] *Lotus-Ford 112.06 mph*
2nd Jackie Stewart [GB] *Tyrrell-Ford*
3rd Peter Revson [USA] *McLaren-Ford*
Fastest lap: Stewart *113.57 mph*

GERMAN Nürburging 30 July
1st Jacky Ickx [Bel] *Ferrari 116.62 mph*
2nd Clay Regazzoni [Switz] *Ferrari*
3rd Ronnie Peterson [Swe] *March-Ford*
Fastest lap: Ickx *117.81 mph*

AUSTRIAN Österreichring 13 Aug
1st Emerson Fittipaldi [Bra] *Lotus-Ford 133.3 mph*
2nd Denny Hulme [NZ] *McLaren-Ford*
3rd Peter Revson [USA] *McLaren-Ford*
Fastest lap: Hulme *134.48 mph*

ITALIAN Monza 10 Sept
1st Emerson Fittipaldi [Bra] *Lotus-Ford 131.61 mph*
2nd Mike Hailwood [GB] *Surtees-Ford*
3rd Denny Hulme [NZ] *McLaren-Ford*
Fastest lap: Jacky Ickx [Bel] *Ferrari 134.15 mph*

CANADIAN Mosport 24 Sept
1st Jackie Stewart [GB] *Tyrrell-Ford 114.27 mph*
2nd Peter Revson [USA] *McLaren-Ford*
3rd Denny Hulme [NZ] *McLaren-Ford*
Fastest lap: Stewart *116.98 mph*

UNITED STATES Watkins Glen 8 Oct
1st Jackie Stewart [GB] *Tyrrell-Ford 117.49 mph*
2nd François Cevert [Fr] *Tyrrell-Ford*
3rd Denny Hulme [NZ] *McLaren-Ford*
Fastest lap: Stewart *119.61 mph*

TARGA FLORIO Piccolo Circuito Madonie 21 May
1st Arturo Merzario [It]/Sandro Munari [It] *Ferrari 75.97 mph*
2nd Helmut Marko [Aus]/Nanni Galli [It] *Alfa-Romeo*
3rd Theo Hezemans [Aus]/Andrea de Adamich [It] *Alfa-Romeo*
Fastest lap: Marko *79.52 mph*

INDIANAPOLIS 500 27 May
1st Mark Donahue [USA] *Sunoco McLaren 162.962 mph*
2nd Al Unser [USA] *Viceroy*
3rd Joe Leonard [USA] *Samsonite*
Fastest qualifier: Bobby Unser [USA] *Olsonite Eagle 195.94 mph*

1973

World Champion: Jackie Stewart [GB]
US National Champion: Roger McCluskey
Fastest Man on Earth: Gary Gabelich (>1970)

GRANDS PRIX

ARGENTINE Buenos Aires 28 January
1st Emerson Fittipaldi [Bra] *Lotus-Ford 102.95 mph*
2nd François Cevert [Fr] *Tyrrell-Ford*
3rd Jackie Stewart [GB] *Tyrrell-Ford*
Fastest lap: Fittipaldi *105.08 mph*

BRAZILIAN Interlagos 11 Feb
1st Emerson Fittipaldi [Bra] *Lotus-Ford 114.22 mph*
2nd Jackie Stewart [GB] *Tyrrell-Ford*
3rd Denny Hulme [NZ] *McLaren-Ford*
Fastest lap: Fittipaldi/Hulme *114.88 mph*

SOUTH AFRICAN Kyalami 3 March
1st Jackie Stewart [GB] *Tyrrell-Ford 117.14 mph*
2nd Peter Revson [USA] *McLaren-Ford*
3rd Emerson Fittipaldi [Bra] *Lotus-Ford*
Fastest lap: Fittipaldi *119.07 mph*

SPANISH Montjuich Park 29 April
1st Emerson Fittipaldi [Bra] *Lotus-Ford 97.86 mph*
2nd François Cevert [Fr] *Tyrrell-Ford*
3rd George Follmer [USA] *Shadow-Ford*
Fastest lap: Ronnie Peterson [Swe] *Lotus-Ford 101.19 mph*

BELGIAN Zolder 20 May
1st Jackie Stewart [GB] *Tyrrell-Ford 107.74 mph*
2nd François Cevert [Fr] *Tyrrell-Ford*
3rd Emerson Fittipaldi [Bra] *Lotus-Ford*
Fastest lap: Cevert *110.51 mph*

MONACO Monte Carlo 3 June
1st Jackie Stewart [GB] *Tyrrell-Ford 80.96 mph*
2nd Emerson Fittipaldi [Bra] *Lotus-Ford*
3rd Ronnie Peterson [Swe] *Lotus-Ford*
Fastest lap: Fittipaldi *83.23 mph*

SWEDISH Anderstorp 17 June
1st Denny Hulme [NZ] *McLaren-Ford 102.63 mph*
2nd Ronnie Peterson [Swe] *Lotus-Ford*
3rd François Cevert [Fr] *Lotus-Ford*
Fastest lap: Hulme *104.33 mph*

FRENCH Paul Ricard 1 July
1st Ronnie Peterson [Swe] *Lotus-Ford 115.12 mph*
2nd François Cevert [Fr] *Tyrrell-Ford*
3rd Carlos Reutemann [Arg] *Brabham-Ford*
Fastest lap: Denny Hulme [NZ] *McLaren-Ford 117.1 mph*

BRITISH Silverstone 14 July
1st Peter Revson [USA] *McLaren-Ford 131.75 mph*
2nd Ronnie Peterson [Swe] *Lotus-Ford*
3rd Denny Hulme [NZ] *McLaren-Ford*
Fastest lap: James Hunt [GB] *March-Ford 134.06 mph*

DUTCH Zandvoort 29 July
1st Jackie Stewart -[GB] *Tyrrell-Ford 114.35 mph*
2nd François Cevert [Fr] *Tyrrell-Ford*
3rd James Hunt [GB] *March-Ford*
Fastest lap: Ronnie Peterson [Swe] *Lotus-Ford 117.71 mph*

GERMAN Nürburging 5 Aug
1st Jackie Stewart [GB] *Tyrrell-Ford 116.79 mph*
2nd François Cevert [Fr] *Tyrrell-Ford*
3rd Jacky Ickx [Bel] *McLaren-Ford*
Fastest lap: Carlos Pace [Bra] *SurteesFord 118.41 mph*

AUSTRIAN Österreichring 9 Aug
1st Ronnie Peterson [Swe] *Lotus-Ford 133.99 mph*
2nd Jackie Stewart [GB] *Tyrrell-Ford*
3rd Carlos Pace [Bra] *Surtees-Ford*
Fastest lap: Pace *135.91 mph*

ITALIAN Monza 9 Sept
1st Ronnie Peterson [Swe] *Lotus-Ford 132.63 mph*
2nd Emerson Fittipaldi [Bra] *Lotus-Ford*
3rd Peter Revson [USA] *McLaren-Ford*
Fastest lap: Jackie Stewart [GB] *Tyrrell-Ford 135.55 mph*

CANADIAN Mosport 23 Sept
1st Peter Revson [USA] *McLaren-Ford 99.13 mph*
2nd Emerson Fittipaldi [Bra] *Lotus-Ford*
3rd Jackie Oliver [GB] *Shadow-Ford*
Fastest lap: Fittipaldi *117.26 mph*

UNITED STATES Watkins Glen 7 Oct
1st Ronnie Peterson [Swe] *Lotus-Ford 118.06 mph*
2nd James Hunt [GB] *March-Ford*
3rd Carlos Reutemann [Arg] *Brabham-Ford*
Fastest lap: Hunt *119.6 mph*

TARGA FLORIO Piccolo Circuito Madonie 13 May
1st Herbert Muller [Switz]/Gijs van Lennep [Hal] *Porsche Carrera 71.11 mph*
2nd Sandro Munari [It]/Jean-Claude Andruet [Fr] *Lancia*
3rd Leo Kinnunen [Fin]/Claude Haldi [SwitzJ *Porsche*
Fastest lap: Rolf Stommelen [Ger] *Alfa-Romeo 78.27 mph*

INDIANAPOLIS 500 28 May
1st Gordon Johncock [USA] *STP Double Oil Filter*
159.036 mph
2nd Bill Vukovich [USA] *Sugaripe Prune*
3rd Roger McCluskey [USA] *Lindsey Hopkins Buick*
Fastest qualifier: Johnny Rutherford [USA] *Gulf McLaren*
198.413 mph

1974

World Champion: Emerson Fittipaldi [Bra]
US National Champion: Bobby Unser
Fastest Man on Earth: Gary Gabelich (1970)

GRANDS PRIX

ARGENTINE Buenos Aires 13 Jan
1st Denny Hulme [NZ] *McLaren-Ford 116.72 mph*
2nd Niki Lauda [Aus] *Ferrari*
3rd Clay Regazzoni [Switz] *Ferrari*
Fastest lap: Regazzoni *119.09 mph*

BRAZILIAN Interlagos 27 Jan
1st Emerson Fittipaldi [Bra] *McLaren-Ford 112.23 mph*
2nd Clay Regazzoni [Switz] *Ferrari*
3rd Jacky Ickx [Bel] *Lotus-Ford*
Fastest lap: Regazzoni *114.1 mph*

SOUTH AFRICAN Kyalami 30 March
1st Carlos Reutemann [Arg] *Brabham-Ford 116.23 mph*
2nd Jean-Pierre Beltoise [Fr] *BRM*
3rd Mike Hailwood [GB] *McLaren-Ford*
Fastest lap: Reutemann *117.46 mph*

SPANISH Jarama 28 April
1st Niki Lauda [Aus] *Ferrari 88.48 mph*
2nd Clay Regazzoni [Switz] *Ferrari*
3rd Emerson Fittipaldi [Bra] *McLaren-Ford*
Fastest lap: Lauda *94.21 mph*

BELGIAN Nivelles 12 May
1st Emerson Fittipaldi [Bra] *McLaren-Ford 113.1 mph*
2nd Niki Lauda [Aus] *Ferrari*
3rd Jody Scheckter [SA] *Tyrrell-Ford*
Fastest lap: Denny Hulme [NZ] *McLaren-Ford 116.82 mph*

MONACO Monte Carlo 26 May
1st Ronnie Peterson [Swe] *Lotus-Ford 80.74 mph*
2nd Jody Scheckter [SA] *Tyrrell-Ford*
3rd Jean-Pierre Jarier [Fr] *Shadow-Ford*
Fastest lap: Peterson *83.42 mph*

SWEDISH Anderstorp 9 June
1st Jody Scheckter [SA] *Tyrrell-Ford 101.11 mph*
2nd Patrick Depailler [Fr] *Tyrrell-Ford*
3rd James Hunt [GB] *Hesketh-Ford*
Fastest lap: Depailler *103 mph*

DUTCH Zandvoort 23 June
1st Niki Lauda [Aus] *Ferrari 114.72 mph*
2nd Clay Regazzoni [Switz] *Ferrari*
3rd Emerson Fittipaldi [Bra] *McLaren-Ford*
Fastest lap: Ronnie Peterson [Swe] *Lotus-Ford*
116.08 mph

FRENCH Dijon-Prenois 7 July
1st Ronnie Peterson [Swe] *Lotus-Ford 119.75 mph*
2nd Niki Lauda [Aus] *Ferrari*
3rd Clay Regazzoni [Switz] *Ferrari*
Fastest lap: Jody Scheckter [SA] *Tyrrell-Ford 122.62 mph*

BRITISH Brands Hatch 20 July
1st Jody Scheckter [SA] *Tyrrell-Ford 115.74 mph*
2nd Emerson Fittipaldi [Bra] *McLaren-Ford*
3rd Jacky Ickx [Bel] *Lotus-Ford*
Fastest lap: Niki Lauda [Aus] *Ferrari 117.63 mph*

GERMAN Nürburging 4 Aug
1st Clay Regazzoni [Switz] *Ferrari 117.33 mph*
2nd Jody Scheckter [SA] *Tyrrell-Ford*
3rd Carlos Reutemann [Arg] *Brabham-Ford*
Fastest lap: Scheckter *118.49 mph*

AUSTRIAN Österreichring 18 Aug
1st Carlos Reutemann [Arg] *Brabham-Ford 134.09 mph*
2nd Denny Hulme [NZ] *McLaren-Ford*
3rd James Hunt [GB] *Hesketh-Ford*
Fastest lap: Clay Regazzoni [Switz] *Ferrari 136.01 mph*

ITALIAN Monza 8 Sept
1st Ronnie Peterson [Swe] *Lotus-Ford 135.1 mph*
2nd Emerson Fittipaldi [Bra] *McLaren-Ford*
3rd Jody Scheckter [SA] *Tyrrell-Ford*
Fastest lap: Carlos Pace [Bra] *Brabham-Ford 137.26 mph*

CANADIAN Mosport 22 Sept
1st Emerson Fittipaldi [Bra] *McLaren-Ford 117.7 mph*
2nd Clay Regazzoni [Switz] *Ferrari*
3rd Ronnie Peterson [Swe] *Lotus-Ford*
Fastest lap: Niki Lauda [Aus] *Ferrari 120.18 mph*

UNITED STATES Watkins Glen 6 Oct
1st Carlos Reutemann [Arg] *Brabham-Ford 119.12 mph*
2nd Carlos Pace [Bra] *Brabham-Ford*
3rd James Hunt [GB] *Hesketh-Ford*
Fastest lap: Pace *120.4 mph*

INDIANAPOLIS 500 26 May
1st Johnny Rutherford [USA] *McLaren Cars 158.589 mph*
2nd Bobby Unser [USA] *Olsonite*
3rd Bill Vukovich [USA] *Suyaripe Prune*
Fastest qualifier: A.J. Foyt [USA] *Gilmore Racing*
191.632 mph

1975

World Champion: Niki Lauda [Aus]
US National Champion: A.J. Foyt
Fastest Man on Earth: Gary Gabelich (>1970)

GRANDS PRIX

ARGENTINE Buenos Aires 12 Jan
1st Emerson Fittipaldi [Bra] *McLaren-Ford 118.6 mph*
2nd James Hunt [GB] *Hesketh-Ford*
3rd Carlos Reutemann [Arg] *Brabham-Ford*
Fastest lap: Hunt *120.37 mph*

BRAZILIAN Interlagos 26 Jan
1st Carlos Pace [Bra] *Brabham-Ford 113.39 mph*
2nd Emerson Fittipaldi [Bra] *McLaren-Ford*
3rd Jochen Mass [Ger] *McLaren-Ford*
Fastest lap: Jean-Pierre Jarier [Fr] *Shadow-Ford 115.5 mph*

SOUTH AFRICAN Kyalami 1 March
1st Jody Scheckter [SA] *Tyrrell-Ford 115.55 mph*
2nd Carlos Reutemann [Arg] *Brabham-Ford*
3rd Patrick Depailler [Fr] *Tyrrell-Ford*
Fastest lap: Carlos Pace [Bra] *Brabham-Ford 118.92 mph*

SPANISH Montjuich Park 27 April
1st Jochen Mass [Ger] *McLaren-Ford 95.54 mph*
2nd Jacky Ickx [Bel] *Lotus-Ford*
3rd Carlos Reutemann [Arg] *Brabham-Ford*
Fastest lap: Mario Andretti [USA] *Pamelli-Ford 99.64 mph*

MONACO Monte Carlo 11 May
1st Niki Lauda [Aus] *Ferrari 75.53 mph*
2nd Emerson Fittipaldi [Bra] *McLaren-Ford*
3rd Carlos Pace [Bra] *Brabham-Ford*
Fastest lap: Patrick Depailler [Fr] *Tyrrell-Ford 82.7 mph*

BELGIAN Zolder 25 May
1st Niki Lauda [Aus] *Ferrari 107.05 mph*
2nd Jody Scheckter [SA] *Tyrrell-Ford*
3rd Carlos Reutemann [Arg] *Brabham-Ford*
Fastest lap: Clay Regazzoni [Switz] *Ferrari 109.89 mph*

SWEDISH Anderstorp 8 June
1st Niki Lauda [Aus] *Ferrari 100.45 mph*
2nd Carlos Reutemann [Arg] *Brabham-Ford*
3rd Clay Regazzoni [Switz] *Ferrari*
Fastest lap: Lauda *101.83 mph*

DUTCH Zandvoort 22 June
1st James Hunt [GB] *Hesketh-Ford 110.48 mph*
2nd Niki Lauda [Aus] *Ferrari*
3rd Clay Regazzoni [Switz] *Ferrari*
Fastest lap: Lauda *115.93 mph*

FRENCH Paul Ricard 6 July
1st Niki Lauda [Aus] *Ferrari 116.6 mph*
2nd James Hunt [GB] *Hesketh-Ford*
3rd Jochen Mass [Ger] *McLaren-Ford*
Fastest lap: Mass *117.51 mph*

BRITISH Silverstone 19 July
1st Emerson Fittipaldi [Bra] *McLaren-Ford 120.02 mph*
2nd Carlos Pace [Bra] *Brabham-Ford*
3rd Jody Scheckter [SA] *Tyrrell-Ford*
Fastest lap: Clay Regazzoni [Switz] *Ferrari 130.47 mph*

GERMAN Nürburging 3 Aug
1st Carlos Reutemann [Arg] *Brabham-Ford 117.73 mph*
2nd Jacques Laffrte [Fr] *Williams-Ford*
3rd Niki Lauda [Aus] *Ferrari*
Fastest lap: Clay Regazzoni [Switz] *Ferrari 119.79 mph*

AUSTRIAN Österreichring 17 Aug
1st Vittorio Brambilla [It] *March-Ford 110.29 mph*
2nd James Hunt [GB] *Hesketh-Ford*
3rd Tom Pryce [GB] *Shadow-Ford*
Fastest lap: Brambilla *116.09 mph*

ITALIAN Monza 7 Sept
1st Clay Regazzoni [Switz] *Ferrari 135.48 mph*
2nd Emerson Fittipaldi [Arg] *McLaren-Ford*
3rd Niki Lauda [Aus] *Ferrari*
Fastest lap: Regazzoni *138.88 mph*

UNITED STATES Watkins Glen 5 Oct
1st Niki Lauda [Aus] *Ferrari 116.1 mph*
2nd Emerson Fittipaldi [Arg] *McLaren-Ford*
3rd Jochen Mass [Ger] *McLaren-Ford*
Fastest lap: Fittipaldi *117.6 mph*

INDIANAPOLIS 500 25 May
1st Bobby Unser [USA] *Jorgensen 149.213 mph*
2nd Johnny Rutherford [USA] *Gatorade*
3rd A.J. Foyt [USA] *Gilmore Racing*
Fastest qualifier: Foyt *193.976 mph*

1976

World Champion: James Hunt [GB]
US National Champion: Gordon Johncock
Fastest Man on Earth: Gary Gabelich (>1970)

GRANDS PRIX

BRAZILIAN Interlagos 25 Jan
1st Niki Lauda [Aus] *Ferrari 112.76 mph*
2nd Patrick Depailler [Fr] *Tyrrell-Ford*
3rd Tom Pryce [GB] *Shadow-Ford*
Fastest lap: Jean-Pierre Jarier [Fr] *Shadow-Ford*
114.83 mph

SOUTH AFRICAN Kyalami 6 March
1st Niki Lauda [Aus] *Ferraro 116.65 mph*
2nd James Hunt [GB] *McLaren-Ford*
3rd Jochen Mass [Ger] *McLaren-Ford*
Fastest lap: Lauda *117.74 mph*

UNITED STATES (WEST) Long Beach 28 March
1st Clay Regazzoni [Switz] *Ferrari 85.57 mph*
2nd Niki Lauda [Aus] *Ferrari*
3rd Patrick Depailler [Fr] *Tyrrell-Ford*
Fastest lap: Regazzoni *87.53 mph*

SPANISH Jarama 2 May
1st James Hunt [GB] *McLaren-Ford 93.01 mph*
2nd Niki Lauda [Aus] *Ferrari*
3rd Gunnar Nilsson [Swe] *Lotus-Ford*
Fastest lap: Jochen Mass [Ger] *McLaren-Ford 94.1 mph*

BELGIAN Zolder 16 May
1st Niki Lauda [Aus] *Ferrari 108.1 mph*
2nd Clay Regazzoni [Switz] *Ferrari*
3rd Jacques Laffite [Fr] *Ligier-Matra*
Fastest lap: Lauda *110.88 mph*

MONACO Monte Carlo 30 May
1st Niki Lauda [Aus] *Ferrari 80.35 mph*
2nd Jody Scheckter [SA] *Tyrrell-Ford*
3rd Patrick Depailler [Fr] *Tyrrell-Ford*
Fastest lap: Clay Regazzoni [Switz] *Ferrari 82.06 mph*

SWEDISH Anderstorp 13 June
1st Jody Scheckter [SA] *Tyrrell-Ford 100.9 mph*
2nd Patrick Depailler [Fr] *Tyrrell-Ford*
3rd Niki Lauda [Aus] *Ferrari*
Fastest lap: Mario Andretti [USA] *Lotus-Ford 102.13 mph*

FRENCH Paul Ricard 4 July
1st James Hunt [GB] *McLaren-Ford 115.84 mph*
2nd Patrick Depailler [Fr] *Tyrrell-Ford*
3rd John Watson [GB] *Penske-Ford*
Fastest lap: Niki Lauda [Aus] *Ferrari 117.09 mph*

BRITISH Brands Hatch 18 July
1st Niki Lauda [Aus] *Ferrari 114.23 mph*
2nd Jody Scheckter [SA] *Tyrrell-Ford*
3rd John Watson [GB] *Penske-Ford*
Fastest lap: Lauda *117.74 mph*

GERMAN Nürburging 1 Aug
1st James Hunt [GB] *McLaren-Ford 117.18 mph*
2nd Jody Scheckter [SA] *Tyrell-Ford*
3rd Jochen Mass [Ger] *McLaren-Ford*
Fastest lap: Scheckter *118.57 mph*

AUSTRIAN Österreichring 15 Aug
1st John Watson [GB] *Penske-Ford 132 mph*
2nd Jacques Laffite [Fr] *Ligier-Matra*
3rd Gunnar Nilsson [Swe] *Lotus-Ford*
Fastest lap: James Hunt [GB] *McLaren-Ford 137.83 mph*

DUTCH Zandvoort 29 Aug
1st James Hunt [GB] *McLaren-Ford 112.68 mph*
2nd Clay Regazzoni [Switz] *Ferrari*
3rd Mario Andretti [USA] *Lotus-Ford*
Fastest lap: Regazzoni *114.46 mph*

ITALIAN Monza 12 Sept
1st Ronnie Peterson [Swe] *March-Ford 124.12 mph*
2nd Clay Regazzoni [Switz] *Ferrari*
3rd Jacques Laffite [Fr] *Ligier-Matra*
Fastest lap: Peterson *128.08 mph*

CANADIAN Mosport 3 Oct
1st James Hunt [GB] *McLaren-Ford 117.84 mph*
2nd Patrick Depailler [Fr] *Tyrrell-Ford*
3rd Mario Andretti [USA] *Lotus-Ford*
Fastest lap: Depailler *119.92 mph*

UNITED STATES Watkins Glen 10 Oct
1st James Hunt [GB] *McLaren-Ford 116.43 mph*
2nd Jody Scheckter [SA] *Tyrrell-Ford*
3rd Niki Lauda [Aus] *Ferrari*
Fastest lap: Hunt *118.2 mph*

JAPANESE Fuji 24 Oct
1st Mario Andretti [USA] *Lotus-Ford 114.09 mph*
2nd Patrick Depailler [Fr] *Tyrrell-Ford*
3rd James Hunt [GB] *McLaren-Ford*
Fastest lap: Masahiro Hasemi [Jap] *KojimaFord 124.64 mph*

INDIANAPOLIS 500 30 May
1st Johnny Rutherford [USA] *Hy-Gain 149.213 mph*
2nd A.J. Foyt [USA] *Gilmore Racing*
3rd Gordon Johncock [USA] *Sinmast*
Fastest qualifier: Mario Andretti [USA] *Cam2 Oil 189.404 mph*

World Champion: Niki Lauda [Aus]
US National Champion: Tom Sneva
Fastest Man on Earth: Gary Gabelich (>1970)

GRANDS PRIX

ARGENTINE Buenos Aires 9 Jan
1st Jody Scheckter [SA] *Wolf-Ford 117.71 mph*
2nd Carlos Pace [Bra] *Brabham-Alfa-Romeo*
3rd Carlos Reutemann [Arg] *Ferrari*
Fastest lap: James Hunt [GB] *McLaren-Ford 120.21 mph*

BRAZILIAN Interlagos 23 Jan
1st Carlos Reutemann [Arg] *Ferrari 112.92 mph*
2nd James Hunt [GB] *McLaren-Ford*
3rd Niki Lauda [Aus] *Ferrari*
Fastest lap: Hunt *115.22 mph*

SOUTH AFRICAN Kyalami 5 March
1st Niki Lauda [Aus] *Ferrari 116.59 mph*
2nd Jody Scheckter [SA] *Wolf-Ford*
3rd Patrick Depailler [Fr] *Tyrrell-Ford*
Fastest lap: John Watson [GB] *Brabham-Alfa-Romeo 118.26 mph*

UNITED STATES (WEST) Long Beach 3 April
1st Mario Andretti [USA] *Lotus-Ford 86.89 mph*
2nd Niki Lauda [Aus] *Ferrari*
3rd Jody Scheckter [SA] *Wolf-Ford*
Fastest lap: Lauda *87.88 mph*

SPANISH Jarama 8 May
1st Mario Andretti [USA] *Lotus-Ford 92.53 mph*
2nd Carlos Reutemann [Arg] *Ferrari*
3rd Jody Scheckter [SA] *Wolf-Ford*
Fastest lap: Jacques Laffite [Fr] *Ligier-Matra 94.24 mph*

MONACO Monte Carlo 22 May
1st Jody Scheckter [SA] *Wolf-Ford 79.61 mph*
2nd Niki Lauda [Aus] *Ferrari*
3rd Carlos Reutemann [Arg] *Ferrari*
Fastest lap: Scheckter *81.35 mph*

BELGIAN Zolder 5 June
1st Gunnar Nilsson [Swe] *Lotus-Ford 96.64 mph*
2nd Niki Lauda [Aus] *Ferrari*
3rd Ronnie Peterson [Swe] *Tyrrell-Ford*
Fastest lap: Nilsson *109.13 mph*

SWEDISH Anderstorp 19 June
1st Jacques Laffite [Fr] *Ligier-Matra 100.87 mph*
2nd Jochen Mass [Ger] *McLaren-Ford*
3rd Carlos Reutemann [Arg] *Ferrari*
Fastest lap: Mario Andretti [USA] *Lotus-Ford 102.59 mph*

FRENCH Dijon-Prenois 3 July
1st Mario Andretti [USA] *Lotus-Ford 113.71 mph*
2nd John Watson [GB] *Brabham-Alfa-Romeo*
3rd James Hunt [GB] *McLaren-Ford*
Fastest lap: Andretti *115.26 mph*

BRITISH Silverstone 16 July
1st James Hunt [GB] *McLaren-Ford 130.35 mph*
2nd Niki Lauda [Aus] *Ferrari*
3rd Gunnar Nilsson [Swe] *Lotus-Ford*
Fastest lap: Hunt *132.6 mph*

GERMAN Hockenheim 31 July
1st Niki Lauda [Aus] *Ferrari 129.57 mph*
2nd Jody Scheckter [SA] *Wolf-Ford*
3rd Hans-Joachim Stuck [Ger] *Brabham-Alfa-Romeo*
Fastest lap: Lauda *130.93 mph*

AUSTRIAN Österreichring 14 Aug
1st Alan Jones [Austral] *Shadow-Ford 122.99 mph*
2nd Niki Lauda [Aus] *Ferrari*
3rd Hans-Joachim Stuck [Ger] *Brabham-Alfa-Romeo*
Fastest lap: John Watson [GB] *Brabham-Alfa-Romeo 131.66 mph*

DUTCH Zandvoort 28 Aug
1st Niki Lauda [Aus] *Ferrari 116.12 mph*
2nd Jacques Laffite [Fr] *Ligier-Matra*
3rd Jody Scheckter [SA] *Wolf-Ford*
Fastest lap: Lauda *118.18 mph*

ITALIAN Monza 11 Sept
1st Mario Andretti [USA] *Lotus-Ford 128.01 mph*
2nd Niki Lauda [Aus] *Ferrari*
3rd Alan Jones [Austral] *Shadow-Ford*
Fastest lap: Andretti *130.92 mph*

UNITED STATES Watkins Glen 2 Oct
1st James Hunt [GB] *McLaren-Ford 100.98 mph*
2nd Mario Andretti [USA] *Lotus-Ford*
3rd Jody Scheckter [SA] *Wolf-Ford*
Fastest lap: Ronnie Peterson [Swe] *Tyrrell 108.69 mph*

CANADIAN Mosport 9 Oct
1st Jody Scheckter [SA] *Wolf-Ford 118.03 mph*
2nd Patrick Depailler [Fr] *Tyrrell-Ford*
3rd Jochen Mass [Ger] *McLaren-Ford*
Fastest lap: Mario Andretti [USA] *Lotus-Ford 120.77 mph*

JAPANESE Fuji 23 Oct
1st James Hunt [GB] *McLaren-Ford 129.15 mph*
2nd Carlos Reutemann [Arg] *Ferrari*
3rd Patrick Depailler [Fr] *Tyrrell-Ford*
Fastest lap: Jody Scheckter [SA] *Wolf-Ford 131.24 mph*

INDIANAPOLIS 500 29 May
1st A.J. Foyt [USA] *Gilmore Racing 161.331 mph*
2nd Tom Sneva [USA] *Norton Spirit*
3rd Al Unser [USA] *American*
Fastest qualifier: Sneva *198.884 mph*

World Champion: Mario Andretti [USA]
US National Champion: Tom Sneva
Fastest Man on Earth: Gary Gabelich (>1970)

GRANDS PRIX

ARGENTINE Buenos Aires 15 Jan
1st Mario Andretti [USA] *Lotus-Ford 119.19 mph*
2nd Niki Lauda [Aus] *Brabham-Alfa-Romeo*
3rd Patrick Depailler [Fr] *Tyrrell-Ford*
Fastest lap: Gilles Villeneuve [Can] *Ferrari 120.78 mph*

BRAZILIAN Rio de Janeiro 29 Jan
1st Carlos Reutemann [Arg] *Ferrari 107.43 mph*
2nd Emerson Fittipaldi [Bra] *Fittipaldi-Ford*
3rd Niki Lauda [Aus] *Brabham-Alfa-Romeo*
Fastest lap: Reutemann *109.19 mph*

SOUTH AFRICAN Kyalami 4 March
1st Ronnie Peterson [Swe] *Lotus-Ford 116.7 mph*
2nd Patrick Depailler [Fr] *Tyrrell-Ford*
3rd John Watson [GB] *Brabham-Alfa-Romeo*
Fastest lap: Mario Andretti [USA] *Lotus-Ford 119.08 mph*

UNITED STATES (WEST) Long Beach 2 April
1st Carlos Reutemann [Arg] *Ferrari 87.1 mph*
2nd Mario Andretti [USA] *Lotus-Ford*
3rd Patrick Depailler [Fr] *Tyrrell-Ford*
Fastest lap: Alan Jones [Austral] *Williams-Ford 88.45 mph*

MONACO Monte Carlo 7 May
1st Patrick Depailler [Fr] *Tyrrell-Ford 80.36 mph*
2nd Niki Lauda [Aus] *Brabham-Alfa-Romeo*
3rd Jody Scheckter [SA] *Wolf-Ford*
Fastest lap: Lauda *83.57 mph*

BELGIAN Zolder 21 May
1st Mario Andretti [USA] *Lotus-Ford 111.38 mph*
2nd Ronnie Peterson [Swe] *Lotus-Ford*
3rd Carlos Reutemann [Arg] *Ferrari*
Fastest lap: Peterson *114.69 mph*

SPANISH Jarama 4 June
1st Mario Andretti [USA] *Lotus-Ford 93.52 mph*
2nd Ronnie Peterson [Swe] *Lotus-Ford*
3rd Jacques Laffite [Fr] *Ligier-Matra*
Fastest lap: Andretti *95.12 mph*

SWEDISH Anderstorp 17 June
1st Niki Lauda [Aus] *Brabham-Alfa-Romeo 104.15 mph*
2nd Riccardo Patrese [It] *Arrows-Ford*
3rd Ronnie Peterson [Swe] *Lotus-Ford*
Fastest lap: Lauda *106.29 mph*

FRENCH Paul Ricard 2 July
1st Mario Andretti [USA] *Lotus-Ford 118.31 mph*
2nd Ronnie Peterson [Swe] *Lotus-Ford*
3rd James Hunt [GB] *McLaren-Ford*
Fastest lap: Carlos Reutemann [Arg] *Ferrai 119.72 mph*

BRITISH Brands Hatch 16 July
1st Carlos Reutemann [Arg] *Ferrari 116.61 mph*
2nd Niki Lauda [Aus] *Brabham-Alfa-Romeo*
3rd John Watson [GB] *Brabham-Alfa-Romeo*
Fastest lap: Lauda *119.71 mph*

GERMAN Hockenheim 30 July
1st Mario Andretti [USA] *Lotus-Ford 129.41 mph*
2nd Jody Scheckter [SA] *Wolf-Ford*
3rd Jacques Laffite [Fr] *Ligier-Matra*
Fastest lap: Ronnie Peterson [Swe] *Lotus-Ford*
 131.35 mph

AUSTRIAN Österreichring 13 Aug
1st Ronnie Peterson [Swe] *Lotus-Ford 118.03 mph*
2nd Patrick Depailler [Fr] *Tyrrell-Ford*
3rd Gilles Villeneuve [Can] *Ferrari*
Fastest lap: Peterson *128.91 mph*

DUTCH Zandvoort 27 Aug
1st Mario Andretti [USA] *Lotus-Ford 116.91 mph*
2nd Ronnie Peterson [Swe] *Lotus-Ford*
3rd Niki Lauda [Aus] *Brabham-Alfa-Romeo*
Fastest lap: Lauda *118.81 mph*

ITALIAN Monza 10 Sept
1st Niki Lauda [Aus] *Brabham-Alfa-Romeo 128.95 mph*
2nd John Watson [GB] *Brabham-Alfa-Romeo*
3rd Carlos Reutemann [Arg] *Ferrari*
Fastest lap: Mario Andretti [USA] *Lotus-Ford 132.08 mph*

UNITED STATES Watkins Glen 1 Oct
1st Carlos Reutemann [Arg] *Ferrari 118.59 mph*
2nd Alan Jones [Austral] *Williams-Ford*
3rd Jody Scheckter [SA] *Wolf-Ford*
Fastest lap: Jean-Pierre Larier [Fr] *Lotus-Ford 122.12 mph*

CANADIAN Montreal 8 Oct
1st Gilles Villeneuve [Can] *Ferrari 99.67 mph*
2nd Jody Scheckter [SA] *Wolf-Ford*
3rd Carlos Reutemann [Arg] *Ferrari*
Fastest lap: Alan Jones [Austral] *Williams-Ford*
 102.64 mph

INDIANAPOLIS 500 28 May
1st Al Unser [USA] *First National City 161.363 mph*
2nd Tom Sneva [USA] *Norton Spirit*
3rd Gordon Johncock [USA] *N. American Van Lines*
Fastest qualifier: Sneva *202.156 mph*

World Champion: Jody Scheckter [SA]
US National Champion: Rick Mears
Fastest Man on Earth: Gary Gabelich (>1970)

GRANDS PRIX

ARGENTINE Buenos Aires 21 Jan
1st Jacques Laffite [Fr] *Ligier-Ford 122.78 mph*
2nd Carlos Reutemann [Arg] *Lotus-Ford*
3rd John Watson [GB] *McLaren-Ford*
Fastest lap: Laffite *124.88 mph*

BRAZILIAN Interlagos 4 Feb
1st Jacques Laffite [Fr] *Ligier-Ford 117.23 mph*
2nd Patrick Depailler [Fr] *Ligier-Ford*
3rd Carlos Reutemann [Arg] *Lotus-Ford*
Fastest lap: Laffite *118.4 mph*

SOUTH AFRICAN Kyalami 3 March
1st Gilles Villeneuve [Can] *Ferrari 117.19 mph*
2nd Jody Scheckter [SA] *Ferrari*
3rd Jean-Pierre Jarier [Fr] *Tyrrell-Ford*
Fastest lap: Villeneuve *123.38 mph*

UNITED STATES (WEST) Long Beach 8 April
1st Gilles Villeneuve [Can] *Ferrari 87.81 mph*
2nd Jody Scheckter [SA] *Ferrari*
3rd Alan Jones [Austral] *Williams-Ford*
Fastest lap: Villeneuve *89.65 mph*

SPANISH Jarama 29 April
1st Patrick Depailler [Fr] *Ligier-Ford 95.97 mph*
2nd Carlos Reutemann [Arg] *Lotus-Ford*
3rd Mario Andretti [USA] *Lotus-Ford*
Fastest lap: Gilles Villeneuve [Can] *Ferrari 99.7 mph*

BELGIAN Zolder 13 May
1st Jody Scheckter [SA] *Ferrari 111.24 mph*
2nd Jacques Laffite [Fr] *Ligier-Ford*
3rd Didier Pironi [Fr] *Tyrrell-Ford*
Fastest lap: Scheckter 114.81 mph

MONACO Monte Carlo 27 May
1st Jody Scheckter [SA] *Ferrari 81.34 mph*
2nd Clay Regazzoni [Switz] *Williams-Ford*
3rd Carlos Reutemann [Arg] *Lotus-Ford*
Fastest lap: Patrick Depailler [Fr] *Ligier-Ford 83.41 mph*

FRENCH Dijon-Prenois 1 July
1st Jean-Pierre Jabouille [Fr] *Renault 118.88 mph*
2nd Gilles Villeneuve [Can] *Ferrari*
3rd Rene Arnoux [Fr] *Renault*
Fastest lap: Arnoux *122.91 mph*

BRITISH Silverstone 14 July
1st Clay Regazzoni [Switz] *Williams-Ford 138.8 mph*
2nd Rene Arnoux [Fr] *Renault*
3rd Jean-Pierre Jarier [Fr] *Tyrrell-Ford*
Fastest lap: Regazzoni *141.87 mph*

GERMAN Hockenheim 29 July
1st Alan Jones [Austral] *Williams-Ford 134.27 mph*
2nd Clay Regazzoni [Switz] *Williams-Ford*
3rd Jacques Laffite [Fr] *Ligier-Ford*
Fastest lap: Gilles Villeneuve [Can] *Ferrari 135.71 mph*

AUSTRIAN Österreichring 12 Aug
1st Alan Jones [Austral] *Williams-Ford 136.52 mph*
2nd Gilles Villeneuve [Can] *Ferrari*
3rd Jacques Laffite [Fr] *Ligier-Ford*
Fastest lap: Rene Arnoux [Fr] *Renault 138.7 mph*

DUTCH Zandvoort 26 Aug
1st Alan Jones [Austral] *Williams-Ford 116.62 mph*
2nd Jody Scheckter [SA] *Ferrari*
3rd Jacques Laffite [Fr] *Ligier-Ford*
Fastest lap: Gilles Villeneuve [Can] *Ferrari 119 mph*

ITALIAN Monza 9 Sept
1st Jody Scheckter [SA] *Ferrari 131.85 mph*
2nd Gilles Villeneuve [Can] *Ferrari*
3rd Clay Regazzoni [Switz] *Williams-Ford*
Fastest lap: Regazzoni *135.71 mph*

CANADIAN Montreal 30 Sept
1st Alan Jones [Austral] *Williams-Ford 105.59 mph*
2nd Gilles Villeneuve [Can] *Ferrari*
3rd Clay Regazzoni [Switz] *Williams-Ford*
Fastest lap: Jones *108.08 mph*

UNITED STATES Watkins Glen 7 Oct
1st Gilles Villeneuve [Can] *Ferrari 106.46 mph*
2nd Rene Arnoux [Fr] *Renault*
3rd Didier Pironi [Fr] *Tyrrell-Ford*
Fastest lap: Nelson Piquet [Bra] *Brabham-Ford*
 121.61 mph

INDIANAPOLIS 500 27 May
1st Rick Mears [USA] *The Gould Charge 158.899 mph*
2nd A.J. Foyt [USA] *Gilmore Racing*
3rd Mike Mosley [USA] *Theodore Racing*
Fastest qualifier: Mears *193.736 mph*

World Champion: Alan Jones [Austral]
US National Champion: Johnny Rutherford
Fastest Man on Earth: Gary Gabelich (>1970)

GRANDS PRIX

ARGENTINE Buenos Aires 13 Jan
1st Alan Jones [Austral] *Williams-Ford 113.99 mph*
2nd Nelson Piquet [Bra] *Brabham-Ford*
3rd Keke Rosberg [Fin] *Fittipaldi-Ford*
Fastest lap: Jones *120.87 mph*

BRAZILIAN Interlagos 27 Jan
1st Rene Arnoux [Fr] *Renault 117.4 mph*
2nd Elio de Angelis [It] *Lotus-Ford*
3rd Alan Jones [Austral] *Williams-Ford*
Fastest lap: Arnoux *119.57 mph*

SOUTH AFRICAN Kyalami 1 March
1st Rene Arnoux [Fr] *Renault 123.19 mph*
2nd Jacques Laffite [Fr] *Ligier-Ford*
3rd Didier Pironi [Fr] *Ligier-Ford*
Fastest lap: Arnoux *125.5 mph*

UNITED STATES (WEST) Long Beach 30 March
1st Nelson Piquet [Bra] *Brabham-Ford 88.45 mph*
2nd Riccardo Patrese [It] *Arrows-Ford*
3rd Emerson Fittipaldi [Bra] *Fittipaldi-Ford*
Fastest lap: Piquet *91.1 mph*

BELGIAN Zolder 4 May
1st Didier Pironi [Fr] *Ligier-Ford 115.82 mph*
2nd Alan Jones [Austral] *Williams-Ford*
3rd Carlos Reutemann [Arg] *Williams-Ford*
Fastest lap: Jacques Laffite [Fr] *Ligier-Ford 117.88 mph*

MONACO Monte Carlo 18 May
1st Carlos Reutemann [Arg] *Williams-Ford 81.2 mph*
2nd Jacques Laffite [Fr] *Ligier-Ford*
3rd Nelson Piquet [Bra] *Brabham-Ford*
Fastest lap: Riccardo Patrese [It] *Arrows-Ford 86.09 mph*

FRENCH Paul Ricard 29 June
1st Alan Jones [Austral] *Williams-Ford 126.15 mph*
2nd Didier Pironi [Fr] *Ligier-Ford*
3rd Jacques Laffite [Fr] *Ligier-Ford*
Fastest lap: Jones *128.11 mph*

BRITISH Brands Hatch 13 July
1st Alan Jones [Austral] *Williams-Ford 125.69 mph*
2nd Nelson Piquet [Bra] *Brabham-Ford*
3rd Carlos Reutemann [Arg] *Williams-Ford*
Fastest lap: Didier Pironi [Fr] *Ligier-Ford 130.02 mph*

GERMAN Hockenheim 10 Aug
1st Jacques Laffite [Fr] *Ligier-Ford 137.22 mph*
2nd Carlos Reutemann [Arg] *Williams-Ford*
3rd Alan Jones [Austral] *Williams-Ford*
Fastest lap: Jones *139.96 mph*

AUSTRIAN Österreichring 17 Aug
1st Jean-Pierre Jabouille [Fr] *Renault 138.69 mph*
2nd Alan Jones [Austral] *Williams-Ford*
3rd Carlos Reutemann [Arg] *Williams-Ford*
Fastest lap: Rene. Arnoux [Fr] *Renault 143.66 mph*

DUTCH Zandvoort 31 Aug
1st Nelson Piquet [Bra] *Brabham-Ford 116.19 mph*
2nd Rene Arnoux [Fr] *Renault*
3rd Jacques Laffite [Fr] *Ligier-Ford*
Fastest lap: Arnoux *119.87 mph*

ITALIAN Imola 14 Sept
1st Nelson Piquet [Bra] *Brabham-Ford 113.98 mph*
2nd Alan Jones [Austral] *Williams-Ford*
3rd Carlos Reutemann [Arg] *Williams-Ford*
Fastest lap: Jones *116.4 mph*

CANADIAN Montreal 28 Sept
1st Alan Jones [Austral] *Williams-Ford 110 mph*
2nd Carlos Reutemann [Arg] *Williams-Ford*
3rd Didier Pironi [Fr] *Ligier-Ford*
Fastest lap: Pironi *111.11 mph*

UNITED STATES Watkins Glen 5 Oct
1st Alan Jones [Austral] *Williams-Ford 126.37 mph*
2nd Carlos Reutemann [Arg] *Williams-Ford*
3rd Didier Pironi [Fr] *Ligier-Ford*
Fastest lap: Jones *129.24 mph*

INDIANAPOLIS 500 25 May
1st Johnny Rutherford [USA] *Pennzoil 142.862 mph*
2nd Tom Sneva [USA] *Bon Jour jeans*
3rd Gary Bettenhausen [USA] *Armstrong Mould*
Fastest qualifier: Rutherford *192.526 mph*

1981

World Champion: Nelson Piquet [Bra]
US National Champion: Rick Mears
Fastest Man on Earth: Gary Gabelich (>1970)

GRANDS PRIX

UNITED STATES (WEST) Long Beach 15 March
1st Alan Jones [Austral] *Williams-Ford 87.6 mph*
2nd Carlos Reutemann [Arg] *Williams-Ford*
3rd Nelson Piquet [Bra] *Brabham-Ford*
Fastest lap: Jones *89.89 mph*

BRAZILIAN Rio de Janeiro 29 March
1st Carlos Reutemann [Arg] *Williams-Ford 96.6 mph*
2nd Alan Jones [Austral] *Williams-Ford*
3rd Riccardo Patrese [It] *Arrows-Ford*
Fastest lap: Marc Surer [Switz] *Ensign-Ford 98.46 mph*

ARGENTINE Buenos Aires 12 April
1st Nelson Piquet [Bra] *Brabham-Ford 124.67 mph*
2nd Carlos Reutemann [Arg] *Williams-Ford*
3rd Alain Prost [Fr] *Renault*
Fastest lap: Piquet *126.81 mph*

SAN MARINO Imola 3 May
1st Nelson Piquet [Bra] *Brabham-Ford 101.21 mph*
2nd Riccardo Patrese [It] *Arrows-Ford*
3rd Carlos Reutemann [Arg] *Williams-Ford*
Fastest lap: Gilles Villeneuve [Can] *Ferrari 104.33 mph*

BELGIAN Zolder 17 May
1st Carlos Reutemann [Arg] *Williams-Ford 112.13 mph*
2nd Jacques Laffite [Fr] *Talbot-Ligier-Matra*
3rd Nigel Mansell [GB] *Lotus-Ford*
Fastest lap: Reutemann *114.45 mph*

MONACO Monte Carlo 31 May
1st Gilles Villeneuve [Can] *Ferrari 82.04 mph*
2nd Alan Jones [Austral] *Williams-Ford*
3rd Jacques Laffite [Fr] *Talbot-Ligier-Matra*
Fastest lap: Jones *84.7 mph*

SPANISH Jarama 21 June
1st Gilles Villeneuve [Can] *Ferrari 92.65 mph*
2nd Jacques Laffite [Fr] *Talbot-Ligier-Matra*
3rd John Watson [GB] *McLaren-Ford*
Fastest lap: Alan Jones [Austral] *Williams-Ford 95.21 mph*

FRENCH Dijon-Prenois 5 July
1st Alain Prost [Fr] *Renault 118.31 mph*
2nd John Watson [GB] *McLaren-Ford*
3rd Nelson Piquet [Bra] *Brabham-Ford*
Fastest lap: Prost *122.95 mph*

BRITISH Silverstone 18 July
1st John Watson [GB] *McLaren-Ford 137.65 mph*
2nd Carlos Reutemann [Arg] *Williams-Ford*
3rd Jacques Laffite [Fr] *Talbot-Ligier-Matra*
Fastest lap: Rene Arnoux [Fr] *Renault 140.62 mph*

GERMAN Hockenheim 2 Aug
1st Nelson Piquet [Bra] *Brabham-Ford 132.54 mph*
2nd Alain Prost [Fr] *Renault*
3rd Jacques Laffite [Fr] *Talbot-Ligier-Matra*
Fastest lap: Alan Jones [Austral] *Williams-Ford 135.07 mph*

AUSTRIAN Österreichring 16 Aug
1st Jacques Laffite [Fr] *Talbot-Ligier-Matra 134.03 mph*
2nd Rene Arnoux [Fr] *Renault*
3rd Nelson Piquet [Bra] *Brabham-Ford*
Fastest lap: Laffite *136.17 mph*

DUTCH Zandvoort 30 Aug
1st Alain Prost [Fr] *Renault 113.72 mph*
2nd Nelson Piquet [Bra] *Brabham-Ford*
3rd Alan Jones [Austral] *Williams-Ford*
Fastest lap: Jones *116.24 mph*

ITALIAN Monza 13 Sept
1st Alain Prost [Fr] *Renault 129.87 mph*
2nd Alan Jones [Austral] *Williams-Ford*
3rd Carlos Reutemann [Arg] *Williams-Ford*
Fastest lap: Reutemann *133.04 mph*

CANADIAN Montreal 27 Sept
1st Jacques Laffite [Fr] *Talbot-Ligier-Matra 85.31 mph*
2nd John Watson [GB] *McLaren-Ford*
3rd Gilles Villeneuve [Can] *Ferrari*
Fastest lap: Watson *90.12 mph*

UNITED STATES Las Vegas 17 Oct
1st Alan Jones [Austral] *Williams-Ford 97.9 mph*
2nd Alain Prost [Fr] *Renault*
3rd Bruno Giacomelli [It] *Alfa-Romeo*
Fastest lap: Didier Pironi [Fr] *Ferrari 101.87 mph*

INDIANAPOLIS 500 24 May
1st Bobby Unser [USA] *The Norton Spirit 139.029 mph*
2nd Mario Andretti [USA] *STP Oil Treatment*
3rd Vern Schuppan [Austral] *Red Roof Inns*
Fastest qualifier: Tom Sneva [USA] *Blue Poly 200.691 mph*

1982

World Champion: Keke Rosberg [Fin]
US National Champion: Rick Mears
Fastest Man on Earth: Gary Gabelich (>1970)

GRANDS PRIX

SOUTH AFRICAN Kyalami 23 Jan
1st Alain Prost [Fr] *Renault 127.82 mph*
2nd Carlos Reutemann [Arg] *Williams-Ford*
3rd Rene Arnoux [Fr] *Renault*
Fastest lap: Prost *134.46 mph*

BRAZILIAN Rio de Janeiro 21 March
1st Alain Prost [Fr] *Renault 113.16 mph*
2nd John Watson [GB] *McLaren-Ford*
3rd Nigel Mansell [GB] *Lotus-Ford*
Fastest lap: Nelson Piquet [Bra] *Brabham-Ford 116.52 mph*

UNITED STATES (WEST) Long Beach 4 April
1st Niki Lauda [Aus] *McLaren-Ford 81.4 mph*
2nd Keke Rosberg [Fin] *Williams-Ford*
3rd Riccardo Patrese [It] *Brabham-Ford*
Fastest lap: Lauda *84.42 mph*

SAN MARINO Imola 25 April
1st Didier Pironi [Fr] *Ferrari 117.3 mph*
2nd Gilles Villeneuve [Can] *Ferrari*
3rd Michele Alboreto [It] *Tyrrell-Ford*
Fastest lap: Pironi *118.64 mph*

BELGIAN Zolder 9 May
1st John Watson [GB] *McLaren-Ford 116.88 mph*
2nd Keke Rosberg [Fin] *Williams-Ford*
3rd Eddie Cheever [USA] *Talbot-Ligier-Matra*
Fastest lap: Watson *119.55 mph*

MONACO Monte Carlo 23 May
1st Riccardo Patrese [It] *Brabham-Ford 82.21 mph*
2nd Didier Pironi [Fr] *Ferrari*
3rd Andrea de Cesaris [It] *Alfa-Romeo*
Fastest lap: Patrese *85.79 mph*

UNITED STATES (EAST) Detroit 6 June
1st John Watson [GB] *McLaren-Ford 78.2 mph*
2nd Eddie Cheever [USA] *Talbot-Ligier-Matra*
3rd Didier Pironi [Fr] *Ferrari*
Fastest lap: Alain Prost [Fr] *Renault 81.28 mph*

CANADIAN Montreal 13 June
1st Nelson Piquet [Bra] *Brabham-Ford 107.94 mph*
2nd Riccardo Patrese [It] *Brabham-Ford*
3rd John Watson [GB] *McLaren-Ford*
Fastest lap: Didier Pironi [Fr] *Ferrari 111.7 mph*

DUTCH Zandvoort 3 July
1st Didier Peroni [Fr] *Ferrari 116.39 mph*
2nd Nelson Piquet [Bra] *Brabham-BMW*
3rd Keke Rosberg [Fin] *Williams-Ford*
Fastest lap: Derek Warwick [GB] *Toleman-Hart 119.23 mph*

BRITISH Brands Hatch 18 July
1st Niki Lauda [Aus] *McLaren-Ford 124.71 mph*
2nd Didier Pironi [Fr] *Ferrari*
3rd Patrick Tambay [Fr] *Ferrari*
Fastest lap: Brian Henton [GB] *Tyrrell-Ford 128.85 mph*

FRENCH Paul Ricard 25 July
1st Rene Arnoux [Fr] *Renault 125.03 mph*
2nd Alain Prost [Fr] *Renault*
3rd Didier Pironi [Fr] *Ferrari*
Fastest lap: Riccardo Patrese [It] *Brabham-BMW 129.88 mph*

GERMAN Hockenheim 8 Aug
1st Patrick Tambay [Fr] *Ferrari 130.43 mph*
2nd Rene Arnoux [Fr] *Renault*
3rd Keke Rosberg [Fin] *Williams-Ford*
Fastest lap: Nelson Piquet [Bra] *Brabham-BMW 133.34 mph*

AUSTRIAN Österreichring 15 Aug
1st Elio de Angelis [It] *Lotus-Ford 138.01 mph*
2nd Keke Rosberg [Fin] *Williams-Ford*
3rd Jacques Laffite [Fr] *Talbot-Ligier-Matra*
Fastest lap: Nelson Piquet [Bra] *Brabham-BMW 141.88 mph*

SWISS Dijon-Prenois 29 Aug
1st Keke Rosberg [Fin] *Williams-Ford 122.29 mph*
2nd Alain Prost [Fr] *Renault*
3rd Niki Lauda [Aus] *McLaren-Ford*
Fastest lap: Prost *125.98 mph*

ITALIAN Monza 12 Sept
1st Rene Arnoux [Fr] *Renault 136.4 mph*
2nd Patrick Tambay [Fr] *Ferrari*
3rd Mario Andretti [USA] *Ferrari*
Fastest lap: Arnoux *138.59 mph*

UNITED STATES Las Vegas 25 Sept
1st Michele Alboreto [It] *Tyrrell-Ford 100.1 mph*
2nd John Watson [GB] *McLaren-Ford*
3rd Eddie Cheever [USA] *Talbot-Ligier-Matra*
Fastest lap: Alboreto *102.52 mph*

INDIANAPOLIS 500 30 May
1st Gordon Johncock [USA] *STP Oil Treatment 162.029 mph*
2nd Rick Mears [USA] *The Gould Charge*
3rd Pancho Carter [USA] *Alex Foods*
Fastest qualifier: Mears *207.004 mph*

1983

World Champion: Nelson Piquet [Bra]
US National Champion: Al Unser
Fastest Man on Earth: Richard Noble [GB] *Black Rock Desert 633.468 mph*

GRANDS PRIX

BRAZILIAN Rio de Janeiro 13 March
1st Nelson Piquet [Bra] *Brabham-BMW 108.93 mph*
2nd Keke Rosberg [Fin] *Williams-Ford* (later disqualified)
3rd Niki Lauda [Aus] *McLaren-Ford*
Fastest lap: Piquet *112.74 mph*

UNITED STATES (WEST) Long Beach 27 March
1st John Watson [GB] *McLaren-Ford 80.65 mph*
2nd Niki Lauda [Aus] *McLaren-Ford*
3rd Rene Arnoux [Fr] *Ferrari*
Fastest lap: Lauda *82.94 mph*

FRENCH Paul Ricard 17 April
1st Alain Prost [Fr] *Renault 124.2 mph*
2nd Nelson Piquet [Bra] *Brabham-BMW*
3rd Eddie Cheever [USA] *Renault*
Fastest lap: Prost *126.37 mph*

SAN MARINO Imola 1 May
1st Patrick Tambay [Fr] *Ferrari 115.26 mph*
2nd Alain Prost [Fr] *Renault*
3rd Rene Arnoux [Fr] *Ferrari*
Fastest lap: Riccardo Patrese [It] *BrabhamBM 119.39 mph*

MONACO Monte Carlo 15 May
1st Keke Rosberg [Fin] *Williams-Ford 80.52 mph*
2nd Nelson Piquet [Bra] *Brabham-BMW*
3rd Alain Prost [Fr] *Renault*
Fastest lap: Piquet *84.89 mph*

BELGIAN Spa 22 May
1st Alain Prost [Fr] *Renault 119.14 mph*
2nd Patrick Tambay [Fr] *Ferrari*
3rd Eddie Cheever [USA] *Renault*
Fastest lap: Andrea de Cesaris [It] *Alfa-Romeo 121.93 mph*

UNITED STATES Detroit 5 June
1st Michele Alboreto [It] *Tyrrell-Ford 81.04 mph*
2nd Keke Rosberg [Fin] *Williams-Ford*
3rd John Watson [GB] *McLaren-Ford*
Fastest lap: Watson *83.6 mph*

CANADIAN Montreal 12 June
1st Rene Arnoux [Fr] *Ferrari 106.05 mph*
2nd Eddie Cheever [USA] *Renault*
3rd Patrick Tambay [Fr] *Ferrari*
Fastest lap: Tambay *108.59 mph*

BRITISH Silverstone 16 July
1st Alain Prost [Fr] *Renault 139.22 mph*
2nd Nelson Piquet [Bra] *Brabham-BMW*
3rd Patrick Tambay [Fr] *Ferrari*
Fastest lap: Prost *142.24 mph*

GERMAN Hockenheim 7 Aug
1st Rene Arnoux [Fr] *Ferrari 130.82 mph*
2nd Andrea de Cesaris [It] *Alfa-Romeo*
3rd Riccardo Patrese [It] *Brabham-BMW*
Fastest lap: Arnoux *133.45 mph*

AUSTRIAN Österreichring 14 Aug
1st Alain Prost [Fr] *Renault 138.88 mph*
2nd Rene Arnoux [Fr] *Ferrari*
3rd Nelson Piquet [Bra] *Brabham-BMW*
Fastest lap: Prost *141.47 mph*

DUTCH Zandvoort 28 Aug
1st Rene Arnoux [Fr] *Ferrari 115.64 mph*
2nd Patrick Tambay [Fr] *Ferrari*
3rd John Watson [GB] *McLaren-Ford*
Fastest lap: Arnoux *119.1 mph*

ITALIAN Monza 11 Sept
1st Nelson Piquet [Bra] *Brabham-BMW 135.19 mph*
2nd Rene Arnoux [Fr] *Ferrari*
3rd Eddie Cheever [USA] *Renault*
Fastest lap: Piquet *137.4 mph*

EUROPEAN Brands Hatch 25 Sept
1st Nelson Piquet [Bra] *Brabham-BMW 123.17 mph*
2nd Alain Prost [Fr] *Renault*
3rd Nigel Mansell [GB] *Lotus-Renault*
Fastest lap: Mansell *126.57 mph*

SOUTH AFRICAN Kyalami 16 Oct
1st Riccardo Patrese [It] *Brabham-BMW 126.11 mph*
2nd Andrea de Cesaris [It] *Alfa-Romeo*
3rd Nelson Piquet [Bra] *Brabham-BMW*
Fastest lap: Piquet *131.25 mph*

INDIANAPOLIS 500 29 May
1st Tom Sneva [USA] *Texaco Star 162.117 mph*
2nd Al Unser [USA] *Hertz*
3rd Rick Mears [USA] *Pennzoil*
Fastest qualifier: Teo Fabi [It] *Skoal Bandit 207.395 mph*

World Champion: Niki Lauda [Aus]
US National Champion: Mario Andretti
Fastest Man on Earth: Richard Noble (>1983)

GRANDS PRIX

BRAZILIAN Rio de Janeiro 25 March
1st Alain Prost [Fr] *McLaren-TAG 111.55 mph*
2nd Keke Rosberg [Fin] *Williams-Honda*
3rd Elio de Angelis [It] *Lotus-Renault*
Fastest lap: Prost *116.63 mph*

SOUTH AFRICAN Kyalami 7 April
1st Niki Lauda [Aus] *McLaren-TAG 128.38 mph*
2nd Alain Prost [Fr] *McLaren-TAG*
3rd Derek Warwick [GB] *Renault*
Fastest lap: Patrick Tambay [Fr] *Renault 133.28 mph*

BELGIAN Zolder 29 April
1st Michele Alboreto [It] *Ferrari 115.23 mph*
2nd Derek Warwick [GB] *Renault*
3rd Rene Arnoux [Fr] *Ferrari*
Fastest lap: Arnoux *120.24 mph*

SAN MARINO Imola 6 May
1st Alain Prost [Fr] *McLaren-TAG 116.36 mph*
2nd Rene Arnoux [Fr] *Ferrari*
3rd Elio de Angelis [It] *Lotus-Renault*
Fastest lap: Nelson Piquet [Bra] *Brabham-BMW 120.87 mph*

FRENCH Dijon-Prenois 20 May
1st Niki Lauda [Aus] *McLaren-TAG 125.54 mph*
2nd Patrick Tambay [Fr] *Renault*
3rd Nigel Mansell [GB] *Lotus-Renault*
Fastest lap: Alain Prost [Fr] *McLaren-TAG 133.25 mph*

MONACO Monte Carlo 3 June
1st Alain Prost [Fr] *McLaren-TAG 62.62 mph*
2nd Ayrton Senna [Bra] *Toleman-Hart*
3rd Stefan Bellof [Ger] *Tyrrell-Ford*
Fastest lap: Senna *64.8 mph*

CANADIAN Montreal 17 June
1st Nelson Piquet [Bra] *Brabham-BMW 108.18 mph*
2nd Niki Lauda [Aus] *McLaren-TAG*
3rd Alain Prost [Fr] *McLaren-TAG*
Fastest lap: Piquet *111.14 mph*

UNITED STATES Detroit 24 June
1st Nelson Piquet [Bra] *Brabham-BMW 81.68 mph*
2nd Elio de Angelis [It] *Lotus-Renault*
3rd Teo Fabi [It] *Brabham-BMW*
Fastest lap: Derek Warwick [GB] *Renault 84.73 mph*

UNITED STATES Dallas 8 July
1st Keke Rosberg [Fin] *Williams-Honda 80.3 mph*
2nd Rene Arnoux [Fr] *Ferrari*
3rd Elio de Angelis [It] *Lotus-Renault*
Fastest lap: Niki Lauda [Aus] *McLaren-TAG 82.83 mph*

BRITISH Brands Hatch 22 July
1st Niki Lauda [Aus] *McLaren-TAG 124.41 mph*
2nd Derek Warwick [GB] *Renault*
3rd Ayrton Senna [Bra] *Toleman-Hart*
Fastest lap: Lauda *128.52 mph*

GERMAN Hockenheim 5 Aug
1st Alain Prost [Fr] *McLaren-TAG 131.61 mph*
2nd Niki Lauda [Aus] *McLaren-TAG*
3rd Derek Warwick [GB] *Renault*
Fastest lap: Prost *133.92 mph*

AUSTRIAN Österreichring 19 Aug
1st Niki Lauda [Aus] *McLaren-TAG 139.12 mph*
2nd Nelson Piquet [Bra] *Brabham-BMW*
3rd Michele Alboreto [It] *Ferrari*
Fastest lap: Lauda *143.11 mph*

DUTCH Zandvoort 26 Aug
1st Alain Prost [Fr] *McLaren-TAG 115.61 mph*
2nd Niki Lauda [Aus] *McLaren-TAG*
3rd Nigel Mansell [GB] *Lotus-Renault*
Fastest lap: Rene Arnoux [Fr] *Ferrari 119.7 mph*

ITALIAN Monza 9 Sept
1st Niki Lauda [Aus] *McLaren-TAG 137.02 mph*
2nd Michele Alboreto [It] *Ferrari*
3rd Riccardo Patrese [It] *Alfa-Romeo*
Fastest lap: Lauda *141.16 mph*

EUROPEAN Nürburging 7 Oct
1st Alain Prost [Fr] *McLaren-TAG 119.15 mph*
2nd Michele Alboreto [It] *Ferrari*
3rd Nelson Piquet [Bra] *Brabham-BMW*
Fastest lap: Piquet *122.2 mph*

PORTUGUESE Estoril 21 Oct
1st Alain Prost [Fr] *McLaren-TAG 112.19 mph*
2nd Niki Lauda [Aus] *McLaren-TAG*
3rd Ayrton Senna [Bra] *Toleman-Hart*
Fastest lap: Lauda *117.25 mph*

INDIANAPOLIS 500 27 May
1st Rick Mears [USA] *Pennzoil Z-7 163.612 mph*
2nd Roberto Guerrero [Col] *Master Mechanics*
3rd Al Unser [USA] *Miller High Life*
Fastest qualifier: Tom Sneva [USA] *Texaco Star 210.019 mph*

World Champion: Alain Prost [Fr]
US National Champion: Al Unser
Fastest Man on Earth: Richard Noble (>1983)

GRANDS PRIX

BRAZILIAN Rio de Janeiro 7 April
1st Alain Prost [Fr] *McLaren-TAG 112.8 mph*
2nd Michele Alboreto [It] *Ferrari*
3rd Elio de Angelis [It] *Lotus-Renault*
Fastest lap: Prost *116.38 mph*

PORTUGUESE Estoril 21 April
1st Ayrton Senna [Bra] *Lotus-Renault 90.2 mph*
2nd Michele Alboreto [It] *Ferrari*
3rd Patrick Tambay [Fr] *Renault*
Fastest lap: Senna *93.46 mph*

SAN MARINO Imola 5 May
1st Elio de Angelis [It] *Lotus-Renault 119.18 mph*
2nd Thierry Boutsen [Bel] *Arrows-BMW*
3rd Patrick Tambay [Fr] *Renault*
Fastest lap: Michele Alboreto [It] *Ferrari 123.95 mph*

MONACO Monte Carlo 19 May
1st Alain Prost [Fr] *McLaren-TAG 86.02 mph*
2nd Michele Alboreto [It] *Ferrari*
3rd Elio de Angelis [It] *Lotus-Renault*
Fastest lap: Alboreto *89.66 mph*

CANADIAN Montreal 17 June
1st Michele Alboreto [It] *Ferrari 108.55 mph*
2nd Stefan Johansson [Swe] *Ferrari*
3rd Alain Prost [Fr] *McLaren-TAG*
Fastest lap: Ayrton Senna [Bra] *Lotus-Renault 112.82 mph*

UNITED STATES Detroit 23 June
1st Keke Rosberg [Fin] *Williams-Honda 81.71 mph*
2nd Stefan Johansson [Swe] *Ferrari*
3rd Michele Alboreto [It] *Ferrari*
Fastest lap: Ayrton Senna [Bra] *Lotus-Renault 85.21 mph*

FRENCH Paul Ricard 17 July
1st Nelson Piquet [Bra] *Brabham-BMW 125.1 mph*
2nd Keke Rosberg [Fin] *Williams-Honda*
3rd Alain Prost [Fr] *McLaren-TAG*
Fastest lap: Rosberg *130.08 mph*

BRITISH Silverstone 21 July
1st Alain Prost [Fr] *McLaren-TAG 146.28 mph*
2nd Michele Alboreto [It] *Ferrari*
3rd Jacques Laffite [Fr] *Ligier-Renault*
Fastest lap: Prost *151.04 mph*

GERMAN Nürburging 4 Aug
1st Michele Alboreto [It] *Ferrari 118.78 mph*
2nd Alain Prost [Fr] *McLaren-TAG*
3rd Jacques Lai-rite [Fr] *Ligier-Renault*
Fastest lap: Niki Lauda [Aus] *McLaren-TAG 122.7 mph*

AUSTRIAN Österreichring 18 Aug
1st Alain Prost [Fr] *McLaren-TAG 143.62 mph*
2nd Ayrton Senna [Bra] *Lotus-Renault*
3rd Michele Alboreto [It] *Ferrari*
Fastest lap: Prost *148.95 mph*

DUTCH Zandvoort 25 Aug
1st Niki Lauda [Aus] *McLaren-TAG 119.99 mph*
2nd Alain Prost [Fr] *McLaren-TAG*
3rd Ayrton Senna [Bra] *Lotus-Renault*
Fastest lap: Prost *124.27 mph*

ITALIAN Monza 8 Sept
1st Alain Prost [Fr] *McLaren-TAG 141.41 mph*
2nd Nelson Piquet [Bra] *Brabham-BMW*
3rd Ayrton Senna [Bra] *Lotus-Renault*
Fastest lap: Nigel Mansell [GB] *Williams-Honda*
146.97 mph

BELGIAN Spa 15 Sept
1st Ayrton Senna [Bra] *Lotus-Renault 117.95 mph*
2nd Nigel Mansell [GB] *Williams-Honda*
3rd Alain Prost [Fr] *McLaren-TAG*
Fastest lap: Prost *127.54 mph*

EUROPEAN Brands Hatch 6 Oct
1st Nigel Mansell [GB] *Williams-Honda 126.54 mph*
2nd Ayrton Senna [Bra] *Lotus-Renault*
3rd Keke Rosberg [Fin] *Williams-Honda*
Fastest lap: Jacques Laffite [Fr] *Ligier-Renault 131.57 mph*

SOUTH AFRICAN Kyalami 19 Oct
1st Nigel Mansell [GB] *Williams-Honda 129.85 mph*
2nd Keke Rosberg [Fin] *Williams-Honda*
3rd Alain Prost [Fr] *McLaren-TAG*
Fastest lap: Rosberg *134.72 mph*

AUSTRALIAN Adelaide 3 Nov
1st Keke Rosberg [Fin] *Williams-Honda 95.71 mph*
2nd Jacques Laffite [Fr] *Ligier-Renault*
3rd Philippe Streiff [Fr] *Ligier-Renault*
Fastest lap: Rosberg *100.9 mph*

INDIANAPOLIS 500 26 May
1st Danny Sullivan [USA] *Miller American 152.982 mph*
2nd Mario Andretti [USA] *Lola*
3rd Roberto Guerrero [Col] *Master Mechanics*
Fastest qualifier: Pancho Carter [USA] *Valvoline Buick
Hawk 212.583 mph*

World Champion: Alain Prost [Fr]
US National Champion: Bobby Rahal
Fastest Man on Earth: Richard Noble (>1983)

GRANDS PRIX
BRAZILIAN Rio de Janeiro 23 March
1st Nelson Piquet [Bra] *Williams-Honda 114.94 mph*
2nd Ayrton Senna [Bra] *Lotus-Renault*
3rd Jacques Laffite [Fr] *Ligier-Renault*
Fastest lap: Piquet *120.39 mph*

SPANISH Jerez 13 April
1st Ayrton Senna [Bra] *Lotus-Renault 104.07 mph*
2nd Nigel Mansell [GB] *Williams-Honda*
3rd Alain Prost [Fr] *McLaren-TAG*
Fastest lap: Mansell *108.23 mph*

SAN MARINO Imola 27 April
1st Alain Prost [Fr] *McLaren-TAG 121.92 mph*
2nd Nelson Piquet [Bra] *Williams-Honda*
3rd Gerhard Berger [Aus] *Benetton-BMW*
Fastest lap: Piquet *123.95 mph*

MONACO Monte Carlo 11 May
1st Alain Prost [Fr] *McLaren-TAG 83.66 mph*
2nd Keke Rosberg [Fin] *McLaren-TAG*
3rd Ayrton Senna [Bra] *Lotus-Renault*
Fastest lap: Prost *85.96 mph*

BELGIAN Spa 25 May
1st Nigel Mansell [GB] *Williams-Honda 126.48 mph*
2nd Ayrton Senna [Bra] *Lotus-Renault*
3rd Stefan Johansson [Swe] *Ferrari*
Fastest lap: Alain Prost [Fr] *McLaren-TAG 130.15 mph*

CANADIAN Montreal 15 June
1st Nigel Mansell [GB] *Williams-Honda 111.39 mph*
2nd Alain Prost [Fr] *McLaren-TAG*
3rd Nelson Piquet [Bra] *Williams-Honda*
Fastest lap: Piquet *16.13 mph*

UNITED STATES Detroit 22 June
1st Ayrton Senna [Bra] *Lotus-Renault 84.97 mph*
2nd Jacques Laffite [Fr] *Ligier-Renault*
3rd Alain Prost [Fr] *McLaren-TAG*
Fastest lap: Nelson Piquet [Bra] *Williams-Honda 88.9 mph*

FRENCH Paul Ricard 6 July
1st Nigel Mansell [GB] *Williams-Honda 117.54 mph*
2nd Alain Prost [Fr] *McLaren-TAG*
3rd Nelson Piquet [Bra] *Williams-Honda*
Fastest lap: Mansell *122.57 mph*

BRITISH Brands Hatch 13 July
1st Nigel Mansell [GB] *Williams-Honda 129.78 mph*
2nd Nelson Piquet [Bra] *Williams-Honda*
3rd Alain Prost [Fr] *McLaren-TAG*
Fastest lap: Mansell *135.22 mph*

GERMAN Hockenheim 27 July
1st Nelson Piquet [Bra] *Williams-Honda 136.59 mph*
2nd Ayrton Senna [Bra] *Lotus-Renault*
3rd Nigel Mansell [GB] *Williams-Honda*
Fastest lap: Gerhard Berger [Aus] *Benetton 143.46 mph*

HUNGARIAN Hungaroring 10 Aug
1st Nelson Piquet [Bra] *Williams-Honda 94.33 mph*
2nd Ayrton Senna [Bra] *Lotus-Renault*
3rd Nigel Mansell [GB] *Williams-Honda*
Fastest lap: Piquet *98.67 mph*

AUSTRIAN Österreichring 17 Aug
1st Alain Prost *McLaren-TAG 141.56 mph*
2nd Michele Alboreto [It] *Ferrari*
3rd Stefan Johansson [Swe] *Ferrari*
Fastest lap: Gerhard Berger [Aus] *Benetton-BMW
148.46 mph*

ITALIAN Monza 7 Sept
1st Nelson Piquet [Bra] *Williams-Honda 141.9 mph*
2nd Nigel Mansell [GB] *Williams-Honda*
3rd Stefan Johansson [Swe] *Ferrari*
Fastest lap: Teo Fabi [It] *Benetton-BMW 147.27 mph*

PORTUGUESE Estoril 21 Sept
1st Nigel Mansell [GB] *Williams-Honda 116.6 mph*
2nd Alain Prost [Fr] *McLaren-TAG*
3rd Nelson Piquet [Bra] *Williams-Honda*
Fastest lap: Mansell *120.22 mph*

MEXICAN Mexico City 12 Oct
1st Gerhard Berger [Aus] *Benetton-BMW 120.14 mph*
2nd Alain Prost [Fr] *McLaren-TAG*
3rd Ayrton Senna [Bra] *Lotus-Renault*
Fastest lap: Nelson Piquet [Bra] *Williams-Honda
124.6 mph*

AUSTRALIAN Adelaide 26 Oct
1st Alain Prost [Fr] *McLaren-TAG 101.63 mph*
2nd Nelson Piquet [Bra] *Williams-Honda*
3rd Stefan Johansson [Swe] *Ferrari*
Fastest lap: Piquet *104.6 mph*

INDIANAPOLIS 500 1 June
1st Bobby Rahal [USA] *Budweiser 170.722 mph*
2nd Kevin Cogan [USA] *7 Eleven*
3rd Rick Mears [USA] *Pennzoil Z-7*
Fastest qualifier: Mears *216.828 mph*

World Champion: Nelson Piquet [Bra]
US National Champion: Bobby Rahal
Fastest Man on Earth: Richard Noble (>1983)

GRANDS PRIX
BRAZILIAN Rio de Janeiro 12 April
1st Alain Prost [Fr] *McLaren-TAG 114.7 mph*
2nd Nelson Piquet [Bra] *Williams-Honda*
3rd Stefan Johansson [Swe] *McLaren-TAG*
Fastest lap: Piquet *119.9 mph*

SAN MARINO Imola 3 May
1st Nigel Mansell [GB] *Williams-Honda 121.29 mph*
2nd Ayrton Senna [Bra] Lotus-*Honda*
3rd Michele Alboreto [It] *Ferrari*
Fastest lap: Teo Fabi [It] *Benetton-Ford 126.33 mph*

BELGIAN Spa 17 May
1st Alain Prost [Fr] *McLaren-TAG 127.8 mph*
2nd Stefan Johansson [Swe] *McLaren-TAG*
3rd Andrea de Cesaris [It] *Brabham-BMW*
Fastest lap: Prost *132.51 mph*

MONACO Monte Carlo 31 May
1st Ayrton Senna [Bra] Lotus-*Honda 82.08 mph*
2nd Nelson Piquet [Bra] *Williams-Honda*
3rd Michele Alboreto [It] *Ferrari*
Fastest lap: Senna *84.9 mph*

UNITED STATES Detroit 21 June
1st Ayrton Senna [Bra] *Lotus-Honda 85.7 mph*
2nd Nelson Piquet [Bra] *Williams-Honda*
3rd Alain Prost [Fr] *McLaren-TAG*
Fastest lap: Senna *89.58 mph*

FRENCH Paul Ricard 5 July
1st Nigel Mansell [GB] *Williams-Honda 117.17 mph*
2nd Nelson Piquet [Bra] *Williams-Honda*
3rd Alain Prost [Fr] *McLaren-TAG*
Fastest lap: Piquet *122.64 mph*

BRITISH Silverstone 12 July
1st Nigel Mansell [GB] *Williams-Honda 146.21 mph*
2nd Nelson Piquet [Bra] *Williams-Honda*
3rd Ayrton Senna [Bra] Lotus-*Honda*
Fastest lap: Mansell *153.06 mph*

GERMAN Hockenheim 26 July
1st Nelson Piquet [Bra] *Williams-Honda 136.95 mph*
2nd Stefan Johansson [Swe] *McLaren-TAG*
3rd Ayrton Senna [Bra] Lotus-*Honda*
Fastest lap: Nigel Mansell [GB] *Williams-Honda
143.83 mph*

HUNGARIAN Hungaroring 9 Aug
1st Nelson Piquet [Bra] *Williams-Honda 95.22 mph*
2nd Ayrton Senna [Bra] Lotus-*Honda*
3rd Alain Prost [Fr] *McLaren-TAG*
Fastest lap: Piquet *99.6 mph*

AUSTRIAN Österreichring 16 Aug
1st Nigel Mansell [GB] *Williams-Honda 146.28 mph*
2nd Nelson Piquet [Bra] *Williams-Honda*
3rd Teo Fabi [It] *Benetton-Ford*
Fastest lap: Mansell *150.5 mph*

ITALIAN Monza 6 Sept
1st Nelson Piquet [Bra] *Williams-Honda 144.55 mph*
2nd Ayrton Senna [Bra] Lotus-*Honda*
3rd Nigel Mansell [GB] *Williams-Honda*
Fastest lap: Senna *149.48 mph*

PORTUGUESE Estoril 20 Sept
1st Alain Prost [Fr] *McLaren-TAG 116.96 mph*
2nd Gerhard Berger [Aus] *Ferrari*
3rd Nelson Piquet [Bra] *Williams-Honda*
Fastest lap: Berger *122.74 mph*

SPANISH Jerez 27 Sept
1st Nigel Mansell [GB] *Williams-Honda 103.67 mph*
2nd Alain Prost [Fr] *McLaren-TAG*
3rd Stefan Johansson [Swe] *McLaren-TAG*
Fastest lap: Gerhard Berger [Aus] *Ferrari 108.47 mph*

MEXICAN Mexico City 18 Oct
1st Nigel Mansell [GB] *Williams-Honda 120.18 mph*
2nd Nelson Piquet [Bra] *Williams-Honda*
3rd Riccardo Patrese [It] *Brabham-BMW*
Fastest lap: Piquet *124.97 mph*

JAPANESE Suzuka 1 Nov
1st Gerhard Berger [Aus] *Ferrari 119.83 mph*
2nd Ayrton Senna [Bra] *Lotus-Honda*
3rd Stefan Johansson [Swe] *McLaren-TAG*
Fastest lap: Alain Prost [Fr] *McLaren-TAG 126.21 mph*

AUSTRALIAN Adelaide 15 Nov
1st Gerhard Berger [Aus] *Ferrari 102.3 mph*
2nd Michele Alboreto [It] *Ferrari*
3rd Thierry Boutsen [Bel] *Benetton-Ford*
Fastest lap: Berger *105.12 mph*

INDIANAPOLIS 500 24 May
1st Al Unser [USA] *Cummins-Holset 162.175 mph*
2nd Roberto Guerrero [Col] *True Valve-STP*
3rd Fabrizio Barbazza [It] *Arciero Winery*
Fastest qualifier: Mario Andretti [USA] *Hanna Auto 215.37 mph*

World Champion: Ayrton Senna [Bra]
US National Champion: Danny Sullivan
Fastest Man on Earth: Richard Noble (>1983)

GRANDS PRIX

BRAZILIAN Rio de Janeiro 3 April
1st Alain Prost [Fr] *McLaren-Honda 117.09 mph*
2nd Gerhard Berger [Aus] *Ferrari*
3rd Nelson Piquet [Bra] *Lotus-Honda*
Fastest lap: Berger *121.09 mph*

SAN MARINO Imola 1 May
1st Ayrton Senna [Bra] *McLaren-Ford 122.3 mph*
2nd Alain Prost [Fr] *McLaren-Honda*
3rd Nelson Piquet [Bra] *Lotus-Ford*
Fastest lap: Prost *122.4 mph*

MONACO Monte Carlo 15 May
1st Alain Prost [Fr] *McLaren-Honda 82.52 mph*
2nd Gerhard Berger [Aus] *Ferrari*
3rd Michele Alboreto [It] *Ferrari*
Fastest lap: Ayrton Senna [Bra] *McLaren-Honda 85.26 mph*

MEXICAN Mexico City 29 May
1st Alain Prost [Fr] *McLaren-Honda 123.08 mph*
2nd Ayrton Senna [Bra] *McLaren-Honda*
3rd Gerhard Berger [Aus] *Ferrari*
Fastest lap: Prost *125.8 mph*

CANADIAN Montreal 12 June
1st Ayrton Senna [Bra] *McLaren-Honda 113.19 mph*
2nd Alain Prost [Fr] *McLaren-Honda*
3rd Thierry Boutsen [Bel] *Benetton-Ford*
Fastest lap: Senna *115.6 mph*

UNITED STATES Detroit 19 June
1st Ayrton Senna [Bra] *McLaren-Honda 82.22 mph*
2nd Alain Prost [Fr] *McLaren-Honda*
3rd Thierry Boutsen [Bel] *Benetton-Ford*
Fastest lap: Prost *85.84 mph*

FRENCH Paul Ricard 3 July
1st Alain Prost [Fr] *McLaren-Honda 116.5 mph*
2nd Ayrton Senna [Bra] *McLaren-Honda*
3rd Michele Alboreto [It] *Ferrari*
Fastest lap: Prost *118.9 mph*

BRITISH Silverstone 10 July
1st Ayrton Senna [Bra] *McLaren-Honda 124.14 mph*
2nd Nigel Mansell [GB] *Williams-Judd*
3rd Alessandro Nannini [It] *Benetton-Ford*
Fastest lap: Mansell *128.3 mph*

GERMAN Hockenheim 24 July
1st Ayrton Senna [Bra] *McLaren-Honda 120.71 mph*
2nd Alain Prost [Fr] *McLaren-Honda*
3rd Gerhard Berger [Aus] *Ferrari*
Fastest lap: Alessandro Nannini [It] *Benetton-Ford 124.3 mph*

HUNGARIAN Hungaroring 7 Aug
1st Ayrton Senna [Bra] *McLaren-Honda 96.56 mph*
2nd Alain Prost [Fr] *McLaren-Honda*
3rd Thierry Boutsen [Bel] *Benetton-Ford*
Fastest lap: Prost *99.06 mph*

BELGIAN Spa 28 Aug
1st Ayrton Senna [Bra] *McLaren-Honda 126.42 mph*
2nd Alain Prost [Fr] *McLaren-Honda*
3rd Ivan Capelli [It] *March-Judd*
Fastest lap: Gerhard Berger [Aus] *Ferrari 128.54 mph*

ITALIAN Monza 11 Sept
1st Gerhard Berger [Aus] *Ferrari 141.96 mph*
2nd Michele Alboreto [It] *Ferrari*
3rd Eddie Cheever [USA] *Arrows-Megatron*
Fastest lap: Alboreto *145.63 mph*

PORTUGUESE Estoril 25 Sept
1st Alain Prost [Fr] *McLaren-Honda 116.15 mph*
2nd Ivan Capelli [It] *March-Judd*
3rd Thierry Boutsen [Bel] *Benetton-Ford*
Fastest lap: Gerhard Berger [Aus] *Ferrari 118.65 mph*

SPANISH Jerez 2 Oct
1st Alain Prost [Fr] *McLaren-Honda 104.07 mph*
2nd Nigel Mansell [GB] *Williams-Judd*
3rd Alessandro Nannini [It] *Benetton-Ford*
Fastest lap: Prost *107.35 mph*

JAPANESE Suzuka 30 Oct
1st Ayrton Senna [Bra] *McLaren-Honda 119.16 mph*
2nd Alain Prost [Fr] *McLaren-Honda*
3rd Thierry Boutsen [Bel] *Benetton-Ford*
Fastest lap: Senna *123.19 mph*

AUSTRALIAN Adelaide 13 Nov
1st Alain Prost [Fr] *McLaren-Honda 102.07 mph*
2nd Ayrton Senna [Bra] *McLaren-Honda*
3rd Nelson Piquet [Bra] *Lotus-Honda*
Fastest lap: Prost *104.12 mph*

INDIANAPOLIS 500 29 May
1st Rick Mears [USA] *Pennzoil Z-7 144.809 mph*
2nd Emerson Fittipaldi [Bra] *Marlboro*
3rd Al Unser [USA] *Hertz*
Fastest qualifier: Mears *219.198 mph*

World Champion: Alain Prost [Fr]
US National Champion: Emerson Fittipaldi [Bra]
Fastest Man on Earth: Richard Noble (>1983)

GRANDS PRIX

BRAZILIAN Rio de Janeiro 26 March
1st Nigel Mansell [GB] *Ferrari 115.73 mph*
2nd Alain Prost [Fr] *McLaren-Honda*
3rd Mauricio Gugelmin [Bra] *March-Judd*
Fastest lap: Riccardo Patrese [It] *Williams-Renault 121.66 mph*

SAN MARINO Imola 23 April
1st Ayrton Senna [Bra] *McLaren-Honda 125.4 mph*
2nd Alain Prost [Fr] *McLaren-Honda*
3rd Alessandro Nannini [It] *Benetton-Ford*
Fastest lap: Prost *129.9 mph*

MONACO Monte Carlo 7 May
1st Ayrton Senna [Bra] *McLaren-Honda 84.21 mph*
2nd Alain Prost [Fr] *McLaren-Honda*
3rd Stefano Modena [It] *Brabham-Judd*
Fastest lap: Prost *87.1 mph*

MEXICAN Mexico City 28 May
1st Ayrton Senna [Bra] *McLaren-Honda 119.39 mph*
2nd Riccardo Patrese [It] *Williams-Renault*
3rd Michele Alboreto [It] *Tyrrell-Ford*
Fastest lap: Nigel Mansell [GB] *Ferrari 122.97 mph*

UNITED STATES Phoenix 4 June
1st Alain Prost [Fr] *McLaren-Honda 87.36 mph*
2nd Riccardo Patrese [It] *Williams-Renault*
3rd Eddie Cheever [USA] *Arrows-Ford*
Fastest lap: Ayrton Senna [Bra] *McLaren-Honda 90.41 mph*

CANADIAN Montreal 18 June
1st Thierry Boutsen [Bel] *Williams-Renault 93.09 mph*
2nd Riccardo Patrese [It] *Williams-Renault*
3rd Andrea de Cesaris [It] *Dallara-Ford*
Fastest lap: Jonathan Palmer [GB] *Tyrrell-Ford 106.83 mph*

FRENCH Paul Ricard 9 July
1st Alain Prost [Fr] *McLaren-Honda 115.5 mph*
2nd Nigel Mansell [GB] *Ferrari*
3rd Riccardo Patrese [It] *Williams-Renault*
Fastest lap: Mauricio Gugelmin [Bra] *March-Judd 118.32 mph*

BRITISH Silverstone 16 July
1st Alain Prost [Fr] *McLaren-Honda 143.69 mph*
2nd Nigel Mansell [GB] *Ferrari*
3rd Alessandro Nannini [It] *Benetton-Ford*
Fastest lap: Mansell *148.47 mph*

GERMAN Hockenheim 30 July
1st Ayrton Senna [Bra] *McLaren-Honda 139.42 mph*
2nd Alain Prost [Fr] *McLaren-Honda*
3rd Nigel Mansell [GB] *Ferrari*
Fastest lap: Senna *143.6 mph*

HUNGARIAN Hungaroring 13 Aug
1st Nigel Mansell [GB] *Ferrari 104.07 mph*
2nd Ayrton Senna [Bra] *McLaren-Honda*
3rd Thierry Boutsen [Bel] *Williams-Renault*
Fastest lap: Mansell *107.41 mph*

BELGIAN Spa 27 Aug
1st Ayrton Senna [Bra] *McLaren-Honda 112.76 mph*
2nd Alain Prost [Fr] *McLaren-Honda*
3rd Nigel Mansell [GB] *Ferrari*
Fastest lap: Prost *117.99 mph*

ITALIAN Monza 10 Sept
1st Alain Prost [Fr] *McLaren-Honda 144.07 mph*
2nd Gerhard Berger [Aus] *Ferrari*
3rd Thierry Boutsen [Bel] *Williams-Renault*
Fastest lap: Prost *147.25 mph*

PORTUGUESE Estoril 24 Sept
1st Gerhard Berger [Aus] *Ferrari 118.81 mph*
2nd Alain Prost [Fr] *McLaren-Honda*
3rd Stefan Johansson [Swe] *Onyx-Ford*
Fastest lap: Berger *123.19 mph*

SPANISH Jerez 1 Oct
1st Ayrton Senna [Bra] *McLaren-Honda 106.44 mph*
2nd Gerhard Berger [Aus] *Ferrari*
3rd Alain Prost [Fr] *McLaren-Honda*
Fastest lap: Senna *109.99 mph*

JAPANESE Suzuka 22 Oct
1st Alessandro Nannini [It] *Benetton-Ford 121.7 mph*
2nd Riccardo Patrese [It] *Williams-Renault*
3rd Thierry Boutsen [Bel] *Williams-Renault*
Fastest lap: Alain Prost [Fr] *McLaren-Honda 126.62 mph*

AUSTRALIAN Adelaide 5 Nov
1st Thierry Boutsen [Bel] *Williams-Renault 82.05 mph*
2nd Alessandro Nannini [It] *Benetton-Ford*
3rd Riccardo Patrese [It] *Williams-Renault*
Fastest lap: Satoru Nakajima [Jap] *Lotus-Judd 86.48 mph*

INDIANAPOLIS 500 28 May
1st Emerson Fittipaldi [Bra] *Marlboro 167.581 mph*
2nd Al Unser, Jr [USA] *Valvoline-Stroh*
3rd Raul Boesel [Bra] *Domino's Pizza*
Fastest qualifier: Rick Mears [USA] *Pennzoil Z-7 223.885 mph*

World Champion: Ayrton Senna [Bra]
US National Champion: Al Unser, Jr
Fastest Man on Earth: Richard Noble (>1983)

GRANDS PRIX

UNITED STATES Phoenix 11 March
1st Ayrton Senna [Bra] *McLaren-Honda 90.58 mph*
2nd Jean Alesi [Fr] *Tyrrell-Ford*
3rd Thierry Boutsen [Bel] *Williams-Renault*
Fastest lap: Gerhard Berger [Aus] *McLaren-Honda*
93.31 mph

BRAZILIAN Interlagos 25 March
1st Alain Prost [Fr] *Ferrari 117.59 mph*
2nd Gerhard Berger [Aus] *McLaren-Honda*
3rd Ayrton Senna [Bra] *McLaren-Honda*
Fastest lap: Berger *121.09 mph*

SAN MARINO Imola 13 May
1st Riccardo Patrese [It] *Williams-Renault 125.99 mph*
2nd Gerhard Berger [Aus] *McLaren-Honda*
3rd Alessandro Nannini [It] *Benetton-Ford*
Fastest lap: Nannini *129.36 mph*

MONACO Monte Carlo 27 May
1st Ayrton Senna [Bra] *McLaren-Honda 85.89 mph*
2nd Jean Alesi [Fr] *Tyrrell-Ford*
3rd Gerhard Berger [Aus] *McLaren-Honda*
Fastest lap: Senna *88.13 mph*

CANADIAN Montreal 10 June
1st Ayrton Senna [Bra] *McLaren-Honda 111.38 mph*
2nd Nelson Piquet [Bra] *Benetton-Ford*
3rd Nigel Mansel [GB] *Ferrari*
Fastest lap: Gerhard Berger [Aus] *McLaren-Honda*
119.65 mph

MEXICAN Mexico City 24 June
1st Alain Prost [Fr] *Ferrari 122.95 mph*
2nd Nigel Mansell [GB] *Ferrari*
3rd Gerhard Berger [Aus] *McLaren-Honda*
Fastest lap: Prost *126.85 mph*

FRENCH Paul Ricard 8 July
1st Alain Prost [Fr] *Ferrari 123.21 mph*
2nd Ivan Capelli [It] *Leyton House-Judd*
3rd Ayrton Senna [Bra] *McLaren-Honda*
Fastest lap: Nigel Mansell [GB] *Ferrari 125.44 mph*

BRITISH Silverstone 15 July
1st Alain Prost [Fr] *Ferrari 145.25 mph*
2nd Thierry Boutsen [Bel] *Williams-Renault*
3rd Ayrton Senna [Bra] *McLaren-Honda*
Fastest lap: Nigel Mansell [GB] *Ferrari 149.98 mph*

GERMAN Hockenheim 29 July
1st Ayrton Senna [Bra] *McLaren-Honda 141.37 mph*
2nd Alessandro Nannini [It] *Benetton-Ford*
3rd Gerhard Berger [Aus] *McLaren-Ford*
Fastest lap: Thierry Boutsen [Bel] *Williams-Honda*
144.08 mph

HUNGARIAN Hungaroring 12 Aug
1st Thierry Boutsen [Bel] *Williams-Renault 103.78 mph*
2nd Ayrton Senna [Bra] *McLaren-Ford*
3rd Nelson Piquet [Bra] *Benetton-Ford*
Fastest lap: Riccardo Patrese [It] *Williams-Renault*
106.08 mph

BELGIAN Spa 26 Aug
1st Ayrton Senna [Bra] *McLaren-Honda 131.51 mph*
2nd Alain Prost [Fr] *Ferrari*
3rd Gerhard Berger [Aus] *McLaren-Honda*
Fastest lap: Prost *134.89 mph*

ITALIAN Monza 9 Sept
1st Ayrton Senna [Bra] *McLaren-Honda 146.83 mph*
2nd Alain Prost [Fr] *Ferrari*
3rd Gerhard Berger [Aus] *McLaren-Honda*
Fastest lap: Senna *150.42 mph*

PORTUGUESE Estoril 23 Sept
1st Nigel Mansell [GB] *Ferrari 120.24 mph*
2nd Ayrton Senna [Bra] *McLaren-Honda*
3rd Alain Prost [Fr] *Ferrari*
Fastest lap: Riccardo Patrese [It] *Williams-Renault*
124.26 mph

SPANISH Jerez 30 Sept
1st Alain Prost [Fr] *Ferrari 106.23 mph*
2nd Nigel Mansell [GB] *Ferrari*
3rd Alessandro Nannini [It] *Benetton-Ford*
Fastest lap: Riccardo Patrese [It] *Williams-Renault*
111.64 mph

JAPANESE Suzuka 21 Oct
1st Nelson Piquet [Bra] *Benetton-Ford 122.34 mph*
2nd Roberto Moreno [Bra] *Benetton-Ford*
3rd Aguri Suzuki [Jap] *Lola-Lamborghini*
Fastest lap: Riccardo Patrese [It] *Williams-Renault*
125.74 mph

AUSTRALIAN Adelaide 4 Nov
1st Nelson Piquet [Bra] *Benetton-Ford 104.07 mph*
2nd Nigel Mansell [GB] *Ferrari*
3rd Alain Prost [Fr] *Ferrari*
Fastest lap: Mansell *108.12 mph*

INDIANAPOLIS 500 27 May
1st Arie Luyendyk [Hol] *Domino's Pizza 185.981 mph*
2nd Bobby Rahal [USA] *STP-Kraco*
3rd Emerson Fittipaldi [Bra] *Marlboro*
Fastest qualifier: Fittipaldi *225.301 mph*

World Champion: Ayrton Senna [Bra]
US National Champion: Michael Andretti
Fastest Man on Earth: Richard Noble (>1983)

GRANDS PRIX

UNITED STATES Phoenix 10 March
1st Ayrton Senna [Bra] *McLaren-Honda 93.34 mph*
2nd Alain Prost [Fr] *Ferrari*
3rd Nelson Piquet [Bra] *Benetton-Ford*
Fastest lap: Jean Alesi [Fr] *Ferrari 95.93 mph*

BRAZILIAN Interlagos 24 March
1st Ayrton Senna [Bra] *McLaren-Honda 116.37 mph*
2nd Riccardo Patrese [It] *Williams-Renault*
3rd Gerhard Berger [Aus] *McLaren-Honda*
Fastest lap: Nigel Mansell [GB] *Williams-Renault*
120.28 mph

SAN MARINO Imola 28 April
1st Ayrton Senna [Bra] *McLaren-Honda 120.27 mph*
2nd Gerhard Berger [Aus] *McLaren-Honda*
3rd J. J. Lehto [Fin] *Dallara-Judd*
Fastest lap: Berger *130.29 mph*

MONACO Monte Carlo 12 May
1st Ayrton Senna [Bra] *McLaren-Honda 85.28 mph*
2nd Nigel Mansell [GB] *Williams-Renault*
3rd Jean Alesi [Fr] *Ferrari*
Fastest lap: Alain Prost [Fr] *Ferrari 88.24 mph*

CANADIAN Montreal 2 June
1st Nelson Piquet [Bra] *Benetton-Ford 115.16 mph*
2nd Stefano Modena [It] *Tyrrell-Ford*
3rd Riccardo Patrese [It] *Williams-Renault*
Fastest lap: Nigel Mansell [GB] *Williams-Renault*
120.28 mph

MEXICAN Mexico City 16 June
1st Riccardo Patrese [It] *Williams-Renault 123.67 mph*
2nd Nigel Mansell [GB] *Williams-Renault*
3rd Ayrton Senna [Bra] *McLaren-Honda*
Fastest lap: Mansell *128.79 mph*

FRENCH Magny-Cours 7 July
1st Nigel Mansell [GB] *Williams-Renault 116.81 mph*
2nd Alain Prost [Fr] *Ferrari*
3rd Ayrton Senna [Bra] *McLaren-Honda*
Fastest lap: Mansell *120.68 mph*

BRITISH Silverstone 14 July
1st Nigel Mansell [GB] *Williams-Renault 131.34 mph*
2nd Gerhard Berger [Aus] *McLaren-Honda*
3rd Alain Prost [Fr] *Ferrari*
Fastest lap: Mansell *135.25 mph*

GERMAN Hockenheim 28 July
1st Nigel Mansell [GB] *Williams-Renault 143.33 mph*
2nd Riccardo Patrese [It] *Williams-Renault*
3rd Jean Alesi [Fr] *Ferrari*
Fastest lap: Patrese *146.91 mph*

HUNGARIAN Hungaroring 11 Aug
1st Ayrton Senna [Bra] *McLaren-Honda 104.48 mph*
2nd Nigel Mansell [GB] *Williams-Renault*
3rd Riccardo Patrese [It] *Williams-Renault*
Fastest lap: Bertrand Gachot [Bel] *Jordan-Ford*
108.85 mph

BELGIAN Spa 25 Aug
1st Ayrton Senna [Bra] *McLaren-Honda 130.41 mph*
2nd Gerhard Berger [Aus] *McLaren-Honda*
3rd Nelson Piquet [Bra] *Benetton-Ford*
Fastest lap: Roberto Moreno [Bra] *Benetton-Ford*
134.81 mph

ITALIAN Monza 8 Sept
1st Nigel Mansell [GB] *Williams-Renault 146.94 mph*
2nd Ayrton Senna [Bra] *McLaren-Honda*
3rd Alain Prost [Fr] *Ferrari*
Fastest lap: Senna *150.76 mph*

PORTUGUESE Estoril 22 Sept
1st Riccardo Patrese [It] *Williams-Renault 120.18 mph*
2nd Ayrton Senna [Bra] *McLaren-Honda*
3rd Jean Alesi [Fr] *Ferrari*
Fastest lap: Nigel Mansell [GB] *Williams-Renault*
124.33 mph

SPANISH Barcelona 29 Sept
1st Nigel Mansell [GB] *Williams-Renault 116.57 mph*
2nd Alain Prost [Fr] *Ferrari*
3rd Riccardo Patrese [It] *Williams-Renault*
Fastest lap: Patrese *128.19 mph*

JAPANESE Suzuka 20 Oct
1st Gerhard Berger [Aus] *McLaren-Honda 125.57 mph*
2nd Ayrton Senna [Bra] *McLaren-Honda*
3rd Riccardo Patrese [It] *Williams-Renault*
Fastest lap: Senna *129.19 mph*

AUSTRALIAN Adelaide 3 Nov
1st Ayrton Senna [Bra] *McLaren-Honda 80.3 mph*
2nd Nigel Mansell [GB] *Williams-Renault*
3rd Gerhard Berger [Aus] *McLaren-Honda*
Fastest lap: Berger *83.6 mph*

INDIANAPOLIS 500 25 May
1st Rick Mears [USA] *Marlboro 176.457 mph*
2nd Michael Andretti [USA] *Kmart+Havoline*
3rd Arie Luyendyk [Hol] *RCA*
Fastest qualifier: Gary Bettenhausen [USA] *Glidden*
224.468 mph

World Champion: Nigel Mansell [GB]
US National Champion: Bobby Rahal
Fastest Man on Earth: Richard Noble (>1983)

GRANDS PRIX

SOUTH AFRICAN Kyalami 1 March
1st Nigel Mansell [GB] *Williams-Renault 118.76 mph*
2nd Riccardo Patrese [It] *Williams-Renault*
3rd Ayrton Senna [Bra] *McLaren-Honda*
Fastest lap: Mansell *123.57 mph*

MEXICAN Mexico City 22 March
1st Nigel Mansell [GB] *Williams-Renault 123.89 mph*
2nd Riccardo Patrese [It] *Williams-Renault*
3rd Michael Schumacher [Ger] *Benetton-Ford*
Fastest lap: Gerhard Berger [Aus] *McLaren-Honda*
127.26 mph

BRAZILIAN Interlagos 5 April
1st Nigel Mansell [GB] *Williams-Renault 118.3 mph*
2nd Riccardo Patrese [It] *Williams-Renault*
3rd Michael Schumacher [Ger] *Benetton-Ford*
Fastest lap: Patrese *121.71 mph*

SPANISH Barcelona 3 May
1st Nigel Mansell [GB] *Williams-Renault 99.02 mph*
2nd Michael Schumacher [Ger] *Benetton-Ford*
3rd Jean Alesi [Fr] *Ferrari*
Fastest lap: Mansell *103.59 mph*

SAN MARINO Imola 17 May
1st Nigel Mansell [GB] *Williams-Renault 127.06 mph*
2nd Riccardo Patrese [It] *Williams-Renault*
3rd Ayrton Senna [Bra] *McLaren-Honda*
Fastest lap: Patrese *130.94 mph*

MONACO Monte Carlo 31 May
1st Ayrton Senna [Bra] *McLaren-Honda 86.86 mph*
2nd Nigel Mansell [GB] *Williams-Renault*
3rd Riccardo Patrese [It] *Williams-Renault*
Fastest Lap: Mansell *91.23 mph*

CANADIAN Montreal 14 June
1st Gerhard Berger [Aus] *McLaren-Honda 117.2 mph*
2nd Michael Schumacher [Ger] *Benetton-Ford*
3rd Jean Alesi [Fr] *Ferrari*
Fastest Lap: Berger *120.37mph*

FRENCH Magny Cours 5 July
1st Nigel Mansell [GB] *Williams-Renault 111.78 mph*
2nd Riccardo Patrese [It] *Williams-Renault*
3rd Martin Brundle [GB] *Benetton-Ford*
Fastest Lap: Mansell *123.36 mph*

BRITISH Silverstone 12 July
1st Nigel Mansell [GB] *Williams-Renault 134.22 mph*
2nd Riccardo Patrese [It] *Williams-Renault*
3rd Martin Brundle [GB] *Benetton-Ford*
Fastest Lap: Mansell *141.63 mph*

GERMAN Hockenheim 26 July
1st Nigel Mansell [GB] *Williams-Renault 146.08 mph*
2nd Ayrton Senna [Bra] *McLaren-Honda*
3rd Michael Schumacher [Ger] *Benetton-Ford*
Fastest Lap: Riccardo Patrese [It] *Williams-Renault 150.06 mph*

HUNGARIAN Hungaroring 16 Aug
1st Ayrton Senna [Bra] *McLaren-Honda 107.33 mph*
2nd Nigel Mansell [GB] *Williams-Renault*
3rd Gerhard Berger [Aus] *McLaren-Honda*
Fastest Lap: Mansell *113.35 mph*

BELGIAN Spa 30 Aug
1st Michael Schumacher [Ger] *Benetton-Ford 118.94 mph*
2nd Nigel Mansell [GB] *Williams-Renault*
3rd Riccardo Patrese [It] *Williams-Renault*
Fastest Lap: Schumacher *137.1 mph*

ITALIAN Monza 13 Sept
1st Ayrton Senna [Bra] *McLaren-Honda 146.28 mph*
2nd Martin Brundle [GB] *Benetton-Ford*
3rd Michael Schumacher [Ge] *Benetton-Ford*
Fastest Lap: Nigel Mansell [GB] *Williams-Renault 150.66 mph*

PORTUGUESE Estoril 27 Sept
1st Nigel Mansell [GB] *Williams-Renault 121.35 mph*
2nd Gerhard Berger [Aus] *McLaren-Honda*
3rd Ayrton Senna [Bra] *McLaren-Honda*
Fastest Lap: Mansell *124.33 mph*

JAPANESE Suzuka 25 Oct
1st Riccardo Patrese [It] *Williams-Renault 124.25 mph*
2nd Gerhard Berger [Aus] *McLaren-Honda*
3rd Martin Brundle [GB] *Benetton-Ford*
Fastest Lap: Nigel Mansell [GB] *Williams-Renault 130.33 mph*

AUSTRALIAN Adelaide 8 Nov
1st Gerhard Berger [Aus] *McLaren-Honda 106.82 mph*
2nd Michael Schumacher [Ger] *Benetton-Ford*
3rd Martin Brundle [GB] *Benetton-Ford*
Fastest Lap: Schumacher *111.14 mph*

INDIANAPOLIS 500 24 May
1st Al Unser, Jr [USA] *Valvoline 134.479 mph*
2nd Scott Goodyear [Can] *Mackenzie*
3rd Al Unser [USA] *Conseco*
Fastest qualifier: Eddie Cheever [USA] *Target+Scotch 229.639 mph*

World Champion: Alain Prost [Fr]
US National Champion: Nigel Mansell [GB]
Fastest Man on Earth: Richard Noble (>1983)

GRANDS PRIX
SOUTH AFRICAN Kyalami 14 March
1st Alain Prost [Fr] *Williams-Renault 115.82 mph*
2nd Ayrton Senna [Bra] *McLaren-Ford*
3rd Mark Blundell [GB] *Ligier-Renault*
Fastest Lap: Prost *119.9 mph*

BRAZILIAN Interlagos 28 March
1st Ayrton Senna [Bra] *McLaren-Ford 102.9 mph*
2nd Damon Hill [GB] *Williams-Renault*
3rd Michael Schumacher [Ger] *Benetton-Ford*
Fastest Lap: Schumacher *120.89 mph*

EUROPEAN Donington Park 11 April
1st Ayrton Senna [Bra] *McLaren-Ford 102.9 mph*
2nd Damon Hill [GB] *Williams-Renault*
3rd Alain Prost [Fr] *Williams-Renault*
Fastest Lap: Senna *115.33 mph*

SAN MARINO Imola 25 April
1st Alain Prost [Fr] *Williams-Renault 122.79 mph*
2nd Michael Schumacher [Ger] *Benetton-Ford*
3rd Martin Brundle [GB] *Ligier-Renault*
Fastest Lap: Prost *130.9 mph*

SPANISH Barcelona 9 May
1st Alain Prost [Fr] *Williams-Renault 124.41 mph*
2nd Ayrton Senna [Bra] *Williams-Renault*
3rd Michael Schumacher [Ger] *Benetton-Ford*
Fastest Lap: Schumacher *131.11 mph*

MONACO Monte Carlo 24 May
1st Ayrton Senna [Bra] *McLaren-Ford 136.83 mph*
2nd Damon Hill [GB] *Williams-Renault*
3rd Jean Alesi [Fr] *Ferrari*
Fastest Lap: Alain Prost [Fr] *Williams-Renault 89.04 mph*

CANADIAN Montreal 13 June
1st Alain Prost [Fr] *Williams-Renault 117.85 mph*
2nd Michael Schumacher [Ger] *Benetton-Ford*
3rd Damon Hill [GB] *Williams-Renault*
Fastest Lap: Schumacher *121.59 mph*

FRENCH Magny Cours 4 July
1st Alain Prost [Fr] *Williams-Renault 115.718 mph*
2nd Damon Hill [GB] *Williams-Renault*
3rd Michael Schumacher [Ger] *Benetton-Ford*
Fastest Lap: Schumacher *119.953 mph*

BRITISH Silverstone 11 July
1st Alain Prost [Fr] *Williams-Renault 134.235 mph*
2nd Michael Schumacher [Ger] *Benetton-Ford*
3rd Riccardo Patrese [I] *Benetton-Ford*
Fastest Lap: Damon Hill *141.674 mph*

GERMAN Hockenheim 25 July
1st Alain Prost [Fr] *Williams-Renault 145.314 mph*
2nd Michael Schumacher [Ger] *Benetton-Ford*
3rd Mark Blundell [GB] *Ligier-Renault*
Fastest lap: Schumacher *149.665 mph*

HUNGARIAN Hungaroring 15 August
1st Damon Hill [GB] *Williams-Renault 105.814 mph*
2nd Riccardo Patrese [I] *Benetton-Ford*
3rd Gerhard Berger [Aus] *Ferrari*
Fastest Lap: Alain Prost *Williams-Renault 111.463 mph*

BELGIAN Spa Francorchamps 29 August
1st Damon Hill [GB] *Williams-Renault 135.331 mph*
2nd Michael Schumacher [Ger] *Benetton-Ford*
3rd Alain Prost [Fr] *Williams-Renault*
Fastest Lap: Prost *140.424 mph*

ITALIAN Monza 12 September
1st Damon Hill [GB] *Williams-Renault 148.597 mph*
2nd Jean Alesi [Fr] *Ferrari*
3rd Michael Andretti [USA] *McLaren-Ford*
Fastest Lap: Hill *Williams-Renault 155.241 mph*

PORTUGUESE Estoril 26 September
1st Michael Schumacher [Ger] *Benetton-Ford 124.118 mph*
2nd Alain Prost [Fr] *Williams-Renault*
3rd Damon Hill [GB] *Williams-Renault*
Fastest Lap: Hill *129.987 mph*

JAPANESE Suzuka 24 October
1st Ayrton Senna [Bra] *McLaren-Ford 115.334 mph*
2nd Alain Prost [Fr] *Williams-Renault*
3rd Mika Hakkinen [Fin] *McLaren-Ford*
Fastest Lap: Prost *129.649 mph*

AUSTRALIAN Adelaide 7 November
1st Ayrton Senna [Bra] *McLaren-Ford 107.611 mph*
2nd Alain Prost [Fr] *Williams-Renault*
3rd Damon Hill [GB] *Williams-Renault*
Fastest Lap: Hill *112.172 mph*

INDIANAPOLIS 31 May
1st Emerson Fittipaldi [Bra] *Penske Chevrolet 157.207 mph*
2nd Arie Luyendyk [Hal] *Lola-Ford Cosworth*
3rd Nigel Mansell [GB] *Lola-Ford Cosworth*
Fastest Lap: Fittipaldi *214.807 mph*

World Champion: Michael Schumacher [Ger]
US National Champion: Al Unser Jnr [US]
Fastest Man on Earth: Richard Noble (>1983)

GRANDS PRIX
BRAZILIAN Interlagos 27 March
1st Michael Schumacher [Ger] *Benetton-Ford 119.695 mph*
2nd Damon Hill [GB] *Williams-Renault*
3rd Jean Alesi [Fr] *Ferrari*
Fastest Lap: Schumacher *123.315 mph*

PACIFIC Aida, Japan 17 April
1st Michael Schumacher [Ger] *Benetton-Ford 108.042 mph*
2nd Gerhard Berger [Aus] *Ferrari*
3rd Rubens Barrichelo [Bra] *Jordan-Hart*
Fastest Lap: Schumacher *111.872 mph*

SAN MARINO Imola 1 May
1st Michael Schumacher [Ger] *Benetton-Ford 123.176 mph*
2nd Nicola Larini [I] *Ferrari*
3rd Mika Hakkinen [Fin] *McLaren-Peugeot*
Fastest Lap: Damon Hill *133.682 mph*

MONACO Monte Carlo 15 May
1st Michael Schumacher [Ger] *Benetton-Ford 88.041 mph*
2nd Martin Brundle [GB] *McLaren-Peugeot*
3rd Gerhard Berger [Aus] *Ferrari*
Fastest Lap: Schumacher *91.821 mph*

SPANISH Barcelona 29 May
1st Damon Hill [GB] *Williams-Renault 119.530 mph*
2nd Michael Schumacher [Ger] *Benetton-Ford*
3rd Mark Blundell [GB] *Tyrell-Yamaha*
Fastest Lap: Schumacher *124.698 mph*

CANADIAN Montreal 12 June
1st Michael Schumacher [Ger] *Benetton-Ford 109.512 mph*
2nd Damon Hill [GB] *Williams-Renault*
3rd Jean Alesi [Fr] *Ferrari*
Fastest Lap: Schumacher *111.937 mph*

FRENCH Magny Cours 3 July
1st Michael Schumacher [Ger] *Benetton-Ford 115.709 mph*
2nd Damon Hill [GB] *Williams-Renault*
3rd Gerhard Berger [Aus] *Ferrari*
Fastest Lap: Hill *119.316 mph*

BRITISH Silverstone 10 July
1st Darnon Hill [GB] *Williams-Renault 125.606 mph*
2nd Jean Alesi [Fr] *Ferrari*
3rd Mika Hakkinen [Fin] *McLaren-Peugeot*
Fastest Lap: Hill *129.875 mph*

GERMAN Hockenheim 31 July
1st Gerhard Berger [Aus] *Ferrari 139.359 mph*
2nd Olivier Panis [Fr] *Ligier-Renault*
3rd Eric Bernard [Fr] *Ligier-Renault*
Fastest Lap: David Coulthard *Williams-Renault*
    143.700 mph

HUNGARIAN Hungaroring 14 August
1st Michael Schumacher [Ger] *Benetton-Ford*
    105.470 mph
2nd Damon Hill [GB] *Williams-Renault*
3rd Jos Verstappen [NL] *Benetton-Ford*
Fastest Lap: Schumacher *109.743 mph*

BELGIAN Spa Francorchamps 28 August
1st Damon Hill [GB] *Williams-Renault 129.360 mph*
2nd Mika Hakkinen [Fin] *McLaren-Peugeot*
3rd Jos Verstappen [NL] *Benetton-Ford*
Fastest Lap: Hill *134.500 mph*

ITALIAN Monza 11 September
1st Damon Hill [GB] *Williams-Renault*
2nd Gerhard Berger [Aus] *Ferrari*
3rd Mika Hakkinen [Fin] *McLaren-Peugeot*
Fastest Lap: Hill *150.985 mph*

PORTUGUESE Estoril 25 September
1st Damon Hill [GB] *Williams-Renault 114.080 mph*
2nd David Coulthard [GB] *Williams-Renault*
3rd Mika Hakkinen [Fin] *McLaren-Peugeot*
Fastest Lap: Coulthard *118.296 mph*

EUROPEAN Jerez Spain 16 October
1st Michael Schumacher [Ger] *Benetton-Ford*
    114.070 mph
2nd Damon Hill [GB] *Williams-Renault*
3rd Mika Hakkinen [Fin] *McLaren-Peugeot*
Fastest Lap: Schumacher *116.429 mph*

JAPANESE Suzuka 6 November
1st Damon Hill [GB:1 *Williams-Renault 94.321 mph*
2nd Schumacher [Ger] *Benetton-Ford*
3rd Jean Alesi [I] *Ferrari*
Fastest Lap: Hill *112.502 mph*

AUSTRALIAN Adelaide 13 November
1st Nigel Mansell [GB] *Williams-Renault 105.834 mph*
2nd Gerhard Berger [Aus] *Ferrari*
3rd Martin Brundle [GB] *McLaren-Peugeot*
Fastest Lap: Schumacher *109.613 mph*

INDIANAPOLIS 500 29 May
1st Al Unsel Jnr [US] *Penske-Mercedes Benz 160.872 mph*
2nd Jacques Villeneuve [Can] *Reynard Ford Cosworth*
3rd Bobby Rahal [US] *Penske Ilmor*
Fastest Lap: Unser Jnr *228.011 mph*

1995

World Champion: Michael Schumacher [Ger]
US National Champion: JacquesVilleneuve [Can]
Fastest Man on Earth: Richard Noble (>1983)

GRANDS PRIX

BRAZILIAN, Interlagos, 26 March
1st Michael Schumacher [Ger] *Benetton-Renault*
    116.145 mph
2nd David Coulthard [GB] *Williams-Renault*
3rd Gerhard Berger [A] *Ferrari*
Fastest Lap: Schumacher *119.537 mph*

ARGENTINEAN, Buenos Aires, 9 April
1st Damon Hill [GB] *Williams-Renault 100.901 mph*
2nd Jean Alesi [F] *Ferrari*
3rd Schumacher [Ger] *Benetton-Renault*
Fastest Lap: Schumacher *105.245 mph*

SAN MARINO, Imola, 30 April
1st Damon Hill [GB] *Williams-Renault 113.040 mph*
2nd Jean Alesi [F] *Ferrari*
3rd Gerhard Berger [A] *Ferrari*
Fastest Lap: Berger *122.250 mph*

SPANISH, Catalunya, 14 May
1st Michael Schumacher [Ger] *Benetton-Renault*
    121.365 mph
2nd Johnny Herbert [GB] *Benetton-Renault*
3rd Gerhard Berger [A] *Ferrari*
Fastest Lap: Hill *125.089 mph*

MONTE CARLO, Monaco, 28 May
1st Michael Schumacher [Ger] *Benetton-Renault*
    85.502 mph
2nd Damon Hill [GB] *Williams-Renault*
3rd Gerhard Berger [A] *Ferrari*
Fastest Lap: Jean Alesi *87.974 mph*

CANADIAN, Montreal, 11 June
1st Jean Alesi [F] *Ferrari 107.059 mph*
2nd Rubens Barrichelo [Br] *Jordan-Peugeot*
3rd Eddie Irvine [GB] *Jordan-Peugeot*
Fastest Lap: Schumacher *111.126 mph*

FRENCH, Magny Cours, 2 July
1st Michael Schumacher [Ger] *Benetton-Renault*
    115.781 mph
2nd Damon Hill [GB] *Williams-Renault*
3rd David Coulthard [GB] *Williams-Renault*
Fastest Lap: Schumacher *123.555 mph*

BRITISH, Silverstone, 16 July
1st Johnny Herbert [GB] *Benetton-Renault 121.591 mph*
2nd Jean Alesi [F] *Ferrari*
3rd David Coulthard [GB] *Williams-Renault*
Fastest Lap: Hill *Williams-Renault 126.037 mph*

GERMAN, Hockenheim, 30 July
1st Michael Schumacher [Ger] *Benetton-Renault*
    138.019 mph
2nd David Coulthard [GB] *Williams-Renault*
3rd Gerhard Berger [A] *Ferrari*
Fastest Lap: Schumacher *140.250 mph*

HUNGARIAN, Hungaroring, 13 August
1st Damon Hill [GB] *Williams-Renault 107.028 mph*
2nd David Coulthard [GB] *Williams-Renault*
3rd Gerhard Berger [A] *Ferrari*
Fastest Lap: Hill *110.610 mph*

BELGIAN, Spa Francorchamps, 27 August
1st Michael Schumacher [Ger] *Benetton-Renault*
    118.187 mph
2nd Damon Hill [GB] *Williams-Renault*
3rd Martin Brundle [GB] *Ligier-Mugen Honda*
Fastest Lap: David Coulthard [GB] *Williams-Renault*
    137.555 mph

ITALIAN, Monza, 10 September
1st Johnny Herbert [GB] *Benetton-Renault 145.285 mph*
2nd Mika Hakkinen [Fin] *McLaren-Mercedes*
3rd Heinz Harald Frentzen [GB] *Red Bull-Sauber*
Fastest Lap: Gerhard Berger [A] *Ferrari 149.354 mph*

PORTUGUESE, Estoril, 24 September
1st David Coulthard [GB] *Williams-Renault 113.288 mph*
2nd Michael Schumacher [Ger] *Benetton-Renault*
3rd Damon Hill [GB] *Williams-Renault*
Fastest Lap: Coulthard *117.195 mph*

EUROPEAN, Nürburgring, 1 October
1st Michael Schumacher [Ger] *Benetton-Renault*
    113.822 mph
2nd Jean Alesi [F] *Ferrari*
3rd David Coulthard [GB] *Williams-Renault*
Fastest Lap: Schumacher *125.540 mph*

PACIFIC, Aida Japan, 22 October
1st Michael Schumacher [Ger] *Benetton-Renault*
    105.286 mph
2nd David Coulthard [GB] *Williams-Renault*
3rd Damon Hill [GB] *Williams-Renault*
Fastest Lap: Schumacher *108.457 mph*

JAPANESE, Suzuka, 29 October
1st Michael Schumacher [Ger] *Benetton-Renault*
    119.519 mph
2nd Mika Hakkinen [Fin] *McLaren-Mercedes*
3rd Johnny Herbert [GB] *Benetton-Renault*
Fastest Lap: Schumacher *127.382 mph*

AUSTRALIAN, Adelaide, 12 November
1st Damon Hill [GB] *Williams-Renault 104.470 mph*
2nd Olivier Danis [F] *Ligier-Mugen Honda*
3rd Gianni Morbidelli [I] *Footwork-Hart*
Fastest Lap: Hill *108.484 mph*

INDIANAPOLIS 500, 28 May
1st Jacques Villeneuve [Can] *ReynardCosworth*
    153.616 mph
2nd Christian Fittipaldi [Br] *Reynard-Cosworth*
3rd Bobby Rahal [USA] *Lola-Mercedes*
Fastest Lap: Scott Brayton [USA] *LolaMenard Buick*
    231.604 mph

1996

World Champion: Damon Hill [GB]
US National Champion : Jimmy Vasser [USA]
Fastest Man on Earth: Richard Noble (>1983)

GRANDS PRIX

AUSTRALIAN, Melbourne, 10 March
1st Damon Hill [GB] *Williams-Renault 123.488 mph*
2nd JacquesVilleneuve [Can] *Williams-Renault*
3rd Eddie Irvine [GB] *Ferrari*
Fastest Lap:Villeneuve *Williams-Renault 126.954 mph*

BRAZILIAN, Interlagos, 31 March
1st Damon Hill [GB] *Williams-Renault 104.187 mph*
2nd Jean Alesi [F] *Benetton-Renault*
3rd Michael Schumacher [Ger] *Ferrari*
Fastest Lap: Hill *Williams-Renault 118.639 mph*

ARGENTINEAN, Buenos Aires, 7 April
1st Damon Hill [GB] *Williams-Renault 99.427 mph*
2nd JacquesVilleneuve [Can] *Williams-Renault*
3rd Jean Alesi [F] *Ferrari*
Fastest Lap: Alesi *Ferrari 106.551 mph*

EUROPEAN, Nürburgring, 28 April
1st Jacques Villeneuve [Can] *Williams-Renault*
    121.792 mph
2nd Michael Schumacher [Ger] *Ferrari*
3rd David Coulthard [GB] *McLaren-Mercedes*
Fastest Lap: Damon Hill [GB] *Williams-Renault*
    125.529 mph

SAN MARINO, Imola, 5 May
1st Damon Hill [GB] *Williams-Renault 120.397 mph*
2nd Michael Schumacher [er] *Ferrari*
3rd Gerhard Berger [A] *Benetton-Renault*
Fastest Lap: Hill *Williams-Renault 123.051 mph*

MONTE CARLO, Monaco, 19 May
1st Olivier Panis [F] *Ligier-Hart 77.059 mph*
2nd David Coulthard [GB] *McLaren-Mercedes*
3rd Johnny Herbert [GB] *Sauber*
Fastest Lap: Jean Alesi [F] *Benetton-Renault 87.371 mph*

SPANISH, Catalunya, 2 June
1st Michael Schumacher [Ger] *Ferrari 95.557 mph*
2nd Jean Alesi [F] *Benetton-Renault*
3rd JacquesVilleneuve [Can] *Williams-Renault*
Fastest Lap: Schumacher *Ferrari 100.211 mph*

CANADIAN Montreal, 16 June
1st Damon Hill [GB] *Williams-Renault 118.396 mph*
2nd JacquesVilleneuve [Can] *Williams-Renault*
3rd Jean Alesi [F] *Benetton-Renault*
Fastest Lap: Villeneuve *Williams-Renault 120.727 mph*

FRENCH, Magny Cours, 30 June
1st Damon Hill [GB] *Williams-Renault 118.174 mph*
2nd JacquesVilleneuve [Can] *Williams-Renault*
3rd Jean Alesi [F] *Benetton-Renault*
Fastest Lap: Villeneuve *Williams-Renault 120.938 mph*

BRITISH, Silverstone, 14 July
1st Jacques Villeneuve [Can] *Williams-Renault 124.011 mph*
2nd Gerhard Berger [A] *Benetton-Renault*
3rd Mika Hakkinen [Fin] *McLaren-Mercedes*
Fastest Lap:Villeneuve *Williams-Renault 127.068 mph*

GERMAN, Hockenheim, 28 July
1st Damon Hill [GB] *Williams-Renault 140.063 mph*
2nd Jean Alesi [F] *Benetton-Renault*
3rd JacquesVilleneuve [Can] *Williams-Renault*
Fastest Lap: Hill *Williams-Renault 143.305 mph*

HUNGARIAN, Hungaroring, 11 August
1st Jacques Villeneuve [Can] *Williams-Renault 107.107 mph*
2nd Damon Hill [GB] *Williams-Renault*
3rd Jean Alesi [F] *Benetton-Renault*
Fastest Lap: Hill *Williams-Renault 110.823 mph*

BELGIAN, Spa Francorchamps, 25 August
1st Michael Schumacher [Ger] *Ferrari 129.570 mph*
2nd Jacques Villeneuve [Can] *Williams-Renault*
3rd Mika Hakkinen [Fin] *McLaren-Mercedes*
Fastest Lap: Gerhard Berger [A] *Ferrari 137.855 mph*

ITALIAN, Monza, 8 September
1st Michael Schumacher [Ger] *Ferrari 146.644 mph*
2nd Jean Alesi [F] *Benetton-Renault*
3rd Mika Hakkinen [Fin] *McLaren-Mercedes*
Fastest Lap: Schumacher *Ferrari 149.891 mph*

PORTUGUESE, Estoril, 22 September
1st Jacques Villeneuve [Can] *Williams-Renault 113.352 mph*
2nd Damon Hill [GB] *Williams-Renault*
3rd Michael Schumacher [Ger] *Ferrari*
Fastest lap: Villeneuve *Williams-Renault 117.686 mph*

JAPANESE, Suzuka, 13 October
1st Damon Hill [GB] *Williams-Renault 122.733 mph*
2nd Michael Schumacher [Ger] *Ferrari*
3rd Mika Hakkinen [Fin] *Benetton-Renault*
Fastest Lap: Jacques Villeneuve [Can] *Williams-Renault 126.076 mph*

INDIANAPOLIS 500 26 May
1st Buddy Lazier [USA] *Reynard-Cosworth 147.956 mph*
2nd Davy Jones [USA] *Lola-Mercedes*
3rd Richie Hearn Reynard-Ford
Fastest Lap: Scott Brayton [USA] *Lola 233.718 mph*

1997

World Champion: Jacques Villeneuve [Can]
US National Champion: Tony Stewart [USA] [I RL]
Fastest Man on Earth:Andy Green [GB] in Thrust SSC at 763.035 mph (>1997).

GRANDS PRIX

AUSTRALIAN, Melbourne, 9 March
1st David Coulthard [GB] *McLaren-Mercedes 126.741 mph*
2nd Michael Schumacher [Ger] *Ferrari*
3rd Mika Hakkinen [Fin] *McLaren-Mercedes*
Fastest Lap: Heinz-Harald Frentzen *Williams-Renault 130.957 mph*

BRAZILIAN, Interlagos, 30 March
1st Jacques Villeneuve [Can] *Williams-Renault 119.854 mph*
2nd Gerhard Berger [A] *Benetton-Renault*
3rd Olivier Panis [F] *Prost-Mugen Honda*
Fastest lap: Villeneuve *Williams-Renault 122.465 mph*

ARGENTINEAN, Buenos Aires, 13 April
1st Jacques Villeneuve [Can] *Williams-Renault 102.616 mph*
2nd Eddie Irvine [GB] *Ferrari*
3rd Raft Schumacher [Ger] *Jordan-Peugeot*
Fastest Lap: Gerhard Berger [A] *Benetton-Renault 108.9 mph*

SAN MARINO, Imola, 27 April
1st Heinz-Harald Frentzen [Ger] *Williams-Renault 125.260 mph*
2nd Michael Schumacher [Ger] *Ferrari*
3rd Eddie Irvine [GB] *Ferrari*
Fastest Lap: Frentzen *Williams-Renault 128.964 mph*

MONTE CARLO, Monaco, 11 May
1st Michael Schumacher [Ger] *Ferrari 65.164 mph*
2nd Rubens Barrichello [Bra] *Stewart-Ford*
3rd Eddie Irvine [GB] *Ferrari*
Fastest Lap: Schumacher *Ferrari 66.836 mph*

SPANISH, Barcelona, 25 May
1st Jacques Villeneuve [Can] *Williams-Renault 124.497 mph*
2nd Olivier Panis [F] *Prost-Mugen Honda*
3rd Jean Alesi [F] *Benetton-Renault*
Fastest Lap: Giancarlo Fisichella [I] *Jordan-Peugeot 128.626 mph*

CANADIAN, Montreal, 15 June
1st Michael Schumacher [Ger] *Ferrari 114.582 mph*
2nd Jean Alesi [F] *Benetton-Renault*
3rd Giancarlo Fisichella [I] *Jordan-Peugeot*
Fastest Lap: David Coulthard [GB] *McLaren-Mercedes 124.1 mph*

FRENCH, Magny Cours, 29 June
1st Michael Schumacher [Ger] *Ferrari 115.372 mph*
2nd Heinz-Harald Frentzen [Ger] *Williams-Renault*
3rd Eddie Irvine [GB] *Ferrari*
Fastest Lap: Damon Hill [GB] *Arrows Yamaha 122.1 mph*

BRITISH, Silverstone, 13 July
1st Jacques Villeneuve [Can] *Williams-Renault 129.191 mph*
2nd Jean Alesi [F] *Benetton-Renault*
3rd Alexander Wurz [Ger] *Benetton-Renault*
Fastest Lap: Michael Schumacher [Ger] *Ferrari 136.9 mph*

GERMAN, Hockenheim, 27 July
1st Gerhard Berger [A] *Benetton-Renault 141.385 mph*
2nd Michael Schumacher [Ger] *Ferrari*
3rd Mika Hakkinen [Fin] *McLaren-Mercedes*
Fastest Lap: Berger *Benetton-Renault 144.331 mph*

HUNGARIAN, Hungaroring, 10 August
1st Jacques Villeneuve [Can] *Williams-Renault 107.648 mph*
2nd Damon Hill [GB] *Arrows Yamaha*
3rd Johnnie Herbert [GB] *Sauber-Petronas*
Fastest Lap: Heinz-Harald Frentzen [Ger] *Williams-Renault 113.256 mph*

BELGIAN, Spa Francorchamps, 24 August
1st Michael Schumacher [Ger] *Ferrari 127.712 mph*
2nd Giancarlo Fisichella [I] *Jordan Peugeot*
3rd Mika Hakkinen [Fin] *McLaren-Mercedes*
Fastest Lap: Jacques Villeneuve [Can] *Williams-Renault 129.12 mph*

ITALIAN, Monza, 7 September
1st David Coulthard [GB] *McLaren-Mercedes 147.912 mph*
2nd Jean Alesi [F] *Benetton-Renault*
3rd Heinz-Harald Frentzen [Ger] *Williams-Renault*
Fastest Lap: Mika Hakkinen [Fin] *McLaren-Mercedes 153.081 mph*

AUSTRIAN, A- I Ring, 21 September
1st Jacques Villeneuve [Can] *Williams-Renault 130.551 mph*
2nd David Coulthard [GB] *McLaren-Mercedes*
3rd Heinz-Harald Frentzen [Ger] *Williams-Renault*
Fastest Lap: Villeneuve *Williams-Renault 134.576 mph*

LUXEMBOURG, Nürburgring, 28 September
1st Jacques Villeneuve [Can] *Williams-Renault 125.036 mph*
2nd Jean Alesi [F] *Benetton-Renault*
3rd Heinz-Harald Frentzen [Ger] *Williams-Renault*
Fastest Lap: Frentzen *Williams-Renault 129.352 mph*

JAPANESE, Suzuka, 12 October
1st Michael Schumacher *Ferrari 128.943 mph*
2nd Heinz-Harald Frentzen [Ger] *Williams-Renault*
3rd Eddie Irvine [GB] *Ferrari*
Fastest Lap: Frentzen *Williams-Renault 132.514 mph*

EUROPEAN, Jerez, Spain, 26 October
1st Mika Hakkinen [Fin] *McLaren-Mercedes 115.11 mph*
2nd David Coulthard [GB] *McLaren-Mercedes*
3rd Jacques Villeneuve [Can] *Williams-Renault*
Fastest Lap: Heinz-Harald Frentzen [Ger] *Williams-Renault 119.15 mph*

INDIANAPOLIS 500
1st Arie Luyendyk *Tredway 201.89 mph*
2nd Scott Goodyear *Nortel*
3rd Jeff Ward *First Plus Team Cheever*
Fastest Lap: Tony Stewart *Glidden Menards Special 215.626 mph*

1998

World Champion: Mika Hakinnen [Swe]
US National Champion [CART]: Alessandro 'Alex' Zanardi [It]
Fastest Man on Earth: Andy Green [GB] in *Thrust SSC at 763.035 mph [>1997]*

GRANDS PRIX

AUSTRALIA Albert Park 8 March
1st Mika Hakinnen [Fin] *West McLaren Mercedes 124.958 mph.*
2nd David Coulthard [GB] *West McLaren Mercedes*
3rd Heinz-Harald Frentzen [Ger] *Winfield Williams*
Fastest Lap: Hakinnen *129.433 mph*

BRAZIL Interlagos 29 March
1st Mika Hakinnen [Fin] *West McLaren Mercedes 118.534 mph*
2nd David Coulthard [GB] *West McLaren Mercedes*
3rd Michael Schumacher [Ger] *Scuderia Ferrari Marlboro*
Fastest Lap: Hakinnen [Fin] *121.014 mph*

ARGENTINA Oscar Galvez 26 April
1st Michael Schumacher [Ger] *Scuderia Ferrari Marlboro 105.200 mph*
2nd Mika Hakinnen [Fin] *West McLaren Mercedes*
3rd Eddie Irvine [GB] *Scuderia Ferrari Marlboro*
Fastest Lap: Alexander Wurz *108.043 mph*

SAN MARINO Imola 26 April
1st David Coulthard [GB] *West McLaren Mercedes 120.619 mph*
2nd Michael Schumacher [Ger] *Scuderia Ferrari Marlboro*
3rd Eddie Irvine [GB] *Scuderia Ferrari Marlboro*
Fastest Lap: Michael Schumacher *123.432 mph*

SPAIN Catalunya 10 May
1st Mika Hakinnen [Fin] *West McLaren Mercedes 122.325 mph*
2nd David Coulthard [GB] *West McLaren Mercedes*
3rd Michael Schumacher [Ger] *Scuderia Ferrari Marlboro*
Fastest Lap: Hakinnen *125.495 mph*

MONACO Monte Carlo 24 May
1st Mika Hakinnen [Fin] *West McLaren Mercedes 87.898 mph*
2nd Giancarlo Fisichella [It] *Mild Seven Benetton Playlife*
3rd Eddie Irvine [GB] *Scuderia Ferrari Marlboro*
Fastest Lap: Hakinnen *90.081 mph*

CANADA Gilles Villeneuve 7 June
1st Michael Schumacher [Ger] *Scuderia Ferrari Marlboro* 112.652 mph
2nd Giancarlo Fisichella [It] *Mild Seven Benetton Playlife*
3rd Eddie Irvine [GB] *Scuderia Ferrari Marlboro*
Fastest Lap: Michael Schumacher *124.586 mph* [Lap Record]

FRANCE Magny-Cours 28 June
1st Michael Schumacher [Ger] *Scuderia Ferrari Marlboro* 118.659 mph
2nd Eddie Irvine [GB] *Scuderia Ferrari Marlboro*
3rd Mika Hakinnen [Fin] *West McLaren Mercedes*
Fastest Lap: David Coulthard McLaren *122.634 mph*

BRITAIN Silverstone 9 July
1st Michael Schumacher [Ger] *Scuderia Ferrari Marlboro* 107.379 mph
2nd Mika Hakinnen [Fin] *West McLaren Mercedes*
3rd Eddie Irvine [GB] *Scuderia Ferrari Marlboro*
Fastest Lap:

AUSTRIA A1-Ring 26 July
1st Mika Hakinnen [Fin] *West McLaren Mercedes* 126.000 mph
2nd David Coulthard [GB] *West McLaren Mercedes*
3rd Michael Schumacher [Ger] *Scuderia Ferrari Marlboro*
Fastest Lap: Coulthard *132.568 mph*

GERMANY Hockenheim 2 August
1st Mika Hakinnen [Fin] *West McLaren Mercedes* 141.671 mph
2nd David Coulthard [GB] *West McLaren Mercedes*
3rd Jacques Villeneuve [Can] Winfield Wiliams
Fastest Lap: Coulthard *143.829 mph*

HUNGARY Hungaroring 16 August
1st Michael Schumacher [Ger] *Scuderia Ferrari Marlboro* 108.157 mph
2nd David Coulthard [GB] *West McLaren Mercedes*
3rd Jacques Villeneuve [Can] *Winfield Wiliams*
Fastest Lap: Michael Schumacher *112.064 mph*

BELGIUM Spa-Francorchamps 20 August
1st Damon Hill [GB] *B&H Jordan Mugen Honda* 110.130 mph
2nd Ralf Schumacher [Ger] *B&H Jordan Mugen Honda*
3rd Jean Alesi [Fr] *Red Bull Sauber Petronas*
Fastest Lap:Michael Schumacher *125.939 mph*

ITALY Monza 13 September
1st Michael Schumacher [Ger] *Scuderia Ferrari Marlboro* 147.632 mph
2nd Eddie Irvine [GB] *Scuderia Ferrari Marlboro*
3rd Ralf Schumacher [Ger] *B&H Jordan Mugen Honda*
Fastest Lap: Mika Hakinnen McLaren *151.560 mph*

LUXEMBOURG Nürburgring 27 September
1st Mika Hakinnen [Fin] *West McLaren Mercedes* 123.363 mph
2nd Michael Schumacher [Ger] *Scuderia Ferrari Marlboro*
3rd David Coulthard [GB] *West McLaren Mercedes*
Fastest Lap: Hakinnen *126.680 mph*

JAPAN Suzuka 1 November
1st Mika Hakinnen [Fin] *West McLaren Mercedes* 127.535 mph
2nd Eddie Irvine [GB] *Scuderia Ferrari Marlboro*
3rd David Coulthard [GB] *West McLaren Mercedes*
Fastest Lap: Michael Schumacher *130.925 mph*

INDIANAPOLIS 500 24 May
1st Eddie Cheever jnr [USA] *Dallara Aurora 145.155 mph*
2nd Buddy Lazier [USA] *Dallara Aurora*
3rd Steve Knapp [USA] *G-Force Aurora*
Fastest Lap: Tony Stewart [USA] *Dallara Aurora 214.746 mph*

World Champion: Mika Hakinnen [Fin]
US National Champion [CART]: Juan Pablo Montoya [Col]
Fastest Man on Earth: Andy Green [GB] in Thrust SSC at 763.035 mph[>1997]

GRANDS PRIX

AUSTRALIA Albert Park 7 March
1st Eddie Irvine [GB] *Scuderia Ferrari Marlboro* 118.590 mph
2nd Heinz-Harad Frentzen [Ger] *Benson & Hedges Jordan*
3rd Ralf Schumacher [Ger] *Winfield Williams*
Fastest Lap: Michael Schumacher *128.783 mph*

BRAZIL Interlagos 11 April
1st Mika Hakinnen [Fin] *West McLaren Mercedes* 119.921 mph
2nd Michael Schumacher [Ger] *Scuderia Ferrari Marlboro*
3rd Heinz-Haral Frentzen [Ger] *Benson & Hedges Jordan*
Fastest Lap: Hakinnen *122.386 mph*

SAN MARINO Imola 2 May
1st Michael Schumacher [Ger] *Scuderia Ferrari Marlboro* 121.466 mph
2nd David Coulthard [GB] *West McLaren Mercedes*
3rd Rubens Barrichello [Br] *Stewart Ford*
Fastest Lap: Michael Schumacher *124.544 mph*

MONACO Monte Carlo 16 May
1st Michael Schumacher [Ger] *Scuderia Ferrari Marlboro* 89.393 mph
2nd Eddie Irvine [GB] *Scuderia Ferrari Marlboro*
3rd Mika Hakinnen [Fin] *West McLaren Mercedes*
Fastest Lap: Hakinnen 91.562 mph

SPAIN Catalunya 30 May
1st Mika Hakinnen [Fin] *West McLaren Mercedes* 121.544 mph
2nd David Coulthard [GB] *West McLaren Mercedes*
3rd Michael Schumacher [Ger] *Scuderia Ferrari Marlboro*
Fastest Lap: Michael Schumacher *124.452 mph*

CANADA Gilles Villeneuve 13 June
1st Mika Hakinnen [Fin] *West McLaren Mercedes* 111.943 mph
2nd Giancarlo Fisichella [It] *Mild Seven Benetton Playlife*
3rd Eddie Irvine [GB] *Scuderia Ferrari Marlboro*
Fastest Lap: Irvine *123.031 mph*

FRANCE Magny-Cours 27 June
1st Heinz-Haral Frentzen [Ger] *Benson & Hedges Jordan* 96.291 mph
2nd Mika Hakinnen [Fin] *West McLaren Mercedes*
3rd Rubens Barrichello [Br] *Stewart Ford*
Fastest Lap: Coulthard *McLaren 119.996 mph*

BRITAIN Silverstone 11 July
1st David Coulthard [GB] *West McLaren Mercedes* 124.256 mph
2nd Eddie Irvine [GB] *Scuderia Ferrari Marlboro*
3rd Ralf Schumacher [Ger] *Winfield Williams*
Fastest Lap: Hakinnen *130.200 mph*

AUSTRIA A1-Ring 25 July
1st Eddie Irvine [GB] *Scuderia Ferrari Marlboro* 129.610 mph
2nd David Coulthard [GB] *West McLaren Mercedes*
3rd Mika Hakinnen [Fin] *West McLaren Mercedes*
Fastest Lap: Hakinnen *133.986 mph*

GERMANY Hockenheim 1 August
1st Eddie Irvine [GB] *Scuderia Ferrari Marlboro* 139.636 mph
2nd Mika Salo [Fin] *Scuderia Ferrari Marlboro*
3rd Heinz-Harald Frentzen [Ger] *Benson & Hedges Jordan*
Fastest Lap: Coulthard *McLaren 144.985 mph*

HUNGARY Hungaroring 15 August
1st Mika Hakinnen [Fin] *West McLaren Mercedes* 107.201 mph
2nd David Coulthard [GB] *West McLaren Mercedes*
3rd Eddie Irvine [GB] *Scuderia Ferrari Marlboro*
Fastest Lap: Coulthard *110.129 mph*

BELGIUM Spa-Francorchamps 29 August
1st David Coulthard [GB] *West McLaren Mercedes* 133.343 mph
2nd Mika Hakinnen [Fin] *West McLaren Mercedes*
3rd Heinz-Haral Frentzen [Ger] *Benson & Hedges Jordan*
Fastest Lap: Hakinnen *136.781 mph*

ITALY Monza 12 September
1st Heinz-Haral Frentzen [Ger] *Benson & Hedges Jordan* 147.848 mph
2nd Ralf Schumacher [Ger] *Winfield Williams*
3rd Mika Salo [Fin] *Scuderia Ferrari Marlboro*
Fastest Lap: Ralf Schumacher *150.821 mph*

EUROPE Nürburgring 26 September
1st Johnny Herbert [GB] *Stewart Ford 110.004 mph*
2nd Jarno Trulli [It] *Gauloises Prost Peugeot*
3rd Rubens Barrichello [Br] *Stewart Ford*
Fastest Lap: Hakinnen *McLaren 125.384 mph*

MALAYSIA Sepang 17 October
1st Eddie Irvine [GB] *Scuderia Ferrari Marlboro 119.727 mph*
2nd Michael Schumacher [Ger] *Scuderia Ferrari Marlboro*
3rd Mika Hakinnen [Fin] *West McLaren Mercedes*
Fastest Lap: Michael Schumacher *123.640 mph*

JAPAN Suzuka 31 October
1st Mika Hakinnen [Fin] *West McLaren Mercedes* 126.821 mph
2nd Michael Schumacher [Ger] *Scuderia Ferrari Marlboro*
3rd Eddie Irvine [GB] *Scuderia Ferrari Marlboro*
Fastest Lap: Michael Schumacher *129.466 mph*

INDIANAPOLIS 500 30 May
1st Kenny Brack [SWE] *Dallara-Aurora 153.176 mph*
2nd Jeff Ward [USA] *Dallara-Aurora*
3rd Billy Boar [USA] *Dallara-Aurora*
Fastest Lap: Greg Ray [USA] *Dallara Aurora 218.882 mph*

World Champion: Michael Schumacher [Ger]
US National Champion [CART]: Gil de Faran [Br]
Fastest Man on Earth: Andy Green [GB] in Thrust SSC at 763.035 mph

GRANDS PRIX

AUSTRALIA Albert Park 12 March
1st Michael Schumacher [Ger] *Scuderia Ferrari Marlboro* 121.946 mph
2nd Rubens Barrichello [Br] *Scuderia Ferrari Marlboro*
3rd Ralf Schumacher [Ger] *BMW Williams*
Fastest Lap: Barrichello *129.671 mph*

BRAZIL Interlagos 26 March
1st Michael Schumacher [Ger] *Scuderia Ferrari Marlboro* 124.524 mph
2nd Giancarlo Fisichella [It] *Mild Seven Benetton Playlife*
3rd Heinz-Harald Frentzen [Ger] *Benson & Hedges Jordan*
Fastest Lap: Michael Schumacher *128.940 mph*

SAN MARINO Imola 9 April
1st Michael Schumacher [Ger] *Scuderia Ferrari Marlboro* 124.301 mph
2nd Mika Hakinnen [Fin] *West McLaren Mercedes*
3rd David Coulthard [GB] *West McLaren Mercedes*
Fastest Lap: Hakinnen *127.536 mph*

BRITAIN Silverstone 23 April
1st David Coulthard [GB] *West McLaren Mercedes* 129.410 mph
2nd Mika Hakinnen [Fin] *West McLaren Mercedes*
3rd Michael Schumacher [Ger] *Scuderia Ferrari Marlboro*
Fastest Lap: Hakinnen *133.385 mph*

SPAIN Catalunya 7 May
1st Mika Hakinnen [Fin] *West McLaren Mercedes*
121.990 mph
2nd David Coulthard [GB] *West McLaren Mercedes*
3rd Rubens Barrichello [Br] *Scuderia Ferrari Marlboro*
Fastest Lap: Hakinnen *125.260 mph*

EUROPE Nürburgring 21 May
1st Michael Schumacher [Ger] *Scuderia Ferrari Marlboro*
111.561 mph
2nd Mika Hakinnen [Fin] *West McLaren Mercedes*
3rd David Coulthard [GB] *West McLaren Mercedes*
Fastest Lap: Michael Schumacher *123.879 mph*

MONACO Monte Carlo 4 June
1st David Coulthard [GB] *West McLaren Mercedes* 89.522
mph
2nd Rubens Barrichello [Br] *Scuderia Ferrari Marlboro*
3rd Giancarlo Fisichella [It] *Mild Seven Benetton Playlife*
Fastest Lap: Mika Hakinnen *92.416 mph*

CANADA Gilles Villeneuve 18 June
1st Michael Schumacher [Ger] *Scuderia Ferrari Marlboro*
112.374 mph
2nd Rubens Barrichello [Br] *Scuderia Ferrari Marlboro*
3rd Giancarlo Fisichella [It] *Mild Seven Benetton Playlife*
Fastest Lap: Mika Hakinnen *125.105 mph*

FRANCE Magny-Cours 2 July
1st David Coulthard [GB] *West McLaren Mercedes*
116.258 mph
2nd Mika Hakinnen [Fin] *West McLaren Mercedes*
3rd Giancarlo Fisichella [It] *Mild Seven Benetton Playlife*
Fastest Lap: Coulthard *119.644 mph*

AUSTRIA A1-Ring 16 July
1st Mika Hakinnen [Fin] *West McLaren Mercedes*
129.737 mph
2nd David Coulthard [GB] *West McLaren Mercedes*
3rd Rubens Barrichello [Br] *Scuderia Ferrari Marlboro*
Fastest Lap: Coulthard *134.808 mph*

GERMANY Hockenheim 30 July
1st Rubens Barrichello [Br] *Scuderia Ferrari Marlboro*
133.806 mph
2nd Mika Hakinnen [Fin] *West McLaren Mercedes*
3rd David Coulthard [GB] *West McLaren Mercedes*
Fastest Lap: Barrichello *146.376 mph*

HUNGARY Hungaroring 13 August
1st Mika Hakinnen [Fin] *West McLaren Mercedes*
108.096 mph
2nd Michael Schumacher [Ger] *Scuderia Ferrari Marlboro*
3rd David Coulthard [GB] *West McLaren Mercedes*
Fastest Laps: Hakinnen *111.108 mph*

BELGIUM Spa-Francorchamps 27 August
1st Mika Hakinnen [Fin] *West McLaren Mercedes*
139.525 mph
2nd Michael Schumacher [Ger] *Scuderia Ferrari Marlboro*
3rd Ralf Schumacher [Ger] *BMW Williams*
Fastest Lap: Barrichello *136.964 mph*

ITALY Monza 10 September
1st Michael Schumacher [Ger] *Scuderia Ferrari Marlboro*
130.665 mph
2nd Mika Hakinnen [Fin] *West McLaren Mercedes*
3rd Ralf Schumacher [Ger] *BMW Williams*
Fastest Lap: Hakinnen *151.394 mph*

UNITED STATES Indianapolis 24 September
1st Michael Schumacher [Ger] *Scuderia Ferrari Marlboro*
118.203 mph
2nd Rubens Barrichello [Br] *Scuderia Ferrari Marlboro*
3rd Heinz-Harald Frentzen [Ger] *Benson & Hedges Jordan*
Fastest Lap: David Coulthard *125.513 mph*

JAPAN Suzuka 8 October
1st Michael Schumacher [Ger] *Scuderia Ferrari Marlboro*
128.820 mph
2nd Mika Hakinnen [Fin] *West McLaren Mercedes*
3rd David Coulthard [GB] *West McLaren Mercedes*
Fastest Lap:Hakinnen *132.246 mph*

MALAYSIA Sepang 22 October
1st Michael Schumacher [Ger] *Scuderia Ferrari Marlboro*
120.669 mph
2nd David Coulthard [GB] *West McLaren Mercedes*
3rd Rubens Barrichello [Br] *Scuderia Ferrari Marlboro*
Fastest Lap: Michael Schumacher *125.826 mph*

2001

World Champion: Michael Schumacher [Ger]
US National Champion [CART]: Gil de Farran [Br]
**Fastest Man on Earth: Andy Green [GB] in Thrust SSC at
763.035 mph**

GRANDS PRIX

AUSTRALIA Albert Park 4 March
1st Michael Schumacher [Ger] *Scuderia Ferrari Marlboro*
116.485 mph
2nd David Coulthard [GB] *West McLaren Mercedes*
3rd Rubens Barrichello [Br] *Scuderia Ferrari Marlboro*
Fastest Lap: Michael Schumacher *134.473 mph*

MALAYSIA Sepang 18 March
1st Michael Schumacher [Ger] *Scuderia Ferrari Marlboro*
105.652 mph
2nd Rubens Barrichello [Br] *Scuderia Ferrari Marlboro*
3rd David Coulthard [GB] *West McLaren Mercedes*
Fastest Lap: Mika Hakinnen *122.811 mph*

BRAZIL Interlagos 1 April
1st David Coulthard [GB] *West McLaren Mercedes*
115.185 mph
2nd Michael Schumacher [Ger] *Scuderia Ferrari Marlboro*
3rd Nick Heidfeld [Ger] *Red Bull Sauber Petronas*
Fastest Lap: Ralf Schumacher *BMW Williams*
127.342 mph

SAN MARINO Imola 15 April
1st Ralf Schumacher [Ger] *BMW Williams 125.555 mph*
2nd David Coulthard [GB] *West McLaren Mercedes*
3rd Rubens Barrichello [Br] *Scuderia Ferrari Marlboro*
Fastest Lap:Ralf Scumacher *129.025 mph*

SPAIN Catalunya 29 April
1st Michael Schumacher [Ger] *Scuderia Ferrari Marlboro*
125.832 mph
2nd Juan Pablo Montoya [Col] *BMW Williams*
3rd Jacques Villeneuve [Can] *Lucky Strike BAR Honda*
Fastest Lap: Michael Schumacher *130.383 mph*

AUSTRIA A1-Ring 13 May
1st David Coulthard [GB] *West McLaren Mercedes*
130.473 mph
2nd Michael Schumacher [Ger] *Scuderia Ferrari Marlboro*
3rd Rubens Barrichello [Br] *Scuderia Ferrari Marlboro*
Fastest Lap: Coulthard *136.597 mph*

MONACO Monte Carlo 27 May
1st Michael Schumacher [Ger] *Scuderia Ferrari Marlboro*
91.268 mph
2nd Rubens Barrichello [Br] *Scuderia Ferrari Marlboro*
3rd Eddie Irvine [GB] *Jaguar Racing*
Fastest Lap: David Coulthard McLaren *94.914 mph*

CANADA Gilles Villeneuve 10 June
1st Ralf Schumacher [Ger] *BMW Williams 120.315 mph*
2nd Michael Schumacher [Ger] *Scuderia Ferrari Marlboro*
3rd Mika Hakinnen [Fin] *West McLaren Mercedes*
Fastest Lap: Ralf Schumacher *128.094 mph*

EUROPE Nürburgring 24 June
1st Michael Schumacher [Ger] *Scuderia Ferrari Marlboro*
126.848 mph
2nd Juan Pablo Montoya [Col] *BMW Williams*
3rd David Coulthard [GB] *West McLaren Mercedes*
Fastest Lap: Montoya *130.069 mph*

FRANCE Magny-Cours 1 July
1st Michael Schumacher [Ger] *Scuderia Ferrari Marlboro*
121.846 mph
2nd Ralf Schumacher [Ger] *BMW Williams*
3rd Rubens Barrichello [Br] *Scuderia Ferrari Marlboro*
Fastest Lap: David Coulthard *124.976 mph*

BRITAIN Silverstone 15 July
1st Mika Hakinnen [Fin] *West McLaren Mercedes*
134.359 mph
2nd Michael Schumacher [Ger] *Scuderia Ferrari Marlboro*
3rd Rubens Barrichello [Br] *Scuderia Ferrari Marlboro*
Fastest Lap: Hakinnen *137.882 mph*

GERMANY Hockenheim 29 July
1st Ralf Schumacher [Ger] *BMW Williams 146.240 mph*
2nd Rubens Barrichello [Br] *Scuderia Ferrari Marlboro*
3rd Jacques Villeneuve [Can] *Lucky Strike BAR Honda*
Fastest Lap: Juan Pablo Montoya *149.959 mph*

HUNGARY Hungaroring 19 August
1st Michael Schumacher [Ger] *Scuderia Ferrari Marlboro*
112.063 mph
2nd Rubens Barrichello [Br] *Scuderia Ferrari Marlboro*
3rd David Coulthard [GB] *West McLaren Mercedes*
Fastest Lap: Mika Hakinnen McLaren *115.895 mph*

BELGIUM Spa-Francorchams 2 September
1st Michael Schumacher [Ger] *Scuderia Ferrari Marlboro*
137 354 mph
2nd David Coulthard [GB] *West McLaren Mercedes*
3rd Giancarlo Fisichella [It] *Mild Seven Benetton Renault*
Fastest Lap: Michael Schumacher *142.012 mph*

ITALY Monza 16 September
1st David Coulthard [GB] *West McLaren Mercedes*
148.471 mph
2nd Rubens Barrichello [Br] *Scuderia Ferrari Marlboro*
3rd Ralf Schumacher [Ger] *BMW Williams*
Fastest Lap: Ralf Schumacher *152.323 mph*

UNITED STATES Indianapolis 30 September
1st Mika Hakinnen [Fin] *West McLaren Mercedes*
123.055 mph
2nd Michael Schumacher [Ger] *Scuderia Ferrari Marlboro*
3rd David Coulthard [GB] *West McLaren Mercedes*
Fastest Lap: Juan Pablo Montoya *125.956 mph*

JAPAN Suzuka 14 October
1st Michael Schumacher [Ger] *Scuderia Ferrari Marlboro*
132.143 mph
2nd Juan Pablo Montoya [Col] *BMW Williams*
3rd David Coulthard [GB] *West McLaren Mercedes*
Fastest Lap: Ralf Schumacher *133.950 mph*
[new record]

INDIANAPOLIS 500 27 May
1st Helio Castroneves [Br] *Dallara-Oldsmobile*
2nd Gil de Farran [Br] *Dallara-Oldsmobile*
3rd Michael Andretti [USA] *Dallara-Olsmobile*
Fastest Lap: Sam Hornish [USA] *219.830 mph*

2002

World Champion: Michael Schumacher [Ger]
US National Champion [CART]: Cristiana da Matta [Br]
Fastest Man on Earth: Andy Green [GB] [>1997]

GRANDS PRIX

AUSTRALIA Albert Park 3 March
1st Michael Schumacher [Ger] *Scuderia Ferrari Marlboro*
119.931 mph
2nd Juan Pablo Motoya [Col] *BMW-Williams*
3rd Kimi Raikonnen [Fin] *West McLaren Mercedes*
Fastest Lap: Raikonnen *133.977 mph*

MALAYSIA Sepang 17 March
1st Ralf Schumacher [Ger] *BMW-Williams 122.832 mph*
2nd Juan Pablo Montoya [Col] *BMW-Williams*
3rd Michael Schumacher [Ger] *Scuderia Ferrari Marlboro*
Fastest Lap: Montoya *126.460 mph*

BRAZIL Interlagos 31 March
1st Michael Schumacher [Ger] *Scuderia Ferrari Marlboro*
124.335 mph
2nd Ralf Schumacher [Ger] *BMW-Williams*
3rd David Coulthard [GB] *West McLaren Mercedes*
Fastest Lap: Juan Pablo Montoya Wiliams *126.696 mph*

SAN MARINO Imola 14 April
1st Michael Schumacher [Ger] *Scuderia Ferrari Marlboro* 127.762 mph
2nd Rubens Barrichello [Br] *Scuderia Ferrari Marlboro*
3rd Ralf Schumacher [Ger] *BMW-Williams*
Fastest Lap: Barrichello *131.101 mph*

SPAIN Catalunya 28 April
1st Michael Schumacher [Ger] *Scuderia Ferrari Marlboro* 126.606 mph
2nd Juan Pablo Montoya [Col] *BMW-Williams*
3rd David Coulthard [GB] *West McLaren Mercedes*
Fastest Lap: Michael Schumacher *131.672 mph*

AUSTRIA A1-Ring 12 May
1st Michael Schumacher [Ger] *Scuderia Ferrari Marlboro* 122.002 mph
2nd Rubens Barrichello [Br] *Scuderia Ferrari Marlboro*
3rd Juan Pablo Montoya [Col] *BMW-Williams*
Fastest Lap: Michael Schumacher *139.642 mph*

MONACO Monte Carlo 26 May
1st David Coulthard [GB] *West McLaren Mercedes* 92.758 mph
2nd Michael Schumacher [Ger] *Scuderia Ferrari Marlboro*
3rd Ralf Schumacher [Ger] *BMW-Williams*
Fastest Lap: Rubens Barichello *96.618 mph*

CANADA Gilles Villeneuve 9 June
1st Michael Schumacher [Ger] *Scuderia Ferrari Marlboro* 121.591 mph
2nd David Coulthard [GB] *West McLaren Mercedes*
3rd Rubens Barrichello [Br] *Scuderia Ferrari Marlboro*
Fastest Lap: Juan Pablo Montoya *128.426 mph*

EUROPE Nürburgring 23 June
1st Rubens Barrichello [Br] *Scuderia Ferrari Marlboro* 121.006 mph
2nd Michael Schumacher [Ger] *Scuderia Ferrari Marlboro*
3rd Kimi Raikinnen West [Fin] *McLaren Mercedes*
Fastest Lap: Michel Schumacher *124.816 mph*

BRITAIN Silverstone 7 July
1st Michael Schumacher [Ger] *Scuderia Ferrari Marlboro* 125.299 mph
2nd Rubens Barrichello [Br] *Scuderia Ferrari Marlboro*
3rd Juan Pablo Montoya [Col] *BMW-Williams*
Fastest Lap: Barichello *138.416 mph*

FRANCE Magny-Cours 21 July
1st Michael Schumacher [Ger] *Scuderia Ferrari Marlboro* 123.737 mph
2nd Kimi Raikinnen West [Fin] *McLaren Mercedes*
3rd David Coulthard [GB] *West McLaren Mercedes*
Fastest Lap: Coulthard *126.712 mph*

GERMANY Hockenheim 28 July
1st Michael Schumacher [Ger] *Scuderia Ferrari Marlboro* 138.029 mph
2nd Juan Pablo Montoya [Col] *BMW-Williams*
3rd Ralf Schumacher [Ger] *BMW-Williams*
Fastest Lap: Michael Schumacher *133.815 mph*

HUNGARY Hungaroring 18 August
1st Rubens Barrichello [Br] *Scuderia Ferrari Marlboro* 112.073 mph
2nd Michael Schumacher [Ger] *Scuderia Ferrari Marlboro*
3rd Ralf Schumacher [Ger] *BMW-Williams*
Fastest Lap: Michael Schumacher *116.680 mph*

BELGIUM Spa-Francorchamps 1 September
1st Michael Schumacher [Ger] *Scuderia Ferrari Marlboro* 140.411 mph
2nd Rubens Barrichello [Br] *Scuderia Ferrari Marlboro*
3rd Juan Pablo Montoya [Col] *BMW-Williams*
Fastest Lap: Michael Schumacher *145.329 mph*

ITALY Monza 15 September
1st Rubens Barrichello [Br] *Scuderia Ferrari Marlboro* 149.806 mph
2nd Michael Schumacher [Ger] *Scuderia Ferrari Marlboro*
3rd Eddie Irvine [GB] *Jaguar Racing*
Fastest Lap: Barrichello *154.901 mph*

UNITED STATES Indianapolis 29 September
1st Rubens Barrichello [Br] *Scuderia Ferrari Marlboro* 125.191 mph
2nd Michael Schumacher [Ger] *Scuderia Ferrari Marlboro*
3rd David Coulthard [GB] *West McLaren Mercedes*
Fastest Lap: Barrichello *128.918 mph*

JAPAN Suzuka 13 October
1st Michael Schumacher [Ger] *Scuderia Ferrari Marlboro* 132.131 mph
2nd Rubens Barrichello [Br] *Scuderia Ferrari Marlboro*
3rd Kimi Raikonnen [Fin] *West McLaren Mercedes*
Fastest Lap: Michael Schumacher *135.461 mph [Lap Record]*

INDIANAPOLIS 500 26 May
1st Helio Castroneve [Br] *Dallara-Chevrolet 166.499 mph*
2nd Paul Tracy [USA] *Dallara-Chevrolet*
3rd Felipe Giaffone [Br] *[G-Force-Chevrolet]*
Fastest Lap: Tomas Scheckter *226.499 mph*

World Champion: Michael Schumacher [Ger]
US World Champion [CART]: Cristiano da Matta [Br]
Fastest Man on Earth: Andy Green [GB] [>1997]

GRANDS PRIX

AUSTRALIA Albert Park 9 March
1st David Coulthard [GB] *West McLaren Mercedes* 121.085 mph
2nd Juan Pablo Montoya [Col] *BMW-Williams*
3rd Kimi Raikonnen [Fin] *West McLaren Mercedes*
Fastest Lap: Raikonnen *135.224 mph*

MALAYSIA Sepang 23 March
1st Kimi Raikonnen [Fin] *West McLaren Mercedes* 125.286 mph
2nd Rubens Barrichello [Br] *Scuderia Ferrari Marlboro*
3rd Fernando Alonso [Sp] *Mild Seven Renault*
Fastest Lap: Michael Schumacher *128.607 mph*

BRAZIL Interlagos 6 April
1st Giancarlo Fisichella [It] *Jordan Ford 95.009 mph*
2nd Kimi Raikonnen [Fin] *West McLaren Mercedes*
3rd Fernando Alonso [Sp] *Mild Seven Renault*
Fastest Lap: Rubens Barrichello *117.502 mph*

SAN MARINO Imola 20 April
1st Michael Schumacher [Ger] *Scuderia Ferrari Marlboro* 129.179 mph
2nd Kimi Raikonnen [Fin] *West McLaren Mercedes*
3rd Rubens Barrichello [Br] *Scuderia Ferrari Marlboro*
Fastest Lap: Michael Schumacher *133.769 mph*

SPAIN Catalunya 4 May
1st Michael Schumacher [Ger] *Scuderia Ferrari Marlboro* 122.173 mph
2nd Fernando Alonso [Sp] *Mild Seven Renault*
3rd Rubens Barrichello [Br] *Scuderia Ferrari Marlboro*
Fastest Lap: Barrichello *132.023 mph [Lap Record]*

AUSTRIA A1-Ring 18 May
1st Michael Schumacher [Ger] *Scuderia Ferrari Marlboro* 132.354 mph
2nd Kimi Raikonnen [Fin] *West McLaren Mercedes*
3rd Rubens Barrichello [Br] *Scuderia Ferrari Marlboro*
Fastest Lap: Michael Schumacher *141.607 mph*

MONACO Monte Carlo 1 June
1st Juan Pablo Montoya [Col] *BMW-Williams 94.928 mph*
2nd Kimi Raikonnen [Fin] *West McLaren Mercedes*
3rd Michael Schumacher [Ger] *Scuderia Ferrari Marlboro*
Fastest Lap: Raikonnen *100.226 mph*

CANADA Gilles Villeneuve 15 June
1st Michael Schumacher [Ger] *Scuderia Ferrari Marlboro* 124.757 mph
2nd Ralf Schumacher [Ger] *BMW-Williams*
3rd Juan Pablo Montoya [Col] *BMW-Williams*
Fastest Lap: Fernando Alonso Renault *128.291 mph*

EUROPE Nürburgring 29 June
1st Ralf Schumacher [Ger] *BMW-Williams 121.561 mph*
2nd Juan Pablo Montoya [Col] *BMW-Williams*
3rd Rubens Barrichello [Br] *Scuderia Ferrari Marlboro*
Fastest Lap: Kimi Raikonnen *124.331 mph*

FRANCE Magny-Cours 6 July
1st Ralf Schumacher [Ger] *BMW-Williams 126.676 mph*
2nd Juan Pablo Montoya [Col] *BMW-Williams*
3rd Michael Schumacher [Ger] *Scuderia Ferrari Marlboro*
Fastest Lap: Montoya *130.669 mph*

BRITAIN Silverstone 20 July
1st Rubens Barrichello [Br] *Scuderia Ferrari Marlboro* 129.715 mph
2nd Juan Pablo Montoya [Col] *BMW-Williams*
3rd Kimi Raikonnen [Fin] *West McLaren Mercedes*
Fastest Lap: Barrichello *139.842 mph [Lap Record]*

GERMANY Hockenheim 3 August
1st Juan Pablo Montoya [Col] *BMW-Williams* 128.646 mph
2nd David Coulthard [GB] *West McLaren Mercedes*
3rd Jarno Trulli [It] *Mild Seven Renault*
Fastest Lap: Montoya *136.574 mph [Lap Record]*

HUNGARY Hungaroring 24 August
1st Fernando Alonso [Sp] *Mild Seven Renault* 115.457 mph
2nd Kimi Raikonnen [Fin] *West McLaren Mercedes*
3rd Juan Pablo Montoya [Col] *BMW-Williams*
Fastest Lap: Montoya *119.374 mph*

ITALY Monza 14 September
1st Michael Schumacher [Ger] *Scuderia Ferrari Marlboro* 153.842 mph
2nd Juan Pablo Montoya [Col] *BMW-Williams*
3rd Rubens Barrichello [Br] *Scuderia Ferrari Marlboro*
Fastest Lap: Michael Schumacher *158.355 mph [Lap Record]*

UNITED STATES Indianapolis 28 September
1st Michael Schumacher [Ger] *Scuderia Ferrari Marlboro* 121.890 mph
2nd Kimi Raikonnen [Fin] *West McLaren Mercedes*
3rd Heinz-Harald Frentzen [Ger] *Sauber Petronas*
Fastest Lap: Michael Schumacher *131.199 mph [Lap Record]*

JAPAN Suzuka 12 October
1st Rubens Barrichello [Br] *Scuderia Ferrari Marlboro* 134.599 mph
2nd Kimi Raikonnen [Fin] *West McLaren Mercedes*
3rd David Coulthard [GB] *West McLaren Mercedes*
Fastest Lap: Ralf Schumacher *139.069 mph*

INDIANAPOLIS 500 25 May
1st Gil de Farran [Br] *Panoz G-Force Toyota 156.291 mph*
2nd Helio Castoneves [Br] *Dallara Toyota*
3rd Tony Kanaan [Br] *Dallara Honda*
Fastest Lap: Tony Kanaan *229.187 mph*

World Champion: Michael Schumacher [Ger]
US National Champion [CART]: Sebastien Bourdais [Fr]
Fastest Man on Earth: Andy Green [GB] [>1997]

GRANDS PRIX

AUSTRALIA Albert Park 7 March
1st Michael Schumacher [Ger] *Scuderia Ferrari Marlboro* 136.086 mph
2nd Rubens Barrichello [Br] *Scuderia Ferrari Marlboro*
3rd Fernando Alonso [Sp] *Mild Seven Renault*
Fastest Lap: Michael Schumacher *141.009 mph [Lap Record]*

MALAYSIA Sepang 21 March
1st Michael Schumacher [Ger] *Scuderia Ferrari Marlboro*
126.998 mph
2nd Juan Pablo Montoya [Col] *BMW-Williams*
3rd Jenson Button [GB] *Lucky Strike BAR Honda*
Fastest Lap: Montoya 131.595 mph [Lap Record]

BAHRAIN Sakhir 4 April
1st Michael Schumacher [Ger] *Scuderia Ferrari Marlboro*
129.851 mph
2nd Rubens Barrichello [Br] *Scuderia Ferrari Marlboro*
3rd Jenson Button [GB] *Lucky Strike BAR Honda*
Fastest Lap: Michael Schumacher 134.262 mph

SAN MARINO Imola 25 April
1st Michael Schumacher [Ger] *Scuderia Ferrari Marlboro*
131.982 mph
2nd Jenson Button [GB] *Lucky Strike BAR Honda*
3rd Juan Pablo Montoya [Col] *BMW-Williams*
Fastest Lap: Michael Schumacher 137.230 mph [Lap Record]

SPAIN Catalunya 9 May
1st Michael Schumacher [Ger] *Scuderia Ferrari Marlboro*
129.994 mph
2nd Rubens Barrichello [Br] *Scuderia Ferrari Marlboro*
3rd Jarno Trulli [It] *Mild Seven Renault*
Fastest Lap: Michael Schumacher 133.638 mph

MONACO Monte Carlo 23 May
1st Jarno Trulli [It] *Mild Seven Renault* 90.456 mph
2nd Jenson Button [GB] *Lucky Strike BAR Honda*
3rd Rubens Barrichello [Br] *Scuderia Ferrari Marlboro*
Fastest Lap: Michael Schumacher 100.369 mph [Lap Record]

EUROPE Nürburgring 30 May
1st Michael Schumacher [Ger] *Scuderia Ferrari Marlboro*
124.373 mph
2nd Rubens Barrichello [Br] *Scuderia Ferrari Marlboro*
3rd Jenson Button [GB] *Lucky Strike BAR Honda*
Fastest Lap: Michael Schumacher 128.713 mph [Lap Record]

CANADA Gilles Villeneuve 13 June
1st Michael Schumacher [Ger] *Scuderia Ferrari Marlboro*
128.726 mph
2nd Rubens Barrichello [Br] *Scuderia Ferrari Marlboro*
3rd Jenson Button [GB] *Lucky Strike BAR Honda*
Fastest Lap: Barrichello 132.505 mph

UNITED STATES Indianapolis 20 June
1st Michael Schumacher [Ger] *Scuderia Ferrari Marlboro*
113.523 mph
2nd Rubens Barrichello [Br] *Scuderia Ferrari Marlboro*
3rd Takuma Sato [Jap] *Lucky Strike BAAR Honda*
Fastest Lap: Barrichello 133.201 mph [Lap Record]

FRANCE Magny-Cours 4 July
1st Michael Schumacher [Ger] *Scuderia Ferrari Marlboro*
127.403 mph
2nd Fernando Alonso [Sp] *Mild Seven Renault*
3rd Rubens Barrichello [Br] *Scuderia Ferrari Marlboro*
Fastest Lap: Michael Schumacher 130.903 mph

BRITAIN Silverstone 11 July
1st Michael Schumacher [Ger] *Scuderia Ferrari Marlboro*
135.709 mph
2nd Kimi Raikonnen [Fin] *West McLaren Mercedes*
3rd Rubens Barrichello [Br] *Scuderia Ferrari Marlboro*
Fastest Lap: Michael Schumacher 146.052 mph [Lap Record]

GERMANY Hockenheim 25 July
1st Michael Schumacher [Ger] *Scuderia Ferrari Marlboro*
134.124 mph
2nd Jenson Button [GB] *Lucky Strike BAR Honda*
3rd Fernando Alonso [Sp] *Mild Seven Renault*
Fastest Lap: Kimi Raikonnen 138.679 mph [Lap Record]

HUNGARY Hungaroring 15 August
1st Michael Schumacher [Ger] *Scuderia Ferrari Marlboro*
119.799 mph
2nd Rubens Barrichello [Br] *Scuderia Ferrari Marlboro*
3rd Fernando Alonso [Sp] *Mild Seven Renault*
Fastest Lap: Michael Schumacher 123.939 mph [Lap Record]

BELGIUM Spa-Francorchamps 29 August
1st Kimi Raikonnen [Fin] *West McLaren Mercedes*
123.589 mph
2nd Michael Schumacher [Ger] *Scuderia Ferrari Marlboro*
3rd Rubens Barrichello [Br] *Scuderia Ferrari Marlboro*
Fastest Lap: Raikonnen 148.465 mph

ITALY Monza 12 September
1st Rubens Barrichello [Br] *Scuderia Ferrari Marlboro*
151.847 mph
2nd Michael Schumacher [Ger] *Scuderia Ferrari Marlboro*
3rd Jenson Button [GB] *Lucky Strike BAR Honda*
Fastest Lap: Barrichello 159.851 mph [Lap Record]

CHINA Shanghai 26 September
1st Rubens Barrichello [Br] *Scuderia Ferrari Marlboro*
127.496 mph
2nd Jenson Button [GB] *Lucky Strike BAR Honda*
3rd Kimi Raikonnen [Fin] *West McLaren Mercedes*
Fastest Lap: Michael Schumacher 132.196 mph

JAPAN Suzuka 10 October
1st Michael Schumacher [Ger] *Scuderia Ferrari Marlboro*
135.784 mph
2nd Ralf Scumacher [Ger] *BMW-Williams*
3rd Jenson Button [GB] *Lucky Strike BAR Honda*
Fastest Lap: Rubens Barrichello 140.082 mph

BRAZIL Interlagos 24 October
1st Juan Pablo Montoya [Col] *BMW-Williams* 129.566 mph
2nd Kimi Raikonnen [Fin] *West McLaren Mercedes*
3rd Rubens Barrichello [Br] *Scuderia Ferrari Marlboro*
Fastest Lap: Montoya 143.861 mph [Lap Record]

INDIANAPOLIS 500 30 May
1st Buddy Rice [USA] *Panoz G-Force Honda* 138.518 mph
2nd Tony Kanaan [Br] *Dallara-Honda]*
3rd Dan Wheldon [GB] *Dallara-Honda*
Fastest Lap: Vitor Meira [Br] *Panoz G-Force Honda*
218.401 mph

2005

World Championship: Fernando Alonso [Sp]
US National Champion [ChampCar]: Sebastien Bourdais [Fr]
Fastest Man on Earth: Andy Green [GB] [>1997]

GRANDS PRIX

AUSTRALIA Albert Park 6 March
1st Giancarlo Fisichella [It] *Mild Seven Renault*
133.698 mph
2nd Rubens Barrichello [Br] *Scuderia Ferrari Marlboro*
3rd Fernando Alonso [Sp] *Mild Seven Renault*
Fastest Lap: Alonso 138.446 mph

MALAYSIA Sepang 20 March
1st Fernando Alonso [Sp] *Mild Seven Renault*
126.391 mph
2nd Jarno Trulli [It] *Panasonic Toyota Racing*
3rd Nick Heidfeld [Ger] *BMW-Williams*
Fastest Lap: Kimi Raikonnen 129.858 mph [Lap Record]

BAHRAIN Sakhir 3 April
1st Fernando Alonso [Sp] *Mild Seven Renault*
128.674 mph
2nd Jarno Trulli [It] *Panasonic Toyota Racing*
3rd Kimi Raikonnen [Fin] *West McLaren Mercedes*
Fastest Lap: Pedro de la Rosa [Sp] *West McLaren
Mercedes* 132.385 mph

SAN MARINO Imola 24 April
1st Fernando Alonso [Sp] *Mild Seven Renault*
129.919 mph
2nd Michael Schumacher [Ger] *Scuderia Ferrari Marlboro*
3rd Alex Wurz [Aus] *West McLaren Mercedes*
Fastest Lap: Michael Schumacher 134.804 mph [Lap Record]

SPAIN Catalunya 8 May
1st Kimi Raikonnen [Fin] *West McLaren Mercedes*
130.391 mph
2nd Fernando Alonso [Sp] *Mild Seven Renault*
3rd Jarno Trulli [It] *Panasonic Toyota Racing*
Fastest Lap: Giancarlo Fisichella [It] *Renault* 136.834 mph [Lap Record]

MONACO Monte Carlo 22 May
1st Kimi Raikonnen [Fin] *West McLaren Mercedes*
92.274 mph
2nd Nick Heidfeld [Ger] *BMW-Williams*
3rd Mark Webber [Australia] *BMW-Williams*
Fastest Lap:Michael Schumacher 98.512 mph

EUROPE Nürburgring 29 May
1st Fernando Alonso [Sp] *Mild Seven Renault* 123.376 mph
2nd Nick Heidfeld [Ger] *BMW-Williams*
3rd Rubens Barrichello [Br] *Scuderia Ferrari Marlboro*
Fastest Lap: Alonso 126.949 mph

CANADA Gilles Villeneuve 12 June
1st Kimi Raikonnen [Fin] *West McLaren Mercedes*
123.500 mph
2nd Michael Schumacher [Ger] *Scuderia Ferrari Marlboro*
3rd Rubens Barrichello [Br] *Scuderia Ferrari Marlboro*
Fastest Lap: Raikonnen 131.147 mph

UNITED STATES Indianapolis 19 June
1st Michael Schumacher [Ger] *Scuderia Ferrari Marlboro*
127.162 mph
2nd Rubens Barrichello [Br] *Scuderia Ferrari Marlboro*
3rd Tiago Monteiro [Port] *Jordan Toyota*
Fastest Lap: Michael Schumacher 131.155 mph

FRANCE Magny-Cours 3 July
1st Fernando Alonso [Sp] *Mild Seven Renault*
125.913 mph
2nd Kimi Raikonnen [Fin] *West McLaren Mercedes*
3rd Michael Schumacher [Ger] *Scuderia Ferrari Marlboro*
Fastest Lap: Raikonnen 129.111 mph

BRITAIN Silverstone 10 July
1st Juan Pablo Montoya [Col] *West Seven Mercedes*
136.060 mph
2nd Fernando Alonso [Sp] *Mild Seven Renault*
3rd Kimi Raikonnen [Fin] *West McLaren Mercedes*
Fastest Lap: Raikonnen 142.854 mph

GERMANY Hockenheim 24 July
1st Fernando Alonso [Sp] *Mild Seven Renault*
132.121 mph
2nd Juan Pablo Montoya [Col] *West Seven Mercedes*
3rd Jenson Button [GB] *Lucky Strike BAR Honda*
Fastest Lap: Kimi Raikonnen 135.654 mph

HUNGARY Hungaroring 31 July
1st Kimi Raikonnen [Fin] *West McLaren Mercedes*
117.351 mph
2nd Michael Schumacher [Ger] *Scuderia Ferrari Marlboro*
3rd Ralf Schumacher [Ger] *Panasonic Toyota Racing*
Fastest Lap: Raikonnen 120.661 mph

TURKEY Istanbul Park 21 August
1st Michael Schumacher [Ger] *Scuderia Ferrari Marlboro*
136.388 mph
2nd Fernando Alonso [Sp] *Mild Seven Renault*
3rd Juan Pablo Montoya [Col] *West Seven Mercedes*
Fastest Lap: Montoya 140.860 mph

ITALY Monza 4 September
1st Juan Pablo Montoya [Col] *West Seven Mercedes*
153.538 mph
2nd Fernando Alonso [Sp] *Mild Seven Renault*
3rd Giancarlo Fisichella [It] *Mild Seven Renault*
Fastest Lap: Kimi Raikonnen 158.992 mph

BELGIUM Spa-Francorchamps 11 September
1st Kimi Raikonnen [Fin] *West McLaren Mercedes*
127.125 mph
2nd Fernando Alonso [Sp] *Mild Seven Renault*
3rd Jenson Button [GB] *Lucky Strike BAR Honda*
Fastest Lap: Ralf Schumacher 140.013 mph

BRAZIL Interlagos 25 September
1st Juan Pablo Montoya [Col] *West Seven Mercedes*
127.654 mph
2nd Kimi Raikonnen [Fin] *West McLaren Mercedes*
3rd Fernando Alonso [Sp] *Mild Seven Renault*
Fastest Lap: Raikonnen 133.378 mph

JAPAN Suzuka 9 October
1st Kimi Raikonnen [Fin] *West McLaren Mercedes*
128.799 mph
2nd Giancarlo Fisichella [It] *Mild Seven Renault*
3rd Fernando Alonso [Sp] *Mild Seven Renault*
Fastest Lap: Raikonnen 141.912 mph

CHINA Shanghai 16 October
1st Fernando Alonso [Sp] *Mild Seven Renault*
113.862 mph
2nd Kimi Raikonnen [Fin] *West McLaren Mercedes*
3rd Ralf Schumacher [Ger] *Panasonic Toyota Racing*
Fastest Lap: Raikonnen 130.779 mph

INDIANAPOLIS 500 29 May
1st Dan Wheldon [GB] *Dallara-Honda 142.033 mph*
2nd Sam Hornish [USA] *Dallara-Toyota*
3rd Tony Kanaan [Br] *Dallara-Honda*
Fastest Lap: Buddy Rice [USA] *Panoz G-Force Honda*
214.691 mph

World Champion: Fernando Alonso [Sp]
US National Champion [ChampCar]: Sebastien Bourdais [Fr]
Fastest Man on Earth: Andy Green [GB] [>1997]

GRANDS PRIX

BAHRAIN Sakhir 12 March
1st Fernando Alonso [Sp] *Mild Seven Renault*
128.014 mph
2nd Michael Schumacher [Ger] *Scuderia Ferrari Marlboro*
3rd Kimi Raikonnen [Fin] *Team McLaren Mercedes*
Fastest Lap: Nico Rosberg 131.009 mph

MALAYSIA Sepang 19 March
1st Giancarlo Fisichella [It] *Mild Seven Renault*
127.628 mph
2nd Fernando Alonso [Sp] *Mild Seven Renault*
3rd Jenson Button [GB] *Lucky Strike Honda Racing*
Fastest Lap: Alonso 130.791 mph

AUSTRALIA Albert Park 2 April
1st Fernando Alonso [Sp] *Mild Seven Renault*
119.297 mph
2nd Kimi Raikonnen [Fin] *Team McLaren Mercedes*
3rd Ralf Schumacher [Ger] *Panasonic Toyota Racing*
Fastest Lap: Raikonnen 137.864 mph

SAN MARINO Imola 23 April
1st Michael Schumacher [Ger] *Scuderia Ferrari Marlboro*
125.717 mph
2nd Fernando Alonso [Sp] *Mild Seven Renault*
3rd Juan Pablo Montoya [Col] *Team McLaren Mercedes*
Fastest Lap: Alonso 131.171 mph

EUROPE Nürburgring 7 May
1st Michael Schumacher [Ger] *Scuderia Ferrari Marlboro*
119.974 mph
2nd Fernando Alonso [Sp] *Mild Seven Renault*
3rd Felipe Massa [Br] *Scuderia Ferrari Marlboro*
Fastest Lap: Michael Schumacher 125.037 mph

SPAIN Catalunya 14 May
1st Fernando Alonso [Sp] *Mild Seven Renault*
131.777 mph
2nd Michael Schumacher [Ger] *Scuderia Ferrari Marlboro*
3rd Giancarlo Fisichella [It] *Mild Seven Renault*
Fastest Lap: Massa 135.037 mph

MONACO Monte Carlo 28 May
1st Fernando Alonso [Sp] *Mild Seven Renault 93.645 mph*
2nd Juan Pablo Montoya [Col] *Team McLaren Mercedes*
3rd David Coulthard [GB] *Red Bull Racing*
Fastest Lap: Michael Schumacher 99.429 mph

BRITAIN Silverstone 11 June
1st Fernando Alonso [Sp] *Mild Seven Renault*
133.886 mph
2nd Michael Schumacher [Ger] *Scuderia Ferrari Marlboro*
3rd Kimi Raikonnen [Fin] *Team McLaren Mercedes*
Fastest Lap: Alonso 140.934 mph

CANADA Gilles Villeneuve 25 June
1st Fernando Alonso [Sp] *Mild Seven Renault*
120.281 mph
2nd Michael Schumacher [Ger] *Scuderia Ferrari Marlboro*
3rd Kimi Raikonnen [Fin] *Team McLaren Mercedes*
Fastest Lap: Raikonnen 128.628 mph

UNITED STATES Indianapolis 2 July
1st Michael Schumacher [Ger] *Scuderia Ferrari Marlboro*
120.619 mph
2nd Felipe Massa [Br] *Scuderia Ferrari Marlboro*
3rd Giancarlo Fisichella [It] *Mild Seven Renault*
Fastest Lap: Michael Schumacher 128.951 mph

FRANCE Magny-Cours 16 July
1st Michael Schumacher [Ger] *Scuderia Ferrari Marlboro*
124.875 mph
2nd Fernando Alonso [Sp] *Mild Seven Renault*
3rd Felipe Massa [Br] *Scuderia Ferrari Marlboro*
Fastest Lap: Michael Schumacher 127.960 mph

GERMANY Hockenheim 30 July
1st Michael Schumacher [Ger] *Scuderia Ferrari Marlboro*
130.039 mph
2nd Felipe Massa [Br] *Scuderia Ferrari Marlboro*
3rd Kimi Raikonnen [Fin] *Team McLaren Mercedes*
Fastest Lap: Michael Schumacher 133.999 mph

HUNGARY Hongaroring 6 August
1st Jenson Button [GB] *Lucky Strike Honda Racing*
101.764 mph
2nd Pedro de la Rosa [Sp] *Team McLaren Mercedes*
3rd Nick Heidfeld [Ger] *BMW-Sauber*
Fastest Lap:Felipe Massa Ferrari 117.343 mph

TURKEY Istanbul Park 27 August
1st Felipe Massa [Br] *Scuderia Ferrari Marlboro*
129.823 mph
2nd Fernando Alonso [Sp] *Mild Seven Renault*
3rd Michael Schumacher [Ger] *Scuderia Ferrari Marlboro*
Fastest Lap:Michael Schumacher 135.683 mph

ITALY Monza 10 September
1st Michael Schumacher [Ger] *Scuderia Ferrari Marlboro*
152.742 mph
2nd Kimi Raikonnen [Fin] *Team McLaren Mercedes*
3rd Robert Kubica [Pol] *BMW-Sauber*
Fastest Lap: Raikonnen 156.961 mph

CHINA Shanghai 1 October
1st Michael Schumacher [Ger] *Scuderia Ferrari Marlboro*
116.597 mph
2nd Fernando Alonso [Sp] *Mild Seven Renault*
3rd Giancarlo Fisichella [It] *Mild Seven Renault*
Fastest Lap: Alonso 124.952 mph

JAPAN Suzuka 8 October
1st Fernando Alonso [Sp] *Mild Seven Renault*
136.690 mph
2nd Felipe Massa [Br] *Scuderia Ferrari Marlboro*
3rd Giancarlo Fisichella [It] *Mild Seven Renault*
Fastest Lap: Alonso 140.165 mph

BRAZIL Interlagos 22 October
1st Felipe Massa [Br] *Scuderia Ferrari Marlboro*
124.107 mph
2nd Fernando Alonso [Sp] *Mild Seven Renault*
3rd Jenson Button [GB] *Lucky Strike Honda Racing*
Fastest Lap: Michael Schumacher 133.574 mph

INDIANAPOLIS 500 28 May
1st Sam Hornish [USA] *Dallara IR4 Honda 157.085 mph*
2nd Marco Andretti [USA] *Dallara IR4 Honda*
3rd Michael Andrett [USA] *Dallara IR4 Honda*
Fastest Lap: Scott Dixon [NZ] *Dallara IR4 Honda*
221.251 mph

First seven races only

GRANDS PRIX

AUSTRALIA Albert Park 18th March
1st Kimi Raikonnen (Fin) *Scuderia Ferrari 134.149 mph*
2nd Fernando Alonso (Sp) *McLaren Mercedes*
3rd Lewis Hamilton (GB) *McLaren Mercedes*
Fastest Lap: Fernando Alonso (Sp) 139.168 mph

MALAYSIA Sepang 8th April
1st Fernando Alonso (Sp) *McLaren Mercedes*
125.451 mph
2nd Lewis Hamilton (GB) *McLaren Mercedes*
3rd Kimi Raikonnen (Fin) *Scuderia Ferrari*
Fastest Lap: Lewis Hamilton 128.214 mph

BAHRAIN Sakhir 15th April
1st Felipe Massa (Br) *Scuderia Ferrari 122.960 mph*
2nd Lewis Hamilton (GB) *McLaren Mercedes*
3rd Kimi Raikonnen (Fin) *Scuderia Ferrari*
Fastest Lap: Felipe Massa 128.665 mph

SPAIN Catalunya 13th May
1st Felipe Massa (Br) *Scuderia Ferrari 125.036 mph*
2nd Lewis Hamilton (GB) *McLaren Mercedes*
3rd Fernando Alonso (Sp) *McLaren Mercedes*
Fastest Lap: Felipe Massa 125.922 mph

MONACO Monte Carlo 27th May
1st Fernando Alonso (Sp) *McLaren Mercedes 96.650 mph*
2nd Lewis Hamilton (GB) *McLaren Mercedes*
3rd Felipe Massa (Br) *Scuderia Ferrari*
Fastest Lap: Fernando Alonso 99.224 mph

CANADA Montreal 10th June
1st Lewis Hamilton (GB) *McLaren Mercedes 109.236 mph*
2nd Nick Heidfeld (Ger) *BMW Sauber*
3rd Alexander Wurz (Austria) *Williams*
Fastest Lap: Fernando Alonso (Sp) 127.704 mph

UNITED STATES Indianapolis 17th June
1st Lewis Hamilton (GB) *McLaren Mercedes 125.145 mph*
2nd Fernando Alonso (Sp) *McLaren Mercedes*
3rd Felip Massa (Br) *Scuderia Ferrari*
Fastest Lap: Kimi Raikonnen (Fin) 128.260 mph

INDIANAPOLIS 500 27th May
1st Dario Franchitti (GB) *Andretti Green 155.774 mph*
2nd Scott Dixon (Aus) *Target Chip Ganassi*
3rd Helio Castroneves (Br) *Team Penske*
Fastest Lap: Tony Kanaan 223.420 mph.

DAYTONA 500

Listed below together with their cars and average speeds, are all
the winners to date of the Daytona 500, the top event of NASCAR
(the National Association for Stock Car Racing, Inc.).

1959: Lee Petty [USA] *Oldsmobile 135.52 mph*

1960: Junior Johnson [USA] *Chevrolet 124.74 mph*

1961: Marvin Panch [USA] *Pontiac 152.53 mph*

1962: Glenn Roberts [USA] *Pontiac 152.53 mph*

1963: Tiny Lund [USA] *Ford 151.57 mph*

1964: Richard Petty [USA] *Plymouth 154.33 mph*

1965: Fred Lorenzen [USA] *Ford 141.54 mph*

1966: Richard Petty [USA] *Plymouth 160.63 mph*

1967: Mario Andretti [USA] *Ford 146.93 mph*

1968: Cale Yarborough [USA] *Mercury 143.25 mph*

1969: Lee Roy Yardborough [USA] *Ford 157.95 mph*

1970: Pete Hamilton [USA] *Plymouth 149.6 mph*

1971: Richard Petty [USA] *Plymouth 144.46 mph*

1972: A.J. Foyt [USA] *Mercury 161.55 mph*

1973: Richard Petty [USA] *Dodge 157.21 mph*

1974: Richard Petty [USA] *Dodge 140.89 mph*

1975: Benny Parsons [USA] *Chevrolet 153.65 mph*

1976: David Pearson [USA] *Mercury 152.18 mph*

1977: Cale Yarborough [USA] *Chevrolet 153.22 mph*

1978: Bobby Allison [USA] *Ford 159.73 mph*

1979: Richard Petty [USA] *Oldsmobile 143.98 mph*

1980: Buddy Baker [USA] *Oldsmobile 177.6 mph*

1981: Richard Petty [USA] *Buick 169.65 mph*

1982: Bobby Allison [USA] *Buick 153.99 mph*

1983: Cale Yarborough [USA] *Pontiac 155.98 mph*

1984: Cale Yarborough [USA] *Chevrolet 150.99 mph*

1985: Bill Elliott [USA] *Ford 172.27 mph*

1986: Geoff Bodine [USA] *Chevrolet 148.12 mph*

1987: Bill Elliott [USA] *Ford 176.26 mph*

1988: Bobby Ellison [USA] *Buick 137.53 mph*

1989: Darrell Waltrip [USA] *Chevrolet 148.47 mph*

1990: Derrike Cope [USA] *Chevrolet 165.76 mph*

1991: Emie Irvan [USA] *Chevrolet 148.15 mph*

1992: Dave Allison [USA] *Ford 160.25 mph*

1993: Dale Jarrett [USA] *Chevrolet 154.97 mph*

1994: Sterling Marlin [USA] *Chevrolet 156.93 mph*

1995: Sterling Marlin [USA] *Chevrolet 141.71 mph*

1996: Dale Jarrett [USA] *Ford Thunderbird 154.30 mph*

1997: Jeff Gordon [USA] *Chevrolet 148.29 mph*

1998: Dale Earnhardt (USA) *Chevrolet 172.71 mph*

1999: Jeff Gordon (USA) *Chevrolet 161.55 mph*

2000: Dale Jarrett (USA) *Ford 155.67 mph*

2001: Michael Waltrip (USA) *Chevrolet 161.78 mph*

2002: Ward Burton (USA) *Dodge 142.97 mph*

2003: Michael Waltrip (USA) *Chevrolet 133.87 mph*

2004: Dale Earnhardt (USA) *Chevrolet 156.35 mph*

2005: Jeff Gordon (USA) *Chevrolet 135.17 mph*

2006: Jimmie Johnson (USA) *Chevrolet 142.67 mph*

INDEX

PHOTOGRAPHIC CREDITS

Agence Vandystadt 358, 359, 360, 361

Allsport 2B, 351 T, 352T, 352B, 353T, 353B, 355, 357

Alfa Romeo 110T, 112B, 122R, 128B, 131B, 133, 135B, 165, 174

Arizona Historical Society 83

Associated Press 219T, 223B, 226T, 237B

BARC 206B, 207B, 217B

Barnaby's Picture Library 110C, 142/3T, 183B, 265T

Neill Bruce / Peter Roberts Collection 13,14/5, 15T, 15B, 55L, 65T, 71T, 74, 75T, 91T, 107B, 107BR, 112/3, 116, 127R, 132T, 132B, 141T, 144B, 150B, 151T, 152T, 157T, 170/1, 175T, 180BL, 184, 188T, 189B, 192T, 192B, 199T, 200T, 201, 209, 210B, 211B, 214T, 221L, 228/9T, 230B, 233T, 237T, 239, 241B, 243BR, 269B, 271B, 300

Cahier 364, 366TL

Cincinnati Historical Society 76/7

Colorsport 290T, 306, 317T, 317B, 319, 322T, 322B, 323T, 325T, 327T, 327B, 328T, 328B, 329T, 329B, 330, 331, 332T, 333T, 383B, 334, 335T, 335BL, 335BR, 336T, 337T, 338B, 339T, 339B, 340/1, 342T, 343T, 343B, 344T, 344B, 345B, 346T, 346B, 347T, 347B, 348, 349T, 349CL, 349BR, 350T, 350B, 351B

CrashNet 369T, 382T

Empics / Hulton 356, 361

Mary Evans Picture Library 12B, 24T, 27T, 33T, 37B, 42B, 52T, 103T, 107T, 123B, 141B, 149L, 152T, 216R

E T Archive 164T

FIAT 50, 56/7T, 63T, 68B, 75B, 96, 97B, 99, 105T, 105B

Ford Picture Library 254B

Formula One Pictures 357, 358

Getty 6, 365T, 366B, 367, 368, 369C, 370, 371, 372, 373, 374B, 375T, 375B, 376, 377, 379B, 380T, 381C, 382B, 383B, 385T

Haymarket Publications 19T, 22/3, 28, 30B, 31L, 31R, 41, 43T, 43B, 46/47, 52B, 60T, 69L, 70T, 92B, 100, 102T, 102B, 110B, 121TR, 125, 129, 130, 132C, 136/7, 138, 145B, 148B, 152/3, 154B, 158/9, 163R, 176, 177, 185B, 204T, 205T, 208T, 215, 226B, 235

David Hodges 161, 163T, 163L, 164BR, 167C, 195B, 212/3, 228/9B, 253T, 270B, 271C, 283B, 288, 301T

Hulton Picture Source 25, 28B, 29, 33B, 34T, 46B, 51B, 53B, 56TL, 58B, 60B, 63B, 68T, 72T, 73T, 101L, 104T, 108T, 116/7, 170, 173B, 186, 199B, 202, 211T, 218T, 218B, 238T, 282B

Robert Hunt Library 88B, 111T, 158T, 190

Indy 500 Photos 4/5, 36T, 44/5, 56/7B, 59, 62, 64/5 (Ron McQueeney) 65C, 66T, 66/7T, 67B, 70/71B, 73C, 78B, 79C, 80/lB, 81T, 82B, 86T, 86B, 88T, 89B, 90T, 94B, 95B, 100L, 101L, 108B, 109T, 117B, 118T, 118B, 122L, 127L, 131L, 149R, 155T, 159B, 162, 164BL, 173T, 180/1, 181, 185T, 194/5, 195T, 205B, 214B, 225R, 233, 241TR, 247T, 257T, 257B, 262T, 262B, 263T, 265B, 286B, 297T, 297B, 301B, 303R, 305, 307T, 307B, 311 T, 313T, 313 (Debbie Young), 316T, 316B, 324/5, 326B, 326T, 326B, 336B, 336M, 342B (Ron McQueeney)

LAT 9, 177, 180, 190B, 197B, 200B, 204B, 208B, 224/5T, 232B, 234B, 236T, 238R, 243BL, 244B, 246, 247B, 248T, 249T, 249B, 250/1, 252, 259T, 259C, 259B, 264T, 266T, 267, 268, 270/1, 276, 277T, 277B, 278, 279, 281T, 281B, 282T, 283T, 284, 285T, 285BR, 287, 289, 290B, 291T, 292/3, 294T, 294B, 295T, 295B, 298, 298B, 299, 302B, 303L, 304T, 304B, 308B, 309, 310T, 310B, 311B, 312, 314, 314/5, 315T, 318, 318/9, 320, 320/1, 321, 363, 365B, 369B, 374T, 375C, 378, 379C, 380B, 381B, 382C, 383T, 384, 385C

Ludvigsen Library 18B, 38, 39B, 91B, 97T, 97CR, 97CL, 112T, 113B, 121TL, 150T

Mercedes Benz Museum 34B, 51, 73B, 146/7, 154T, 155B, 157B, 192

NASCAR 144

National Motor Museum 12T, 16T, 16B, 16/7, 17B, 18T, 19B, 21, 23, 24B, 26, 32, 35T, 35B, 36/7, 39T, 40T, 40/41, 42T, 48, 48/9B, 49B, 51T, 53T, 54/5T, 55R, 65B, 69R, 71B, 79B, 84/5, 86/7, 93C, 94/5T, 98/9T, 98B, 103B, 104B, 106, 119, 120, 121B, 124T, 126T, 134/5,140, 143L, 156, 159R, 172B, 184/5, 190T, 198T, 222/3, 232T

Free Library of Philadelphia / Automotive Reference Collection 78/9, 89T, 126B, 128T, 131R, 145T, 166/7T, 210T, 220B, 263B

David Phipps 217T, 220T, 221R, 222B, 224B, 225L, 227R, 228, 230T, 231L, 231R, 234T, 236B, 240, 241TL, 243B, 244T, 244C, 245B, 248B, 253B, 254/5, 254T, 255B, 256B, 260, 261T, 261B, 264B, 266B, 269T, 269C, 272T, 272/3B, 273T, 273B, 274/5T, 274/5B, 274, 278/9, 280, 285BL, 286T, 288/9, 291B

Popperfoto 2T, 123, 124B, 134B, 139B, 146B, 152L, 166B, 178B, 179, 182T, 182B, 183T, 216L, 354-5

Quadrant Picture Library 10/11, 27C, 30T, 58/9T, 92/3, 93R, 109B, 114/5, 117T, 139T, 142B, 143R, 147, 148T, 166/7B, 168/9, 172T, 178T, 186/7, 187, 188B, 198B, 203T, 203B, 206/7, 22L,

RAC 315B

Renault 47

Security Pacific Archives, Los Angeles Public Library 61

Sporting Pictures UK 354, 355

Sutton Images 366TR

Topham Picture Source 20, 27B, 171, 189T, 196, 242/2, 256T, 296T, 296B

David Ward 14